2020
Guidebook to
NORTH CAROLINA
TAXES

D0989179

William W. Nelson, J.D.

Wolters Kluwer Editorial Staff

Reviewing Editors .... Carol Kokinis-Graves, Timothy Bjur
Production Coordinator .... Govardhan L
Production Editors .... Ravikishore M, Shashikant G

This publication is designed to provide accurate and authoritative information in regard to the subject matter covered. It is sold with the understanding that the publisher is not engaged in rendering legal, accounting, or other professional service and that the authors are not offering such advice in this publication. If legal advice or other expert assistance is required, the services of a competent professional person should be sought.

ISBN 978-0-8080-5310-1

Do not send returns to the above address. If for any reason you are not satisfied with your book purchase, it can easily be returned within 30 days of shipment. Please go to *support.cch.com/returns* to initiate your return. If you require further assistance with your return, please call: (800) 344-3734 M-F, 8 a.m. – 6 p.m CT.

Printed in the United States of America

PREFACE

This *Guidebook* is designed for practitioners and students of North Carolina state and local taxes. It explains the background and operation of each tax and provides many helpful hints to practitioners to help solve their everyday tax problems. Because of this design, the *Guidebook* can be used as both a textbook for students and as a tool for the tax practitioner.

The author fully appreciates the frustrations when answers to North Carolina tax questions are either ambiguous or difficult to find. Thus, he has attempted to provide explanations, examples, hints, cautions, and answers to the commonly encountered real life problems, while stressing areas for tax planning.

The administration of taxes and the appeals process are complex in North Carolina. In many instances, a taxpayer with a valid claim for tax relief is denied such relief because of a failure to follow the proper procedures. For this reason, the *Guidebook* stresses the appropriate procedures to be followed, and gives practical tips toward obtaining appropriate relief.

All 2019 legislative amendments, administrative guidance and judicial decisions received as of press time are reflected, and references to North Carolina and federal laws are to the laws as of the date of publication of this book.

The emphasis is on the law applicable to the filing of income tax returns in 2020 for the 2019 tax year. However, if legislation has made changes effective after 2019, the author has tried to note this also, with an indication of the effective date to avoid confusion.

The *Guidebook* is not designed to eliminate the necessity of referring to the law and regulations for answers to complicated problems, nor is it intended to take the place of detailed reference works such as the CCH NORTH CAROLINA TAX REPORTS. The *Guidebook* is able to provide a concise, readable treatment of North Carolina taxes that will supply a complete answer to most questions and will serve as a time-saving aid where it does not provide the complete answer.

In addition, the author has provided the reader with the sources of authority to consult whenever a problem arises that may need further clarification. The reader is strongly encouraged to consider the original source before making important tax decisions.

SCOPE OF THE BOOK

This *Guidebook* is designed to do three things:

1. Give a general picture of the impact and pattern of taxes levied by the state of North Carolina.

2. Provide a readable quick-reference work for both the major and minor taxes levied in North Carolina. As such, it explains what the North Carolina law provides and indicates whether the North Carolina provision is the same as federal law.

3. Analyze and explain the differences (especially corporation income tax and individual income taxes), in most cases, between North Carolina and federal law.

HIGHLIGHTS OF 2019 NORTH CAROLINA TAX CHANGES

The most important 2019 North Carolina tax changes received by press time are noted in the "Highlights of 2019 North Carolina Tax Changes" section of the *Guidebook*, beginning on page 11. This useful reference gives the practitioner up-to-the-minute information on changes in tax legislation and recent relevant judicial decisions.

FINDERS

The practitioner may find the desired information by consulting the general Table of Contents at the beginning of the *Guidebook,* the Table of Contents at the beginning of each chapter, or the Topical Index at the end of the *Guidebook.*

The Law and Rule Locator is an equally useful finder's tool. Beginning on page 597, this finding list shows where sections of North Carolina statutory law and administrative rules referred to in the *Guidebook* are discussed.

November 2019

ABOUT THE AUTHOR

William W. Nelson is a partner in the law firm of Smith, Anderson, Blount, Dorsett, Mitchell & Jernigan, L.L.P. in Raleigh, North Carolina. Mr. Nelson's principal practice areas are federal and state tax planning for businesses. He also assists taxpayers with federal and state tax controversies and has been active in numerous state tax legislative reform efforts. He received his undergraduate (1982 Phi Beta Kappa) and law (1985, with high honors) degrees from the University of North Carolina at Chapel Hill. He is a past Chair of the Tax Section of the North Carolina Bar Association, an occasional lecturer at Duke University School of Law, a former adjunct Professor of Law at the University of North Carolina School of Law, a member of the UNC Tax Institute Board of Advisors, the Chair of the North Carolina Chamber Tax Committee, and a Fellow of the American College of Tax Counsel.

CONTENTS

HIGHLIGHTS OF 2019 NORTH CAROLINA TAX CHANGES

The most important statutory changes to North Carolina's tax law enacted in 2019 are noted below.

IRC Conformity

The North Carolina Constitution prohibits automatic conformity to the Internal Revenue Code. As a result, the General Assembly annually updates the reference to the Code in the North Carolina Revenue Act in order to incorporate some or all of the changes made to the Code during the preceding year. The 2019 General Assembly updated the Code reference from February 9, 2018 to January 1, 2019. As a result, North Carolina conforms to the following statutes amending the Code enacted after February 9, 2018:

Public Law No.	Title	Date of Enactment
115-141	Consolidated Appropriations Act of 2018	March 23, 2018
115-243	Tribal Social Security Fairness Act of 2018	September 20, 2018
115-250	Airport and Airway Extension Act of 2018 (Part II)	September 29, 2018
115-254	FAA Reauthorization Act of 2018	October 5, 2018
115-271	SUPPORT for Patients and Communities Act	October 24, 2018

Individual Income Tax

• *Increase in Standard Deduction*

The standard deduction has been increased by 7.5% for the 2020 and later tax years. *See* ¶ 202.

• *Qualified Charitable Distributions*

North Carolina has conformed to the federal exclusion of qualified charitable IRA charitable distributions, effective for the 2019 and later tax years. *See* ¶ 202.

Apportionment

• *Market-based Sourcing*

The General Assembly has enacted market-based sourcing for apportioning the corporate income tax base and the franchise tax net worth base, effective for taxable years beginning on or after January 1, 2020. Under market-based sourcing, receipts are sourced to the location of the taxpayer's market. If the market cannot be determined, receipts are sourced based on a method of reasonable approximation. If the source of a receipt cannot be reasonably approximated, the receipt must be excluded from the denominator of the apportionment fraction. Special market-based sourcing rules are provided for broadcasters, banks, natural gas pipeline companies and electric power companies. A corporation with a state net loss at the end of 2019 may elect to continue sourcing receipts from services under the income producing activities test of former law until its losses are used up or expire. The election must be made on the 2020 tax return and is irrevocable. The election applies only for income tax purposes, and the franchise tax net worth base is apportioned as if the election had not been made. The Department of Revenue issued proposed market-based sourcing rules in 2017, the effectiveness of which was contingent on future enactment of market-based sourcing legislation. These rules will now become effective beginning in 2020, but the Department is required to revise the rules to reflect differences between the market-based sourcing legislation proposed in 2017 and the market-based sourcing rules that have been enacted. *See* ¶ 1007.

Sales Tax

• *Wayfair Codification*

The General Assembly has codified the Department's directive issued in response to the Supreme Court's decision in *South Dakota v. Wayfair* requiring a remote seller with more than $100,000 in North Carolina sales or at least 200 separate sales transactions sourced to North Carolina to collect North Carolina sales or use tax. *See* ¶ 1707.

• *Marketplace Facilitators*

The sales and use tax law has been extended to impose sales and use tax collection responsibility on marketplace facilitators. A "marketplace facilitator" is defined as a person who owns or operates a physical or electronic platform or other marketplace on which the items of another person are listed or made available for sale and who facilitates the sales of the marketplace seller's items. A marketplace facilitator must collect sales and use tax on all facilitated sales if it satisfied the $100,000/200 transaction threshold for the current or the preceding calendar year. These provisions are effective February 1, 2020 and apply to sales that occur on or after that date. *See* ¶ 1707.

• *Accommodation Facilitators*

The rules regarding the rental of accommodations through accommodation facilitators have been clarified. The definition of "accommodation facilitator" has been expanded to cover persons who list accommodations for a fee as well as persons who accept payment or credit card information from renters. The term also specifically includes real estate brokers. Each facilitator and provider of the accommodation must collect tax on that portion of the rental payment it collects. Special provisions apply to accommodation facilitators that are operated by or on behalf of a hotel. These provisions are effective February 1, 2020. *See* ¶ 1726.

• *Highway Use Tax on Vehicle Subscriptions*

The Highway Use Tax has been amended to provide a new 5% rate applicable to vehicle subscription arrangements. *See* ¶ 2901.

Credits and Incentives

• *Non-shareholder Contributions to Capital*

The income tax law has been amended to allow corporate and individual taxpayers to deduct grants from the state's Job Maintenance and Capital Development Fund, Job Development and Investment Grant Program and the One North Carolina Fund in computing state net income. These changes are effective for amounts received after 2018. *See* ¶ ¶ 202 and 903.

• *Sunset Extensions*

The following provisions, formerly scheduled to sunset on January 1, 2020, have been extended until January 1, 2024: (1) the historic rehabilitation tax credits, (2) the sales tax exemption for aviation gasoline and jet fuel sold to an interstate air business for use in commercial aircraft, (3) the sales tax exemption for sales of engines, engine parts, service contracts and repair, maintenance and installation services and certain other items to a professional motorsports racing team or sanctioning body or to persons providing engines to a professional motorsports racing team, (4) the refund for sales taxes paid by a professional motorsports racing team or sanctioning body on aviation gasoline and jet fuel, and (5) the refund for 50% of the sales taxes paid by a professional motorsports racing team on tangible personal property (other than tires or accessories) that comprise a part of a professional motorsports vehicle. *See* ¶ ¶ 1104, 1804, 1809 and 1905.

Property Tax

• *Builder Inventory Property Tax Exclusion*

The annual application for the property tax exclusion for increases in the value of builder-owned real property inventory attributable to the builder's improvements has been replaced with a one-time application. *See* ¶ 2202.

Compliance and Administration

• *Powers of Attorney*

The Department has been directed to update its electronic data systems to store and recognize power of attorney registrations to ensure that notices are sent to a taxpayer's representative at the same time they are sent to the taxpayer. The Department is required to report its progress on achieving this goal by January 31, 2020.

• *Taxation of Out-of-State Businesses and Workers Engaged in Disaster Relief*

Relief provisions have been enacted for out-of-state businesses and nonresident employees that enter the state temporarily to help restore critical infrastructure following a declared disaster at the request of a critical infrastructure company. A majority of the states have enacted similar relief provisions. Eligible businesses and employees are exempt from the corporate and individual income taxes, the franchise tax, the unemployment tax and the requirement to obtain a certificate of authority to transact business. These provisions are effective for disasters declared on or after August 1, 2019. *See* ¶ 3312.

• *Innocent Spouse Relief*

North Carolina's innocent spouse statute has been amended to conform to the federal statute, which provides relief for both understatements and underpayments of tax, effective for taxable years beginning on or after January 1, 2018. *See* ¶ 503.

• *Contingent Refund Claims*

The law permitting taxpayers to file contingent refund claims has been amended to permit such claims after the general limitation period has expired if the period has been extended due to another exception. This change is effective July 26, 2019. *See* ¶ 3203.

• *Federal Determinations*

If a taxpayer's federal tax return is corrected as a result of a federal determination in a manner that affects the taxpayer's state tax liability, the taxpayer must file an amended North Carolina return reflecting the federal change. The definition of a "federal determination" has been amended to clarify that the determination must be final. *See* ¶ 3202.

PART I

TABLES

TAX RATES

¶10 Individual Income Tax

The individual income tax rate is 5.25% for years beginning in or after 2019 (see ¶ 104).

¶11 Estate and Trust Income Tax

A tax is imposed on the taxable income of an estate or trust that is for the benefit of a North Carolina resident, derived from North Carolina sources or derived from a North Carolina trade or business at the rates applicable to individuals (see ¶ 701).

¶15 Corporation Income Tax

The North Carolina corporate income tax rate is 2.5% for years beginning in or after 2019 (see ¶ 801).

¶20 Franchise Tax

The franchise tax is imposed at the rate of $1.50 per $1,000 of the franchise tax base. The minimum franchise tax is $200. (see ¶ 1401). For special rules applicable to holding companies, see ¶ 1304. For special rules applicable to S corporations, see ¶ 1401.

¶25 Sales and Use Taxes

The general sales and use tax rate is 4.75%. The local sales and use tax rate ranges from 2% to 2.75% depending on the county to which the sale is sourced. The combined general rate (applicable to sales of electricity, piped natural gas, video programming services, telecommunication services, spirituous liquor and aviations gasoline and jet fuel) is 7% (see ¶¶ 1605 and 1607).

CREDITS, REFUNDS AND SPECIAL RATES

¶36 Credits, Refunds and Special Rates

The table below lists the most significant credits available against the personal income tax, corporate income tax and franchise tax and the most significant special rates and refunds available with respect to the sales and use tax. Sales and use tax exemptions are too numerous to be included in the table but are discussed in Chapter 18. Many credits, special rates and refund provisions have sunsetted or are scheduled to sunset, and the table below groups these special provisions by their sunset date.

Income and Franchise Tax Credits

G.S. § 105-	Provision	Sunset Reference
Credits Expired January 1, 2018		
130.45	Credit for Manufacturing Cigarettes for Exportation	S.L. 1999-333, § 10, as amended by S.L. 2003-435, § 5.1
130.46	Credit for Manufacturing Cigarettes for Exportation While Increasing Employment and Using State Ports	S.L. 2003-435, § 6.2
Credits Expiring January 1, 2024		
129.100	Historic Rehabilitation Credit for Rehabilitating Income—Producing Historic Structures	G.S. § 105-129.105
129.101	Historic Rehabilitation Credit for Rehabilitating—Non-Income Producing Historic Structures	G.S. § 105-129.105
Credits Expiring January 1, 2038		
129.95-99	Tax Incentives for Railroad Intermodal Facilities	G.S. § 105-129.99
Credits With No Expiration Date		
163.10	Credit for Withheld Income Taxes	
129.25-27	Tax Incentives for Recycling Facilities	
130.25	Credit for Construction of Cogenerating Power Plants	
122.1	Credit for Additional Annual Report Fee Paid by LLCs	
131.8	Credit for Net Income Taxes Paid to Other States by S Corporations	
153.9	Credit for Income Taxes Paid to Other States by Individuals	
160.4	Credit for Income Taxes paid to Other States by Estates and Trusts	

Sales Tax Special Refunds (Exemptions are discussed at Chapter 18)

G.S. § 105-	Provision	Sunset Reference
Sales Tax Refunds Expiring January 1, 2024		
164.14A(a)(4)	Sales Tax Refund for Motorsports Team or Sanctioning Body	S.L. 2013-316, § 3.5.(a)
164.14A(a)(5)	Sales Tax Refund for Professional Motorsports Team	S.L. 2013-316, § 3.5.(a)
Sales Tax Refunds Expiring January 1, 2038		
164.14A(a)(7)	Sales Tax Refund for Railroad Intermodal Facility	G.S. § 105-164.14A(a)(7)
Sales Tax Refunds With No Expiration Date		
164.14(a)	Sales Tax Refund for Interstate Carriers	
164.14(a2)	Sales Tax Refund for Utility Companies	
164.14(c)	Sales Tax Refunds for Government Entities	
164.14(e)	Sales Tax Refunds for State Agencies	
164.14A(a)(2)	Sales Tax Refund for Major Recycling Facilities	

PART II

INDIVIDUAL INCOME TAX

CHAPTER 1

IMPOSITION OF TAX, RATES, EXEMPTIONS

¶101 History, Sources of Authority, and Administration

North Carolina has imposed some form of income tax on individuals since 1848, when the General Assembly levied a tax on interest, dividends, business profits, and salaries and fees [Laws of the State of North Carolina: Session 1848-49, C. 77]. In 1868, however, North Carolina voters approved a Constitution that included a provision prohibiting the taxation of income derived from property that had been subject to the property tax, and prior to 1921, the income tax in North Carolina produced little revenue.

In November 1920, North Carolina voters approved an amendment to the State Constitution that authorized the North Carolina General Assembly to levy a State income tax on all sources of income [Article V, § 3, 1868 Constitution of North Carolina]. This constitutional amendment specified a maximum income tax rate of six percent and minimum personal exemptions. Subsequent constitutional amendments raised the maximum rate to ten percent and eliminated reference to minimum personal exemptions. Article V, § 2(6) of the North Carolina Constitution now reads as follows:

> The rate of tax on incomes shall not in any case exceed ten percent, and there shall be allowed personal exemptions and deductions so that only net incomes are taxed [Constitution of North Carolina, 1970].

The current North Carolina individual income tax is imposed by Article 4 of Chapter 105 of the North Carolina General Statutes (G.S.). The individual income tax withholding and estimated tax provisions are contained in Article 4A of Chapter 105. Rules for taxation of estates, trusts, and beneficiaries are in Part 3 of Article 4. The income tax regulations are contained in Title 17 of the North Carolina Administrative Code (NCAC).

The North Carolina individual income tax is based on North Carolina taxable income. The starting point for the computation of North Carolina taxable income is federal adjusted gross income, which is then modified to arrive at North Carolina taxable income. See ¶ 103 for details.

North Carolina residents pay tax on their entire taxable income (from wherever derived) [G.S. § 105-153.4(a)]; but nonresidents must pay tax only on taxable income derived from North Carolina sources [G.S. § 105-153.4(b)]. Part-year residents must pay tax on their entire taxable income (from wherever derived) for the period during which they were North Carolina residents but only on taxable income derived from North Carolina sources for the period during which they were not North Carolina residents [G.S. § 105-153.4(c)].

The North Carolina individual income tax is administered by the Personal Taxes Division of the North Carolina Department of Revenue. For more detail, see Part XIV, "Administration and Procedure."

¶102 Persons Subject to Tax

The North Carolina individual income tax is imposed on the North Carolina taxable income of resident individuals, nonresident individuals, and part-year resident individuals. As discussed below, North Carolina taxable income is defined differently for each type of individual taxpayer. For the income taxation of estate and trusts, see Chapter 7.

• *Residents*

The term resident includes (1) any individual who is domiciled in North Carolina at any time during the taxable year, or (2) any individual who resides within North Carolina during the taxable year for other than a temporary or transitory purpose [G.S. § 105-153.3(15)]. An individual who lives in North Carolina for more than 183 days of a tax year is presumed to be a resident for income tax purposes in the absence of factual proof to the contrary; but the absence of an individual from the State for more than 183 days raises no presumption that he is not a resident. The fact of marriage does not raise any presumption as to domicile or residence [17 NCAC 6B.3901].

• *Nonresidents*

A nonresident taxpayer is one who (a) lives in North Carolina for a temporary or transitory purpose but is a domiciliary of another state or (b) lives outside North Carolina and is a domiciliary of another state, but receives income from sources in North Carolina [17 NCAC 6B.3902].

• *Part-year residents*

A part-year resident is one who (1) moved into the state and became a domiciliary during the taxable year or (2) moved out of North Carolina *and* became a domiciliary of another state during the taxable year [17 NCAC 6B.3903]. Note that simply moving out of North Carolina does not automatically make one a nonresident. North Carolina residents who leave North Carolina during the taxable year do not become nonresidents until they have *both* (1) established a definite domicile elsewhere and (2) abandoned any North Carolina domicile.

• *Domicile*

The key word in the definition of residency is domicile. A domicile and an abode are not necessarily the same thing. A residence is a place where one lives; an abode is a settled place of residence. An individual may have several places of abode during a taxable year, but at no time can an individual have more than one domicile. A domicile is a legal residence and is specifically defined by North Carolina income tax regulations:

> Domicile means the place where an individual has a true, fixed permanent home and principal establishment, and to which place, whenever absent, the individual has the intention of returning. In many cases, a determination must be made as to when or whether a domicile has been abandoned. A long-standing principle in tax administra-

tion, repeatedly upheld by the courts, is that an individual can have but one domicile; and, once established, it is not legally abandoned until a new one is established. A taxpayer may have several places of abode in a year, but at no time can an individual have more than one domicile. A mere intent or desire to make a change in domicile is not enough; voluntary and positive action must be taken.

The taxpayer has the burden of proving that his domicile has changed. To carry that burden, the taxpayer must show: (1) that he has abandoned the first domicile with an intention not to return, (2) that he has acquired a new domicile by residing at another place, and (3) that he intends to make the new residence his permanent home. For an example of taxpayers who carried this burden and successfully transferred their domicile to Florida two weeks before the sale of their business despite maintaining significant ties to North Carolina, *See Fowler v. N.C. Dept. of Revenue,* 242 N.C. App. 404, 775 S.E.2d 350 (2015). *See also, Secretary's Decision No.* 2003-220, (August 14, 2003), and *Secretary's Decision No.* 2003-318 (November 19, 2003).

• *Tests of legal residence*

Some of the tests or factors to be considered in determining the legal residence of an individual for income tax purposes are as follows [17 NCAC 6B.3901(b)]:

(1) Place of birth.

(2) Permanent residence of parents.

(3) Family connections.

(4) Close friends.

(5) Address given for military purposes.

(6) Civic ties.

(7) Church membership.

(8) Club or lodge membership.

(9) Payment of State income taxes.

(10) Listing of "legal" or "permanent" address on federal tax returns.

(11) Continuous car registration and driver's license.

(12) Voting by absentee ballot.

(13) Occasional visits or spending one's leave "at home" if a member of the armed services.

(14) Home ownership.

(15) Professional ties (*e.g.,* certification as teacher, lawyer, or CPA).

(16) Attendance of children at State-supported colleges or universities on a basis of residence—taking advantage of lower tuition fees.

(17) Execution of approved certificates or other statements indicating permanent resident.

(18) Expression of intention.

The following events are indications that residency has changed: [17 NCAC 6B.3901(c)]

(1) Selling an old house/buying a new one.

(2) Directing the U.S. Postal Service to forward mail.

(3) Picking up or forwarding family medical records.

(4) Notifying senders of statements, bills, or subscriptions of a new address.

(5) Obtaining new local utilities, subscriptions, *etc.*, discontinuing old ones.

(6) Transferring titles to vehicles.

(7) Applying for new state certifications (*e.g.*, joining a new bar).

• *Members of the U.S. Armed Forces*

A legal resident of North Carolina who is a member of the Armed Forces is subject to the North Carolina individual income tax and to the withholding of North Carolina individual income tax whether the individual is stationed in North Carolina or some other state or country. Any individual who enters military service while a resident of North Carolina is presumed to be a North Carolina resident for income tax purposes. North Carolina residency is not abandoned until residency is established elsewhere. To establish residency elsewhere, an individual in military service must not only be present in the new location with the intention of making it a new domicile, but must also factually establish that the individual has done so [17 NCAC 6B.3901 (a), (d), (e)]. Merely filling out a Department of Defense Form 2058 ("State of Legal Residence Certificate") is not sufficient to establish a new residency outside North Carolina. *See* Final Agency Decision 10 REV 3634 (October 19, 2010). There is no presumption as to the residence of a spouse of a member of the armed forces because of marriage. Legal residency is determined by the facts and circumstances of individual cases [17 NCAC 6B.3902(c)].

An individual who is a legal resident of another state stationed in North Carolina by virtue of military orders is not subject to North Carolina individual income tax on service. However, other income from employment, a business, or tangible property in North Carolina is subject to North Carolina individual income tax [17 NCAC 6B.3902(b)].

Military Spouses

The income earned for services performed in North Carolina by the spouse of a service member who is legally domiciled in a state other than North Carolina is exempt from North Carolina income tax if (1) the service member is present in North Carolina solely in compliance with military orders; (2) the spouse is in North Carolina solely to be with the service member; and (3) the spouse is domiciled in the same state as the service member. All three conditions must be met to qualify for exemption [Frequently Asked Questions Regarding the Military Spouses Residency Relief Act, North Carolina Department of Revenue].

IRC § 692 provides that in the case of any individual who dies while in active service as a member of the Armed Forces of the United States, if such death occurred while serving in a combat zone (as determined under IRC § 112) or as a result of wounds, disease, or injury incurred while so serving is not subject to the federal individual income tax. Furthermore, any federal income tax for taxable years preceding the date of death that is unpaid at the date of death (including interest, additions to the tax, and additional amounts) shall not be assessed, and if assessed the assessment shall be abated, and if collected shall be credited or refunded as an overpayment. G.S. § 105-158 provides that any income excludable from federal income tax under IRC § 692 for a taxable year is not subject to the North Carolina individual income tax for that same taxable year.

The Secretary of Revenue is required to cancel and abate all assessments made after October 16, 1940, for taxes owed by veterans of the U.S. Armed Forces, as of the date of their entry into military service, who were killed while on active duty or who have a compensable service-connected disability. If the tax has been paid, the amount of assessment without interest must be refunded [G.S. § 105-244.1].

¶103 Tax Base—North Carolina Taxable Income

• *Adjusted gross income*

The starting point for determination of North Carolina taxable income is federal adjusted gross income as defined under IRC § 62 [G.S. § 105-153.3(1)]

Residents [G.S. § 105-153.4(a)]: For residents of North Carolina, the term "North Carolina taxable income" means the taxpayer's federal adjusted gross income as modified in G.S. § § 105-153.5 and 105-153.6.

Nonresidents [G.S.§ 105-153.4(b)]: For nonresidents, the term "North Carolina taxable income" means the taxpayer's federal adjusted gross income as modified in G.S. § § 105-153.5 and 105-153.6 multiplied by a fraction, the numerator of which is the amount of the taxpayer's federal gross income as so modified that is derived from North Carolina sources and is (a) attributable to the ownership of any interest in real or tangible personal property in North Carolina, (b) derived from a business, trade, profession, or occupation carried on in North Carolina, or (c) derived from gambling activities in North Carolina, and the denominator of which is the taxpayer's federal gross income as so modified.

Part-year residents [G.S. § 105-153.4(c)]: For part-year residents the term "North Carolina taxable income" means the taxpayer's federal adjusted gross income as modified in G.S. § § 105-153.5 and 105-153.6 multiplied by a fraction, the numerator of which is the taxpayer's federal gross income as so modified (from all sources) during the portion of the year the taxpayer was a North Carolina resident and the denominator of which is the taxpayer's federal gross income as so modified (from all sources) for the entire year.

S corporations and partnerships [G.S. § 105-153.4(d)]: The amount of a shareholder's pro rata share of S corporation income that is included in the numerator of the nonresident fraction (as defined in G.S. § 105-153.4(b)) is the shareholder's pro rata share of the S corporation's income (as modified in G.S. § § 105-153.5 and 105-153.6) attributable to North Carolina, as defined in G.S. § 105-131(b)(4). If a partnership or other unincorporated business has one or more nonresident partners or members and operates in one or more other states, the amount of a partner's or member's distributive share of the total net income of the business (as modified in G.S. § § 105-153.5 and 105-153.6) plus, in the case of a partnership, any guaranteed payments made to the partner that is includible in the nonresident fraction is determined under the provisions of G.S. § 105-130.4). The total net income of the business is its entire gross income less all expenses, taxes, interest, and other deductions allowable under the Internal Revenue Code that were incurred in the operation of the business. The taxation of pass-through entities is discussed in Chapter 6.

• *References to the IRC in the North Carolina statutes*

Each year the North Carolina General Assembly updates G.S. § 105-228.90(b)(1b), which specifies the version of the Internal Revenue Code that is referenced. These updates are necessary because the North Carolina Constitution, Art. V, § 2(1), provides that the power of taxation "shall never be surrendered, suspended, or contracted away." If the individual income tax were based on federal taxable income as determined under the Internal Revenue Code, as it might from time to time be amended by the Congress, the North Carolina legislature would have contracted away or surrendered its taxing power. Thus, the Legislature must approve by affirmative action, in the form of an update of the Internal Revenue Code reference, any changes that have been made in the Internal Revenue Code each year. G.S. § 105-228.90(b)(1b) currently defines the "Code" as the Internal Revenue Code as enacted as of February 9, 2018, including any provisions enacted as of that date, that become effective either before or after that date. Thus, the Code reference does not include, and North Carolina does not conform to, federal tax legislation enacted after January 1, 2019.

• *Computation of North Carolina taxable income*

The computation of North Carolina taxable income is discussed in Chapter 2.

¶104 Tax Rate

North Carolina has a flat tax rate of 5.25% for taxable years beginning on or after January 1, 2019 [G.S. § 105-153.7(a)].

• *Tax tables*

The Secretary may provide tables that compute the amount of tax due for a taxable year. The tables do not apply to (1) an individual who files a federal tax return for a period of less than 12 months due to a change in annual accounting period; (2) estates; or (3) trusts [G.S. § 105-153.7(b)].

¶105 Accounting Periods

A taxpayer must compute North Carolina taxable income on the basis of the taxable year used in computing the taxpayer's federal income tax liability [G.S. § 105-153.4(e)].

INDIVIDUAL INCOME TAX

CHAPTER 2

COMPUTATION OF TAXABLE INCOME

¶201 In General

This chapter explains the computation of North Carolina taxable income. The starting point for determination of North Carolina taxable income is federal adjusted gross income as defined under the Internal Revenue Code (¶103). Federal adjusted gross income is adjusted by the additions and deductions described in ¶202 and ¶203 to arrive at North Carolina taxable income.

¶202 Adjustments to Federal Adjusted Gross Income

Taxpayers must make the adjustments described below to federal adjusted gross income in computing North Carolina taxable income. Except with respect to the standard or itemized deduction, an amount may be deducted from federal adjusted gross income only to the extent the amount is included in the taxpayer's adjusted gross income, and amounts must be added back to federal adjusted gross income only to the extent they are not included in the taxpayer's adjusted gross income [G.S. § 105-153.5(b) and (c)].

• *Deduction for standard deduction or itemized deductions*

A taxpayer may deduct either the North Carolina standard deduction for the taxpayer's filing status (see table below) or the itemized deductions allowed for North Carolina tax purposes. The North Carolina standard deduction is shown in the table below. Note that a person who is not eligible for a standard deduction under Code § 63 (e.g., a nonresident alien) has a North Carolina standard deduction of zero. The itemized deduction amount, which is not subject to the overall limitation on itemized deductions under Code § 68, is an amount equal to the sum of (1) the amount allowed as a charitable contribution deduction under Code § 170 for the taxable year (provided that for the 2014-2018 taxable years a taxpayer who elected the Code § 408(d)(8) income exclusion for a qualified charitable distribution from an individual retirement plan by a person who has reached age $70^{1}/_2$ may deduct the amount that would have been allowed as a charitable deduction under Code § 170 but for the income exclusion election), (2) the amount allowed as a deduction for interest paid or accrued during the taxable year under Code § 163(h) with respect to any qualified residence (provided that for 2014, 2015, 2016 and 2017 the qualified residence interest deduction does not include mortgage insurance premiums treated as qualified residence interest) plus the amount allowed as a deduction for property taxes paid or accrued on real estate under Code § 164 for the taxable year, (3) the amount allowed as a deduction for medical and dental expenses under Code § 213, and (4) the amount repaid during the taxable year that was included in income in an earlier taxable year under a claim of right, provided the repayment was not deducted in computing federal adjusted gross income (and provided that this amount is subject to Code §67 limitation if the repayment did not exceed $3,000 and further provided that the taxpayer did not calculate his federal income tax under Code §1341(a)(5)). The itemized deduction amount for qualified residence interest and real property taxes may not exceed $20,000. For taxpayers filing as married filing separately or married filing jointly, the total mortgage interest and real estate taxes claimed by both spouses may not exceed $20,000. For spouses filing as married filing separately with a joint obligation for mortgage interest and real estate taxes, the deductions for these items is allowed to the spouse who actually paid them. If the amount of mortgage interest and real estate taxes paid by both spouses exceeds $20,000, the deductions must be prorated based on the percentage paid by each spouse. For joint obligations paid from joint accounts, the proration is based on the income reported by each spouse for the taxable year. A taxpayer may not deduct both the standard deduction amount and the itemized deductions amount [G.S. §105-153.5(a)].

Standard Deduction Chart

Filing Status	Standard Deduction	
	2019	2020
Married filing jointly/surviving spouse	$20,000	$21,500
Head of household	$15,000	$16,125
Single	$10,000	$10,750
Married filing separately	$10,000	$10,750

• Deduction for Children

For taxable years beginning on or after January 1, 2018, a taxpayer who is allowed a federal child tax credit under IRC §24 for the taxable year is allowed a deduction in computing North Carolina taxable income for each qualifying child for whom the taxpayer is allowed the federal credit. The amount of the credit is based on the taxpayer's federal adjusted gross income for the taxable year [G.S. §105-153.5(a1)]. This deduction replaces the North Carolina child tax credit, which was available for years before 2018.

Filing Status	AGI	Deduction Amount
Married Filing Jointly	Up to $40,000	$2,500
	Over $40,000 up to $60,000	$2,000
	Over $60,000 up to $80,000	$1,500
	Over $80,000 up to $100,000	$1,000
	Over $100,000 up to $120,000	$500
	Over $120,000	$0
Head of Household	Up to $30,000	$2,500
	Over $30,000 up to $45,000	$2,000
	Over $45,000 up to $60,000	$1,500
	Over $60,000 up to $75,000	$1,000
	Over $75,000 up to $90,000	$500
	Over $90,000	$0
Single	Up to $20,000	$2,500
	Over $20,000 up to $30,000	$2,000
	Over $30,000 up to $40,000	$1,500
	Over $40,000 up to $50,000	$1,000
	Over $50,000 up to $60,000	$500
	Over $60,000	$0
Married Filing Separately	Up to $20,000	$2,500
	Over $20,000 up to $30,000	$2,000
	Over $30,000 up to $40,000	$1,500
	Over $40,000 up to $50,000	$1,000
	Over $50,000 up to $60,000	$500
	Over $60,000	$0

• *Deduction for interest on government obligations*

A taxpayer may deduct interest on obligations of the following entities to the extent included in federal adjusted gross income: (1) the United States or its possessions; (2) the State of North Carolina, its political subdivisions, or a commission, an authority, or other agency of the State or its political subdivisions; (3) a nonprofit educational institution organized or chartered under the laws of North Carolina; and (4) a hospital authority created by a city or county pursuant to G.S. § 131E-17 [G.S. § 105-153.5(b)(1)]. The Department of Revenue takes the position that interest on United States obligations is deductible only if the obligation is a direct obligation of the United States or its possessions. Interest on obligations that are merely backed or guaranteed by the United States Government does not qualify for the deduction. The following items may not be deducted: (a) distributions that represent gains from the sale or other disposition of government obligations; (b) interest paid in connection with repurchase agreements issued by banks and savings and loan associations; or (3) any portion of a distribution from an individual retirement account (IRA) *See 2009-2010 Individual Income Tax Rules and Bulletins* § III.3.a.

• *Deduction of gain on obligations issued before July 1, 1995*

A taxpayer may deduct gain from the disposition of obligations issued before July 1, 1995 if the North Carolina law under which the obligations were issued specifically exempts the gain from tax [G.S. § 105-153.5(b)(2); *2009-2010 Individual Income Tax Rules and Bulletins* § III.3.c].

• *Deduction of taxable portion of Social Security benefits*

A taxpayer may deduct Social Security benefits received under Title II of the Social Security Act and amounts received from retirement annuities or pensions received under the Railroad Retirement Act of 1937 [G.S. § 105-153.5(b)(3); *2009-2010 Individual Income Tax Bulletins,* § III.3.d].

• *Deduction of tax refunds*

A taxpayer may deduct refunds of state, local, and foreign income taxes [G.S. § 105-153.5(b)(4)].

• *Deduction of certain government retirement plan payments*

A taxpayer may deduct amounts received during the taxable year from one or more federal, state or local government retirement plans to the extent the amounts are exempt from tax pursuant to a court order in settlement of any of the following cases: (1) *Bailey v. State,* 92 CVS 10221, 94 CVS 6904, 95 CVS 6625, 95 CVS 8230; (2) *Emory v. State,* 98 CVS 0738; or (3) *Patton v. State,* 95 CVS 0436 [G.S. § 105-153.5(b)(5)]. The settlements reached in these cases generally prohibit the State from taxing government retirement benefits if the retiree was vested in the retirement system as of August 12, 1989. Under most government retirement systems, a person was vested as of August 12, 1989 if he had at least five years of creditable service as of such date. *See generally 2009-2010 Individual Income Tax Rules and Bulletins* § IV. For the treatment of rollover distributions to or from a tax qualified Bailey retirement account, *see* Directives PD-03-1, PD-04-1 and PD-14-1.

• *Deduction of certain income by members of Indian tribes*

A taxpayer may deduct income that is (1) earned or received by an enrolled member of a federally recognized Indian tribe and (2) derived from activities on a federally recognized Indian reservation while the member resides on the reservation.

Income from intangibles having a situs on the reservation and retirement income associated with activities on the reservation are considered income derived from activities on the reservation [G.S. § 105-153.5(b)(6)].

• *Deduction of excess of state basis over federal basis*

A taxpayer may deduct the amount by which the North Carolina tax basis of property disposed of during the taxable year exceeds the property's federal tax basis [G.S. § 105-153.5(b)(7)].

• *Deduction related to federal decoupling adjustments*

A taxpayer may deduct the amount allowed under G.S. § 105-153.6 resulting from an add-back of federal accelerated depreciation and expensing deductions when the State decouples from these federal provisions [G.S. § 105-153.5(b)(8)]. These adjustments are discussed at ¶ 203.

• *Deduction for eugenics compensation payments*

Effective for taxable years beginning on or after January 1, 2015 and before January 1, 2016, a taxpayer may deduct an amount paid to the taxpayer during the taxable year from the Eugenics Sterilization Compensation Fund as compensation to a qualified recipient under the Eugenics Asexualization and Sterilization Compensation Program [G.S. § 105-153.5(b)(9)].

• *Deduction related to federal COD income deferral*

Under Code § 108(i)(1), a taxpayer that realized cancellation of indebtedness (COD) income by reacquiring its own debt instrument in 2009 or 2010 may defer recognition of the income for four years (for 2010 reacquisitions) or five years (for 2009 reacquisitions) and then recognize the income ratably over a five year period. North Carolina did not conform to these deferrals and required the deferred amounts to be added back to federal adjusted gross income in computing North Carolina taxable income. As a result, taxpayers recognizing the COD income for federal purposes beginning in 2014 may deduct the federal inclusions in computing North Carolina taxable income [G.S. § 105-153.5(b)(10); *see* S.L. 2016-5, § 2.1.(b)].

• *Deduction related to federal credit in lieu of deduction*

If a taxpayer's federal ordinary and necessary business expense deductions are reduced because the taxpayer claimed a federal credit with respect to an expense in lieu of a deduction, the taxpayer may deduct the expense in computing North Carolina taxable income as long as North Carolina does not allow a similar credit [G.S. § 105-153.5(b)(11); *see* S.L. 2016-5, § 2.1.(c)].

• *Deduction for personal education savings account deposits*

Effective for taxable years beginning on or after January 1, 2018, a taxpayer may deduct the amount deposited during the taxable year in a personal education savings account established under North Carolina's Personal Education Savings Account Program to hold scholarship funds awarded by the State Education Assistance Authority [G.S. § 105-153.5(b)(12)].

• *Deduction for Qualified Opportunity Zone inclusions*

A taxpayer may deduct the amount of deferred Qualified Opportunity Zone gains included in federal gross income to the extent such amount was previously required to be added back in computing North Carolina taxable income [G.S. § 105-153.5 (c2) (6)].

¶202

• *Deduction for hurricane relief payments*

A taxpayer may deduct amounts received during the year (other than in payment for goods or services) from the State Emergency Response and Disaster Relief Reserve Fund for hurricane relief or assistance to the extent included in federal taxable income [G.S. § 105-153.5(b)(13)].

• *Deduction for economic incentives*

A taxpayer may deduct amounts received as economic incentives under the state's Jobs Development Investment Grant or Job Maintenance and Capital Development Fund programs [G.S. § 105-153.5(b)(14)].

• *Add-back for interest on obligations of states other than North Carolina*

A taxpayer must add back interest on the obligations of states other than North Carolina, their political subdivisions, and agencies of those states and their political subdivisions [G.S. § 105-153.5(c)(1)]. This includes that portion of an exempt interest dividend from a regulated investment company (mutual fund) that represents interest on direct obligations of states other than North Carolina. *2009-2010 Individual Income Tax Rules and Bulletins* § III.2.a.

• *Add-back related to S corporation built-in gains tax*

For federal income tax purposes, certain S corporations are subject to an entity-level tax on built-in gains. This corporate level tax reduces the amount of S corporation income passed-through to the S corporation's shareholders. Because North Carolina does not subject S corporations to these entity-level taxes, an individual taxpayer must add back an amount equal to the amount by which the taxpayer's share of the S corporation's income was reduced because of the built-in gains tax [G.S. § 105-153.5(c)(2)].

• *Add-back for excess federal basis over state basis*

A taxpayer must add back the amount by which the federal tax basis of property disposed of during the taxable year exceeds the property's North Carolina tax basis [G.S. § 105-153.5(c)(3)].

• *Add-back of unabsorbed federal NOL carryover*

A taxpayer must add back the amount of any federal NOL carryover to the current year that is not absorbed in the current year but carried forward to future years [G.S. § 105-153.5(c)(6); *see* S.L. 2016-5, § 2.2.(a)].

• *Add-back for non-qualified 529 plan withdrawals*

A taxpayer must add back the amount of any prior year deductions for contributions to the state's 529 plan to the extent such amounts were withdrawn from the plan and not used for educational expenses unless the withdrawal was not subject to the additional tax under Code Section 529(c)(6) (because, e.g., the non-qualified use was due to the beneficiary's death or disability) or the withdrawal was rolled over to an ABLE account [G.S. § 105-153.5(c)(7)].

• *Add-back for Qualified Opportunity Zone deferrals and exclusions*

A taxpayer must add back the amount of any gains deferred or excluded from federal gross income because reinvested in Qualified Opportunity Zones [G.S. §§ 105-153.5(c2)(5) and (7)].

• *Add-back for discharge of indebtness income exclusions*

For taxable years 2014, 2015, 2016 and 2017 a taxpayer must add-back any amount excluded under Code § 108 with respect to the discharge of qualified principal residence indebtedness (provided that if the taxpayer is insolvent the amount required to be added back is limited to the amount of the federal exclusion in excess of the amount by which the taxpayer is insolvent) [G.S. § 105-153.5(c2)1].

• *Add-back for qualified charitable distribution exclusions*

For taxable years 2014, 2015, 2016, 2017 and 2018, a taxpayer must add-back any amount excluded under Code § 408(d)(8) with respect to a qualified charitable distribution from an individual retirement plan by a person who has reached age 70^1/$_2$. [G.S. § 105-153.5(c2)(3)].

• *Add-back for qualified tuition deduction*

For taxable years 2014, 2015, 2016 and 2017, a taxpayer must add-back any amount deducted under Code § 222 with respect to qualified tuition and related expenses [G.S. 105-153.5(c2)].

• *Add-back related to federal decoupling adjustment*

A taxpayer must add back the amount required under G.S. § 105-153.6 when the State decouples from federal accelerated depreciation and expensing [G.S. § 105-153.5(c)(5)]. These adjustments are discussed at ¶ 203.

¶203 Federal Decoupling Adjustments

• *Special accelerated depreciation*

A taxpayer who takes a federal special depreciation deduction under Code § 168(k) (relating to bonus depreciation for property placed in service between 2008 and 2013) or Code § 168(n) (relating to additional depreciation for certain disaster assistance property) must add back 85% of those special depreciation deductions to federal taxable income (for taxable years before 2012) or federal adjusted gross income (for taxable years after 2011) in determining North Carolina taxable income. The taxpayer is then allowed to deduct 20% of the add-back in each of the first five years following the year of the add-back [G.S. § 105-153.6(a)].

A taxpayer who placed property in service in the 2009 taxable year and whose North Carolina taxable income reflected a special accelerated depreciation deduction for such property under Code § 168(k) was required to add back 85% of the federal deduction in computing North Carolina taxable income for the 2010 taxable year. Such a taxpayer may deduct the add-back in five annual 20% installments commencing in the 2011 taxable year [G.S. § 105-153.6(b)].

• *Expensing elections*

A taxpayer who places in service section 179 property (*i.e.*, property eligible for the federal expensing election under Code § 179) during a taxable year must add-back 85% of the amount by which the federal expensing deductions under Code § 179 exceeded the dollar and investment limitation for that year. For taxable years begin-ning in or after 2013, the dollar limitation is $25,000 and the investment limitation is $200,000.

The taxpayer may deduct 20% of the add-back in each of the first five taxable years following the year of the add-back [G.S. § 105-153.6(c)].

- *Asset basis*

The federal decoupling adjustments for special accelerated depreciation and expensing do not create a difference in the basis of the assets depreciated or expensed for federal and state tax purposes, except in the case of an actual or deemed transfer of an asset on or after January 1, 2013 where the transferee takes a carryover basis for federal tax purposes. In that case, the transferee must add any remaining deductions related to the special accelerated depreciation add-back to the basis of the asset for state tax purposes and depreciate the adjusted basis over the asset's remaining life. The transferor (and any owner in the transferor) is not allowed any remaining special accelerated depreciation deductions with respect to the transferred asset. Each trans-feror (and each owner in the transferor) must certify in writing to the transferee that the transferor (and any owner of the transferor) will not take any remaining bonus depreciation deductions associated with the transferred asset [G.S. § 105-153.6(d) and (e)]. A "transferor" for this purpose is an individual, a partnership, corporation, S corporation, limited liability company or estate or trust that does not fully distribute income to its beneficiaries, and an "owner in a transferor" is a partner, shareholder, member or beneficiary that is subject to income tax as an individual, estate or trust [G.S. § 105-153.6(h)].

For carryover basis transfers before January 1, 2013, the transferor and transferee may elect to make the basis adjustment described above on the transferee's 2013 tax return to the extent the transferor (and any owner in the transferor) has not taken the special accelerated depreciation deductions on a prior return and provided each transferor (or owner in the transferor) certifies in writing to the transferee that the transferor (or owner in the transferor) will not take any remaining deductions with respect to the add-back attributable to the transferred assets for the tax years beginning on or after January 1, 2013. The amount of the transferee's basis adjust-ment may not exceed the total remaining bonus depreciation deductions forfeited by the transferor (and any owner in the transferor). If the asset has been disposed of or has no remaining useful life on the transferee's books, the transferee may claim any remaining bonus depreciation deductions on its 2013 return [G.S. § 105-153.6(f)].

Where these transferor basis adjustments have been made, adjusted gross in-come must be adjusted to account for any difference in the amount of depreciation, amortization, or gains or losses applicable to the property that has been depreciated or amortized by use of a different basis or rate for State income tax purposes than used for federal purposes [G.S. § 105-153.6(g)].

¶204 Nonresidents and Part-Year Residents

Nonresidents and part-year residents must prorate their federal taxable income to determine the portion that is taxable in North Carolina.

- *Nonresidents*

North Carolina taxable income for nonresidents means the taxpayer's federal adjusted gross income with North Carolina adjustments multiplied by an apportion-ment fraction. The apportionment fraction for nonresidents is the amount of gross income with North Carolina adjustments derived from North Carolina sources and attributable to the ownership of any interest in real or tangible personal property in North Carolina; the conduct of a business, trade or occupation within the state, or gambling activities within the state divided by the taxpayer's gross income with North Carolina adjustments (see ¶202 and ¶203) [G.S. §105-153.4(b)]. "Gross income" for this purpose is defined by reference to Code §61 [G.S. §105-153.3(6)].

- *Part-year residents*

A part-year resident is an individual who resided in North Carolina for only part of the taxable year, having moved into or out of North Carolina during the year. The North Carolina taxable income of a part-year resident is determined by multiplying federal adjusted gross income with North Carolina adjustments by an apportionment fraction. The apportionment fraction is gross income with North Carolina adjustments derived from all sources during the period of residency divided by gross income with North Carolina adjustments [G.S. §105-153.4(c)]. Federal gross income for this purpose is *total income* reported on the federal return. "Gross income" for this purpose is defined by reference to Code §61 [G.S. §105-153.3(6)].

- *Nonresident spouses*

An individual who files a joint federal return with a spouse but cannot qualify to file a joint North Carolina return because the spouse is a nonresident and had no North Carolina taxable income may file the State return as either married filing jointly or married filing separately. However, once the individual files a joint return, they cannot choose to file as married filing separately for that tax year after the due date of the return. An individual who files a joint federal income tax return and chooses to file a separate State return must calculate the individual's federal taxable income on a federal income tax form as a married person filing a separate federal income tax return and attach it to the individual's North Carolina return to show how the separate federal taxable income was determined. The individual filing the separate federal return must report only the individual's income, exemptions, and deductions [17 NCAC 6B.3904(b)].

Alternative Calculation

In lieu of making the calculation on a federal form, a taxpayer may submit a schedule showing the computation of taxpayer's separate federal taxable income. A taxpayer who submits a schedule must attach a copy of pages 1 and 2 of the joint federal return if the federal return reflects and address outside North Carolina [17 NCAC 6B.3904(b)].

- *S corporations and partnerships*

Nonresidents and part-year residents who are shareholders in an S corporation or partners in a partnership must apportion their income from those entities [G.S. §105-153.4(d)]. This is explained in Chapter 6.

- *Professional athletes*

The North Carolina-source income of a nonresident individual who is a member of a professional athletic team is determined by multiplying the individual's total compensation for services rendered as a member of a professional athletic team during the taxable year multiplied by an apportionment fraction. The apportionment fraction is the number of duty days spent in North Carolina rendering services for the team in any manner during the taxable year divided by the total number of duty days

¶204

spent both within and without North Carolina during the taxable year [17 NCAC 6B.3905(a)(1)]. For definition of these terms, see 17 NCAC 6B.3905(a)(3).

Teams employing a nonresident athlete must withhold 7.75% of the athlete's North Carolina-source income with no withholding allowances [17 NCAC 6B.3905(b)]. If a team properly withholds and the athlete has no other North Carolina income, the nonresident athlete is not required to file a North Carolina return. In order to get a refund, however, a return must be filed. Withholding requirements for resident team members are the same as for other resident individuals (see Chapter 5).

INDIVIDUAL INCOME TAX

CHAPTER 3

WITHHOLDING AND ESTIMATED TAX PAYMENTS

¶301 In General

• *General requirement to withhold*

Employers and others must withhold State income tax from salaries and wages of all North Carolina residents (whether for services performed inside or outside North Carolina) and nonresidents and Individual Taxpayer Identification Number (ITIN) holders who perform services for compensation in North Carolina. The statutory rules governing withholding are in Article 4A of Chapter 105 of the North Carolina General Statutes [§§ 105-163.1—105-163.24]. Terms used in this chapter are defined below. Payers of amounts subject to withholding must remit the amount of State income held to the Department. These requirements are explained in the booklet, *Income Tax Withholding Tables and Instructions for Employers* (Form NC-30), which is available from the Department of Revenue.

• *Amount to be withheld*

For employees, the amount to be withheld must approximate the employee's North Carolina individual income tax liability [G.S. § 105-163.2(a)]. Withholding of income tax is also required from non-wage compensation paid to nonresidents for personal services performed in North Carolina. See ¶304 for details on withholding from nonresidents' non-wage compensation. The amount of State income tax withheld by an employer is considered held in trust until it is paid to the Department of Revenue [G.S. § 105-163.2(a)]. A pension payer required to withhold federal taxes under IRC § 3505 is required to withhold State income taxes. An employer who pays non-wage compensation of more than $1,500 during the calendar year to a nonresident contractor for personal services performed in North Carolina must withhold NC income tax at the rate of 4% from this non-wage compensation. See discussion at ¶304.

• *Definition of terms*

For purposes of Article 4A of Chapter 105 of the North Carolina General Statutes, the following definitions apply [G.S. § 105-163.1]:

(1) *Compensation:* Consideration a payer pays a payee.

(2) *Dependent:* An individual for whom a dependency exemption can be claimed under the Internal Revenue Code.

(3) *Employee:* An individual, whether a resident or a nonresident of North Carolina, who performs services in North Carolina for wages or an individual who is a resident of North Carolina and performs services outside North Carolina for wages. The term includes an ordained or licensed member of the clergy who elects to be considered an employee under G.S. § 105-163.1A, an officer of a corporation, and an elected public official.

(4) *Employer:* A person for whom an individual performs services for wages. In applying the requirements to withhold income taxes from wages and pay the withheld taxes, the term includes the following persons:

(a) One who controls the payment of wages to an individual for services performed for another.

(b) One who pays wages on behalf of a person who is not engaged in trade or business in North Carolina.

(c) One who pays wages on behalf of a unit of government that is not located in North Carolina.

(d) One who pays wages for any other reason.

(5) *Individual:* A human being.

(6) *Individual Taxpayer Identification Number (ITIN):* A taxpayer identification number issued by the IRS to an individual who is required to have a U.S. taxpayer identification number but who does not have or is ineligible for a social security number.

(7) *ITIN contractor:* An ITIN holder who performs services in North Carolina for non-wage compensation.

(8) *ITIN holder:* A person whose taxpayer identification number is an ITIN (including applied-for and expired numbers).

(9) *Miscellaneous payroll period:* A payroll period other than a daily, weekly, biweekly, semimonthly, monthly, quarterly, semiannual, or annual payroll period.

(10) *Nonresident contractor:* Either one of the following:

(a) A nonresident individual who performs personal services in North Carolina for non-wage compensation in connection with a performance, an entertainment, an athletic event, a speech, or the creation of a film, radio, or television program.

(b) A nonresident entity that provides for the performance of such services in North Carolina.

(11) *Nonresident entity:* Any of the following:

¶301

(a) A foreign limited liability company, defined using the definition of "foreign LLC" in G.S. § 57D-1-03, that has not obtained a certificate of authority from the Secretary of State pursuant to Article 7 of Chapter 57D of the General Statutes.

(b) A foreign limited partnership as defined in G.S. § 59-102 or a general partnership formed under the laws of any jurisdiction other than North Carolina, unless the partnership maintains a permanent place of business in North Carolina for compensation.

(c) A foreign corporation, as defined in G.S. § 55-1-40, that has not obtained a certificate of authority from the Secretary of State pursuant to Article 15 of Chapter 55 of the General Statutes.

(12) *Pass-through entity:* An entity or business, including a limited partnership, a joint venture, a subchapter S corporation, or a limited liability company, all of which is treated as owned by individuals or other entities under the federal tax laws and in which the owners report their share of the income, losses, and credits from the entity or business on their income tax returns filed with this State. For the purpose of this section, an owner of a pass-through entity is an individual or entity who is treated as an owner under the federal tax laws [G.S. §§ 105-163.1(9), 105-228.90(b)(4d)].

(13) *Payee:* (1) a nonresident contractor, (2) an ITIN contractor, (3) a person who performs services in North Carolina for compensation and who either fails to provide the payer with a taxpayer identification number, or provides the payer with a number that the Secretary has informed the payer is invalid.

(14) *Payer:* A person who, in the course of a trade or business, pays compensation to a nonresident individual or a nonresident entity compensation for personal services performed in North Carolina or an ITIN holder who is a contractor and not an employee for services performed in North Carolina.

(15) *Payroll period:* A period for which an employer ordinarily pays wages to an employee of the employer.

(16) *Pension payer:* A payor or a plan administrator with respect to a pension payment under IRC § 3505.

(17) *Pension payment:* A periodic payment or a nonperiodic distribution as those terms are defined in IRC § 3505.

(18) *Taxable year:* Defined in IRC § 441(b).

(19) *Taxpayer identification number (TIN):* An identification number issued by the Social Security Administration or the IRS other than TINs for pending U.S. adoptions and preparer TINs.

(20) *Wages:* The term has the same meaning as in Code section 3401.

(21) *Withholding agent:* An employer or a payer.

¶ 302 Employers

• *Definition of employer*

An employer is any person or organization for whom an individual performs any service as an employee (see ¶ 303). The term includes federal, state, and local government agencies as well as religious, charitable, educational, and other nonprofit organizations even though they may be exempt for other tax purposes [G.S. § 105-163.1(5); *2009—2010 Individual Income Tax Bulletins,* § XVII:10].

Withholding Does Not Create Nexus

A nonresident employer's act in compliance with North Carolina withholding requirements does not in itself constitute evidence that the nonresident is doing business in North Carolina [G.S. § 105-163.4]; *2009—2010 Individual Income Tax Bulletins,* § XVII:10.]

• *Liability of withholding agents*

A withholding agent (see definition at ¶ 301) who withholds the proper amount of taxes and remits the withheld amount to the Department of Revenue is not liable to any person for the amount paid. A withholding agent who fails to withhold the proper amount of taxes or remit the amount withheld to the Department is liable for the amount of tax not withheld or not remitted and is subject to penalties [G.S. § 105-163.8].

• *Withholding identification numbers*

New employers required to withhold North Carolina individual income tax must complete and file with the Department of Revenue a Registration Application for Withholding Identification Number (Form NC-BR). This form is also used to apply for a sales and use tax number. The employer will be assigned a unique withholding identification number that should be used on all reports and correspondence about withholding. Employers *may not* use the number of another employer from whom they acquired a business or their federal identification numbers [NC-30, Income Tax Withholding Tables and Instructions for Employers]. Each employer should have *only one* withholding identification number. Employers who operate distinct businesses and maintain completely separate payrolls should register each and file separate reports for each business, including separate wage and tax statements at the end of the year. However, if an employer has several operations that are treated together as one entity, the employer may file a single report for total payroll.

Each employer corporation is required to apply for a withholding identification number, and each must maintain separate records. Changing a proprietorship or partnership to a corporation requires a new withholding identification number, but a new withholding identification number usually is not required merely to change a trade name or show partial changes of ownership in a partnership (*e.g.,* adding or removing the name of a partner). Instead, the details and date of such changes should be reported to the Department of Revenue by letter.

Some employees are exempt from withholding but may enter into a voluntary withholding agreement with their employers. These are discussed at ¶ 303. Methods of withholding are discussed at ¶ 307. Withholding returns and payment of withheld tax are discussed at ¶ 308.

• *Employee withholding allowance certificates—employer's responsibilities*

New employees must furnish their employers with withholding allowance certificates (Form NC-4). See discussion at ¶ 303. An employer is not required to ascertain whether or not the total amount of allowances is greater than the total number to which the employee is entitled. If, however, the employer has reason to believe that the employee is claiming too many allowances, the employer is requested to notify the Department of Revenue immediately. The employer must withhold on the basis of the certificate until written notice is received from the Department that the certificate is defective. As part of the written notice, the Department will advise the employer to ignore the allowance certificate filed and to withhold on a number specified [17 NCAC 6C.0126(d)]. The employer must promptly furnish the employee a copy of the written notice [17 NCAC 6C.0126(e)].

An employer is required to submit copies of any withholding allowance certificates on which an employee claims more than 10 withholding allowances or claims exemption from withholding and the employee's wages would normally exceed $200 [17 NCAC 6C.0126(a)]. If an employee claims total exemption from withholding and does not complete a new certificate, the employer must withhold on the basis of a single individual with zero withholding allowances [17 NCAC 6C.0126(i)].

¶303 Employees

• *Who are employees?*

For North Carolina individual income tax withholding purposes, an employee is either a resident individual legally domiciled in North Carolina who performs services within or outside North Carolina for wages or a nonresident of North Carolina who performs services within North Carolina for wages. To prevent double withholding and to anticipate any tax credits allowable to a North Carolina resident, withholding of North Carolina tax is not required from wages paid for services performed in another state if that state requires withholding. This relief from double withholding does not, however, relieve a resident taxpayer of the obligation to file a North Carolina individual income tax return and pay any balance due after credits. However, all wages received by a nonresident for services performed in North Carolina are subject to North Carolina withholding. Any relief from double withholding must be granted by the taxpayer's state of residence [17 NCAC 6C.0107].

• *Employee-employer relationship*

Anyone who performs services subject to the will and control of an employer, both as to what shall be done and how it shall be done, is an employee. An employer-employee relationship exists when the person for whom the services are performed *has the right* to control and direct the individual performing the services. It is irrelevant that the employer may not actually control and direct the manner in which the services are performed; if the employer has the right to do so, and employee-employer relationship exists and the employee's wages are subject to withholding. It does not matter that the employee is called by some name other than employee (*e.g.*, partner, agent, independent contractor); if the employer has the right to control and direct the individual performing the services, the individual is an employee for withholding purposes. It also does not matter whether the individual works full-time or part-time or how payments are measured, paid, or what they are called.

Lawyers, physicians, contractors, and others who follow an independent trade, business, or profession in which they offer their services to the public generally are not employees. If an individual is subject to the control and direction of another *only* as to the results of his work and not as to the methods of accomplishing the results, the individual is an independent contractor, not an employee [17 NCAC 6C.0108].

• *Special situations*

Ministers: An ordained or licensed person of the clergy who performs services for a church of any religious denomination may file an election with the Department and the church he or she serves to be considered an employee of the church instead of self-employed. Unless a clergy person files an election, his or her compensation is not subject to withholding [G.S. § 105-163.1A].

Common carriers: The Amtrak Reauthorization and Improvement Act of 1990 provides that the compensation paid to an employee of an interstate railroad subject to the jurisdiction of the Surface Transportation Board (STB) is subject to income tax or income tax withholding *only* in the state of the employee's residence when the employee regularly performs assigned duties in more than one state. The Act also prohibits the taxation of compensation paid by an interstate motor carrier subject to the jurisdiction of the STB or to an employee of a private motor carrier performing services in two or more states except by the state of the employee's residence. Therefore, compensation paid to nonresident employees of these common carriers for services performed in North Carolina is not subject to the North Carolina individual income tax or income tax withholding.

Under the Federal Aviation Act (49 USCS § 40116), a nonresident airline employee rendering service on an aircraft is not liable for North Carolina individual income tax unless the employee's scheduled flight time in North Carolina is more than 50% of his or her total scheduled flight time during the calendar year. If the employee's flight logs show that more than 50% of the scheduled flight time is in North Carolina, the amount of North Carolina reportable income is based on the percentage that North Carolina flight time is to total flight time for the year [*2009— 2010 Individual Income Tax Bulletins*, § XVII:14].

Federal employees: Under an agreement with North Carolina, federal agencies withhold North Carolina income tax from the military pay of members of the Armed Forces designated as legal residents of North Carolina and from the pay of civilian federal employees whose regular place of employment is in North Carolina.

Seamen: The Vessel Worker Tax Fairness Act [46 U.S.C. 11108] prohibits withholding of state income tax from the wages of a seaman on a vessel engaged in foreign, coastwide, intercoastal, interstate, or noncontiguous trade. Vessels engaged in other activity do not come under the restriction, but any seaman who is employed in coastwide trade between ports in North Carolina may have tax withheld if it is pursuant to a voluntary agreement between the seaman and his employer [17 NCAC 6C.0112(a)].

With respect to income obtained while (1) engaged as a licensed pilot on a vessel performing duties in more than one state or (2) performing regularly assigned duties as a master, officer, or crewman on a vessel operating in the navigable waters of more than one state, an individual is subject to income tax only in the state and political subdivision in which the individual resides [17 NCAC 6C.0112(b)].

¶303

Exemption from Withholding Does Not Necessarily Mean Exemption from Estimated Tax

Seamen and fishing boat crewmen exempt from withholding under these rules should determine whether they meet the requirements for making payments of estimated income tax [17 NCAC 6C.0112(b)].

Professional athletes: Professional athletic teams must withhold income tax from the North Carolina source income of a nonresident member of the team at the rate of 7.75% of the income with no allowance for any withholding exemption. See discussion at ¶204. Taxes are withheld from the income of a resident member of the team in the same way taxes are withheld from other residents.

Nonresident members of professional athletic teams are not required to file a North Carolina individual income tax return if the only North Carolina source income is the compensation received for services rendered as a member of the team and the team has met the withholding requirements. See ¶308. Individuals are liable for any additional tax, penalty, or interest due if their team does not properly determine his/her North Carolina source income or properly withhold tax from that income [*2009—2010 Individual Income Tax Bulletins,* §XVII:18].

Domestic employees: Employers are not required to withhold State income tax from the wages of domestic employees. However, the employer and employee may enter into a voluntary agreement to withhold. The amount to withhold is based on the employee information shown on the employee's withholding allowance certificate (Form NC-4). Employers may wish to contact the Division of Employment Security regarding any employment insurance liability [*2009—2010 Individual Income Tax Bulletins,* §XVII:19].

Farm labor: Compensation paid by a farmer for services performed on the farmer's farm in producing or harvesting agricultural products or in transporting the agricultural products to market is subject to North Carolina withholding *if* the compensation is subject to federal withholding. Generally, wages paid to agricultural workers are subject to federal income tax withholding if the worker is paid $150 or more during the year or the employer pays $2,500 or more to all agricultural workers during the year [*2009—2010 Individual Income Tax Bulletins,* §XVII:20].

North Carolina state lottery winnings: Winnings of $600 or more paid by the North Carolina State Lottery Commission are subject to State withholding at the rate of 7% [*2009—2010 Individual Income Tax Bulletins,* §XVII:21].

• *Employee's withholding allowance certificate*

New employees, before beginning employment, must fill out and sign withholding allowance certificates and give them to their employers. North Carolina Withholding allowance certificates are filed on Form NC-4. Withholding allowance certificates become effective upon the first payment of wages and remain in effect until a new one is furnished [G.S. §105-163.5(c)]. If an employee fails to furnish a withholding allowance certificate, the employer must withhold tax as if the employee is single with zero allowances [G.S. §105-163.5(b)]. An employee who works for two or more employers should claim all allowable allowances with only one employer and claim zero allowances with the other employer(s) [17 NCAC 6C.0126(h)]. See ¶302 for employer's responsibilities with respect to withholding allowances.

If an employee's allowances should decrease, requiring more tax to be withheld, the employee is required to furnish his employer with an amended certificate within 10 days after the change. If an employee's allowances increase, requiring less tax to be withheld, the employee may furnish his or her employer with an amended certificate at any time after the change occurs [G.S. § 105-163.5(d); *2009—2010 Individual Income Tax Bulletins*, § XVII:6]. An employee who claims total exemption from withholding must complete a new certificate by February 15 [17 NCAC 6C.0126(i)].

Federal/State Difference

Although State and federal definitions of dependent, single person, married, head of household, and qualifying widow(er) are the same, the number of allowances to which an individual is entitled will differ. Federal exemption certificates *are not acceptable* [*2009—2010 Individual Income Tax Bulletins*, § XVII:6].

• *Additional withholding allowances [17 NCAC 6C.0124]*

Additional withholding allowances may be claimed by taxpayers who expect to have allowable itemized deductions exceeding the standard deduction or allowable adjustments to income. For most taxpayers, one additional allowance may be claimed for each $2,500 that the itemized deductions are expected to exceed the standard deduction and for each $2,500 of adjustments reducing income. For taxpayers whose annual income equals or exceeds the applicable threshold for their filing status (see table below), an additional allowance may be claimed for each $2,000 that their itemized deductions are expected to exceed the standard deduction and for each $2,000 of adjustments reducing income. Employees who are entitled to a tax credit may claim one additional allowance for each $175 of tax credit, unless the employee's annual income equals or exceeds the applicable threshold for filing status (see table below). If an employee's annual income equals or exceeds the applicable threshold, the employee may claim an additional allowance of only $140 for each credit.

Filing Status	Applicable Threshold
Head of household	$80,000
Married	50,000
Single	60,000

¶304 Nonresident or ITIN Contractors

• *Generally*

Payers who, pay more than $1,500 during a calendar year to a payee are required to withhold North Carolina income tax at the rate of 4% from compensation paid to the payee [G.S. § 105-163.3(a); Directive PD-10-1 (January 13, 2010). See "Definition of terms" at ¶301. A payer required to withhold from a payee's compensation must pay the withheld taxes and report the withheld amount at the time and in the manner required for wage withholding [G.S. § 105-163.3(d)].

- *Exceptions to withholding [G.S. § 105-163.3; Tax Directive PD-10-1]*

Nonresident entities with certificates of authority: Tax is not required to be withheld from compensation paid to a nonresident entity if the entity is a corporation or a limited liability company that has obtained a certificate of authority from the Secretary of State. The payer must obtain from the entity and retain in its records the entity's identification number issued by the Secretary of State.

Nonprofit corporations: A nonprofit corporation that is exempt from North Carolina corporation income tax under G.S. § 105-130.11 is not subject to withholding. This includes any organization that is exempt from federal income tax under the Internal Revenue Code. The entity must provide documentation of its tax exemption to the payer (*e.g.,* a copy of the organization's federal determination letter of tax exemption; copy of a letter of tax exemption from the Department of Revenue).

Partnerships: If an entity is a partnership, no tax is required to be withheld if the partnership has a permanent place of business in North Carolina. The payer must obtain from the partnership and retain in its records the partnership's address and taxpayer identification number.

Clergy: Tax is not required to be withheld from personal services income paid to an individual who is an ordained or licensed member of the clergy.

Residents: Individuals who are North Carolina residents are exempt from the requirement of withholding on personal services income. Payers must obtain from any resident to whom they pay compensation for personal services the individual's address and social security number and retain this information in their records.

- *Threshold*

If, at the time payment is made, a payer does not believe that the total compensation to be paid to a contractor during the year will exceed $1,500, no withholding is required. If additional compensation paid later in the year causes total compensation for the year to exceed $1,500, the payer must withhold tax from the additional compensation, but is not required to withhold extra tax from the additional compensation to make up for the earlier compensation from which no tax was withheld [Tax Directive PD-98-3].

- *Payer registration*

A payer who withholds tax from personal services income who is not already registered with the Department of Revenue for wage withholding must register by completing Form NC-BR. A payer who withholds tax from compensation paid to nonresident or ITIN contractors and who also withholds from wages must file a return and pay the withholding from the nonresident or ITIN contractors with the wage withholding. The payment of tax withheld from the nonresident or ITIN contractor is due at the time the withholding from wages is due, and the payer is subject to penalties and interest on both types of withholding based on that due date. Separate quarterly payments of withholdings from payments made to nonresident or ITIN contractors is no longer permitted.

- *Overwithholding*

If a payer makes an error and withholds too much tax from a person's compensation (because the person was not a payee, the amount paid was not compensation, or the amount was otherwise excessive), the payer may refund the overwithholding to the payee if the refund is made before the end of the calendar year and before the payer furnishes the person the annual statement of tax withheld. The payer should not report the refund on the annual statement or remit the amount refunded to the Department. If the amount refunded has already been remitted, the payer must reduce the next payment of tax withheld from compensation paid to that person by the amount refunded, [IG.S. § 105-163.3(f)]. If no additional compensation is due to be paid to that contractor and the amount withheld in error has already been remitted, the payer cannot refund the tax withheld in error. The contractor must file an income tax return and claim credit for the tax withheld [*2009—2010 Individual Income Tax Bulletins*, § XVI:8].

¶305 Pension Payers

- *Generally*

A pension payer required to withhold federal taxes under IRC § 3405 on a pension payment to a North Carolina resident must deduct and withhold from the payment the State income taxes payable on the payment. If a payee has provided a North Carolina address to a pension payer, the payee is presumed to be a North Carolina resident, and the payer must withhold State tax unless the payee elects not to have tax withheld (see below). A pension payer for this purpose is a payor or a plan administrator with respect to a pension payment under IRC § 3405 [G.S. § 105-163.1(11a)]. A pension payment for this purpose is a periodic payment or a nonperiodic distribution as those terms are defined in IRC § 3405 [G.S. § 105-163.1(11b)]. Unless otherwise specified, the definitions, provisions, and requirements of IRC § 3405 with respect to withholding on pensions apply to North Carolina withholding on pensions [*Tax Directive PD-00-2*, July 20, 2000].

The person who is liable under IRC § 3405 for withholding federal taxes on the payment is also liable for withholding State taxes [G.S. § 105-163.2A(b)]. A pension payer that either fails to withhold tax when required to do so or to remit that tax that is withheld is liable for the tax [*Tax Directive PD-00-2*, July 20, 2000].

- *Amount of withholding*

In the case of a periodic payment, a pension payer must treat a pension payment paid to an individual as if it were an employer's payment of wages to an employee and withhold the amount that would be required to be withheld if the payment were a payment of wages by an employer to an employee for the appropriate payroll period. If the pension payer has more than one arrangement under which distributions may be made to an individual, each arrangement must be treated separately. Form NC-4P, Withholding Certificate for Pension or Annuity Payments, is used by recipients of pensions payments to report correct filing status, number of allowances, and any additional amount the recipient wants withheld from the pension payment or to elect not to have State income tax withheld. Taxpayers may use substitute forms for Form NC-4P *if* it contains all the provisions included on Form NC-4P [G.S. § 105-163.2A(b), (c); *Tax Directive PD-00-2*, July 20, 2002]. In the case of a nonperiodic distribution, as defined in IRC § 3405(e)(3), the amount to be withheld is 4% of the distribution [G.S. § 105-163.2A(c)].

• *Election of no withholding*

A recipient may elect not to have State taxes withheld on pension payments *to the extent permitted by IRC § 3405* [G.S. § 105-163.2A(d)]. Under IRC § 3405 a recipient of eligible rollover distributions does not have the option of electing not to have federal tax withheld. Therefore, a recipient of a pension payment that is an eligible rollover distribution does not have the option of electing not to have State tax withheld from the distribution. In the case of a periodic distribution, an election not to have tax withheld from a pension payment remains in effect until revoked by the recipient. In the case of a nonperiodic distribution, the election applies on a distribution-by-distribution basis unless it meets conditions prescribed by the Department for it to apply to subsequent nonperiodic distributions by the pension payer. An election is void if the recipient does not furnish a tax identification number to the payer or until the pension payer is notified by the Department that the tax identification number furnished by the recipient is incorrect. In the case of a void election, the payer must withhold on periodic payments as if the recipient were married claiming three allowances and on nonperiodic distributions at the rate of 4%.

• *Notification procedures*

A pension payer must notify recipients of the right to elect not to have taxes withheld [G.S. § 105-163.2A(d)]. The notice requirements for North Carolina purposes are the same as the federal notice requirements, which are provided in IRC § 3405(e)(10). Section D of Federal Regulation 35.3405-1 contains sample notices that may be modified for State purposes to satisfy the notice and election requirements for periodic payments and nonperiodic distributions. Under federal law, instead of notification that tax will be withheld unless the recipient chooses not to have tax withheld, pension payers may notify recipients whose annual payments are less than $5,400 that no federal tax will be withheld unless the recipient chooses to have federal withholding apply. This notice may be provided when making the first payment. The same provision applies for any purpose with respect to State withholding from recipients whose annual payments are less than $5,400 [*Tax Directive PD-00-2*, July 20, 2002].

• *Exemptions from withholding*

Payers are not required to withhold tax from the following pension payments [G.S. § 105-163.2A(e)]:

(1) A pension payment that is wages within the meaning of Article 4 of Chapter 105 of the General Statutes of North Carolina.

(2) Any part of a pension payment that meets *both* of the following conditions:

(a) It is not a distribution or payment from an individual retirement as defined in IRC §7701.

(b) The pension payer reasonably believes it is not taxable to the recipient under Article 4 of Chapter 105.

(3) A distribution described in IRC §404(k)(2), relating to dividends on corporate securities.

(4) A pension payment that consists only of securities of the recipient's employer corporation plus cash not in excess of $200 in lieu of securities of the employer corporation.

(5) Distributions of retirement benefits from North Carolina State and local government retirement systems and federal retirement systems identified as qualifying retirement systems under the terms of the *Bailey/Emory/Patton* settlement that are paid to retirees who were vested in the retirement system as of August 12, 1989.

¶306 Lottery Commission

The North Carolina State Lottery Commission is required to deduct and withhold state income taxes at the individual income tax rate in effect under G.S. §105-153.7 from the payment of winnings in an amount of $600 or more. The Commission must file a return, pay over the taxes withheld, and report the amount withheld as if it were an employer and as if the winnings were wages [G.S. §105-163.2B]. The Court of Appeals has rejected arguments that the legislation establishing the North Carolina lottery was not validly enacted because not read and passed on three separate days as required of revenue bills. See *Heatherly v. State*, 189 N.C. App. 213, 658 S.E.2d 11 (2008). On appeal, the North Carolina Supreme Court was evenly divided, with the result that the decision of the Court of Appeals was left undisturbed but without precedential value [*Heatherly v. State*, 363 N.C. 115, 678 S.E.2d 656 (2009)].

¶307 Methods of Withholding

• *Generally*

Income tax must be withheld according to tables prepared by the North Carolina Department of Revenue or by using an acceptable alternate method. In calculating an employee's anticipated income tax liability, the employer must allow for the additions the employee is required to make to federal adjusted gross income and the deductions and credits to which the employee is entitled. Two alternate methods are acceptable to the Department: the percentage method and the annualized method. Formula tables for both the percentage and annualized wages methods are contained in *Income Tax Withholding Tables and Instructions for Employers* (NC-30) issued by the Department of Revenue.

If one of the three approved methods would impose an unreasonable burden on an employer or produce substantially incorrect results, the Secretary may authorize or require an employer to use some other method to compute the amounts to be withheld. The authorized alternative method must reasonably approximate the predicted income tax liability of the affected employees. In addition, with the agreement of the employer and employee, the Secretary may authorize an employer to use an alternative method that results in withholding of a greater amount than otherwise required [G.S. §105-163.2(e)].

Withholding if no payroll period: If wages are paid for a period that is not a payroll period, the amount to be withheld shall be that applicable in the case of a miscellaneous payroll period containing a number of days, excluding Sundays and holidays, equal to the number of days in the period for which wages are paid [G.S. § 105-163.2(c)].

• *Supplemental wage payments*

Generally: Supplemental wage payments include items of compensation that are not regular (*e.g.,* bonuses, commissions, overtime pay). The method used to withhold tax from supplemental wage payments depends partly on whether tax has been withheld from regular wages [17 NCAC 6C.0117(a)].

Tax withheld on regular wages: If tax has been withheld on the regular wages and the supplemental amount is not paid in a single payment together with the wages, the employer may treat the supplemental wages as wholly separate from the regular wages and apply a flat rate of 6% to the supplemental wage payment without making any allowance for exemptions. Alternatively, the supplemental wages are added to the regular wages for the most recent payroll period. The income tax is figured as if the regular wages and supplemental wages constitute a single payment, and the tax already withheld from the regular is subtracted from this amount to arrive at the amount of withholding for the supplemental payment [17 NCAC 6C.0117(b)].

Tax not withheld on regular wages: If an employer has not withheld income tax from the employee's regular wages, the employer must add the supplemental wages to the employee's regular wages paid for the current or last preceding payroll period and withhold tax as though the supplemental wages and regular wages were one payment [17 NCAC 6C.0117(c)].

Tips treated as supplemental wages: An employer withholds income tax on tips from wages or from funds an employee makes available. If an employee receives regular wages and reports tips, the employer figures the amount of withholding as if the tips were supplemental wages. If the employer has not withheld tax from the regular wages, the employer adds the tips to the regular wages and withholds income tax on the total. If the employer withheld income tax from the regular wages, the employer can withhold on tips as explained above [17 NCAC 6C.0117(d)].

Vacation pay: If an employer pays an employee vacation pay in addition to regular wages, the vacation pay is treated as supplemental wages [*Income Tax Withholding Tables and Instructions for Employers* (NC-30)].

¶308 Returns and Payment

• *Generally*

Each new employer who is required to withhold North Carolina income tax must complete and file with the Department an application for a withholding identification number. See ¶302.

North Carolina does not use a deposit system for income tax withheld similar to the federal system. Withheld taxes are paid quarterly, monthly, or semiweekly [G.S.

§ 105-163.6]. If the Secretary finds that collection of the amount of taxes required to be withheld is in jeopardy, the Secretary may make a jeopardy assessment (see ¶ 3209).

• *Electronic Filing*

The Department of Revenue allows withholding tax forms NC-5, Withholding Return, and NC-5P, Withholding Payment Voucher, to be filed electronically. Details on electronic filing of these returns can be found at <http://www.dornc.com/electronic/index.html>.

• *Adjustments*

Employers are liable to report and pay the correct amount of tax to the Department even if less than the correct amount was inadvertently deducted from employees. Employers who discover such an error must report and pay the correct amount of tax and recover the amount due the employee by deducting it from later payments or adjusting in any other way agreeable to both employer and employee. An employer who reported an incorrect amount of tax must amend the return. If an employer deducts too much tax from an employee's wage payment, the employer must report and pay to the Department the *actual amount withheld* unless the over-deducted amount is repaid to the employee or otherwise adjusted. Records to show that this has been done must be maintained by the employer [*Income Tax Withholding Tables and Instructions for Employers* (NC-30)].

Reports Required Even If No Tax Due

Employers who owe no taxes for a filing period must still file a return with zeros entered on the appropriate lines.

• *Quarterly returns*

Quarterly reports and payments are due by the last day of the month following the end of the calendar quarter [G.S. § 105-163.6(b)]. Quarterly payers use Form NC-5. Reports can be amended on Form NC-5X. Required annual reports are discussed below. Only employers who withhold an average of less than $250 per month may file quarterly returns [G.S. § 105-163.6(b)].

• *Monthly returns*

An employer who withholds an average of at least $250 but less than $2,000 from wages each month must file and pay withheld taxes on a monthly basis [G.S. § 105-163.6(c)].

Employers who withhold an average of at least $250 but less than $2,000 from wages each month must file a return and pay the withheld taxes on a monthly basis (Form NC-5). Monthly reports for January through November are due by the 15th day of the month following the end of the month covered by the return. Monthly reports for December are due by January 31 of the following year [G.S. § 105-163.6(c)]. Required annual reports are discussed below.

¶308

• *Semiweekly returns*

An employer who withholds an average of $2,000 or more of North Carolina income tax per month must file withholding tax reports and pay the tax withheld at the same time the employer is required to file the reports and pay the tax withheld on the same wages for federal income purposes. The due date for reporting and paying North Carolina income tax withheld is determined by the due date for depositing federal employment taxes (income tax withheld and FICA). Some employers are required to pay taxes by electronic funds transfer (discussed below).

Semiweekly payers must file North Carolina Quarterly Income Tax Withholding Return (Form North Carolina-5Q), which reconciles the tax paid for the quarter with the tax withheld for the quarter. The due dates for Form NC-5Q are the same as for the federal quarterly return (Federal Form 941), *i.e.*, on or before the last day of the month following the close of the quarter. An employer has 10 additional days to file the return if all required payments were made during the quarter and no additional tax is due [2009—2010 *Individual Income Tax Bulletins*, § XVIII:2]. Required annual reports are discussed below. Amended returns are filed on blank copies of Form NC-5Q. Required annual reports are discussed below.

• *Electronic funds transfer (EFT)*

Employers who remit an average of at least $20,000 per month must pay taxes by electronic funds transfer. The $20,000 threshold applies separately to each tax [G.S. § 105-241(b)]. Employers who are required to remit payments by EFT will be notified in writing at least sixty (60) days prior to the first month that EFT payment is due. Every 12 months the Department must determine whether, during the applicable period for that tax, the average amount of the taxpayer's required payments of the tax was at least $20,000 a month. If it was not, the Department must suspend the requirement that the taxpayer pay by EFT and give the taxpayer written notice that the requirement has been suspended [G.S. § 105-241(b)]. Voluntary participation is offered for all employers who are interested in remitting funds by electronic funds transfer. For questions concerning electronic funds transfer, contact the EFT Section at (919) 733-7307 [2009—2010 *Individual Income Tax Bulletins*, § XVIII:4].

• *Annual reports*

Employee wage and tax statements: Employers must furnish wage and tax statements (Form W-2) to employees [G.S. § 105-163.7]. Two copies must be furnished to the employee, and one copy must the furnished to the Department. The Internal Revenue Service supplies a six-part Form W-2 that will produce the required federal and North Carolina statements in one packet. Copies of the wage and tax statements must be filed with the employer's Annual Reconciliation of North Carolina Income Tax Withheld (Form NC-3).

Personal services income paid to nonresidents: A payer that withholds tax from compensation paid to a nonresident contractor must provide the nonresident contractor with a statement (Form NC-1099PS) showing the total compensation and the amount withheld during the calendar year on or before January 31 following the calendar year, or if the contractor requests the statement before then, within 45 days after the last payment of compensation to the contractor. Federal form 1900-MISC may be used in lieu of Form NC-1099PS [2009—2010 *Individual Income Tax Bulletins*, § XVI:6]. Form NC-1099PS must also be filed with the Department of Revenue.

Sales of real property by nonresidents: Sales of real property by nonresidents must be reported by the buyer on Form NC-1099NRS, reporting the seller's name, address, and social security number, or federal employer identification number; the location of the property; the closing date; and the gross sales price of the real property and its associated tangible personal property. Within 15 days of the closing date, the buyer must file one copy of the report with the Department of Revenue and also furnish a copy of the report to the seller. This requirement applies to individuals, fiduciaries, partnerships, corporations, or units of government buying real property located in North Carolina from a nonresident individual, partnership, estate, or trust [17 NCAC 6B.3804(c)].

Other 1099 Income

Other reports of 1099 information (interest, rents, premium, dividends, annuities, *etc.*) are not required to be reported to North Carolina *unless* the payments have not been reported to the Internal Revenue Service.

- *Responsible person liability*

Each responsible person in a business entity is personally liable for the principal amount of all income taxes required to be withheld from the wages of the entity's employees (see ¶3211).

¶309 Estimated Tax

- *Who must file*

An individual is required to pay estimated income tax if the tax shown due on the income tax return for the taxable year, reduced by the North Carolina tax withheld and allowable credits, is $1,000 or more without regard to the amount of income the individual has that is not subject to withholding [G.S. §105-163.15(f), (g); *2009—2010 Individual Income Tax Bulletins*, §XIX:2].

- *Due dates*

Estimated payments for calendar-year taxpayers are required to be paid in four installments, on the following dates [G.S. §105-163.15(c)]:

    (1) April 15 of the taxable year.

    (2) June 15 of the taxable year.

    (3) September 15 of the taxable year.

    (4) January 15 of the following taxable year.

If a taxpayer files a North Carolina individual income tax return (Form D-400) by January 31 of the following taxable year and pays the entire balance due, the January 15 payment does not have to be made [G.S. §105-163.15(h)]. When the due date for the estimated income tax payment falls on a Saturday, Sunday, or holiday, the payment is due on or before the next business day [*2009-2010 Individual Income Tax Bulletins*, §XX:6].

¶309

The due dates for fiscal-year taxpayers are the 15th day of the 4th, 6th, and 9th months of the fiscal year and the 1st month of the following fiscal year [G.S. § 105-163.15(j)].

• *Estimated income tax filing and payment*

Forms: The form for payment of estimated individual income tax (Form NC-40) is available from the Department of Revenue in the form of personalized payment vouchers or a four-part nonpersonalized payment form. Both types of forms include the necessary vouchers and instructions for making payments. An individual can also make estimated payments online at www.dornc.com [*2009—2010 Individual Income Tax Bulletins,* § XIX:1].

Taxpayers who do not file electronically, should use the correct estimated income tax form (Form NC-40) when remitting payments. Each form has been preprinted with the date that payment is due for calendar-year taxpayers. Fiscal-year taxpayers should change the calendar-year dates to the corresponding fiscal-year dates. If forms are preprinted with the taxpayer's name, address, and social security number, the taxpayer should make changes to the form because corrected forms will not be available until the following year. If a spouse's name is not indicated on the form, and the taxpayers wish to make a joint payment, the taxpayers should add the spouse's name and social security number on each of the forms.

Required installments: The required installment for any payment period is the lesser of (1) 22.5% of the tax shown on the current-year return or (2) 25% of the tax shown on the prior-year return *if* the prior-year return covered all 12 months of the year [17 NCAC 6D.0209(b)]. See "Safe harbors," below.

Married taxpayers: Married individuals can make joint payments of estimated income tax even if they are not living together, but they may not make a joint estimated income tax payment if they are separated under a decree of divorce or of separate maintenance. Also, they cannot file joint estimated income tax returns if either spouse is a nonresident alien or if either spouse has different tax years. The decision to make joint estimated income tax payments does not affect a couple's choice of filing a joint return or separate returns. If they make joint payments and then file separate returns, they may divide the estimated income tax payments between them [17 NCAC 6D.0102(d)].

• *Short periods*

A taxpayer filing a short period return because of a changed income year must make estimated income tax payments on the installment dates that fall within the short period and 15 days after the close of the short period that would have been due had the taxpayer not changed income year. Underpayment penalties for short periods are computed for the period of underpayment based on the tax shown due on the short period return and computed in the same manner as it would have been computed had the taxpayer not changed income year [17 NCAC 6D.0102].

• *Interest*

In the case of any underpayment of estimated tax by an individual, the Secretary must assess interest at the rate applicable to overpayments and assessments. (discussed at ¶3205) [G.S. § 105-163.15(a)]. Interest is computed separately for each payment period. Therefore, a taxpayer may owe interest for an early period even if that taxpayer later paid enough to make up the underpayment. If a taxpayer did not pay enough tax by the due date of each of the payment periods, he may owe interest even if the taxpayer is due a refund when the return is filed [*2007—2008 Individual Income Tax Bulletins,* § XX:1].

Interest Not Waivable

G.S. § 105-163.15 was amended in 2005 to reclassify additions for underpayments of estimated income tax as interest rather than penalties. The reclassification has the effect of making the additions nonwaivable and payable to the General Fund rather than to the Civil Penalty and Forfeiture Fund. See *N.C. School Bd. Ass'n. v. Moore*, 359 N.C. 474, 614 S.E.2d 504 (2005). However, interest may not be imposed with respect to 2014 underpayments resulting from changes to the standard and itemized deductions enacted by S.L. 2014-3, § 2.2 [S.L. 2015-6, § 2.9].

• *Safe harbors*

Interest on underpayments of estimated tax can be avoided if the taxpayer had no tax liability for the preceding year or if the total tax shown on the current year return less credits and amounts paid through withholding is less than $1,000 or the taxpayer makes payments of estimated income on each installment date for 25% of one of the safe harbor amounts discussed below [G.S. § 105-163.15(d), (e) and (f)].

(1) 90% of the tax (after tax credits) on the current year's return.

Example: Angela, a single taxpayer, has a final North Carolina individual income tax liability for the current year of $4,074. In order to avoid underpayment interest, Angela must have had made quarterly payments of at least $916.65 (90% of $4,074 divided by 4) to avoid underpayment interest under this safe harbor. If she wanted to, Angela could have paid her estimated income tax in one lump sum in the amount of at least $3,666.60 (90% of $4,074) on the due date for the first quarter of her taxable year.

(2) 100% of the tax on the preceding year's return (provided it was a taxable year of 12 months and the individual filed a return for that year).

(3) 90% of the tax determined by annualizing the income received during the year up to the month in which the installment is due. If a taxpayer's income varied during the taxable year (*e.g.*, taxpayer's business is seasonal), the taxpayer may be able to lower or eliminate the amount of the required installments by using the annualized income installment method [Form D-422A (Annualized Income Installment Worksheet)]. A taxpayer who uses the Annualized Income Installment Worksheet for any payment date must use it for all payment dates. The worksheet automatically selects the smaller of the annualized income installment or the regular installment increased by the amount saved by using the annualized income installment method in determining earlier installments. Taxpayers who were required to complete the Itemized Deductions Worksheet for federal income tax purposes must fill out the second page of Form D-422A.

Irrevocable Election

A taxpayer may elect to have an income tax refund applied to estimated income tax for the following year. For example, a taxpayer due a refund for taxable Year 1 may elect to have all or any portion of the refund applied to estimated income tax for Year 2. The

¶309

election is made on the return showing the refund, which must be filed by the last allowable date for making estimated tax payments for the following year [17 NCAC 6D.0102(c)]. This is an irrevocable election. Once a valid election is made, the taxpayer cannot revoke the election and have the amount refunded or applied in any other manner (*e.g.*, to offset any subsequent determined tax liability) [G.S. § 105-269.4; 17 NCAC 6D.0102(d)].

• Underpayments

An *underpayment* is the excess of the required installment (or, if lower, the annualized income installment) for a payment period over the portion of the amount paid by the due date that is not applied to an underpayment for an earlier payment period. Payments include income tax withheld and are considered payments of estimated income tax in equal installments on the required installment dates (usually four), unless the individual can prove otherwise. A payment of estimated tax is credited against unpaid installments in the order in which the installments are required to be paid [*2009—2010 Individual Income Tax Bulletins*, § XX:3].

Determining an underpayment: The required installment for any payment period is the lesser of (1) 22.5% of the tax shown on the current year return (90% ÷ 4) or (2) 25% of the tax shown on the prior-year return *if* the prior-year return covered all 12 months of the year. If the annualized income installment for any period is less than the required installment for the same period and the annualized income installment is used to determine the underpayment, add the difference between the annualized income installment and the required installment to the required installment for the next period. If the annualized income installment for the next period is used, add the difference between the annualized income installment for that period and the required installment (as increased) for that period to the required installment for the following payment period. There will be no underpayment for any payment period in which the estimated income tax payments, reduced by any amounts applied to underpayments in earlier periods, were paid by the due date for the period and were at least as much as the annualized income installment for the period [*2009—2010 Individual Income Tax Bulletins*, § XX:5].

Period of underpayment: The interest accrues with respect to the number of days that the installment was not paid. Start counting with the date *after* the due date and include the earlier of (1) the date of payment or (2) the due date of the current payment. If the 15th of the month is on a weekend, the payment is due on the next business day.

> **Example:** Alex forgot to make his first quarterly estimated income tax payment until May 8. If April 15 falls on a Saturday, Alex's period of underpayment is 21 days (from April 17 to May 9). Arlene forgot to make her second quarterly estimated income tax payment until July 8. If June 15 is a business day, Arlene's period of underpayment is 23 days (from June 15 to July 8).

If a payment of estimated tax is applied to an underpayment for an earlier period, but the payment is less than the underpayment, there will be more than one period of underpayment for the earlier period. The first period of underpayment for any payment period will be from the day after the due date for the payment period to the date of the first applied payment. Later periods of underpayment for that payment period will be from the day after the due date for the payment period to the date of the next applied payment. To determine interest for a payment period with more than one period of underpayment, compute interest separately for each of the periods of underpayment [*2009—2010 Individual Income Tax Bulletins,* § XX:6].

• *Overpayments*

An overpayment for any period occurs when the withholding and estimated income tax payments are more than the total of any underpayments for an earlier period plus the lesser of the required installment or the annualized income installment for the period. If there is an overpayment for a period, it should be carried to the next period and added to the withholding and estimated income tax paid for that later period to determine any underpayment or overpayment for that later period [*2009—2010 Individual Income Tax Bulletins,* § XX:4].

• *Farmers and fishermen*

An individual who is a farmer or fisherman for a taxable year is subject to the following provisions [G.S. § 105-163.15(i)]:

(1) *One installment:* The farmer or fisherman is required to make only one installment payment of tax for that taxable year. The installment is due on January 15 of the following year. The amount of the required installment payment is the lesser of:

(a) $66^2/3\%$ of the tax shown on the return for the taxable year, or, if no return is filed, $66^2/3\%$ of the tax for that year.

(b) 100% of the tax shown on the return of the individual for the preceding taxable year, if the preceding taxable year was a taxable year of 12 months and the individual filed a return for that year [G.S. § 105-163.15(i)(1)].

(2) *Exception:* If, on or before March 1 of the following taxable year, the taxpayer files a return for the taxable year and pays in full the amount payable, no addition to tax is imposed with respect to any underpayment of the required installment for the taxable year [G.S. § 105-163.15(i)(2)].

(3) *Eligibility:* An individual is a farmer or fisherman for any taxable year if the individual's gross income from farming or fishing (including oyster farming) for the taxable year is at least $66^2/3\%$ of the total gross income from all sources for the taxable year, or the individual's gross income from farming or fishing (including oyster farming) shown on the individual's return for the preceding is at least $66^2/3\%$ of the total gross income from all sources shown on the return [G.S. § 105-163.15(i)(3)].

INDIVIDUAL INCOME TAX

CHAPTER 4

CREDITS AGAINST TAX

¶401 Tax Credits—In General

North Carolina has repealed most of its income tax credits. The only remaining income tax credits available to individuals are the credit for withheld income taxes, the credit for taxes paid to other states or countries, the credit for dependent children and the historic rehabilitation tax credits. These credits are discussed below. Also discussed below are credits allowed under prior law. See also the tax credit chart at ¶ 36.

¶402 Credit for Withholding and Estimated Income Tax for Individuals

North Carolina allows credits against North Carolina individual income tax for amounts withheld from wages and for payments of estimated tax for both residents and nonresidents for taxable years beginning in that calendar year. Amounts withheld from compensation paid to nonresident entities may be taken as a credit against the North Carolina individual income tax. If the nonresident entity is a pass-through entity (*e.g.*, limited partnership, general partnership, joint venture, S corporation, limited liability company), the entity must pass through and allocate to each owner the owner's share of the credit. If more than one taxable year begins in the calendar year during which the withholding occurred, the credit may be claimed for the last taxable year beginning in the calendar year. To claim the credit for withholding or estimated income tax, the individual or nonresident entity must file with the Secretary one copy of the withholding statement required by G.S. § 105-163.3 or G.S. § 105-163.7 [G.S. § 105-163.10]. Withholding is discussed in more detail in Chapter 3.

¶403 Credit for Taxes Paid to Other States or Countries by North Carolina Residents

North Carolina resident individuals may take a credit for income taxes imposed by and paid to another state or country on income that is also taxed by North Carolina. Nonresidents must look to their own states for relief from double taxation

[*2009—2010 Individual Income Tax Bulletins*, § XVII:24]. This credit is subject to the following conditions:

(1) The income must have been derived from sources in the other state or country and must have been taxed under the laws of that state or country without regard to the legal residence of the taxpayer. An exception is provided for an individual who is deemed to be both a resident of North Carolina and a resident of another state or country under the laws of that state or country. For an individual with dual residency, the Secretary may allow a credit against the taxes imposed by and paid to the other jurisdiction on income taxed in North Carolina.

(2) The credit allowable is the smaller of either (a) the tax paid the other state or country on income also taxed by North Carolina or (b) the product obtained by multiplying the North Carolina tax computed before credit by a fraction the numerator of which is the part of the North Carolina income, as adjusted, that is taxed in the other state or country and the denominator of which is the total income, as adjusted, received while a resident of North Carolina. This fraction rule can be stated as follows:

$$\frac{\text{Portion of total federal income, as adjusted, taxed in another state or country}}{\text{Total federal income, as adjusted, while a resident of North Carolina}} \cdot = \frac{\text{NC tax credit}}{\text{(if not greater than the tax paid to other jurisdiction)}}$$

If credits are claimed for taxes paid to more than one state or country, a separate computation must be made for each state or country; and the separate credits must be combined to determine the total credit. See examples of computations below.

(3) The taxpayer must submit (with the North Carolina return) a receipt or other proof showing payment of income tax to the other state or country and a true copy of the return filed with the other state or country [G.S. § 105-153.9; 17 NCAC 6B.0607; *2009—2010 Individual Income Tax Bulletins*, § XI:2].

Examples of computation of credit for taxes paid to other states or countries: The following examples are adapted from *2009—2010 Individual Income Tax Bulletins*, § XI:2:

> **Example 1:** Adam Alford, a full-year resident of North Carolina, filed a 2008 North Carolina return as a single individual. His total income is $37,000. He worked temporarily in South Carolina, earning $5,000, on which he paid tax of $131 to South Carolina. Adam claimed the standard deduction in computing his federal taxable income, which was $28,800. The credit against his North Carolina income tax is determined as follows:

Federal taxable income	$28,800.00
State standard deduction and personal exemption adjustment	2,700.00
North Carolina taxable income	$31,500.00
North Carolina tax due	$2,079.00

Less tax credit (computed using fraction rule in (2) above):

$$\frac{\$5,000}{\$37,000} \times \$2,079.00 = \$281.00$$

Since the $131.00 tax paid to South Carolina is less than the computed tax credit of $281.00, Adam's allowable tax credit is $131.00	131.00
Net North Carolina tax due	$1,948.00

¶403

Example 2: Barbara and Barney Barnes are both residents of North Carolina and filed a joint 2008 North Carolina income tax return. Their total income is $40,000. $5,500 of their total income was received from jointly owned rental property in Virginia. Barney received $2,000 for temporary employment in South Carolina. Barbara and Barney claimed the standard deduction in computing their federal taxable income, which was $23,600. They paid $290 on the income earned in Virginia, and Barney paid tax of $102 on his income reported to South Carolina. The credit against their North Carolina income tax is determined as follows:

Federal taxable income	$23,600.00
State standard deduction and personal exemption adjustment	5,400.00
North Carolina taxable income	$29,000.00
North Carolina tax due	$ 1,819.00

Less tax credit for tax paid to Virginia (computed using fraction rule in (2) above):

$$\frac{\$5,500}{\$40,000} \times \$1,819.00 = \$250.00$$

Less tax credit for tax paid to South Carolina (computed using fraction rule in (2) above):

$$\frac{\$2,000}{\$40,000} \times \$1,819.00 = \$91.00$$

Total tax credit ($250.00 + $91.00)	341.00
Net North Carolina tax due	$ 1,478.00

Example 3: Caitlin Cabot, a single taxpayer, became a North Carolina resident on June 1, 2008. Prior to moving to North Carolina, she earned $4,000 in South Carolina. From June 1 through December 31, she earned $6,000 in South Carolina and $10,000 in North Carolina. She paid income tax to South Carolina of $400 on the $10,000 South Carolina income. Caitlin claimed the standard deduction in computing her 2008 federal taxable income, which was $11,000. Her tax credit is determined as follows:

Federal taxable income	$11,000.00
State standard deduction and personal exemption adjustment	2,700.00
North Carolina taxable income before part-year resident adjustment	$14,500.00
North Carolina taxable income after part-year resident adjustment	$11,600.00

[$16,000 × $14,500 = $11,600]

North Carolina tax on $11,600	$698.00

Less tax credit
(computed using fraction rule in (2) above):
$6,000 × $698 = $262

However, since part of the tax paid to South Carolina was on income not taxed by North Carolina, a further computation is necessary to determine that portion of the $400 South Carolina tax that was paid on income also taxed by North Carolina.

$$\frac{\text{S.C. income taxed by N.C.}}{\text{Total S.C. income}} = \frac{\$6,000}{\$10,000} \times \$400 = \$240$$

		240.00
Net tax due North Carolina		$458.00

Governmental entities: No credit is allowed for income taxes paid to a city, county, or other political subdivision of a state or to the federal government.

S corporation shareholders: Resident shareholders of S corporation are considered to have paid a tax imposed on the shareholder in an amount equal to their pro rata share of any net income tax (*i.e.*, any tax imposed on or measured by a corporation's net income) paid by the S corporation to a state that does not measure the income of S corporation shareholders by the income of the S corporation]. Each shareholder of an S corporation is allowed as a credit against the North Carolina individual income tax

¶403

an amount equal to the shareholder's pro rata share of the tax credits for which the S corporation is eligible [G.S. § 105-131.8(a)]. S corporations are discussed in more detail in Chapter 6.

Estates, trusts, and beneficiaries: There are special provisions for estates and trusts [G.S. § 105-160.4]. Subject to restrictions provided by G.S. § 105-160.3, credits allowed to individuals are also allowed to the same extent to an estate or a trust. Any credit computed as a percentage of income received must be apportioned by the estate or trust and the beneficiaries based on the distributions made during the taxable year. See ¶ 703 for details of credits allowed to estates and trusts and their beneficiaries.

Refunds

If any taxes paid to another state or country for which a taxpayer has been allowed a credit against their North Carolina income tax return is at any time credited or refunded to the taxpayer, a tax equal to the portion of the credit credited or refunded is due and payable from the taxpayer and is subject to the penalties and interest provided in Subchapter I of Chapter 105 of the North Carolina General Statutes [G.S. § 105-153.9(b)]. Taxpayers must pay the tax due to a credit or refund by another jurisdiction within 30 days of the date of receipt of the refund or notice of the credit [*2009—2010 Individual Income Tax Bulletins*, § XI:2].

¶404 Credit for Dependent Children

Repeal

This credit has been repealed effective for taxable years beginning on or after January 1, 2018 and replaced by the deduction for children discussed at ¶202. The discussion below relates to prior law.

A taxpayer who is allowed a federal child tax credit under IRC § 24 for the taxable year is allowed a credit against the North Carolina individual income tax for each dependent child for whom the individual is allowed the federal credit. The amount of the credit is based on the taxpayer's federal adjusted gross income for the taxable year [G.S. § 105-153.10(a)].

Filing Status	*AGI*	*Credit Amount*
Married Filing Jointly	Up to $40,000	$125
	Over $40,000 up to $100,000	$100
	Over $100,000	$0
Head of Household	Up to $32,000	$125
	Over $32,000 up to $80,000	$100
	Over $80,000	$0
Single	Up to $20,000	$125
	Over $20,000 up to $50,000	$100
	Over $50,000	$0
Married Filing Separately	Up to $20,000	$125
	Over $20,000 up to $50,000	$100
	Over $50,000	$0

Limitation: The amount of this credit cannot exceed the amount of income tax imposed for the taxable year reduced by the sum of all credits allowed, except payments of tax made by or on behalf of the taxpayer [G.S. § 105-153.10(b)].

Carryforward: There is no carryforward provision for this credit.

Nonresidents: A nonresident who claims the credit for dependent children must reduce the amount of the credit by multiplying it by the appropriate apportionment fraction [G.S. § 105-153.10(b)]. See ¶ 204 for discussion of apportionment for nonresidents.

Part-year residents: A part-year resident who claims the credit for dependent children must reduce the amount of the credit by multiplying it by the appropriate apportionment fraction [G.S. § 105-153.10(b)]. See ¶ 204 for discussion of apportionment for part-year residents.

¶405 Historic Rehabilitation Tax Credit

The historic rehabilitation tax credit is discussed at ¶ 1104.

INDIVIDUAL INCOME TAX

CHAPTER 5

RETURNS, PAYMENT, AND ADMINISTRATION

¶501 In General

The minimum gross income filing requirements under North Carolina law are different from the federal filing requirements because North Carolina law does not adjust the standard deduction and personal and dependency exemptions for inflation as required by the Internal Revenue Code. North Carolina requirements for due dates are similar to federal requirements. See Chapter 6 for filing requirements for pass-through entities.

¶502 Returns—Time and Place for Filing

• *When*

Returns of taxpayers reporting on a calendar-year basis are due on or before April 15 in each year at the place and in the form prescribed by the Secretary. The returns of taxpayers reporting on a fiscal-year basis are due on or before the 15th day of the 4th month following the close of the fiscal year [G.S. § 105-155(a)].

Information returns: Information returns must be filed at times prescribed by the Secretary [G.S. § 105-155(a)].

Nonresident aliens: The returns of nonresident aliens whose federal income tax returns are due at a later date under IRC § 6072(c), are due on or before the 15th day of the 6th month following the close of the taxable year [G.S. § 105-155(a)].

Extension of time: A taxpayer may ask the Secretary for an extension of time to file a return under G.S. § 105-263 [G.S. § 105-155(a)]. See ¶505.

Caution! Don't Omit Information

An income tax return from which information required to calculate the taxpayer's individual income tax liability has been omitted is not a return for the purpose of determining the applicable statute of limitations. The determining date is the date a return is filed that contains sufficient information upon which to determine tax liability [*2007—2008 Individual Income Tax Bulletins,* § XII:1].

If a due date falls on a Saturday, Sunday, or holiday, returns are due on or before the next business day. Information returns are due at the times prescribed by the Secretary. See ¶ 502.

See Chapter 6 for requirements for *pass-through entities.* See ¶ 309 for due dates of *declarations of estimated tax* and ¶ 509 for discussion of *amended returns.*

- *Where*

If a refund is due, returns are filed with the North Carolina Department of Revenue, P.O. Box R, Raleigh, NC 27634-0001. If no refund is due, returns are filed with the North Carolina Department of Revenue, P.O. Box 25000, Raleigh, NC 27640-0640. Refunds are discussed at ¶ 3203.

- *Failure to file*

For penalties for failure to file returns, see ¶ 3204.

¶503 Persons Required to File

The following individuals must file a North Carolina individual income tax return for the taxable year:

(1) North Carolina residents with federal gross income in excess of the North Carolina standard deduction amount [G.S. § 105-153.8(a)(1)].

(2) Nonresidents who both (1) derived gross income from North Carolina sources during the taxable year attributable to the ownership of any interest in real or tangible personal property in North Carolina, derived from a business, trade, profession, or occupation carried in North Carolina or derived from gambling activities in North Carolina and (2) had federal gross income in excess of the North Carolina standard deduction amount [G.S. § 105-153.8(a)(2)].

(3) Part-year residents who received income while a resident or who received income while a nonresident attributable to the ownership of any interest in real or tangible personal property in North Carolina, derived from a business, trade, profession, or occupation carried in North Carolina or derived from gambling activities in North Carolina [*2009-2010 Individual Income Tax Bulletins* § II:2.6].

(4) Any individual whom the Secretary believes to be liable for North Carolina individual income tax when so notified by the Secretary and requested to file a return [G.S. § 105-153.8(a)(3)].

(5) *Deceased taxpayers and taxpayers unable to file:* If an individual who was required to file a North Carolina individual income tax return for the taxable year while living has died before making the return, the administrator or executor of the estate must file the return in the decedent's name and behalf, and

the tax will be levied upon and collected from the estate. If a taxpayer is unable to file a North Carolina individual income tax return, the return must be filed by a duly authorized agent or by a guardian or other person charged with the care of the person or property of the taxpayer [G.S. § 105-153.8(b)].

(6) *Filing for refund purposes:* Taxpayers who are not required to file a return because their incomes are below the minimum amounts should nevertheless file returns if any tax was withheld during the taxable year. Refunds will not be made in the absence of a filed return.

• *Filing status*

A taxpayer must claim the same filing status for North Carolina individual income purposes as for federal income tax purposes. If either the taxpayer or the taxpayer's spouse is a nonresident and had no North Carolina taxable income for the taxable year, they may choose to file a joint State return if they filed a joint federal return; they, however, still have the option of filing separate returns. Once a joint return is filed, separate returns may not be filed for that year after the due date of the return. Prior to the 2006 taxable year, such taxpayers were required to utilize the Married Filing Separately filing status [*2009—2010 Individual Income Tax Bulletins*, § I:3.f].

Joint Returns for Nonresidents

A couple, only one of whom is a North Carolina resident or who has North Carolina income, may file a joint North Carolina return [G.S. § 105-153.8(e)].

Only spouses can file joint returns. All other individuals must file separate returns. See also *Bryant v. Bowers*, 182 N.C. App 338, 641 S.E.2d 855 (2007) (holding that the provisions of G.S. § 105-153.8(e) regarding a surviving spouse's right to refunds of joint estimated tax overpayments are inapplicable where joint estimated taxes are paid by the estate, in which case G.S. §§ 28A-15-8 and 28A-15-9 govern). On joint returns, both spouses are jointly and severally liable for the tax due. If, however, a spouse qualifies for relief of liability for federal income tax as an "innocent spouse" that spouse is not liable for the corresponding North Carolina income tax [G.S. § 105-153.8(e)]. For the recognition of same-sex marriages for personal income tax purposes, *see* Directive PD-14-3 (October 24, 2014).

Joint federal and separate State returns: If a taxpayer files a joint federal return but files a separate North Carolina return, the taxpayer must complete a separate federal return and attach it to the North Carolina individual income tax return to show how federal taxable income would be determined on a separate federal return. In lieu of completing a separate federal return, a taxpayer may submit a schedule showing the computation of the separate federal taxable income. Taxpayers who choose this alternative (submitting a schedule) must attach a copy of the joint federal return *if* the federal return *does not* reflect a North Carolina address.

In determining the federal taxable income on the separate federal return, deductions are allowable only to the spouse responsible for payment of the item and who actually paid the amount during the tax year. In the case of a joint obligation, nonbusiness deductions (except for medical expenses) are allowable to the spouse who actually paid the item. In determining the amount of medical expenses paid by each spouse from a joint checking account, each spouse is considered to have paid his or her own medical expenses. However, the Secretary of the Department of Revenue has ruled that deductible expenses paid out of the spouses' joint bank account will be allocated between the spouses based on their respective adjusted gross incomes, absent evidence supporting a more accurate allocation [*Secretary's Decision No. 2001-545 (December 6, 2001)*].

Married taxpayers domiciled in community property state: If spouses who are domiciled in a community property state or country recognized as such for federal income tax purposes file separate North Carolina returns and each spouse reports one-half of the salary and wages received while domiciled in the community property state or country, each spouse is entitled to claim one-half of the credit for the income tax withheld with respect to such community wages. A schedule or statement must be attached to the North Carolina return showing the name and social security number of each spouse and that they were domiciled in a community property state and as such, 50% of each spouse's income tax withheld is allocated to the other spouse's income tax return [17 NCAC 6B.0113(a), (b)].

- *Estates and trusts; pass-through entities*

See Chapter 7 for filing requirements for estates and trusts and Chapter 6 for filing requirements for pass-through entities.

¶504 Forms for Filing Individual Income Tax Returns

North Carolina individual income tax returns and affirmations must be filed on the form prescribed by the Secretary [G.S. § 105-155(d)]. Forms and additional schedules prescribed by the Secretary of Revenue are available from the North Carolina Department of Revenue in Raleigh or from any of the branch offices located throughout the State. Forms may also be obtained by calling (919) 715-0397 or downloading them from the Department of Revenue website [http://www.dor.state.nc.us/forms]. Taxpayers may also request forms to be mailed to them at the Department's website at http://www.dor.state.nc.us/request. Individuals who qualify may also file electronically (see below).

- *Form D-400*

This is the form used by most North Carolina taxpayers. AA joint return should show the name and social security number of both spouses. Both spouses are jointly and severally liable for the tax due on a joint return unless one spouse has been relieved of any liability for federal income tax purposes as a result of the federal "innocent spouse" provisions [IRC § 6015]. All individuals must use Form D-400; Form D-200EZ (Short Form) has been discontinued.

Tax Preparers Not Required to Sign by Hand

Paid tax return preparers are no longer required to sign returns by hand [17 NCAC 6B.0104(l)].

¶505 Extension of Time to File

The Secretary may extend the time in which a person must file a return, but an extension of time for filing does not extend the time for paying the tax due or the time when a penalty attaches for failure to pay the tax [G.S. § 105-263(b)]. A final return may be filed at any time within the extension period, but it must be filed before the end of the extension period to avoid the late filing penalty [17 NCAC 6B.0107(d)].

Effect of Extension

An extension of time to file does not extend the time to pay the tax or extend the time when a penalty attaches in the case of a franchise tax return or an income tax return. An extension of time to file *does* extend the time to pay the tax or extend the time when a penalty attaches in the case of any return other than a franchise tax return or an income tax return [G.S. § 105-263]. For an exception to this rule, see "Individuals living outside the United States and Puerto Rico," below.

- *Application for extension to file*

If an individual income tax return cannot be filed by the due date, an individual may apply for an automatic six-month extension of time to file the return. To receive the extension, an individual must file Form D-410 (Application for Extension for Filing Individual Income Tax Return) by the original due date of the return, and a partnership, estate, or trust must file Form D-410P (Application for Filing Partnership, Estate, or Trust Tax Return) [17 NCAC 6B.0107(a)].

- *Penalties [17 NCAC 6B.0107(b)]*

Late application: Taxpayers who do not file an application for extension by the original due date of the return are subject to both the 5% per month filing penalty ($5 minimum; 25% maximum) and the 10% late payment penalty ($5 minimum) on the remaining balance due.

Late payment: A 10% late payment penalty applies to the remaining balance due if the tax paid by the original due date of the return is less than 90% of the total amount of tax due. If the 90% rule is met, any remaining balance due, including interest, must be paid with the income tax return before the expiration of the extension period to avoid the late payment penalty [17 NCAC 6B.0107(b)].

- *Individuals living outside the United States and Puerto Rico*

Individuals who are U. S. citizens or residents and are "out of the country" on the regular due date of the return (April 15) are granted an automatic 4-month extension for filing a North Carolina income tax return if they attach a statement to their return to explain that they were out of the country on the due date of the return. The individual marks the "out of the country" indicator on page 1 of Form D-400. The extension application, Form D-410, does not have to be filed. The time for payment of the tax is also extended; however, interest is due on any unpaid tax from the original due date of the return until the tax is paid.

If an individual is unable to file the return within the automatic 4-month extension period, an additional 2-month extension may be obtained by filing Form D-410 by August 15 and marking the "out of country" indicator on the form. For this purpose, "Out of the Country" means (1) the individual lives outside the United States and Puerto Rico, and his or her main place of work is outside the United States and Puerto Rico, or (2) the individual is in military service outside the United States and Puerto Rico [2009—2010 *Individual Income Tax Bulletins*, § I:6].

- *Members of the Armed Forces*

Service in a combat zone: Members of the United States Armed Forces and qualifying support personnel serving in a combat zone who receive an extension of time to file a federal income tax return are entitled to the same extension of time for filing, and the same relief from accrual of penalty and interest, for North Carolina individual income tax purposes [G.S. § 105-249.2].

Deferred payment: A member of the armed forces may defer payment of income tax for a period of 180 days after military service ends if the service member's inability to pay the tax was caused by military service. No penalty or interest accrues during the period of deferment [17 NCAC 6B.3407].

¶506 Payment of Tax

- *When*

The full amount of the tax payable as shown on a return must be paid by the due date of the return. If, however, the amount shown to be due is less than one dollar ($1.00), no payment need be made [G.S. § 105-157(a)]. Payments of estimated income tax are discussed at ¶309. If the average amount of a taxpayer's required payment of tax is at least $20,000 a month, the taxpayer is required to pay by electronic funds transfer (EFT). Electronic fund transfers are discussed at ¶3210.

- *Where*

Remittances are made payable to the North Carolina Department of Revenue and are remitted to the Department in Raleigh. If the taxpayer is due a refund, the return should be sent to P.O. Box R, Raleigh, NC 27634-0001. Returns for which an amount is due are sent to P.O. Box 25000, Raleigh, NC 27640-0640.

Electronic Payment of Tax (E-Pay)

The North Carolina Department of Revenue has initiated an on-line payment program called E-Pay as an alternative to mailing the Individual Income Payment Voucher, Form D-400V [http://www.dor.state.nc.us/electronic/epay.html]. Taxpayers who choose to pay North Carolina individual income taxes electronically can pay by credit card (MasterCard and Visa) or by bank draft. This payment method should be used only for the payment of tax owed on an original North Carolina individual income tax return for the current year. It should not be used to pay estimated tax, tax owed on prior year returns, or tax billed on assessment notices. D-400V Amended may be used to pay tax due on an amended return. Taxpayers who need assistance with the E-Pay service can phone (877) 308-9103.

- *Designation of refund to go to Nongame and Endangered Wildlife Fund*

A taxpayer may elect to contribute all or any portion of his/her income tax refund (minimum of $1) to the North Carolina Nongame and Endangered Wildlife Fund. This is an irrevocable election. Contributions to this fund are used to assist in the management and protection of North Carolina's many nongame species, including endangered wildlife. The Nongame and Endangered Wildlife Fund is the primary source of money to support much needed research, public education, and management programs designated specifically to benefit nongame wildlife [*2009-2010 Individual Income Tax Bulletins,* § XIV:4]. Refunds are discussed at ¶3203.

¶506

Direct Deposit of Refunds

If a taxpayer's return is E-filed by an approved tax preparer or an approved on-line service provider and is entitled to a refund, the refund can be deposited directly into the taxpayer's checking or savings account [http://www.dor.state.nc.us/electronic/directdeposit.html]. Direct deposits can be made only to one account. If for any reason (*e.g.*, inadequate information provided by taxpayer, rejection by the financial institution, discretion of the Department of Revenue based on review of the return) direct deposit cannot be made, the Department of Revenue will issue a check to the taxpayer. Direct deposit is available only for an original refund and is not available to taxpayers who file a paper return. E-filing is discussed at ¶510.

¶507 Information Returns

Information returns are required to be filed with the Department of Revenue to report payments of income by a person who is a resident, has a place of business in North Carolina, or has an employee, an agent, or another representative in any capacity in North Carolina if the person directly or indirectly pays or controls the payment of any income to any taxpayer [G.S. § 105-154(b)]. Reportable income includes interest, rents, premiums, dividends, annuities, remunerations, emoluments, fees, gains, profits, taxable meal reimbursements, and other determinable annual or periodic gains during a calendar year. For penalties for failure to file returns, see ¶3204.

Information returns must be made on Information at the Source Reports, Form NC-1099, if the payments have not otherwise been reported. Form NC-1099 reports are not required to be filed if the payments have been reported to the Internal Revenue Service, the payments have otherwise been reported to the Department, or no North Carolina income tax was withheld from the payments.

Exception

Reports of the sale of real property located in North Carolina by nonresidents must be filed even if the sale is reported to the Internal Revenue Service [17 NCAC 6B.3804(c)]. A buyer who buys real property from a nonresident seller (individual, estate, or trust) must file Form 1999-NRS within 15 days of the closing date of the sale. The return is remitted to the North Carolina Department of Revenue, Nonresident Property Sales, P.O. Box 871, Raleigh, NC 27602-0871. Note that it is the purchaser who must file this return. A seller, however, who sells property at a gain has North Carolina taxable income from the sale and may be liable for payment of estimated income tax on the recognizable gain. See ¶309 for discussion of estimated income tax.

Partnerships: Partnerships doing business in North Carolina are required to file information returns specifically stating the items of federal gross income and deductions and the required North Carolina adjustments. Partnership filing is discussed in Chapter 6.

¶508 Federal Changes

If a taxpayer's federal adjusted taxable income, filing status, personal exemptions, standard or itemized deductions or federal tax credit is changed or corrected by the Commissioner of Internal Revenue or other officer of the United States or competent authority, and the change or correction affects the amount of state tax payable, the taxpayer must file an income tax return reflecting each change or correction from a federal determination within six months after being notified of each change or correction. The Secretary must then propose an assessment or issue a refund. If a taxpayer files a federal amended return that would increase the tax-payer's state tax liability, the taxpayer must file an amended state return within six months. If the federal amended return would decrease the taxpayer's state tax liability, the taxpayer may file an amended state return within the time period set forth in G.S. § 105-241.6, discussed at ¶3203. If the taxpayer fails to timely file an amended return reflecting the federal correction or determination, the taxpayer is subject to penalties and forfeits the right to any refund based on the federal change. [G.S. § 105-159]. See ¶3202 for the definition of federal determination.

¶509 Amended Returns

North Carolina individual income tax returns may be amended by filing an amended tax return, Form D-400X [17 NCAC 6B.0108]. A separate Form D-400X must be filed for each return that is being amended. Generally, an amended return must be filed within three years after the date the original return was due to be filed or within six months of the date the tax was paid, whichever is later. Amended returns should be mailed to the North Carolina Department of Revenue, P.O. Box 25000, Raleigh, NC 27640-0640. A return filed early is considered filed on the due date. If changes on the D400-X are applicable to the taxpayer's Federal return, the taxpayer must include a copy of Federal form 1040X [Form D-400X].

Federal changes: If a taxpayer's federal taxable income is corrected or otherwise determined by the federal government, the taxpayer must, within two years after being notified of the correction or final determination by the federal government, file an amended income tax return with the Secretary reflecting the corrected or deter-mined taxable income. Federal changes are discussed at ¶508.

¶510 Electronic Filing

• *Generally*

A taxpayer may file a tax return with the Department of Revenue electronically only when the Department has established and implemented procedures permitting electronic filing of a specific tax return. A return may be filed electronically only by using the procedures established by the Department for the particular return [17 NCAC 01C.0702]. The name and identification number of the taxpayer constitutes the taxpayer's signature when transmitted as part of a tax return filed electronically by the taxpayer or at the taxpayer's direction [17 NCAC 01C.0702].

E-File is an electronic method of filing a tax return by using a computer, a modem, and approved software. The Internal Revenue Service and the North Caro-lina Department of Revenue approve software products that individuals and tax professionals can purchase or use to file federal and state tax returns electronically [www.dor.state.nc.us/electronic/e-file.html].

• *Who Can E-File?*

Taxpayers who request a refund, have a zero balance due, or owe tax may file a North Carolina individual income tax return (Form D-400) or a Form D-400TC (Individual Tax Credits) electronically. Taxpayers may be full year residents, part-year residents, or nonresidents of North Carolina. Some tax forms may not be filed electronically (*e.g.*, amended returns, prior year returns, returns for non-calendar year filers). A complete list of forms that cannot be filed electronically is contained in the *North Carolina Handbook for Electronic Filers,* [Chapter 9].

• *Locating professionals that offer electronic filing*

A taxpayer can obtain a list of authorized E-file providers in their area that offer electronic filing by going to http://www.dor.state.nc.us/electronic/individual/professional.html and entering their zip code.

PART III

INCOME TAX TREATMENT OF PASS-THROUGH ENTITIES

CHAPTER 6

INCOME TAX TREATMENT OF PASS-THROUGH ENTITIES

PASS-THROUGH ENTITIES

¶601 Introduction

A "pass-through entity" is an entity or business, including a limited partnership, a general partnership, a joint venture, a subchapter S corporation, or a limited liability company, all of which are treated as owned by individuals or other entities under the federal tax laws, in which the owners report their share of the income, losses, and credits from the entity or business on their income tax returns filed with

North Carolina. An owner of a pass-through entity is an individual or entity who is treated as an owner under the federal tax laws [G.S. § 105-228.90(b)].

¶602 North Carolina Tax Treatment of Pass-Through Entities

The Internal Revenue Service's "check-the-box" regulations provide a method of elective classification for partnerships and limited liability companies. Pursuant to the federal "check-the-box" regulations, for North Carolina income tax purposes, a partnership that does not elect to be classified as a corporation will be classified by default as a partnership if it has more than one member. If a partnership or limited liability company has only one member, it is disregarded as an entity separate from its owners.

This chapter discusses the tax treatment of pass-through entities classified as partnerships rather than corporations. A foreign partnership or limited liability company that does not elect to be classified as a corporation is classified as a partnership if it has two or more members and any member has unlimited liability. It is classified as an association if no member has unlimited liability and is disregarded as an entity separate from its owner if it has a single owner who has unlimited liability [*Technical Advice Memorandum*, No. 97-3, January 27, 1997].

For tax treatment of corporations, see Part V of this *Guidebook*; for tax treatment of individuals, see Part II of this *Guidebook*.

¶603 Doing Business in North Carolina

While partnerships and LLCs treated as partnerships are not subject to income or franchise taxes, it is often important to determine whether the partnership or LLC is doing business in North Carolina. Most importantly, if the partnership or LLC is doing business in the State, its business activities and assets may be attributed to its partners or members, creating nexus with the state for such partners or members for North Carolina income and franchise tax purposes. With respect to partnerships, 17 NCAC 5C.0102(b) states that a corporate member of a partnership "operating" in North Carolina will be treated as doing business in the State. Similarly, 17 NCAC 5C.1701 states that a corporate member of a partnership "doing business" in North Carolina will be treated as doing business in the State. (In practice, the term "operating" in 17 NCAC 5C.0102(b) has been treated as synonymous with "doing business." See *Secretary's Decision No. 97-548* (April 24, 1998).)

Investment Partnerships

A partnership whose only activity is as an investment partnership is not considered to be doing business in North Carolina. An "investment partnership" for this purpose is a partnership that is not a dealer in securities under IRC § 475(c)(1) and that derives income exclusively from buying, holding, and selling securities for its own account. An investment partnership is not required to file an income tax return in North Carolina or pay income tax in North Carolina on behalf of its nonresident partners [17 NCAC 6B.3503(c)].

With respect to LLCs, the Department of Revenue has issued a directive clarifying its views when an LLC's business activities will create nexus and return filing obligations between the State and the LLC's members [*Tax Directive* CD-02-1 (May 31,

2002)]. The Directive first states that a corporate member of an LLC doing business in North Carolina has nexus in North Carolina, regardless of whether the LLC is classified as a corporation or partnership or is a disregarded entity for tax purposes.

Although the Department treats a corporate member of an LLC doing business in North Carolina as having nexus with the State, regardless of the LLC's tax classification, the Directive goes on to state that the corporate member has no return filing obligation unless the LLC is classified as a partnership or a disregarded entity for tax purposes, in which case the business of the LLC is attributed to the member in the same way that the business of a partnership is attributed to its partners under 17 NCAC 5C.0102(b) and 5C.1701. If the LLC is classified as a corporation for tax purposes, the LLC's activities are not attributed to its corporate members who, thus, have no return filing obligations as a result of their membership interest in the LLC. Of course, the corporate member of an LLC classified as a corporation for tax purposes may be required to file a North Carolina return if it has other activities that subject it to the North Carolina income or franchise tax. See ¶ 641 regarding when an LLC will be classified as a corporation, partnership, or disregarded entity.

Comment on Tax Directive CD-02-1

The Department's statement that the corporate members of an LLC taxed as a corporation have nexus with the State is curious. The corporate income tax law imposes the tax on every corporation "doing business" in the State and requires every such corporation to file a return. See G.S. § § 105-130.3 and 105-130.16. Thus, there is no distinction in the law between nexus and return filing obligations. Moreover, the Directive itself states that a member of an LLC classified as a corporation will not be required to file a return unless it conducts other activities that "subject it" to income or franchise tax. Thus, the Directive itself presupposes that a corporate member of such an LLC is not "subject to" the tax solely by virtue of its membership interest, *i.e.*, it has no nexus solely by virtue of its membership interest.

S CORPORATIONS

¶605 S Corporations in General

Part 1A of Chapter 105 of the G.S. ("S Corporation Income Tax") provides the definitions and rules affecting North Carolina S corporations. In general, an S corporation is taxed like a partnership. Many of the provisions of the corporation income tax and the individual income tax, however, also apply to S corporations.

The North Carolina S corporation closely conforms to federal law in many respects. In general the terms used in the North Carolina S corporation status have the same meaning as when used in a comparable context in the Internal Revenue Code. Due consideration must be given to applicable sections of the Internal Revenue Code in effect and to federal rulings and regulations interpreting them unless the North Carolina S corporation provisions specifically conflict with federal provisions [G.S. § 105-131(c)].

S Corporations Must Pay Franchise Tax

S corporations are exempt from the corporation income tax but are subject to the franchise tax.

- *Definitions of G.S. §105-131*

    C corporation: A corporation that is not an S corporation and is subject to the corporation income tax [G.S. § 105-131(b)(2)].

    Code: The meaning given in G.S. § 105-228.90 [G.S. § 105-131(b)(1)]. See discussion at ¶ 103.

    Department: The North Carolina Department of Revenue [G.S. § 105-131(b)(3)].

    Income attributable to the State: Items of income, loss, deduction, or credit of the S corporation apportioned and allocated to North Carolina under the corporation income tax rules of G.S. § 105-130.4 [G.S. § 105-131(b)(4)].

    Income not attributable to the State: All items of income, loss, deduction, or credit of the S corporation other than income attributable to North Carolina [G.S. § 105-131(b)(5)].

    Post-termination transition period: That period defined in IRC § 1377(b)(1) [G.S. § 105-131(b)(6)].

    Pro rata share: The share determined with an S corporation shareholder for a taxable period in the manner provided in IRC § 1377(a) [G.S. § 105-131(b)(7)].

    S corporation: A corporation for which a valid election under IRC § 1362(a) is in effect [G.S. § 105-131(a)(8)].

    Secretary: The Secretary of Revenue [G.S. § 105-131(b)(9)].

    Taxable period: Any taxable year or portion of a taxable year during which a corporation is an S corporation [G.S. § 105-131(b)(10)].

¶606 Income of S Corporations and Shareholders

A North Carolina S corporation is not subject to the corporation income tax [G.S. § 105-131(a)]. For corporation income tax purposes, the income of the S corporation is passed through to its shareholders. Resident shareholders must report all of their pro rata shares of North Carolina S corporation income on their individual income tax returns. Nonresident shareholders report only North Carolina source income on their individual income tax returns [G.S. § 105-131.1].

- *Adjustment of shareholder income*

    Each shareholder's pro rata share of an S corporation's income is subject to the adjustments for individuals provided in G.S. §§ 105-153.5 and 105-153.6 [G.S. § 105-131.2(a)]. In addition, the S corporation must add any amount deducted under § 164 of the Code as state, local or foreign income tax [G.S. § 105-153.5 (c1)].

¶606

• *Characterization of shareholder income*

North Carolina S corporation items of income, loss, deduction, and credit passed through to shareholders retain their characterization in the shareholders' hands [G.S. § 105-131.2(b)].

• *Part-year resident shareholders*

If an S corporation shareholder is both a North Carolina resident and a nonresident during any taxable period, the shareholder's pro rata share of the S corporation's income attributable to North Carolina and income not attributable to North Carolina for the taxable period must be further prorated between the shareholder's periods of residence and nonresidence, based on the number of days in each period [G.S. § 105-131.5].

• *No loss carryforward*

An S corporation is not entitled to claim a net economic loss deduction. In Secretary's Decision No. 2006-314 (July 20, 2007), the taxpayers were S corporation shareholders. The S corporation incurred losses in 2001, which resulted in a net operating loss for the taxpayers for federal income tax purposes. The taxpayers carried these NOLs back to an earlier year for federal purposes but failed to amend their North Carolina returns for the carryback year to reflect the reduction in their North Carolina taxable income as a result of the federal NOL carryback. Instead, after the carryback year was closed, the taxpayers claimed that the S corporation's 2001 loss was a net economic loss for North Carolina tax purposes, which the corporation was entitled to carry forward to later years pursuant to G.S. § 105-130.8(a) and which passed through to the taxpayers in the carryforward years. The Secretary ruled that Article 4 of Chapter 105 "viewed as a whole" did not permit S corporations to claim net economic loss deductions and that the taxpayers' only remedy was the (now foreclosed) opportunity to amend their North Carolina returns for the carryback year.

¶607 Basis of S Corporation Stock

• *Initial basis*

The initial basis of a resident shareholder in a North Carolina S corporation and in any indebtedness of the corporation owed to that shareholder is determined as required by the Internal Revenue Code on the later of (1) the date the stock is acquired or (2) the effective date of the S corporation election or the date the shareholder becomes a North Carolina resident. The initial basis of a nonresident shareholder in the stock and indebtedness of an S corporation is zero [G.S. § 105-131.3(a), (c)]. A shareholder is considered to have acquired stock or indebtedness received by gift at the time the donor acquired the stock or indebtedness, if the donor was a North Carolina at the time of the gift [G.S. § 105-131.3(g)].

• *Basis adjustments*

The stock basis of all shareholders is reduced by their pro rata shares of losses and deductions.

Resident shareholders: A resident shareholder's basis in stock and indebtedness of an S corporation is adjusted as required by IRC § 1011 with the following two exceptions [G.S. § 105-131.3(b)]:

(1) Any adjustments required by G.S. § 105-131.2 (other than for income exempt from the federal income tax).

(2) Any adjustment required by IRC § 1367 for a taxable period during which North Carolina did not measure S corporation shareholder income by reference to the corporation's income, which are disregarded.

A resident shareholder's basis is adjusted as required by IRC § 1376 [G.S. § 105-131.3(d)].

Nonresident shareholders: A nonresident shareholder's basis in stock and indebtedness of an S corporation is adjusted as required by IRC § 1367, except that adjustments to basis are limited to the income taken into account by the shareholder for North Carolina income tax purposes [G.S. § 105-131.3(d)].

¶608 Carryforwards and Carrybacks

Carryforwards and carrybacks to and from an S corporation are restricted in the manner provided in IRC § 1371(b) [G.S. § 105-131.4(a)].

¶609 Limitations on Losses and Deductions

• *Losses and deductions limited by basis*

The aggregate amount of losses or deductions of an S corporation taken into account by a shareholder may not exceed the combined adjusted bases of the shareholder in the stock and indebtedness of the S corporation. Losses or deductions that are disallowed to a shareholder for a taxable period due to limitation are treated as if they were incurred by the corporation in the succeeding taxable period with respect to that shareholder [G.S. § 105-131.4(b), (c)].

• *Disallowed losses and deductions limited by basis*

Losses or deductions that are disallowed for a taxable period due to basis limitations are treated as incurred by the corporation in the succeeding taxable period with respect to the shareholders who were denied the losses or deductions [G.S. § 105-131.4].

• *Disallowed losses and deductions for last taxable S corporation year*

Losses or deductions disallowed by basis limitations for the corporation's last taxable period as an S corporation are treated as incurred by the shareholder on the last day of any post-termination transition period [G.S. § 105-131.4(d)(1)].

¶610 Distributions

In general, distributions with respect to its stock made to resident shareholders of North Carolina S corporations are characterized as (1) a dividend or (2) gain from the sale or exchange of property pursuant to IRC § 1368. Distributions of money during a post-termination transition period are not taxable to the shareholder to the extent the distribution is applied against and reduces the shareholder's adjusted stock basis in accordance with IRC § 1371(e) [G.S. § 105-131.6]. "Adjusted basis of the stock" and "adjusted stock basis" mean the adjusted basis of the shareholder's stock after required adjustments.

The accumulated adjustments account maintained for each resident shareholder must be equal to, and adjusted in the same manner as, the corporation's accumulated adjustments account defined in IRC § 1368(e)(1)(A) with the following two exceptions:

(1) The accumulated adjustments account must be modified in the manner required by G.S. § 105-131.3(b)(1).

(2) The amount of the corporation's federal accumulated adjustments account that existed on the day North Carolina began to measure the S corporation shareholders' income by reference to the income of the S corporation is ignored and treated as additional accumulated earnings and profits of the corporation.

¶611 Returns

S corporations incorporated or doing business in North Carolina must file annual returns on or before the due date prescribed for C corporation returns, which is on or before the 15th day of the 4th month following the close of the taxable year [G.S. § 105-131.7(a)]. S corporations use Form CD-401S for North Carolina returns. This is a franchise tax return that is also an information return for income tax purposes. All corporations doing business or having employees in North Carolina must report any payments made of wages, rent, interest, or dividends [G.S. § 105-130.21].

• *Nonresident shareholders*

The Department of Revenue *must* permit S corporations to file composite returns and make composite payments of tax on behalf of some or all nonresident shareholders and *may* allow S corporations to file composite returns and make composite payments of tax on behalf of some or all resident shareholders [G.S. § 105-131.7(b)]. An S corporation must file with the Department the agreement of each nonresident shareholder to file a return and timely pay all taxes imposed on the shareholder with respect to the S corporation's income and the shareholder's agreement to be subject to personal jurisdiction in North Carolina for the collection of any unpaid taxes. If the corporation fails to file such an agreement, the corporation must pay an estimate of the tax due with respect to such nonresident shareholders. The corporation is empowered to collect the amount of any such payment from the shareholder on whose behalf it was paid [G.S. § 105-131.7(c)]. The agreement is due with the annual return for the first taxable year in which a corporation becomes an S corporation or for the first taxable year in which the S corporation has a nonresident shareholder [G.S. § 105-131.7(d)].

¶612 Tax Credits

Each shareholder of an S corporation is entitled to a credit against his income tax in an amount equal to his pro rata share of the tax credits for which the S corporation is eligible (subject to the limitations on credits for estates and trusts under G.S. § 105-160.3(b)) [G.S. § 105-131.8(b)].

Individuals as well as estates and trusts are entitled to credits against the individual income tax or the income tax on estates and trusts, as the case may be, for income taxes paid to another state. *See* G.S. §§ 105-153.9 and 105-160.4. If an S corporation's income is subject to tax in another state, any shareholders of the S corporation that are residents of North Carolina are entitled to a credit for their pro rata shares of the tax paid [G.S. § 105-131.8].

A shareholder claiming the credit must attach a schedule to his income tax return that reflects the total amount of tax paid to the other state or country and explains how his pro rata share of the tax was determined A separate tax credit must be calculated for each state or country to which the S corporation paid tax. Nonresident shareholders are not allowed credit for tax paid to another state or country [*2009–2010 Individual Income Tax Bulletins, § VII:4*].

¶613 Qualified Subchapter S Subsidiaries (QSSSs)

The Federal Small Business Job Protection Act of 1996 allows S corporations to own qualified subchapter S corporation subsidiaries (QSSSs). A parent must elect QSSS treatment for its 100%-owned subsidiary. For federal income tax purposes, a QSSS is not treated as a separate corporation. Instead, all the subsidiary's assets, liabilities, and items of income, deductions and credits are treated as those of the S corporation parent [IRC § 1361(b)(3)(A)]. North Carolina follows the federal treatment for income tax purposes and recognizes all the income and expense items as belonging to the parent corporation.

All of the subsidiary's activities are attributed to the parent for purposes of determining whether the parent is doing business in North Carolina. The S corporation must aggregate and include the subsidiary's items of income, loss, and deductions before determining the parent's apportionable or allocable income. The S corporation parent must also include the subsidiary's sales in determining the parent's apportionment factor [CTAM 97-13].

Each QSSS doing business in North Carolina and each parent S corporation doing business in North Carolina must file a separate franchise tax return for each taxable period based on their own separate attributes. The assets, liabilities, income, deductions, or credits of the parent and the QSSS are *not* combined for this purpose. A franchise tax return must be filed even if the resulting liability is the minimum franchise tax [CTAM 97-13].

PARTNERSHIPS

¶622 Partnership Income

The starting point in the determination of a partnership's taxable income is the partnership's taxable income for federal income tax purposes. The same additions, deductions, and transitional adjustments to federal taxable income required of individuals apply to partnerships [17 NCAC 6B.3501]. See Chapter 2 for discussion of additions, deductions, and transitional adjustments required of individual taxpayers. In addition, the partnership must add back any amounts deducted under § 164 of the Code as state, local or foreign income taxes [G.S. § 105-153.5(c1)].

• *Limited partnerships*

The North Carolina Uniform Limited Partnership Act provides that domestic and foreign limited partnerships and their owners are classified for North Carolina income tax purposes in accordance with their classification for federal income tax purposes [G.S. § 59-1107].

¶613

• *Segregation of multiple business activities*

The business activities of a partnership are not segregated if it does not employ a method that clearly reflects the income or loss of its separate activities. A partnership must allocate to North Carolina the income derived from its business activities in North Carolina that are segregated from its other business activities [17 NCAC 6B.3513(d)].

• *Guaranteed payments*

In the determination of gross income and deductible business expenses, partnerships may treat guaranteed payments to partners for services or for use of capital as if they were paid to a nonpartner. For other tax purposes, however, guaranteed payments are treated as partners' distributive shares of partnership income [17 NCAC 6B.3513(a)].

• *Interest expense*

Interest income that passes through to partners retains its same character as when received by the partnership, but the expenses incurred in earning interest are deductible by the partnership. It is net interest income after expenses that is reflected in a partner's pro rata share of the partnership income.

• *Investment partnerships*

The general rule discussed at ¶603 that any partnership operating in North Carolina is doing business in the state does not apply to an investment partnership. Therefore, an investment partnership is not required to file a North Carolina income tax return or pay the income tax due on each nonresident partner's share of partnership income derived from North Carolina [17 NCAC 6B.3503(c); *Tax Directive PD-02-1*(November 4, 2004); *2009—2010 Individual Income Tax Bulletins,* §IX:13].

"Investment partnership" defined: An "investment partnership" is a partnership that is not a dealer in securities (as defined in IRC §475(c)(1)) and that derives income exclusively from buying, holding, and selling securities for its own account. If any of the partnership's income is from other activities, either within or outside North Carolina or either received directly or flowing through from other pass-through entities, the partnership is not an investment partnership for North Carolina tax purposes. Other activities include, but are not limited to, providing services or products to customers and holding real property for appreciation and income [17 NCAC §6B.3503(c); *2009—2010 Individual Income Tax Bulletins,* §IX:13]. *See also,* PTPLR 2019-1 (partnership deriving income from short-term commercial loans not an investment partnership).

The Department of Revenue has further interpreted the term "investment partnership" under 17 NCAC 6B.3503(c) and *Tax Directive PD-02-1* (November 6, 2002) to mean a partnership in which *all* income or loss is derived from changes in the value of its investments in intangible assets (capital appreciation) or from intangible income derived from the assets in which the partnership invests (*i.e.,* dividends or interest) and such income is solely for the benefit of the partnership's owners [*Tax Directive PD-04-2* (November 4, 2004)].

¶622

¶623 Allocation and Apportionment

Apportionable (business) income is apportioned; nonapportionable (nonbusiness) income is allocated. See the discussions at ¶1004, ¶1005, and ¶1006. Income from an intangible source (including gain realized from the sale of intangible property) that is received in the course of doing business in North Carolina so as to have a taxable situs in North Carolina is included in the numerator of the fraction used in determining the portion of federal taxable income that is taxable to North Carolina by a nonresident [17 NCAC 6B.3501]. Income from an intangible source that is not received in the course of doing business in North Carolina is allocated to the state where the intangible property has situs. For example, a nonresident partner in a partnership that holds securities for capital appreciation and income with only occasional sales of stocks and bonds has nonbusiness income that is not allocable to North Carolina [17 NCAC 6B.3503(d)].

The North Carolina Department of Revenue has issued a policy directive to announce a change regarding the apportionment and allocation of income by a multistate partnership for corporate income tax purposes. A partnership that is doing business in North Carolina and at least one other state and has corporate or nonresident individual partners must determine the portion of the partners' shares of the partnership's distributive net income subject to North Carolina tax by using the statutory allocation and apportionment provisions. The partnership will no longer account separately for income from segregated activities that are part of the partnership's unitary business unless the Department has authorized the use of an alternative apportionment formula [*Policy Directive PD-14-2* (October 10, 2014)].

¶624 Returns and Payment of Tax

- *Partnerships required to file*

Partnerships (including publicly traded partnerships; see G.S. § 105-154(e)) that (1) do business in North Carolina and (2) are required to file federal partnership returns must file North Carolina partnership returns. "Doing business" in North Carolina means the operation of any activity within North Carolina regularly, continuously, and systematically for the purpose of income or profit. A sporadic activity, hobby, or amusement diversion does not come within the definition of a business carried on in North Carolina [17 NCAC 6B.3503(a)]. The phrases (1) "carrying on business," (2) "doing business," and (3) "business activity" all refer to the same concept—nexus. "Doing business" is discussed in detail at ¶803.

- *Forms and schedules*

Partnerships must file Form D-403 (Partnership Income Tax Return). This is an information return.

The return must include the names and addresses of the individuals entitled to share in the net income of the partnership and must be signed by one of the partners and the individual preparing the return [17 NCAC 6B.3503(a)].

If the partnership claims a tax credit and there are nonresident partners whose share of the tax due is being paid by the manager of the partnership, the partnership must file a Form D-403TC (Partnership Tax Credit Summary). Partnerships should not file Form D-403TC if all partners are North Carolina residents or nonresidents whose share of tax is not being paid by the manager.

Schedule NC K-1 is used by the partnership to report each partner's share of the partnership's income, adjustments, tax credits, tax paid, *etc.* Schedule NC K-1 must reflect the net tax paid by the partnership. The partnership must also provide a completed Schedule NC K-1 (or other schedule containing the same information) to each person who was a partner in the partnership at any time during the year on or before the due date of the partnership return. When reporting the distributive share of tax credits, a list of the amount and type of tax credits should be provided to each partner [G.S. § 105-154(c); 17 NCAC 6B.3503(b)]. Publicly traded partnerships are only required to provide schedules NC K-1 to partners whose distributive share of the partnership's net income during the tax year was more than $500 [G.S. § 105-154(e)(1)].

• *Due date and extensions of time*

Partnership returns of calendar-year partnerships are due on or before April 15 of the year following the close of the taxable year. Partnership returns of fiscal-year partnerships are due on or before the 15th day of the fourth month following the close of the taxable fiscal year [G.S. § 105-155(a)]. Partnerships are not required to remit tax on their income; they are not taxable entities for income tax purposes. The partnership income "passes through" the partnership to the partners, who pay the tax in their capacities as individuals.

• *Estimated income tax*

Partnerships are not required to make estimated tax payments. Individual partners subject to the North Carolina individual income tax must pay estimated income tax on Form North Carolina-40. Nonresident individual partners are not required to pay estimated tax on their distributive shares of partnership income. Partnerships may, however, make prepayments of tax, which must be reported on the partnership income tax return.

¶625 Income of Partners

• *Adjustments to federal taxable income*

Partners must adjust federal taxable income as necessary for partnership income reflected in federal taxable income. Adjustments to federal taxable income (additions and subtractions) are discussed at ¶202 and ¶203. Deductions from federal taxable income do not include a partner's salary (guaranteed payment), interest on a partner's capital account, partner relocation and mortgage interest differential payments, or payments to a retired partner regardless of whether they were determined without regard to current profits. Even those guaranteed payments for services or use of capital are considered partnership expenses for purposes of determining a partnership's income; these types of payments are treated as part of the partnership income on a partner's individual income tax return [17 NCAC 6B.3513(b)].

• *Interest income*

"Net interest income" is interest passed through to partners after the partnership has deducted interest expense. If net interest income is subject to the federal income tax, a partner's federal gross income reflects interest income after expenses.

Interest income not subject to federal income tax is not reflected in a partner's federal taxable income. In these cases, a partner must increase or decrease federal taxable income as required for the net amount of interest attributable to the partnership [*2009-2010 Individual Income Tax Rules and Bulletins* § IX.9].

• *Withholding*

When an established business in North Carolina is owned by a partnership having one or more nonresident members, the managing partner must compute and pay the tax due for each nonresident partner. If the nonresident partner is a corporation, partnership, trust or estate, the managing partner is not required to pay the tax on that partner's share of the partnership income provided the partner files Form North Carolina-NPA, Nonresident Partner Affirmation, which affirms that the partner will pay the tax with its corporation, partnership, trust or estate income tax return. In such cases, a copy of Form NC-NPA must be attached to the partnership return when it is filed. Note that this provision does not extend to grantor trusts because no tax is paid on grantor trust returns.

Payment of the tax due from each nonresident partner's share of partnership net income by the managing partner on behalf of corporations, partnerships, trusts and estates that are partners does not relieve the partner from filing an income tax return. However, credit for the tax paid by the managing partner may be claimed on the partner's income tax return [G.S. § 105-154(d); *2009—2010 Individual Income Tax Bulletins*, § IX:5]. Publicly traded partnerships are not required to pay tax on behalf of nonresident partners [G.S. § 105-154(e)(2)].

• *Resident partners*

Resident partners must pay tax on their pro rata shares of partnership income whether or not distributed, including income from business activities outside of North Carolina. However, income derived from a partnership's business activities outside of North Carolina that are segregated from its other business activities are not includible in determining the tax due for nonresident partners [17 NCAC 6B.3513(d)].

• *Part-year resident partners*

Part-year residents with distributive income from a partnership doing business in North Carolina and in one or more other states must prorate their shares of partnership income attributable and not attributable to North Carolina between their periods of residence and nonresidence in accordance with the number of days in each period [17 NCAC 6B.3528]. See also ¶ 102.

• *Nonresident partners*

A nonresident individual partner is not required to file a North Carolina individual income tax return when the only income from North Carolina sources is the nonresident's share of income from a partnership doing business in North Carolina, and the manager of the partnership has reported the income of the nonresident partners and paid the tax due. A nonresident partner may, however, file an individual income tax return and claim credit for the tax paid by the manager of the partnership if the payment is properly identified on the individual income tax return [17 NCAC 6B.3513(c)]. For the treatment of investment partnerships, see ¶ 622.

¶625

Manager's responsibility: In a partnership having one or more nonresident partners, the managing partner is responsible for reporting the share of the income of nonresident partners and is required to compute and pay the tax due for each nonresident partner. If the nonresident partner is a corporation, partnership, trust or estate, the managing partner is not required to pay the tax on that partner's share of the partnership income if the non-individual partner signs an affirmation that it will pay the tax with its corporation, partnership, trust or estate income tax return. A copy of the affirmation must be attached to the partnership return when it is filed [G.S. § 105-154(d); *2009—2010 Individual Income Tax Bulletins,* § IX:5].

• *Corporate partners*

A "corporation" is defined as a joint-stock company or association, an insurance company, a domestic corporation, a foreign corporation, or a limited liability company [G.S. § 105-130.2(1a)]. A corporation that is a member of a partnership doing business in North Carolina is subject to tax and is required to include in total net income subject to allocation and apportionment its share of partnership net income or net loss to the same extent required for federal income tax purposes [17 NCAC 5C.1701]. This is true even if the corporate partner itself transacts no business outside North Carolina. Conversely, a foreign corporation that owns an interest in a partnership transacting taxable business in North Carolina is subject to corporate taxation in North Carolina even if it transacts no business on its own in North Carolina (see ¶ 803). The "doing business" rule is applicable for all tiers of a partnership structure and applies to both general and limited partners [*Secretary of Revenue of North Carolina v. Perkins Restaurants, Inc.,* TRB Admin. Dec. No. 351 (1999)].

Classification of corporate partner's share of partnership income: Whether a corporate partner's share of the partnership's net income is classified as apportionable income or nonapportionable income depends upon the facts in each case. In general, all income from transactions and activities that are dependent upon or contribute to the operations of a taxpayer is apportionable. Income from unrelated business activities that make up a discrete business enterprise is nonapportionable. When classified as apportionable income, the corporate partner's apportionment factors include its proportionate share of the partnership's property, payroll, and sales. If income is classified as nonapportionable income, it is included in the corporate partner's net taxable income and allocated in accordance with the allocation provisions of G.S. § 105-130.4 [*Corporate Income, Franchise, and Insurance Tax Bulletin, II. Q.2(2018)*].

• *Limited partners*

Nexus: In the *Perkins Restaurant* case, the corporation (Taxpayer) held an ownership interest in a limited partnership that in turn held the ownership interest in a limited partnership that owned and operated restaurants in North Carolina. Taxpayer was subject to North Carolina franchise and corporation income tax. The Tax Review Board ruled that corporations that are partners in partnerships doing business in North Carolina are considered to be doing business in North Carolina without regard to the tier of partnership structure in which the corporation's ownership is located. It does not matter, either, whether the corporation is a general partner or a limited partner [*Secretary of Revenue of North Carolina v. Perkins Restaurants, Inc.,* TRB Admin. Dec. No. 351, January 28, 1999].

¶626 Partnership Tax Credits

A partnership that engages in an activity that is eligible for a tax credit qualifies for the credit as an entity and then passes through to each of its partners the partner's distributive share of the credit for which the partnership entity qualifies [G.S. § 105-269.15(a)].

• *Limitations on credits*

Maximum dollar limits and other limitations that apply in determining the amount of a tax credit available to a taxpayer apply to the same extent in determining the amount of a tax credit for which a partnership entity qualifies, with the one exception that the tax credit cannot exceed the amount of tax imposed on the taxpayer [G.S. § 105-269.15(a)]. All limitations on an income tax credit apply to each partner to the extent of the partner's distributive share of the credit, except that a corporate partner's distributive share of an individual income tax credit is allowed as a corporation income tax credit to the extent the corporate partner could have qualified for a corporation income tax credit if it stood in the position of the partnership. All limitations on an income tax credit apply to the sum of the credit passed through to the partner plus the credit for which the partner qualifies directly [G.S. § 105-269.15(b)].

• *Allowance of credit to partner*

A partner's distributive share of an income tax credit passed through by a partnership is allowed to the partner only to the extent the partner would have qualified for the credit if the partner stood in the position of the partnership [G.S. § 105-269.15(b)]. A partner's distributive share of an income tax credit is determined in accordance with IRC §§ 702 and 704 [G.S. § 105-269.15(c)].

¶627 Disposition of Partnership Interest by a Partner

An interest in a partnership is intangible personal property. Gain from the sale of a nonresident partner's interest in a partnership is not included in the numerator of the fraction used to determine the amount of income taxable in North Carolina unless the sale of the partnership interest conveys title to tangible partnership property. If a partnership owning an interest in another partnership sells its interest in that partnership, the nonresident partners of the selling partnership do not include their distributive shares of the gain realized from the sale of the partnership interest in the numerator unless the selling partnership is carrying on a trade or business in North Carolina [17 NCAC 6B.3527(a)].

• *Nonresident partners*

Nonresident partners must include their distributive shares of the gains or losses from the sale or other disposition of the partnership's assets in the numerator of the fraction used to determine North Carolina taxable income. If the sale of partnership interests conveys title to tangible partnership property instead of to limited interests in the partnership, the transaction is considered a sale of partnership assets for purposes of determining North Carolina taxable income [17 NCAC 6B.3527(b)].

LIMITED LIABILITY COMPANIES

¶641 Income Tax Treatment of LLCs

A limited liability company (LLC), a foreign limited liability company authorized to transact business in North Carolina, and a member of one of these companies are subject to income taxation in accordance with their classification for federal income tax purposes [CTAM-97-3 (January 27, 1997)]. For federal income tax purposes, an LLC may be classified as a partnership, a C corporation, an S corporation, or a disregarded entity. Thus, an LLC classified as a partnership and its members will be taxed as a partnership and as partners for North Carolina income tax purposes [G.S. § 105-153.9 and (13)]. Similarly, an LLC classified as a C corporation for federal income tax purposes is subject to the North Carolina corporation income tax [G.S. §§ 105-130.2(4) and (11) and 105-130.3]. An LLC classified as an S corporation for federal income tax purposes will be treated as an S corporation for North Carolina S corporation income tax purposes [G.S. § 105-131(b)(8) and (c)]. An LLC treated as a disregarded entity for federal income tax purposes will be treated as a disregarded entity for North Carolina income tax purposes as well. An LLC is not required to obtain an administrative ruling from the Internal Revenue Service on its federal income tax classification in order to determine its North Carolina income tax classification [CTAM-97-3 (January 27, 1997)].

Franchise Tax Treatment of LLCs and Their Members

An LLC classified as a C corporation for federal income tax purposes is subject to the North Carolina franchise tax on corporations. In addition, certain direct or indirect corporate members of LLCs may be subject to the franchise tax on a proportionate share of assets and liabilities of a limited liability company in which they are members. These provisions are discussed at ¶ 1305.

• *Annual report for Secretary of State*

Each domestic limited liability company other than a professional limited liability company governed by G.S. § 57D-2-02 and each foreign limited liability company authorized to transact business in North Carolina must file an annual report with the Secretary of State on a form prescribed by the Secretary and in the manner required by the Secretary [G.S. § 57D-2-24].

PART IV

INCOME TAX ON ESTATES AND TRUSTS

CHAPTER 7

ESTATES AND TRUSTS

¶701 In General

The provisions of the income tax on estates and trusts are found at G.S. § 105-160 et seq. All income of an estate or trust is taxed to the fiduciary or the beneficiary. The conduit rules for taxing estates and trusts are applicable for North Carolina individual income tax purposes. Under the conduit rules the income retains its same character as when received by the estate or trust without regard to who is taxed on the income [*2007—2008 Individual Income Tax Bulletins,* § VIII:1]. The tax rate for estates and trusts is the same as the tax rates for individuals. The additions and deductions to federal taxable income of an estate or trust must be apportioned between the estate or trust and the beneficiaries based on the distributions of income made during the taxable year. In general, estates and trusts are allowed all tax credits allowed to individuals, with some exceptions (see ¶703).

¶702 Basis and Computation of Tax

This tax is imposed on the North Carolina taxable income of estates and trusts at the same rates as levied on single taxpayers [G.S. § 105-160.2]. The starting point for the computation of the North Carolina taxable income of an estate or trust is federal taxable income from the federal return (federal Form 1041) of the estate or trust (line 22 of federal Form 1041). The required adjustments (additions, subtractions, and transitional adjustments) must be apportioned between the beneficiaries and the fiduciary. Only the amount apportioned to the fiduciary is subtracted from federal taxable income in the computation of North Carolina taxable income. If none of the federal taxable income, as adjusted, is (1) from dividends, interest, gains, losses, other intangibles or (2) from sources outside North Carolina for the benefit of a nonresident beneficiary, the total income of the estate or trust (after deduction of adjustments apportioned to the estate or trust) is taxable to the fiduciary. If, however, there are nonresident beneficiaries and the fiduciary's income after adjustments includes (1) any intangible income (*i.e.*, income from interest, dividends, gains, losses), or other intangible property or (2) income from sources outside North Carolina for the benefit of a nonresident beneficiary, those amounts are deducted to arrive at North Carolina taxable income. In *N. C. Department of Revenue v. Kimberley Rice Kaestner 1992 Family Trust*, ___ U.S. ___ (2019), the United States Supreme Court affirmed the decision of the North Carolina Supreme Court that G.S. § 105-160.2 was unconstitutional under the Due Process Clause of the U.S. Constitution and Article I, § 19 of the North Carolina Constitution to the extent it purported to subject to tax a trust with no connection to North Carolina other than a resident beneficiary who could not compel trust distributions and who did not in fact receive trust distributions while she was a resident of the state.

• *Allocation of undistributed income from intangible property*

If there are no nonresident beneficiaries, all undistributed income from intangibles (*e.g.*, dividends, interest) is taxable to the estate or trust. All of the adjusted federal taxable income, therefore, is taxable to the estate or trust, since North Carolina residents are taxed on all income from all sources. If there are any nonresident beneficiaries, the amount of undistributed income from intangible property that is held for the benefit of a beneficiary (resident or nonresident) is determined on the basis of the ratio that the beneficiary's interest for the taxable year bears to the interests of both resident and nonresident income beneficiaries for the taxable year [17 NCAC 6B.3724(b)]. The amount of income of the estate or trust that is undistributed income from intangible property held for the benefit of a nonresident beneficiary (from any source) can be deducted from adjusted federal taxable income to arrive at North Carolina taxable income.

Where Does the Beneficiary Live on the Last Day of the Year?

A beneficiary's state of residence is based on the beneficiary's state of residence on the last day of the taxable year of the trust [17 NCAC 6B.3724(b)].

• *Allocation of income attributable to nonresidents (other than undistributed income from intangibles)*

If there are nonresident beneficiaries, the nonresident beneficiaries are taxable only on their North Carolina source income. The North Carolina source income of a nonresident beneficiary includes income (1) that is derived from North Carolina sources and is attributable to the ownership of any interest in real or tangible property in North Carolina or (2) that is derived from a business, trade, profession, or occupation carried on in North Carolina [G.S. § 105-160.2]. Any non-North Carolina source income held for the benefit of a nonresident is subtracted from adjusted taxable income to arrive at the North Carolina taxable income.

¶703 Credits Against Tax

Credits against tax allowed to individuals (see Chapter 4) are allowed to the same extent for estates and trusts except for the credit for taxes paid to other states (discussed at ¶403) [G.S. § 105.160.3].

Any credit computed as a percentage of income received must be apportioned between the estate and the beneficiaries on the basis of the distributions made during the taxable year. No amount of credit may exceed the amount of the tax liability reduced by the sum of all credits allowable, except for payments of tax made by or on behalf of the estate or trust [G.S. § 105-160.3(a)].

● *Taxes paid to other states by estates and trusts*

If a fiduciary is required to pay North Carolina income tax for an estate or trust, the fiduciary is allowed a credit against the tax for income taxes imposed by and paid to another state or country on income derived from sources within that other state or county [G.S. § 105-160.4(a)]. This calculation requires two steps:

(1) Determine the fraction of the gross income for North Carolina individual income tax purposes that is derived from sources with and subject to income tax in another state or country.

(2) Multiply the North Carolina income tax before credit by the fraction determined in step (1).

The credit allowed is the *smaller* of (1) the product so calculated or (2) the income tax actually paid the other state or country [G.S. § 105-160.4(b)].

Documentation: Receipts showing the payment of income taxes to another state or country and a true copy of the return upon the basis of which the taxes are assessed must be filed with the Secretary of Revenue at or before the time the credit is claimed. If credit is claimed due to a deficiency assessment, a true copy of the notice assessing or proposing to assess the deficiency, as well as a receipt showing the payment of the deficiency, must be filed with the Secretary [G.S. § 105-160.4(c)].

Refunds: If any taxes paid to another state or country for which the fiduciary has been allowed a credit are at any time credited or refunded to the fiduciary, a tax equal to that portion of the credit allowed for the taxes so credited or refunded shall be due and payable from the fiduciary and shall be subject to the penalties and interest on delinquent payments. See ¶3204 and ¶3205 for a discussion of penalties and interest.

● *Resident beneficiaries*

Resident beneficiaries of an estate or trust may claim a credit against their North Carolina tax for their share of the tax paid by the fiduciary to another state or country [17 NCAC 6B.3714]. Before computing the tax credit allowable to the estate or trust, the credit must be allocated between the estate or trust and its beneficiaries. This first requires allocations of (1) the tax paid and (2) the gross income of the estate or trust on which tax was paid to another state or country so that the allocation computations can be made. The beneficiary's share of the gross income on which tax has been paid to another state or country is determined by the governing instrument. The fiduciary's share of the total gross income to be used in the computation of the tax credit is total gross income from federal Form 1041. If additional tax credits are claimed, a separate schedule must be attached to the fiduciary return showing how the credits were determined and how they are allocated between the beneficiaries and the fiduciary.

If at any time any taxes paid to another state or country for which a beneficiary has been allowed credit are credited or refunded to the beneficiary, a tax equal to that portion of the credit allowed for the credited or refunded taxes becomes due and payable from the beneficiary and is subject to penalties and interest on delinquent payments [G.S. § 105-160.4(b)]. Penalties are discussed at ¶ 3204.

¶704 Additions to and Subtractions from Federal Taxable Income

Generally, estates and trust are subject to the same adjustments allowed to individuals. These are discussed at ¶ 202 and ¶ 203. In addition, an estate or trust must add back any amount deducted under § 164 of the Code as state, local or foreign income taxes [G.S. § 105-153.5 (c1)]. The additions and deductions (adjustments) to federal taxable income of an estate or trust, however, must be apportioned between the estate or trust and the beneficiaries based on the distributions of income made during the taxable year. Unless the trust instrument or will that created the estate or trust specifically provides for the distribution of certain classes of income to different beneficiaries, the apportionment of adjustments to the beneficiaries is determined on the basis that each beneficiary's share of the "income for regular tax purposes" from Schedule K-1, federal Form 1040 relates to "adjusted total income" from federal Form 1041. If the trust instrument or will specifically provides for the distribution of certain classes of income to different beneficiaries, any adjustments directly attributable to a particular class of income must be apportioned to the beneficiary to which that class of income is distributed [17 NCAC 6B.3723(a)].

In allocating the adjustments for state purposes, the amount of "income for regular tax purposes" on federal Schedule K-1 must be adjusted for distributions to the beneficiary that are not reflected in "income for regular purposes" [17 NCAC 6B.3723(b)]. The "adjusted total income" on federal Form 1041 must be adjusted as follows:

(1) Exclude classes of income that are not part of the distribution to the beneficiary.

(2) Include classes of income that are a part of the distribution to the beneficiary but are not included in adjusted total income.

¶705 Returns, Payment, and Penalties

• *Forms*

Estates and trusts file North Carolina returns on North Carolina Form D-407 (Estates and Trusts Income Tax Return). The starting point for preparing the income tax return of an estate or trust is the estate or trust's federal taxable income from federal Form 1041. Then the required adjustments to federal taxable income must be made. These adjustments are the same as for individuals except that they must be apportioned between fiduciary and beneficiary. The fiduciary of the estate or trust is required to file an income tax return for the estate or trust for which she/he acts if she/he is required to file a federal return for estates and trusts and (1) the estate or trust derives income from North Carolina sources or (2) the estate or trust derives any come that is for the benefit of a North Carolina resident [G.S. § 105-160.5; *2007—2008 Individual Income Tax Bulletins,* § VIII:2]. Fiduciaries of estates and trusts are required to report federal corrections or determinations of taxable income [G.S. § 105-160.8]. Federal changes are discussed at ¶ 508.

¶704

Exception for Grantor Trusts

With respect to grantor trust returns, North Carolina has access to the federal information contained in the federal grantor trust returns. Therefore, a North Carolina grantor trust return is not required to be filed when the entire trust is treated as a grantor trust for federal tax purposes [*2007—2008 Individual Income Tax Bulletins,* § VIII:2].

• *Due dates*

The return must be filed on or before April 15 for calendar year taxpayers and on or before the 15th day of the 4th month following the end of the fiscal year for fiscal year taxpayers [G.S. § 105-155(a)]. A fiduciary may request an extension of time to file a return [G.S. § 105-160.6]. Extensions are discussed at ¶ 505.

• *Payment*

The full amount of the tax payable as shown on the return must be paid within the time allowed for filing the return. If, however, the amount shown to be due after all credits is less than $1, no payment need be made [G.S. § 105-160.7(a)].

• *Penalties*

The penalty for failure to file an estate or trust return by the due date is 5% of the tax per month (minimum $5; maximum 25% of the tax).

The penalty for failure to pay the tax by the due date is 10% of the tax (minimum $5).

Other penalties for fraud, negligence, and criminal penalties for willful failure to comply with the income tax laws are similar to those applicable to individuals [*2007—2008 Individual Income Tax Bulletins,* § VIII:4]. Penalties are discussed more fully at ¶ 3204.

PART V

CORPORATION INCOME TAX

CHAPTER 8

IMPOSITION OF TAX, RATES, EXEMPTIONS

¶801 Base, Rates, Methods, and Periods

North Carolina has imposed a corporation income tax since 1921. The present law is codified as Part I of Article 4, Chapter 105, General Statutes of North Carolina, as amended to date. The estimated income tax provisions for corporations are contained in Article 4, Part 1A. The corporation income tax is administered by the Corporate Tax Division of the North Carolina Department of Revenue.

Except for those corporations that are specifically exempt (see ¶ 804), the corporation income tax is imposed directly on the net income of domestic corporations and foreign corporations doing business in North Carolina [G.S. § 105-130.1]. The franchise tax, which is a privilege tax, is imposed in addition to the corporation income tax. The franchise tax is discussed in Part VI. S corporations, which are not subject to the corporation income tax, are discussed in Chapter 6.

Federal taxable income is used as the starting point in determining the corporation's taxable income for North Carolina purposes (see ¶ 901).

• *Definition of terms*

The following definitions apply to all sections of the North Carolina corporation income tax law [G.S. § 105-130.2]:

Affiliate: A corporation is an affiliate of another corporation when both are directly or indirectly controlled by the same parent corporation or by the same or associated financial interests by stock ownership, interlocking directors, or by any other means whatsoever, whether the control is direct or through one or more subsidiary, affiliated, or controlled corporations.

Corporation: A joint-stock company or association, an insurance company, a domestic corporation, a foreign corporation, or a limited liability company.

C corporation: A corporation that is not an S corporation.

Domestic corporation: A corporation organized under the laws of North Carolina.

¶801

Fiscal year: An income year that ends on the last day of any month other than December. A corporation that has elected to compute its federal income tax on a 52-53-week basis must use the same taxable year for North Carolina purposes as for federal purposes.

Foreign corporation: Any corporation other than a domestic corporation.

Gross income: Same as the federal income tax definition of IRC § 61.

Income year: The taxable year the corporation uses to compute state net income. If no fiscal year has been established, the income year is the calendar year. In the case of a return made for a fractions part of year, the income year is the period for which the return is made.

Limited liability company: A company classified as a corporation for federal income tax purposes that is either a limited liability company organized under Chapter 57D of the General Statutes or a foreign limited liability company authorized by that Chapter to transact business in North Carolina. In this context the term "shareholder" means a member of the limited liability company and the term "corporate officer" means a member or manager of the limited liability company.

Parent: A corporation is a parent of another corporation when, directly or indirectly, it controls the other corporation by stock ownership, interlocking directors, or by any other means whatsoever exercised by the same or associated financial interests, whether the control is direct or through one or more subsidiary, affiliated, or controlled corporations.

S corporation: A corporation for which a valid election under IRC § 1362(a) is in effect [G.S. § 105.130.2 (5a) and G.S. § 105.131(b)].

State net income: The taxpayer's federal taxable income, adjusted as required (see ¶902 and ¶905). In the case of a corporation that has income from business activity that is taxable both within and without North Carolina, state net income must be allocated and apportioned to North Carolina as required (see Chapter 10).

Taxable year: Income year.

- *Tax Base*

The North Carolina corporation income tax is imposed on state net income (defined above) or that portion of state net income that is allocated and apportioned to North Carolina. Corporations that do not allocate or apportion income are subject to tax on their entire state net income. For a discussion of allocation and apportionment, see Chapter 10.

- *Tax rates*

The corporation income tax rate is 2.5% for taxable years beginning on or after January 1, 2019 [G.S. § 105-130.3].

- *Accounting periods and methods*

For North Carolina purposes, corporations must compute net income in accordance with the method of accounting regularly employed in keeping their books, and the method must be consistent with respect to both income and deductions and must follow as nearly as practicable the federal practice, unless it is contrary to the context

¶801

and intent of the North Carolina corporation income tax statutes. In general, because the starting point for the computation of state net income is federal taxable income, North Carolina adopts the accounting periods and methods used for federal purposes. The Secretary may adopt federal rules and regulations of the Internal Revenue Service unless they are contrary to the context and intent of the North Carolina corporation income tax [G.S. § 105-130.15(a)].

Change of accounting period (i.e., income year): A corporation may change its accounting period without the prior approval of the Secretary of Revenue if the change is approved by or acceptable to the Internal Revenue Service and the period is used for filing federal returns. The taxpayer must notify the Secretary about the change after the change as been approved by the IRS. If federal approval is not required, the corporation must submit notification of the change with the short-period return. If a corporation wants to change its accounting period without IRS approval, it may make such change with the approval of the Secretary, provided the approval is requested at least 30 days prior to the end of its new income year [G.S. § 105-130.15(b)(1)].

Short-period return: A short-period return (*i.e.,* a return for a period of less than 12 months) must be made when a corporation changes its income year. A short period begins on the day after the close of the former taxable year and ends at the close of the day before the day designated as the first day of the new taxable year. If, however, a corporation is changing from or to a 52–53 week accounting period, it does not have to file a short-period return if the change results in a short period of 359 days or more or less than seven days. Short-period returns must be filed within the same period following the end of the short period as that required for full-year returns [G.S. § 105-130.15(b)(2)].

Installment method of reporting: A foreign corporation cannot use the installment method of reporting income for North Carolina purposes unless it files a bond with the Secretary in the amount of the sureties required by the Secretary [G.S. § 105-130.15(c)]. A domestic corporation that is dissolved, whether voluntarily, administratively, or judicially, or a foreign corporation that withdraws from the State or has its certificate of authority revoked, must file all tax reports and returns due and pay all taxes due. The final return of a corporation that has been dissolved, has withdrawn, or has had its certificate of authority revoked must include in income any unrealized or unreported profit from installment sales [G.S. § 105-130.15(d); 17 NCAC 5C.2101].

¶802 Corporations Subject to Tax

All domestic corporations (those chartered in North Carolina) and all foreign corporations doing business in North Carolina (see below) are subject to the North Carolina corporation income tax, and are required to file annual income tax returns [G.S. § § 105-130.3, 105-130.16]. Even for a year in which it was inactive or did not earn any net income, a corporation must file an income tax [17 NCAC 5C.0101(b)]. Note that a corporation that is inactive or has no assets is subject to an annual minimum franchise tax of $35 (see discussion at ¶1302)].

Because the concept of "doing business" for income tax purposes differs from the concept of "qualification" under the North Carolina Business Corporation Act, a foreign corporation operating in North Carolina may be subject to income tax even though it is not required to obtain a certificate of authority to do business in North Carolina [17 NCAC 5C.0101(a)].

Example: A Virginia corporation engaged in the general contracting business that obtains a single job in North Carolina to be completed within six months, would not, under the Business Corporation Act, be required to obtain a certificate of authority to do business in North Carolina, but would be subject to income tax.

¶803 Doing Business in North Carolina

The power of a state to tax its own residents is not subject to the limitations placed on interstate commerce by federal law. The question of whether a domestic corporation is doing business in North Carolina does not depend on how much business it does but whether it does *any* business in North Carolina. Thus, the question of whether or not a corporation is "doing business" in North Carolina almost always arises in the context of taxation of a foreign corporation, and it usually involves the carrying on of interstate commerce by the foreign corporation. The term "doing business" is not defined in the North Carolina tax statutes. The North Carolina Department of Revenue, however, has defined the term broadly in the regulatory rule of 17 NCAC 5C.0102 (see "Regulatory definition of 'doing business in North Carolina'," below). The best information on what the term means can be obtained by examining the authority on constitutionally permissible state taxation of interstate commerce.

"Doing Business" and "Business Activity" Synonymous

To be eligible for allocation and apportionment, a corporation must have income from business activity in another state. The Department of Revenue treats "doing business" and "business activity" as synonymous terms.

• *Regulatory definition of "doing business in North Carolina"*

The current position of the North Carolina Department of Revenue with respect to nexus is set forth in 17 NCAC 5C.0102 [*Frequently Asked Questions About N.C. Corporate, Excise, & Insurance Tax*, North Carolina Department of Revenue http:// www.dor.state.nc.us/faq/corporate.html]. This regulation states that, for income tax purposes, the term "doing business" means the operation of any business enterprise or activity in North Carolina for economic gain, including (but not limited to) the following:

(1) The maintenance of an office or other place of business in North Carolina [17 NCAC 5C.0102(a)(1)].

(2) The maintenance in North Carolina of an inventory of merchandise or material for sale, distribution, or manufacture, regardless of whether kept on the taxpayer's premises or in a public or rental warehouse [17 NCAC 5C.0102(a)(2)].

(3) The selling or distributing of merchandise to customers in North Carolina directly from a company-owned or company-operated vehicle when title to the merchandise is transferred from the seller or distributor to the customer at the time of the sale or distribution [17 NCAC 5C.0102(a)(3)].

¶803

(4) The rendering of a service to clients or customers in North Carolina by agents or employees of a foreign corporation [17 NCAC 5C.0102(a)(4)].

(5) The owning, renting, or operating of business or income-producing property in North Carolina, including (but not limited to) the following [17 NCAC 5C.0102(a)(5)]:

(a) Realty.

(b) Tangible personal property.

(c) Trademarks, trade names, franchise rights, computer programs, copyrights, patented processes, licenses.

Activities in North Carolina conducted by agent: The Secretary of Revenue has ruled that a corporation with no property or employees in North Carolina was nevertheless doing business in the State, because all of the corporation's operations and administrative functions were carried out by an unrelated consulting firm located in North Carolina. The corporation was therefore deemed to "maintain an office or other place of business" in the State for purposes of this rule [*Secretary's Decision No. 2001-289* (December 21, 2001)].

• *State taxation of income from interstate commerce*

The Commerce Clause of the U.S. Constitution prohibits any state taxation that imposes a burden on interstate commerce. At one time it was believed that this clause placed significant restrictions on the ability of states to tax corporations engaged in interstate commerce, particularly those engaged *solely* in interstate commerce. Prior to 1977, the U.S. Supreme Court had ruled that, under the Commerce Clause, it was unconstitutional for a state to levy a tax upon the privilege of carrying on a business that was exclusively interstate in character, no matter how fairly it was apportioned to business done within the state [*Spector Motor Service, Inc. v. O'Connor,* 340 U.S. 602 (1951)]. In North Carolina, however, the North Carolina Supreme Court upheld the North Carolina corporate income tax as it applied to a foreign corporation engaged in interstate business within the State. The court concluded that the tax, unlike the Connecticut tax at issue in *Spector,* was not a tax on the privilege of engaging in interstate business. Rather, the tax was imposed on the taxpayer's net income earned within and reasonably attributable to the taxpayer's business performed within the North Carolina [*ET & WNC Transp. v. Currie,* 248 NC 560, 104 S.E.2d 403 (1958), *aff'd per curiam,* 359 U.S. 28 (1959)].

In 1977, the U.S. Supreme Court overturned its decision in *Spector.* In *Complete Auto Transit v. Brady, Inc.,* 430 U.S. 274, *reh. denied* 430 U.S. 976 (1977), the Court ruled that a state tax on interstate commerce is not unconstitutional if it meets the following four criteria:

(1) The tax is applied to an activity with a substantial nexus with the taxing state.

(2) The tax is fairly apportioned.

(3) The tax does not discriminate against interstate commerce.

(4) The tax is fairly related to the services provided by the State.

• *Interstate Income Act of 1959 [P.L. 86-272, 15 U.S.C. §381]*

The major restriction on the taxation of corporations engaged in interstate commerce now is the Interstate Income Act of 1959. Public Law 86-272 prohibits imposition of a state net income tax on foreign corporations whose only activity in the state consists of the following:

(1) Solicitation of orders for sales of tangible personal property when the orders are approved and filled from a point outside the state.

(2) Solicitation of orders for a prospective customer if the customer's orders are approved outside the state and filled from a stock of goods outside the state.

"Solicitation" Not Defined

Public Law 86-272 does not define the term "solicitation," so the boundaries of the term are not clear. Moreover, different states have arrived at different conclusions with respect to what constitutes "mere solicitation." According to the U.S. Supreme Court, "mere solicitation" includes only those activities that are *entirely ancillary* to the solicitation of orders [*Wisconsin Dep't of Revenue v. William Wrigley, Jr., Co.*, 505 U.S. 214 (1992)]. Entirely ancillary (*i.e.,* immune) activities are those that serve no independent business function apart from the solicitation of orders (*e.g.,* recruiting, training, and evaluating sales personnel; use of hotels or homes for sales-related meetings; management involvement in tax credit disputes; providing a car and stock of free samples to salespersons). The Court recognized that there is a *de minimis* exception to the "mere solicitation" rule that applies to protect trivial nonimmune activities. However, in the *Wrigley* case, replacement of stale gum, restocking display racks, and storage of gum in Wisconsin were not considered ancillary activities and fell outside the scope of mere solicitation. In addition, Wrigley's nonimmune activities, taken together, constituted a more than trivial nexus with the state and thus were not protected by the *de minimis* exception.

Note that the protection of P.L. 86-272 is extended only to the sale of *tangible* personal property. For example, the sale of real or intangible property or the provision of services is not afforded the protection of P.L. 86-272. Note, also, that domestic corporations are subject to the North Carolina corporation income tax by virtue of their incorporation in North Carolina, regardless of the extent of their activities in the State.

In *Tax Directive CD-98-2* (April 27, 1998), the Department of Revenue confirmed its long-standing position that a foreign corporation sending agents or employees into North Carolina to solicit sales on behalf of a foreign manufacturer is not entitled to the protection afforded by P.L. 86-272. The sales agent cannot rely on P.L. 86-272 because the agent is rendering a service within the State (soliciting sales for the manufacturer) rather than making sales of tangible personal property.

Other Taxes Differ

Because P.L. 86-272 applies only to taxes that are measured by net income, it is possible that a corporation may be exempt from the corporate net income tax but not exempt from the capital stock/franchise tax or the sales and use tax.

¶803

• *Corporate partners in partnerships*

Corporations that are partners in a partnership or joint venture doing business in North Carolina are considered to be "doing business" [17 NCAC 5C.0102(b)]. This is true if the corporation owns an interest in a partnership that owns an interest in a partnership doing business in North Carolina. See *Secretary's Decision No. 97-548* (April 24, 1998), in which the Secretary ruled that a foreign corporation was doing business in North Carolina by virtue of holding a limited partnership interest in a limited partnership that in turn held a limited partnership interest in a partnership that was doing business in North Carolina. The decision confirms that a foreign corporation will be considered to be doing business within the State if it holds a partnership interest in a partnership doing business in the State regardless of whether the interest is a general or limited partnership interest and regardless of the presence of one or more intervening partnerships between the taxpayer and the partnership doing business in North Carolina.

Corporate Members of LLCs

The Department treats a corporate member of an LLC doing business in North Carolina as having nexus with the State, regardless of whether the LLC is classified as a corporation or as a partnership. However, the Department takes the position that the corporate member has no return-filing obligation unless the LLC is classified as a partnership or a disregarded entity for tax purposes, in which case the business of the LLC is attributed to the member in the same way that the business of a partnership is attributed to its partners under 17 NCAC 5C.0102(b) and 5C.1701 [*Tax Directive CD-02-1* (May 31, 2002)]. See discussion of *Tax Directive CD-02-1* at ¶603.

• *Rental of tangible personal property*

In *Secretary's Decision No. 98-299* (September 28, 1998), the Secretary ruled that a foreign corporation making sales and rentals of videos into North Carolina was doing business in the State, notwithstanding the fact that it had no facilities or sales or delivery force in the state. However, the Wake County Superior Court has held that an out-of-state corporation that sells and rents videotapes in North Carolina is not subject to the corporate income tax, the corporate franchise tax, or the sales and use tax because its activities, under the Commerce Clause of the U.S. Constitution as interpreted in the Supreme Court's now overruled decision in *Quill Corp. v. North Dakota*, 504 U.S. 298 (1992), do not create a "substantial nexus" that justifies North Carolina's attempts to collect the use tax, corporate income tax, and franchise tax. The corporation's activities in this case were limited to sending mail-order catalogs advertising its videos into North Carolina and filling orders placed by North Carolina residents by shipping the videos into North Carolina by common carrier [*Educational Resources, Inc. v. Tolson*, Wake County Superior Court, Nos. 00-CVS-14723 & 00-CVS-14724 (February 20, 2003)].

• *Licensing of trademarks*

The North Carolina Court of Appeals has held that a Delaware corporation that owned trademarks licensed to affiliates doing business in North Carolina was doing business within the state [*A&F Trademark, Inc. v. Tolson*, 167 N.C. App. 150, 605 S.E.2d 187 (2004), appeal dismissed, 359 N.C. 320 (2005), *cert. den.*, 546 U.S. 821 (2005)]. The court specifically endorsed the administrative interpretation of "doing business" set forth in 17 NCAC 5C.0102(a) and rejected the taxpayer's contention that the physical presence standard of *Quill Corp. v. North Dakota* applied to income taxes.

- *Out-of-state mortgage lenders*

A mortgage lender corporation that does not maintain a place of business in North Carolina is "doing business" in North Carolina (and is thus subject to the corporate income and franchise taxes) if (1) it makes more than $5,000,000 of loans secured by real property in North Carolina regardless of the location of the borrower and (2) it uses employees, agents, or independent contractors to perform services or activities in North Carolina for the purpose of soliciting or finalizing the loans (*e.g.*, accepting loan applications, collecting payments from customers, closing loans, foreclosing on real property in North Carolina).

An out-of-state corporation that acquires title to real property located in North Carolina as a result of foreclosure has nexus with North Carolina because it owns property located in North Carolina, and the income from the property must be allocated and apportioned. A corporation that invests in a loan by buying it from another person does not make the loan and therefore does not have nexus with North Carolina. Similarly, an out-of-state corporation that invests in State and/or local obligations does not have nexus. An out-of-state corporation that is not a mortgage lender corporation that makes a loan to an affiliate secured by real property located in North Carolina does not have nexus with North Carolina based on the loan to the affiliate. See *Tax Directive No.* CD-99-1 (February 19, 1999).

- *Royalty payments*

Royalty payments received for the use of intangible property in North Carolina are classified as income derived from doing business in North Carolina [G.S. § 105-130.7A(a)], which creates nexus with North Carolina. "Intangible property" for this purpose means copyrights, patents, and trademarks [G.S. § 105-130.7A(1a)]. See discussion of "Royalty payments" at ¶ 902.

Options: These royalty payments can be either (1) deducted by the payer and included in the income of the recipient or (2) added back to the income of the payer and excluded from the income of the recipient [G.S. § 105-130.7A(a)]. Note, however, that electing the add-back option does not prevent the recipient from having nexus with North Carolina [G.S. § 105-130.7A(a)].

- *Interstate motor carriers*

The regulations provide a special definition of "doing business" for interstate motor carriers. "Doing business" by an interstate motor carrier is defined as the performance of any of the following business activities in North Carolina [17 NCAC 5C.0102(c)]:

    (1) Maintenance of an office in North Carolina.

    (2) Operation of a terminal or other place of business in North Carolina.

    (3) Having an employee working out of the office or terminal of another company.

    (4) Dropping off or gathering up shipments in North Carolina.

¶804 Exempt Corporations

The following corporations are exempt from the corporate income tax:

(1) Fraternal beneficiary societies, orders, or associations that operate under the lodge system and provide life, sick, accident, or other benefits to members or their dependents [G.S. § 105-130.11(a)(1)].

(2) Cooperative banks without capital stock organized and operated for mutual purposes and without profit [G.S. § 105-130.11(a)(2)].

(3) Electric and telephone membership corporations organized under Chapter 117 of the General Statutes (relating to rural electrification) [G.S. § 105-130.11(a)(2)].

(4) Corporations organized for religious, charitable, scientific, or educational purposes, or for the prevention of cruelty to children and animals, including cemetery corporations [G.S. § 105-130.11(a)(3)]. Such organizations organized as trusts are also exempt [2007-2008 Corporate Income Tax Technical Bulletins, § II, T, 3.b]. For an example of a corporation denied exemption for private inurement, see *Secretary's Decision No. 2001-289* (December 21, 2001).

(5) Business leagues, chambers of commerce, merchants associations, and boards of trade not organized for profit if no net earnings inure to the benefit of any private stockholder or individual [G.S. § 105-130.11(a)(4)].

(6) Civic leagues or organizations not organized for profit and operated exclusively for the promotion of civic welfare [G.S. § 105-130.11(a)(5)].

(7) Clubs organized and operated exclusively for pleasure, recreation, and other non-profit purposes if no net earnings inure to the benefit of any private stockholder or individual [G.S. § 105-130.11(a)(6)].

(8) Mutual hail, cyclone, and fire insurance companies; mutual ditch or irrigation companies; mutual or cooperative telephone companies; and like organizations of a purely local character that derive their entire income from assessments, dues, or fees collected from members for the sole purpose of meeting expenses [G.S. § 105-130.11(a)(7)].

(9) Farmers', fruit growers' or like organizations organized and operated as sales agents to market the products of members, and to return to them the proceeds, less the necessary selling expenses, on the basis of the quantity of product furnished by them [G.S. § 105-130.11(8)].

(10) Mutual associations formed to conduct agricultural business on the mutual plan and marketing associations organized under G.S. § 54-129 through § 54-158 [G.S. § 105-130.11(9)].

(11) Insurance companies subject to the tax on gross premiums [G.S. § 105-130.11(a)(10)]. The tax on gross premiums is discussed in Chapter 28.

(12) Condominium associations, homeowner associations, or cooperative housing corporations not organized for profit (but only with respect to membership income) [G.S. § § 105-130.11(a)(11) and 105-130.11(c)].

(13) Pension, profiti-sharing, stock bonus and annuity trusts established by employers to distribute principal and income exclusively to employees and beneficiaries [2007-2008 Corporate Income Tax Technical Bulletins, § II, T, 3.h].

(14) Federally qualified real estate mortgage investment conduits (except for net income from prohibited transactions) [G.S. § 105-130.4(d)].

(15) Federally qualified regulated investment companies and real estate investment trusts that file an election with the Department (but only with respect to net income distributed or declared for distribution to shareholders during the income year or before the return for the income year is due) [2007-2008 Corporate Income Tax Technical Bulletins, § II, T, 5]. *See also* G.S. § 105-130.12 for the taxation of captive REITS.

(16) S corporations [G.S. § 105-130.3]. Taxation of S corporations is discussed in detail in Chapter 6.

• *Unrelated business income*

Organizations exempt from federal income tax as well as organizations specifically exempt from North Carolina income tax (other than those described in G.S. § 105-130.11(a)(2) cooperative banks and electric and telephone membership corporations), (a)(10) (insurance companies), (a)(11) (condominium/homeowner/corporations having associations) and S corporations are subject to tax on their unrelated business income as defined by Code § 512, adjusted by the allowable additions and deductions [G.S. § 105-130.11(b)]. Income derived from the following activities is not taxable as unrelated business income [G.S. § 105-130.11(b)]: (i) research performed by a college, university, or hospital; (ii) research performed for the United States or its instrumentality or for a state or its political subdivision; or (iii) research performed by an art organization operated primarily to carry on fundamental research, the results of which are freely available to the general public. In addition, amounts paid or incurred by 501(c)(3) organizations for a qualified parking facility that increase unrelated business taxable income for federal purposes do not create unrelated business taxable income for North Carolina purposes [G.S. § 105-130.11(b)(4)].

• *Proof of exemption*

A corporation is not exempt from tax merely because it is not organized and operated for profit. Nor does the fact that it is formed under Chapter 55A of the General Statutes (Nonprofit Corporation Act) automatically entitle a corporation to exemption [*Corporate Income, Franchise and Insurance Tax Bulletin*, II.T.8 (2018)].

Every corporation claiming exemption as a nonprofit organization or as cooperative or mutual association must furnish the Secretary with a copy of its Articles of Incorporation and bylaws, and any other document of information (e.g., trust agreement) that may be requested. After reviewing the evidence submitted, the Secretary will notify the corporation whether or not it qualifies for exemption. The principal factors that are considered in determining taxable status are the following [*Corporate Income, Franchise and Insurance Tax Bulletin*, II.T.8 (2018)]:

(1) The corporation's character.

(2) The corporation's purpose (the activities in which it will engage).

(3) The sources and disposition of its income.

(4) Whether any of its net income may inure to any private individual.

(5) What disposition will be made of its assets in event of dissolution.

¶804

Department Requires Specific Stipulation

It is the policy of the Department of Revenue, except when the nonprofit nature and intent of the corporation is otherwise clearly indicated, to require that the Articles of Incorporation or bylaws of the corporation contain a specific stipulation that no part of its net income will inure to the benefit of any private member, shareholder, or other individual, either during the existence of the corporation or in the event of its dissolution.

• *Notification of change in purpose or operation*

If any change is made in its purposes or method of operation that affects its taxable status, the corporation should promptly notify the Department of Revenue of the change [*Corporate Income, Franchise and Insurance Tax Bulletin*, II.T.9 (2018)].

CORPORATION INCOME TAX

CHAPTER 9

COMPUTATION OF TAXABLE INCOME

¶901 In General

• *Base*

The North Carolina corporation income tax is imposed on the state net income of every domestic corporation and foreign corporation doing business in North Carolina [G.S. § 105-130.1]. State net income is the taxpayer's federal taxable income adjusted as provided in G.S. § 105-130.5 and, in the case of a corporation that has income from business activity that is taxable both within and without North Carolina, allocated and apportioned to North Carolina as provided in G.S. § 105-130.4. Corporations doing business solely within North Carolina or not subject to tax in another state are taxed on their entire net income. Allocation and apportionment are discussed in Chapter 10. S corporations are exempt from the corporation income tax [G.S. § 105-131.1(a)]. Shareholders of S corporation pay tax on their pro rata shares of the corporation's income. S corporations are discussed in Chapter 6.

• *Computation of state net income*

The starting point for the determination of state net income for corporations is federal taxable income as defined under the Internal Revenue Code with required North Carolina adjustments. Each year the General Assembly updates the definition of Internal Revenue Code to take into account federal tax legislation. See ¶103 for the current definition. To compute state net income, a corporation starts with federal taxable income and adds or deducts items required by North Carolina law. Additions are discussed in ¶902; deductions are discussed in ¶903; and other adjustments (which may be either additions or deductions) are discussed in ¶905.

Note that in computing state net income the starting point is federal taxable income before the NOL deduction (*see* Form CD-405).

• *Special situations*

Certain homeowner associations: Nonprofit corporations or organizations operated for the benefit of its members (*e.g.,* condominium associations, homeowner associations, cooperative housing corporations) are subject to income tax on gross income (net of allowable deductions) that is not membership income. Membership income means the income from assessments, fees, charges, or similar amounts received from members of the organization for expenditure in the preservation, maintenance, and management of the common areas and facilities of, or the residential units in, the condominium or housing development [G.S. § 105-130.11(c)]. See also ¶ 804.

Real estate mortgage investment conduit: An entity that qualifies as a real estate mortgage investment conduit as defined in IRC § 8601 is taxable on any North Carolina net income derived from a prohibited transaction, as defined in IRC § 8601. Note, however, that holders of a regular or residual interest in a real estate mortgage investment conduit are subject to tax on income from that interest [G.S. § 105-130.11(d)].

¶ 902　North Carolina Additions to Federal Taxable Income

The following items must be added back to federal taxable income in computing state net income:

• *Capital gains offset by capital losses*

The amount by which gains have been offset by the capital loss carryover allowed under the Internal Revenue Code. All gains recognized on the sale or other disposition of assets must be included in determining state net income or loss in the year of disposition [G.S. § 105-130.5(a)(5)].

• *Deferred cancellation of indebtedness income*

The amount of cancellation of indebtedness (COD) income the taxpayer has elected to defer under § 108(i)(1) of the Code in connection with a debtor's reacquisition of its own debt instrument [G.S. § 105-130.5(a)(21)]. Deferred COD income added to federal taxable income under this provision may be subtracted from federal taxable income in computing state net income [G.S. § 105-130.5(b)(25)].

• *Depreciation for utility plants acquired by natural gas distributors*

The amount allowed for federal purposes or as an expense in lieu of depreciation for a utility plant acquired by a natural gas local distribution company, to the extent the plant is included in the company's rate base at zero cost in accordance with G.S. § 62-158 [G.S. § 105-130.5(a)(12)].

• *Disaster-related work payments*

Payments made to an affiliate or subsidiary that are not taxable pursuant to the relief provisions for disaster-related work on critical infrastructure must be added back to the extent deducted in computing federal taxable income. [G.S. § 105-130.5(a)(30)]. For a discussion of the relief provisions, see ¶ 3312.

• *Dividend deduction paid to captive REIT*

The dividend paid deduction allowed under the Code to a captive REIT, as defined in G.S. § 105-130.12 [G.S. § 105-130.5(a)(19)].

• *Federal contributions deduction*

Contributions deducted on the federal income tax return [G.S. § 105-130.5(a)(3)]. See ¶ 907 for discussion of the deductions for contributions.

• *Federal decoupling adjustment*

The amount required to be added under G.S. § 105-130.5B when the State decouples from federal accelerated depreciation and expensing [G.S. § 105-130.5(a)(24)]. The federal decoupling adjustments are discussed at ¶ 904.

• *Foreign-derived intangible income deduction*

The amount deducted for federal purposes under Code section 250 to lower the effective federal rate on foreign-derived intangible income [G.S. § 105-130.5(a)(28)].

• *Global intangible low-taxed income deduction*

The amount deducted for federal purposes under Code section 250 to lower the effective federal rate on global intangible low-taxed income [G.S. § 105-130.5(a)(28)].

• *Interest on state and local obligations of other states*

Interest income earned on bonds and other obligations of other states or their political subdivisions, less allowable amortization on any bond acquired on or after January 1, 1963 [G.S. § 105-130.5(a)(4)]. Gain or loss realized on the sale or other disposition of any type of obligation of the United States or its possessions, the State of North Carolina (unless exempted by the specific obligation), or its political subdivisions, or of any other government is taxable and must be included in the computation of a corporation's state net income [17 NCAC 5C.0404(a)]. Gain or loss realized on the sale or other disposition of obligations is not included in taxable income if the law under which the obligations were issued specifically exempts the gain or interest from taxation [17 NCAC 5C.0404(b)]. The following are examples of such obligations:

(1) Indebtedness issued under G.S. § 131E-28 by the North Carolina Hospital Authorities (both interest and gain exempt).

(2) Obligations issued by the North Carolina Housing Finance Agency under G.S. § 122A-19 (both interest and gain exempt).

(3) Bonds issued under the joint Municipal Electric Power and Energy Act under G.S. § 159B-26 (both interest and gain exempt).

• *Interest paid to incur tax-exempt income*

Interest paid in connection with income exempt from the corporate income tax [G.S. § 105-130.5(a)(2)].

• *Net interest paid to related members*

Net interest expense paid to a related member as determined under G.S. § 105-130.5(a)(25). For more detail see ¶ 910.

¶ 902

• *NOL deduction*

Any amount allowed as a net operating loss deduction (NOL) under the Code [G.S. § 105-130.5(a)(6)]. *See* ¶ 906 for deductions for state net losses and net economic losses.

• *OID deducted on AHYDOs*

The amount of original issue discount (OID) on an applicable high-yield discount obligation (AHYDO) allowed as a deduction under § 163(e)(5)(F) of the Code [G.S. § 105-130.5(a)(22).

• *Payments to affiliates*

Payments to or charges by a parent, subsidiary, or affiliated corporation in excess of fair compensation in all intercompany transactions of any kind whatsoever [G.S. § 105-130.5(a)(9)].

• *Percentage depletion*

Percentage depletion in excess of cost depletion applicable to mines, oil and gas wells, and other natural deposits [G.S. § 105-130.5(a)(11)].

This rule, however, does not apply to depletion deductions for solid minerals or rare earths extracted from the soil or waters of North Carolina (*e.g.,* clay, gravel, phosphate rock, lime, shells, stone, sand, feldspar, gemstones, mica, talc, lithium compounds, tungsten, coal, peat, olivine, pyrophyllite).

Corporations required to apportion income to North Carolina must first add to federal taxable income the amount of all percentage depletion in excess of cost depletion that was subtracted from its gross income in computing its federal income and then subtract from the taxable income apportioned to North Carolina the amount by which the percentage depletion allowance for solid minerals or rare earths extracted from the soil or waters of North Carolina exceeds the cost depletion allowance for these items.

• *Qualified Opportunity Zone deferrals and exclusions*

Gains deferred or excluded from federal taxable income because reinvested in Qualified Opportunity Zones [G.S. § § 105-130.5(a)(26) and (27)].

• *Repatriation deduction*

The amount deducted for federal purposes pursuant to Code section 965(c) to lower the effective federal tax rate on deemed repatriations [G.S. § § 105-130.5(a)(29)].

• *Royalty payments*

General Rule: Royalty payments made to, or in connection with transactions with, a related member during the taxable year to the extent deducted in computing federal taxable income [G.S. § § 105-130.5(a)(14) and 105-130.7A(c)].

Exceptions: This addition is not required for an amount of royalty payments that meets any of the following conditions:

¶902

(1) The related member includes the amount as income on its North Carolina income tax return for the same taxable year that the amount is deducted by the taxpayer *and* the related member does not elect to deduct the amount pursuant to G.S. § 105-130.5(b)(20) [G.S. § 105-130.7A(c)(1)].

(2) The taxpayer can establish that the related member during the same taxable year directly or indirectly paid, accrued, or incurred the amount to a person who is not a related member [G.S. § 105-130.7A(c)(2)].

(3) The taxpayer can establish that the related member to whom the amount was paid is organized under the laws of a foreign country that has a comprehensive income tax treaty with the United States and that imposes a tax on the royalty income of the related member at a rate that equals or exceeds the North Carolina corporation income tax rate [G.S. § 105-130.7A(c)(3)].

Royalty Payment: The term "royalty payment" means expenses, losses, and costs paid, accrued, or incurred for "North Carolina royalties" to the extent allowed as deductions or costs in the determination of federal taxable income before the operating loss deduction and special deductions for the taxable year (as well as interest and similar charges deductible under IRC § 163 and otherwise deductible under North Carolina law paid, accrued, or incurred for the late payment of such royalties) [G.S. § 105-130.7A(b)(6)]. A "North Carolina royalty" is an amount charged that is for, related to, or in connection with the "use" of "intangible property" in North Carolina and includes royalty and technical fees, licensing fees, and other similar charges [G.S. § 105-130.7A(b)(2)]. "Intangible property" means copyrights, patents, and "trademarks" [G.S. § 105-130.7a(1a)]. A "trademark" is a trademark, trade name, service mark, or other similar type of intangible asset [G.S. § 105-130.7A(b)(7)]. The "use" of intangible property includes direct or indirect maintenance, management, ownership, sale, exchange, or disposition of the asset [G.S. § 105-130.7A(b)(8)].

Related Member: A "related member" is a person that, with respect to the taxpayer during any part of the taxable year, is one or more of the following: (1) a "related entity"; (2) a component member (as defined in IRC § 1563(b)); (3) or a person to or from whom there would be attribution of stock ownership under IRC § 1563(e) if the phrase "5 percent or more" were replaced by "twenty percent (20%) or more" each place it appears in that section [G.S. § 105-130.7A(b)(5) and (b)(1)]. A "related entity" is any of the following [G.S. § 105-103.7A(b)(4)]: (1) a stockholder who is an individual, or a member of the stockholder's family enumerated in IRC § 318, if the stockholder and the members of the stockholder's family own in the aggregate at least 80% of the value of the taxpayer's outstanding stock; (2) a stockholder, or a stockholder's partnership, limited liability company, estate, trust, or corporation, if the stockholder and the stockholder's partnerships, limited liability companies, estates, trusts, and corporations own in the aggregate at least 50% of the value of the taxpayer's outstanding stock; or (3) a corporation, or a party related to the corporation in a manner that would require an attribution of stock from the corporation to the party or from the party to the corporation under the attribution rules of IRC § 318 if the taxpayer owns at least 80% of the value of the stock. For purposes of these definitions, the term "own" means to own directly, indirectly, beneficially, or constructively, and the attribution rules of IRC § 318 apply in determining ownership [G.S. § 105-130.7A(b)(3)].

"Doing Business": The royalty reporting statute also codifies the Department's long-standing administrative interpretations that income from the use of intangible property in North Carolina is income derived from doing business in North Carolina

¶902

[G.S. § 105-130.7A(a); *see also* 17 NCAC 5C.0102(a)(5) and S.D. 97-990; *A&F Trademark v. Tolson*, 167 N.C. App. 150, 605 S.E.2d 187 (2004), *appeal dismissed*, 359 N.C. 320 (2005), *cert. den.*, 546 U.S. 821 (2005)].

Indirect transaction: For purposes of the royalty reporting statute, an indirect transaction or relationship has the same effect as if it were direct [G.S. § 105-130.7A(d)].

• *Subchapter R exclusions*

The amount excluded from gross income under Subchapter R of Chapter 1 of the Code (relating to the federal alternative tax on qualifying shipping activities) [G.S. § 105-130.5(a)(16)].

• *Tax credits*

The total amount of all income tax credits allowed under North Carolina law during the taxable year as a credit against the corporation's income tax liability [G.S. § 105-130.5(a)(10)]. A corporation that apportions part of its income to North Carolina must add back the credits after it determines the amount of its income that is apportioned and allocated to North Carolina and cannot apply the apportionment factor used in determination of its apportioned income to the amount of the North Carolina credits. Tax credits for corporations are discussed in Chapter 11.

• *Taxes based on net income and excess profits tax*

Taxes based on or measured by net income by whatever name called and excess profits taxes to the extent allowed for federal purposes [G.S. § 105-130.5(a)(1)].

¶903 North Carolina Deductions from Federal Taxable Income

The following items may be deducted from federal taxable income in computing state net income:

• *911 charges*

To the extent included in federal taxable income, the amount of 911 charges collected under G.S. § 62A-5 and remitted to a local government under G.S. § 62A-6, and the amount of wireless Enhanced 911 service charges collected under G.S. § 62A-23 and remitted to the Wireless Fund under G.S. § 62A-24 [G.S. § 105-130.5(b)(17)].

• *Capital losses*

The amount of losses realized on the sale or other disposition of assets not allowable under IRC § 1211(a), relating to limitations on capital losses. All losses recognized on the sale or other disposition of assets must be included in determining state net income or loss in the year of disposition [G.S. § 105-130.5(b)(8)].

• *Contributions*

Contributions or gifts made by the corporation within the taxable year to the extent provided under G.S. § 105-130.9 [G.S. § 105-130.5(b)(5)]. For more detail, see ¶906.

• *Controlled foreign corporation*

The amount of any Subpart F income required to be included in the taxpayer's income for federal purposes under IRC § 951, net of related expenses, and the amount of any foreign taxes deemed paid by the taxpayer and treated as a dividend under IRC § 78, net of any related expenses [G.S. § 105-130.5(b)(3b)].

• *Deferred COD income*

Cancellation of indebtedness (COD) income deferred for federal purposes under Code § 108(i)(1) and added to federal taxable income under G.S. § 105-130.5(a)(21) [G.S. § 105-130.5(b)(25)].

• *Dividends from captive REITs*

A dividend received from a captive REIT, as defined in G.S. § 105-130.12 [G.S. § 105-130.5(b)(23)].

• *Economic incentives*

Amounts received as an economic incentive under the state's Jobs Development Investment Grant or Job Maintenance and Capital Development Fund programs to the extent such amounts were included in federal taxable income [G.S. § 105-130.5 (b)(31)].

• *Excessive payments received from affiliated corporations*

Payments received from a parent, subsidiary, or affiliated corporation in excess of fair compensation in intercompany transaction that were not allowed as a deduction under North Carolina's revenue laws [G.S. § 105-130.5(b)(2)].

• *Federal basis reduced by tax credit*

The amount by which the basis of a depreciable asset has been reduced on account of a tax credit allowed for federal tax purposes because of a tax credit allowed against the corporation's federal income tax liability or because of a grant allowed under § 1603 of the American Recovery and Reinvestment Tax Act of 2009 [P.L. 111-3]. This deduction may be claimed only in the year in which the Internal Revenue Code requires that the asset's basis be reduced. In computing gain or loss on the asset's disposition, this deduction is considered to be depreciation [G.S. § 105-130.5(b)(14)].

• *Federal decoupling adjustment*

The amount required to be added under G.S. § 105-130.5B when the State decouples from federal accelerated depreciation and expensing [G.S. § 105-130.5(a)(24)]. The federal decoupling adjustments are discussed at ¶ 904.

• *Foreign-source dividends*

Dividends treated as received from sources outside the United States (as determined under IRC § 862), net of related expenses, may be subtracted to the extent included in federal taxable income [G.S. § 105-130.5(b)(3a)].

• *Global intangible low-taxed income inclusions*

The amount included in federal taxable income under Code section 951A as global intangible low-taxed income [G.S.§ 105-130.5(b)(3b)].

• *Hurricane relief payments*

The amount paid to the taxpayer during the year (other than in payment for goods or services) from the State Emergency Response and Disaster Relief Reserve Fund for hurricane relief or assistance to the extent included in federal taxable income [G.S. § 105-130.5(b)(29)].

• *Interest on federal obligations*

Interest on the obligations of the United States or its possessions to the extent provided in federal taxable income. However, federal interest is not deductible for North Carolina purposes unless interest upon obligations of the State of North Carolina or any of its political subdivisions is exempt from income tax imposed by the United States [G.S. § 105-130.5(b)(1)]. Market discount income on federal bonds is not deductible under this provision, because market discount income on North Carolina obligations is subject to federal taxation. *See* Final Agency Decision 08 REV 2665 (January 22, 2010), *aff'd Fidelity Bank v. N.C. Dept. of Revenue*, 2013 NCBC 27 (N.C. Super., May 3, 2013), *aff'd in part*, ___ N.C. ___ (2017).

• *Interest on State obligations and State-chartered or organized educational institutions*

Interest on the obligations of any of the following, net of related expenses, to the extent included in federal taxable income [G.S. § 105-130.5(b)(1a)]:

(1) North Carolina, a political subdivision of North Carolina, or a commission, an authority, or another agency of North Carolina or of a political subdivision of North Carolina.

(2) Nonprofit educational institutions organized or chartered under the laws of North Carolina.

(3) A hospital authority created by a city or county pursuant to G.S. § 131E-17.

• *Natural gas expansion surcharges*

The amount of natural gas expansion surcharges collected by a natural gas local distribution company under G.S. § 62-158 (relating to public utilities) [G.S. § 105-130.5(b)(16)].

• *Net economic loss carryforward*

For taxable years beginning before January 1, 2015, corporations were entitled to deduct net economic losses as calculated under former G.S. § 105-130.8 incurred by the corporation in any or all of the 15 preceding years. Corporations required to allocate and apportion net income were required to deduct only the allocable and apportionable net economic loss from total income allocable and apportionable to North Carolina [G.S. § 105-130.5(b)(4)]. For taxable years beginning on or after January 1, 2015, corporations are allowed to deduct state net losses [G.S. § 105-130.5(b)(4a)]. However, corporations may continue to deduct any unused portion of a net economic loss incurred in years before 2015 in computing state net income for taxable years beginning before January 1, 2030 [G.S. § 105-130.5(b)(4)]. For more detail, see ¶ 906.

¶903

• *Ordinary and necessary business expenses*

The amount by which a deduction or an ordinary and necessary business expense on the corporation's federal income tax return was reduced and not allowable as a deduction because the corporation claimed a federal tax credit in lieu of a federal deduction for the taxable year [G.S. § 105-130.5(b)(11)].

• *Qualified interest expense*

The amount of qualified interest expense to a related member as determined under G.S. § 105-130.7B [G.S. § 105-130.5(b)(28)]. For more detail see ¶ 910.

• *Qualified Opportunity Zone inclusions*

The amount of deferred Qualified Opportunity Zone gain included in federal taxable income to the extent such amount was previously required to be added back in computing state net income [G.S.§ 105-130.5(b)(30)].

• *Repatriation inclusions*

The amount included in federal taxable income under Code section 965 as a deemed repatriation of deferred foreign income [G.S. § 105-130.5(b)(3b)].

• *Royalty payments*

Royalty payments received from a related member who added the payments to income for the same taxable year [G.S. § 105-130.5(b)(20)]. *See* ¶ 902 for discussion of royalty payments added to income.

• *State net losses*

The allocable and apportionable state net loss [G.S. § 105-130.5(b)(4a)]. For discussion see ¶ 906.

• *Undistributed capital gains of regulated investment companies (RICs)*

With respect to a shareholder of a regulated investment company, the portion of undistributed capital gains of RICs included in federal taxable income and on which the federal tax paid by the RIC is allowed as a credit or refund to the shareholder under IRC § 852 [G.S. § 105-130.5(b)(9)].

¶904 Federal Decoupling Adjustments

• *Special Accelerated Depreciation*

A taxpayer that takes a federal special depreciation deduction under Code § 168(k) (relating to bonus depreciation for property placed in service after 2007) or Code § 168(n) (relating to additional depreciation for certain disaster assistance property) must add back 85% of those special depreciation deductions in determining state net income. The taxpayer is then allowed to deduct 20% of the add-back in each of the first five years following the year of the add-back [G.S. § 105-130.5B(a)].

A taxpayer who placed property in service in the 2009 taxable year and whose state net income reflected a special accelerated depreciation deduction for such property under Code § 168(k) was required to add back 85% of the federal deduction in computing state net income for the 2010 taxable year. Such a taxpayer may deduct the add-back in five annual 20% installments commencing in the 2011 taxable year [G.S. § 105-130.5B(b)].

• *Expensing Elections*

A taxpayer who places in service section 179 property (*i.e.,* property eligible for the federal expensing election under Code § 179) during a taxable year must add-back 85% of the amount by which the federal expensing deductions under Code § 179 exceeded the dollar and investment limitation for that taxable year. For taxable years beginning in or after 2013, the dollar limitation is $25,000 and the investment limitation is $200,000.

The taxpayer may deduct 20% of the add-back in each of the first five taxable years following the year of the add-back [G.S. § 105-130.5B(c)].

• *Asset Basis*

The federal decoupling adjustments for special accelerated depreciation and expensing do not create a difference in the basis of the assets depreciated or expensed for federal and state tax purposes, except in the case of an actual or deemed transfer of an asset on or after January 1, 2013 where the transferee takes a carryover basis for federal tax purposes. In that case, the transferee must add any remaining deductions related to the special accelerated depreciation add-back to the basis of the asset for state tax purposes and depreciate the adjusted basis over the asset's remaining life. The transferor is not allowed any remaining special accelerated depreciation deductions with respect to the transferred asset [G.S. § 105-130.5B(d) and (e)].

For carryover basis transfers before January 1, 2013, the transferor and transferee may elect to make the basis adjustment described above on the transferee's 2013 tax return to the extent the transferor has not taken the special accelerated depreciation deductions on a prior return and provided the transferor certifies in writing to the transferee that the transferor will not take any remaining deductions with respect to the add-back attributable to the transferred assets for the tax years beginning on or after January 1, 2013. If the asset has been disposed of or has no remaining useful life on the transferee's books, the transferee may take the remaining bonus depreciation deduction on its 2013 return [G.S. § 105-130.5B(f)].

Where the transferee is permitted to increase the basis of an asset received in a carryover basis transaction as described above, federal taxable income must be adjusted to account for any difference in the amount of depreciation, amortization, gain or loss resulting from differences in federal and state depreciation and amortization [G.S. § 105-130.5B(g)].

¶905 Other Adjustments

The following adjustments do not fit automatically into either the addition category or the deduction category. They may be additions or deductions.

    (1) With respect to any bond acquired prior to January 1, 1963, the amount of premium paid is deductible only in the year of sale or other disposition. No

deduction is allowed for North Carolina purposes for annual amortization of bond premiums applicable to bonds acquired prior to January 1, 1963 [G.S. § 105-130.5(c)(1)].

(2) Federal taxable income must be increased or decreased to account for any difference in the amount of depreciation, amortization, or gains or losses applicable to property that has been depreciated or amortized by using a different basis or rate for North Carolina income tax purposes than for federal purposes [G.S. § 105-130.5(c)(2)]. This adjustment would be required only for property acquired before North Carolina conformed to the federal Internal Revenue Code.

(3) No deduction is allowed for any direct or indirect expenses related to income not taxed for North Carolina corporation income tax purposes, except for adjustments allowed by G.S. § 105-130.5(a) and (b). For dividends received that are not taxed, the adjustment for expenses may not exceed 15% of the dividend amount [G.S. § 105-130.5(c)(3)]. But see ¶ 909.

(4) Federal taxable income must be adjusted where the recovery of previously deducted amounts causes different changes in state net income and federal taxable income. For example, an item previously deducted may have reduced a taxpayer's North Carolina tax but not the taxpayer's federal tax. If this item is not included in federal taxable income in the year of recovery, it must be added back for North Carolina purposes. On the other hand, an item previously deducted may have reduced a taxpayer's federal tax but not the taxpayer's North Carolina tax. If this item is included in federal taxable income in the year of recovery, it may be subtracted for North Carolina purposes [G.S. § 105-130.5(c)(4)].

(5) A corporation that uses the installment method of accounting and that withdraws from North Carolina, dissolves, merges, or consolidates its business, or terminates its business in North Carolina in any other way, must include in state net income on its final return all unrealized or unreported income from installment sales made while doing business in North Carolina. A final income tax return must be filed within 75 days after the close of business [G.S. § 105-130.15(d)].

¶906 State Net Losses and Net Economic Losses

• *Generally*

For taxable years beginning on or after January 1, 2015, a corporation may deduct a state net loss. For taxable years beginning before January 1, 2015, a corporation was permitted to deduct a net economic loss. A corporation that had an unused net economic loss at the end of its last taxable year beginning before January 1, 2015 may carry the unused net economic loss forward as an additional deduction from federal taxable income for taxable years beginning before January 1, 2030 [G.S. § 105-130.5(b)(4) and (4a)].

• *State net loss defined*

A taxpayer's state net loss for a taxable year is the amount by which allowable deductions for the year other than prior year losses exceed its gross income for the year as determined under the Code and as adjusted pursuant to G.S. § 105-130.5 [G.S. § 105-130.8A(a)].

- *Allocation and apportionment of loss*

In the case of a corporation with income from business activities within and without the State, the State net loss must be allocated and apportioned to North Carolina in the year the loss is incurred [G.S. § 105-130.8A(a)].

- *Carryforward*

A state net loss may be carried forward for 15 taxable years following the year the loss was incurred, provided that any loss carried forward must be applied to the next succeeding taxable year before any portion is applied to a subsequent taxable year [G.S. § 105-130.8A(b)]. In addition, the extent to which a state net loss survives a merger or acquisition is to be determined by the Secretary applying standards contained in the Treasury Regulations adopted under Code sections 381 and 382 [G.S. § 105-130.8A(c)].

- *Books and records*

A taxpayer claiming a state net loss deduction must maintain all records necessary to determine and verify the amount of the deduction and must make such research available to the Secretary for inspection [G.S. § 105-130.8A(d)].

- *Statute of limitations*

Either the taxpayer or the Secretary may redetermine a loss originating in a closed year in order to determine the amount of the loss that can be carried forward to an open year [G.S. § 105-130.8A(d)].

- *Net economic losses*

Unused net economic losses incurred in taxable years beginning before January 1, 2015 may be carried forward to taxable years beginning before January 1, 2030 [G.S. § 105-130.8A(e)]. In determining and verifying the amount of a net economic loss incurred in taxable years beginning before January 1, 2015, the provisions of former G.S. § 105-130.8 will continue to apply [G.S. § 105-1308A(e)].

¶907 Contributions Deduction

Subject to certain limitations, contributions or gifts made by a corporation in a taxable year to qualified donees are deductible in determining net income [G.S. § 105-130.9].

- *Contributions limited to 5% of net income*

5% donees: For this purpose, charitable contributions are defined in IRC § 170(c). Such contributions made to these organizations (except those listed below) are limited to an amount not exceeding 5% of the corporation's net income as determined before the deductions for contributions. No carryover of unused contributions to subsequent years is permitted [G.S. § 105-130.9(1)].

¶907

• *Contributions fully deductible*

100% donees: Contributions by any corporation to (1) the State of North Carolina, (2) any county of North Carolina, (3) any municipality of North Carolina (or to any of their institutions, instrumentalities, or agencies), and (4) any educational institution located in North Carolina are fully deductible.

For this purpose "educational institution" means only an educational institution that normally maintains a regular faculty and curriculum and normally has a regularly organized body of students in attendance at the place where the educational activities are carried on. This definition includes the institution's departments, schools, and colleges, as well as a group of educational institutions and an organization (corporation, trust, foundation, association, or other entity) organized and operated exclusively to receive, hold, invest, and administer property and to make expenditures to or for the sole benefit of an educational institution or groups of such institutions [G.S. § 105-130.9(2)].

The following example, from *Corporate Income, Franchise, and Insurance Tax Bulletin*, II.K.4. (2018), illustrates the computation of the contributions deduction.

> *Example:* Corporation deducted contributions of $100 to a North Carolina county agency, $50 to a college located in North Carolina, and $50 to other qualified donees (subject to the 5% limitation) in determining net income of $1,000 before deduction of a net economic loss (or state net loss) of $500.

Net income		$1,000
Add: Contributions		200
Net income before net economic loss deductions		$1,200
Less: Net economic loss (or state net loss) brought forward		500
Net income before contributions deductions		$ 700
Less allowable contributions:		
Deductions subject to the 5% limitation (5% of $700)	$ 35	
College located in North Carolina	50	
North Carolina county agency	100	185
Net taxable income		$ 515

• *Contributions by corporations subject to allocation and apportionment*

A corporation subject to allocation and apportionment must deduct from total net income allocable to North Carolina the contributions it made to North Carolina 100% donees. However, contributions made to 5% donees (see above) are limited to 5% of the total net income allocated to North Carolina as computed before the contributions deduction. For this purpose, total net income allocated to North Carolina is income apportionable to North Carolina plus income directly allocable to North Carolina less the allowable portion of the net economic loss deduction. See example below. Allocation and apportionment are discussed in Chapter 10.

No Contribution Deduction from Apportioned Business Income

The contributions that qualify as a direct deduction from total net income allocated to North Carolina cannot be deducted in arriving at the corporation's total net income subject to apportionment [G.S. § 105-130.9(3)].

¶907

The following example, from *Corporate Income, Franchise, and Insurance Tax Bulletin*, II.K.5. (2018), illustrates the computation of the contributions deduction for a corporation subject to allocation and apportionment:

Example: Corporation has net income of $114,000 before the net economic loss (or state net loss) deduction and contributions deduction. Contributions total $6,200 and include $200 to a North Carolina agency, $2,000 to other North Carolina donees, and $4,000 to qualified donees located outside North Carolina.

Net income before contributions and net economic loss deduction		$114,000
Less: Contributions to donees outside North Carolina		4,000
Total		$110,000
Less: Total nonapportionable income		10,000
Total apportionable income		$100,000
Apportionable to North Carolina (35%)		$ 35,000
Add: Nonapportionable income directly allocable to North Carolina		1,000
Total income allocated to NC		$ 36,000
Less: Allowable portion of net economic loss (or state net loss) deduction		6,000
Total income allocated to North Carolina before contributions to donees		$ 30,000
Less contributions:		
North Carolina donees (not to exceed 5% of $30,000)		$ 1,500
North Carolina county agency	200	1,700
Net taxable income		$ 28,300

¶908 Rapid Amortization of OSHA-Mandated Equipment

In lieu of depreciation, a corporation may opt to amortize the cost of any equipment mandated by the Occupational Safety and Health Act (OSHA), including the cost of planning, acquiring, constructing, modifying, and installing such equipment [G.S. § 105-130.10A(a)].

Equipment mandated by OSHA: "Equipment mandated by the Occupational Safety and Health Act" is any tangible personal property and other buildings and structural components of buildings that are acquired, constructed, reconstructed, modified, or erected after January 1, 1979, and that the taxpayer must acquire, construct, install, or make available in order to comply with the occupational and health standards required by the United States Secretary of Labor or the Commissioner of Labor of North Carolina [G.S. § 105-130.10A(b)].

Occupational safety and health standards: "Occupational safety and health standards" includes, but is not limited to, interim federal standards, consensus standards, any proprietary standards or permanent standards, as well as temporary emergency standards that may be adopted by the United States Secretary of Labor and that are published in the Code of Federal Regulations or otherwise properly promulgated under the Occupational Safety and Health Act of 1970 or any alternative rule, regulation, or standard promulgated by the Commissioner of Labor of North Carolina [G.S. § 105-130.10A(b)].

¶909 Attribution of Expenses to Nontaxable Income and to Nonapportionable Income

All expenses directly connected with the production of income that is not taxable in North Carolina (untaxed income) must be used to compute the net amount of such untaxed income [17 NCAC 5C.0304(a)].

¶908

- *Interest expenses*

When a corporation earns untaxed income or holds property that does or will produce untaxed income and incurs interest expense that is not specifically related to any particular income or property, it must attribute a portion of the interest to untaxed income and property in the determination of taxable income reported to North Carolina according to the formula set forth in 17 NCAC 5C.0304(b).

- *Examples of untaxed income*

The following are examples of untaxed income:

(1) Dividend income classified as nonapportionable [17 NCAC 5C.0304(c)(1)].

(2) Dividend income excludable by statute [17 NCAC 5C.0304(c)(2)].

(3) Interest income classified as nonapportionable [17 NCAC 5C.0304(c)(3)].

(4) Interest income earned on United States obligations and North Carolina obligations [17 NCAC 5C.0304(c)(4)].

(5) Other nonapportionable income or exempt income [17 NCAC 5C.0304(c)(5)].

- *Interest income and expenses*

When a corporation earns income not taxable in North Carolina or holds property that does or will produce untaxed income and incurs interest expense that is not specifically related to any particular income or property, it must attribute a portion of the interest expense to the untaxed income and/or property in determining state net income [17 NCAC 5C.0304(b)]. The formula (called in this text the attribution formula) used for computing the amount of interest expense to be attributed to untaxed income and property is prescribed in 17 NCAC 5C.0304(b). The application of this principle is illustrated in the following example:

> *Example:* Morse Corporation has total tax return balance sheet assets of $3,000,000. The value of its assets that produce untaxed income is $90,000. Morse's gross untaxed income is $5,000; its total gross profits are $200,000. During the taxable year, Morse had interest income of $9,000 that is not specifically related to any particular income or property. Morse must attribute $338 of this interest income to untaxed income and property. The attribution formula must be used, as follows:

(1)	Determine asset ratio:		
	(A)	Value of tax return balance sheet assets that produce or would produce untaxed income	$ 90,000
	(B)	Value of all assets on the tax return balance sheet	$ 3,000,000
	(C)	Asset ratio ($90,000/$3,000,000)	0.0300
(2)	Determine income/profit ratio:		
	(A)	Gross untaxed income	$ 9,000
	(B)	Total gross profits	$ 200,000
	(C)	Income/profit ratio ($9,000/$200,000)	0.0450
(3)	Add asset ratio and income/profit ratio (0.0300 + 0.0450)		0.0750
(4)	Average percentage (0.0750/2)		0.0375
(5)	Interest expense attributable to untaxed income (0.0375 × $9,000)		$338

Taxpayers Who Use the Equity Method

When the equity method of accounting is used (1) the increase or decrease in value as a result of using the equity method may be excluded from the value in (1)(A), above, and

(2) equity included in the value in (1)(B), above, may be excluded and the reserve for depreciation reflected on the balance sheet may be restored to the asset value [17 NCAC 5C.0304].

• *Expenses connected with interest income from United States obligations*

Interest income from obligations of the United States or its possessions is excludable from state net income to the extent such income is included in federal taxable income. Expenses incurred in producing the exempt income must be determined and subtracted from the gross amount earned during a taxable period before the deduction is made in computing state net income. In the computation of expenses related to income from United States obligations, the attribution formula described above may be used [17 NCAC 5C.0304(d)].

• *Expenses related to dividends received*

Dividend income may be either apportionable income or nonapportionable income, depending on its nature. A dividend is considered apportionable income if any of the following circumstances apply [*CTAM 97-14* (September 15, 1997)]:

(1) The dividend arises out of or is acquired in the regular course of the corporation's trade or business.

(2) The purpose of the corporation in acquiring or holding the stock that gives rise to the dividend is related to the corporation's trade or business.

(3) The dividend is paid by a unitary subsidiary.

If a dividend is not apportionable income, it is nonapportionable income. Attribution of expenses is required for nonapportionable dividends for both domestic and foreign corporations. Nonapportionable dividends (less related expenses) are allocated to the corporation's state of commercial domicile. Note that attribution of expenses is not required for apportionable dividends.

• *Other expenses attributed to nontaxable income and to nonapportionable income and property*

In the determination of expenses other than interest expense attributed to untaxed income, the procedure set forth in the Code for determining expenses related to foreign source income (generally referred to as stewardship and supportive expenses) may be used to determine the expenses allocated to untaxed income and property producing or that would produce untaxed income. Alternatively, the attribution formula described above can be used to determine the amount of supportive function expenses attributable to untaxed income. In the determination of "supportive function expenses," direct expenses incurred exclusively in a specific identifiable taxable or nontaxable activity must be determined and excluded before applying the attribution percentage to expenses. If direct expenses are determinable for a particular activity resulting in an accurate computation of the net income or loss for such activity, the values of this activity must be removed as elements of the ratio when applying the attribution formula [17 NCAC 5C.0304(e)].

¶909

¶910 Interest Paid or Accrued to Related Members

For taxable years beginning on or after January 1, 2016, in computing its state net income a corporation must add back to federal taxable income its "net interest expense" and deduct its "qualified interest expense" [G.S. § 105-130.7B(a)].

• *Net interest expense*

Net interest expense is the excess of the interest paid or accrued by the taxpayer to each related member during the taxable year over the amount of interest from each related member includible in the gross income of the taxpayer for the taxable year. A "related member" for this purpose is defined in G.S. § 105-130.7A (see discussion of royalty payments in ¶902) [G.S. § 105-130.7B(b)(3)].

• *Qualified interest expense*

Qualified interest expense is the amount of net interest expense paid or accrued to a related member in a taxable year not to exceed the taxpayer's proportionate share of interest paid or accrued to a person who is not a related member during the same taxable year. A taxpayer's proportionate share of interest paid or accrued to a person who is not a related member is the amount of the taxpayer's net interest expense paid or accrued to, or through a related member to, an ultimate payer divided by the total net interest expense of all related members that is paid or accrued directly to, or through a related member to, the same ultimate payer. An amount that is distributed, paid or accrued directly or through a related member that is not treated as interest does not qualify. In determining whether an instrument is a debt instrument, the Secretary is not permitted to apply the covered debt instrument rules promulgated under Code § 385. An "ultimate payer" is a related member that receives or accrues interest from related members directly or through a related member and pays or accrues interest to a person who is not a related member [G.S. § 105-130.7B(b)(4), (5) and (6)].

• *Exceptions*

The limitation on the deduction of net interest expense paid or accrued to a related member does not apply if (1) North Carolina imposes an income tax on the interest income of the related member, (2) another state imposes an income or gross receipts tax on interest income of the related member (not including interest income eliminated by combined or consolidated return requirements), (3) the related member is organized under the laws of a foreign country that has a comprehensive income tax treaty with the United States, and that country taxes the interest income at a rate equal to or greater than the North Carolina corporate income tax rate, or (4) the related member is a bank [G.S. § 105-130.7B(b)(4)].

A bank for purposes of the exception described above is one or more of the following, or a subsidiary or affiliate of one or more of the following: (1) a bank holding company as defined in the federal Bank Holding Company Act, or (2) one or more of the following entities incorporated or chartered under the laws of North Carolina, another state, or the United States: (a) a bank (as defined in G.S. § 53C-1-4), (b) a savings bank (as defined in G.S. § 54C-4), (c) a savings and loan association (as defined in G.S. 54B-4), or (d) a trust company (as defined in G.S. § 53C-1-4) [G.S. § 105-130.7B(b)(2)].

CORPORATION INCOME TAX

CHAPTER 10

ALLOCATION AND APPORTIONMENT

¶1001 In General

When a taxpayer has income from sources both within North Carolina and outside North Carolina, the determination of the portion of the taxpayer's entire net income that has a North Carolina source must be made pursuant to the allocation and apportionment provisions of G.S. §105-130.4 and rules set forth in 17 NCAC 5C. A taxpayer must have income from business activity taxable by North Carolina and at least one other state to allocate and apportion income [17 NCAC 5C.0701(a)].

Division of income: Allocation and apportionment are methods of assigning the income of a corporation among states. Allocation is the assignment in its entirety of nonapportionable income to a particular jurisdiction. Apportionment is the division of apportionable income among jurisdictions, using a formula containing apportionment factors [17 NCAC 5C.0701(c)]. A taxpayer must determine which portion of its entire net income constitutes "apportionable income" and which portion constitutes "nonapportionable income."

The various items of nonapportionable income are directly allocated to specific jurisdictions pursuant to the provisions of G.S. §105-130.4(d) to (h). The apportionable income of a taxpayer other than those subject to special rules must be divided among the jurisdictions in which the business is conducted pursuant to sales factor apportionment [17 NCAC 5C.0701(a)]. Income must be classified as apportionable or nonapportionable income on a consistent basis. If a taxpayer is not consistent in reporting, it must disclose in its return to North Carolina the nature and extent of the inconsistency [17 NCAC 5C.0701(b)].

Proration of deductions: Any allowable deduction that is applicable both to apportionable and nonapportionable income or to more than one "trade or business" of the taxpayer must be prorated to those classes of income or trades or businesses in determining income subject to tax. A taxpayer is required to be consistent in the proration of deductions [17 NCAC 5C.0704].

¶1002 Basic Definitions

The following definitions apply for the purposes of allocation and apportionment:

Apportionable income: All income that is apportionable under the United States Constitution including income that arises from transactions or activities in the regular course of the taxpayer's business or from property the acquisition, management, employment, development or disposition of which is or was related to that trade or business [G.S. § 105-130.4(a)(1)].

Business activity: Any activity by a corporation that would establish nexus except as limited by 15 U.S.C. § 381 (Public Law 86-272) [G.S. § 105-130.4 (a)(2)].

Casual sale of property: The sale of any property that was not purchased, produced, or acquired primarily for sale in the corporation's regular trade or business [G.S. § 105-130.4(a)(3)].

Commercial domicile: The principal place from which the trade or business of the taxpayer is directed or managed [G.S. § 105-130.4(a)(4)].

Compensation: Wages, salaries, commissions, and any other form of remuneration paid to employees for personal services [G.S. § 105-130.4(a)(5)].

Nonapportionable income: All income other than apportionable income [G.S. § 105-130.4(a)(6)].

Sales: All gross receipts of the corporation except receipts from any of the following:

(1) Receipts from a casual sale of property [G.S. § 105-130.4(a)(7)a].

(2) Receipts allocated under subsections (c) through (h) of G.S. § 105-130.4 (relating to rents and royalties from property; gains and losses from dispositions of property; interest and dividends; royalties from intellectual property, and income from other nonbusiness activities or investments not otherwise specified [G.S. § 105-130.4(a)(7)b].

(3) Receipts exempt from taxation [G.S. § 105-130.4(a)(7)c].

(4) The portion of receipts realized from the sale or maturity of securities or other obligations that represents a return of principal [G.S. § 105-130.4(a)(7)d].

(5) The portion of receipts from financial swaps and similar financial derivatives representing the derivative's notional principal amount [G.S. § 105-130.4(a)(7)e].

(6) Receipts in the nature of dividends excluded for federal tax purposes or included for federal tax purposes but subtracted in computing state net income [G.S. § 105-130.4 (a)(7) f].

State: Any state of the United States, the District of Columbia, the Commonwealth of Puerto Rico, any territory or possession of the United States, and any foreign country or political subdivision thereof [G.S. § 105-130.4(a)(8)].

¶1003 Condition Precedent to the Use of Allocation and Apportionment

A taxpayer is entitled and required to allocate and apportion income if the taxpayer's business activity makes the taxpayer (1) subject to tax, (2) in another state, (3) on or with respect to its net income [G.S. § 105-130.4(b)]. Some corporations are subject to special apportionment rules.

• *Subject to tax (taxable in another state)*

The concept of taxability in another state (see "In another state," below) is based upon the premise that every state in which the taxpayer is engaged in business activities may impose an income tax even though every state does not do so. In some states other types of taxes may be imposed as a substitute for an income tax, but only those taxes that may be considered as basically revenue raising rather than regulatory are considered in determining whether the taxpayer is taxable in another state or not [*Corporate Income, Franchise, and Insurance Tax Bulletin*, II.H.4.b (2018)].

For purposes of allocation and apportionment, a corporation is taxable in another state if its activity in the other state meets either one of the following criteria [G.S. § 105-130.4(b)]:

(1) The corporation's business activity in that state subjects it to a net income tax or a tax measured by net income.

(2) That state has jurisdiction based on the corporation's business activity in the state to subject the corporation to a tax measured by net income regardless of whether that state exercises its jurisdiction or not.

Tax Must Be Measured by Net Income

In some states other types of taxes may be imposed as a substitute for an income tax. However, if the tax in the other state, even though not called an income tax, is measured by net income, that tax must be considered in determining whether the taxpayer is taxable in another state for purposes of the North Carolina corporation income tax. On the other hand, an "income tax" that is not measured by net income is not considered in determining whether the taxpayer is taxable in another state for purposes of the North Carolina corporation income tax.

Business activity in North Carolina and another state: A taxpayer must have income from business activity taxable by North Carolina and at least one other state in order to allocate and apportion income. Income from business activity includes apportionable or nonapportionable income. Thus, if a taxpayer has nonapportionable income taxable by one state and apportionable income taxable by another state, the taxpayer's income must be allocated in accordance with the allocation and apportionment rules of G.S. § 105-130.4. If a corporation is not taxable in another state on its apportionable income but is taxable in another state only because of nonapportionable income, all apportionable income must be attributed to North Carolina [17 NCAC 5C.0601].

Voluntary payment of tax in another state: If the taxpayer voluntarily files and pays an income tax to another state when not required to do so by the laws of that state or pays a minimal fee for qualification, organization, or for the privilege of doing business in that state but (1) does not actually engage in business activities in that state or (2) does actually engage in some activity, but not sufficient activity to establish nexus, and the minimum tax bears no relation to the corporation's activities with that state, the taxpayer is not subject to tax within that state and is, therefore, not taxable in another state [17 NCAC 5C.0604(a)].

Unitary Combined Return

The filing of a unitary combined return in another state with other related corporations does not, standing alone, constitute business for purposes of determining if a corporation is entitled to allocate and apportion in North Carolina [17 NCAC 5C.0604(a)].

Examples: The following examples, from *Corporate Income, Franchise, and Insurance Tax Bulletin,* II.H.4.b (2018), illustrate the application of the concept of "taxable in another state."

Example 1: State A requires all nonresident corporations that qualify or register in State A to pay an annual license fee or tax for the privilege of doing business in the state, even if the privilege is not exercised. The amount paid is determined according to the total authorized capital stock of the corporation; the rates are progressively higher by bracketed amounts. State A sets a minimum fee of $50 and a maximum fee of $500. Failure to pay the tax bars a corporation from utilizing State A's courts for enforcement of its rights. State A also imposes a corporation income tax. Corporation X, a nonresident corporation in State A, is qualified in State A and pays the required annual fee, but X has never carried on any activities in State A except utilization of the courts of State A. Corporation is not taxable in State A.

Example 2: Corporation X (from Example 1) has sufficient business activities in State A to establish nexus under State A's criteria. Corporation X is subject to and pays State A's corporation income tax. Therefore, X is taxable in State A.

Example 3: State B requires all nonresident corporations qualified or registered in State B to pay an annual permit fee or tax for doing business in State B. The base of the fee or tax is the sum of (1) outstanding capital stock and (2) surplus and undivided profits and is determined by a three-factor apportionment formula. Corporation X (a nonresident corporation in State B) operates a plant in State B and pays the required fee or tax. Corporation X is taxable in State B because of its business activities there. Note that in this example, the fee or tax is measured, in part, by net income.

Example 4: State C has a corporation franchise tax for the privilege of doing business in State C. State C's corporation franchise tax is measured by net income. Corporation X files a return based on its business activities in State C, but the amount of computed liability is less than the minimum tax. X pays the minimum tax. Corporation X is subject to State C's corporation franchise tax that is measured by net income, and therefore is taxable in State C.

• *In another state*

A state includes any state of the United States, the District of Columbia, the Commonwealth of Puerto Rico, any territory or possession of the United States, and any foreign country or political subdivision thereof [G.S. § 105-130.4(a)(9)].

The Department takes the position that the same criteria are used to determine if a domestic corporation has business activity in another state (and thus taxable nexus) that are used to determine whether a corporation is doing business in North Carolina [*CTAM 97-15* (September 16, 1997)]. In *Secretary's Decision No.* 2001-289 (December 21, 2001), the Secretary ruled that the presence in another state of a third party providing contractual services to the taxpayer was not sufficient to establish business activity in that state. See ¶ 803 for discussion of "doing business." In the case of a jurisdiction other than a state of the United States or political subdivisions of such state, the

¶1003

determination of whether jurisdiction to subject the taxpayer to a net income is made as though the jurisdictional standards applicable to a state of the United States apply in that jurisdiction. If, after applying these standards, jurisdiction is present, the other jurisdiction is not considered as without jurisdiction by reason of the provisions of a treaty between that jurisdiction and the United States [17 NCAC 5C.0605].

• *Corporate partners*

A corporation that is a member of a partnership or joint venture doing business in North Carolina is subject to the North Carolina corporation income tax and is required to include in its total net income subject to apportionment and allocation its share of the partnership's net income or net loss to the same extent required for federal income tax purposes [17 NCAC 5C.1701]. This is true even if the corporate partner itself transacts no business outside North Carolina. Conversely, a foreign corporation that owns an interest in a partnership transacting taxable business in North Carolina is subject to corporate taxation in North Carolina even if it transacts no business on its own in North Carolina (see ¶803). The "doing business" rule is applicable for all tiers of a partnership structure and applies to both general and limited partners [*Secretary of Revenue of North Carolina v. Perkins Restaurants, Inc.*, Tax Review Board Administrative Decision No. 351 (1999) See also Secretary's Decision No. 2007-28].

Situs of Intangible Assets

In general, intangible assets have a taxable situs in the domiciliary state of the owner. However, if intangible assets have acquired a "business situs" in North Carolina (*i.e.*, they are used in a trade or business in North Carolina), they are subject to tax in North Carolina even if owned by a foreign corporation. On the other hand, if a North Carolina taxpayer owns intangible assets that have acquired a business situs in another state, the income is not taxable in North Carolina but in the state in which the intangible has situs. Situs is a place that is or is held to be the location of something (*e.g.*, property) and that commonly determines jurisdiction over it.

¶1004 Classification of Income

Corporations that meet the conditions precedent (have income from business activity in another state and are taxable in another state) may allocate and apportion income. The first step in the allocation and apportionment process is to separate net income into two parts: (1) apportionable income and (2) nonapportionable income. Classification of income by labels (*e.g.*, manufacturing income, compensation for services, sales income, interest, dividends, rents, royalties, capital gains, operating income) is of no aid in determining whether income is apportionable income or nonapportionable income. In practice this means that all income is presumptively apportionable income unless a corporation can prove that it is not.

• *Apportionable income*

"Apportionable income" for North Carolina corporate income tax purposes means all income that is apportionable under the United States Constitution [G.S. § 105-130.4(a)(1)].

The definition of apportionable income permits the State to require apportionment of any income apportionable under the United States Constitution. The Supreme Court has held that both the Due Process and Commerce Clauses of the Constitution limit the state's power to require apportionment of income earned by a multistate business. In arguing for nonapportionable income classification under the statutory definition, taxpayers will generally need to argue that income is either derived from a non-unitary business or is otherwise earned in the course of activities unrelated to those carried out in the taxing state. *See, e.g., Allied-Signal, Inc. v. Director, Div. of Taxation,* 504 U.S. 768, 787 (1992). In Final Agency Decision 09 REV 5669 (April 21, 2011), the Department ruled that a Texas corporation's gain from the sale of a minority limited partnership interest was nonapportionable income where there were no functional integration, centralization of management or economies of scale and thus no unitary relationship between the corporation and the partnership.

Constitutional Issues

The definition of apportionable income as all income apportionable under the Constitution means that any classification of income will raise constitutional issues. The courts have ruled that Constitutional objections to a proposed assessment are for the courts alone, and the Secretary (as well as the former Tax Review Board) are without power to rule on Constitutional issues. *See, e.g., Great American Ins. Co. v. Gold,* 254 NC 168, 173, 118 S.E.2d 792, 796 (1961); *Secretary's Decision No. 97-990, §V* (September 9, 2000). However, while the Office of Administrative Hearings is required to dismiss a tax case for lack of subject matter jurisdiction where the sole issue is the constitutionality of a statute, it is expressly permitted to hear and decide cases involving the constitutionality of the application of a statute [G.S. §105-241.17(3); *see also* 26 NCAC 03.0127(c)]. The Office of Administrative Hearings (and the Department on review of a hearing decision) may thus address the constitutional issues raised by cases involving the classification of income as apportionable or nonapportionable. *See* Final Agency Decision 09 REV 5669 (April 21, 2011).

Apportionable income of corporations is apportioned to North Carolina by use of single sales factor apportionment [G.S. §105-130.4(i)].

• *Nonapportionable income*

Nonapportionable income is all income other than apportionable income [G.S. §105-130.4(a)(5)]. Nonapportionable income is directly allocated to a particular state. The most common items of nonapportionable income are (1) rents and royalties from tangible personal property; (2) gains and losses from dispositions of tangible property; (3) interest; (4) dividends; and (5) royalties from patents and copyrights. See ¶1005 for discussion of allocation of these items.

¶1005 Allocation of Nonapportionable Income

After a corporation has determined which portion of its entire net income constitutes "apportionable income" and which portion constitutes "nonapportionable income" (see classification of income at ¶1004), it must allocate various items of nonapportionable income directly to specific jurisdictions pursuant to the provisions of G.S. §105-130.4(d) to G.S. §105-130.4(h) [17 NCAC 5C.0701(a)]. Specific items of nonapportionable income are discussed below. Allocation and apportionment of income from partnership interest are explained at ¶623.

• *Rents and royalties*

Realty: Net rents and royalties from real property are allocable to the state in which the real property in question is located. If the real property is located in North Carolina, the income from the property is allocable to North Carolina [G.S. §105-130.4(d)(1)].

¶1005

Example: McFarland Corporation owns two buildings that it rents—one located in Charlotte, North Carolina, and one located in Richmond, Virginia. The rental income from these buildings is properly classified as nonapportionable income. The rental income from the building in Richmond is allocation to Virginia; the rental income from the building in Charlotte is allocable to North Carolina.

Tangible personal property: Net rents and royalties from tangible personal property are entirely allocable to North Carolina if the taxpayer's commercial domicile is in North Carolina and the taxpayer is not organized under the laws of or taxable in the state in which the property is located [G.S. § 105-130.4(d)(2)b]. Otherwise, net rents and royalties from tangible personal property are allocable to North Carolina if and *to the extent* that the property is utilized in North Carolina [G.S. § 105-130.4(d)(2)a]. The extent of utilization of tangible personal property in North Carolina is determined by multiplying the rents and royalties by a fraction, the numerator of which is the number of days of physical location of the property in North Carolina during the rental or royalty period in the taxable year and the denominator of which is the number of days of physical location of the property everywhere during all rental or royalty periods in the taxable year. If the physical location of the property during a rental or royalty period is unknown or unascertainable, the tangible personal property is considered to be utilized in the state in which the property was located at the time the rental or royalty payer obtained possession [G.S. § 105-130.4(d)(3)].

Example: Mitchell Corporation acquired all the assets of Minor Corporation, including a large piece of construction equipment. Mitchell rented the equipment until it could find a suitable buyer. During taxable year 2003, Mitchell rented to equipment to Max Corporation in Greenville, South Carolina, from July 17 to October 18 and to Min corporation in Asheville, North Carolina, from October 20 to December 16. Assume the rental income is nonapportionable income and that net rental income from this piece of equipment is $5,000. The income is allocated as follows:

Income allocable to North Carolina = 58/152 × $5,000 = $1,908

Income allocable to South Carolina = 94/152 × $5,000 = $3,092

- *Gains and losses from disposition of property*

Realty: Gains and losses from sales or other dispositions of real property are allocable to the state in which the realty is located [G.S. § 105-130.4(e)(1)].

Tangible personal property: Gains and losses from sales or other dispositions of tangible personal property are allocable to North Carolina if (1) the property had a situs in North Carolina at the time of the disposition or (2) the taxpayer's commercial domicile is in North Carolina and the taxpayer is not taxable in the state in which the property has a situs [G.S. § 105-130.4(e)(2)].

Intangible personal property: Gains and losses from sales or other dispositions of intangible personal property are allocable to North Carolina if the corporation's commercial domicile is in North Carolina [G.S. § 105-130.4(e)(3)].

- *Interest and net dividends*

Interest and net dividends are allocable to North Carolina if the corporation's commercial domicile is in North Carolina. For this purpose, the term "net dividends" means gross dividend income received less related expenses [G.S. § 105-130.4(f)]. A dividend will be considered apportionable income if *any* of the following circumstances apply [*CTAM 97-14* (September 15, 1997)]:

(1) The dividend arises out of or is acquired in the regular course of the corporation's trade or business.

(2) The purpose of the corporation in acquiring or holding the stock that gives rise to the dividend is related to the corporation's trade or business.

(3) The dividend is paid by a unitary subsidiary.

• *Income from intellectual property*

Royalties or similar income items received from the use of patents, copyrights, secret processes, and other similar intangible property are allocable to North Carolina (1) if and to the extent that the patent, copyright, secret process or other similar intangible property is utilized in North Carolina or (2) if and to the extent that the patent, copyright, secret process or other similar intangible property is utilized in a state in which the taxpayer is not taxable and the taxpayer's commercial domicile is in North Carolina [G.S. § 105-130.4(g)(1)].

Patents, secret processes, and similar assets: A patent, secret process or other similar intangible property is utilized in a state to the extent that it is employed in production, fabrication, manufacturing, processing, or other use in the state or to the extent that a patented product is produced in the state. If the basis of receipts from such intangible property does not permit allocation to states or if the accounting procedures do not reflect states of utilization, the asset is considered utilized in the state in which the taxpayer's commercial domicile is located [G.S. § 105-130.4(g)(2)].

Copyrights: A copyright is utilized in a state to the extent that printing or other publication originates in the state. If the basis of receipts from copyright royalties does not permit allocation to sales or if the accounting procedures do not reflect states of utilization, the copyright is utilized in the state in which the taxpayer's commercial domicile is located [G.S. § 105-130.4(g)(3)].

• *Other nonbusiness activities or investments*

The income less related expenses from any other nonbusiness activities or investment not otherwise specified in G.S. § 105-130.4 is allocable to North Carolina if the business situs of the activities or investments is located in North Carolina [G.S. § 105-130.4(h)].

• *Proration of deductions related to apportionable and nonapportionable income*

Any allowable deduction that is applicable to apportionable and nonapportionable income or to more than one "trade or business" of the taxpayer must be prorated to those classes of income or trades or businesses in determining North Carolina taxable income [17 NCAC 5C.0704].

Consistency required: A taxpayer must be consistent in the proration of deductions between apportionable and nonapportionable income when filing returns [17 NCAC 5C.0704].

¶1006 Apportionment of Apportionable Income

Corporations engaged in multistate activity (other than certain corporations subject to the special apportionment rules discussed at ¶1008) are required to apportion to North Carolina all apportionable income by using single sales factor apportionment. [G.S. § 105-130.4(i)].

Not taxable in another state: If a corporation is not taxable in another state on its apportionable income but is taxable in another state only because of nonapportionable income, all apportionable income must be attributed to North Carolina [17 NCAC 5C.0601].

¶1006

Alternate apportionment methods: If a corporation believes that use of the statutory apportionment formula will result in too much tax on its income reasonably attributable to business or earnings within North Carolina, it may petition the Secretary of Revenue for permission to use an alternate apportionment method. For more detail, see ¶ 1009.

• *Special formulas and methods*

Some corporations are subject to special apportionment formulas. These are discussed at ¶ 1008. Corporations are not permitted to use any unapproved alternative formula or method. See discussion at ¶ 1009.

• *Income earned through partnerships*

Where the business of a partnership is directly or integrally related to the business of the corporate partner, the corporate partner's share of the partnership's net income is classified as apportionable income, and the corporate partner's apportionment factor includes its proportionate share of the partnership's sales. If the corporate partner is a holding company, its business is considered to be integrally related to that of the partnership in which it holds an interest, even where that interest is a minority interest [17 NCAC 5C.1702; Secretary's Decision No. 2007-28 (September 14, 2007)].

¶1007 Sales Factor

• *Adoption of market-based sourcing*

The General Assembly has adopted proposed market-based sourcing rules under which gross receipts from sales of tangible personal property, services and intangibles are sourced for purposes of computing the sales factor based on the location of the taxpayer's market.

The Department adopted rules to implement market-based sourcing on January 4, 2017. The General Assembly has directed that these rules are effective for taxable years beginning on or after January 1, 2020 and has directed the Department to revise the rules to make them consistent with legislation adopted in 2019. *See* S.L. 2019-246, § 3.(F).

• *Sales factor defined*

The sales factor is a fraction, the numerator of which is the total sales of the corporation in North Carolina during the taxable year and the denominator of which is the total sales of the corporation everywhere during the taxable year. An exception is made for the receipts from any casual sale of property, which is excluded from both the numerator and the denominator of the sales factor. If a corporation is not taxable in another state on its income but is taxable in another state only because of nonapportionable income, all sales are attributable to North Carolina [G.S. § 105-130.4(*l*)].

• *Market-based sourcing*

Receipts are sourced to North Carolina if the taxpayer's market for the receipts is in North Carolina. If the market for a receipt cannot be determined, the receipt must be sourced using a method of reasonable approximation. If the source of the receipt cannot be determined by reasonable approximation, the receipt must be excluded from the denominator of the sales fraction [G.S. § 105-130.4(*l*)].

• *Rules for determining the market for a receipt*

The following rules apply in determining the market for a receipt [G.S. § 105-130.4(*l*):

Real property. Receipts from the sale, rental, lease, or license of real property are sourced to North Carolina if the property is located in North Carolina.

Tangible personal property rentals or licenses. Receipts from the rental, lease, or license of tangible personal property are sourced to North Carolina if the property is located in North Carolina.

Tangible personal property sales. Receipts from the sale of tangible personal property are sourced to North Carolina if the property is received by the purchaser (or its designee) in North Carolina, i.e., the place at which the goods are ultimately received after all transportation has been completed.

Services. Receipts from the sale of a service are sourced to North Carolina if the service is delivered to a location in North Carolina.

Intangible property rentals, licenses and contingent sales. Receipts from the rental, lease or license of intangible property is sourced to North Carolina if the property is used in North Carolina. Intangible property used in marketing a good or service to a consumer is used in North Carolina if the good or service is purchased by a consumer who is in North Carolina. Note that for this purpose, a sale of intangible property the receipts from which are contingent on the productivity, use, or disposition of the property is treated as a rental or license.

Intangible property noncontingent sales. Receipts from the sale of intangible property are sourced to North Carolina if the property is used in North Carolina. A contract right, government license, or similar intangible property that authorized the holder to conduct a business activity in a specific geographic area is used in North Carolina if the geographic area includes all or part of North Carolina. All other receipts from a sale of intangible property are excluded from the numerator and denominator of the sales factor.

¶1008 Corporations Subject to Special Apportionment

• *Railroad companies*

The apportionable income of a railroad company is apportioned to North Carolina by multiplying the income by a fraction, the numerator of which is the "railway operating revenue" from business done in North Carolina and the denominator of which is the "total railway operating revenue" from all business done by the company as shown by its records kept in accordance with generally accepted accounting principles [G.S. § 105-130.4(m)].

Definitions: The following definitions apply to the apportionment of the income of railroad companies [G.S. § 105-130.4(m)]:

(1) *Equal mileage proportion:* Equal mileage proportion is the ratio of the distance of movement of property and passengers over lines in North Carolina to the total distance of movement of property and passengers over lines of the company receiving revenue.

(2) *Railway operating revenue:* Railway operating revenue from business done in North Carolina means railway operating revenue from business wholly within North Carolina plus the equal mileage proportion within North Carolina of each item of railway operating revenue received from the company's interstate business.

(3) *Interstate business:* Interstate business is railway operating revenue from the interstate transportation of persons or property into, out of, or through North Carolina.

Incomplete or inaccurate records: If the Secretary of Revenue finds that a particular company's accounting records are not kept so as to reflect with exact accuracy the division of revenue by North Carolina lines as to each transaction involving interstate revenue, the Secretary may adopt regulations that use an apportionment formula that approximates with reasonable accuracy the proportion of interstate revenue actually earned upon lines in North Carolina [G.S. § 105-130.4(m)].

Operation by partnerships taxed as corporations: If a railroad is being operated by a partnership that is treated as a corporation for income tax purposes and pays income tax to North Carolina, or if located in another state would be so treated and so pay as if located in North Carolina, each partner's share of the net profits is considered as dividends paid by a corporation for this purpose and is treated as dividends for inclusion in gross income, deductibility, and separate allocation of dividend income [G.S. § 105-130.4(m)].

• *Motor carriers*

Apportionable income of a motor carrier of property or people is apportioned by multiplying the income by a fraction, the numerator of which is the number of vehicle miles in North Carolina and the denominator of which is the total number of vehicle miles of the company everywhere. "Vehicles miles" are the miles traveled by vehicles owned or operated by the company based upon miles on a scheduled route, miles hauling property for a charge or miles carrying passengers for hire [G.S. § 105-130.4(o)].

• *Transportation corporations*

Apportionable income of air or water transportation corporations is apportioned by a fraction, the numerator of which is the corporation's revenue ton miles in North Carolina and the denominator of which is the corporation's revenue ton miles everywhere. A "revenue ton mile" is one ton of passengers, freight, mail, or other cargo carried one mile by aircraft, motor vehicle or vessel. For this purpose, a passenger is considered to weigh 200 pounds [G.S. § 105-130.4(s)].

Special rules are provided for qualified air freight forwarders. A qualified air freight forwarder is an air freight forwarding business that is an affiliate of an air carrier and whose business is primarily carried on with the affiliated air carrier. An air carrier is an air transportation corporation that operates in interstate commerce provided the majority of its revenue ton miles are attributed to transportation by aircraft. A qualified air freight forwarder uses the revenue ton mile fraction of its affiliated air carrier. G.S. § 105-130.4(s).

• *Pipeline companies*

Receipts from the transportation or transmission of petroleum-based liquids or natural gas by a company subject to rate regulation by the Federal Energy Regulatory Commission are apportioned by multiplying the income by a fraction the numerator of which is the number of traffic units in North Carolina during the taxable year and the denominator is the number of traffic units everywhere during the taxable year. A "traffic unit" is either one barrel of liquid transported one mile or one cubic foot of gas transported one mile [G.S. § 105-130.4(s2)].

• *Wholesale content distributors*

Wholesale content distributor. A "wholesale content distributor" is a broadcast television network, a cable program network, or any television distribution company owned by, affiliated with, or under common ownership with any such network. The term does not include a multichannel video programming distributor or a distributor of subscription-based Internet programming services [G.S. § 105-130.4A(a)(3)].

Receipts factor. The receipts factor of a wholesale content distributor is a fraction, the numerator of which is the taxpayer's gross receipts from transactions and activity in the regular course of its trade or business from sources within North Carolina and the denominator of which is its gross receipts from such transactions and activity everywhere [G.S. § 105-130.4A(b)].

Customer-location sourcing rule. A wholesale content distributor's receipts from transactions and activities in the regular course of its business, including advertising, licensing, and distribution activities, but excluding receipts from the sale of real property or tangible personal property, are sourced to North Carolina if they are derived from a business customer whose commercial domicile is in North Carolina or from an individual customer whose billing address is in North Carolina [G.S. § 105-130.4A(b)].

Customer. A customer, for this person, is a person who has a direct contractual relationship with the wholesale content distributor, including an advertiser or program licensee and an individual subscriber [G.S. § 105-130.4A(a)(1)].

Minimum apportionment. The amount of a wholesale content distributor's income apportioned to North Carolina may not be less than 2% of the taxpayer's total domestic gross receipts from advertising and licensing activities [G.S. § 105-130.4(*l* 1)].

• *Banks*

Bank. A "bank" includes a bank, a bank holding company, a savings bank, a savings and loan association, a trust company, and a subsidiary or affiliate of any of the foregoing [G.S. § § 105-130.4B(a)(1) and 105-130.7B(b)(2)].

Receipts factor. The receipts factor of a bank is a fraction, the numerator of which is the total receipts of the taxpayer in North Carolina during the income year, and the denominator of which is the total receipts of the taxpayer everywhere during the income year [G.S. § 105-130.4B(b)].

Amounts excluded from receipts factor. The following receipts are excluded from both the numerator and the denominator of the receipts factor: (1) receipts from casual sales; (2) receipts exempt from tax; (3) receipts that constitute a return of capital; (4) dividends not subject to tax; (5) the notional principal amount of swaps and other derivatives [G.S. § 105-130.4B(b)].

Special sourcing rules. Special rules are provided for determining the source of receipts from (1) the sale, lease or rental of tangible personal property; (2) the sale, lease or rental of transportation property; (3) interest, fees and penalties from loans secured by real property; (4) interest, fees and penalties from loans not secured by real property; (5) net gains from the sale of loans secured by real property; (6) net gains from the sale of loans not secured by real property; (7) interest, fees and penalties received from cardholders; (8) ATM fees; (9) net gains from the sale of credit card receivables and (10) miscellaneous receipts [G.S. § 105-130.4B(c) –(*l*)].

¶1008

¶1009 Other Methods of Allocation and Apportionment

• *Request to use alternative method*

A corporation that believes the statutory apportionment method that otherwise applies subjects a greater portion of its income to tax than is attributable to its business in North Carolina may make a written request to the Secretary of Revenue for permission to use an alternative method [G.S. § 105-130.4(t1)]. The request must set out the reasons for the corporation's belief and propose an alternative method. The statutory apportionment method that otherwise applies to a corporation is presumed to be the best method of determining the portion of the corporation's income that is attributable to its business in North Carolina. A corporation has the burden of establishing by clear, cogent, and convincing proof that the proposed alternative method is a better method of determining the amount of the corporation's income attributable to the corporation's business in North Carolina [G.S. § 105-130.4(t1)].

• *Secretary's decision*

The Secretary must issue a written decision on a corporation's request for an alternative apportionment method. If the decision grants the request, it must describe the alternative method the corporation is authorized to use and state the tax years to which the alternative method applies. A decision may apply to no more than three (3) tax years. A corporation may renew a request to use an alternative apportionment method by making another written request.

A decision of the Secretary on a request for an alternative apportionment method is final and is not subject to administrative or judicial review. A corporation authorized to use an alternative method may apportion its income in accordance with the alternative method or the statutory method. A corporation may not use an alternative apportionment method except upon written order of the Secretary, and any return in which any alternative apportionment method not authorized by the Secretary is used is not considered a lawful return [G.S. § 105-130.4(t1)].

• *Alternative apportionment methods*

If the Secretary of the North Carolina Department of Revenue determines that the statutory formula does not fairly represent a corporation's business activity in North Carolina, the Secretary may require one of the following apportionment methods (determined on an individual basis) [17 NCAC 5D.0114]:

(1) Separate accounting.

(2) Exclusion of one or more apportionment factor.

(3) Inclusion of one or more additional factors that will fairly represent the taxpayer's business activity in North Carolina.

(4) Employment of any other method that results in an equitable allocation and apportionment of the taxpayer's income.

• *Statutory apportionment presumed equitable*

There is a presumption that the statutory apportionment formula is the best method of determining the portion of a corporation's income attributable to its in-state business and the burden is on the corporation to show that it is not by clear, cogent and convincing evidence. A corporation must use the statutory formula unless the Secretary orders in writing that it is entitled to use an alternative formula. Any return in which a formula or method other than the statutory formula is used without permission of the Secretary is not considered a lawful return [G.S. § 105-130.4(t1)].

CORPORATION INCOME TAX

CHAPTER 11

CREDITS AND GRANTS

CREDITS

¶1101 Tax Credits—In General

North Carolina has repealed most of its income tax credits. The only remaining income tax credits available to corporations are the credits for recycling facilities, railroad inter-model facilities, historic rehabilitation, cogenerating equipment, and cigarette exports. These credits are discussed below. Also discussed below are the credits allowed under prior law. See also the tax credit chart at ¶36.

¶1102 Tax Credit for Recycling Facility

Article 3C provides a tax credit for purchasing machinery and equipment for a large or major recycling facilities [G.S. § 105-129.27].

• *Definitions*

Machinery and equipment: Engines, machinery, tools, and implements used or designed to be used in the business for which the tax credit is claimed. The term does not include real property or rolling stock [G.S. § 105-129.25(4)].

Major recycling facility: A recycling facility that meets both of the following criteria [G.S. § 105-129.25(5); G.S. § 105-129.26(a)]:

(1) The facility is located in an area that, at the time the owner began construction of the facility, was a development tier one area (as defined in G.S. § 143B-437.08).

(2) The Secretary of Commerce has certified that the owner will, by the end of the fourth year after the year the owner begins construction of the recycling facility, invest at least $300,000,000 in the facility and create at least 250 new, full-time jobs at the facility.

Owner: A person who owns or leases a recycling facility [G.S. § 105-129.25(6)].

Post-consumer waste material: : Any product that was generated by a business or consumer, has served its intended end use, and has been separated from the solid waste stream for the purpose of recycling. This term includes material acquired by a recycling facility either directly or indirectly, such as through a broker or an agent [G.S. § 105-129.25(7)].

Purchase: An acquisition as defined by IRC § 179 [G.S. § 105-129.25(8)].

Recycling facility: A manufacturing plant at least three-fourths of whose products are made up of at least 50% post-consumer waste material measured by weight or volume. The term includes real and personal property located at or on land in the same county and reasonably near the plant site and used to perform business functions related to the plant or to transport materials and products to or from the plant, and utility infrastructure and transportation infrastructure to and from the plant [G.S. § 105-129.25(9)].

• *Amount of credit*

An owner that purchases or leases machinery and equipment for a major recycling facility in North Carolina during the taxable year is eligible for a tax credit for investing in large or major recycling facilities [G.S. § 105-129.27(a)]. The amount of the credit depends on whether the facility is a "large recycling facility" or a "major recycling facility."

Major recycling facility: An owner that purchases machinery and equipment for a major recycling facility in North Carolina during the taxable year is eligible for a credit equal to 50% of the amount payable by the owner during the taxable year to purchase or lease the machinery and equipment [G.S. § 105-129.27(a)].

• *Application of credit*

The tax credit for investing in a large or major recycling facility is allowed against the franchise tax and the corporation income tax. Any other nonrefundable credits allowed the owner are subtracted before the large or major recycling facility credit [G.S. § 105-129.27(b)].

The sale, merger, consolidation, conversion, acquisition, or bankruptcy of a recycling facility, or any transaction by which the facility is reformulated as another business, does not create new eligibility for a succeeding owner with respect to a credit for which the predecessor was not eligible. A successor business may, however, take any carried-over portion of a credit that its predecessor could have taken if it had a tax liability [G.S. § 105-129.27(d)].

• *Forfeiture*

Failure to make required minimum investment or create required number of new jobs: If the owner of a major recycling facility fails to make the required minimum investment or create the required number of new jobs within the period certified by the Secretary of Commerce, the facility no longer qualifies for the credit and the owner forfeits all tax benefits previously received [G.S. § 105-129.26(c)]. Forfeiture, however, does not occur if the failure was due to events beyond the owner's control. When the tax benefits are forfeited, the owner is liable for a tax equal to the amount of all past corporate franchise tax, corporation income tax, and sales and use taxes previously avoided as a result of the tax benefits received plus interest at the established rate (see ¶ 3205), computed from the date the taxes would have been due if the tax benefits had not been received. The tax and interest are due 30 days after the forfeiture date, and an owner that fails to pay the tax and interest is subject to the penalties provided in G.S. § 105-236 (discussed at ¶ 3204).

Failure to place machinery or equipment in service: If any machinery or equipment for which a recycling facility credit was allowed is not placed in service within 30 months after the credit was allowed, the credit is forfeited [G.S. § 105-129.27(e)]. A taxpayer that forfeits a recycling facility credit is liable for all past taxes avoided as a result of the credit plus interest at the established rate (see ¶ 3205), computed from the date the taxes would have been due if the credit had not been allowed. The past taxes and interest are due 30 days after the date of forfeiture, and a taxpayer that fails to pay the past taxes and interest by the due date is subject to penalties provided in G.S. § 105-236 (discussed at ¶ 3204).

• *Substantiation and recordkeeping*

In order to claim a recycling facility credit, an owner must provide any information required by the Secretary of Revenue [G.S. § 105-129.26(d)]. An owner that claims a recycling facility credit must maintain and make available for inspection by the Secretary of Revenue any records the Secretary considers necessary to determine and verify the amount of credit to which the owner is entitled. The burden of proving eligibility for the credit and the amount of the credit rests upon the owner, and no credit will be allowed to an owner that fails to maintain adequate records or to make them available for inspection.

¶1103 Tax Credit for Railroad Intermodal Facilities

A taxpayer that constructs or leases an eligible railroad intermodal facility in North Carolina and places it in service during the taxable year is allowed a tax credit [G.S. § 105-129.95(a)]. A "railroad intermodal facility" is an intermodal facility whose primary purpose is to transfer freight between a railroad and another mode of transportation [G.S. § 105-129.95(4)]. An "intermodal facility" is a facility where freight is transferred from one mode of transportation to another [G.S. § 105-129.95(30)]. An "eligible railroad intermodal facility" is one whose costs of construction exceed $30,000,000 [G.S. § 105-129.95(2)].

Amount of credit: The credit is equal to 50% of all amounts payable by the taxpayer towards the costs of construction or under the lease for the railroad intermodal facility in North Carolina [G.S. § 105-129.96(a)].

Application: A taxpayer may apply a railroad intermodal facilities tax credit against the franchise tax, the corporate income tax, or the individual income tax. The taxpayer must elect the tax against which the credit will be claimed when filing the return on which the first installment of the credit is claimed [G.S. § 105-129.96(b)].

Limitations: The credit may not exceed 50% of the tax against which it is applied [G.S. § 105-129.96(b)]. In addition, the credit is not allowed to the extent the cost of the facility was provided by public funds [G.S. § 105-129.96(a)].

No double credit: If the taxpayer is the lessee of the facility, the taxpayer must obtain the lessor's written certification that the lessor will not claim the credit [G.S. § 105-129.96(c)].

Carryforwards: Any unused portion of a credit may be carried forward for the succeeding 10 years. Any carryforwards of a credit must be claimed against the same tax [G.S. § 105-129.96(b)].

Substantiation: To claim a tax credit for railroad intermodal facilities must provide any information required by the Secretary of Revenue. The taxpayer must also maintain and make available for inspection by the Secretary any records the Secretary considers necessary to determine and verify the amount of credit to which the taxpayer is entitled. The burden of proving eligibility for a credit and the amount of the credit rests upon the taxpayer, and no credit will be allowed to a taxpayer that fails to maintain adequate records or to make them available for inspection [G.S. § 105-129.97].

Sunset: This credit is scheduled to expire effective for taxable years beginning on or after January 1, 2038 [G.S. § 105-129.99].

¶1104 Historic Rehabilitation Tax Credit

Effective for qualified rehabilitation expenditures made on or after January 1, 2016 (but see below for a special rule for income-producing historic structures), a taxpayer is allowed a credit for rehabilitating an income-producing historic structure and a credit for rehabilitating a non-income-historic structure [S.L. 2015-241, § 32.3].

• *Credit for income-producing historic structures [G.S. § 105-129.105]*

Base amount. A taxpayer who is allowed a federal income tax credit under Code § 47 for making qualified rehabilitation expenditures (as defined in Code § 47) for a certified historic structure (as defined in Code § 47) located in North Carolina is allowed a credit equal to 15% of the first $10 million of qualified rehabilitation expenditures and 10% of the second $10 million of such expenditures.

Development tier bonus amount. If the historic structure is located in a development tier one or two area (as defined in G.S. § 143B-437.08), the taxpayer is allowed an additional credit amount equal to 5% of the first $20 million in qualified rehabilitation expenditures.

Targeted investment bonus amount. If the historic structure is located on an eligible targeted investment site, the taxpayer is allowed an additional credit amount equal to 5% of the first $20 million in qualified rehabilitation expenditures. An eligible target investment site is a site located in North Carolina that: (1) was used as a manufacturing facility (or for ancillary purposes), a warehouse for selling agricultural products, or as a public or private utility, (2) is a certified historic structure, and (3) has been at least 65% vacant for a period of at least two years immediately before the date the State Historic Preservation Officer certifies that the site comprises an eligible targeted investment site.

Cap. The total credit amount, i.e., the total of the base amount, the development tier bonus amount and the targeted investment bonus amount with respect to a single income-producing certified historic structure, may not exceed $4,500,000.

Pass-through entities. Notwithstanding the provisions of G.S. § 105-131.8 (requiring pro rata credit allocations among S corporation shareholders) and G.S. § 105-269.15 (requiring partnership credit allocations to conform to the requirements of §§ 702 and 704 of the Code), a pass-through entity that qualifies for the income-producing historic structure credit may allocate the credit among any of its owners in its discretion as long as an owner's adjusted basis in the pass-through entity, as determined for federal income tax purposes, at the end of the taxable year in which the certified historic structure is placed in service, is at least 40% of the amount of credit allocated to that owner. Owners to whom a credit is allocated are allowed the credit as if they had qualified for the credit directly. A pass-through entity and its owners must include with their tax returns for every taxable year in which an allocated credit is claimed a statement of the allocation made by the pass-through entity and the allocation that would have been required under G.S. § 105-131.8 or G.S. § 105-269.15.

• *Credit for non-income-producing historic structures*

Credit amount. A taxpayer who is not allowed a federal income tax credit under Code § 47 and who has rehabilitation expenses of at least $10,000 for a State-certified historic structure located in North Carolina is allowed a credit equal to 15% of the rehabilitation expenses [G.S. § 105-129.106(a)].

State-certified historic structure. A State-certified historic structure is a structure that is individually listed in the National Register of Historic Places or is certified by the State Historic Preservation Officer as contributing to the historic significance of a National Register Historic District or a locally designated historic district certified by the United States Department of the Interior [G.S. § 105-129.106(c)(5)].

Rehabilitation expenses. Rehabilitation expenses are defined as expenses incurred in the certified rehabilitation of a certified historic structure and added to the property's basis. The expenses must be incurred within any 24-month period per discrete property parcel. The term does not include the cost of acquiring the property, the cost attributable to the enlargement of an existing building, the cost of site work expenditures, or the cost of personal property [G.S. § 105-129.106(c)(4)].

Placed in service. A property is placed in service on the later of the date on which the rehabilitation is completed or the date on which the property is used for its intended purpose [G.S. § 105-129.106(c)(3)].

Certified rehabilitation. A certified rehabilitation consists of repairs or alterations consistent with the Secretary of the Interior's Standards for Rehabilitation and certified as such by the State Historic Preservation Officer [G.S. § 105-129.106(c)(1)].

Discrete property parcel. A discrete property parcel is a lot or tract described by metes and bounds, a deed or plat of which has been recorded in the deed records of the county in which the property is located, and on which a State-certified historic structure is located, or a single condominium unit in a State-certified historic structure [G.S. § 105-129.106(c)(2)].

Limitations. The amount of the historic rehabilitation credit for a non-income-producing historic structure may not exceed $22,500 per discrete property parcel (i.e., the credit can be claimed for rehabilitation expenses up to $150,000). If the taxpayer is the transferee of a State-certified historic structure for which rehabilitation expenses were made, the taxpayer as transferee is allowed a credit for the rehabilitation expenses made by the transferor only if the transfer occurs before the structure is placed in service. In this event, the transferor must provide the transferee documentation of the rehabilitation expenses and credit. No other taxpayer may claim the credit. A taxpayer is allowed to claim an historic rehabilitation credit for non-income – producing property only once in any five-year period, carryovers notwithstanding [G.S. § 105-129.106(b)].

• *Taxes creditable*

The historic rehabilitation credits are allowed against the franchise, the individual and corporate income taxes, or the insurance company gross premiums tax. The taxpayer may take a credit against only one of these taxes and must elect the tax against which a credit will be claimed when filing the return on which the credit is claimed. Once made, the election is binding. Any carryforwards of a credit must be claimed against the same tax [G.S. § 105-129.108(a)].

• *Cap and carryforward; no double credits*

An historic rehabilitation credit may not exceed the amount of the tax against which it is claimed for the taxable year reduced by the sum of all credits allowed (except credits for tax payments). Any unused portion of the credit may be carried forward for the succeeding nine years [G.S. § 105-129.108(c)]. The taxpayer may not claim an historic rehabilitation credit and a credit under the former historic rehabilitation tax credit regime or a mill rehabilitation credit for the same activity [G.S. § 105-129.108(i)].

• *When claimed*

A taxpayer may claim an historic rehabilitation credit on a return filed for the taxable year in which the certified historic structure is placed in service. When an income-producing certified historic structure is placed in service in two or more phases in different years, the amount of credit that may be claimed in a year is the amount based on the qualified rehabilitation expenditures associated with the phase placed into service during that year [G.S. § 105-129.108(b)].

• *Substantiation*

To claim an historic rehabilitation credit, the taxpayer must provide any information required by the Secretary, including a copy of the certification obtained from the State Historic Preservation Office verifying that the historic structure has been rehabilitated in accordance with the applicable requirements, and, if the target investment bonus is claimed, a copy of the eligibility certification. The taxpayer must also maintain and make available for inspection by the Secretary any records the Secretary considers necessary to determine and verify the amount of the credit. The burden of proving eligibility for the credit and the amount of the credit rests upon the taxpayer, and no credit may be allowed to a taxpayer that fails to maintain adequate records or to make them available for inspection [G.S. § 105-219.108(h)].

• *Forfeitures of the credit for rehabilitating income-producing historic structures*

Forfeiture for disposition. A taxpayer who is required under Code § 50 to recapture all or part of the federal credit for rehabilitating an income-producing historic structure located in North Carolina forfeits the corresponding part of the North

Carolina historic rehabilitation credit with respect to that historic structure. If the credit was allocated among the owners of a pass-through entity, the forfeiture applies to the owners in the same proportion that the credit was allocated [G.S. § 105-129.108(d)].

Forfeiture for change in ownership. If an owner of a pass-through entity that has qualified for the historic rehabilitation credit for income-producing historic structures disposes of all or a portion of the owner's interest in the pass-through entity within five years from the date the rehabilitated historic structure is placed in service and the owner's interest in the pass-through entity is reduced to less than two-thirds of the owner's interest in the pass-through entity at the time the historic structure was placed in service, the owner forfeits a portion of the credit. The amount forfeited is determined by multiplying the amount of the credit by the percentage reduction in ownership and then multiplying that product by the forfeiture percentage. The forfeiture percentage equals the recapture percentage found in the table in Code § 50(a)(1)(B) [G.S. § 105-129.108(e)]. No change-of-ownership forfeiture is required if the change in ownership is the result of (1) the death of the owner or (2) a merger, consolidation, or similar transaction requiring approval by the shareholders, partners, or members of the taxpayer under applicable state law, but only to the extent the taxpayer does not receive cash or tangible property in the merger, consolidation, or other similar transaction [G.S. § 105-129.108(f)].

Liability for forfeiture. A taxpayer or an owner of a pass-through entity that forfeits a credit is liable for all past taxes avoided as a result of the credit plus interest computed from the date the taxes would have been due if the credit had not been allowed. The past taxes and interest are due 30 days after the date the credit is forfeited. A taxpayer or owner of a pass-through entity that fails to pay the taxes and interest by the due date is subject to the penalties provided in G.S. § 105-236 [G.S. § 105-129.108(g)].

• *Rules and fees*

The North Carolina Historical Commission, in consultation with the State Historic Preservation Officer, may adopt rules to administer any certification process required in administering the historic rehabilitation credits and may adopt a schedule of fees for providing such required. An application fee may not exceed 1% of the completed qualifying rehabilitation expenditures [G.S. § 105-129.107].

• *State historic preservation officer*

The State historic rehabilitation officer is the Deputy Secretary of the Office of Archives and History of the North Carolina Department of Cultural Resources or the Deputy Secretary's designee [G.S. § 105-129.105(c)(7)].

• *Sunset*

The historic rehabilitation credits for both income- and non-income-producing properties expire for qualified rehabilitation expenditures and rehabilitation expenses incurred on or after January 1, 2024. For qualified rehabilitation expenditures and rehabilitation expenses incurred before this date, the credits expire for property not placed in service by January 1, 2032 [G.S. § 105-129.110].

¶1105 Tax Credit for Cogenerating Equipment

A corporation or a partnership, other than a public utility, that constructs a cogenerating power plant in North Carolina is allowed a credit against the corporation income tax in an amount equal to 10% of the costs paid during the taxable year to purchase and install the electrical or mechanical power generation equipment of that plant if the corporation or partnership owns or controls the power plant at the time of construction. A "cogenerating power plant" for this purpose is a power plant that sequentially produced electrical or mechanical power and use thermal energy using natural gas as its primary energy source [G.S. § 105-130.25(b)].

The tax credit cannot be taken for the year in which the costs are paid, but must be taken for the taxable year beginning during the calendar year following the taxable year in which the costs were paid. This tax credit cannot exceed the amount of the taxpayer's corporation income tax for the year reduced by the sum of all tax credits allowed, except payments of tax made by or on behalf of the taxpayer [G.S. § 105-130.25(a)].

• *Alternative method*

A taxpayer eligible for the tax credit for construction of cogenerating power plants may elect to treat the costs paid during an earlier year as if they were paid during the year in which the plant becomes operational [G.S. § 105-130.25(c)]. This election must be made on or before April 15 following the year in which the plant becomes operational. This is an irrevocable election. An election with respect to costs paid by a partnership must be made by the partnership and is binding on any partners to whom the tax credit is passed through.

If a taxpayer makes this election, the tax credit may not exceed one-fourth the amount of the taxpayer's corporation income tax for the year reduced by the sum of all tax credits allowed, except payments of tax by or on behalf of the taxpayer. Any unused portion of the tax credit may be carried forward for the next 10 taxable years.

• *Application*

A taxpayer must file an application for the tax credit with the Secretary on or before April 15 following the calendar year in which the costs were paid. Application for the tax credit must be made in order to become eligible for the tax credit. An application with respect to costs paid by a partnership must be made by the partnership on behalf of its partners [G.S. § 105-130.25(d)].

• *Ceiling*

The total amount of tax credits allowed to all taxpayers for construction of cogenerating power plants in a calendar year may not exceed $5,000,000. If the total tax credits claimed in a calendar year exceed $5,000,000, the Secretary will allocate the total allowable amount among all taxpayers claiming the tax credits in proportion to the size of the tax credit claimed by each taxpayer. If a tax credit is reduced by this allocation, the Secretary will notify the taxpayer of the amount of the reduction on or before December 31 of the year the taxpayer applied for the tax credit.

The amount of the reduction may be carried forward and claimed for the next 10 taxable years if the taxpayer reapplies for a tax credit in the amount of the reduction. The Secretary's allocations are final and will not be adjusted to account for tax credits applied for but not claimed [G.S. § 105-129.25(e)].

¶1106 Tax Credit for Exporting Cigarettes to Foreign Countries [Repealed]

Repeal

This credit has been repealed effective for taxable years beginning on or after January 1, 2018 [S.L. 2003-435, §5.1]. The discussion below relates to prior law.

A corporation engaged in the business of manufacturing cigarettes for exportation is allowed a credit against the corporation income tax [G.S. § 105-130.45(b)].

Definition of "exportation": For this purpose, exportation means the shipment of cigarettes manufactured in the United States to any of the following sufficient to relieve the cigarettes in the shipment of federal excise tax on cigarettes [G.S. § 105-130.45(a)(2)]:

(1) A foreign country.

(2) A possession of the United States.

(3) A commonwealth of the United States that is not a state.

Comment: State Ports Requirement

The credit applies to all tobacco products but is only available to manufacturers that waterborne export cigarettes through the North Carolina State Ports during the taxable year [G.S. § 105-130.45(b)]. However, the calculation of the credit is not limited to just cigarettes that are waterborne exported. The amount of credit available is based on the current year's exportation volume compared to the base year's exportation volume [G.S. § 105-130.45(b); *Corporate Income, Franchise, and Insurance Tax Bulletin*, IV.B.11.a (2018).

• *Amount of tax credit*

The amount of the tax credit is determined by comparing the corporation's export volume in the year for which the tax credit is claimed with its export volume in 2003. The amount of the credit is computed as follows:

Percentage Increase Over Base Year Volume	*Amount of Tax Credit Per Thousand Cigarettes Exported*
120% or more	40¢
100% — 119%	35¢
80% — 99%	30¢
60% — 79%	25¢
50% — 59%	20¢
Less than 50%	No tax credit

• *Limitation*

The tax credit is limited to the lesser of $6 million or 50% of the amount of corporation income tax imposed for the taxable year, reduced by all other allowable tax credits, except tax payments made by or on behalf of the taxpayer [G.S. § 105-130.45(c)]. Unused credits may be carried forward to the next succeeding ten (10) years. The limitation on the amount of the tax credit applies to the cumulative amount of the tax credit claimed in any tax year, including the amount of any tax credit carried forward from previous tax years.

• *Documentation*

A corporation claiming the tax credit must include on its tax return (1) a statement of the base year exportation volume; (2) a statement of the exportation volume on which the credit is based; and (3) a list of the corporation's monthly export volume, as shown on its monthly reports to the Alcohol and Tobacco Tax and Trade Bureau of the United States Treasury, for the months in the year for which the tax credit is claimed [G.S. § 105-130.45(d)].

Comment: No Double Credit

A taxpayer may not claim this credit and the enhanced cigarette exportation tax credit (discussed at ¶1107) for the same activity [G.S. § 105-130.45(e)].

• *Computation of credit of successor in business*

In the case of a successor in business, the amount of credit allowed is determined by comparing the exportation volume of the corporation in the year for which the credit is claimed with all of the predecessor corporation's combined base year exportation volume, rounded to the nearest whole percentage [G.S. § 105-130.45(b)]. A "successor in business" is a corporation that through amalgamation, merger, acquisition, consolidation, or other legal succession becomes invested with the rights and assumes the burdens of the predecessor corporation and continues the cigarette exportation business [G.S. § 105-130.45(a)(3)].

• *Sunset*

The credit is repealed effective for cigarettes exported on or after January 1, 2018 [S.L. 1993-333,§10, as amended by S.L. 2003-435,§5.1].

¶1107 Enhanced Cigarette Exportation Tax Credit [Repealed]

Repeal

This credit has been repealed, effective for exports occurring on or after January 1, 2018 [S.L. 2003-435, §6.2]. The discussion below relates to prior law.

• *Eligibility for credit*

A corporation is eligible for an enhanced cigarette exportation tax credit if it meets the following conditions [G.S. § 105-130.46(d)]:

(1) It satisfies the employment level requirement (see below).

(2) It is engaged in the business of manufacturing cigarettes for exportation.

(3) It exports cigarettes and other tobacco products through the North Carolina State Ports during the taxable year.

"Exportation: means the shipment of cigarettes manufactured in the United States to a foreign country sufficient to relieve the cigarettes in the shipment of the federal excise tax on cigarettes [G.S. § 105-130.46(b)(2)].

• *Employment level requirement*

Required employment level: In order to be eligible for a full credit, a corporation must maintain an employment level in North Carolina for the taxable year that exceeds the corporation's employment level in North Carolina at the end of the 2004 calendar year by at least 800 full-time jobs [G.S. § 105-130.46(c)]. A "full-time job" is a position that requires at least 1,600 hours of work per year and is intended to be held by one employee during the entire year [G.S. § 105-130.46(b)(3)]. A taxpayer's employment level is the total number of full-time jobs and part-time jobs converted into full-time equivalents. A job is included in the employment level for a year only if that job is located within North Carolina for more than six (6) months of the year. A job is located in North Carolina if more than 50% of the employee's duties are performed in North Carolina [G.S. § 105-130.46(b)(1)].

Successor in business: In the case of a successor in business, the corporation must maintain a North Carolina employment level that exceeds all its predecessor corporations' combined North Carolina employment levels at the end of the 2004 calendar year by at least 800 full-time jobs [G.S. § 105-130.46(c)]. A "successor in business" is a corporation that through amalgamation, merger, acquisition, consolidation, or other legal succession becomes invested with the rights and assumes the burdens of the predecessor corporation and continues the cigarette exportation business [G.S. § 105-130.46(b)(4)].

• *Amount of credit*

The enhanced cigarette exportation tax credit is equal to 40¢ per thousand (1,000) cigarettes exported [G.S. § 105-130.46(d)].

Ceiling: The total amount of credit that may be taken in a taxable year may not exceed the lesser of (2) $10,000,000 or (2) 50% of the amount of tax against which the credit is taken for the taxable year reduced by the sum of all other credits allowable, except tax payments made by or on behalf of the taxpayer. This limitation applies to the cumulative amount of the credit allowed in any tax year, including carryforwards [G.S. § 105-130.46(g)].

• *Application and allocation of credit*

The enhanced cigarette exportation credit may be applied against the corporation income tax and the franchise tax. When a taxpayer claims an enhanced cigarette exportation tax credit, the taxpayer must elect the percentage of the credit to be applied against the corporation income tax, with the remaining percentage to be applied against the franchise tax. This election is binding for the year in which it is made and for any carryforwards. However, a taxpayer may elect a different allocation for each year in which the taxpayer qualifies for a credit [G.S. § 105-130.46(f)].

• *Partial credit*

A corporation that has previously qualified for the credit but fails to satisfy the employment level requirement in a succeeding year may still claim a partial credit for the year in which the employment level requirement is not satisfied. The partial credit is equal to the full credit multiplied by a fraction. The numerator of the fraction is the number of full-time jobs by which the corporation's employment level in North Carolina for the taxable year exceeds the corporation's employment level in North Carolina at the end of the 2004 calendar year. The denominator of the fraction is 800.

Example: Xebec Corporation exported 10,000,000 cigarettes and had 2,000 employees during the current taxable year. It previously qualified for the enhanced cigarette exportation tax credit. Its employment level at the end of 2004 was 1,500. Since its current employment level exceeds the end-of-2004 level by only 500 jobs, Xebec qualifies for only a partial credit of $250, computed as follows:

Full credit = $4,000 [(10,000,000 ÷ 1,000) × $0.40]

Partial credit = $2,500 [((2,000 – 1,500) ÷ 800) × $4,000]

In the case of a successor in business, the numerator of the fraction is the number of full-time jobs by which the corporation's employment level in North Carolina for the taxable year exceeds all its predecessor corporations' combined employment levels in North Carolina at the end of the 2004 calendar year.

• *Carryforward*

Any unused portion of a credit may be carried forward for the next succeeding 10 years and must be taken against the tax against which the credit was originally claimed. A successor in business (defined above) may take the carryforwards of a predecessor corporation as if they were carryforwards of a credit allowed to the successor in business [G.S. § 105-130.46(h)].

• *Documentation of credits*

Corporations that claim this credit must include the following with their tax return [G.S. § 105-130.46(i)]:

(1) A statement of the exportation volume on which the credit is based.

(2) A list of the corporation's export volume shown on its monthly reports to the Alcohol and Tobacco Tax and Trade Bureau of the United States Treasury for the months in the tax year for which the credit is claimed.

(3) Any other information required by the Department of Revenue.

Comment: No Double Credit

A taxpayer may not claim both an enhanced cigarette exportation tax credit and the tax credit for exporting cigarettes to foreign countries (discussed at ¶1106) for the same activity [G.S. § 105-130.46(j)].

• *Reports*

A corporation that claims this credit must submit an annual report by May 1 of each year to (1) the Senate Finance Committee; (2) the House of Representatives Finance Committee; (3) the Senate Appropriations Committee; (4) the House of Representatives Appropriations Committee; and (5) the Fiscal Research Division of the General Assembly. The report must state (1) the amount of credit earned by the corporation during the previous year; (2) the amount of credit (including carryforwards) claimed by the corporation during the previous year; and (3) and the percentage of domestic leaf content in cigarettes produced by the corporation during the previous year [G.S. § 105-130.46(k)].

• *Sunset*

The credit is repealed for exports occurring on or after January 1, 2018 [S.L. 2003-435, § 6.2].

¶1108 Tax Credit for Investing in Renewable Energy Property [Repealed]

Repeal

This credit is generally repealed effective for renewable energy property placed into service on or after January 1, 2016 [G.S. § 105-129.16A(e)]. The discussion below relates to prior law. The credit has been extended until January 1, 2017 (or May 5, 2017 for renewable biomass resources property) for a taxpayer who incurred at least 50% of the costs and completed at least 50% of the physical construction of a project before January

1, 2016 (or 80% of the costs and physical construction if the project has a total size of less than 65 megawatts of direct current capacity). In order to qualify for the extension, the taxpayer must have applied for the extension by October 1, 2015 and must have paid the application fee of $1,000 per megawatt of capacity (with a $5,000 minimum fee). The taxpayer must also provide certain verification information to the Department by March 1, 2016 [G.S § 105-129.16A(f)].

A taxpayer who constructs, purchases (as defined in IRC § 79), or leases renewable energy property and places it in service in North Carolina during a taxable year is allowed a tax credit equal to 35% of the cost of the property. The tax credit for renewable energy property that serves a nonbusiness purpose must be taken for the taxable year in which the property is placed in service. The entire tax credit for all other renewable energy property, however, cannot be taken for the taxable year in which it is placed in service but must be taken in five equal installments, beginning with the taxable year in which the property is placed in service. Upon request of a taxpayer that leases renewable energy property, the lessor of the property must give the taxpayer a statement that describes the renewable energy property and states the cost of the property [G.S. § 105-129.16A(a)].

- *Renewable energy property defined*

Renewable energy property is any of the following machinery and equipment or real property [G.S. § 105-129.15(7)]:

(1) Biomass equipment that uses "renewable biomass resources" for biofuel production of ethanol, methanol, and biodiesel; anaerobic biogas production of methane utilizing agricultural and animal waste or garbage; or commercial thermal or electrical generation. The term also includes related devices for converting, conditioning, and storing the liquid fuels, gas, and electricity produced with biomass equipment. "Renewable biomass resources" are organic matter produced by terrestrial and aquatic plants and animals such as standing vegetation, aquatic crops, forestry and agricultural residues, spent pulping liquor, landfill wastes, and animal wastes.

(2) Combined heat and power system property as defined in IRC § 48.

(3) Geothermal equipment that meets either of the following descriptions:

(a) It is a heat pump that uses the ground or groundwater as a thermal energy source to heat a structure or as a thermal energy sink to cool a structure.

(b) It uses the internal heat of the earth as a substitute for traditional energy for water heating or active space heating or cooling.

(4) "Hydroelectric generators" located at existing dams or in free-flowing waterways, and related devices for water supply and control, and converting, conditioning, and storing the electricity generated. A "hydroelectric generator" is a machine that produces electricity by water power or by the friction of water or steam [G.S. § 105-129.15(4d)].

(5) Solar energy equipment that uses solar radiation is a substitute for traditional energy for water heating, active space heating and cooling, passive heating, daylighting, generating electricity, distillation, desalination, detoxification, or the production of industrial or commercial process heat. The term also includes related devices necessary for collecting, storing, exchanging, conditioning, or converting solar energy to other useful forms of energy [G.S. § 105-129.15(e)].

(6) Wind equipment required to capture and convert wind energy into electricity or mechanical power, and related devices for converting, conditioning, and storing the electricity produced or relaying the electricity by cable from the turbine motor to the power grid [G.S. § 105-129.15(f)].

• *Installation of renewable energy property*

"Installation of renewable energy property:" means renewable energy property that, standing alone or in combination with the machinery, equipment, or real property, is able to produce energy on its own [G.S. § 105-129.15(4b)].

• *Cost defined*

In the case of property owned by the taxpayer, cost is determined pursuant to regulations adopted under IRC § 1012, subject to the limitation on cost provided in IRC § 179. In the case of property the taxpayer leases from another, cost is value as determined pursuant to G.S. § 105-130.4(j)(2) unless the property is renewable energy property for which the taxpayer claims either a federal energy credit under IRC § 48 or a federal grant in lieu of that credit and makes a lease pass-through election under the Internal Revenue Code. In this circumstance, the cost of the leased renewable energy property is the cost determined under the Internal Revenue Code [G.S. § 105-129.15(2)].

• *Ceiling for nonbusiness property*

The following ceilings apply to a renewable energy property placed in service for a nonbusiness purpose:

(1) $1,400 per dwelling unit for solar energy equipment for domestic water heating. This $1,400 ceiling also applies to solar energy equipment used for heating pools [G.S. § 105-129.16A(c)(2)a].

(2) $3,500 per dwelling unit for solar energy equipment for active space heating, combined active space and domestic hot water systems, and passive space heating [G.S. § 105-129.16A(c)(2)b].

(3) $8,400 for each installation of geothermal equipment [G.S. § 105-129.16A(c)(2)c].

(4) $10,500 for each installation of any other renewable energy property [G.S. § 105-129.16A(2)c].

• *Ceiling for business property*

A ceiling of $2,500,000 applies to each installation of renewable energy property for a business purpose. Renewable energy property is placed in service for a business purpose if the useful energy generated by the property is offered for sale or is used on-site for a purpose other than providing energy to a residence [G.S. § 105-129.16A(c)(1)].

• *Ceiling for eco-industrial parks*

A ceiling of $5,000,000 applies to each installation of renewable energy property placed in service for a business purpose at an Eco-Industrial Park certified under G.S. § 143B-437.08 [G.S. § 105-129.16A(c)(3)]. See ¶ 1115 for discussion of Eco-Industrial Park.

• *No credit for property purchased with public funds*

No credit is allowed to the extent the cost of the renewable energy property was provided by public funds. However, this limitation does not apply to renewable energy property purchased with grants made under § 1603 of the American Recovery and Reinvestment Tax Act of 2009 [G.S. § 105-129.16A(a)].

• *Application and election*

The tax credits authorized by Article 3B apply to the franchise tax, the corporation income tax, the individual income tax, and the income tax on estates and trusts. The credit for investment in renewable energy property is also creditable against the insurance company gross premiums tax. Taxpayers make an irrevocable election of the tax against which the tax credits will be claimed when filing the return on which the first installment of a tax credit is claimed [G.S. § 105-129.17(a)].

• *Cap*

The business and energy tax credits may not exceed 50% of the tax against which they are claimed for the taxable year, reduced by the sum of all other tax credits allowed against that tax, except tax payments made by or on behalf of the taxpayer. This limitation applies to the cumulative amount of business and energy tax credits, including carryforwards, claimed by the taxpayer against each tax for the taxable year [G.S. § 105-129.17(b)].

• *Carryforwards*

Any unused portion of the business and energy tax credits may be carried forward for the succeeding five years [G.S. § 105-129.17(b)].

• *Substantiation*

To claim the credit, a taxpayer must be able to prove that he is eligible for the credit and establish the proper amount of the credit. He must also maintain whatever records the Secretary determines are necessary to verify the amount of the credit and make such records available for inspection [G.S. § 105-129.18].

¶1109 Credit for Rehabilitation of Income-Producing Historic Structures [Repealed]

Repeal

This credit has been repealed effective for qualified rehabilitation expenditures incurred on or after January 1, 2015. For qualified rehabilitation expenditures incurred before this date, the credit expires for property not placed in service by January 1, 2023 [G.S. § 105-129.39]. The discussion below relates to prior law.

A taxpayer who is allowed a federal income tax credit under IRC § 47 for making qualified rehabilitation expenditures for a certified historic structure located in North Carolina is allowed a tax credit equal to 20% of the expenditures that qualify for the federal tax credit. If the certified historic structure is a facility that at one time served as a State training school for juvenile offenders, the amount of the credit is equal to 40% of the expenditures that qualify for the federal credit [G.S. § 105-129.35(a)].

A "certified historic structure" is any building (and its structural components) that is (1) listed in the National Register or (2) located in a registered historic district and (3) certified by the U.S. Secretary of the Interior to the U.S. Secretary of the Treasury as being of historic significance to the district [IRC § 47(c)(3); G.S. § 105-129.35(c)(1)].

"Qualified rehabilitation expenditures are any amounts properly chargeable to capital account for certified historic structures (including additions and improvements) for which depreciation is allowable under IRC § 168 [IRC § 47(c)(2); G.S. § 105-129.35(c)(3)].

- *Forfeiture in the event of IRC § 50 recapture*

A taxpayer who is required under IRC § 50 to recapture all or part of the federal tax credit for rehabilitating an income-producing historic structure located in North Carolina forfeits the corresponding part of the North Carolina tax credit. If the tax credit was allocated among the owners of a pass-through entity, the forfeiture applies to the owners in the same proportion that the tax credit was allocated [G.S. § 105-129.37(c)].

- *Pass-through entity allocation*

A pass-through entity that qualifies for this tax credit may allocate the tax credit among any of its owners in its discretion as long as an owner's federal adjusted basis in the pass-through entity. as determined at the end of the taxable year in which the certified historic structure is placed in service, is at least 40% of the amount of credit allocated to that owner. Owners to whom a tax credit is allocated are allowed the tax credit as if they qualified for the tax credit directly. A pass-through entity and its owners must include with their tax returns for every taxable year in which an allocated tax credit is claimed a statement of the allocation made by the pass-through entity and the allocation that would have been required under G.S. § 105-131.8 or § 105-269.15 [G.S. § 105-129.35(b)].

A "pass-through entity" for this purpose is an entity or business (including a limited partnership, a joint venture, a Subchapter S Corporation, or a limited liability company), that is treated as owned by individuals or other entities under the federal tax laws and in which the owners report their share of the income, losses, and credits from the entity or business on their income tax returns filed with this State An owner of a pass-through entity is an individual or entity that is treated as an owner under the federal tax laws [G.S. § 105-129.35(c)(2), 105-228.90(b)(4d)].

- *Forfeiture rules for pass-through entities*

If an owner of a pass-through entity that has qualified for a credit for rehabilitating an income-producing historic structure disposes of all or a portion of the owner's interest in the pass-through entity within five years from the date the rehabilitated structure is placed in service and the owner's interest in the pass-through entity is reduced to less than two-thirds of the owner's interest in the pass-through entity at the time the historic structure was placed in service, the owner forfeits a portion of the tax credit. The amount forfeited is determined by multiplying the amount of tax credit by the percentage reduction in ownership and then multiplying that product by the forfeiture percentage. The forfeiture percentage equals the recapture percentage found in the table in IRC § 50(a)(1)(B). The remaining allowable tax credit is allocated equally among the five years in which the tax credit is claimed [G.S. § 105-129.37(d)].

Exception: Forfeiture is not required if the change in ownership is the result of (1) the death of the owner or (2) a merger, consolidation, or similar transaction requiring approval by the shareholders, partners, or members of taxpayer under applicable state law, to the extent that the taxpayer does not receive cash or tangible property in the transaction [G.S. § 105-129.37(e)].

Liability from forfeiture: A taxpayer or an owner of a pass-through entity that forfeits a tax credit (either from disposition or change in ownership) is liable for all past taxes avoided as a result of the tax credit plus interest at the established rate (see ¶3203) computed from the date the taxes would have been due if the tax credit had not been allowed. The past taxes and interest are due 30 days after the date the tax credit is forfeited. A taxpayer or owner of a pass-through entity that fails to pay the taxes and interest by the due date is subject to penalties (see ¶3204) [G.S. §105-129.37(f)].

- *Substantiation*

A taxpayer claiming this credit must attach to the return a copy of the certification obtained from the State Historic Preservation Officer verifying that the historic structure has been properly rehabilitated [G.S. §105-129.35(a); *Corporate Income, Franchise, and Insurance Tax Bulletin*, IV.F.2.g (2018). Certification is discussed at ¶1130.

¶1110 Credit for Rehabilitating Nonincome-Producing Historic Structures [Repealed]

Repeal

This credit has been repealed effective for rehabilitation expenses incurred on or after January 1, 2015. For rehabilitation expenses incurred before this date, the credit expires for property not placed in service by January 1, 2023. [G.S. §105-129.39]. The discussion below relates to prior law.

A taxpayer that is not allowed a federal income tax credit under IRC §47 and who incurs *rehabilitation expenses* for a *state-certified historic structure* located in North Carolina is eligible for a tax credit equal to 30% of the rehabilitation expenses. If the certified historic structure is a facility that at one time served as a State training school for juvenile offenders, the amount of the credit is equal to 40% of the expenditures that qualify for the federal credit [G.S. §105-129.36(a)].

"Certified rehabilitation" means repairs or alterations consistent with the U.S. Secretary of the Interior's Standards for Rehabilitation and certified as such by the North Carolina Historic Preservation Officer prior to the commencement of the work [G.S. §105-129.35(b)(1)]. "Rehabilitation expenses" are expenses incurred in the certified rehabilitation of a certified structure and added to the property's basis. This term does not include (1) the cost of acquiring the property; (2) the cost attributable to the enlargement of an existing building; (3) the cost of sitework expenditures; or (4) the cost of personal property [G.S. §105-120.36(b)(2)].

"State-certified historic structures" are structures that are individually listed in the National Register of Historic Places or are certified by the State Historic Preservation Officer as contributing to the historic significance of a National Register Historic District or a locally designated historic district certified by the U.S. Department of the Interior [G.S. §105-120.36(b)(3)].

"State Historic Preservation Officer" is the Deputy Secretary of Archives and History or the Deputy Secretary's designee who acts to administer the historic preservation programs within North Carolina [G.S. §105-129.36(b)(4)].

- *Eligibility*

To qualify for this tax credit, the taxpayer's rehabilitation expenses must exceed $25,000 within a 24-month period [G.S. §105-129.36(a)].

- *Substantiation*

To claim this credit, a taxpayer must attach to the return a copy of the certification issued by the State Historic Preservation Officer (see ¶1130) [G.S. §105-129.36(a)]. The rehabilitation must be certified prior to the commencement of the work [*Corporate Income, Franchise and Insurance Tax Bulletin*, IV F.3.c (2018)].

¶1111 Mill Rehabilitation Tax Credits [Repealed]

Repeal

These credits have been repealed effective for projects for which an application for an eligibility certification is submitted on or after January 1, 2015. Eligibility certifications expire January 1, 2023 [G.S. §105-129.75]. The discussion below relates to prior law.

There are two mill rehabilitation tax credits: (1) a credit for making qualified rehabilitation expenditures for income-producing eligible sites in North Carolina (discussed at ¶1151) and (2) a credit for making rehabilitation expenditures for nonincome-producing eligible sites in North Carolina (discussed at ¶1152).

The material in this paragraph applies to both credits for income-producing property (discussed at ¶1151) and for nonincome-producing property (discussed at ¶1152).

Comment: No Double-Dipping

A taxpayer that claims a mill rehabilitation credit may not also claim a historic rehabilitation tax credit with respect to the same activity [G.S. §105-129.74].

- *Application of credits*

The mill rehabilitation tax credits discussed in ¶1151 and ¶1152 may be claimed against the franchise tax, the corporation income tax, the personal income tax, the income tax on estates and trusts, or the gross premiums tax on insurance companies. However, the taxpayer may take a credit against only one of the taxes against which it is allowed. The taxpayer must elect the tax against which a credit will be claimed when filing the return on which is claimed; and this election is binding. Any carryforwards of a credit must be claimed against the same tax [G.S. §105-129.73].

- *Definition of terms*

For purposes of Article 3H of the North Carolina General Statutes, the following definitions apply [G.S. §105-129.70]

(1) *Certified historic structure:* Defined in IRC §47 (relating to rehabilitation credit) [G.S. §105-129.70(1)].

(2) *Certified rehabilitation:* Defined in G.S. §105-129.36 (see ¶1157) [G.S. §105-129.79(2)].

(3) *Cost certification:* The certification obtained by the State Historic Preservation Officer from the taxpayer of the amount of the qualified rehabilitation expenditures or the rehabilitation expenses incurred with respect to a certified rehabilitation of an eligible site [G.S. §105-129.70(3)].

(4) *Development tier area:* Defined in G.S. §143B-437.08 [G.S. §105-129.70(3a)].

(5) *Eligibility certification:* The certification obtained from the State Historic Preservation Officer that the applicable facility comprises an eligible site and that the rehabilitation is a certified rehabilitation [G.S. § 105-129.70(4)].

(6) *Eligible site:* A site located in North Carolina that satisfies *all* of the following conditions [G.S. § 105-129.70(5)]:

(a) It was used as a manufacturing facility or for purposes ancillary to manufacturing as a warehouse for selling agricultural products, or as a public or private utility.

(b) It is a certified historic structure or a State-certified historic structure.

(c) It has been at least 80% vacant for a period of at least two years immediately preceding the date the eligibility certification is made.

(7) *Pass-through entity:* An entity or business all of which is treated as owned by individuals or other entities under the federal tax laws (*e.g.,* partnership, joint venture, S corporation, limited liability company), in which the owners report their shares of the income, losses, and credits from the entity or business on their North Carolina income tax returns [G.S. § 105-129.70(7); G.S. § 105-228.90(b)(4d)].

(8) *Qualified rehabilitation expenditures:* Defined in IRC § 47 [G.S. § 105-129.70(8)].

(9) *Rehabilitation expenses:* Defined in G.S. § 105-129.36 (see ¶ 1157) [G.S. § 105-129.70(9)].

(10) *State-certified historic structure:* Defined in G.S. § 105-129.36 (see ¶ 1157) [G.S. § 105-129.70(10)].

(11) *State Historic Preservation Officer:* Defined in G.S. § 105-129.36 (see ¶ 1157)].

• *Rules and fees*

The North Carolina Historical Commission, in consultation with the State Historic Preservation Officer is authorized to adopt a schedule of fees and rules needed to administer the certification process for tax credits for historic structures [G.S. § 105-129.36A]. The rules and fee schedule adopted under G.S. § 105-129.36A also apply to mill rehabilitation credits [G.S. § 105-129.74].

¶1112 Mill Rehabilitation Tax Credits for Income-Producing Eligible Sites [Repealed]

Repeal

This credit has been repealed effective for projects for which an application for an eligibility certification is submitted on or after January 1, 2015. Eligibility certifications expire January 1, 2023 [G.S. § 105-129.75]. The discussion below relates to prior law. Despite repeal of the credit, in 2019 a special, very narrowly-tailored expansion of the credit was enacted for the cost of rehabilitating a manufacturing facility used as or adjacent to a railroad station. This credit may be claimed in two installments in 2021 and 2022 [G.S.§ 105- 129.110].

• *Eligibility for credit*

A taxpayer who is allowed a credit under IRC § 47 for making qualified rehabilitation expenditures of at least $3,000,000 with respect to a certified rehabilitation of an eligible site is allowed a credit equal to a percentage of the expenditures that qualify for the federal credit. In order to be eligible for a mill rehabilitation credit, the taxpayer must provide to the Secretary a copy of the eligibility certification and the cost certification [G.S. § 105-129.71(a)].

- *Amount of credit*

The amount of the credit is determined as follows [G.S. § 105-129.71(a)]:

If Eligible Site Is Located In	Amount of Credit Is[1]
Development Tier One Area[1]	40% of qualified rehabilitation expenditures
Development Tier Two Area	40% of qualified rehabilitation expenditures
Development Tier Three Area	30% of qualified rehabilitation expenditures

[1]The credit may not exceed the amount of the tax against which if it claimed for the taxable year reduced by the sum of all credits allowed, except payment of tax made by or on behalf of the taxpayer [G.S. § 105-129.73(b)].

Carryover of credit: If the amount of credit exceeds the amount allowable, any unused portion of the credit may be carried forward for the succeeding nine years [G.S. § 105-129.73(b)].

- *Timing of credit*

The credit may be claimed in the year in which the eligible site is placed into service. When the eligible site is placed into service in two or more phases in different years, the amount of credit that may be claimed in a year is the amount based on the qualified rehabilitation expenditures associated with the phase placed into service during that year [G.S. § 105-129.71(a)].

- *Pass-through entities*

Allocation of credits: Notwithstanding the provisions of G.S. § 105-131.8 (relating to S corporation tax credits) or G.S. § 105-269.15 (relating to tax credits for partnerships), a pass-through entity that qualifies for a mill rehabilitation credit may allocate the credit among any of its owners in its discretion as long as an owner's adjusted basis in the pass-through entity (as determined under the Internal Revenue Code) at the end of the taxable year in which the eligible site is placed in service is at least 40% of the amount of credit allocated to that owner. Owners to whom a credit is allocated are allowed the credit as if they had qualified for it directly. A pass-through entity and its owners must include with their tax returns for every taxable year in which an allocated credit is claimed a statement of the allocation made by the pass-through entity and the allocation that would have been required under G.S. § 105-131.8 or G.S. § 105-269.15 [G.S. § 105-129.71(b)].

Forfeiture for change in ownership: If an owner of a pass-through entity that has qualified for a mill rehabilitation credit disposes of all or a portion of the owner's interest in the pass-through entity within five years from the date the eligible site is placed in service and the owner's interest in the pass-through entity is reduced to less than two-thirds of the owner's interest in the pass-through entity at the time the eligible site was placed in service, the owner forfeits a portion of the credit. The amount of the forfeiture is determined by multiplying the amount of credit by the percentage reduction in ownership and then multiplying that product by the forfeiture percentages. The forfeiture percentage equals the recapture percentage found in the table in IRC § 50(a)(1)(B) [G.S. § 105-129.71(c)].

Exceptions to forfeiture: Forfeiture is not required is the change in ownership is the result of (1) the death of the owner or (2) a merger, consolidation, or similar transaction requiring approval by the shareholders, partners, or members of the taxpayer under applicable State law, to the extent the taxpayer does not receive cash or tangible property in the merger, consolidation, or other similar transaction [G.S. § 105-129.71(d)].

Liability from forfeiture: A taxpayer or an owner of a pass-through entity that forfeits a mill rehabilitation credit is liable for all past taxes avoided as a result of the credit plus interest at the established rate (see ¶ 3205), computed from the date the taxes would have been due if the credit had not been allowed. The past taxes and interest are due 30 days after the date the credit is forfeited; and a taxpayer or owner of a pass-through entity that fails to pay the taxes and interest by the due date is subject to the penalties provided in G.S. § 105-236 (see ¶ 3204) [G.S. § 105-171(e)].

¶1113 Mill Rehabilitation Tax Credits for Nonincome-Producing Eligible Sites [Repealed]

Repeal

This credit has been repealed effective for projects for which an application for an eligibility certification is submitted on or after January 1, 2015. Eligibility certifications expire January 1, 2023 [G.S. § 105-129.75]. The discussion below relates to prior law.

• *Eligibility for credit*

A taxpayer who is not allowed a federal income tax credit under IRC § 47 and who makes rehabilitation expenses of at least $3,000,000 with respect to a certified rehabilitation of an eligible site is allowed a credit equal to a percentage of the rehabilitation expenses. In order to be eligible for a mill rehabilitation credit, the taxpayer must provide to the Secretary a copy of the eligibility certification and the cost certification [G.S. § 105-129.72(a)].

• *Amount of credit*

The amount of the credit is determined as follows [G.S. § 105-129.72(a)]:

If Eligible Site Located In	Amount of Credit Is
Development Tier One Area	40% of rehabilitation expenses
Development Tier Two Area	40% of rehabilitation expenses
Development Tier Three Area	No credit

Carryover of credit: If the amount of credit exceeds the amount allowable, any unused portion of the credit may be carried forward for the succeeding nine years [G.S. § 105-129.73(b)].

• *Timing of credit*

The entire credit may not be taken for the taxable year in which the property is placed in service but must be taken in five equal installments beginning with the taxable year in which the property is placed in service. When the eligible site is placed into service in two or more phases in different years, the amount of credit that may be claimed in a year is the amount based on the rehabilitation expenses associated with the phase placed into service during that year [G.S. § 105-129.72(a].

• *Pass-through entities*

Allocation of credits: Notwithstanding the provisions of G.S. § 105-131.8 (relating to S corporation tax credits) or G.S. § 105-269.15 (relating to tax credits for partnerships), a pass-through entity that qualifies for a mill rehabilitation credit may allocate the credit among any of its owners in its discretion as long as an owner's adjusted basis in the pass-through entity (as determined under the Internal Revenue Code) at the end of the taxable year in which the eligible site is placed in service is at least 40% of the amount of credit allocated to that owner. Owners to whom a credit is allocated are allowed the credit as if they had qualified for it directly. A pass-through entity and its owners must include with their tax returns for every taxable year in which an allocated credit is claimed a statement of the allocation made by the pass-through entity and the allocation that would have been required under G.S. § 105-131.8 or G.S. § 105-269.15 [G.S. § 105-129.72(b)].

Forfeiture for change in ownership: If an owner of a pass-through entity that has qualified for a mill rehabilitation credit disposes of all or a portion of the owner's interest in the pass-through entity within five years from the date the eligible site is placed in service and the owner's interest in the pass-through entity is reduced to less than two-thirds of the owner's interest in the pass-through entity at the time the eligible site was placed in service, the owner forfeits a portion of the credit. The amount of the forfeiture is determined by multiplying the amount of credit by the percentage reduction in ownership and then multiplying that product by the forfeiture percentages. The forfeiture percentage equals the recapture percentage found in the table in IRC § 50(a)(1)(B) [G.S. § 105-129.72(c)].

Exceptions to forfeiture: Forfeiture is not required is the change in ownership is the result of (1) the death of the owner or (2) a merger, consolidation, or similar transaction requiring approval by the shareholders, partners, or members of the taxpayer under applicable State law, to the extent the taxpayer does not receive cash or tangible property in the merger, consolidation, or other similar transaction [G.S. § 105-129.72(d)].

Liability from forfeiture: A taxpayer or an owner of a pass-through entity that forfeits a mill rehabilitation credit is liable for all past taxes avoided as a result of the credit plus interest at the established rate (see ¶ 3205), computed from the date the taxes would have been due if the credit had not been allowed. The past taxes and interest are due 30 days after the date the credit is forfeited; and a taxpayer or owner of a pass-through entity that fails to pay the taxes and interest by the due date is subject to the penalties provided in G.S. § 105-236 (see ¶ 3204) [G.S. § 105-172(e)].

GRANTS

¶ 1114 Job Development Investment Grant Program

The Job Development Investment Grant (JDIG) Program is intended to foster job creation in North Carolina [G.S. § 143B-437.52(a)]. The program is administered by the Economic Development Committee, which includes the Secretaries of Commerce and Revenue, the Director of the Office of State Budget and Management and a representative of each of the North Carolina House and Senate [G.S. § 143B-437.51(4)]. The program authorizes the Committee to make grants to businesses that promise to create new jobs. The grants are based on the amount of income taxes withheld from the wages of the employees holding the new jobs. Grants are awarded and administered under Community Economic Development Agreements entered into between the Committee and the grantee business.

• *Eligibility*

A business may apply to the Committee for a grant for any project that creates the minimum number of eligible positions as set out in the table below (if the project will be located in more than one development tier area, the location with the highest development tier area designation determines the minimum number of eligible positions that must be created) [G.S. § 143B-437.53(a)]:

Development Tier Area	Number of Eligible Positions
Tier One	10
Tier Two	20
Tier Three	50

A project that consists solely of retail facilities or that consists of a professional or semiprofessional sports team or club, other than a professional motorsports racing team, is not eligible for a JDIG grant [G.S. § 143B-437.53(b)]. In addition, to be eligible, a business must satisfy certain health insurance and health and safety standards [G.S. § 143B-437.53(c) and (e)].

• *Grant awards and grant terms*

The amount of a JDIG grant is a percentage of the withholdings of eligible positions (i.e., new full-time positions in North Carolina). The percentage may not be more than 80% of the withholdings of the eligible positions for a development tier one area and not more than 75% for any other area. The percentage ceiling is increased to 100% for a high-yield project (i.e., a project requiring investment of at least $500,000,000 in private funds and the creation of at least 1,750 eligible positions) [G.S. § 143B-437.56(a) and (a1)]. The amount of a grant associated with any specific eligible position (other than in transformative projects) may not exceed $6,500 in any year [G.S. § 143B-437.56(f)].

A business that is receiving any other North Carolina grant may not receive a JDIG grant that, when combined with any other grants, exceeds seventy-five percent (75%) of the withholdings of the business, unless the Committee makes an explicit finding that the additional grant is necessary to secure the project [G.S. § 143B-437.56(e)].

The maximum amount of total annual liability for JDIG grants awarded in any single calendar year is $35,000,000. The authorized maximum is increased to $45,000,000 for any year in which a grant is made for a high-yield project [G.S. § 143B-437.52(c)(1)]. Not more than half the authorized maximum may be awarded in any calendar semiannual period, provided that this limitation does not apply to unawarded amounts rolled over from the first half of the year or amounts awarded to high-yield projects [G.S. § 143B-437.52(c)(2)]. Certain geographical limitations also apply [G.S. § 143B-437.52(c)(3)].

The term of the grant may not exceed 12 years starting with the first year a grant payment is made. This limitation is increased to 20 years for certain high-yield projects and to 30 years after the end of the base period (*i.e.*, the period during which the eligible positions are to be filled). The first grant payment must be made within six years after the date on which the grant was awarded. The number of years in the base period for which grant payments may be made may not exceed five years (10 years for transformative projects) [G.S. § 143B-437.56(b)].

• *Community Economic Development Agreements*

Each Community Economic Development Agreement must include a list of provisions set forth in the statute, which include a description of the project, the grant term, the number and locations of the positions to be filled, the grant amount, a requirement that the business maintain operations at the project location (or another location approved by the Committee) for 150% of the grant term, and clawback and other enforcement provisions [G.S. § 143B-437.57].

- *Failure to comply with agreement*

If the business fails to comply with any condition or requirement set forth in the agreement, the Committee may terminate the agreement or reduce the amount of the grant or the grant term. The reduction in the amount or the term must, at a minimum, be proportional to the failure to comply measured relative to the condition or criterion with respect to which the failure occurred [G.S. § 143B-437.59].

- *Sunset*

The authority of the Committee to award new grants expires January 1, 2019 [G.S. § 143B-437.62].

¶1115 NC Green Business Fund and Grant Program

- *Establishment of fund*

The NC Green Business Fund is a special fund in the Department of Commerce and is administered by the Department of Commerce [G.S. § 143B-437.4(a)].

- *Purpose*

Grants are made from the Fund to private businesses with fewer than 100 employees, nonprofit organizations, local governments, and North Carolina agencies to help grow a green economy in North Carolina and must be used for projects that focus on priority areas specified in the statute. The Department of Commerce may cap grants and may require a private business to provide matching funds. A project that is located in an Eco-Industrial Park certified under G.S. § 143B-437.08 has priority over a comparable project that is not located in a certified Eco-Industrial Park and grants to such projects are not subject to cap and matching fund requirements [G.S. § 143B-437.4(b)].

- *Eco-Industrial Park defined*

An Eco-Industrial Park is an industrial park that the Secretary of Commerce has certified meets the following requirements [G.S. § 143B-437.08(j)]:

(1) It has at least 100 developable acres.

(2) It is located in a county that is not required under G.S. § 143-215.107A to perform motor vehicle emissions inspections.

(3) Each building located in the industrial park is constructed in accordance with energy-efficiency and water-use standards established in G.S. § 143-135.37 for construction of a major facility.

(4) Each business located in the park is in a clean-industry sector according to the Toxic Release Inventory by the United States Environmental Protection Agency.

- *Agreements*

Funds may be disbursed from the Fund only in accordance with an agreement between the Department of Commerce and the grantee that (1) describes the use of grand proceeds, (2) allows the Department of Commerce to inspect the grantee's books and records and confirm compliance, (3) establishes a method for confirming compliance, (4) establishes a fund disbursement schedule, (5) require a recapture of funds if there is a compliance failure and (6) includes other provisions necessary to ensure proper use of grant funds [G.S. § 143B-437.6].

¶1116 One North Carolina Fund

- *Establishment of fund*

The One North Carolina Fund is a special fund in the Department of Commerce from which money is allocated to local governments to help them recruit, expand, or retain new and existing businesses [G.S. § 143B-437.71(a)].

- *Purposes*

Allocated funds may only be used for: (1) installation or purchase of equipment, (2) structural repairs, improvements, or renovations to existing buildings to be used for expansion, (3) construction of or improvements to new or existing water, sewer, gas, or electric utility distribution lines or equipment for existing buildings, (4) construction of or improvements to new or existing water, sewer, gas, or electric utility distribution lines or equipment for new or proposed buildings to be used for manufacturing and industrial operations or (5) any other purposes specifically provided by an act of the General Assembly [G.S. § 143B-437.71(b)].

- *Agreements*

Money may be disbursed from the fund only in accordance with a Local Government Grant Agreement between the State and one or more local governments and a Company Performance Agreement between the local government and the grantee business [G.S. § 143B-437.72(a)].

A Company Performance Agreement must include [G.S. § 143B-437.72(b)]:

(1) A commitment to create or retain a specified number of jobs within a specified salary range at a specific location and commitments regarding the time period in which the jobs will be created or retained and the minimum time period for which the jobs must be maintained.

(2) A commitment to provide proof satisfactory to the local government and the State of new jobs created or existing jobs retained and the salary level of those jobs.

(3) A provision that funds received under the agreement may be used only for a permitted purpose.

(4) A provision allowing the State or the local government to inspect all records of the business to confirm compliance.

(5) A provision establishing the method for determining compliance with the agreement.

(6) A provision establishing a fund disbursement schedule.

(7) Provisions requiring a timely notices and requests for disbursements.

(8) A provision requiring recapture of grant funds in the event of a compliance failure.

(9) Any other provision the State or the local government finds necessary to ensure the proper use of State or local funds.

A Local Government Grant Agreement must include [G.S. § 143B-437.72(c)]:

(1) A commitment on the part of the local government to match the funds allocated by the State. A local match may include cash, fee waivers, in-kind services, the donation of assets, or the provision of infrastructure. The State match may not exceed $3.00 for each $1.00 provided by the local government if

the local government is in a development tier one area; $2.00 for each $1.00 provided by the local government if the local government is in a development tier two area; or $1.00 for each $1.00 provided by the local government if the local government is in a development tier three area.

(2) A provision requiring the local government to recapture any funds to which the local government is entitled under the Company Performance Agreement.

(3) A provision requiring the local government to reimburse the State for any funds improperly disbursed or recaptured.

(4) A provision allowing the State access to all records possessed by the local government necessary to ensure compliance.

(5) A fund disbursement schedule consistent with the disbursement schedule in the Company Performance Agreement.

(6) Any other provision the State finds necessary to ensure the proper use of State funds.

• *Disbursement*

Funds may be disbursed from the One North Carolina Fund to the local government only after the local government has demonstrated that the business has complied with the terms of the Company Performance Agreement [G.S. § 143B-437.72(d)].

¶1117 North Carolina SBIR/STTR Incentive and Matching Funds Programs

The One North Carolina Fund (see ¶1116) includes a special account, the One North Carolina Small Business Account, to be used for the North Carolina SBIR/STTR Incentive Program and the North Carolina SBIR/STTR Matching Funds Program.

• *North Carolina SBIR/STTR Incentive Program*

The North Carolina SBIR/STTR Incentive Program is administered by the North Carolina Board of Science, Technology, and Innovation and is intended to foster job creation and economic development in North Carolina. The Board may provide grants to eligible businesses to offset costs associated with applying to the United States Small Business Administration for Small Business Innovative Research (SBIR) grants or Small Business Technology Transfer Research (STTR) grants [G.S. § 143B-437.80(a)].

• *Purpose*

Grants are made from the Fund to private businesses with fewer than 100 employees, nonprofit organizations, local governments, and North Carolina agencies to help grow a green economy in North Carolina and must be used for projects that focus on priority areas specified in the statute. The Department of Commerce may cap grants and may require a private business to provide matching funds. A project that is located in an Eco-Industrial Park certified under G.S. § 143B-437.08 has priority over a comparable project that is not located in a certified Eco-Industrial Park and grants to such projects are not subject to cap and matching fund requirements [G.S. § 143B-437.4(b)].

In order to be eligible for a grant under the North Carolina SBIR/STTR Incentive Program, a business must: (1) be a for-profit, North Carolina-based business; (2) have submitted a qualified SBIR/STTR Phase I proposal to a participating federal agency in response to a specific federal solicitation; (3) satisfy all federal SBIR/STTR requirements; (4) not receive concurrent funding support from other sources that duplicates the purpose of the North Carolina SBIR/STTR Incentive Program; (5) certify that at least 51% of the research described in the federal SBIR/STTR Phase I proposal will be conducted in North Carolina and that the business will remain a North Carolina-based business for the duration of the SBIR/STTR Phase I project; and (6) demonstrate its ability to conduct research in its SBIR/STTR Phase I proposal [G.S. § 143B-437.80(b)].

The Board may award grants to reimburse an eligible business for up to 50% of the costs of preparing and submitting a SBIR/STTR Phase I proposal, up to a maximum of $3,000. Limitations on the number of grants a business may receive and the costs that may be reimbursed apply [G.S. § 143B-437.80(c)].

• *North Carolina SBIR/STTR Matching Funds Program*

The North Carolina SBIR/STTR Matching Funds Program is administered by the North Carolina Board of Science, Technology, and Innovation and is intended to foster job creation and economic development in North Carolina. The Board may provide grants to eligible businesses to match funds received by a business as a SBIR or STTR Phase I award and to encourage businesses to apply for Phase II awards [G.S. § 143B-437.81(a)].

In order to be eligible for a grant under this section, a business must: (1) be a for-profit, North Carolina-based business; (2) have received a SBIR/STTR Phase I award from a participating federal agency in response to a specific federal solicitation (to receive the full match, the business must also have submitted a final Phase I report, demonstrated that the sponsoring agency has interest in the Phase II proposal, and submitted a Phase II proposal to the agency); (3) satisfy all federal SBIR/STTR requirements; (4) not receive concurrent funding support from other sources that duplicates the purpose of the matching funds program; (5) certify that at least 51% of the research described in the federal SBIR/STTR Phase II proposal will be conducted in this State and that the business will remain a North Carolina-based business for the duration of the SBIR/STTR Phase II project; and (6) demonstrate its ability to conduct research in its SBIR/STTR Phase II proposal [G.S. § 143B-437.81(b)].

The Board may award grants to match the funds received by a business through a SBIR/STTR Phase I proposal up to a maximum of $100,000. The business is entitled to 75% of the total grant upon receipt of the SBIR/STTR Phase I award. The remaining 25% of the grant is disbursed to the business upon submission by the business of the Phase II application to the funding agency and acceptance of the Phase I report by the funding agency. Limitations on the number of grants a business may receive apply [G.S. § 143B-437.81(c)].

¶1118 Job Maintenance and Capital Development Fund

The Job Maintenance and Capital Development Fund is a fund in the Department of Commerce used to encourage businesses to maintain high-paying jobs and make capital investments in North Carolina [G.S. § 143B-437.012(b)].

• *Eligibility*

A business is eligible for a grant under this program if (1) it is a major employer or a large manufacturing employer, (2) all newly hired employees of the business are citizens or legal residents of the United States and (3) it satisfies wage, health insurance, safety and environmental standards [G.S. § 143B-437.012].

A major employer is a business (1) that the Department of Commerce has certified has invested or intends to invest, over a six-year period, at least $200,000,000 of private funds in real property improvements and tangible personal property in a project located in a development tier one area and (2) that employs (and agrees to continue to employ) at least 2,000 full-time employees or equivalent full-time contract employees at the project that is the subject of the grant [G.S. § 143B-437.012(d)(1)].

A large manufacturing employer is a business (1) that is engaged in manufacturing and is converting its manufacturing process to change the product it manufactures or is investing in its manufacturing process by enhancing pollution controls or transitioning the manufacturing process from using coal to using natural gas for the purpose of becoming more energy efficient or reducing emissions, (2) that the Department of Commerce has certified has invested or intends to invest, over a five-year period, at least $50,000,000 of private funds in real property improvements and tangible personal property, (3) that employs (and agrees to continue to employ) a specified minimum number of full time employees for the term of the grant in a development tier one area or a development tier two area with a population of less than 60,000. The specified minimum number of employees is 320 if the project is in a development tier one area and 800 if the project is in a development tier two area with a population of less than 60,000 [G.S. § 143B-437.012(d)(2)].

- *Agreements*

Grants are disbursed pursuant to an agreement between the Department of Commerce and the grantee. The grant agreement must include performance criteria, remedies, and other safeguards set forth in the statute or required by the Department of Commerce and provide for the State to disburse the grant over a period of up to 10 years [G.S. § 143B-437.012(j)].

- *Grant amount*

The amount of the grant is based on consideration of a number of factors including: (1) 95% of the grantee's privilege and sales and use taxes paid on machinery and equipment installed at the project that is the subject of the agreement; (2) 95% of the grantee's sales and use taxes paid on building materials used to construct, renovate, or repair facilities at the project that is the subject of the agreement; (3) 95% of the additional income and franchise taxes attributable to the grantee's investment in machinery and equipment and real property at the project that are not offset by tax credits; (4) 95% of the sales and use taxes paid on electricity and the excise tax paid on piped natural gas; (5) 100% of worker training expenses, including wages paid for on-the-job training, associated with the project; and (6) 100% of any State permitting fees associated with the capital expansion at the project [G.S. § 143B-437.012(l)].

- *Limitations*

The total aggregate cost of all agreements entered into under this grant program may not exceed $79,000,000, and the total annual cost of any one agreement may not exceed $6,000,000 [G.S. § 143B-437.012(n)].

¶1119 Utility Account

The Industrial Development Fund Utility Account, otherwise known as the "Utility Account," is a special fund in the Department of Commerce used to help local government units in the State's poorest counties create jobs. Utility Account funds must be used for construction of or improvements to new or existing water, sewer, gas, telecommunications, high-speed broadband, electrical utility distribution lines or equipment, or transportation infrastructure for existing or new or proposed buildings. The funds may only be used by the city and county governments for projects that are reasonably anticipated to result in the creation of new jobs, but there is no maximum funding amount per new job to be created or per project. Funds may not be used for retail, entertainment or sports projects and may be used for a nonmanufacturing project only if the project meets a wage standard. Priority is given to projects involving "eligible industries" (i.e., a company headquarters or a person engaged in the business of air courier services, information technology and services, manufacturing, or warehousing and wholesale trade). The Secretary of Commerce may use up to $100,000 of Utility Account funds to provide emergency assistance in any county that is experiencing a major economic dislocation [G.S. § 143B-437.01].

¶1120 Site Infrastructure Fund

The Site Infrastructure Development Fund is a special fund in the Department of Commerce to be used only for site development or to acquire and hold options to purchase land for an anticipated industrial site. To be eligible for consideration for site development for a project, (1) a business must invest at least $100,000,000 of private funds in the project, (2) the project must employ at least 100 new employees, and (3) the business must satisfy certain health insurance, safety and environmental standards. Funds are disbursed pursuant to a site development agreement with the business that include performance criteria, remedies, and other safeguards to secure the State's investment [G.S. § 143B-437.02].

¶1121 Film and Entertainment Grant Fund

The Film and Entertainment Grant Fund is a special fund in the Department of Commerce used to encourage the production of motion pictures, television shows, movies for television, productions intended for online distribution and commercials and to develop the filmmaking industry within North Carolina. Grants made from the fund are paid out over a period of time, not to exceed three years [G.S. § 143B-437.02A(a)].

* *Eligibility*

To be eligible for a grant, a production company must have qualifying expenses of at least $3,000,000 for a feature-length theatrical film or $1,000,000 for a feature-length television movie, $1,000,000 (per episode) for a television series, or $250,000 for a commercial for theatrical or television viewing [G.S. § 143B-437.02A(a)(1)]. In addition, funds may not be used for a production that: (1) contains material that is obscene or harmful to minors; (2) has the primary purpose of political advertising, fundraising, or marketing, other than by commercial, a product, or service; (3) is news programming, including weather, financial market, and current events reporting; (5) is live sporting event programming, including pre-event and post-event coverage and scripted sports entertainment; (6) is a radio production; (7) is a talk, game, or awards show or other gala event; or (8) fails to credit North Carolina [G.S. § 143B-437.02A(a)(4)]. No grant may be made with respect to any qualifying expenses for which a taxpayer received a credit under North Carolina's former film production credit program [S.L. 2014-100, § 15.14B.(c)].

* *Limitations*

Funds may not be used to provide a grant in excess of 25% of the qualifying expenses for the production or in excess of $7,000,000 for a feature-length film, $12,000,000 for a single season series or $250,000 for a commercial for theatrical or television viewing or online distribution [G.S. § 143B-437.02A(a)(2)]. Qualifying expenses, generally, are production expenses spent in North Carolina with exceptions for certain amounts paid to highly compensated individuals [G.S. § 143B-437.02A(b)(7)]. In addition, funds may not be used to provide a grant to more than one production company for a single production [G.S. § 143B-437.02A(a)(3)].

• *Sunset*

This grant program expires July 1, 2020 [S.L. 2014-100, § 15.14B.(c)].

CORPORATION INCOME TAX

CHAPTER 12

RETURNS, PAYMENT OF TAX, ADMINISTRATION AND PROCEDURES

¶1201 Requirement to File

Every corporation doing business in North Carolina must file an annual income tax return showing specifically the items of gross income and the deductions allowed and any other facts the Secretary requires. A corporate return must be signed by an officer, and the officer signing the return must furnish an affirmation, in the required form, verifying the return [G.S. § 105-130.16]. The return must be signed by one of the following officers:

(1) President.

(2) Vice-president.

(3) Treasurer.

(4) Chief financial officer.

Annual Report Fee

A corporation is required to submit a $25 annual report fee with its combined corporate income tax and franchise tax return [G.S. § 55-1-22(a)(23)].

- *Electronic filing*

The Department of Revenue participates in the Federal/State Electronic Filing Program and accepts corporation income tax returns filed under that program [17 NCAC 5C.1905]. A taxpayer may file a tax return with the Department of Revenue electronically only when the Department has established and implemented procedures permitting electronic filing of a specific tax return. A return may be filed electronically only by using the procedures established by the Department for the particular return [17 NCAC 1C.0701]. The latest information regarding what forms may be e-filed and the latest procedures may be found on the Department's Web site at: http://www.dor.state.nc.us/electronic/index.html.

Electronic signature: The name and identification number of the taxpayer constitutes the taxpayer's signature when transmitted as part of a tax return filed electronically by the taxpayer or at the taxpayer's direction [17 NCAC 1C.0702].

• *Identification numbers*

Corporations do not need to apply for corporate identification numbers. For corporate income and franchise tax purposes, taxpayers are identified by the federal identification number and the number assigned by the Secretary of State [*Frequently Asked Questions About NC Corporate, Excise, and Insurance Tax, North Carolina Department of Revenue, http://www.dor.state.nc.us/faq/corporate.html*].

• *Exempt corporations*

Tax-exempt organizations that are required to file a return under G.S. § 105-130.11(b) to report unrelated business income must file a calendar year return on or before May 15 of the following year and a fiscal year return on or before the 5th day of the fifth month following the close of the fiscal year [*Corporate Income, Franchise, and Insurance Tax Bulletin*, II.R.1 (2018)].

¶1202 Combined Returns and Redeterminations

Current law replaces the "true earnings" standard of former G.S. § 105-130.6 with an "economic substance" standard similar in some ways to that found in Code § 7701(o). For cases decided under the true earnings standard, *see Sam's East, Inc. v. Hinton*, 197 N.C. App. 229, 676 S.E.2d 654 (2009); *Delhaize America, Inc. v. Lay*, 222 N.C. App. 336, 731 S.E.2d 486 (2012). The Department announced that agreements entered into with taxpayers under its 2009 Resolution Initiative, many of which established a methodology for filing future returns, are void for tax years beginning on or after January 1, 2012 if (i) the Secretary has reason to believe that the taxpayer's state net income is not accurately reported on a separate return and (ii) the Secretary and the taxpayer are unable to agree on a future filing methodology. *Department of Revenue, Important Notice* (October 12, 2011).

Interpretation of G.S. §105-130.5A

Following the enactment of G.S. § 105-130.5A, the Department of Revenue, on November 16, 2011, issued *Directive CD-11-01*, Part Two of which explained the Secretary's authority under the new law to redetermine a corporation's state net income by adjusting intercompany transactions or requiring the corporation to file a combined return for taxable years beginning on or after January 1, 2012. On April 17, 2012, the Department issued a new *Directive CD-12-02*, which replaced and superseded Part Two of the earlier directive. However, on June 20, 2012, S.L. 2012-43 (S.B. 824) was enacted, which:

(1) superseded *Directive CD-12-02* [S.L. 2012-43 (S.B. 824) § 5],

(2) prohibited the Secretary from interpreting G.S. § 105-130.5A through a bulletin or directive [G.S. § 105-262.1(a)],

(3) prohibited the Secretary from redetermining the State net income of a corporation properly attributable to business carried on in this State under G.S. § 105-130.5A (except for a voluntary redetermination under G.S. § 105-130.5A(c))

until the Secretary adopts a rule to administer G.S. § 105-130.5A, [G.S. § 105-262.1(a)], and

(4) provided an expedited procedure for the adoption of such a rule [G.S. § 105-262.1].

Further, S.L. 2012-43 provided that a rule adopted under this expedited procedure will be effective only on the last day of the month the Codifier of Rules enters the rule in the North Carolina Administrative Code [G.S. § 105-262.1(k)]. After the rule becomes effective, however, the Secretary may issue a proposed assessment or a proposed denial of a refund request under the authority of G.S. § 105-130.5A for any taxable year beginning on or after January 1, 2012, subject to the applicable statute of limitations [S.L. 2012-43 (S.B. 824), § 6].

S.L. 2012-43 also provided that although CD-12-02 has been superseded, a taxpayer who relied on the interpretation set forth in the Directive and whose North Carolina taxable income for 2012 is less under that interpretation than under the rule eventually adopted is entitled to rely on the Directive for the 2012 taxable year [S.L. 2012-43 (S.B. 824), § 5].

The Secretary adopted a rule to administer G.S. § 105-130.5A effective January 31, 2013. *See* 17 NCAC 05F.

• *Notice*

If the Secretary has "reason to believe" that a corporation is conducting its trade or business in a manner that fails to accurately report its State net income properly attributable to its business carried on in the State the Secretary may issue a written notice to the corporation requiring it to provide additional information. The Secretary may have reason to believe a corporation is not accurately reporting its income attributable to its in-state business if the corporation has engaged in intercompany transactions that lack economic substance or that are not at fair market value. The notice issued to the corporation may request "any information reasonably necessary" to determine whether the corporation's intercompany transactions have economic substance and are at fair market value and for the accurate computation of the corporation's State net income properly attributable to its business carried on in the State. The corporation must provide the information requested within 90 days of the date of the notice [G.S. § 105-130.5A(a)].

• *Factual finding and voluntary redeterminations*

The Secretary must review the information provided and, based on such information, may make a factual finding that the corporation's intercompany transactions lack economic substance or are not at fair market value. Such a finding of fact is a prerequisite for redetermining the corporation's income or requiring the corporation to file a combined return. In determining whether the corporation's intercompany transactions lack economic substance or are not at fair market value, the Secretary must consider each taxable year separately [G.S. § 105-130.5A(b)]. In determining whether transactions between members of the affiliated group of entities are not at fair market value, the Secretary must apply the standards contained in the regulations adopted under section 482 of the Code [G.S. § 105-130.5A(h)]. In making this determination, the Secretary must consider all the facts and circumstances relative to the transactions, including any transfer pricing studies provided by the taxpayer (though the mere fact that the taxpayer has such a study will not suffice to establish that the transaction was made at fair market value) and must apply any federal or state case law developed under Code Sec. 482 [17 NCAC 05F.0301].

If the Secretary has reason to believe that a corporation is conducting its trade or business in a manner that fails to accurately report its State net income properly attributable to its in-state business, without making a finding of fact that the corporation's intercompany transactions lack economic substance or are not at fair market value, the Secretary and the corporation may agree to an alternative filing methodology that accurately reports state net income using any reasonable method for redetermining the corporation's income attributable to its in-state business [G.S. § 105-130.5A(c)]. The Department of Revenue has ruled that an alternative filing method may not be approved under this provision without a finding that intercompany transactions are not at fair value or do not have economic substance even where the taxpayer has asserted that the amount of tax paid to the state is not appropriate primarily because of the application of the statutory apportionment factor. *See* Voluntary Determination Request Letter (August 11, 2017).

• *Redetermining income*

If the Secretary makes a factual finding that the corporation's intercompany transactions lack economic substance or are not at fair market value, the Secretary may redetermine the corporation's State net income properly attributable to its in-state business by adding back, eliminating, or otherwise adjusting intercompany transactions. The corporation may propose a method for redetermining its net income attributable to its in-state business, and the Secretary must consider and is authorized to use any such reasonable method [G.S. § 105-130.5A(b)]. The Secretary's adjustments may include (1) disallowing deductions, (2) attributing income to related corporations, (3) disregarding transactions and (4) reclassifying income as apportionable or allocable [17 NCAC 05F.0401].

• *Combined return*

If, and only if, the Secretary determines that such adjustments are not adequate under the circumstances to redetermine the corporation's State net income, the Secretary may require the corporation to file a combined return with all members of its affiliated group that are conducting a unitary business, regardless of whether the members of the affiliated group are doing business in North Carolina [G.S. § 105-130.5A(b) and (f)]. For this purpose, a unitary business means one or more related business organizations where there is a unity of ownership, operation and use. A unitary business can also exist where there is interdependence in the functions of the related business organizations. A determination of whether two corporations are part of a unitary business is to be based on all the facts and circumstances of the case [17 NCAC 05F. 0102(6)].

If the Secretary determines that a combined return is required, it must issue written notice to the corporation requiring the corporation to submit the combined return. The corporation must submit the combined return within 90 days of the date of the notice. The submission by the corporation of the combined return required by the Secretary is not deemed to be a return and is not construed as an agreement by the corporation that an assessment based on the combined return is correct or that additional tax is due by the Secretary's deadline for submitting the combined return. The Secretary or the corporation may propose a combination of fewer than all members of the unitary group, and the Secretary is authorized to consider whether such proposed combination is a reasonable means of redetermining State net income. However, the Secretary may not require a combination of fewer than all members of the unitary group without the consent of the corporation [G.S. § 105-130.5A(d)]. The combined state net income of the corporation and the members of the affiliated group of entities included in the combined return must be apportioned to North Carolina using an apportionment formula that accurately reports the state net income properly attributable to the corporation's in-state business and which fairly reflects the apportionment formula in G.S. § 105-130.4 applicable to the corporation and each member of the affiliated group included in the combined return [G.S. § 105-130.5A(i)].

• *Corporations filing consolidated returns for federal income tax purposes*

Any corporation electing or required to file a consolidated income tax return with the Internal Revenue Service must determine its North Carolina net income as if the corporation had filed a separate federal return and shall not file a consolidated or combined return with the North Carolina Secretary of Revenue unless one of the following applies [G.S. § 105-130.140]:

(1) The corporation is specifically directed in writing by the Secretary under G.S. § 105-130.5A to file a consolidated or combined return.

(2) Pursuant to a written request from the corporation under G.S. § 105-130.5A, the Secretary has provided written advice to the corporation stating that the Secretary will allow a consolidated or combined return under the facts and circumstances set out in the request and the corporation files a consolidated or combined return in accordance with that written advice.

• *Notice of proposed assessment or refund*

If the Secretary redetermines a corporation's stated net income by making adjustments or requiring a combined return, the Secretary must issue a proposed assessment or refund upon making such redetermination in accordance with the procedures set forth in Article 9 of Chapter 105 of the General Statutes (discussed in Chapter 32) [G.S. § 105-130.5A(k)]. Within 90 days of issuing any proposed assessment, the Secretary must provide the corporation with a written statement containing details of the facts, circumstances, and reasons supporting the Secretary finding of fact that the corporation did not accurately report its State net income properly attributable to its in-state business and the Secretary's proposed method for computing the corporation's State net income [G.S. § 105-130.5A(e)].

• *Economic substance*

A transaction has economic substance if (i) the transaction, or the series of transactions of which it is a part, has one or more reasonable business purposes other than the creation of state income tax benefits and (ii) the transaction, or the series of transactions of which it is a part, has economic effects beyond the creation of state income tax benefits. In determining whether a transaction has economic substance, all of the following apply [G.S. § 105-130.5A(g)]:

(1) Reasonable business purposes and economic effects include, but are not limited to, any material benefit from the transaction (other than state income tax benefits not allowable under (3) below).

(2) In determining whether to require a combined return, whether the transaction has economic effects beyond the creation of state income tax benefits may be satisfied by demonstrating material business activity of the entities involved in the transaction. A material business activity is an activity that is an

integral part of the unitary group's business and that is performed on a regular and continuous basis [17 NCAC 05F. 0102(4)].

(3) If state income tax benefits resulting from a transaction, or a series of transactions of which it is a part, are consistent with legislative intent, such state income tax benefits shall be considered in determining whether such transaction has business purpose and economic substance.

(4) Centralized cash management of an affiliated group is not evidence of an absence of economic substance. "Centralized cash management" for this purpose means a process by which an affiliated group of businesses makes all or most cash management decisions from one location, such as a headquarters or designated subsidiary, that results in individual affiliates having little autonomy in making decisions concerning how cash is managed [17 NCAC 05F.0102(1)]. Although the existence of a centralized cash management system is not conclusive evidence that a transaction lacks economic substance, if the Secretary finds that the cash management transaction, or series of transactions of which the transaction is a part, results in the creation of unreasonably excessive interest expense when compared to industry practice, the shifting of assets, or the reclassification of income as nonapportionable or nonallocable, the Secretary may determine the transaction to lack economic substance [17 NCAC 05F.0207].

(5) Achieving a financial accounting benefit may not be taken into account as a reasonable business purpose for entering into a transaction if the origin of the financial accounting benefit is a reduction of state income tax.

- *How the taxpayer is to establish economic substance*

Burden of proof. The taxpayer has the burden of proving that a transaction meets both the reasonable purpose and economic effects prongs of the economic substance test [17 NCAC 05F.0201].

Proving business purpose. In proving that a transaction has a reasonable business purposes the taxpayer must show: (1) that the asserted business purpose was valid and realistic; (2) that the transaction was a reasonable and realistic means to accomplish that purpose; (3) that there is evidence that the taxpayer took steps to achieve that purpose; and (4) that the value of the non-State income tax benefits reasonably anticipated by the taxpayer from the transaction exceeds the additional cost associated with the transaction. Generally, reasonable business purpose is supported by contemporaneous documentation. Though not conclusive, the absence of contemporaneous documentation weakens the contention that the asserted business purpose is valid [17 NCAC 05F.0202].

Proving economic effect. In proving that a transaction has economic effects beyond the creation of State income tax benefits, the taxpayer must show by objective evidence that (1) when the transaction was initiated there was a reasonable likelihood that it would produce a material benefit other than State income tax benefits and that (2) the transaction in fact produced a material benefit apart from State income tax benefits [17 NCAC 05F.0203]. For this purpose a "material benefit" means an improvement in the economic position of the taxpayer on a pre-tax basis [17 NCAC 05F.0102(3)] and "economic position" means the status of a taxpayer's assets, liabilities, and equity (whether actual, contingent, or potential) and their interrelationship to one another [17 NCAC 05F.0102(2)]. In analyzing whether a transaction has an economic effect, the Secretary must analyze the economic effect on the taxpayer and on all the parties to the transaction in the aggregate.

• *How the Secretary is to apply the economic substance rules*

Common law principles. In applying the economic substance doctrine, the Secretary is required to rely on general principles of the common law economic substance doctrine as established under federal and state case law, except where such case law conflicts with the statute. General principles of the economic substance doctrine include the following principles: (1) economic substance is a prerequisite to any provision allowing deductions; (2) the taxpayer has the burden of proving that a transaction has both purpose and substance; (3) the taxpayer has the burden of showing that the form of the transaction accurately reflects its substance and that deductions claimed are permissible; (4) the economic substance of a transaction is determined based on documentation and data rather than the taxpayer's subjective opinions; and (5) the transactions, not the entities, are to be examined for economic substance 17 NCAC 05F.0204].

Facts to be considered. In applying the economic substance test, the Secretary must consider or analyze all the facts and circumstances including the following: (1) the reasons for the transaction; (2) whether the transaction was a reasonable means to accomplish the asserted purposes; (3) the expected benefits from the transactions; (4) the effects the transaction had on the taxpayer's profits; (5) whether there was a reasonable or realistic potential for profit from the transaction; (6) the objective economic impact of the transaction other than State income tax savings; (7) the transaction's effect on the taxpayer's State income tax liability; (8) the transaction's effect on the taxpayer's tax liability in other states; (9) the transaction's effect on the taxpayer's federal tax liability; (10) whether the method of determining the amount of a payment is an industry practice; (11) the change in the business operations of the parties, if any, after the transaction; (12) whether assets were transferred between or among related parties; (13) whether the business operations related to specific assets changed after any transfer of those assets; (14) whether the transferor of assets retained control over the assets; (15) the tax consequences of the transfer of assets; (16) the party or parties who created or developed the ideas which led to the transaction; (17) the party or parties who presented the ideas concerning the transaction to the taxpayer; (18) whether the contemporaneous documentation explaining the transaction to the taxpayer discussed profit potential in addition to tax benefits; (19) the party or parties who drafted the agreements relating to the transaction; (20) the party or parties who negotiated the agreements relating to the transaction; (21) the party or parties who dictated the terms of the agreements relating to the transaction; (22) cost-benefit analyses or other studies conducted related to the transaction; (23) non-tax benefits obtained by the taxpayer as a result of the transaction; and (24) whether the intercompany transaction resulted in a circular cash flow [17 NCAC 05F.0205].

Consideration of state tax benefits. The Secretary is required to consider state income tax benefits resulting from a transaction in determining whether a transaction has reasonable business purposes and economic substance when the state income tax benefits are consistent with legislative intent. For instance, state deductions and credits are consistent with legislative intent when the General Assembly enacted the deductions and credits to encourage the activities that generated the deductions or credits. When a transaction that generates targeted tax incentives is, in form and substance, consistent with the state income tax benefits designed by the General

Assembly, the Secretary must consider the state income tax benefits in determining whether the transaction has reasonable business purposes and economic substance [17 NCAC 05F.0206].

• *Procedure for filing a combined return*

Form CD-405. When a combined return is to be filed, the "principal member" of the combined group must file Form CD-405, The North Carolina C Corporation Tax Return, and all required schedules. The combined return replaces the separate entity returns filed by the members of the group that are doing business in North Carolina [17 NCAC 05F.0502].

Principal member. The "principal member" of the group is the member that acts in the group's name in all matters relating to the group's income tax liability, and that is responsible for preparing the corporate income tax return and making corporate income tax payments for the group [17 NCAC 05F.0102(5)].

Schedules. The combined return must include the following schedules: (1) a computation of the North Carolina taxable income of each corporation in the combined return that would have been reported if the member had filed a North Carolina income tax return on a separate company basis; (2) a schedule detailing all intercompany eliminations made by and between the members of the unitary group; (3) a schedule of all North Carolina income tax estimated payments made by each member of the group; (4) a schedule reflecting the computation of the combined apportionment factor as required in 17 NCAC 05F.0501(6) (taxpayers may not use Schedule O of the CD-405); (5) a schedule of eligible net economic losses and the use of such losses by member entities and the combined group; and (6) a schedule of eligible tax credits and the use of such credits by member entities and the combined group [17 NCAC 05F.0502].

Credit information. Any member of the combined group that has activities that qualify for a North Carolina income tax credit must provide all required information to determine and support the amount of the credit on a separate company basis. This information must be included with the combined return in each year the qualifying member becomes eligible to claim a credit or an installment of a credit, even if the group's income tax liability for that tax year is not sufficient for the combined group to benefit from the income tax credit. Combined groups eligible to claim income tax credits must complete Form CD-425, Corporate Tax Credit Summary, on a combined basis and file it with the group's income tax return. If a member of the combined group is eligible to claim an income tax credit limited by statute to 50 percent of tax, the combined group must also complete Form NC-478, Summary of Tax Credits Limited to 50 Percent of Tax [17 NCAC 05F.0503].

• *Combined return methodology*

The following methodology must be employed in preparing a combined return [17 NCAC 05F.0501]:

Determine combined federal taxable income. The starting point is the federal taxable income shown on a pro forma IRS Form 1120 for each corporation. These 1120s must represent each corporation's federal taxable income as if it were not part of a consolidated federal 1120. The taxpayer must then combine the pro forma 1120s of the corporations to be included in the combined group. This results in a combination of each corporation's line items in determining combined income. The taxpayer must

¶1202

eliminate the intercompany transactions between members of the combined group in arriving at combined federal taxable income.

Make North Carolina modifications. The taxpayer then makes North Carolina modifications (additions and subtractions) as provided in G.S. § 105-130.5 to determine combined income subject to apportionment.

Apportion the combined income. The taxpayer then apportions the combined income by including in the apportionment sales factor of all corporations included in the combined group as provided in G.S. § 105-130.4. All sales into North Carolina by entities within the combined group must be included in the sales factor numerator. Where an intercompany transaction has occurred and been eliminated in the calculation of combined income, the amount eliminated must also be eliminated from the numerator and denominator of the sales factor.

Only one apportionment factor is to be calculated for the combined group. The standard sales factor apportionment formula generally must be used. However, if more than 50 percent of the group's combined income subject to apportionment is generated from a business activity subject to special apportionment under subsections (m) through (s1) of G.S. § 105-130.4, then that apportionment formula must be used for the entire group. If the taxpayer believes the statutory apportionment method that otherwise applies to the combined group subjects a greater portion of the group's income to tax than is attributable to its business in North Carolina, the taxpayer may propose, and the Secretary must consider, an alternative method of apportionment. The taxpayer must apply the combined apportionment factor to the combined apportionable income to determine income apportioned to North Carolina.

Add nonapportionable income. The taxpayer must add any nonapportionable income allocated to North Carolina to the income apportioned to North Carolina to determine total income subject to North Carolina tax.

Apply NELs. The combined group's income subject to tax is reduced by net economic losses sustained by a corporation that becomes a member of the group, but not fully used by that corporation before becoming a member of the combined group, subject to the provisions of G.S. § 105-130.8. NELs brought by a corporation into the group remain with that corporation and, to the extent not used by the group during the years the corporation is part of the group, may be claimed by the corporation in the tax years after the corporation ceases to be a part of the group. The tax years that the corporation is part of the combined group count toward the 15-year carryforward period authorized in G.S. § 105-130.8. An NEL sustained by the group in a combined return year must be allocated among the members of the group that reported losses on their pro forma 1120s, after elimination of intercompany transactions between members of the combined group. The amount allocated to each member must be determined by dividing that member's loss (after elimination of intercompany transactions) by the total losses (after elimination of intercompany transactions) of all members of the combined group in that tax year. To the extent not used by the group during the years the corporation is part of the group, the group's NELs allocated to a corporation that is a member of the group may be claimed by the corporation in the tax years after the corporation ceases to be a part of the group. Net economic losses must be used in order beginning with earliest tax year. If more than one corporation brought NELs from the same tax year into the combined group and a portion of the losses from that year is used, the amount of used NELs must be prorated among the members bringing losses from that year based on the percentage of each member's losses to the total losses carried forward from that year. See ¶906 for a discussion of net economic losses, which are replaced by state net losses for taxable years beginning on or after January 1, 2015.

Application of credits. The combined group's income tax may be reduced by tax credits earned by a member of the group, but not fully used by that entity prior to becoming a member of the group, subject to the provisions of the specific credits involved. Because the eligibility for a tax credit is determined at the separate entity level, any unused installment or carryforward of a tax credit earned by a member of the group remains with that entity if that entity is no longer a member of the combined group or the group is no longer required to file a combined return. This rule applies whether the credit was earned by the entity before becoming a member of the group or while a member of the group. For franchise tax purposes, the tax credits may only be used by the entity generating the credit unless the group also files a combined return for franchise tax purposes.

- *Franchise tax returns*

Unless the Secretary authorizes a group to file a combined franchise tax return pursuant to G.S. § 105-122, each member of the group that is doing business in North Carolina must file a separate North Carolina franchise tax return and pay any franchise tax due. Any corporation that is included in a combined income tax return but that is not doing business in North Carolina is not subject to North Carolina franchise tax. The principal member must file its franchise tax return on the combined group's CD-405. All other members' separate returns should show zero dollars ($0) on the "Net Taxable Income" and "NC Net Income Tax" lines on the CD-405 and include a statement with the return that its income is included in the combined income tax return filed by the principal member and that identifies the name and Federal Employer Identification Number of the principal member. If the corporation filing a franchise tax return is a multistate taxpayer, then it must calculate an apportionment factor to be used in calculating its capital stock base using its separate entity sales before intercompany eliminations. Schedule O of the CD-405 must reflect the entity's apportionment factor for franchise tax purposes [17 NCAC 05F.0601].

- *Affiliated group*

An affiliated group is defined as a group of two or more corporations or noncorporate entities in which more than fifty percent (50%) of the voting stock of each member corporation or ownership interest of each member noncorporate entity is directly or indirectly owned or controlled by a common owner or owners, either corporate or noncorporate, or by one or more of the member corporations or noncorporate entities. The following entities may not be included in a combined return [G.S. § 105-130.5A(j)]:

(1) A corporation not required to file a federal income tax return.

(2) An insurance company, other than a captive insurance company, (i) which is subject to tax under Article 8B of this Chapter, (ii) whose premiums are subject to tax under Article 21 of Chapter 58 or a similar tax in another state, (iii) which is licensed as a reinsurance company, (iv) which is a life insurance company as defined in Section 816 of the Code, or (v) which is an insurance company subject to tax imposed by Section 831 of the Code. A "captive insurance company" means an insurer that is part of an affiliated group where the

insurer receives more than fifty percent (50%) of its net written premiums or other amounts received as compensation for insurance from members of the affiliated group.

(3) A corporation exempt from taxation under section 501 of the Code.

(4) An S corporation.

(5) A foreign corporation as defined in section 7701 of the Code, other than a domestic branch of a foreign corporation.

(6) A partnership, limited liability company, or other entity not taxed as a corporation.

(7) A corporation at least eighty percent (80%) of the gross income of which from all sources in the tax year is active foreign business income as defined in section 861(c)(1)(B) of the Code as in effect as of July 1, 2009.

Nothing in the definition of affiliated group may be construed to limit or negate the Secretary's authority to add back, eliminate, or otherwise adjust intercompany transactions involving the entities listed above to accurately compute the corporation's state net income properly attributable to its in-state business.

• *Penalties*

If a corporation does not file a combined return by the time required, then the corporation is subject to the penalties provided in G.S. § 105-236(a)(3). Penalties may not be imposed on an assessment under this provision except as expressly authorized in G.S. §§ 105-130.5A and 105-236(a)(5)f [G.S. § 105-130.5A(l)].

• *Advice*

A corporation may request the Secretary in writing to provide specific advice regarding whether a redetermination of the corporation's state net income or a combined return would be required under certain facts and circumstances. The Secretary may request that the taxpayer provide information necessary to provide the specific advice. The Secretary must provide the specific advice within 120 days of the receipt of the requested information from the taxpayer. G.S. § 105-264 governs the effect of this advice [G.S. § 105-130.5A(m)].

• *Extensions of time*

The Secretary and the taxpayer may extend any time limit included in these procedures by mutual agreement [G.S. § 105-130.5A(n)].

• *Other adjustments*

Nothing in these procedures may be construed to limit or negate the Secretary's authority to make tax adjustments as otherwise permitted by law, except that the Secretary may not make adjustments under these procedures that limit a corporation's options for reporting royalty payments under G.S. § 105-130.7A [G.S. § 105-130.5A(o)]. The Department has stated that it is authorized to adjust a taxpayer's income under other law, including judicially created doctrines such as economic substance. Department of Revenue, *Important Notice Regarding the Secretary's Authority to Adjust the Net Income of a Corporation or to Require a Corporation to File a Combined Return.*

• *Appeals*

If the corporation appeals a final determination by the Department under these procedures to the Office of Administrative Hearings in a contested tax case, the administrative law judge shall review *de novo* (i) whether the separate income tax returns submitted by the taxpayer failed to report state net income properly attributable to its in-state business through the use of intercompany transactions that lack economic substance or are not at fair market value between members of an affiliated group of entities; (ii) whether the Department's means of determining the corporation's State net income under this section was an appropriate means of determining the corporation's State net income properly attributable to North Carolina; and (iii) if a combined return was required by the Department, whether adjustments other than requiring the corporation to file a return on a combined basis are adequate under the circumstances to redetermine state net income [G.S. § 105-130.5A(p)].

¶1203 Time and Place for Filing Returns

• *Due dates*

In general, franchise and income taxes are returned on a single form (CD-405) that is due on or before the 15th day of the 4th month following the close of the taxable year. A taxable year ending on any day other than the last day of the month is deemed to end on the last day of the calendar month ending nearest to the last day of a taxpayer's actual taxable year [G.S. § 105-130.17(b)]. In the case of non-U.S. corporations that file federal returns pursuant to IRC § 6072(c), a return must be filed on or before the 15th day of the 6th month following the close of its income year [G.S. § 105-130.17(g); IRC § 6072(c)].

Returns of *agricultural cooperatives* are due on or before the 15th day of the 9th month following the close of the taxable year (September 15th for calendar-year taxpayers) [G.S. § 105-130.17(c)]. *Tax-exempt corporations* (under G.S. § 105-130.11) that file on a calendar-year basis must file returns on or before May 15 of the following year; and tax-exempt corporations that file on a fiscal-year basis must file returns on or before the 15th day of the 5th month following the end of the fiscal year [G.S. § 105-130.17(d)].

Cessation of operations: A corporation that ceases operation in North Carolina before the end of its taxable year for any reason (including consolidation) must file its return for the short taxable year within 105 days after the date it terminates its business in North Carolina [G.S. § 105-130.17(e)].

Information at the source: Information returns must be filed by a corporation having a place of business or having one or more employees, agents or other representatives in North Carolina, in whatever capacity acting, including lessors or mortgagors of real or personal property, or having the control, receipt, custody, disposal, or payment of interest (other than interest coupons payable to the bearer), rent, salaries, wages, premiums, annuities, compensations, remunerations, emoluments or other fixed or determinable annual or periodical gains or profits paid or payable during any year to any taxpayer. The return must be made under regulations prescribed by the Secretary [G.S. § 105-130.21(a)]. The filing of a report in compliance of this requirement does not act in evidence of and is not to be deemed to be evidence that the filing corporation is doing business in North Carolina [G.S. § 105-130.21(a)].

Every corporation doing business or having a place of business in North Carolina must file an annual report with the Secretary of Revenue that includes the names and addresses of all taxpayers/residents to whom dividends have been paid and the amount of such dividends during the income year [G.S. § 105-130.21(b)].

Business Corporation Annual Report

All corporations authorized to transact business in North Carolina (except insurance companies and professional corporations must deliver an annual report to the Secretary of State by the 15th day of the fourth month following the close of the corporation's fiscal year [G.S. § 55-16-22]). The former option to file the annual report with the corporation's income tax return was repealed effective August 11, 2017 [S.L. 2017-204, § 1.13].

• *Interest and penalties*

Interest accrues at the established rate (discussed at ¶3205). A penalty for failure to file of 5% of the total taxes due is incurred each month a return is delinquent (minimum $5; maximum 25%). A penalty of 10% for failure to pay by the due date is also imposed. Penalties are discussed in more detail at ¶3204.

• *Where to file*

Returns should be filed with the North Carolina Department of Revenue, P.O. Box 25000, Raleigh, NC 27640-0500, or at one of the Department's local branch offices located in principal cities throughout North Carolina [G.S. § 105-130.17(a)].

• *Extensions of time to file*

A corporation can receive a six-month (seven-month prior to January 1, 2008) extension of time to file its corporate franchise and income tax return if the corporation timely files a request for a refund on Form CD-410 (Application for Extension of Time to File Corporate Franchise and Income Tax Return). The application must be filed on or before the 15th day of the 3rd month following the end of the taxpayer's taxable year. An extension of time to file does not extend the time to pay. An extension may be granted even if the request of the extension is not accompanied by payment. However, the failure to pay penalty applies to the amount not paid by the original due date of the return, and interest accrues at the applicable rate on the amount not paid by the original due date of the corporate return [17 NCAC 5C.2004]. See ¶3204 for more on penalties.

¶1204 Payment of Tax

In general, the full amount of corporation income tax is payable within the time allowed for filing the return [G.S. § 105-130.19(a)]. Taxes are payable in the national currency. The Secretary shall prescribe whether taxes must be paid in cash, by check (payable to "North Carolina Department of Revenue"), by electronic funds transfer, or by another method [G.S. § 105-241(a)]. Taxpayers who, during the applicable period for a tax, have average required payments of at least $20,000 a month are required to pay by electronic funds transfer (EFT). The threshold ($20,000) applies separately to each tax [G.S. § 105-241(b)]. For more information about electronic funds transfer, see ¶3210. Payments are remitted to the Department of Revenue, P.O. Box 25000, Raleigh, NC 27640-0640.

¶1205 Estimated Tax

Corporations with an estimated income tax liability of $500 or more are required to file declarations of estimated tax. The number of declarations that must be filed depends on the quarter in which the corporation first estimates its income tax liability will be equal to or more than the threshold amount of $500 [G.S. §§ 105-163.69, 105-163.40(a)]. Declarations of estimated income tax for corporations are filed on Form CD-429 unless a corporation is required to pay estimated income tax by EFT. See below.

Online Payment of Estimated Tax

Taxpayers who file corporate estimated income taxes can now pay online through the North Carolina Department of Revenue's web site at www.dornc.com. Taxpayers can pay corporate estimated income taxes by credit or debit card (MasterCard or Visa) or by bank draft. They receive an acknowledgement from the Department so they know their payments have been received [*Press Release*, North Carolina Department of Revenue, September 6, 2005]. Electronic services provided by the Department of Revenue are discussed at ¶3309.

• *Due dates*

The due dates for and the amounts of payment installments depend on when the corporation first meets the $500 threshold. For example, if the $500 threshold is met during the first quarter of the taxable year, the corporation must pay its estimated income tax in four equal installments of 25% of the estimated income tax. The table below contains the information on required payments.

If the date of first required payment is:	The number of installments to be made is:	*The following percentages of the estimated tax must be paid on or before the 15th day of the:*			
		4th month	6th month	9th month	12th month
Before the 1st day of the 4th month of the taxable year	4	25	25	25	25
After the last day of the 3rd month and before the 1st day of the 6th month of the taxable year	3	—	33	33	33
After the last day of the 5th month and before the 1st day of the 9th month of the taxable year	2	—	—	50	50
After the last day of the 8th month and before the 1st day of the 12th month of the taxable year	1	—	—	—	100

• *Payment of tax*

Payment of estimated income tax should accompany the declaration of estimated income tax. Checks should be made payable to North Carolina Department of Revenue and mailed to North Carolina Department of Revenue, P.O. Box 25000,

Raleigh, NC 27640-0650. Some corporations must make estimated income tax payments by EFT. Notify the Department of Revenue of any change of address by completing Form NC-AC (Business Address Correction). Mailing for the next year will be corrected, but corporations will not receive a new coupon book for the current year [*Instructions*, Form CD-429A].

• *Electronic funds transfer*

Corporations with total estimated income tax payments to North Carolina in a 12-month period that exceed $240,000 (an average of $20,000 monthly) or those that are required to make federal estimated income tax payment by EFT are required to pay North Carolina estimated income tax by EFT [G.S. § 105-163.40(d)]. See also ¶ 1204 and ¶ 3210.

EFT Eliminates Need to File Form CD-429

Corporations that are required to pay estimated income tax by EFT are not required to file Form CD-429.

• *Amended declarations*

When a corporation files an amended declaration after making one or more installment payments on its estimated tax, the amount of each remaining installment is the amount that would have been payable if the estimate in the original declaration was the original estimate, increased or decreased as appropriate, by the amount computed by dividing as follows:

$$\frac{\text{Absolute difference between the amount paid and the amount that would have been paid if the estimate in the amended declaration was the original estimate}}{\text{The number of remaining installments}}$$

Example: Vaasa Corporation, a calendar-year corporation, estimated its North Carolina corporation income tax for 2008 would be $20,000. Vaasa timely made required payments of $5,000 in the 1st and 2nd quarters. In July, Vaasa Corporation realized that the slump in sales that began early in the year was likely to last at least until the end of the year; so Vaasa filed an amended declaration of estimated tax. Vaasa's revised estimate of its 2008 tax liability was $15,000, which would have required quarterly payments of $3,750. Vaasa's two remaining payments will be in the amount of $1,250 each, computed as follows:

$$\frac{(\$10,000 - \$7,500)}{2} = \$1,250$$

Note that Vaasa has already made total payments of $10,000 during the first two quarters. If it makes two more payments of $1,250 each, it will have paid a total of $15,000 (the amount required under the revised estimate).

• *Overpayments*

If a taxpayer pays more estimated tax than the actual tax for its taxable year, the excess is considered an overpayment by the taxpayer and is refunded [G.S. § 105-163.43]. See ¶ 3203 for discussion of refunds.

Overpayments applied to next year: A corporation may elect to have an income tax refund applied to estimated income tax for the following tax year. A return reflecting an election to apply a refund to estimated tax for the following year must be filed by the last allowable date for making estimated tax payments for that year for the election to be valid. If a corporation makes a valid election, that corporation may not revoke the election after the return has been filed in order to have the amount refunded or applied in any other manner (e.g., an offset against any subsequently determined tax liability) [17 NCAC 5C.1904].

• *Interest*

Underpayment: Interest is assessed on underpayments of estimated tax. The interest is assessed at the applicable interest rate for the underpayment period. Interest is discussed at ¶3205. In general, an installment of estimated tax is considered underpaid in an amount equal to the difference between 90% of the corporation's tax liability for the taxable year and the amount, if any, of the installment timely paid by the corporation [G.S. § 105-163.41(b)]. The period of underpayment runs from the date the installment was due to the earlier of (1) the 15th day of the fourth month following the close of the taxable year or (2) the date of actual payment [G.S. § 105-163.41(c)].

Additions Reclassified as Interest Rather than Penalties

G.S. § 105-163.41 was amended in 2005 to reclassify additions for underpayments of estimated income tax as interest rather than penalties. The reclassification has the effect of making the additions nonwaivable and payable to the General Fund rather than to the Civil Penalty and Forfeiture Fund. *See N.C. Sch. Bds. Ass'n v. Moore*, 359 N.C. 474, 614 S.E.2d 504 (2005).

Safe harbors: No interest will be due if the total amount of all payments of estimated tax made on or before the due dates equals or exceeds the amount that would have been required if the estimated tax were equal to the least of the following safe-harbor amounts [G.S. § 105-163.41(d)]:

(1) The tax shown on the corporation's return for the preceding taxable year if the preceding year was a taxable year of 12 months.

(2) An amount equal to the tax computed at the rates applicable to the current taxable year but otherwise applicable based on the facts and the law for the preceding taxable year.

(3) An amount equal to 90% of the tax for the taxable year determined by placing on an annualized basis the taxable income for the appropriate installment period being reported. The taxable income is placed on an annualized basis by multiplying by 12 the taxable income for the period under consideration and dividing by the number of months in the period under consideration [G.S. § 105-163.41(d)(3)]. The denominator is determined as follows:

(a) If the payment is required to be paid in the 4th month, the denominator is 3.

(b) If the payment is required to be paid in the 6th month, the denominator will be 3 or 5.

(c) If the payment is required to be paid in the 9th month, the denominator will be 6 or 8.

(d) If the payment is required to be paid in the 12th month, the denominator will be 9 or 11.

¶1205

Large Corporations

Large corporations, as defined in IRC § 6655, cannot use the first two safe harbors above [G.S. § 105-163.41(d)(5)]. A corporation for this purpose is a large corporation if it (or any predecessor corporation) had taxable income of $1,000,000 or more for any taxable year during the three taxable years immediately preceding the taxable year involved [IRC § 6655(g)(2)(A) and (B)(i)].

¶1206 Federal Changes

Requirement to file amended return when federal changes made: If a taxpayer's federal taxable income or a federal tax credit is changed or corrected by the Commissioner of Internal Revenue or other officer of the United States or other competent authority, and the change or correction affects the amount of state tax payable, the taxpayer must file an income tax return reflecting each change or correction from a federal determination within six months of being notified of each change or correction. The Secretary must then propose an assessment of any additional tax due or refund any overpayment (see ¶3208) and refund any overpayment of tax. If a taxpayer files a federal amended return that would increase the taxpayer's state tax liability, the taxpayer must file an amended state return within six months. If the federal amended return would decrease the taxpayer's state tax liability, the taxpayer may file an amended state return within the time period set forth in G.S. § 105-241.6, discussed at ¶3203. A taxpayer that fails to comply with this section is subject to penalties (see ¶3204) and forfeits its rights to any refund due by reason of the determination [G.S. § 105-130.20].

Assessments and refunds: When a corporation files an amended return reflecting a federal change, the Secretary must propose an assessment for any additional tax due or refund any overpayment [G.S. 105-130.20]. Proposed assessments and refund claims are discussed at ¶¶3208 and 3203.

Fraud provisions: When a federal adjustment is made in a corporation's income tax return and a fraud penalty assessed by the federal government, North Carolina may open the year for adjustments on the basis of either fraud or the federal assessment. The penalty for fraud is 50% of the total deficiency. If the corporation has not filed a North Carolina return, the fraud penalty and the delinquency penalty of 5% per month ($5 minimum; 25% maximum) may be assessed. The fact that no return has been filed, either State or federal, does not prevent North Carolina from opening the taxable year on the basis of federal changes [*2007—2008 Technical Bulletins* II, U].

¶1207 Recordkeeping

Although penalties are provided for failure to provide any records required by the Department [G.S. § 105-235(9)], the corporation income tax provisions do not specify any recordkeeping requirements, nor do the income tax regulations issued by the Department of Revenue. There is, however, a penalty for failure to provide any records required by the Department. See ¶3204 for discussion of penalties. The Business Corporation Act, however, requires corporations to maintain appropriate accounting records in written form or in another form capable of conversion into written form within a reasonable time [G.S. § 55-16-01].

PART VI

FRANCHISE TAX

CHAPTER 13

IMPOSITION OF TAX

¶1301 In General

• *Nature of tax*

North Carolina levies a series of franchise taxes upon corporations (both domestic and foreign). The franchise tax law is codified as Article 3 of Chapter 105 of the General Statutes of North Carolina. The taxes levied upon domestic corporations (corporations organized under the laws of North Carolina) are for the corporate rights and privileges granted by their charters, and the enjoyment of corporate powers, rights, privileges, and immunities under the laws of North Carolina [G.S. § 105-114(a1)(1)]. The taxes levied upon foreign corporations (corporations not organized under the laws of North Carolina) are for the privilege of doing business in North Carolina and for the benefit and protection they receive from the government and laws of North Carolina [G.S. § 105-114(a1)(2)]. Certain corporations are subject to special franchise taxes.

• *Base and rate*

In general, the franchise tax is measured by the corporation's capital stock, surplus and undivided profits (or, beginning in 2017, the corporation's net worth). Holding companies are subject to special franchise taxes. See ¶ 1304. Corporations that allocate and apportion net income for corporation income tax purposes apportion capital stock, surplus and undivided profits to North Carolina. Apportionment is discussed in Chapter 14. The franchise tax (other than for specially taxed entities) is imposed at the rate of $1.50 per $1,000 of valuation. See ¶ 1401.

• *Payment required to continue in corporate form*

The payment of the franchise tax is a condition precedent to the right to continue in the corporate form of organization (for domestic corporations) and a condition precedent to the right to continue to engage in doing business in North Carolina (for foreign corporations) [G.S. § 105-114(a)(2)].

Identification Numbers

Corporations do not need to apply for corporate identification numbers. For corporate income and franchise tax purposes, taxpayers are identified by the federal identification number and the number assigned by the Secretary of State [*Frequently Asked Questions About NC Corporate, Excise, and Insurance Tax, North Carolina Department of Revenue , http://www.dor.state.nc.us/faq/corporate.html*].

• *Definition of terms*

The following definitions apply to the franchise tax.

City: A city as defined by G.S. § 160A-1(2). The term also includes an urban service district defined by the governing board of a consolidated city-county, as defined by G.S. § 160B-2(1)[G.S. § 105-114(b)(1)].

Code: For purpose of the franchise tax, the "Code" is defined by reference to G.S. § 105-228.90 [G.S. § 105-114(b)(1a)]. For the current definition, see ¶ 103.

Corporation: A domestic corporation, a foreign corporation, an electric membership corporation organized under Chapter 117 of the General Statutes or doing business in North Carolina, or an association that is organized for pecuniary gain, has capital stock represented by share, whether with or without par value, and has privileges not possessed by individuals or partnerships. The term includes a mutual or capital stock savings and loan association or building and loan association chartered under the laws of any state or of the United States. The term includes a limited liability company or a partnership that elects to be taxed as a C corporation under the Internal Revenue Code but does not include noncorporate limited liability companies or partnerships (*i.e.*, limited liability companies or partnerships that do not elect to be taxed as corporations under the Internal Revenue Code) [G.S. § 105-114(b)(2); G.S. § 105-114.1(a)(5) *Corporate Income, Franchise, and Insurance Tax Bulletin*, I.A.2. (2018)].

Unincorporated Entities

An unincorporated entity can be subject to the franchise tax if it is organized for pecuniary gain, has capital stock represented by shares and has privileges not possessed by individuals or partnerships, Thus a business trust has been held to be a corporation for franchise tax purposes. *See First Carolina Investors v. Lynch,* 78 N.C. App. 583, 337 S.E.2d 691 (1985). However, despite the language of G.S. § 105-114 that the franchise tax is imposed upon "persons and partnerships", partnerships not otherwise falling within the franchise tax definition of corporation are not subject to the tax.

Doing business: Each and every act, power, or privilege exercised or enjoyed in North Carolina, as an incident to, or by virtue of the powers and privileges granted by the laws of North Carolina [G.S. § 105-114(b)(3)].

Income year: The calendar year or the fiscal year upon the basis of which the net income is computed for tax purposes. If no fiscal year has been established, the income year is the calendar year. In the case of a return made for a fractional part of a year or under rules adopted by the Secretary, the income year is the period for which the return is made [G.S. § § 105-114(b)(4) and 105-130.2(10)].

¶ 1301

Total assets: The sum of all cash, investments, furniture, fixtures, equipment, receivables, intangibles, and any other items of value owned by a person or business entity [G.S. § 105-114(b)(5)].

¶ 1302 Corporations Subject to Tax

All domestic corporations and foreign corporations that have qualified to do business or are doing business in North Carolina, unless specifically exempt, are subject to the franchise tax [G.S. §§ 105-122(a), 105-114]. See definition of corporation in ¶ 1301.

• *Nexus*

A corporation has nexus for franchise tax if it is doing business in this state.

This definition of "doing business" is broader than "doing business" for corporation income tax purposes. The levy of income taxes is subject to the limitations of P.L. 86-272, which prohibits a state from imposing an income tax on income derived in the state by a corporation if the corporation's only activity in the state is the solicitation of sales of tangible property. See ¶ 803 for discussion of P.L. 86-272. The franchise tax is a privilege or excise tax [G.S. § 105-114(a)], not an income tax; so P.L. 86-272 does not apply to the franchise tax.

A corporation that is protected from payment of income tax under P.L. 86-272 is not protected from the payment of franchise tax. A corporation that is subject to franchise tax but not income tax due to P.L. 86-272 apportions its capital stock, surplus, and undivided profits base by the use of the apportionment formula that would have applied to the corporation's business income if that income had been subject to income tax. In computing the amount due under the formula, the sales factor is to be computed without regard to P.L. 86-272 [*Tax Directive CD 98-4* (November 19, 1998)].

• *S corporations*

S corporations are subject to the franchise tax. The election of S corporation status for corporation income tax purposes does not affect the franchise tax liability of S corporations doing business and/or incorporated or domesticated in North Carolina. The income taxation of S corporations is discussed in Chapter 6.

• *Inactive corporations*

Inactive corporations without assets are subject annually to a minimum franchise tax of $200. Failure to file and pay the minimum tax results in suspension of the Articles of Incorporation or Certificate of Authority [17 NCAC 5B.0104]. A corporation that intends to dissolve or withdraw through suspension for nonpayment of franchise tax should indicate its intention in writing to the Department of Revenue [*Corporate Income, Franchise, and Insurance Tax Bulletin*, I.A.5 (2018)].

Validity of Action During Suspension

A corporation or LLC may be suspended for failure to file a return or pay a tax due if the failure has continued for 90 days. A suspended corporation or LLC loses all the powers, privileges, and franchises conferred upon it by its articles of incorporation or articles of organization, or, in the case of a foreign entity, its authorization to transact business in North Carolina. Where a suspended corporation or LLC is reinstated, upon entry of reinstatement, the suspension is deemed never to have occurred, so that any act performed or attempted to be performed during the period of suspension will be valid. However, the validity of these actions may not affect the rights of any person who reasonably relied to that person's prejudice on the suspension [S.L. 2001-387, §§152 and 153; G.S. §105-232(a)].

• *Reinstatement after suspension*

In order to be reinstated after suspension, a corporation must file all returns for all tax schedules and pay all tax, penalty, and interest due and pay a $25 reinstatement fee. When the Department of Revenue determines that all of these requirements have been met, the Department of Revenue will notify the office of the Secretary of State [G.S. §105-232].

• *Dissolution or withdrawal*

Corporations are not subject to franchise tax after the end of the income year in which articles of dissolution or withdrawal are filed with the Secretary of State unless they engage in business activities not incidental to winding up their affairs. Therefore no franchise tax is required with the income return filed for the year in which the application is filed or with any subsequent income returns that may be required in connection with winding up the affairs of the corporation [17 NCAC 5B.0105].

¶1303 Exempt Corporations

The following corporations are specifically exempt from the franchise tax. If, however, the Secretary requests, an exempt corporation must establish its claim for exemption in writing [G.S. §105-125(a)].

(1) Charitable, religious, fraternal, benevolent, scientific, or educational corporations not operated for profit [G.S. §105-125(a)(1)].

(2) Insurance companies subject to the gross premiums tax levied by Article 8B of Chapter 105 [G.S. §§105-125(a)(2), 105-228.5(a)].

(3) Certain mutual or cooperative associations including (a) mutual ditch or irrigation association, (b) mutual or cooperative telephone associations or companies (c) mutual canning associations, (d) cooperative breeding associations, (e) similar corporations of a purely local character deriving receipts solely from assessments, dues, or fees collected from members for the sole purpose of meeting expenses [G.S. §105-125(a)(3)].

(4) A cooperative marketing association that operates solely for the purpose of marketing products of members or other farmers and returns to the members and farmers the proceeds of sales (less the association's necessary operating expenses, including interest and dividends on capital stock) on the basis of the quantity of product furnished by them. The association's operations may include activities directly related to these marketing activities [G.S. §105-125(a)(4)].

(5) A production credit association organized under the federal Farm Credit Act of 1933 [G.S. §105-125(a)(5)].

(6) A club organized and operated exclusively for pleasure, recreation, or other nonprofit purposes; a civic league operated exclusively for the promotion of social welfare; a business league; or a board of trade [G.S. §105-125(a)(6)].

(7) A chamber of commerce or merchants' association not organized for profit if no part of its net earnings inures to the benefit of a private stockholder, an individual, or another corporation [G.S. § 105-125(a)(7)].

(8) An organization (*e.g.,* condominium association, homeowners' association, cooperative housing corporation) not organized for profit, the membership of which is limited to the owners or occupants of residential units in the condominium, housing development, or cooperative housing corporation. To qualify for the exemption, the organization must meet two criteria: (a) It must be operated exclusively for the management, operation, preservation, maintenance, or landscaping of the residential units owned by the organization or its members or of the common areas and facilities that are contiguous to the residential units and owned by the organization or by its members and (b) no part of its net earnings may insure, other than through the performance of related services for the members of the organization, to the benefit of any person [G.S. § 105-125(a)(8)].

(9) Except as otherwise provided by law, an organization exempt from federal income tax under the Internal Revenue Code [G.S. § 105-125(a)(9)].

(10) An entity that qualifies as a real estate mortgage investment conduit as defined in IRC § 860D. A real estate mortgage investment conduit must establish in writing its qualification for this exemption [G.S. § 105-125(a)].

¶1304 Holding Companies

Holding companies are subject to special franchise tax rules.

• *Imposition*

Every corporation (domestic and foreign) incorporated or domesticated in North Carolina or doing business in North Carolina that is, at the close of its taxable year, a holding company is subject to a franchise tax under G.S. § 105-120.2 in lieu of the regular franchise tax imposed by G.S. § 105-122 [G.S. § 105-114(a4)]. A holding company for this purpose is any corporation that satisfies at least one of the following conditions [G.S. § 105-120.2(c)]:

(1) It has no assets other than ownership interests in corporations in which it owns, directly or indirectly more than 50% of the outstanding voting stock or voting capital interests. (Note that the ownership of *any* asset other than an equity interest in a controlled subsidiary will apparently result in failure of this condition.)

(2) It receives during its taxable year more than 80% of its gross income from corporations in which it owns (directly or indirectly) more than 50% of the outstanding voting stock or voting capital interests or ownership interests. (Note that a corporation with no gross income may not be able to satisfy this condition.)

(3) It owns copyrights, patents and trademarks that comprise more than 80% of its assets or it derives more than 80% of its gross income from royalty and license fee revenues and, in either case, it is wholly-owned by a manufacturing company with more than $5 billion in manufacturing revenues and that includes in its net worth franchise tax base an investment in a subsidiary that owns copyrights, patents or trademarks.

If a holding company has an ownership interest in an LLC doing business in the State and the LLC is treated as a C Corporation for federal income tax purposes, the holding company's share of the income of the LLC is included in the denominator and, if the corporation owns more than fifty percent (50%) of the voting capital interest in the LLC, the holding company's share of the income of the LLC is included in the numerator when computing the holding company test [*Corporate Income, Franchise, and Insurance Tax Bulletin*, I.B.1 (2018)]. The Department of Revenue has ruled that "gross income" for purposes of gross income test, includes total income under code § 61 as reported on Form 1120, including income of a disregarded entity [Directive CD-18-1].

Counties, cities, and towns may not levy a franchise tax on holding corporations [G.S. § 105-120.2(e)].

Filing returns and apportionment: Holding companies file returns, determine the amounts of their net worth, and apportion their net worth to North Carolina under the provisions of G.S. § 105-122, like other corporations. See Chapter 14.

Computation of tax: The statute provides two formulas for computing the franchise tax of holding companies:

(1) Tax computed at the rate of $1.50 per $1,000 of the amount of the company's apportioned net worth, with a minimum of $200 and a maximum of $150,000 (note that for taxes due before January 1, 2017, the minimum and maximum holding company franchise tax amounts were $35 and $75,000 respectively).

(2) Tax computed at the rate of $1.50 per $1,000 on the greater of (a) 55% of the appraised value as determined for ad valorem taxation of all the real and tangible personal property in North Carolina or (b) the total actual investment in North Carolina of the corporation as computed under G.S. § 105-122(d).

If the amount of tax computed under formula (2) is greater than the tax computed under formula (1), the taxpayer must use formula (2) [G.S. § 105-120.2(b)(2)].

¶ 1305 Corporate-Controlled LLCs

• *Background*

LLCs are generally excluded from the definition of a "corporation" for franchise tax purposes and so are not generally subject to the tax. There are, however, two major exceptions to this general rule.

• *"Corporate" LLCs*

First, any LLC that elects to be taxed as a corporation for federal income tax purposes is treated as a corporation for franchise tax purposes and so becomes directly liable for the franchise tax [G.S. § § 105-114(b)(2), 105-114.1 and 105-122.1].

• *Corporate Controlled LLCs*

Second, if a corporation or an "affiliated group" of corporations owns 50% or more of the "capital interests" in a noncorporate limited liability company (i.e., one that has checked the box to be treated as a corporation), the corporation or group of corporations must include in its three tax bases (discussed at ¶ 1401) the same percentage of (1) the noncorporate limited liability company's net worth; (2) 55% of the noncorporate limited liability company's appraised ad valorem tax value of property; and (3) the noncorporate limited liability company's actual investment in tangible property in North Carolina, as appropriate [G.S. § 105-114.1(b)]. For this purpose, an "affiliated group" means an affiliated group as defined in IRC § 1504 [G.S. § 105-114.1(a)(1)] and a "capital interest" means the right under a limited liability company's "governing law" to receive a percentage of the company's assets upon dissolution after payments to creditors [G.S. § 105-114.1(a)(2)]. A limited liability company's governing law is the law under which it is organized [G.S. § 105-114.1(a)(4)].

Affiliated group: If the assets of a noncorporate limited liability company are to be attributed to an affiliated group of corporations, the percentage to be attributed to a particular group member that is doing business in North Carolina is determined by multiplying the capital interests in the noncorporate limited liability company owned by the affiliated group by a fraction, the numerator of which is the capital interest in the noncorporate limited liability company owned by the group member and the denominator of which is the capital interest in the noncorporate limited liability company owned by all group members that are doing business in North Carolina [G.S. § 105-114.1(e)].

• *Rules for Determining Capital Interests*

Constructive ownership: Ownership of the capital interests in a noncorporate limited liability company is determined by reference to the constructive ownership rules for partnerships, estates, and trusts in IRC § 318(a)(2)(A) and (B), with the following three modifications [G.S. § 105-114.1(c)]:

(1) The term "capital interest" is substituted for "stock" each place it appears (since it is the constructive ownership of LLC capital interests that is being determined).

(2) A noncorporate limited liability company and any noncorporate entity other than a partnership, estate, or trust is treated as a partnership (to ensure that the franchise tax is not avoided by interposing such a noncorporate entity between the LLC and its ultimate corporate owners).

(3) The operating rule of IRC § 318(a)(5) applies without regard to IRC § 318(a)(5)(C) (to ensure that the franchise tax is not avoided by interposing multiple tiers of noncorporate entities between the LLC and its ultimate corporate owners).

Timing: Ownership of the capital interest in a noncorporate limited liability company is determined as of the last day of the LLC's taxable year. The inclusion in the owner's tax bases must be made to the owner's next following franchise tax return. If a noncorporate limited liability company and a corporation or an affiliated group of corporations have engaged in a pattern of transferring assets between them so that neither of them owned capital interests on the last day of the taxable year, the ownership of the capital interests in the noncorporate limited liability company must be determined as of the last day of the taxable year of the corporation or group of corporations [G.S. § 105-114.1(g)].

Threshold Determined by Rights on Dissolution

Note that the attribution rules determine the 50% capital-interest ownership threshold by reference to the right to receive the LLC's assets on dissolution of the LLC, which may be different from the ratio by which the members share in the LLC's profits and losses.

Exemption

The requirements of G.S. § 105-114.1 do not apply to assets owned by a noncorporate limited liability company if the total book value of its assets never exceeds $150,000 during its taxable year [G.S. § 105-114.1(f)]. This exemption is premised on the fact that the $200 annual fee payable by noncorporate LLCs pursuant to G.S. § 57D-1-22 was intended as a substitute for the franchise tax.

No Double Counting

If a corporation is required to include a percentage of a noncorporate limited liability company's assets in its tax bases, its investment in the noncorporate limited liability company is not included in the computation of the net worth base under G.S. § 105-122(b) (discussed at ¶ 1401) [G.S. § 105-114.1(d)].

• *Penalty*

A taxpayer that, because of fraud with intent to evade tax, underpays the North Carolina franchise tax on assets attributable to it under the new law is guilty of a Class H felony [G.S. § 105-114.1(d)]. Penalties are discussed at ¶ 3204.

• *Filing and nexus issues*

An LLC that is treated as a corporation reports income and franchise tax as a corporate entity. Therefore, the attributes of the LLC do not flow through to a corporate member for purposes of apportioning the corporate member's franchise tax base under G.S. § 105-122(c)(1), and a corporate member that has no connection with North Carolina other than its ownership interest in the LLC does not have a corporate income or franchise tax filing obligation, *even if the corporate member is entitled to receive 50% or more of the LLC's assets upon dissolution.* However, if the corporate member (1) has activities in North Carolina (in addition to its ownership interest in the LLC) that make it subject to the franchise tax and (2) is entitled to receive 70% or more of the LLC's assets upon dissolution, it must file a corporate income and franchise tax return and include the applicable percentage (see "Attribution," above) of the LLC's assets in its "Investment in Tangible Property in NC" franchise tax base [*Tax Directive CD-02-2* (May 31, 2002)].

• *Annual Report Fee Credit*

LLCs are subject to an annual report fee of $200 while corporations are subject to an annual report fee of only $25. The higher LLC annual report fee was intended to offset the revenue loss resulting from LLCs' exemption from the franchise tax. Therefore, an LLC that becomes subject to the franchise tax may claim a credit against its franchise tax liability equal to the difference between the LLC and corporation annual report fees [G.S. § 105-122.1].

¶ 1305

FRANCHISE TAX

CHAPTER 14

BASE AND RATE

¶1401 Base and Rate

The North Carolina franchise tax is imposed on the highest of three bases: (1) net worth (2) 55% of the appraised value of real and tangible personal property in the State and (3) total actual investment in tangible property in the State. These bases are described in ¶¶ 1402, 1403 and 1404.

• *Rate*

The franchise tax rate for C corporations is $1.50 per $1,000 of tax base. The franchise tax rate for S corporations is $200 for the first $1,000,000 of tax base and $1.50 per $1,000 of tax base in excess of $1,000,000 [G.S. § 105-122(d2)]. The special franchise tax rate for S corporations is effective for taxable years beginning on or after January 1, 2019 (reported on the 2018 and later year income tax returns).

• *Minimum tax*

A corporation's franchise tax can never be less than $200 [G.S. § 105-122(d2)].

¶1402 Net Worth

A corporation's net worth base is equal to its total assets (without regard to the deduction for accumulated depreciation, depletion, or amortization) less its total liabilities, with the three adjustments discussed below for depreciation and amortization, the cost of treasury stock and affiliated indebtedness [G.S. § 105-122(b)].

• *Computation of net worth*

A corporation's net worth is computed in accordance with generally accepted accounting principles as of the end of the corporation's taxable year. If the corporation does not maintain its books and records in accordance with generally accepted accounting principles, then its net worth is computed in accordance with the accounting method used by the corporation for federal tax purposes. The determination of a corporation's net worth must be made on the basis of its books and records as of the close of its income year [G.S. § 105-122(b)]. A corporation's net worth must be adjusted for the items described below.

• *Depreciation and amortization*

A corporation may deduct accumulated depreciation, depletion, and amortization as determined in accordance with the method used for federal tax purposes [G.S. § 105-122(b)(1)]. Assets for which such a deduction is allowed must be valued in accordance with the method used to compute federal depreciation, depletion and amortization [G.S. § 105-122(b)(1b)].

• *Treasury stock*

A corporation may deduct the cost of treasury stock [G.S. § 105-122(b)(3)].

• *Affiliated indebtedness*

A corporation must add back indebtedness it owes to a parent, a subsidiary, an affiliate, or a noncorporate entity in which the corporation or an affiliated group of corporations owns directly or indirectly more than 50% of the capital interests [G.S. § 105-122(b)(2)]. For purposes of the affiliated indebtedness adjustment, the following definitions apply:

Affiliate. A corporation is an affiliate of another corporation when both are directly or indirectly controlled by the same parent corporation or by the same or associated financial interests by stock ownership, interlocking directors, or by any other means whatsoever, whether the control is direct or through one or more subsidiary, affiliated, or controlled corporations [G.S. § 105-122(b1)(1)].

Affiliated group. An affiliated group has the meaning set forth in G.S. § 105-114.1 (see discussion at ¶ 1305) [G.S. § 105-122(b1)(2)].

Capital interest. A capital interest refers to the right, under the law under which the entity was organized, to receive a percentage of the entity's assets upon dissolution after payments to creditors [G.S. § 105-122(b1)(3) and (4)].

Indebtedness. Indebtedness includes all loans, credits, goods, supplies, or other capital of whatsoever nature furnished by a parent, subsidiary or affiliate or a noncorporate entity in which the corporation or an affiliated group of corporations owns directly or indirectly more than 50% of the capital interests. The term does not include indebtedness endorsed, guaranteed, or otherwise supported by one of these related parties [G.S. § 105-122(b1)(5)].

Noncorporate entity. A noncorporate entity is any person that is neither a human being nor a corporation [G.S. § 105-122(b1)(6)].

Parent and subsidiary. A parent-subsidiary relationship exists between two corporations if one corporation directly or indirectly controls the other by stock ownership, interlocking directors, or by any other means whatsoever exercised by the same or associated financial interests, whether the control is direct or through one or more subsidiary, affiliated, or controlled corporations [G.S. § 105-122(b1)(7) and (8)].

• *Further adjustment for borrowed capital*

If a corporation is required to add back affiliated indebtedness as described above, the amount added back may be reduced if part of the capital of the creditor entity was borrowed from someone other than a parent, a subsidiary, or an affiliate. Specifically, in computing its net worth the debtor corporation may deduct a proportionate part of the indebtedness based on the ratio of the creditor entity's borrowed capital to its total assets. Borrowed capital does not include indebtedness incurred by a bank arising out of the receipt of a deposit and evidenced by a certificate of deposit, a passbook, a cashier's check, a certified check, or other similar document [G.S. § 105-122(b)(2)].

¶1402

• *Adjustment for creditor corporation*

If the creditor corporation is subject to the North Carolina franchise tax, it may deduct the amount of indebtedness owed to it by a parent, subsidiary, or affiliated corporation to the extent that such indebtedness was added back by the debtor corporation to its own net worth [G.S. § 105-122(b)(2a)].

¶1403 Appraised Value of Property in North Carolina

The appraised valuation of property base is 55% of the appraised value (as determined for ad valorem taxation) of all of a corporation's real and tangible personal property in North Carolina. The appraised value of tangible property, including real estate, is the ad valorem valuation from the calendar year preceding the due date of the return [G.S. § 105-122(d)(2)]. Also included is the appraised value of all vehicles for which the county tax assessor has issued a billing during the income year [*Corporate Income, Franchise, and Insurance Tax Bulletin*, I.G. (2018)]. If property is included in the investment in tangible property base (see ¶1404), that property must also be included in the appraised valuation base [17 NCAC 5B.1406].

¶1404 Investment in Tangible Property in North Carolina

The "total actual investment in tangible property" base is the total original purchase price or consideration to the reporting taxpayer of its tangible properties (both real and personal) in North Carolina plus additions and improvements less reserve for depreciation permitted for income tax purposes. For franchise taxes reported with 2019 and later income tax returns, corporations may also deduct indebtedness specifically incurred and existing solely for and as a result of the purchase of real property and permanent improvements thereon [G.S. § 105-122(d)(3)].

With respect to taxes due before January 1, 2017, the following additional deductions against the total actual investment base are allowed: (1) any indebtedness incurred and existing by virtue of the purchase of any real estate and any permanent improvements made on the property; (2) reserves for the entire cost of any air-cleaning device or sewage or waste treatment plant (including waste lagoons) and pollution abatement equipment approved by the Department of Environmental Quality or a local air pollution control program; and (3) the cost of constructing facilities of any private or public utility built for the purpose of providing sewer service to residential and outlying areas [G.S. § 105-122(d)].

¶1405 Apportionment

• *Apportionment*

A corporation that is doing business in North Carolina and in one or more other states must apportion its net worth to this State [G.S. § 105-122(c1)].

• *Methods of apportionment*

Statutory method: A corporation must use one of the following apportionment methods unless the Department has authorized it to use an alternative method under G.S. § 105-122(c1)(2) [G.S. § 105-122(c1)]:

(1) A corporation that is subject to the North Carolina corporation income tax must apportion its net worth by using the fraction it applies in apportioning its income for corporation income tax purposes provided that a wholesale content distributor's apportionment may not be less than 2% [G.S. § 105-122(c1)(1)]. Note that a corporation with a state net loss that has elected to apportion its income by sourcing receipts from services under the income – producing activities test of former law must nevertheless apportion its net worth franchise tax base as if such election had not been made [G.S. § 105-122(c1)].

(2) A corporation that is not subject to the North Carolina corporation income tax must apportion its net worth by using the fraction it would be required to apply in apportioning its income as if it were subject to the corporation income tax [G.S. § 105-122(c1)(1)].

Alternative methods: The statutory method is presumed to be the best method of apportionment [G.S. § 105-122(c1)(1)]. Nevertheless, a corporation that believes that the statutory apportionment method subjects a greater portion of its net worth to tax than is attributable to its business in North Carolina may make a written request to the Secretary for permission to use an alternative method. The request must set out the reasons for the corporation's belief and propose an alternative method. The corporation has the burden of establishing by clear, cogent, and convincing proof that the statutory apportionment method subjects a greater portion of the corporation's net worth to tax than is attributable to its business in North Carolina and that the proposed alternative method is a better method of determining the amount of the corporation's net worth attributable to its business in North Carolina. The Secretary must issue a written decision on a corporation's request for an alternative apportionment method. If the decision grants the request, it must describe the alternative method the corporation is authorized to use and the tax years to which the alternative method applies. A decision may apply to no more than three (3) tax years. A corporation may renew its request to use an alternative method by making another written request. A decision of the Secretary on a request for an alternative apportionment method is final and is not subject to administrative or judicial review. A corporation authorized to use an alternative method may apportion its net worth in accordance with the alternative method or the statutory method [G.S. § 105-122(c1)(2)].

¶1406 Tax Credits

North Carolina has repealed most of its franchise tax credits. The only remaining franchise tax credits are (1) the credit for additional annual report fees paid by limited liability companies subject to the franchise tax (discussed at ¶1305), (2) the enhanced cigarette exportation credit (discussed at ¶1107), (3) the historic rehabilitation credit (discussed at ¶1104), (4) the credit for railroad intermodal facilities (discussed at ¶1103), and (5) the credit for recycling facilities (discussed at ¶1102). *See* also the tax credit chart at ¶36.

FRANCHISE TAX

CHAPTER 15

RETURNS, PAYMENT OF TAX, ADMINISTRATION AND PROCEDURES

¶1501 Returns

• *Returns*

The franchise tax is levied for the income year of the corporation in which the taxes become due [G.S. § 105-114(a3)]. For corporations (domestic and foreign) the franchise tax return is filed in a combined report with the corporation income tax on Form CD-405 and is due on or before the 15th day of the 3rd month following the end of the corporation's income year. For details see ¶ 1203. Franchise and income taxes are payable as of the filing due date to the North Carolina Department of Revenue. The franchise tax must be paid in full with the return. The procedure for obtaining an extension of time to file corporate franchise and income tax returns is also discussed at ¶ 1203. The tax paid represents an advance payment for the ensuing income year. For corporations filing combined income tax returns, see ¶ 1202.

• *Electronic filing*

The Department of Revenue participates in the Federal/State Electronic Filing Program and accepts general business franchise tax returns filed under that program [17 NCAC 5B.0108]. A taxpayer may file a tax return with the Department of Revenue electronically only when the Department has established and implemented procedures permitting electronic filing of a specific tax return. A return may be filed electronically only by using the procedures established by the Department for the particular return [17 NCAC 1C.0701].

Electronic signature: The name and identification number of the taxpayer constitutes the taxpayer's signature when transmitted as part of a tax return filed electronically by the taxpayer or at the taxpayer's direction [17 NCAC 1C.0702].

• *Change of accounting period*

A change of accounting period automatically establishes a new franchise year. A combined franchise and income tax return is required for the short income period. If the new franchise year overlaps the old year, credit is permitted against the franchise tax to the extent of the overlap [17 NCAC 5B.1501].

Example: Corporation changes its income year from a calendar year to one ending July 31. A combined franchise and income return is required for the short period January 1, 2017, through July 31, 2017 (7 months). Franchise tax paid on the 2016 return applicable to the calendar year 2017 was $240. Franchise tax on the short period would be applicable to the year August 1, 2017, through July 31, 2018 and would be computed as follows [*Corporate Income, Franchise and Insurance Tax Bulletin*, I.I.1 (2018)]:

Total tax due per return	$268
Less credit for portion of prior year's tax:	
Total tax paid on 2016 return	$240
Less amount applicable to short period ($^{7}/_{12}$ of $240)	140
Amount applicable beyond short period	100
Net franchise tax due on short period return	$168

• Mergers

Because franchise tax is prepaid, a special computation is sometimes required to prevent a duplication of tax when two or more corporations with different accounting periods (*i.e.,* income years) merge or otherwise transfer the entire assets from one corporation to the other [17 NCAC 5B.1502(a)]. In such a situation, the surviving corporation is allowed to deduct the amount of franchise tax paid by the submerged corporation applicable to overlapping accounting periods [17 NCAC 5B.1502(b)].

• Inactive corporations

A corporation that is inactive and without assets must file an annual return and pay a minimum franchise tax. The annual return of an inactive corporation must contain a statement of the status of the corporation. Failure to file a return and pay the minimum tax results in suspension of the articles of incorporation or certificate of authority [17 NCAC 5B.0104].

• Dissolution or withdrawal

Corporations that have filed articles of dissolution or withdrawal with the Secretary of State are not subject to franchise tax after the end of the income year in which the articles are filed unless they engage in business activities not incidental to winding up their affairs [17 NCAC 5B.0105].

• Corporations in bankruptcy

Corporations in bankruptcy are required to file returns even though they are not required to pay pre-petition tax penalty and interest [*Frequently Asked Questions About N.C. Corporate, Excise & Insurance Tax,North Carolina Department of Revenue, http://www.dor.state.nc.us/faq/corporate.html*].

¶1502 Estimated Tax

There are no provisions requiring payment of estimated franchise tax. However, if an electric power company's liability is consistently at least $10,000 per month, the electric power company must prepay the next month's tax liability at the same time that it is paying the current month's liability. See discussion at ¶1501.

¶1502

¶1503 Payment of Tax

Taxpayers file a combined franchise tax and corporation income tax return. Payment of the tax is due with the return. The utility franchise tax liability, dependent on various law requirements, may be monthly or quarterly.

- *Electronic funds transfer (EFT)—utility companies*

All utility companies with an average franchise utility tax of $20,000 or more per month are required to remit the utility tax by EFT. See ¶3210 for discussion of electronic funds transfer.

¶1504 Administration

The franchise tax is administered by the Corporate Tax Division of the North Carolina Department of Revenue.

- *Administrative provisions*

The franchise tax, like the corporation income tax, is governed by the provisions of Article 9 of Chapter 105 of the North Carolina General Statutes. See Chapter 12 for details of the corporate provisions. See also Chapter 32 for details on administrative provisions in general.

PART VII

SALES AND USE TAXES

CHAPTER 16

IMPOSITION, BASE AND RATES, CREDITS

¶1601 In General

The North Carolina sales and use taxes are imposed by Article 5 of Chapter 105 of the General Statutes, known as the "North Carolina Sales and Use Tax Act." The taxes levied under Article 5 are to provide revenue for the support of the North Carolina public school system and for other necessary uses and purposes of the government and State of North Carolina [G.S. § 105-164.2].

• *Administration*

The North Carolina sales and use taxes are administered by the Sales and Use Tax Division of the North Carolina Department of Revenue.

• *Sales tax*

The sales tax is levied on retail sales of tangible personal property, digital property and certain services. A list of taxable items can be found at ¶1605.

• *Use tax*

The North Carolina use tax has been in existence since 1939. It is levied on tangible personal property purchased or received from within or without North Carolina for storage, use, or consumption in North Carolina at the same Rate applicable to the sale or lease of the property. Note that the mere ordering of tangible personal property is not sufficient to make the property subject to the use tax. A use tax cannot take effect before the use begins, which may be after the date of the order. See, for example, *Atwater-Waynick Hosiery Mills, Inc. v. Clayton*, 268 N.C. 673, 151 S.E.2d 574 (1966).

Residents are responsible for paying the use tax on purchases for which no North Carolina sales or use tax has been charged. The use tax applies to transactions that would be subject to sales tax if the purchase were made in North Carolina.

• *Federal Internet Tax Freedom Act*

The Federal Internet Tax Freedom Act (ITFA) (P.L. 105-277, Division C, Title XI, 112 Stat. 2681-719 (1998)) bars state and local governments from imposing (1) multiple taxes on electronic commerce, (2) discriminatory taxes on electronic commerce, or (3) taxes on Internet access. The moratorium on such taxes began on October 1, 1998, expired on October 20, 2001, and was revived and extended until November 1, 2003, by the Internet Tax Nondiscrimination Act (H.R. 1552). The moratorium did not apply to Internet access taxes that were imposed and enforced before October 1, 1998. On November 19, 2004, S. 150 (a bill to make permanent the moratorium on taxes on Internet access) was passed by the U.S. Senate and cleared for the White House. S. 150 extends the moratorium on taxes on Internet access and multiple and discriminatory taxes on electronic commerce imposed by the Internet Tax Freedom Act (ITFA) until November 1, 2007. S. 150 also does the following:

(1) Expands the definition of exempt Internet access to include telecommunications services to the extent they are purchased, used, or sold by an Internet access provider [S. 150, § 2(c)(1)].

(2) Permits Internet access taxes that were generally imposed and actually enforced prior to October 1, 1998 [S. 150, § 2(b)(3)].

(3) Permits until November 1, 2005, other Internet access taxes that were generally imposed and actually enforced as of November 1, 2003 [S. 150, § 3].

(4) Provides that taxation of charges for voice or similar service using Voice Over Internet Protocol (VOIP) is not affected by S. 150.

NOTE: Items (1) and (3) combine to phase out taxes on digital subscriber line services.

• *Streamlined Sales Tax Project (SSTP)*

The Streamlined Sales Tax Project (SSTP) is a project created by participating state governments and the District of Columbia. Its mission is to develop measures to design, test, and implement a sales and use tax system that radically simplifies sales and use taxes. North Carolina is an "implementing state" in the SSTP. An "implementing state" is one that has the right to vote on the terms of the Interstate Agreement among the states (*i.e.*, the Streamlined Sales and Use Tax Agreement (SSUTA)). For more details, visit the web site of the National Streamlined Sales Tax Project at http://www.streamlinedsalestax.org/.

• *Streamlined Sales and Use Tax Agreement (SSUTA)*

The SSUTA was adopted November 12, 2002, and amended on November 19, 2003, November 16, 2005, and April 16, 2005. As a implementing state, North Carolina now has the right to vote on the terms of the SSUTA. A copy of the SSUTA can be found at http://www.streamlinedsalestax.org/.

SSUTA information: The North Carolina Department of Revenue has posted on its web site information related to the Streamlined Sales and Use Tax Agreement (SSUTA), including a database of the sales and use tax rates by jurisdiction. The rate database and list of data elements can be found at http://www.dor.state.nc.us/taxes/sales/streamlined.html.

Registration under SSUTA: Registration under SSUTA satisfies the registration requirements for sales and use tax purposes [G.S. § 105-164.42K]. Sales and use tax registration is discussed at ¶1604. A seller who registers under the Agreement within 12 months after the State becomes a member of the Agreement and who meets the following conditions is not subject to assessment for sales tax for any period before the effective date of the seller's registration:

(1) The seller was not registered with the State during the 12-month period before the effective date of this State's participation in the Agreement.

(2) When the seller registered, the seller had not received a letter from the Department notifying the seller of an audit.

(3) The seller continues to be registered under the Agreement and to remit tax to the State for at least 36 months.

More Information

For more details, see *North Carolina Information For Streamlined Sales Tax Participants* (North Carolina Department of Revenue, July 1, 2012), Also, see *Streamlined Sales and Use Tax* (North Carolina Department of Revenue, August 2012) in which The North Carolina Department of Revenue has updated information related to the Streamlined Sales and Use Tax (SST) Agreement. A revised Certificate of Compliance was issued August 1, 2012, and the taxability matrix, which defines the tax treatment of the definitions included in the SST Agreement and includes changes effective August 1, 2012, has been updated.

¶1602 Sourcing Rules

When sales involve a buyer and a seller located in different states, a frequent question that arises is, "In which state is the transaction taxable?" Determination of the answer to this question is referred to as "sourcing" sales. In general, sales are sourced based on destination [G.S. § 105-164.4B(a)].

• *General sourcing rules*

The rules described below apply in determining where a seller should source the sale of an item. Except as otherwise provided, a service is sourced to the place where the purchaser can potentially first make use of the service. These rules apply regardless of the nature of the item, except as otherwise noted [G.S. § 105-164.4B(a)]:

(1) When a purchaser receives an item at a business location of the seller, the sale is sourced to that business location [G.S. § 105-164.4B(a)(1)].

(2) If a purchaser or purchaser's donee receives an item, at a location specified by the purchaser and the location is not a business location of the seller, the sale is sourced to the location where the purchaser or the purchaser's donee receives the item [G.S. § 105-164.4B(a)(2)].

(3) When items (1) and (2) above do not apply, the sale is sourced to the location indicated by an address for the purchaser that is available from the business records of the seller that are maintained in the ordinary course of the seller's business when use of this access does not constitute bad faith [G.S. § 105-194.4B(a)(3)].

(4) When items (1), (2), and (3) above do not apply, the sale is sourced to the location indicated by an address for the purchaser obtained during the consummation of the sale including the address of a purchaser's payment instrument, if no other address is available, when use of this address does not constitute bad faith [G.S. § 105-164.4B(a)(4)].

(5) When items (1), (2), (3), and (4) above do not apply (including the circumstance in which the seller is without sufficient information to apply the rules) the location will be determined based on one of the following [G.S. § 105-164.4B(a)(5)]:

(a) Address from which the tangible personal property was shipped.

(b) Address from which the digital good or the computer software delivered electronically was first available for transmission by the seller.

(c) Address from which the service was provided.

• *Periodic rental payments for leased or rented property*

When a lease or rental agreement requires recurring periodic payments, the payments are sourced as follows:

(1) The first payment is sourced in accordance with the general sourcing rules discussed above, and each subsequent payment is sourced to the primary location of the leased or rented property for the period covered by the payment. This rule applies to all property except (a) a motor vehicle, (b) an aircraft, (c) transportation equipment (as defined below); and (d) a utility company railway car [G.S. § 105-164.4B(b)(1)].

(2) For a leased or rented motor vehicle or aircraft that is not transportation equipment (as defined below), all payments are sourced to the primary location of the leased or rented property for the period covered by the payment [G.S. § 105-164.4B(b)(2)].

(3) For leased or rented property that is transportation equipment (as defined below), all payments are sourced in accordance with the general sourcing rules discussed above [G.S. § 105-164.4B(b)(3)].

(4) For a railway car that is leased or rented by a utility company and that would be transportation equipment if it were used in interstate commerce, all payments are sourced in accordance with the general sourcing rules discussed above [G.S. § 105-164.4B(b)(4)].

"Transportation equipment" defined: For purposes of sourcing periodic rental equipment payments, "transportation equipment" means any of the following that are used to carry persons or property in interstate commerce: a locomotive, a railway car, a commercial motor vehicle as defined in G.S. § 20-4.01, or an aircraft [G.S. § 105-164.4B(c)]. The term includes a container designed for use on the equipment and a component part of the equipment.

• *Admissions*

Gross receipts derived from admissions charges to entertainment activities (discussed at ¶ 1728) are sourced to the place where a person gains admission to the activity. If this location is not known when the gross receipts are received, the general sourcing rules discussed above apply [G.S. §§ 105-164.4B(h) and 105-164.4G(g)].

• *Prepaid meal plans*

Gross receipts derived from a prepaid meal plan are sourced to the location where the food or prepared food is available to be consumed [G.S. § 105-164.4B(g)].

¶1602

- *Computer software renewals*

Receipts from the renewal of a service contract for pre-written software are sourced under the general sourcing rules discussed above. However, the seller may source the renewal receipts to the same address where the purchaser received the underlying software if the seller has not received information from the purchaser indicating a change in the location of the software [G.S. § 105-164.4B(i)].

- *Telecommunications services*

Telecommunications services are sourced in accordance with G.S. § 105-164.4C. See ¶ 1719 for discussion of sourcing rules for telecommunications services.

- *Direct mail*

Direct mail is sourced under rules that distinguish between advertising and promotional direct mail and other direct mail. Advertising and proportional direct mail is sourced to the place of delivery if it is purchased under a direct pay permit or an exemption certificate claiming direct mail and bearing the direct mail permit number, or if the purchaser provides the seller with information showing the jurisdictions where the direct mail is to be delivered. In other cases advertising and promotional direct mail is sourced to the place of shipment. All other direct mail is sourced to the purchaser's address as disclosed in the seller's business records or to the place of delivery if purchased pursuant to a direct pay permit or exemption certificate [G.S. § 105-164.4E]. In the absence of bad faith, a seller is relieved of liability for failing to collect, pay or remit tax on any direct mail transaction where the purchaser uses a direct pay permit or an exemption certificate claiming direct mail and bearing the direct mail permit number. A purchaser is also relieved of liability to collect any further additional tax on the sale of advertising and promotional direct mail where the seller sources the mail according to delivery information provided by the purchaser [G.S. § 105-164.4E(c)].

- *Accommodations*

The rental of an accommodation (see definition at ¶1603) is sourced to the location of the accommodation [G.S. § 105-164.4B(e)].

- *Certain Digital property*

A purchaser receives certain digital property when the purchaser takes possession of the property or makes first use of the property, whichever comes first [G.S. § 105-164.4B(f)]. Certain digital property is sourced under the general sourcing role discussed above, provided that if rules (1) through (4) of the general sourcing rules do not apply, the location of the sale will be determined based on the address from which the digital property was first available for transmission by the seller. North Carolina Department of Revenue Important Notice: Sourcing for Certain Digital Property Subject to Sales and Use Tax (August 2013).

¶1603 Definition of Terms

In order to provide a guide to the important sales and use tax terms, a glossary is provided in this paragraph for quick reference. All definitions are contained in G.S. § 105-164.3 unless otherwise indicated. Some definitions specific only to certain situations are defined in context when discussing the situation.

• *Accommodation*

A hotel room, a motel room, a residence, a cottage, or a similar lodging facility for occupancy by an individual [G.S. § 105-164.3(1)].

• *Accommodation facilitator*

A person that contracts with the provider of an accommodation to market the accommodation and accept payment or payment information for the rental or to list the accommodation for rent on a forum, platform or application for a consideration [G.S. § 105-164.3(1a)].

• *Admission charge*

The gross receipts derived for the right to attend an entertainment activity. The term includes a charge for a single ticket, a multioccasional ticket, a season or annual pass, a membership fee that provides for admission, a cover charge, a surcharge, a convenience fee, a processing fee, a facility fee, a facilitation fee or similar charge or any other charges included in gross receipts derived from admission [G.S. § 105-164.3(1b)].

• *Admission facilitator*

A person who accepts payment of an admission charge to an entertainment activity but who is not the operator of the entertainment venue [G.S. § 105-164.3(1c)].

• *Advertising and promotional direct mail*

Direct mail the primary purpose of which is to attract public attention to an item, person, or business or organization or to attempt to sell, popularize, or secure financial support for an item, person, business or organization. [G.S. § 105-164.3(1d)].

• *Amenity*

An amenity is a feature that increases the value or attractiveness of an entertainment activity that allows a person access to items that are not subject to sales tax and are not available with the purchase or admission to the same event without the feature. Amenities include parking privileges, special entrances, access to areas other than general admission, mascot visits and merchandise discounts. Amenities do not include any charge for food, prepared food and alcoholic beverages subject to sales tax [G.S. § 105-164.3(1f)].

• *Ancillary service*

A service associated with or incidental to the provision of a telecommunications service. The term includes detailed communications billing, directory assistance, vertical service, and voice mail service. A vertical service is a service that allows a customer to identify a caller or manage multiple calls and call connections (*e.g.*, call forwarding, caller ID, three-way calling, conference bridging) [G.S. § 105-164.3(1h)].

• *At retail*

The term "at retail" means the sale, lease, or rental for any purpose other than for resale, sublease, or subrent [G.S. § 105-164.3(34)].

• *Aviation gasoline and jet fuel*

These terms have the same meaning used for motor fuels tax purpose [G.S. § 105-164.3(1k) and (16b)].

¶1603

• *Business*

The term "business" includes any activity a person engages in or causes another to engage in with the object of direct or indirect gain, profit, benefit, or advantage, but it does not include an occasional and isolated sale or transaction by a person who does not claim to be engaged in business [G.S. § 105-164.3(1m)]. An entity is treated as engaged in a "business" whether or not it holds itself out to the general public or limits its transactions to selected customers. Thus, a husband and wife were treated as engaged in a leasing business where they leased equipment solely to their wholly owned corporation [*Tax Review Board Administrative Decision No. 382* (2002)].

Casual Sales

This definition of "business" clearly indicates that what are customarily called "casual sales" are not taxable.

• *Cable service*

The one-way transmission to subscribers of video programming or other programming service and any subscriber interaction required to select or use the service [G.S. § 105-164.3(1n)].

• *Candy*

The term "candy" means a preparation of sugar, honey, or other natural or artificial sweeteners in combination with chocolate, fruits, nuts, or other ingredients or flavorings in the form of bars, drops, or pieces that do not require refrigeration. "Candy" does not include any preparation that contains flour [G.S. § 105-164.3(2)].

• *Capital improvement*

A capital improvement consists of one or more of the following [G.S. § 105-164.3(2c)]:

(1) New construction, reconstruction, or remodeling.

(2) The performance of work that requires the issuance of a permit under the State Building Code except for the repair or replacement of electrical components, gas logs, water heaters, and similar individual items that are not part of new construction, reconstruction, or remodeling.

(3) The installation of a transmission, distribution or other network asset on land owned by a service provider or on a right-of-way or easement in favor of a service provider. A service provider is any person, including a state agency, the federal government, or a government entity entitled to state tax refunds under G.S. § 105-164.14(c), providing telecommunications (or ancillary) services, video programming services, electricity or piped natural gas services or water or sewer services. These installations are capital improvements even though any separately stated charges for repair, maintenance or installation services or a contribution in aid of construction are included in gross receipts subject to the combined general rate.

(4) The installation of equipment or a fixture that is attached to real property and that (i) is capitalized and depreciated under Generally Accepted Accounting Principles or International Financial Reporting Standards, (ii) is depreciated for federal income tax purposes, or (iii) is expensed under Code Section 179.

¶1603

(5) The painting or wallpapering of real property, except where such painting or wallpapering is incidental to a repair, maintenance, and installation service.

(6) The replacement or installation of a septic tank system, siding, roof, plumbing, electrical, commercial refrigeration, irrigation, sprinkler, or other similar system, but excluding the repair, replacement, or installation of electrical or plumbing components, water heaters, gutters, and similar individual items that are not part of new construction, reconstruction, or remodeling.

(7) The replacement or installation of a heating or air conditioning unit or a heating, ventilation, or air conditioning system, but excluding the repair, replacement, or installation of gas logs, water heaters, pool heaters, and similar individual items that are not part of new construction, reconstruction, or remodeling.

(8) The replacement or installation of roads, driveways, parking lots, patios, decks, and sidewalks.

(9) Punch-list services performed to resolve an issue that was part of a real property contract if the services are performed within six months of completion of the real property contract or, for new construction, within 12 months of the new structure being occupied for the first time.

(10) Landscaping. *See* SUPLR 2018-0004.

(11) An addition or alteration to real property that is permanently affixed or installed to real property and is not specifically included within the definition of a repair, maintenance, and installation service.

● *Certain digital property*

An audio work; audiovisual work; a book, magazine, newsletter, report, or other publication; or a photograph or greeting card that is delivered or acquired electronically and that is not considered tangible personal property. Certain digital property does not include an information service [G.S. § 105–164.3(2f)]. *See also* SUPLR-0001 (digital certificates, authentication and resolution services provided on a subscription basis are not certain digital property).

● *Clothing*

All human wearing apparel suitable for general use [G.S. § 105-164.3(3)].

● *Computer*

An electronic device that accepts information in digital or similar form and manipulates it for a result based on a sequence of instructions [G.S. § 105-164.3(4a)].

● *Computer software*

A set of coded instructions designed to cause a computer or automatic data processing equipment to perform a task [G.S. § 105-164.3(4b)].

● *Consumer*

A "consumer" is any person who stores, uses, or otherwise consumes in North Carolina an item purchased or received from a retailer or supplier either within or without North Carolina [G.S. § 105-164.3(5)].

• *Custom computer software*

Computer software that is not prewritten computer software. The term includes a user manual or other documentation that accompanies the sale of the software [G.S. § 105-164.3(5b)].

• *Datacenter*

A "datacenter" is a facility that provides infrastructure for hosting or data processing services. The facility must have power and cooling systems that are capable of having any capacity component or distribution element serviced or repaired on a planned basis without interrupting or impeding the performance of the computer equipment. The facility must also include redundant capacity components (*i.e.,* components beyond those required to support the computer equipment) and multiple distribution paths (configured to ensure that failure on one path does not interrupt or impede other paths) serving the computer equipment at the facility. Although the facility must have multiple distribution paths serving the computer equipment, a single distribution path may serve the computer equipment at any one time [G.S. § 105-164.3(5c)].

• *Delivery charges*

"Delivery charges" are charges imposed by a retailer for preparation and delivery of an item to a location designated by the consumer [G.S. § 105-164.3(4a)].

• *Development tier*

Development tier is the classification assigned to an area pursuant to G.S. § 143B-437.08 [G.S. § 105-164.3(6a)].

• *Diaper*

An absorbent garment worn by humans who cannot control or have difficulty controlling bladder or bowel movement [G.S.§ 105-164.3(6b)].

• *Dietary supplement*

A "dietary supplement" a product that is intended to supplement the diet of humans and is required to be labeled as a dietary supplement under federal law, identifiable by the "Supplement Facts" box found on the label [G.S. § 105-164.3(4b)].

• *Digital code*

"Digital code" is a code that gives a purchaser of the code a right to receive an item by electronic delivery or electronic access. A digital code may be obtained electronically or in a tangible medium, but does not include a gift certificate or gift card [G.S. § 105-164.3(7a)].

• *Direct mail*

Printed material delivered or distributed by the United States Postal Service or other delivery service to a mass audience or to addresses on a mailing list provided by the purchaser or at the direction of the purchaser when the cost of the items is not billed directly to the recipients. The term includes tangible personal property supplied directly or indirectly by the purchaser to the direct mail seller for inclusion in the package containing the printed materials. The term does not include multiple items of printed material delivered to a single address [G.S. § 105-164.3(7c)].

- *Direct-to-home satellite service*

Programming transmitted or broadcast by satellite directly to the subscribers' premises without the use of ground equipment or distribution equipment, except equipment at the subscribers' premises or the uplink process to the satellite.

- *Drug*

A compound, substance, or preparation or a component of one of these that (1) is not a food, a dietary supplement, or an alcoholic beverage and (2) meets any of the following descriptions:

(a) It is recognized in the United States Pharmacopoeia, Homeopathic Pharmacopoeia of the United States, or National Formulary [G.S. § 105-164.3(8a)a].

(b) It is intended for use in the diagnosis, cure, mitigation, treatment, or prevention of disease [G.S. § 105-164.3(8a)b].

(c) It is intended to affect the structure or function of the body [G.S. § 105-164.3(8a)c].

- *Durable medical equipment*

Equipment that meets the following conditions:

(1) It can withstand repeated use [G.S. § 105-164.3(8b)a].

(2) It is primarily and customarily used to serve a medical purpose [G.S. § 105-164.3(8b)b].

(3) It is generally not useful to a person in the absence of an illness or injury [G.S. § 105-164.3(8b)c].

(4) It is not worn in or on the body [G.S. § 105-164.3(8b)d].

The term "durable medical equipment" includes repair and replacement parts for the equipment but does not include mobility-enhancing equipment.

- *Durable medical supplies*

Supplies that are eligible to be covered under Medicare or Medicaid and that are related to use with durable medical equipment [G.S. § 105-164.3(8c)].

- *Electronic*

Relating to technology having electrical, digital, magnetic, wireless, optical, electromagnetic, or similar capabilities [G.S. § 105-164.3(8d)].

- *Engaged in business*

The following activities constitute being "engaged in business" [G.S. § 105-164.3(9)].

(1) *Maintaining a place of business:* Maintaining, occupying, or using any office or other place of business (*e.g.,* distribution facility, sales or sample room, warehouse, storage place) in North Carolina, whether temporarily or permanently and whether directly or indirectly.

(2) *Solicitation of sales:* Having any representative, agent, sales representative, marketplace facilitator or solicitor operating in North Carolina or transacting business by mobile phone application or other applications in North Carolina, whether temporarily or permanently and whether directly or indi-

rectly. Thus, an out-of-state seller of well-drilling rigs was found to be engaged in business in North Carolina where (1) it engaged a local non-employee sales representative to solicit customers in North Carolina, (2) it sent employees into the state to make repairs, and (3) its president made annual trips to North Carolina to attend trade shows [*Secretary's Decision No. 2005-75* (October 26, 2005)]. See also, Secretary's Decision No. 2006-177 (January 16, 2007) (taxpayer whose employees delivered and installed window shutters in North Carolina held to be engaged in business in North Carolina). The fact that any corporate retailer, agent, or subsidiary engaged in business in North Carolina may not be legally domesticated or qualified to do business in North Carolina is immaterial.

(3) *Maintaining tangible personal property for lease or sale:* Maintaining tangible personal property or certain digital property in North Carolina for the purpose of lease or rental, whether temporarily or permanently and whether directly or through a subsidiary.

(4) *Shipping wine to North Carolina customers:* Shipping wine directly to a purchaser in North Carolina as authorized by G.S. § 18B-1001.1.

(5) *Remote sales:* Making a remote sale or a marketplace-facilitated sale to a customer in North Carolina. See ¶1707.

• *Entertainment Activity*

An entertainment activity is a (1) live performance or other live event of any kind the purpose of which is entertainment, (2) a movie, motion picture or film, (3) a museum, cultural site, garden, exhibit, show or similar attraction, or a guided tour at any such museum, cultural site, garden, exhibit, show or similar attraction or (4) a guided tour at any of the foregoing [G.S. § 105-164.4G(a)(3)]. For an example of an activity not treated as an entertainment activity, see SUPLR 2016-0005 (trampoline jumping).

• *Facilitator*

An accomodation facilitator, an admission facilitator or a service contract facilitator [G.S. § 105-164.3(9e)].

• *Food*

The term "food" includes substances that are sold for ingestion or chewing by humans and are consumed for their taste or nutritional value. The substances may be in liquid, concentrated, solid, frozen, dried, or dehydrated form. The term "food" does not include alcoholic beverages or tobacco products [G.S. § 105-164.3(10)].

• *Food sold through vending machines*

The term "food sold through a vending machine" means food dispensed from a machine or other mechanical device that accepts payment [G.S. § 105-164.3(5b)].

• *Freestanding appliance*

A machine commonly thought of as an appliance operated by gas or electricity, such as a dishwasher, washing machine, clothes dryer, refrigerator, freezer, microwave, or slide-in or drop-in range [G.S. § 105-164.3(1d)].

• *Gross sales*

"Gross sales" means the sum total of all sales of tangible personal property, digital property and services [G.S. § 105-164.3(12)].

• *Hub*

The term "hub" means either of the following:

(1) An interstate air courier's principal airport within North Carolina for sorting and distributing letters and packages and from which the interstate air courier has, or expects to have upon completion of construction, no fewer than 150 departures a month under normal operating conditions [G.S. § 105-164.3(13)a].

(2) An interstate passenger air carrier's hub is the airport in North Carolina that meets both of the following conditions:

(a) The air carrier has allocated to the airport more than sixty percent (60%) of its aircraft value apportioned to North Carolina [G.S. § 105-164.3(13)b.1].

(b) The majority of the air carrier's passengers boarding at the airport are connecting from other airports rather than originating at that airport [G.S. § 105-164.3(13)b.2].

• *Incontinence underpad*

An absorbent product not worn on the body but designed to protect tangible personal property from soiling or damage due to human incontinence [G.S. § 105-164.3(14a)].

• *Information service*

An "information service" is a service that generates, acquires, stores, processes, or retrieves data and information and delivers it electronically to or allows electronic access by a customer whose primary purpose for using the service is to obtain the processed data or information [G.S. § 105-164.3(14b)].

• *In this State*

The phrases "in this State" or "in North Carolina" mean within the exterior limits of the State of North Carolina and include all territory within such limits owned or ceded to the United States of America [G.S. § 105-164.3(14)].

• *Interstate air business*

An "interstate air business" is (1) an interstate air courier, (2) an interstate freight air carrier, or (3) an interstate passenger air carrier [G.S. § 105-164.3(14c)].

• *Interstate air courier*

A person whose primary business is the furnishing of air delivery of individually addressed letters and packages for compensation, in interstate commerce, except by the United States Postal Service [G.S. § 105-164.3(15)].

• *Interstate freight air carrier*

A person whose primary business is scheduled freight air transportation, as defined in the North American Industry Classification System adopted by the United States Office of Management and Budget, in interstate commerce [G.S. § 105-164.3(16)].

¶1603

- *Interstate passenger air carrier*

A person whose primary business is scheduled passenger air transportation in interstate commerce [G.S. § 105-164.3(15)].

- *Item*

Tangible personal property, digital property or a service unless the context requires otherwise [G.S. § 105-164.3(16a)].

- *Landscaping service*

A service that modifies the living elements on a piece of land including installation of plants on land, tree trimming, mowing, seeding, mulching, and fertilizing. The term does not include services to plants in pots or buildings [G.S. § 105-164.3(16e)].

- *Lease or rental*

Defined at ¶ 1706.

Exclusions: The term "lease or rental" does not include any of the following:

(1) A transfer of possession or control of property under a security agreement or deferred payment plan that requires the transfer of title upon completion of the required payments [G.S. § 105-164.3(17)a].

(2) A transfer of possession or control of property under an agreement that requires the transfer of title upon completion of required payments and payment of an option price that does not exceed the greater of $100 or 1% of the total required payments [G.S. § 105-164.3(17)b].

(3) The providing of tangible personal property along with an operator for a fixed or indeterminate period of time if the operator is necessary for the equipment to perform as designed. For this purpose, an operator must do more than maintain, inspect, or set up the tangible personal property [G.S. § 105-164.3(17)c]. *See* SUPLR-2018-0013 (lease of barricades and other lane-closure items taxable because taxpayer's employee's who installed, maintained and removed such items were not "operators").

- *Major recycling facility*

A recycling facility that qualifies under G.S. § 105-129.26(a) [G.S. § 105-164.3(19)].

- *Manufactured home*

A structure that is designed to be used as a dwelling and is manufactured in accordance with the specifications for manufactured homes issued by the United States Department of Housing and Urban Development [G.S. § 105-164.3(20)]. This definition is for sales and use tax purpose; for definition of "manufactured home" for property tax purposes, see ¶ 2105. A modular home is not considered a manufactured home. See discussion of modular homes at ¶ 1730.

- *Marketplace*

A physical or electronic place, forum, platform, application, or other method by which a marketplace seller sells or offers to sell items, the delivery of or first use of which is sourced to this State [G.S. § 105-164.3(20a)].

- *Marketplace-facilitated sale*

    The sale of an item by a marketplace facilitator on behalf of a marketplace seller that occurs through a marketplace [G.S. § 105-164.3(20b)].

- *Marketplace facilitator*

    A person that (1) owns or operates a marketplace, (2) directly or indirectly lists or makes available for sale a marketplace seller's items through such marketplace and (3) collects the sales of the marketplace seller's items or otherwise processes payment or makes payment processing services available to purchasers for the sale of a marketplace seller's items [G.S. § 105-164.3(20c)].

- *Marketplace seller*

    A person that sells or offers to sell items through a marketplace regardless of whether the person (1) has a physical presence in North Carolina, (2) is registered as a North Carolina retailer, or (3) would or would not have been required to collect sales tax if the sale had not been made through a marketplace [G.S. § 105-164.3(20d)].

- *Mixed transaction contract*

    A contract that includes a real property contract for a capital improvement and an unrelated repair, maintenance and installation service for real property [G.S. § 105-164.3(20e)].

- *Mobile telecommunications service*

    A radio communication service carried on between mobile stations communicating among themselves that includes all three of the following:

    (1) Both one-way and two-way radio communications [G.S. § 105-164.3(21)a].

    (2) A mobile service that provides a regularly interacting group of base, mobile, portable, and associated control and relay stations for private one-way or two-way land mobile radio communications by eligible users over designated areas of operation [G.S. § 105-164.3(21)b].

    (3) Any service for which a federal license is required in a personal communications service [G.S. § 105-164.3(21)c].

- *Mobility-enhancing equipment*

    Equipment that meets all of the following conditions:

    (1) It is primarily and customarily used to provide or increase the ability of an individual to move from one place to another [G.S. § 105-164.3(21a)a].

    (2) It is appropriate for use in either a home or a motor vehicle [G.S. § 105-164.3(21a)b].

    (3) It is not generally used by a person with normal mobility [G.S. § 105-164.3(21a)c].

    (4) It is not normally provided on a motor vehicle by a motor vehicle manufacturer [G.S. § 105-164.3(21a)d].

- *Modular home*

    A factory-built structure that is designed to be used as a dwelling, is manufactured in accordance with the specifications for modular homes under the North

Carolina State Residential Building Code, and bears a seal or label issued by the Department of Insurance [G.S. § 105-164.3(21a)]. See discussion of modular homes at ¶ 1730.

• *Modular homebuilder*

A person that furnishes for consideration a modular home to a purchaser who will occupy the modular home. The purchaser can be a person that will lease or rent the unit as real property [G.S. § 105-164.3(21b)].

• *Moped*

A vehicle other than a motor-driven or electric-assisted bicycle that has two or three wheels, no external shifting device, and a motor that does not exceed 50 cubic centimeters piston displacement and cannot propel the vehicle at a speed greater than 30 miles per hour on a level surface. The motor may be powered by electricity, alternative fuel, motor fuel or a combination of each [G.S. § 105-164.3(22) and G.S. § 20-4.01(27)d1].

• *Motor vehicle*

A vehicle that is designed primarily for use upon the highways and is either self-propelled or propelled by a self-propelled vehicle [G.S. § 105-164.3(22)]. The term "motor vehicle," however, does not include the following:

(1) A moped [G.S. § 105-164.3(22)a].

(2) Special mobile equipment [G.S. § 105-164.3(22)].

(3) A tow dolly that is exempt from motor vehicle title and registration requirements [G.S. § 105-164.3(22)c].

(4) A farm tractor or other implement of husbandry [G.S. § 105-164.3(22)d].

(5) A manufactured home, a mobile office, or a mobile classroom [G.S. § 105-164.3(22)e].

(6) Road construction or road maintenance machinery or equipment [G.S. § 105-164.3(22)f].

• *Motor vehicle service contract*

A service contract for a motor vehicle (or a component, system or accessory) sold by (i) a motor vehicle dealer (as defined in G.S. § 20-286) (ii) a motor vehicle service agreement company (defined as a person other than a motor vehicle dealer that is the obligor under a motor vehicle service contract and who is not an insurer) or (iii) a motor vehicle dealer on behalf of a motor vehicle service agreement company [G.S. § 105-164.3(23a)].

• *NAICS*

The North American Industry Classification System [G.S. § § 105-164.3(23c) and 105-228.90].

• *Net taxable sales*

The gross sales or gross receipts of a retailer or another person subject to the sales tax after deducting exempt sales and nontaxable sales [G.S. § 105-164.3(24)].

• *New Construction*

Construction of or site preparation for a permanent new building, structure or fixture on land or an increase in the square footage of an existing building, structure or fixture on land [G.S. § 105-164.3(24a)].

• *Nonresident retail or wholesale merchant*

A "nonresident retail or wholesale merchant" is a person who does not have a place of business in North Carolina, is registered for sales or use tax purposes in another jurisdiction, and is engaged in the business of acquiring, by purchase, consignment, or otherwise, tangible personal property or certain digital property and selling the property outside North Carolina or in the business of providing a service.

• *Operator*

A person (1) provided with the lease or rental of tangible personal property or a motor vehicle to operate, drive or maneuver the property or vehicle (2) whose presence, skill, knowledge and expertise are necessary to bring about a desired or appropriate effect and (3) who does more than calibrate, test, analyze, research, probe or monitor the property or vehicle [G.S. § 105-164.3(25a)].

• *Other direct mail*

Any direct mail that is not advertising or promotional direct mail regardless of whether advertising or promotional direct mail is included in the same mailing [G.S. § 105-164.3(25a)].

• *Over-the-counter drug*

A drug that has a label that identifies the product as a drug. The label must include either of the following [G.S. § 105-164.3(25b)]:

(1) A "Drug Facts" panel.

(2) A statement of its active ingredients contained in the compound, substance, or preparation.

• *Person*

An individual, a fiduciary, a firm, an association, a partnership, a limited liability company, a corporation, a unit of government, or another group acting as a unit. The term includes an officer or employee of a corporation, a member, a manager, or an employee of a limited liability company, and a member or employee of a partnership who, as officer, employee, member, or manager, is under a duty to perform an act in meeting the requirements of Subchapter I, V, or VIII of Chapter 105, of G.S. § 55-16-22, of Article 81 of Chapter 106 of the General Statutes, or of Article 3 of Chapter 119 of the General Statutes [G.S. § § 105-164.3(26), 105-228.90(b)(5)].

• *Place of primary use*

The street address representative of where the use of a customer's telecommunications service primarily occurs. The street address must be the customer's residential street address or primary business street address. For mobile telecommunications service, the street address must be within the licensed service area of the service provider. If the customer who contracted with the telecommunications provider for the telecommunications service is not the end user of the service, the end user is considered the customer for the purpose of determining the place of primary use [G.S. § 105-164.3(26a)].

¶1603

• *Prepaid meal plan*

A plan offered by an institution of higher education that (1) entitles a person to food or prepared food, (2) must be billed or paid for in advance, and (3) provides for predetermined units of or unlimited access to food or prepared food but does not include a dollar value that declines with use [G.S. § 105-164.3(27a)].

• *Prepared food*

"Prepared food" is food that meets at least one of the following conditions:

(1) It is sold in a heated state or is heated by the retailer [G.S. § 105-164.3(28)a].

(2) It consists of two or more foods mixed or combined by the retailer for sale as a single item except for foods containing raw eggs, fish, meat, or poultry that require cooking by the consumer as recommended by the Good and Drug Administration to prevent food-borne illnesses [G.S. § 105-164.3(28)b].

(3) It is sold with eating utensils provided by the retailer (*e.g.,* plates (not including packaging or containers used to transport the food), knives, forks, spoons, glasses, cups, napkins, straws) [G.S. § 105-164.3(28)b].

Exception

Prepared food does not include food the retailer sliced, repackaged, or pasteurized but did not heat, mix, or sell with eating utensils [G.S. § 105-164.3(28)].

• *Prescription*

An order, formula, or recipe issued orally, in writing, electronically, or by another means of transmission by a physician, dentist, veterinarian, or another person licensed to prescribe drugs [G.S. § 105-164.3(29)].

• *Prewritten computer software*

Computer software (including prewritten upgrades) that is not designed and developed by the author or another creator to the specifications of a specific purchaser. The term includes software designed and developed to the specifications of a specific purchaser when it is sold to a person other than the specific purchaser [G.S. § 105-164.3(29a)].

• *Production company*

A person engaged in the business of making original motion picture, television, or radio images for theatrical, commercial, advertising, or educational purposes [G.S. § 105-164.3(30)].

• *Professional motorsports racing team [G.S. § 105-164.3(30a)]*

A racing team that satisfies all of the following conditions:

(1) The team is operated for profit.

(2) The team does not claim a deduction under IRC § 183 (relating to activities not engaged in for profit).

(3) The team competes in at least 66% of the races sponsored in a race series in a single season by a motorsports sanctioning body.

¶ 1603

• *Property management contract*

A written contract obligating a person to provide five or more real property management services [G.S. § 105-164.3].

• *Prosthetic device*

A replacement, corrective, or supporting device worn on or in the body (including repair and replacement parts for the device) that meets one of the following conditions:

(1) It artificially replaces a missing portion of the body [G.S. § 105-164.3(30d)a].

(2) It prevents or corrects a physical deformity or malfunction [G.S. § 105-164.3(30d)b].

(3) It supports a weak or deformed portion of the body [G.S. § 105-164.3(30d)c].

• *Purchase*

"Purchase" means acquired for a consideration or consideration in exchange for a service whether (1) the transfer was effected by a transfer of title and/or possession or a license to use or consume; (2) the transfer was absolute or conditional regardless of the means by which it was effected; and (3) the consideration is a price or rental in money or by way of exchange or barter. The term "purchase" also includes the procuring of a retailer to erect, install, or apply tangible personal property for use in North Carolina [G.S. § 105-164.3(32)].

• *Purchase price*

When applied to an item subject to use tax, the term "purchase price" has the same meaning as the term "sales price" [G.S. § 105-164.3(12a)].

• *Qualified aircraft*

A qualified aircraft is an aircraft with a maximum take-off weight of more than 9,000 and less than 15,000 pounds [G.S. § 105-164.3(33a)].

• *Qualified jet engine*

A qualified jet engine is an engine certified pursuant to Part 33 of Title 14 of the Code of Federal Regulation [G.S. § 105-164.3(33b)].

• *Qualifying datacenter*

A qualifying datacenter is a datacenter that meets certain wage and health insurance requirements. In addition, the Secretary of Commerce must have made a written determination that at least $75 million in private funds has been or will be invested in the datacenter over a five year period beginning on or after January 1, 2012 [G.S. § 105-164.3(33c)].

• *Real property*

Real property means land, buildings or structures on land, permanent fixtures on land and manufactured or modular homes on land [G.S. § 105-164.3(33d)].

¶1603

- *Real property contract*

A contract between a real property contractor and another person to perform a capital improvement to real property [G.S. § 105-164.3(33e)].

- *Real property contractor*

A real property contractor is a person that contracts to perform a real property contract in accordance with G.S. § 105-164.4H, including a general contractor, a subcontractor or a builder [G.S. § 105-164.3(33f)].

- *Reconstruction*

Reconstruction means the rebuilding or constructing again of a prior existing permanent building, structure or fixture on land, including where there is a change in the square footage of the building, structure or fixture [G.S. § 105-164.3(33g)].

- *Related member*

A person that, with respect to the taxpayer during any part of the taxable year, is one or more of the following [G.S. §§ 105-164.3(33h) and 105-130.7(a)(5)]:

(1) A related entity.

(2) A component member.

(3) A person to or from whom there would be attribution of stock ownership in accordance with Section 1563(e) of the Code if the phrase "5 percent or more" were replaced by "twenty percent (20%) or more" each place it appears in that section.

- *Remodeling*

A remodeling is a transaction comprised of multiple services performed by one or more persons to restore, improve, alter, or update real property, including a transaction where the internal structure or design of one or more rooms or areas within a room or building are substantially changed. The term does not include a single repair, maintenance, and installation service. The term also does not include a transaction involving a repair, maintenance and installation service and an ancillary service where the true purpose of the transaction is a repair, maintenance, and installation service. Examples of such a transaction include (i) sheetrock repair that includes the application of paint as an ancillary service, (ii) the replacement of cabinets that includes the installation of caulk or molding as an ancillary service, and (iii) the installation of hardwood floors that includes installation of shoe molding as an ancillary service [G.S. § 105-164.3(33i)].

- *Renovation*

A renovation means the same thing as a remodeling [G.S. § 105-164.3 (33k)].

- *Rental agent*

A rental agent includes a real estate broker (as defined in G.S. § 93A-2) [G.S. § 105-164.4F(a)(3)]. An example of a rental agent is a real estate company that handles accommodation rentals [*Notice*, Sales and Use Tax Division, North Carolina Department of Revenue, December 2010].

• *Repair, maintenance and installation services*

Repair, maintenance and installation services include five different activities applied to tangible personal property, motor vehicles, certain digital property and real property. The term does not include a service used to fulfill a real property contract [G.S. § 105-164.3(33m)]:

(1) *Maintenance activities:* activities to keep property or a motor vehicle in working order to avoid breakdown and prevent deterioration or repairs, including cleaning, washing and polishing.

(2) *Repair activities:* activities to calibrate, refinish or restore (or attempt to calibrate, refinish or restore) property or a motor vehicle to proper working order or good condition, including replacing or putting together what is broken or torn.

(3) *Diagnostic activities:* activities to troubleshoot or identify (or attempt to identify) the source of a problem in order to determine what is needed to restore property or a motor vehicle to proper working order or good condition (other than activities that may lead to the issuance of an inspection report).

(4) *Installation activities:* activities to install, apply, connect, adjust or set into position tangible personal property or certain digital property. Installation services include floor installation and refinishing, carpet installation, floor covering installation, installation of doors, windows, cabinets, countertops, and installation of items to replace similar existing items, and the replacement of multiple like-kind items, but do not include installations that are part of (and substantiated as) a capital improvement.

(5) *Inspection activities:* activities to inspect or monitor property or install, apply or connect tangible personal property or certain digital property on a motor vehicle or adjust a motor vehicle.

For general guidance on repair, maintenance and installation services, see Directive SD-16-2 and Directive SD-16-4. See also Directive SD-18-5 (photographic tinting services are taxable repair, maintenance or installation services); SUPLR 2018-0009 (non-self-service car washes are repair, maintenance and installation services); SUPLR 2018-0008 (auto detailing services are repair, maintenance and installation services). For repair, maintenance and installation services exempt from tax, see ¶1809.

• *Retail sale*

A "retail sale" or "sale at retail" is the sale, lease, or rental for any purpose other than for resale, sublease, or subrent [G.S. § 105-164.3(34)].

• *Retailer*

"Retailer" means (1) a person engaged in the business of making sales at retail, offering to make sales at retail, or soliciting sales at retail, of items sourced to North Carolina, (2) a person other than a real property contractor engaged in the business of delivering, erecting, installing, or applying tangible personal property or certain digital property for use in North Carolina, (3) a person engaged in the business of making a remote sale if one of the conditions of G.S. § 105-164.8(b) is met, (4) a person required to collect the sales tax; or (5) a marketplace facilitator or other facilitator required to collect tax [G.S. § 105-164.3(35)]. The term "retailer" includes a person who, by written contract, agrees to be the rental agent for the provider of an accommodation is considered a retailer under this Article and is liable for the tax imposed by this subdivision [G.S. § 105-164.4F(d)]. Retailers also include operators of hotels, motels, tourist homes, tourist camps, bed and breakfast inns, persons who rent private residences and cottages, and similar type businesses providing accommodations [Notice, Sales and Use Division, North Carolina Department of Revenue, December 2010].

• *Retailer-contractor*

A retailer-contractor is a person that acts as a retailer when it makes a sale at retail and as a real property contractor when it performs a real property contract [G.S. § 105-164.3(35a)].

• *Sale at retail*

The term "sale at retail" has the same meaning as the term "retail sale" [G.S. § 105-164.3(34)].

• *Sale or selling*

The term "sale or selling" means the transfer of title, license to use or consume, or possession of tangible personal property or certain digital property for consideration or the performance of a service for consideration. The transfer or performance may be conditional in any manner and by any means [G.S. § 105-164.3(36)]. The term applies to the following:

(1) Fabricating tangible personal property for consumers by persons engaged in business who directly or indirectly furnish the materials used in the fabrication.

(2) Furnishing or preparing tangible personal property (a) consumed on the premises of the person furnishing or preparing the property, or (b) consumed at the place at which the property is furnished or prepared.

(3) Transferring possession of property where the seller retains title or security for payment of the consideration.

(4) A lease or rental.

(5) Transfer of digital code.

(6) An accommodation.

(7) A service contract.

(8) Any other subject to tax under Article 5 of Subchapter I of Chapter 105.

• *Sales price*

In general, "sales price" means the total amount or consideration for which an item is sold, leased, or rented. The consideration may be in the form of cash, credit, property, or services, but the sales price must be valued in money, regardless of the form in which it is received [G.S. § 105-164.3(37)]. See ¶1704 for a detailed discussion of "sales price."

• *Satellite digital audio radio service*

A radio communication service in which audio programming is digitally transmitted by satellite to an earth-based receiver, whether directly or via a repeater station [G.S. § 105-164.3(37a)].

¶1603

- *Secondary metal recycle*

A person that gathers and obtains ferrous and nonferrous metals and products that have served their original economic purpose and converts them into new and different products of prepared grades for sale [G.S. § 150-164.3(37g)].

- *Secretary*

The Secretary of Revenue of the North Carolina Department of Revenue [G.S. § 105-164.3(38)].

- *Service contract*

A contract under which the obligor agrees to maintain, monitor, inspect, repair or provide another service within the definition of a repair, maintenance and installation service to certain digital property, tangible personal property or real property for a period of time or some other defined measure, including a warranty agreement other than manufacturer's or dealer's warranty provided at no charge to the customer, a maintenance agreement, a repair agreement or a similar agreement. The term includes a service contract for a pool, fish tank or similar aquatic feature. The term does not include a single repair, maintenance or installation service but does include a contract where a repair, maintenance or installation service may be provided as a condition of the contract [G.S. § 105-164.3(38b)].

- *Service contract facilitator*

A person who contracts with the obligor of a service contract to market the service contract and who accepts payment from the purchaser of the service contract [G.S. § 105-164.3(38c)].

- *Soft drink*

A "soft drink" is a nonalcoholic beverage that contains natural or artificial sweeteners [G.S. § 105-164.3(40)]. The term "soft drink" does not include beverages that contain one or more of the following ingredients:

(1) Milk or milk products [G.S. § 105-164.3(40)a].

(2) Soy, rice, or similar milk substitutes [G.S. § 105-164.3(40)b].

(3) More than fifty percent (50%) vegetable or fruit juice [G.S. § 105-164.3(40)c].

- *Special mobile equipment*

"Special mobile equipment" is any of the following:

(1) A vehicle that (a) has a permanently attached crane, mill, well-boring apparatus, ditch-digging apparatus, air compressor, electric welder, feed mixer, grinder, or other similar apparatus; (b) is driven on the highway only to get to and from a nonhighway job; and (c) is not designed or used primarily for the transportation of persons or property [G.S. § 105-164.3(41)a].

(2) A vehicle that has permanently attached special equipment and is used only for parade purposes [G.S. § 105-164.3(41)b].

(3) A vehicle that (a) is privately owned; (b) has permanently attached fire-fighting equipment; and (c) is used only for fire-fighting purposes [G.S. § 105-164.3(41)c].

(4) A vehicle that (a) has permanently attached playground equipment and (b) is used only for playground purposes [G.S. § 105-164.3(41)d].

- *State agency*

"State agency" means a unit of the executive, legislative, or judicial branch of State government (*e.g.*, a department, a commission, a board, a council, or The University of North Carolina). A local board of education, however, is not a State agency [G.S. § 105-164.3(43)].

- *Storage*

"Storage" means the keeping or retention in North Carolina of tangible personal property or certain digital property for any period of time purchased from a person in business for any purpose *except* for the purpose of sale in the regular course of business [G.S. § 105-164.3(44)]. The former exceptions for temporary storage prior to removal outside North Carolina have been repealed. *See* S.L. 2016-5, § 3.2.(b), effective January 1, 2017.

- *Streamlined Agreement*

The Streamlined Sales and Use Tax Agreement (SSUTA), as amended as of December 14, 2018 [G.S. § 105-164.3(45a)]. The SSUTA is discussed at ¶ 1601.

- *Tangible personal property*

"Tangible personal property" means personal property that may be seen, weighed, felt, or touched, or is in any other manner perceptible to the senses and includes electricity, water, gas, steam, and prewritten computer software [G.S. § 105-164.3(46)]. Note that certain services, such as the lease of lodgings, dry cleaning services, and telecommunications services are also taxable. For more detail on tangible personal property, see ¶ 1705.

- *Taxpayer*

Any person liable for the North Carolina sales and use tax [G.S. § 105-164.3(47)].

- *Telecommunications service*

The electronic transmission, conveyance, or routing of voice, transmission, conveyance, or routing of voice, data, audio, video, or any other information or signals to a point or points. The term includes any transmission, conveyance, or routing in which a computer processing application is used to act on the form, code, or protocol of the content for purposes of the transmission, conveyance, or routing, regardless of whether it is referred to as voice-over Internet protocol or the Federal Communications Commission classifies it as enhanced or value added. The term does not include (1) an information service; (2) the sale, installation, maintenance, or repair of tangible personal property; (3) advertising (including directory advertising); (4) billing and collection services provided to a third party; (5) Internet access service; (6) radio and television audio and video programming service; (7) ancillary service; or (8) certain digital property [G.S. § 105-164.3(48)].

- *Tobacco product*

A cigarette, a cigar, or any other product that contains tobacco and is intended for inhalation or oral use [G.S. § § 105-164.3(10), 105-113.4(11a)].

• Use

"Use" means the exercise of any right, power, or dominion whatsoever over an item by the purchaser of the item. The term and includes withdrawal from storage, distribution, installation, affixation to real or personal property, and exhaustion or consumption of the item by the owner or purchaser. "Use", however, does not include the sale of an item in the regular course of business [G.S. § 105-164.3(49)]. Property purchased by a federal government contractor and accounted for in overhead but title to which passed to the government pursuant to federal law was held not subject to use tax because the transfer of title to the government was held to be in the regular course of the taxpayer's business. See FINAL AGENCY DECISION 09 REV 5695 (November 4, 2011).

Held to Be Taxable Uses

The use of construction materials (*e.g.*, lumber, steel) in components that become part of structures in North Carolina has been held to be a taxable "use," even though the materials were purchased and stored outside North Carolina [*Morton Bldgs., Inc. v. Tolson*, 172 N.C. App. 119, 615 S.E.2d 906 (2005). *See also Department of Revenue v. First Petroleum Services, Inc.*, 17 CVS 1663 (N.C. Business Court 2018).] The use of film prints, negatives, and other items by a land surveying company that provided mapping services inside and outside North Carolina has been held to be a taxable "use" [*Tax Review Board Administrative Decision No.* 451 (2004)]. The consumption by an advertising agency of film used to produce printed matter for customers has been held to be a taxable "use" [*Secretary's Decision Nos.* 2001-462 (September 18, 2002) and 2001-463 (September 18, 2002)]. See also *Secretary's Decision Nos.* 2004-303 (September 13, 2004) and 2004-304 (September 13, 2004); Tax Review Board Administrative Decision No 479 (2005)]. The installation of repair parts by a taxpayer engaged in providing helicopter repair and maintenance services to a hospital was a taxable "use" of such parts. *See Secretary's Decision No.* 2005-52(June 8, 2005). The Secretary has held that the addition of the word "distribution" in the definition of a taxable use, effective January 1, 2002 (S.L. 2001-347 (H.B. 144), §2.6), subjects North Carolina purchasers to use tax on the delivered price of printed material (including advertising material) printed and mailed from outside the state by third parties to the purchaser's North Carolina customers. *See Secretary's Decision Nos.* 2003-442(March 12, 2004) and 2003-443 (June 30, 2004). See also Secretary's Decision No. 2006-243 (January 11, 2007) (payments for advertising circulars to out-of-state printer held to be payments for tangible personal property rather than for advertising services). On the state's power to tax such uses under the Commerce Clause, see *D.H. Holmes Co. v. McNamara*, 486 U.S. 24 (1988).

• Use tax

The tax imposed by Part 2 of Article 5 of Chapter 105 of the North Carolina General Statutes [G.S. § 105-164.3(50)].

• Video programming

Programming provided by, or generally considered comparable to programming provided by, a television broadcast station, regardless of the method of delivery [G.S. § 105-164.3(50c)].

• Water

Water delivered by or through main lines or pipes for either commercial or domestic use or consumption is exempt [G.S. § 105-164.13(51)].

¶1603

- *Wholesale merchant*

A "wholesale merchant" is a person engaged in any of the following businesses: (1) making wholesale sales, (2) of buying or manufacturing items and selling them to a registered person or nonresident retail or wholesale merchants for resale, (3) manufacturing, producing, processing, or blending any articles of commerce and maintaining a store, warehouse, or any other place that is, separate and apart from the place of manufacture or production, for the sale or distribution of the articles (*except* bakery products) to another for the purpose of resale [G.S. § 105-164.3(51)].

- *Wholesale sale*

A "wholesale sale" is a sale of an item for the purpose of resale. The term includes a sale of certain digital property for reproduction into certain digital or tangible personal property offered for sale. The term, however, *does not* include a sale to users or consumers not for resale or, in the case of certain digital property, not for reproduction and sale of the reproduced property [G.S. § 105-164.3(52)].

¶1604 Imposition, Registration, and Responsibility for Collecting and Remitting Tax

- *Imposition of sales tax*

The North Carolina sales tax is a privilege tax that is imposed on retailers engaged in business in North Carolina. The sales tax is levied on the "net taxable sales" or "gross receipts," as appropriate, from sales or rentals of tangible personal property, digital property and certain specified services. For this purpose the term "gross receipts" has the same meaning at "sales price" [G.S. § 105-164.4(a)]. Sales price is discussed at ¶1704. The applicable rates are discussed at ¶1605.

Liability. The sales tax is collected from the retailer or facilitator. The tax is based on the retailer's or facilitator's net taxable sales if the taxpayer keeps proper books showing taxable and nontaxable sales. Otherwise, the tax is based on gross sales without allowance for exemptions and exclusions. The sales tax is in addition to any other license, privilege, excise or other tax that may be levied [G.S. § 105-164.4(b)].

- *Imposition of use tax*

The North Carolina use tax is an excise tax imposed at the applicable rate and maximum tax (if any) on the storage, use, or consumption in North Carolina of (1) tangible personal property purchased, leased or rented inside or outside North Carolina for storage, use, or consumption in North Carolina [G.S. § 105-164.6(a)(1)]; (2) certain digital property purchased inside or outside North Carolina for storage, use, or consumption in North Carolina [G.S. § 105-164.6(a)(2)]; and (3) services sourced to North Carolina [G.S. § 105-164.6(a)(3)]. When applied to an item subject to use tax, the term "purchase price" has the same meaning as the term "sales prices" (discussed at ¶1704) [G.S. § 105-164.3(33)]. Rates are discussed at ¶1605.

Liability: The use tax is payable by the person who purchases, leases, or rents the taxable items described above. If the purchased item becomes part of real property in North Carolina, the real property contractor, the retailer-contractor, the subcontractor, the lesee and the owner are jointly and severally liable for the tax (absent substantiation that a capital improvement is involved). The liability of a real property contractor, retailer-contractor, subcontractor, lessee or an owner who did not purchase the item is satisfied by receipt of an affidavit from the purchaser certifying that the tax has been paid [G.S. § 105-164.6(b)].

Credit: A credit is allowed against the use tax for the following [G.S. § 105-164.6(c)]:

(1) The amount of sales or use tax due or paid on the item to North Carolina, provided the tax is stated and charged separately on the invoice or other document of the retailer given to the purchaser at the time of sale (except for vending machine sales or where the retailer displays a statement that the sales price includes the tax) or provided the purchaser obtains documentation that the retailer remitted the tax after the sale. Payment of sales or use tax to North Carolina on an item by a retailer extinguishes the liability of a purchaser for the North Carolina use tax.

(2) The amount of sales or use tax paid on the item to another state. If the amount of tax paid to the other state is less than the amount of North Carolina use tax, the difference is payable to North Carolina. This credit does not apply to tax paid to a state that does not grant a similar credit for sales or use taxes paid in North Carolina.

• *Registration*

A person who (i) engages in business in North Carolina as a wholesaler or retail merchant (ii) engages in business in North Carolina selling or delivering items for storage, use, or consumption in North Carolina or (iii) is a facilitator who is liable for tax, must obtain a certificate of registration from the North Carolina Department of Revenue [G.S. §§ 105-164.4(c), 105-164.6(f) and 105-164.29].

To obtain a certificate of registration, a person must register with the Department. A person who has more than one business must only obtain one certificate for each legal entity to cover all operations of each business throughout the State. An application for registration must be signed (1) if the owner is an individual, by the individual, (2) if the owner is a limited liability company, by a manager, member or company official, (3) if the owner is a partnership, by a manager, member or partner, or (4) if the owner is a corporation, by an executive officer or other specifically authorized person (provided written evidence of such person's authority is attached to the application) [G.S. § 105-164.29(a)].

A certificate of registration is not assignable and must be displayed at each place of business [G.S. § 105-164.29(b)]. A certificate remains valid unless it is revoked by the Secretary for a compliance failure or becomes void because the holder of the certificate files no returns (or files returns showing no sales) for a period of eighteen months. There is an exception to this rule for certain sellers who contract with a certified service provider under the Streamlined Agreement where the service provider files returns for the seller showing no tax due for an eighteen month period. [G.S. § 105-164.29(c)]. Before the Secretary revokes a certificate for a compliance failure, the Secretary must notify the holder and inform the holder that the revocation will become final unless the holder files a request for Departmental review within the time specified in G.S. § 105-241.11 for requesting Departmental review of a proposed assessment (see ¶ 3210) [G.S. § 105-164.29(d)].

¶1604

SSUTA Registration

Registration under the Streamlined Sales and Use Tax Agreement satisfies the North Carolina sales and use tax requirements [G.S. § 105-164.42K]. See discussion at ¶1601.

• *Collecting and remitting tax*

Responsibility of seller: The sales tax is primarily a privilege or license tax on retailers or facilitators and not a tax on consumers. The intent of the law, however, is that the sales tax be passed on to the consumer [*Rent-A-Car Co. v. Lynch*, 39 N.C. App 709, 251 S.E.2d 917, 297 N.C. 455, 251 S.E.2d 919, *rev'd on other grounds*, 298 N.C. 559, 259 S.E.2d 564 (1979)]. Vendors are required to collect the sales tax on taxable transactions and remit them to the Department. The tax must be stated and charged separately on the invoices or other documents of the retailer or facilitator given to the purchaser at the time of the sale except for either of the following [G.S. § 105-164.7]:

(1) Vending machine sales.

(2) Where a retailer displays a statement indicating the sales price includes the tax.

The sales tax must be added to the purchase price and constitutes a debt from the purchaser to the retailer or facilitator. However, failure to charge or collect the tax from the purchaser does not relieve the retailer or facilitator from the liability to remit the tax [*Piedmont Canteen Service, Inc. v. Johnson*, 256 N.C. 155, 161, 123 S.E.2d 582, 586 (1962)]. See, also, *Secretary's Decision No.* 2003-441 (February 25, 2004). A vendor is considered to act as a trustee on behalf of the state when it collects tax from the purchaser of a taxable item [G.S. § 105-164.7]. "Vendor" is used in the discussion of the sales and use taxes to include retailers, lodging operators, lessors, or any other person who engages in taxable transactions. Returns and payment are discussed in detail in ¶1901. See also ¶1811 and ¶1812 for discussion of direct pay permits.

Responsibility of purchaser: The use tax is the responsibility of the purchaser [G.S. § 105-164.6(b)]. An individual who is not engaged in the business of selling tangible personal property at retail and who purchases taxable tangible personal property for a non-business purpose must report and remit the tax due.

Voluntary collection of use tax: The Secretary may enter into agreements with sellers pursuant to which the seller agrees to collect and remit on behalf of its customers State and local use taxes due on items the seller sells. [G.S. § 105-164.6A]. See ¶1707 for a discussion of the contents of voluntary collection agreements.

• *Excessive and erroneous collections*

Over-collections remitted to Secretary: When the tax collected for any period on a taxable sale is in excess of the total amount that should have been collected, or where tax is erroneously collected on an exempt or nontaxable sale, the total amount collected must be remitted to the Secretary.

Seller's remedies: Where the seller has over-collected the sales tax and remitted the tax to the Secretary, the Secretary may take one of two remedial actions. First, the Secretary may refund the tax if the seller gives the purchaser a credit or refund of the tax paid. Second, if the Secretary determines that the seller is liable for a use tax on a related transaction, the Secretary may allow the seller to offset the use tax liability with the over-collected sales tax (without affecting the seller's liability to the purchaser). The offset remedy is available with respect to tax liabilities that accrue on or after July 1, 2011 [S.L. 2011-293 (H.B. 93) §2]. For the exclusiveness of the refund remedy before this date, *see* Final Agency Decision 08 REV 2880 (Feb. 23, 2010), *rev'd, Technocom Bus. Sys., Inc. v. N.C. Dept. of Revenue*, 2011 NCBC 1 (N.C. Super., Jan. 4, 2011). However, an offset remedy was applied to earlier periods in reliance on former G.S. § 105-164.41. *See Technocom Bus. Sys., Inc. v. N.C. Dept. of Revenue*, 219 N.C. App. 207, 723 S.E.2d 151 (2012). The refund and offset remedies are mutually exclusive [G.S. § 105-164.11(a)].

Purchaser's remedies—Refund procedures: The customer refund procedures provided in Chapter 105 or otherwise provided by administrative rule, bulletin, or directive on the law issued by the Secretary provide the first course of remedy available to purchasers seeking a refund of over-collected sales or use taxes from the seller [G.S. § 105-164.11(b); *Sales and Use Tax Technical Bulletins*, § 34-21.I.a]. Procedures for claiming refunds and credits for overpayment of sales and use tax are contained in *Sales and Use Tax Technical Bulletins*, § 34-21]. For special procedures available to retailers making taxable retail sales of items on which tax has been paid, see ¶ 1906.

Purchaser's remedies—Cause of action against seller: A cause of action against the seller for over-collected sales or use taxes does not accrue until a purchaser has provided written notice to a seller and the seller has had 60 days to respond. The notice to the seller must contain the information necessary to determine the validity of the request [G.S. § 105-164.11(c)].

Presumption of reasonable business practice: In connection with a purchaser's request from the seller of over-collected sales or use taxes, a seller is presumed to have a reasonable business practice if, in the collection of sales and use taxes, the seller uses either a provider or a system (including a proprietary system) that is certified by the State and the seller has remitted to the State all taxes collected less any deductions, credits, or collection allowances [G.S. § 105-164.11(d)]. The SSUTA is discussed at ¶ 1601.

Seller's reliance on written advice: A seller who requests and relies on specific written advice from the Secretary in collecting and remitting sales tax is not liable to a purchaser for any overcollected sales or use tax [G.S. § 105-164.11(e)].

¶ 1605 Rates

• *General rate of tax*

The general sales and use tax rate is 4.75% [G.S. § 105-164.4(a)].

The general rate of tax applies unless another rate applies [G.S. § 105-164.4(a)(1)].

Simultaneous state and local changes: When state and local sales and use tax rates change on the same date because one increases and the other decreases but the combined rate does not change, sales and use taxes payable on the following periodic payments are reportable in accordance with the changed state and local rates, as follows [G.S. § 105-164.16(e)]:

(1) Lease or rental payments *billed* after the effective date of the changes.

(2) Installment sale payments *received* after the effective date of the changes by a taxpayer who reports the installment sale on a cash basis.

Effective date of tax changes for general rate items: For a taxable item that is provided and billed on a monthly or other periodic basis, a new tax or a tax rate increase applies to the first billing period that is at least 30 days after enactment and that starts on or after the effective date of the change [G.S. § 105-164.15A(a)(1)]. See also Directive SD-18-2.

For a taxable item that is not billed on a monthly or other periodic basis, a tax change applies to amounts received for items provided on or after the effective date of the change, except amounts received for items purchased to fulfill a real property contract for a capital improvement entered into or awarded before the effective date or entered into or awarded pursuant to a bid made before the effective date [G.S. § 105-164.15A(a)(2)].

Effective date of tax changes for combined rate items: The effective date of a rate change for an item that is taxable at the combined general rate is as follows: (1) for a taxable item that is not billed on a periodic basis, a rate change applies to amounts received for items provided on or after the effective date of a change in the State general rate of tax set forth in G.S. § 105-164.4; (2) for a taxable item that is provided and billed on a periodic basis, a tax increase applies to the first billing period that is at least 30 days after enactment and that starts on or after the effective date of the rate increase; (3) a rate decrease applies to bills rendered on or after the effective date; (4) with respect to an increase in the authorization for local sales and use taxes, the date on which local sales and use taxes authorized for every county become effective in the first county or group of counties to levy the authorized taxes; and (5) for a repeal in the authorization for local sales and use taxes, the effective date of repeal [G.S. § 105-164.15A(b)].

- *Table of tax rates*

The rates on net taxable sales or gross receipts, as appropriate, are established in G.S. § 105-164.4 and are shown in the table below.

CGR

"CGR" in the rate column of the table below means the "combined general rate." "Combined general rate" means the State's general rate of tax set in G.S. § 105-164.4(a) (currently 4.75%)) plus the sum of the rates of the applicable local sales and use taxes authorized to be levied by all counties. The current combined general rate is 7%. Local sales and use taxes are discussed at ¶ 1607.

Table of Rates[1]				
Taxable Item or Activity	*Rate (and cap)*	*Base*	*G.S. §*	*Comments*
Accommodations	4.75%	GR	105-164.4F(b)	Discussed at ¶ 1726.
Aircraft, including all attached accessories	4.75% ($2,500)	SP	105-164.4(a)(1a)	
Aviation gasoline and jet fuel	CGR	GR	105-164.4(a)(15)	Certain sales to intastate air businesses are exempt. See discussion at ¶ 1804.
Boats, including all attached accessories	3% ($1,500)	SP	105-164.4(a)(1b)	
Certain digital property	4.75%	SP	105-164.4((1)b)	Discussed at ¶ 1725.

Taxable Item or Activity	Rate (and cap)	Base	G.S. §	Comments
Electricity	CGR	GR	105-164.4(a)(9)	Includes separate charges for repair, maintenance and installation services and contributions in aid of construction. Sales of electricity to manufacturers are exempt. See discussion at ¶1809.
Entertainments	4.75%	GR	105-164.4(a)(10)	Discussed at ¶1728.
Lease or rental of tangible person property	Applicable percentage rate		105-164.4(a)(2)	Applies to gross receipts. The applicable percentage rate is the rate that applies to sales of the leased or rented property.
Linens, apparel, etc. rented to customers by laundries	4.75%	GR	105-164.4(a)(4)	Applies to gross receipts. Does not apply to receipts from coin-operated washers & dryers.
Manufactured homes, including all attached accessories	4.75%	SP	105-164.4(a)(1a)	Sales made after September 1, 2014 are 50% exempt. See ¶1730.
Modular homes, including all accessories attached when it is delivered to the purchaser	4.75%	SP	105-164.4(a)(1a)	Sales made after September 1, 2014 are 50% exempt. See ¶1730.
Piped natural gas	CGR	GR	105-164.4(a)(9)	Includes separate charges for repair, maintenance and installation services and contributions in aid of construction. Sales of piped natural gas to manufacturers are exempt. See discussion at ¶1809.
Prepaid meal plans	4.75%	SP or GP	105-164.4(a)(12)	
Prepaid telephone calling service	4.75%	GR	105-164.4(a)(4d)	Applies to sale or recharge.
Qualified jet engines	4.75%	SP	105-164.4(a)(1a)	The tax is capped at $2500 if the purchaser has a direct pay permit [G.S. § 105-164.27A.(a2)].
Real property contractors	4.75%	SP	105-164.4H	Applies to taxable property or services sold to real property contractors to fulfill a real property contract. Discussed at ¶1709.
Repair, maintenance and installation services	4.75%	SP or GR	105-164.4(a) (1)c and (16)	Applies regardless of whether the tangible personal property or certain digital property is subject to a maximum tax. Includes tangible personal property and certain digital property that becomes part of or is applied to the purchaser's property.
Video programming service	CGR	GR	105-164.4(a)(6)	Discussed at ¶1721
Satellite digital audio radio service	4.75%	GR	105-164.4(a)(6a)	Includes services received by a mobile or portable station.
Service contracts	4.75%	SP or GR	105-164.4(a)(11)	Discussed at ¶1729
Specialty market or other event articles	5.75%	SP	105-164.4(a)(4b)	Does not apply to person's own household personal property.
Spirituous liquor	CGR	SP	105-164.4(a)(7)	Also applies to antique spirituous liquor upon the adoption of implementing rules by the ABC Commission. Does not apply to mixed beverages.

¶1605

Taxable Item or Activity	Rate (and cap)	Base	G.S. §	Comments
		Table of Rates[1]		
Tangible personal property	4.75%	SP	105-164.4(a)(1)a	Includes all retail sales not subject to another rate. Does not apply to repair, maintenance and installation services for real property.
Telecommunications service	CGR	GR	105-164(a)(4c)	See ¶ 1719 for discussion of telecommunications service.

NOTES

[1] Abbreviations: SP = Sales Price; GR = Gross Receipts; CGR - Combined General Rate; AP – Admissions Price.

• *Use tax rates*

Items subject to the North Carolina use tax are taxed at the rate and maximum tax, if any, that would apply to the sale of the product [G.S. § 105-164.6(a)]. Imposition of the use tax is discussed at ¶ 1604.

• *Tax computations*

A sales and use tax computation must be carried to the third decimal place and must round up to the next cent whenever the third decimal place is greater than four. The taxpayer may compute the tax due on a transaction on an item or invoice basis. The rounding rule is applied to the aggregate tax due. For the convenience of the retailer in collecting the tax due under Article 5, the Secretary prescribes tables that compute the tax due on sales. The Secretary must issue a separate table for each rate of tax that may apply to a sale. Retailers are not required to collect tax based on the bracket system. [G.S. § 105-164.10].

¶ 1606 Tax Credits, Deductions, and Refunds

• *Credit for tax paid to another state*

If a retail sales and use tax is due and has been paid with tangible personal property in another state, the tax is credited upon the North Carolina use tax. A person who sells a modular home at retail is allowed a credit for tax paid to another state on tangible personal property incorporated in the modular home [G.S. § 105-164.4(a)(1a)]. If the amount of tax paid to another state is less than the amount of North Carolina use tax, the taxpayer must pay to North Carolina an amount sufficient to make the tax paid to the other state and North Carolina equal to that of the North Carolina tax. The Secretary requires proof of payment of tax to another State as the Secretary deems necessary. No credit will be given for taxes paid in another state if that state does not grant similar credit for sales taxes paid in North Carolina [G.S. § 105-164.6(c)]. The local sales and use tax provisions also allow a credit upon the local use tax for retail sales taxes paid to the State and a credit upon the local use tax for taxes paid to another state. The local use tax is not subject to credit for payment of any State sales or use tax not imposed for the benefit and use of counties and municipalities. The State credit provision and the local credit provision must be applied separately.

• *Deduction for worthless accounts*

Accounts of purchasers, representing taxable sales, on which the tax has been paid, that are found to be worthless and actually charged off for income tax purposes may, at a corresponding period, be deducted from gross sales. However, if they are later collected, they must be added to gross sales [G.S. § 105-164.13(15)]. In *Home Depot U.S.A., Inc. V. NCDOR*, 11 CVS 2261 (November 6, 2015) (N.C. Bus. Ct.), the court denied a worthless account deduction to a retailer for worthless accounts charged off by an unrelated lender under a private label credit card program, finding that the party claiming the deduction must be the holder of the purchaser account.

• *Refund on returned merchandise*

If an article sold is returned and the sale is rescinded by a refund of the entire amount paid including tax, the vendor is entitled to obtain a refund of or credit for the sales or use taxes paid to the Department by reason of the initial sale of such merchandise. The records of the taxpayer must clearly reflect and support his claim for any such refund or credit [17 NCAC 7B.3003].

• *Use tax credits*

A credit is allowed against the use tax for the following [G.S. § 105-164.6(c)]:

(1) The amount of sales or use tax paid on the item to North Carolina. Payment of sales or use tax to North Carolina on an item by a retailer extinguishes the liability of a purchaser for the North Carolina use tax.

(2) The amount of sales tax paid on the item to another state. If the amount of tax paid to the other state is less than the amount of North Carolina use tax, the difference is payable to North Carolina. This credit does not apply to tax paid to a state that does not grant a similar credit for sales or use taxes paid in North Carolina.

¶1607 Local Sales and Use Taxes

• *Overview*

All counties, as well as transportation authorities throughout the state, are authorized to adopt and levy local government sales and use taxes by the following articles of Chapter 105 of the North Carolina General Statutes:

(1) **Article 39**: The First One Cent (1¢) Local Government Sales and Use Tax [G.S. §§ 105-463 et seq.]. This Article applies to all 100 counties of North Carolina [G.S. § 105-464].

(2) **Article 40**: The First One-Half Cent ($1/2$ cent) Local Government Sales and Use Tax [G.S. §§ 105-480 et seq.]. This Article applies only to counties that levy the one-cent local government sales and use tax [G.S. § 105-482].

(3) **Article 42**: The Second One-Half Cent ($1/2$ cent) Local Government Sales and Use Tax [G.S. §§ 105-495 et seq.]. This Article applies only to counties that levy (a) the one-cent local government sales and use tax and (b) the first$1/2$ cent local government sales and use tax [G.S. § 105-497].

(4) **Article 43**: One-Half Cent ($1/2$ cent) and One-Quarter Cent ($1/4$ cent) Local Government Public Transportation Sales and Use Tax [G.S. §§ 105-506 et seq.] This Article includes $1/2$ cent provisions that apply separately to Mecklenburg County, the Triangle and the Triad, and a $1/4$ cent provision that applies to all other counties.

(5) **Article 46**: The One-Quarter Cent ($1/4$ cent) County Sales and Use Tax [G.S. §§ 105-535 et seq.]. This Article applies only to counties that levy (a) the one cent (1¢) sales and use tax, (b) the first one-half cent ($1/2$ cent) local

government sales and use tax and (c) the second one-half cent ($^1/_2$ cent) local government sales and use tax [G.S. § 105-536].

• *Rates*

As of October 1, 2019, the state and local sales tax rate was 7% in Alexander, Anson, Ashe, Buncombe, Cabarrus, Catawba, Cherokee, Clay, Cumberland, Davidson, Duplin, Edgecombe, Gaston, Graham, Greene, Halifax, Harnett, Haywood, Hertford, Jackson, Jones, Lee, Lincoln, Martin, Montgomery, Moore, New Hanover, Onslow, Pasquotank Pitt, Randolph, Robeson, Rockingham, Rowan, Rutherford, Sampson, Stanly, Surry, Swain and Wilkes Counties; 7.25% in Mecklenburg and Wake counties; 7.5% in Durham and Orange Counties; and 6.75% in all other counties.

• *Purpose and use of revenues*

Counties were authorized to levy the one-cent local government sales and use tax "to obtain an added source of revenue with which to meet their growing financial needs" [G.S. § 105-464]. The first and second half-cent local government sales and use taxes were intended for similar purposes as well as to reduce the counties' dependence on other revenues such as property taxes [G.S. § § 105-481 and 105-496]. In addition, for a specified period of time after enactment of the levy, counties are required to use specified portions of the revenue generated by the first and second half-cent local government sales and use taxes for public school capital outlays or to retire indebtedness associated with public school capital outlays [G.S. § § 105-487 and 105-502].

The local government public transportation sales and use tax provides counties and transportation authorities an additional source of revenue to finance local public transportation systems [G.S. § 105-505]. A county or transportation authority may not levy the local government public transportation sales and use tax unless the county (or a local government unit within the county) or the transportation authority operates a public transportation system and the county or the transportation authority has developed a financial plan for the equitable allocation or use of the revenue generated by the tax, and, in the case of a plan developed by a transportation authority, the plan has been approved by the county commissioners of each county and the Metropolitan Planning Organizations (as defined in Article 16 of Chapter 136 of the General Statutes) within the special taxing district created by the authority [G.S. § § 105-507, 105-510.6 and 105-510.13]. A taxing county must allocate the tax revenue in accordance with the plan and the county or transportation authority must use the revenue only for the financing, construction, operation and maintenance of local transportation systems. The funds generated by the tax may not be used to replace existing revenues or other resources for public transportation [G.S. § § 105-510(b), 105-510.7 and 105-510.16(b)].

• *Procedure for levy and repeal*

Article 39 of Chapter 105 contains rules for the approval and repeal of levies of all the local government sales and use taxes [G.S. § § 105-465, 105-466, 105-473, 105-483, 105-498, 105-508, 105-510.15, and 105-538]. Generally, there are two ways of levying the tax, although the local government public transportation sales and use tax is subject to special rules discussed below. First, a special election to approve the levy of the tax may be held on the request of the county commissioners or the request of voters pursuant to a petition [G.S. § 105-465]. If the levy is approved in the special election, the county commissioners may proceed to levy the tax by resolution [G.S. § 105-466(a)]. Alternatively, except in the case of the quarter-cent local government sales and use tax, the county commissioners may levy the tax without a special election, provided the tax has not been defeated in a special election within five years [G.S. §§105-466(b) and 105-537]. If the tax is levied, a special election may also be held upon the request of the county commissioners or of the voters by petition to repeal the tax. If the voters vote to repeal, the county commissioners must proceed to terminate the levy. If the tax was imposed by the county commissioners acting without a special election, the commissioners may also terminate the levy without a special election [G.S. §105-473].

Local government public transportation sales and use taxes may be levied by any county other than Durham, Forsyth, Guilford, Orange and Wake and only after voter approval in an advisory referendum [G.S. §§105-505, 105-508, and 105-510.14(a)]. If the voters approve the tax, the county commissioners may levy the tax by resolution [G.S. §§105-509 and 105-510.15]. Local government public transportation sales and use taxes may also be levied by a regional transportation authority for the benefit of a special district. The Triangle Transit Authority may create a special district consisting of one or more of Durham, Orange and Wake Counties. The Piedmont Authority for Regional Transportation may create a special district consisting of one or both of Forsyth and Guilford Counties [G.S. §§105-510.8(a) and 105-510.10(a)]. If the voters of the special district approve the tax, the board of trustees of the transportation authority may levy the tax by resolution [G.S. §§105-510.9 and 105-510.11]. Any repeal of a tax levied by a transportation authority must be accomplished in the same manner as its enactment [G.S. §§105-510.9 and 105-510.11].

• *Scope*

The local government sales and use taxes apply to items subject to the State sales and use tax under G.S. §105-164.4 at the general rate. Thus, items subject to state sales tax at special rates are not subject to the local sales tax. This includes items subject to the combined general rate. In addition, modular and manufactured homes, aircrafts and qualified jet engines, which are subject to state tax at the general rate, are exempt from the local sales tax [G.S. §105-467(a)(1)]. In addition, the following items that are exempt from the State sales tax are subject to the local government sales and use taxes: (1) sales of food exempt from the State sales tax under G.S. §105-164.13B, (2) food sold as part of a bundled transaction if the price of the food exceeds 10% of the price of the bundle. The local government sales and use tax also applies to the presumed price of an item of tangible personal property transferred as part of a conditional contract under G.S. §105-164.12B [G.S. §105-467(a)(8)].

• *Exemptions and refunds*

The State sales tax exemptions and exclusions apply to the local sales and use tax authorized to be levied and imposed except for the state exemption for food. The State refund provisions contained in G.S. §§105-164.14 and 105-164.14A (*see* ¶¶1903, 1904 and 1905) apply to the local sales and use tax as well. However, the aggregate annual refund allowed an entity under G. S. §105-164.14(b) (*see* ¶1903) for a fiscal year may not exceed $13,300,000. A refund of an excessive or erroneous State sales tax collection allowed under G.S. §105-164.11 and a refund of State sales tax paid on a rescinded sale or cancelled service contract under G.S. §105-164.11A apply to the local sales and use tax as well [G.S. §105-467(b)].

A local school administrative unit is entitled to an annual refund of local government sales and use taxes on direct purchases of items. This refund provision extends to a joint agency created by interlocal agreement among local school administrative units to jointly purchase food service related materials, supplies and equipment on their behalf. It also extends to local government sales taxes indirectly incurred by a local school administrative unit (or joint agency) on purchases of building materials, supplies, fixtures and equipment that become part of or annexed to a structure that is owned by or leased to the entity and that is being erected, altered or repaired for use by the entity. The refund does not apply to purchases of electricity, telecommunications services, ancillary services, piped natural gas, video programming or a prepaid meal plan. Refund requests are due in the same time and manner as requests for refunds of state sales and use taxes [G.S. § 105-467(b)].

- *Sourcing rules*

The general sourcing rules that apply to the State sales and use tax also apply to the local government sales and use tax [G.S. § 105-467(c)]. These rules are discussed at ¶ 1602. The Sales and Use Tax Technical Bulletins provide that the tax is due in the county where the purchaser or its agent takes delivery of the items purchased, even where the purchaser's order was submitted or accepted at a business location maintained by the seller in another county. Where property is shipped to the purchaser, the tax is collected for the destination county. *Sales and Use Tax Technical Bulletins*, § 48-1. If the seller does not know where the property was received by the purchaser, the tax is collected for the county where the first of the following addresses is known to the seller: (1) the business or home address of the purchaser, (2) the billing address of the purchaser (or, for prepaid wireless calling service, the location associated with the mobile telephone number), and (3) the address from which the property was shipped or the service provided. *Sales and Use Tax Technical Bulletins*, § 48-2.A.3.

- *Sourcing of digital property and computer software delivered electronically*

The North Carolina Department of Revenue has specified the sourcing provision applicable to the sale of certain digital property and computer software delivered electronically relative to provisions of N.C. Gen. Stat § 105-164.4B(a)(3), where the delivery address is unknown and the seller cannot ascertain an address of the purchaser. The seller should source the sale of such to the location from which the digital property or the computer software delivered electronically was first available for transmission by the seller [*Important Notice: Sourcing of Digital Property and Computer Software Delivered Electronically*, North Carolina Department of Revenue, November 2011].

- *Local use tax*

A purchaser who purchases taxable property for use, storage or consumption in a taxing county from vendors located outside North Carolina or outside the purchaser's county on which the local tax was not required to be collected must report and remit the tax to the Secretary [G.S. § 105-468; Sales and Use Tax Technical Bulletins, § 48-2.A.1]. Retailers, including out-of-state retailers, who collect use tax on sales to North Carolina residents are required to ascertain the county of residence of each buyer and provide that information to the Secretary along with any other information necessary for the Secretary to allocate the use tax proceeds to the correct taxing county [G.S. § 105-469(b); Sales and Use Tax Technical Bulletins, § 48-3.B.1].

Where a local sales or use tax was due and has been paid with respect to tangible personal property by the purchaser in another taxing county within North Carolina, or where a local sales or use tax was due and has been paid in a taxing jurisdiction outside North Carolina where the purpose of the tax is similar in purpose and intent to the local tax, the tax paid may be credited against the local use tax due the North Carolina taxing county. No credit, however, will be given for tax paid to another jurisdiction outside North Carolina if the jurisdiction does not grant similar credit for North Carolina taxes. If the amount of sales or use tax paid is less than the amount of use tax due the taxing county, the difference between the amount paid and the amount due the taxing county must be paid to the Secretary, who may require proof of payment in another taxing county or jurisdiction [G.S. § 105-468]. A purchaser is not entitled to a credit against a local government use tax for any sales or use taxes paid to another state not imposed for the benefit and use of counties and municipalities. Sales and Use Tax Technical Bulletins, § 48-2.B.

• *Administration*

The local government sales and use taxes are administered by the Department of Revenue [G.S. § § 105-469(a) and 105-164.13B(b)].

To the extent not inconsistent with the local government sales and use tax provisions, the following State sales and use tax provisions apply to the local government sales and use taxes: (1) the definitions and other provisions of Article 5 of Chapter 105 (the State sales and use tax article), (2) the provisions of Article 9 of Chapter 105 (general administrative, penalty and remedy provisions) as they relate to State sales and use taxes, and (3) the administrative interpretations made by the Secretary with respect to State sales and use taxes [G.S. § 105-474].

SALES AND USE TAXES

CHAPTER 17

TAXABLE SALES AND USES

¶1701 Introduction

North Carolina imposes a sales tax on retailers who make sales of tangible personal property in North Carolina and a use tax on the "use" of tangible personal property in North Carolina. The sales tax is characterized as a privilege tax [G.S.

§ 105-164.4(a)]; and the use tax is characterized as an excise tax [G.S. § 105-164.6(a)]. Both taxes are imposed at varying rates (see ¶ 1605). The use tax is imposed on the "storage, use, or consumption" of tangible personal property in North Carolina. The term "use" is commonly used as a convenience to mean "storage, use, or consumption," and it has that meaning in this chapter unless the context clearly indicates otherwise.

The use tax supplements the sales tax by imposing tax on taxable purchases on which no sales tax has been paid. Retailers are responsible for collecting and remitting sales tax on taxable sales, and purchasers are responsible for remitting use tax on taxable purchases unless the vendor collects the use tax. If an out-of-state vendor does not have a physical location or other type of physical representation (*i.e.*, nexus) in North Carolina, North Carolina cannot require the out-of-state vendor to collect North Carolina's tax. Some out-of-state vendors, however, who do not have taxable nexus with North Carolina, voluntarily collect the use tax as a convenience to their customers.

The sales tax is imposed on (1) retailers at applicable percentage rates of the "sales price" of taxable tangible personal property; (2) on lessors and renters at the applicable percentage rate of the "gross receipts" from leasing or renting; and (3) on utilities at the applicable rate of "gross receipts" from the sales of electricity and telecommunications. The use tax is imposed on purchasers at the appropriate rates on the "cost price" of taxable tangible personal property. Applicable percentage rates are discussed in ¶ 1605. See ¶ 1704 for discussion of sales price.

Whether referring to the sales tax or the use tax, a taxable transaction involves both a sale by a vendor and a purchase by a customer. For convenience, in this chapter, the term "sale" means a sale/purchase that may be subject to the North Carolina sales tax, and the term "purchase" means a purchase/sale that may be subject to the North Carolina use tax, unless the context clearly indicates otherwise. A taxable purchase may require that the purchaser remit use tax to North Carolina. However, if an out-of-state vendor is required to collect or voluntarily collects the use tax for North Carolina customers, the purchaser is not required to remit use tax to North Carolina.

Definitions

Consult ¶ 1603 for definitions applicable to the sales and use taxes that are not provided in this chapter.

¶ 1702 Taxable Sales and Uses

• *Criteria for taxability*

In order to be a taxable sale, a transaction must satisfy five criteria:

    (1) It must be a "sale" [G.S. § 105-164.3(36)].

    (2) The sale must be made by a "retailer" [G.S. § 105-164.4(a)].

    (3) The sale must be made "at retail" [G.S. § 105-164.3(35)].

(4) The sale must be of "tangible personal property," "digital property" or specified services [G.S. § 105-164.3(35)].

(5) The sale must not qualify for an exemption [G.S. § 105-164.13]. See definition of terms at ¶ 1603.

¶ 1703 Retailers

- *"Retailer" defined*

The term "retailer" is defined in ¶ 1603. In addition, when, in the opinion of the Secretary, it is necessary for the efficient administration of the sales and use tax, the Secretary may regard the following as retailers [G.S. § 105-164.3(35)]: (1) salesmen, solicitors, representatives, consignees, peddlers, truckers, or canvassers as agents of the dealers, distributors, consignors, supervisors, employers, or persons under whom they operate or from whom they obtain the tangible personal property sold by them without regard to whether they are making sales on their own behalf or on behalf of the dealers, distributors, consignors, supervisors, employers or persons under whom they operate; and (2) the dealers, distributors, consignors, supervisors, employers, or persons with whom these agents deal.

Wholesale Sales

The sales and use tax does not apply to wholesale sales. Most wholesale merchants, however, are required to be licensed even if they do not make retail sales.

- *Engaged in business*

"Engaged in business" for sales and use tax purposes means (1) maintaining, occupying, or using permanently or temporarily, directly or indirectly, or through a subsidiary or agent, by whatever name called, any office, place of distribution, sales or sample room or place, warehouse or storage place, or other place of storage, use, or consumption in North Carolina; (2) permanently or temporarily, directly or through a subsidiary, having any representative, agent, salesman, canvasser or solicitor operating in North Carolina in such selling or delivering; (3) maintaining in North Carolina, either permanently or temporarily, directly or through a subsidiary, tangible personal property for the purpose of lease or rental; or (4) making a mail order sale. The fact that any corporate retailer, agent, or subsidiary engaged in business in North Carolina may not be legally domesticated or qualified to do business in North Carolina is immaterial [G.S. § 105-164.3(5)]. For a potentially far-reaching administrative application of the definition of "engaged in business," see *Tax Review Board Administrative Decision No. 443* (June 2, 2004), holding that a New York specialty transmission retailer was engaged in business in North Carolina where it received orders in New York, purchased transmissions in New York, shipped the transmissions to subcontractors in North Carolina for modification and arranged for the subcontractors to deliver the modified transmissions to customers in North Carolina. The Board concluded that the subcontractors, by delivering property on the taxpayer's behalf, became the taxpayer's agents and that the presence of the taxpayer's transmissions at the subcontractors' North Carolina locations constituted the storage of inventory in North Carolina by the taxpayer. The Board seemed influenced by the fact that one of the subcontractors was a proprietorship owned by the son of the taxpayer's president.

¶1704 Sales Price

"Sales price" means the total amount or consideration for which an item is sold, leased, or rented. The consideration may be in the form of cash, credit, property, or services. The sales price must be valued in money, regardless of whether it is received in money [G.S. § 105-164.3(37)]. The term includes all of the following:

(1) The retailer's cost of the item sold, including the cost of materials, labor, interest, taxes, and other expenses [G.S. § 105-164.3(37)a.1 and 2.].

(2) Charges by the retailer for any services necessary to complete the sale [G.S. § 105-164.3(37)a.3.].

(3) Delivery charges (including postage paid to have items delivered directly to customers; see Secretary's Decision No. 2004-220 (October 4, 2004)) [G.S. § 105-164.3(37)a.4.].

(4) Installation charges [G.S. § 105-164.3(37)a.5.].

(5) The amount of any credit for trade-in does not reduce the sales price [G.S. § 105-164.3(37)a.7.]. (Note that a dealer's resale of items taken in trade is not exempt from sales tax even though no credit is allowed for the trade-in on the sale of the new item). *See Secretary's Decision No. 2007-69* (September 6, 2007).

(6) Discounts that are reimbursable by a third party and can be determined at the time of sale through (a) presentation by the consumer of a coupon or other documentation; (b) identification of the consumer as a member of a group eligible for a discount; or (c) the invoice the retailer gives the consumer [G.S. § 105-164.3(37)a.8.].

Items not included in "sales price": The term "sales price" does not include the following [G.S. § 105-(37)b.]:

(1) Discounts that are not reimbursable by a third party, are allowed by the retailer, and are taken by a consumer on a sale. For the treatment of discounts for early payment, *see* SUPLR 2017-0003.

(2) Interest, financing, and carrying charges from credit extended on the sale, if the amount is separately stated on the invoice, bill of sale, or a similar document given to the consumer.

(3) Any taxes imposed directly on the consumer that are separately stated on the invoice, bill of sale, or similar document given to the consumer.

• *Service charges*

In general, service charges must be included in the taxable sales price of tangible personal property sold, leased, or rented [G.S. § 105-164.3(37)]. For example, the taxpayer's charges for creative services, design labor, and other services made in connection with the sale of trade booths, displays, and printed material were considered part of the sales price of the tangible personal property, even though the service charges were separately stated, where the creative services were an integral, necessary and inseparable function of the fabrication process that produced the tangible personal property sold [*Secretary's Decision No. 2003-262 (October 9, 2003)*]. A "drop-

¶1704

off" caterer was required to collect tax on the service fee it charged customers for delivering and setting up food and post-event retrieval and cleaning [Final Agency Decision 08 REV 2563 (January 14, 2010)]. See also, *Sales and Use Tax Technical Bulletins,* § 24-1.B which provides that where advertising agencies make retail sales of tangible personal property (*e.g.,* catalogs, magazines, handbills, brochures, programs, pamphlets) sold and delivered to clients or others on behalf of their clients, the sales price to which the tax applies includes all charges for services rendered in the production, fabrication, manufacture, or delivery of the property (*e.g.,* charges for commissions, supervision, research, transportation, postage, telephone messages, film, negatives, models' fees, stage props, printing), even though the service charges may be separately stated on the invoice sent to the client and in the taxpayer's records.

- *"Sales price" of items sold through coin-operated vending machines*

The "sales price" of tangible personal property sold through coin-operated vending machines (except tobacco products) is considered to be 50% of the total amount for which the property is sold in the vending machine [G.S. § 105-164.13(50)].

- *Gift wrap*

For the taxation of gift wrap items and services provided to purchasers of items sold at retail, see Directive SD-18-3.

- *Shop supplies*

Separately stated charges for shop supplies are part of the sales price of tangible personal property sold at retail to repair tangible property, a motor vehicle or a boat. Additionally, any charge for shop supplies in conjunction with taxable repair, maintenance and installation services is part of the sales price of such services [Directive SD-18-4].

¶ 1705 Tangible Personal Property—Special Topics

- *Art objects and supplies*

Unless specifically exempt by statute, retail sales of objects of art and art supplies are subject to the general rate of State tax and any applicable local sales or use tax [*Sales and Use Tax Technical Bulletins,* § 32-1]. For information on sales by advertising artists, see Sales and Use Tax Technical Bulletins, § 24-2.

- *Freestanding appliances*

A sale of a freestanding appliance is treated as a sale of tangible personal property [G.S. § 105-164.4(a)(1)]. Thus, the sale of a freestanding appliance is taxable even if the sale is pursuant to a real property contract.

- *Mailing lists on computer disks*

Computer disks containing mailing list information are tangible personal property. Thus, the rental of computer disks containing mailing list information for storage, use, or consumption within North Carolina is subject to the general State and local rates of use tax [*Secretary's Decision No. 97-591* (November 18, 1997)].

- *Photographs, blue prints, photostatic copies*

Blueprints and photostatic copies: Sales of photostatic copies or blueprints to consumers or users (including sales to architectural or engineering firms if not for resale) are subject to the general rate of State tax and any applicable local sales or use tax [*Sales and Use Tax Technical Bulletins,* § 32-7.A, § 32-7.B]. Architects are liable for sales tax on blueprints or plans when they reproduce plans or drawings and sell them. No tax is due when plans and specifications are instruments of service and title remains with the architect [*Sales and Use Tax Technical Bulletins,* § 32-7.C].

Developing negatives: Charges by photo finishers for developing customers' film into negatives that are returned to the customers only on the exposed film furnished by the customer are not subject to sales or use tax [*Sales and Use Tax Technical Bulletins,* § 32-6].

Equipment and supplies: Sales of printing equipment and supplies, including paper and ink, to consumer or captive printers are subject to the general rate of State tax and any applicable local sales or use tax [*Sales and Use Tax Technical Bulletins,* § 32-4].

Frames and other articles: Sales of frames, films, and other articles by photographers, photo finishers, or others to users or consumers are subject to the general rate of State tax and any applicable local sales or use tax [*Sales and Use Tax Technical Bulletins,* § 32-2.A].

Photographs and other images: Photographs delivered in a tangible format (*e.g.,* photographic paper) are tangible personal property for North Carolina sales and use tax purposes. Photographs delivered in an electronic or digital format via Internet download of e-mail are not tangible personal property for North Carolina sales and use tax purposes. See, for example, *Secretary's Decision No.* 2003-171 (August 29, 2003). The provision of ultrasonic images delivered to customers in the form of still images or DVD videos are taxable retail sales and not the provision of medical diagnostic services. Final Agency Decision 09 REV 1582 (August 10, 2010).

Tinting or coloring: The tinting or coloring of photographs for a customer constitutes a service, and the receipts for the service are not taxable. Sales to photographers and photo finishers of materials to be used by them in performing tinting or coloring services are subject to the general rate of State tax and any applicable local sales or use tax [*Sales and Use Tax Technical Bulletins,* § 32-3].

- *Provision of both goods and services*

In some cases a taxpayer may provide both goods and services to customers, and the taxability of the transaction may depend on whether the goods or services were the customers' true object in entering into the transactions. If the goods were the true object, the transfer of these goods pursuant to the transaction will be treated as taxable sales. If services were the true object, the taxpayer will be treated as consuming the goods used in the transaction and will be liable for a use tax on the cost of such goods. See, *e.g., Tax Review Board Administrative Decision No.* 451 (September 9, 2004), considering the true object of aerial photography supply contract; *Secretary's Decision No.* 2002-410 (March 18, 2003), *rev'd Tax Review Board Administrative Decision No.* 429 (March 9, 2004), considering the true object of a cost-per-page copier maintenance agreement. *Secretary's Decision No.* 2003-441 (February 25, 2003) (true object of a portable toilet rental agreement); *Secretary's Decision No.* 2003-442 (March 12, 2003)

¶1705

(true object of advertising material printing and distribution agreement); *Secretary's Decision No. 2003-124* (December 2, 2003) (true object of photography sitting, retouching and copyright services); *Secretary's Decision No. 2003-317* (January 9, 2004) (true object of custom printing contracts); *Secretary's Decision No. 2004-199* (September 1, 2004) (true object of wedding video production transaction); *Secretary's Decision No. 2004-348* (May 18, 2005) (true object of video and photography transactions). *See also Carolina Photography, Inc. v. Hinton*, 196 N.C. App 337, 674 S.E.2d 724 (2009) (photographer's sitting fee part of fabrication cost of photograph). See also ¶1715.

¶1706 Leases and Rentals of Tangible Personal Property

• *Lease receipts*

The gross receipts or gross proceeds derived from or the total amount agreed to be paid for the lease or rental, within North Carolina, of all kinds and types of tangible personal property not specifically exempt by statute are subject to the sales or use tax at the same rate that is applicable to the retail sale of such property. The tax is computed gross receipts, gross proceeds, or rental payable without any deduction whatsoever for any expense incident to the conduct of business including, but not limited to, property taxes, interest, insurance fees, maintenance fees, delivery charges, *etc.* The tax is due and payable at the time the lessor bills the lessee for rent whether billing is for the lump-sum rental or on a monthly or other periodic basis [17 NCAC 7B.4401].

• *Lease or rental defined*

A "lease or rental" is a transfer of possession or control of tangible personal property for a fixed or indeterminate term for consideration [G.S. § 105-164.3(17)]. See ¶1602 for sourcing rule for periodic lease payments.

Exclusions: The term "lease or rental" does not include any of the following:

(1) A transfer of possession or control of property under a security agreement or deferred payment plan that requires the transfer of title upon completion of the required payments [G.S. § 105-164.3(17)a].

(2) A transfer of possession or control of property under an agreement that requires the transfer of title upon completion of required payments and payment of an option price that does not exceed the greater of $100 or 1% of the total required payments [G.S. § 105-164.3(17)b].

(3) The providing of tangible personal property along with an operator for a fixed or indeterminate period of time if the operator is necessary for the equipment to perform as designed. For this purpose, an operator must do more than maintain, inspect, or set up the tangible personal property [G.S. § 105-164.3(17)c]. The operator must do more than maintain, inspect and set up the equipment to qualify for the exemption. North Carolina Department of Labor Administrative Rules that specify that personnel in charge of equipment must maintain control of the equipment during operation may provide evidence that such personnel do more than maintain, inspect and set up the equipment. *See Secretary's Decision No. 2007-161* (December 11, 2007).

• *Royalties*

Royalties paid, or agreed to be paid, either on a lump-sum or production basis, for tangible personal property used in this State are rentals subject to the applicable State and local sales or use tax [*Sales and Use Tax Technical Bulletins*, § 23-2; 17 NCAC 7B.4402].

• *Taxes on leased property*

Local property taxes imposed on tangible personal property being leased are an expense of conducting business incurred by the owner-lessor. Payments by the lessee to the lessor for property taxes constitute a part of the total consideration paid by the lessee for the lease of the property and, therefore, are includable as a part of the lessor's gross receipts that are subject to sales tax [*Sales and Use Tax Technical Bulletins*, § 23-3].

• *Insurance on leased property*

Insurance premiums on insurance that lessees purchase on their own property or to insure themselves against liability for damages to the property or person of others are exempt from tax, whether paid directly to the insurer or to the lessor as agent for transmittal to the insurer. Insurance premiums paid by lessees directly to the lessor as agent for transmittal to the insurer are exempt if they are separately stated from the charges for the lease or rental of tangible personal property in the lessor's records and on the invoice given to the lessee. If the insurance premiums are not separately stated, they are part of the taxable base [*Sales and Use Tax Technical Bulletins*, § 23-4].

• *Maintenance on leased property*

Sales of tangible personal property to registered lessors or retailers for the purpose of lease or rental exclusively are wholesale sales and not subject to tax provided properly executed certificates of resale are provided to vendors of this type of property. Sales of lubricants, repair parts, and accessories to lessors or retailers who use them to repair, recondition, or maintain leased or rented personal property are also wholesale sales when properly executed certificates of resale are provided to the vendors. Lessors are responsible for payment of any applicable State and local tax on the cost price of such items if they are used for a purpose other than repairing or maintaining leased or rented property or if they are resold as such [17 NCAC 7B.4403(a)]. When lessees purchase lubricants and repair parts to maintain tangible personal property being leased or rented, the lessee is liable for payment of the applicable State and local sales or use tax on the cost price [17 NCAC 7B.4403(b)].

• *Optional maintenance agreements on the lease of property*

A maintenance agreement is optional when the lessee is not required to purchase the maintenance agreement from the lessor and is free to contract with anyone he or she chooses to maintain the leased property [*Sales and Use Tax Technical Bulletins*, § 23-5.C.1.a]. If a lessor enters into a maintenance agreement to maintain leased property at the option of its customer (lessee) for a flat fee, whether the agreement is a separate contract or a part of the lease of the property and a separate charge is made to the customer for parts and supplies that are used in maintaining the leased property, receipts from the maintenance agreement are not subject to tax. The lessor is deemed to be using the repair parts or supplies in the performance of a service, and tax is due on the cost price of the repair parts or supplies used in performing the

¶1706

service. If, however, in connection with maintenance agreements, the lessor charges for parts or supplies not covered by the maintenance agreement and bills the customer for the parts or supplies, the lessor would be liable for collecting and remitting the applicable State and local sales or use tax on such transactions [*Sales and Use Tax Technical Bulletins*, § 23-5.C.2]. See also Secretary's Decision No. 2007-14 (June 26, 2007) (lessor of copier machines liable for use tax on materials and supplies consumed in performance of cost-per-copy optional maintenance agreement).

• *Mandatory maintenance agreements on the lease of property*

A maintenance agreement is mandatory if the lessee, as a condition of the lease, is required to purchase the maintenance agreement from the lessor [*Sales and Use Tax Technical Bulletins*, § 23-5.C.2]. If a maintenance agreement is mandatory, whether it is a separate agreement or a part of the lease of the property, the charge for the maintenance agreement is subject to the applicable State and local sales or use tax [*Sales and Use Tax Technical Bulletins*, § 23-5.C.3].

• *Equipment furnished with operator*

If owners of tangible personal property furnish operators or crews to operate the property, the owner is deemed to be rendering a service, and the receipts from the transaction are not subject to sales or use tax. Repair parts, lubricants, and other tangible personal property purchased by persons for use in providing tangible personal property with operator are subject to sales tax on the purchase price [17 NCAC 7B.4404].

• *Lease with an option to purchase*

Sales or use tax is due on the gross receipts derived from or the total amount agreed to be paid for the lease or rental of tangible personal property under a lease agreement with an option to purchase. If the agreement provides that the lessee will pay a stipulated amount at the time the option is exercised less a credit for a portion or all of the lease payments, the tax is due on the amount actually paid [17 NCAC 7B.4405].

> **Example:** X leases tangible personal property with an option to purchase from Y. X makes lease payments under the agreement of $200, on which tax has been paid. X decides to exercise the purchase option and pay $700 for the property. Additional tax is due on $500 at the time the option is exercised.

• *Sale of leased property*

When tangible personal property that has been leased is sold at retail, the retail sale is subject to the applicable rate of tax without regard to any tax which has been collected and remitted to the Department on receipts from the lease or rental of the property.

• *Conditional sales contracts*

Lease agreements with an option to purchase may contain some provisions which make the instrument a conditional sales contract even though denominated a lease with option to purchase. Such instruments may contain any one of the following provisions [17 NCAC 7B.4413]:

¶1706

(1) The risk of the property during the term of the lease is that of the lessee.

(2) That the lessee is to maintain, restore, or replace the property if damaged or destroyed during the term of the lease.

(3) The lessee is to pay the taxes and insurance on the property during the term of the lease. When any of these elements appear, the lease should be mailed to the Taxpayer Assistance Section of the Office Services Division for determination as to whether the instrument is a lease with an option to purchase or a conditional sales contract.

• *Extension of leases*

When tangible personal property, the sale of which is subject to a maximum tax, is leased for a definite period of time, the lease payments during the term of the lease are subject to the maximum tax. If the original lease contains provisions for extension, the extended term of the lease is part of the original lease, and the maximum tax applies to the extended period. However, if the original lease does not contain provision for extension, but a new lease agreement is subsequently entered into granting an extension or a new lease, the second lease (the extension agreement) does not have the benefit of the maximum tax by reason of the first lease [17 NCAC 7B.4411].

More information on leases can be obtained in §23 of the *Sales and Use Tax Technical Bulletins* and §4400 of Subchapter 7B of Title 17 of the North Carolina Administrative Code.

¶1707 Remote Sales

• *Wayfair*

The extent to which North Carolina or any other state can compel a person outside its borders to collect its tax is limited by federal constitutional provisions, the most important of which is the Commerce Clause. In *South Dakota v. Wayfair, Inc.*, 585 U.S. (2018), the Supreme Court overruled its decisions in *National Bellas Hess v. Department of Revenue of Illinois*, 386 U.S. 753 (1967), and *Quill Corp. v. North Dakota*, 504 U.S. 298 (1992) and eliminated the requirement that a remote seller have physical presence in a state to be subject to sales or use tax collection obligations. The Department of Revenue quickly announced that remote sellers with more than $100,000 in gross sales sourced to North Carolina or at least 200 separate transactions sourced to North Carolina in the current or previous calendar year must collect and remit North Carolina sales and use tax effective the later of November 1, 2018 or sixty days after meeting the gross sales or transaction threshold [Directive SD-18-6]. As discussed below, these economic thresholds have now been codified.

• *Remote sales*

North Carolina requires retailers engaged in business in North Carolina to collect tax on remote sales. A "remote" sale is a sale (1) of an item (2) by a retailer who receives the order outside North Carolina and (3) delivers the item or causes it to be delivered or makes it accessible to a person in North Carolina or performs a service sourced to North Carolina if (4) the purchaser is in North Carolina and (5) the order is placed by mail, by telephone, over the Internet, mobile phone application or by another method [G.S. § 105-164.3(33j)].

¶1707

• *Engaged in business*

A retailer making a remote sale will be treated as engaged in business in North Carolina and thus required to collect North Carolina sales tax on remote ales if the retailer satisfies any of the conditions described below:

(1) The retailer is a corporation engaged in business in North Carolina or a person domiciled in, a resident of, or a citizen of North Carolina [G.S. § 105-164.8(b)(1)].

(2) The retailer maintains retail establishments or offices in North Carolina regardless of whether the remote sales are connected with such establishments or offices [G.S. § 105-164.8(b)(2)].

(3) The retailer solicits or transacts business in North Carolina through employees, independent contractors, agents, or other representatives. A retailer is presumed to be soliciting or transacting business through an independent contractor or agent if the retailer enters into an agreement with a person of North Carolina under which the person directly to indirectly refers potential customers to the retailer for a commission or other consideration. Such referrals specifically include referrals via a link (or "clickthrough") on a web site. This presumption applies only if referrals from all North Carolina persons with such referral agreements result in gross receipts from sales to North Carolina customers of more than $10,000 during the preceding four quarterly periods [S.L. 2009-451, § 27A.3.(a) and (w)]. The law includes a rather unnecessary provision that the presumption may be rebutted by proof that the activities of North Carolina referral source were insufficient to establish nexus under the United States Constitution [G.S. § 105-164.8(b)(3)].

(4) The retailer creates nexus with North Carolina by purposefully or systematically exploiting the market provided by North Carolina by any media-assisted, media-facilitated, or media-solicited means, including the following [G.S. § 105-164.8(b)(5)]:

(a) Direct mail advertising.

(b) Distribution of catalogs.

(c) Computer-assisted shopping.

(d) Television, radio, or other electronic media.

(e) Telephone solicitation.

(f) Magazine or newspaper advertisement.

(g) Other media.

A retailer who purchases advertising (in any medium) is not considered to be engaged in business in North Carolina solely as a result of such purchases.

(5) Through compact or reciprocity with another jurisdiction of the United States, that jurisdiction uses its taxing power and its jurisdiction over the retailer in support of North Carolina's taxing power [G.S. § 105-164.8(b)(6)].

(6) The retailer consents expressly or by implication to the imposition of the sales and use tax [G.S. § 105-164.8(b)(7)].

(7) The retailer holds a wine shipper permit [G.S. § 105-164.8(b)(8)].

¶1707

(8) The retailer had gross sales of over $100,000 from remote sales sourced to North Carolina or at least 200 separate remote sales transactions sourced to North Carolina during the current or immediately preceding calendar year [G.S. § 105-164.8(b)(9)].

(9) The retailer is a marketplace facilitator and had gross sales of over $100,000 from remote sales sourced to North Carolina or at least 200 separate remote sales transactions sourced to North Carolina during the current or immediately preceding calendar year. For purposes of calculating these thresholds, direct sales by the marketplace facilitator and marketplace-facilitated sales for all sales by marketplace sellers are counted [G.S. § 105-164.8(b)(10)].

• *Special rules for marketplace-facilitated sales*

Payment of tax. A marketplace facilitator that meets the gross sales or transaction threshold necessary to be considered engaged in business in North Carolina is considered a retailer and must collect and remit tax on each marketplace-facilitated sale it makes regardless of whether a marketplace seller for whom it makes a marketplace-facilitated sale (1) has a physical presence in North Carolina, (2) is required to be registered to collect sales tax in North Carolina, or (3) would or would not have been required to collect sales tax in North Carolina had the sale not been made through a marketplace [G.S. § 105-164.4J(b)].

Report. A marketplace facilitator must inform each marketplace seller for whom it facilitates a sale sourced to North Carolina information regarding the gross sales from such sales and the number of facilitated transactions made on behalf of such seller. The information may be provided in any format and must be provided or made available no later than 10 days after the end of each calendar month [G.S. § 105-164.4J(c)].

Liability relief. The Department is prohibited from assessing a marketplace facilitator for failure to collect the correct amount of tax due if the marketplace facilitator can demonstrate that the failure to collect the correct amount of tax was due to incorrect information given to the marketplace facilitator by the marketplace seller (provided the marketplace facilitator did not receive specific written advice from the Secretary for the transaction at issue). This relief provision does not apply to a marketplace-facilitated sale for which the marketplace facilitator is the marketplace seller or if the marketplace facilitator is affiliated with the marketplace seller. If a marketplace facilitator is protected from assessment under this provision, the marketplace seller is liable for the tax due if the marketplace seller is engaged in business in North Carolina [G.S. § 105-164.4J(d)].

Refund of tax. If a marketplace facilitator who collected tax on a sale makes a refund to the purchaser of any portion of the sales price, the marketplace facilitator can seek a refund of tax paid on the refunded sales price under the provisions of G.S. 105-164.11A(a) (discussed at ¶ 1903) [G.S. § 105-164.4J(e)].

Class actions. No class action may be brought against a marketplace facilitator in North Carolina on behalf of customers arising from or related to an overpayment of sales or use tax collected on facilitated sales by a marketplace facilitator, regardless of how the claim is characterized [G.S. § 105-164.4J(f)].

Agreements. Marketplace facilitators and marketplace sellers are free to enter into agreements with each other regarding the collection and remittance of North Carolina

¶1707

sales tax on facilitated sales sourced to North Carolina, except that an a marketplace seller cannot be required to collect and remit sales and use tax on marketplace-facilitated sales [G.S. § 105-164.4J(g)].

Use tax obligation. Any purchaser in a marketplace-facilitated sale remains liable for use tax on the sale if the marketplace facilitator fails to collect and remit the tax due [G.S. § 105-164.4J(h)].

Limitation. This section does not apply to an accommodation facilitator, an admission facilitator, or a service contract facilitator whose collection and remittance requirements are set out in G.S. 105-164.4F, 105-164.4G, and 105-164.4I, respectively [G.S. § 105-164.4J(i)].

- *Local use taxes*

A retailer who is required to collect the State sales and use taxes must also collect a local use tax on a transaction if a local sales tax does not apply to the transaction [G.S. § 105-164.8(c)]. The sourcing principles discussed at ¶ 1602 determine whether a local sales tax or a local use tax applies to a transaction. Local sales and use taxes are discussed at ¶ 1607.

- *Voluntary collection of use tax by sellers*

The Secretary may enter into agreements with sellers pursuant to which the seller agrees to collect and remit on behalf of its customers State and local use taxes due on items the seller sells. For this purpose a "seller" is a person who is engaged in the business of selling items for use in North Carolina and who does not have sufficient nexus with North Carolina to be required to collect U.S. tax on the sales [G.S. § 105-164.6A(a)]. The agreement *must* contain certain mandatory provisions and *may* contain certain optional provisions as listed below.

(1) *Mandatory provisions:* The agreements *must* contain the following provisions:

(a) The seller is not liable for use tax not paid to it by a customer [G.S. § 105-164.6A(b)(1)].

(b) A customer's payment of a use tax to the seller relieves the customer of liability for the use tax [G.S. § 105-164.6A(b)(2)].

(c) The seller must remit all use taxes it collects from customers on or before the due date specified in the agreement, which may not be later than 31 days after the end of a quarter or other collection period. The collection period cannot be more often than annually if the seller's state and local tax collections are less than $1,000 in a calendar year [G.S. § 105-164.6A(b)(3)].

(d) A seller who fails to remit use taxes collected on behalf of its customers by the due date specified in the agreement is subject to interest and penalties provided in Article 9 of Chapter 105 [G.S. § 105-164.6A(b)(4)]. See Chapter 32.

(2) *Optional provisions:* The agreements *may* contain the following provisions:

(a) The seller will collect the use tax only on items that are subject to the general rate of tax [G.S. § 105-164.6A(c)(1)].

(b) The seller will collect local use taxes only to the extent they are at the same rate in every unit of local government in North Carolina [G.S. § 105-164.6A(c)(2)].

(c) The seller will remit the tax and file reports in the form prescribed by the Secretary [G.S. § 105-164.6A(c)(3)].

(d) Other provisions establishing the types of transactions on which the seller will collect tax and prescribing administrative procedures and requirements [G.S. § 105-164.6A(c)(4)].

¶1708 Food and Beverages

• *Food sales*

Food is exempt from the state sales and use taxes and is subject only to local sales and use taxes unless the food is specifically taxable [G.S. § § 105-164.13B(a) and 105-467(a)(5)].

"Food" is defined broadly as substances that are sold for ingestion or chewing by humans and are consumed for their taste or nutritional value. The substances may be in liquid, concentrated, solid, frozen, dried, or dehydrated form. The term does not include an alcoholic beverage (as define in G.S. § 105-113.68) or a tobacco product (as defined in G.S. § 105-113.4) [G.S. § 105-164.3(10)]. Food that is exempt from the State sales and use tax is subject to the 2% county tax. The additional $^1/2$% Mecklenburg County tax and the additional 1% Dare County tax (repealed effective July 1, 2006) do not apply to sales of good that is exempt from the State tax [Notice, North Carolina Department of Revenue, June 2006].

Specifically taxable food items: The following food items are subject to tax:

(1) Dietary supplements [G.S. § 105-164.13B(a)(2)].

(2) Food sold through vending machines [G.S. § 105-164.13B(a)(3)], although 50% of the sales price is exempt from tax [G.S. § 105-164.13(50)].

(3) Prepared food, other than bakery items sold without eating utensils by an artisan bakery. The term "bakery item" includes bread, rolls, buns, biscuits, bagels, croissants, pastries, donuts, danish, cakes, tortes, pies, tarts, muffins, bars, cookies, and tortillas. An "artisan bakery" is a bakery that meets all of the following requirements: (a) it derives over 80% of its gross receipts from bakery items; (b) its annual gross receipts (combined with the gross receipts of all related persons do not exceed $1,800,000 (a related person is a person described in Section 267(b) or Section 707(b) of the Code) [G.S. § 105-164-13B(a)(4)].

(4) Soft drinks [G.S. § 105-164.13B(a)(5)], although 50% of the sales price of canned or bottled soft drinks sold through vending machines is exempt from tax [G.S. § 105-164.13(50)].

(5) Candy [G.S. § 105-164.13B(a)(7)].

• *Prepared food*

Prepared food does not qualify for the state sales tax exemption and so is subject to state and local sales tax [G.S. § 105-164.13B(a)(4)].

¶1708

"Prepared food" defined: Food that meets at least one of the following conditions [G.S. § 105-164.3(28)]:

(1) It is sold in a heated state, or it is heated by the retailer.

(2) It consists of two or more goods mixed or combined by the retailer for sale as a single item. This does not include foods containing raw eggs, fish, meat, or poultry that require cooking by the consumer as recommended by the Food and Drug Administration to prevent food-borne illnesses.

(3) It is sold with eating utensils provided by the retailer (e.g., plates, knives, forks, spoons, glasses, cups, napkins, straws).

Not prepared food: Prepared food does not include food the retailer sliced, repackaged, or pasteurized but did not heat, mix, or sell with eating utensils [G.S. § 105-164.3(28)].

Items given away by merchant: If a retailer engaged in the business of selling prepared food or drink for immediate or on-premises consumptions also gives prepared food or drink to its patrons or employees free of charge, the food or drink given away is considered sold along with the food or drink sold [G.S. § 105-164.12C]. See also ¶ 1727.

• *Prepared food examples*

Breads, cakes, and similar bakery items: These items are not subject to the State tax unless they are considered to be prepared foods. For example, bread selected from a shelf on the bread aisle of a grocery store is not subject to the State tax. However, bread purchased in a grocery store is subject to the State tax if the retailer made the bread [*Notice*, North Carolina Department of Revenue, June 2006; see also Secretary's Decision Nos. 2007-12 (January 7, 2007) and 2007-13 (January 7, 2007) (bakeries liable for general state sales tax on baked goods sold through their thrift stores)].

Bakeries: Bakeries that make the items they sell (e.g., bread, pie, cake, pastry) must collect the general State tax and applicable local tax without regard to whether they are consumed on the premises or taken off the premises for home consumption [*Notice*, North Carolina Department of Revenue, June 2006].

Bakery thrift stores: The sales price of bread, rolls and buns sold at a bakery thrift store are exempt from North Carolina sales and use tax. Such baked goods are, however, subject to local sales and use taxes. A "bakery thrift store" is a retail outlet of a bakery that sells at wholesale over 90% of the items it makes and sells at the retail outlet day-old bread, rolls and buns returned to it by retailers that acquired these items from the bakery [G.S. § 105-164.13(27a); § 105-467(a)(5b)].

Resale of bakery items: Sales of bakery items that a bakery purchases from a third part and resells without alteration or heating are not subject to the State tax unless eating utensils are provided to the customer [*Notice*, North Carolina Department of Revenue, June 2006].

Prepared items: Items like pimiento cheese, cole slaw, and potato salad are not subject to the State tax unless they are considered to be prepared food. For example, potato salad selected from the refrigeration section of a grocery store is not subject to the State tax, but potato salad purchased in the deli section of a grocery store is subject to the State tax if the retailer made the potato salad [*Notice*, North Carolina Department of Revenue, June 2006].

Fried chicken: Fried chicken purchased in the frozen foods section of a grocery store is not subject to the State tax, but fried chicken is subject to the State tax as a prepared food if the retailer either combined two or more foods or sells it in a heated state or if the chicken is cooked by the retailer [*Notice,* North Carolina Department of Revenue, June 2006].

• *Prepared food sold to college students*

The sale of prepared food to college students in dining rooms operated by educational institutions or student organizations is subject to state and local sales tax. The retailer may be the educational institution or a third party food service provider depending on the terms of the contract between the two. *See generally* Directive SD-13-1.

• *Meals on transportation company diners*

Sales of prepared foods or meals by railroads, Pullman cars, steamships, airlines, or other transportation company diners are subject to the general rate of State tax and any applicable local sales or use tax while within North Carolina [17 NCAC 7B.2204].

• *Caterers*

All charges by persons engaged in the catering business that are connected with the furnishing, preparing, or serving of meals, foods, and other tangible personal property to users or consumers are subject to the 4% State tax and any applicable local sales or use tax. If caterers perform other services that are not a part of the charges for the furnishing, preparing, or serving of meals, foods, or other tangible personal property, the charges for such services are exempt *if separately stated* from taxable charges on the customer's invoice given at the time of the sale and in the vendor's records. If not separately stated, the otherwise exempt charges are taxable [17 NCAC 7B.2207]. See Secretary's Decision No. 2007-41 (June 26, 2007) (caterer liable for use tax on rental fees paid to lessor of tables, chairs and other items used for catering and was not permitted to treat the provision of such items to its customers as a taxable re-lease of the items).

• *Service charges or gratuity imposed of food, beverages, or prepared food*

Service charge of 20% or less: When a service charge is imposed on food, beverages, or prepared food, an amount that does not exceed 20% of the sales price is considered a tip and specifically exempt if it (1) is separately stated in the price list, menu, or written proposal and also in the invoice or bill; *and* (2) it is turned over to the service personnel directly providing service [G.S. § 105-164.13A; *Sales and Use Tax Technical Bulletins,* § 19-13.A]. If any part of the 20% gratuity is shared with personnel not directly involved in the service of food, beverages, or prepared food, the 20% gratuity is a part of the taxable sales price. For example, the exemption does not apply to service charges if any part is distributed to chefs, bartenders, bus boys, hosts, maitres d', valets, coat checkers, managers, and supervisors even if they may occasionally serve food or drinks directly to customers [*Sales and Use Tax Technical Bulletins,* § 19-13.B].

Service charge in excess of 20%: If a service charge exceeds 20%, and 20% of the gratuity is given to the personnel directly involved in the service of the food, beverages, or prepared food, the 20% given to food service personnel is exempt from tax when the other statutory conditions for exemption are met; and the amount of the gratuity in excess of 20% is taxable as part of the sales price. If persons other than those directly involved in the service of food share in the 20% service charge or gratuity, the total amount of the gratuity is taxable as part of the sales price [*Sales and Use Tax Technical Bulletins*, § 19-13.C].

Warning

Note that only the amount of gratuities in excess of 20% can be shared with employees other than the food and beverage staff (*e.g.,* coat checkers, maitres d'hotel, bell hops, bus boys) without resulting in inclusion of the entire gratuity in the taxable sales price.

- *Administration of local food tax*

The Secretary of Revenue administers local sales and use taxes imposed on food as if they were State taxes [G.S. § 105-164.13B(b)].

¶1709 Real Property Contractors

- *Real property contractors*

A real property contractor (see ¶1603 for definition) is considered to be the consumer of the tangible personal property or certain digital property that the contractor purchases, installs or applies for others to fulfill a real property contract and that is used to fulfill that contract or that becomes part of the real property. Consequently, a North Carolina retailer must collect tax on the sales price of an item sold at retail to a real property contractor unless a specific exemption applies [G.S. § 105-164.4H(a)]. If a retailer does not collect tax on retail sales to a real property contractor, the contractor and the real property owner may be jointly and severally liable for the tax due (see G.S. § 105-164.6(b)) or the real property contractor may be considered a retailer-contractor (see below) [G.S. § 105-164.4H(a)]. Because a real property contractor is considered the consumer of the items the contractor purchases and installs, the real property contractor's invoice or other documentation to a person should not include a separate amount for tax for the real property contract. If it does, the amount of tax shown is treated as an erroneous collection and must be remitted to the Secretary [G.S. § 105-164.4H(c)].

See also *Directive SD-15-1* (2015), *revised*, October 25, 2016, and Directive SD-16-3 and Directive SD-18-1.

- *Substantiation*

Services to real property will be treated as sales of taxable repair, maintenance, and installation services unless the taxpayer can establish an exemption or substantiate that the transaction is a real property contract or a mixed transaction contract. A taxpayer may substantiate that a transaction is a real property contract or a mixed transaction contract by the receipt of an affidavit of capital improvement, although other records may also be used. An affidavit of capital improvement will be sufficient to substantiate that the contract should be taxed as a real property contract absent fraud or other egregious activities. The issuer of the affidavit (and not the recipient) is liable for any additional tax due on the transaction if it is determined that the transaction does not involve a capital improvement. The Secretary is authorized to establish guidelines for transactions where an affidavit of capital improvement is not required [G.S. § 105-164.4H(a1)].

- *Retailer-contractors*

A retailer-contractor (see ¶ 1603 for definition) acts as a retailer when it makes a sale at retail. A retailer-contractor that contracts to perform a real property contract acts as a real property contractor. In such cases, when the retailer-contractor purchases tangible personal property or certain digital property to be installed or applied to real property or to fulfill the contract, those items may be purchased under an exemption certificate if the retailer-contractor also purchases inventory or services from the seller for resale. When the retailer-contractor withdraws the items from inventory and installs or applies them to real property the retailer contractor must accrue and pay use tax on the retailer-contractor's purchase price of the items. Property that the retailer-contractor withdraws from inventory that does not become part of the real property is also subject to use tax [G.S. § 105-164.4H(b)]. See also *Directive SD-15-1* (2015).

- *Subcontractor of a retailer-contractor*

If a retailer-contractor subcontracts any part of a real property contract to a subcontractor, and the subcontractor purchases tangible personal property or digital property that is installed or applied to real property or a service used to fulfill the contract, the subcontractor must pay tax on the property at the time of purchase. If the subcontractor does not pay tax on the purchase of the property, the subcontractor, the retailer-contractor, the real property owner and any lessee of the real property are jointly and severally liable for the tax. The liability of any of these parties who did not purchase the property or service may be satisfied by getting an affidavit from the purchaser certifying that the tax has been paid [G.S. § 105-164.4H(b)].

- *Mixed transaction contracts*

A mixed transaction contract is taxed as follows [G.S. § 105-164.4H(d)].

De minimis rule. If the allocated sales price of the taxable repair, maintenance, and installation services included in the contract does not exceed 25% of the contract price, then the entire contract is taxed as a real property contract [G.S. § 105-164.4H(d)(1)].

Bifurcation. If the allocated sales price of the taxable repair, maintenance, and installation services included in the contract exceeds 25% of the contract price, then the contract is bifurcated into a real property contract and a contract for the provision of repair, maintenance and installation services. Any purchase of tangible personal property or certain digital property to fulfill the real property contract are taxed under the rules for real property contracts. Any taxable repair, maintenance, and installation services are taxed in accordance with the rules for repair, maintenance and installation services. The taxpayer must determine the price for each taxable repair, maintenance, and installation service in the contract based on a reasonable allocation of revenue that is supported by the taxpayer's records kept in the ordinary course of business [G.S. § 105-164.4H(d)(2)].

¶1709

¶1710 [Reserved]

¶1711 Property Management Contracts

Real property management services have never been subject to sales tax in North Carolina. However, real property managers often provide repair, maintenance and installation services with respect to the properties they manage, and distinguishing between nontaxable property management services from taxable repair, maintenance and installation services can be difficult. The following rules have been enacted to provide greater clarity on this issue.

• *Property management contract*

A property management contract is a written contract obligating a person (the real property manager) to provide five or more of the following real property management services: (1) hiring and supervising employees for real property; (2) providing a person to manage real property; (3) receiving and applying revenues received from real property owners or tenants; (4) providing repair, maintenance, and installation services to comply with obligations of a homeowners' association or a landlord under a lease, rental, or management agreement; (5) arranging for a third party to provide repair, maintenance, and installation services; (6) incurring and paying expenses for the management, repair, and maintenance of the real property; (7) handling administrative affairs for the real property [G.S. § 105-164.3].

• *General rule of nontaxability*

As a general rule, repair, maintenance and installation services provided by a real property manager as part of the services rendered under a property management contract are not taxable [G.S. § 105-164.4K]. Where a real property manager provides repair, maintenance and installation services that are not taxable, the real property manager is treated as the consumer of the items that he purchases, installs, applies, or otherwise uses to fulfill the property management contract. Retailers must therefore collect tax on the sales price of such items sold to a real property manager unless an exemption is available [G.S. § 105-164.4K(d)].

• *Exceptions*

Repair, maintenance, and installation services provided by a real property manager under a property management contract are taxable in the circumstances described below [G.S.§ 105-164.4K(a)]. In these circumstances, the real property manager is treated as a retailer unless an exemption is available [G.S. § 105-164.4K(d)].

Additional charge. Repair, maintenance, installation services provided by the real property manager are taxable if they are provided for an additional charge.

Mark-up. Repair, maintenance, installation services provided by the real property manager are taxable if the real property manager arranges for a third party to provide the services and the real property manager imposes an additional contract amount or charge for arranging these services.

25% threshold. Repair, maintenance, installation services provided by the real property manager are taxable if more than 25% of the time spent managing the real property for a billing or invoice period is attributable to otherwise taxable repair, maintenance, and installation services.

Where services are taxable because the 25% threshold has been exceeded, the real property manager must determine an allocated sales price for the repair, maintenance, and installation services portion of the property management contract based on a reasonable allocation of revenue supported by the manager's business records kept in the ordinary course of business. The charges for the taxable repair, maintenance, and installation services must be separately stated on the invoice or similar billing document given to the customer at the time of the sale.

• *Specific exclusions*

The following repair, maintenance, and installation services provided by a real property manager pursuant to a property management contract are specifically not taxable [G.S. § 105-164.4K(b)]: (1) services to inspect, identify or attempt to identify the source of a problem in order to determine what is needed to restore the real property to working order or good condition, and (2) services to inspect or monitor the real property, including the normal operation of all systems that are part of the real property.

• *Substantiation*

A real property manager must substantiate that repair, maintenance and installation services rendered are not taxable, whether because they do not exceed the 25% threshold, are specifically excluded or otherwise exempt. With respect to the 25% threshold, the substantiation must be based on a reasonable approximation of the real property management services provided, supported by the manager's business records kept in the ordinary course of business, contemporaneously provided for each billing or invoice period and maintained in the manager's business records [G.S. § 105-164.4K(c)].

• *Grace Period*

The Department is prohibited from taking any action to assess any tax due on repair, maintenance and installation services rendered by a real property manager for a filing period beginning on or after January 1, 2019, and ending before January 1, 2021, unless the retailer received specific written advice from the Secretary for the transactions at issue. The grace period provisions of G.S. § 105-244.3 (see ¶ 1906) are also available [G.S. § 105-164.4K(f)].

¶1712 [Reserved]

¶1713 Canned Computer Software

"Custom computer software" is exempt from the sales and use tax. See ¶ 1809. Prewritten software (*i.e.*, canned software) that is not designed to the specifications of a particular customer is specifically excluded from the definition of "custom computer software" and is, therefore taxable. Before July 15, 2003, canned software that had been modified to a customer's specifications was considered nontaxable custom software. On and after July 15, 2003, only the cost of the custom modifications is exempt [G.S. § 105-164.13]. License fees for upgrades in software delivered on a storage medium are taxable under this rule even though the upgrades are accessed through alphanumeric codes delivered over the Internet [*Secretary's Decision No. 2002-141 (August 9, 2002)*].

¶1714 Drop Shipments

A drop shipment is a shipment of tangible personal property from a seller directly to the purchaser's customer, at the direction of the purchaser. Drop shipments are also known as third-party drop shipments [*Sales and Use Tax Technical Bulletins, §42-4*]. Generally, a retailer accepts an order from a customer and, at the direction of the customer/purchaser, places this order with a third party (usually a manufacturer or wholesale distributor) and directs the third party to ship the goods directly to the purchaser's customer. Drop shipments are examined as two transactions: (1) the sale from the primary seller to the customer/purchaser and (2) the sale from the customer/purchaser to the purchaser's customer.

• *All parties located in North Carolina*

When all the parties are located in North Carolina, the original order from a retailer is not taxable if the retailer furnishes a resale certificate to the primary seller. The retailer (the secondary seller) then collects sales tax on its secondary sale to its customer. However, different considerations arise if all the parties are not located in North Carolina.

• *At least one party located outside North Carolina*

A North Carolina wholesaler is not required to collect North Carolina sales tax on its sales to an out-of-state retailer or an out-of-state wholesaler properly registered in another taxing jurisdiction when it drop ships taxable tangible personal property to the out-of-state retailer's or out-of-state wholesaler's customers in North Carolina. The purchaser is liable for reporting the applicable State and county use tax on these purchase [*Sales and Use Tax Technical Bulletins, §42-4.A*].

This position is based on the decision by the North Carolina Court of Appeals in the case of *VSA, Inc. v. Faulkner*, 126 N.C. App. 421, 485 S.E. 2d 348 (1997). The facts in *VSA* were as follows:

(1) Taxpayer was a North Carolina wholesaler.

(2) Taxpayer was properly registered for North Carolina sales and use tax purposes.

(3) Taxpayer sold its products to vendees located in another state.

(4) Taxpayer's vendees were not engaged in business in North Carolina.

(5) Taxpayer's vendees were properly registered in their taxing jurisdictions.

(6) Taxpayer's vendees resold the products to North Carolina customers.

(7) Taxpayer delivered the products to its vendees' customers in North Carolina.

Drop shipments to North Carolina locations of the original customer/purchaser: In-state retailers or in-state wholesalers and out-of-state retailers or wholesalers engaged in business in North Carolina making retail sales of taxable tangible personal property to out-of-state users or consumers where property is drop shipped to purchaser's locations in North Carolina continue to be subject to the sales tax [*Sales and Use Tax Technical Bulletins,* § 42-4.B].

¶1715 Bundled Transactions

• *Bundled transactions*

Defined: A "bundled transaction" is a retail sale of two or more distinct and identifiable items, at least one of which is taxable and one of which is nontaxable, for one nonitemized price. The term does not apply to real property or services to real property. Items are not sold for one nonitemized price if an invoice or another sales document made available to the purchaser separately identifies the price of each item [G.S. § 105-164.3(1*l*)].

Not bundled transactions: A bundled transaction does not include the retail sale of the following:

(1) An item and any packaging item that accompanies the item and is exempt under G.S. § 105-164.13(23) [G.S. § 105-164.3(1i)(a)].

(2) A sale of two or more items whose combined price varies or is negotiable, depending on the items the purchaser selects [G.S. § 105-164.3(1i)(b)].

(3) A sale of an item accompanied by a transfer of another item with no additional consideration [G.S. § 105-164.3(1i)(c)].

(4) An item and the delivery or installation of the item [G.S. § 105-164.3(1i)(d)].

(5) An item and any service necessary to complete the sale [G.S. § 105-164.3(1i)(e)].

(6) The sale of tangible personal property and a service (or of two services) where the property (or one service) is essential to the use of the service (or the second service), is provided exclusively in connection with the service (or the second service) and the service (or the second service) is the true object of the transaction [*Sales and Use Tax Directive SD-07-1* (October 1, 2007)].

• *Tax application*

Tax applies to the sales price of a bundled transaction unless one of the following applies [G.S. § 105-164.4D(a)]:

(1) *50% test:* All of the items in the bundle are tangible personal property; the price of the taxable items in the bundle does not exceed 50% of the price of the bundle; and the bundle includes one or more of the following exempt items:

(a) Food that is exempt under G.S. § 105-164.13B.

(b) Drugs exempt under G.S. § 105-164.13(13).

(c) Medical devices, equipment, or supplies exempt under G.S. § 105-164.13(12).

If more than half of the bundle consists of exempt food items, the total price of the bundle is subject to the 2% local food tax. *See Sales and Use Tax Directive SD-07-1* (October 1, 2007). If more than half of the bundle is attributable to exempt medical products, the total price of the bundle is exempt, provided that the other items in the bundle are limited to prescription medical items and prosthetic devices. *See Sales and Use Tax Directive SD-07-1* (October 1, 2007).

(2) *Allocation:* The bundle includes a service, and the retailer determines an allocated price for each item in the bundle based on a reasonable allocation of revenue that is supported by the retailer's business records kept in the ordinary course of business. In this circumstance, tax applies to the allocated price of each taxable item in the bundle.

(3) *10% test:* The price of the items in the bundle does not exceed 10% of the price of the bundle, and the 50% test and allocation do not apply.

(4) *Prepaid meal plan:* The bundle includes a prepaid meal plan and a dollar value that declines with use. In this case, tax applies to the allocated price of the prepaid meal plan. The tax applies to the dollar value that declines with use as the dollar value is presented for payment.

(5) *Tuition, room and meals:* The bundle includes tuition, room and meals offered by an institution of higher education. In this case tax applies to the allocated price of the meals as determined by the institution of higher education based on a reasonable allocation of revenue that is supported by the institution's business records kept in the ordinary course of business.

Determining threshold: A retailer of a bundled transaction may use either the retailer's purchase price or the retailer's sales price to determine if the transaction meets the 50% test or the 10% test but cannot use a combination of purchase price and sales price to make this determination. If a bundled transaction subject to the 10% test includes a service contract, the retailer must use the full term of the contract in determining whether the transaction meets the 10% threshold [G.S. § 105-164.12B(b)].

- *Tangible personal property sold below cost with conditional contract*

Conditional contract defined: A conditional contract is one in which all of the following conditions are met [G.S. § 105-164.12B(a)]:

(1) A seller transfers an item of tangible personal property to a consumer on the condition that the consumer enter into an agreement to purchases on an ongoing basis for a minimum period of at least six (6) months.

(2) The agreement requires the consumer to pay a cancellation fee to the seller if the consumer cancels the contract for services within the minimum period.

(3) For the item transferred, the seller charges the consumer a price that, after any price reduction, is below the purchase price the seller paid for the item. The seller's purchase price is presumed to be no greater than the price the seller paid, as shown on the seller's purchase invoice, for the same item within 12 months before the seller entered into the conditional contract.

Sales price: If a seller transfers an item of tangible personal property as part of a conditional contract, a sale has occurred, and the sales price of the item is presumed to be the retail price at which the item would sell in the absence of the conditional contracts. Sales tax is due at the general rate at the time of the transfer on the following: (1) any part of the presumed sales price the consumer pays at that time, if the service in the contract is taxable at the combined general rate; (2) the presumed sales price, if the service in the contract is not taxable at the combined general rate; or (3) if any part of the service contract is not taxable at the combined general rate, the percentage of the presumed sales price equal to the percentage of the service in the contract that is not taxable at the combined general rate [G.S. § 105-164.12B(b)].

¶1716 Warranties

• *Manufacturer's warranty*

A "manufacturer's warranty" is an explicit warranty the manufacturer of an item extends to the purchaser of the item as part of the purchase price of the item. If an item is defective, the warranty allows the purchaser to return the item and receive either a replacement for the defective item or the repair of the defective item. Whether the cost of the replacement item or any parts used to repair the defective item is taxable depends on whether the manufacturer charges the purchaser for the replacement item or the repair parts [*Sales and Use Tax Technical Bulletins*, § 41-1.A].

Manufacturer charges: If the manufacturer charges the purchaser for the replacement item or the repair parts, sales or use tax is due on the amount paid for the replacement item or repair parts.

Manufacturer does not charge: If the manufacturer does not charge the purchaser for the replacement item or repair parts, no tax is due on the cost of the replacement item or on the cost of repair parts. This applies when the manufacturer makes the repairs and when the manufacturer contracts with a dealer or another person to make the repairs on behalf of the manufacturer. A small, fixed deductible fee a manufacturer charges a purchaser who receives a replacement item or repair of a defective item is not considered a charge; this fee is unrelated to the cost of the replacement item or repair part and is a nontaxable service fee.

• *Dealer's warranty*

A "dealer's warranty" is an explicit warranty the seller of an item extends to the purchaser of the item as part of the purchase price of the item. If the item is defective, the warranty allows the purchaser to return the item and receive either a replacement for the defective item or the repair of the defective item. This type of warranty normally occurs when there is no manufacturer's warranty. The same principles that apply to a manufacturer's warranty apply to a dealer's warranty. Thus, if the dealer charges the purchaser for the replacement item or the repair parts, sales or use tax is due on the amount paid for the replacement item or repair parts. If the dealer does not charge the purchaser for the replacement item or the repair parts, no tax is due on the replacement item or on the cost of repair parts [*Sales and Use Tax Technical Bulletins*, § 41-1.B].

• *After-warranty adjustment*

An "after-warranty adjustment" is an arrangement between a customer, a dealer, and a manufacturer. Under the arrangement, the dealer and the manufacturer agree to replace or repair an item purchased by a customer that is of the type made by the manufacturer and sold by the dealer for a percentage of the amount they would charge in the absence of the arrangement. The arrangement can apply to charges for labor as well as for parts and materials [*Sales and Use Tax Technical Bulletins*, § 41-1.C].

¶1716

If a replacement is made under the arrangement, the dealer supplies the replacement from the dealer's inventory. If a repair is made under the arrangement, the dealer supplies the parts from its inventory and performs the required labor needed to accomplish the repair. The manufacturer then reimburses the dealer for the agreed upon portion of the total charges, and the dealer absorbs the remaining unpaid amounts the dealer incurred. For either a replacement or repair, the dealer uses tangible personal property withdrawn from its inventory and is liable for sales or use tax on the dealer's cost of the property used.

• *Manufacturer recall*

A manufacturer recall is an action by a manufacturer of an item or a component part of an item to replace the item or component part for all customers who have purchased the item due to a defect or other problem, even if the manufacturer's warranty has expired. A recall is generally made due to health or safety reasons. The same principles that apply to a manufacturer's warranty apply to a manufacturer recall. If a charge is made for the replacement item or part, sales or use tax is due on the amount paid for the replacement item or part. If no charge is made for the replacement item or part, no tax is due on the cost of the replacement item or part. These principles apply for both mandatory and voluntary recalls and also apply when the manufacturer makes the repairs or contracts with a dealer or another person to make the repairs on behalf of the manufacturer [*Sales and Use Tax Technical Bulletins*, § 41-1.D].

¶1717 Aircraft—Boats—Qualified Jet Engines

• *Boats*

A 3% tax is imposed on the sales price of each boat, including all attached accessories at the time of delivery to the purchaser. The maximum tax on such items is $1,500 [G.S. § 105-164.4(1b)].

• *Aircraft*

Aircraft are subject to tax at the general rate, but the maximum tax is $2,500 per article [G.S. § 105-164.4(a)(1a)].

• *Qualified jet engines*

Qualified jet engines (*i.e.*, engines certified under Part 33 of Title 14 of the Code of Federal Regulations) are subject to tax at the general rate, but the purchaser may apply for a direct pay permit to exempt the purchase from sales tax and cap the use tax on the engine at $2,500 [G.S. § 105-164.27A(a2)].

• *Refunds*

Refunds for special entities are discussed at ¶1903.

¶1718 Motor Vehicles

Motor vehicles are not subject to the sales and use tax; they are taxable under the provisions of the highway use tax. See ¶2901.

¶1719 Telecommunications Services

The gross receipts derived from providing telecommunications service and ancillary service, including any separately stated charges billed to a customer for repair, maintenance and installation services or a contribution in aid of construction, are subject to the combined general rate of 7% for all transactions sourced to North Carolina [G.S. § 105-164.4(a)(4c)].

• *Definition of terms*

The following definitions apply in the context of the tax on telecommunications services:

Ancillary service: "Ancillary service" is a service associated with or incidental to the provision of telecommunications service, including detailed billing, directory assistance, voicemail, caller ID, call forwarding, three-way and conference calling [G.S. § 105-164.3(1b)].

Call-by-call basis: "Call-by-call basis" is a method of charging for a telecommunications service whereby the price of the service is measured by individual calls [G.S. § 105-164.4C(h)(1a)].

Call center: "Call center" is a business that is primarily engaged in providing support services to customers by telephone to support products or services of the business. A business is primarily engaged in providing support services by telephone if at least 60% of its calls are incoming [G.S. § § 105-164.4C(h)(2), 105-164.27A(b)].

Mobile telecommunications service: "Mobile telecommunications service" is a radio communication service carried on between mobile stations or receivers and land stations and by mobile stations communicating among themselves and includes all of the following: (1) both one-way and two-way radio communication services; (2) a mobile service that provides a regularly interacting group of base, mobile, portable, and associated control and relay stations for private one-way or two-way land mobile radio communications by eligible users over designated areas of operation; and (3) any service for which a federal license is required in a personal communications service [G.S. § § 105-164.4C(h)(3), 105-164.3(21)].

Place of primary use: "Place of primary use" is the street address representative of where the use of a customer's telecommunications service primarily occurs. The street address must be the customer's residential street address or primary business street address. For mobile telecommunications service the street address must be within the licensed service area of the service provider. If the customer who contracted with the telecommunications provider for the telecommunications service is not the end user of the service, the end user is considered the customer for the purpose of determining the place of primary use [G.S. § § 105-164.4C(h)(4), 105-164.3(26a)].

Postpaid calling service: "Postpaid calling service" is a telecommunications service that is charged on a call-by-call basis and is obtained by making payment at the time of the call either through the use of a credit or payment mechanism (*e.g.*, bank card, travel card, credit card, debit card) or by charging the call to a telephone number that is not associated with the origination or termination of the telecommunications service. A postpaid calling service includes a service that meets all the requirements of a prepaid telephone calling service, except the exclusive use requirement [G.S. § 105-164.4C(h)(5)].

Prepaid telephone calling service: "Prepaid telephone calling service" is defined at ¶ 1720.

Private telecommunications service: "Private telecommunications service" is a telecommunications service that entitles a subscriber of the service to exclusive or priority use of a communications channel or group of channels [G.S. § 105-164.4C(h)(7)].

Telecommunications service: "Telecommunications service" is the transmission, conveyance, or routing of voice, data, audio, video, or any other information or signals to a point, or between or among points, by or through any electronic, radio, satellite, optical, microwave, or other medium, regardless of the protocol used for the transmission, conveyance, or routing. The term includes mobile telecommunications service and vertical services [G.S. § 105-164.3(48)].

• *Base and rate*

The gross receipts derived from providing telecommunications service or ancillary service in North Carolina are taxed at the combined general rate [G.S. § 105-164.4C(a)]. Telecommunications service is provided in North Carolina if the service is sourced to North Carolina under the sourcing principles of G.S. § 105-164.4C(a1) and (a2). See "General sourcing principles," below. Ancillary services are provided in North Carolina if the telecommunications service to which it is ancillary is provided in North Carolina.

Federal Definitions Apply to Mobile Telecommunications

The definitions and provisions of the federal Mobile Telecommunications Sourcing Act apply to the sourcing and taxation of mobile telecommunications services [G.S. § 105-164.4C(a)].

• *General sourcing principles*

The following general sourcing principles apply to telecommunications services. If a service falls within one of the exceptions (see "Sourcing exceptions," below), the service is sourced in accordance with the exception instead of the general sourcing principle [G.S. § 105-164.4C(a1)].

(1) *Flat rate:* A telecommunications service that is not sold on a call-by-call basis is sourced to North Carolina if the primary use is in North Carolina [G.S. § 105-164.4C(a1)(1)].

(2) *General call-by-call:* A telecommunications service that is sold on a call-by-call basis and is not a postpaid calling service is sourced to North Carolina in the following circumstances:

(a) The call both originates and terminates in North Carolina [G.S. § 105-164.4C(a1)(2)a].

(b) The call either originates or terminates in North Carolina and the telecommunications equipment from which the call originates or terminates and to which the call is charged is located in North Carolina. This rule applies regardless of where the call is billed or paid [G.S. § 105-164.4C(a1)(2)b.].

(3) *Postpaid:* A postpaid calling service is sourced to the origination point of the telecommunications signal as first identified by either the seller's telecommunications system or, if the system used to transport the signal is not the seller's system, by information the seller receives from its service provider [G.S. § 105-164.4C(a1)(3)].

• *General sourcing exceptions*

The following telecommunications services and products are sourced in accordance with special rules specified in G.S. § 105-164.4C. The special rules for exceptions are as follows [G.S. § 105-164.4C(a2)]:

(1) Mobile telecommunications service is sourced to the place of primary use, unless the service (a) is a prepaid wireless calling service or (b) is air-to-ground radiotelephone service.

(2) Prepaid telephone calling service is sourced in accordance with G.S. § 105-164.4B. See ¶ 1720.

(3) Private telecommunications service is sourced in accordance with G.S. § 105-164.4C(e). See "Private lines," below.

• *Sourcing rules for private lines*

The gross receipts derived from private telecommunications service are sourced as follows [G.S. § 105-164.4C(e)]:

(1) If all the customer's channel termination points are located in North Carolina, the service is sourced to North Carolina.

(2) If all the customer's channel termination points are not located in North Carolina and the service is billed on the basis of channel termination points, the charge for each channel termination point located in North Carolina is sourced to North Carolina.

(3) If all the customer's channel termination points are not located in North Carolina and the service is billed on the basis of channel mileage, the following rules apply:

(a) A charge for a channel segment between two channel termination points located in North Carolina is sourced to North Carolina.

(b) Fifty percent (50%) of a charge for a channel segment between a channel termination point located in North Carolina and a channel termination point located in another state is sourced to North Carolina.

(4) If all the customer's channel termination points are not located in North Carolina and the service is not billed on the basis of channel termination points or channel mileage, a percentage of the charge for the service is sourced to North

Carolina. The percentage is determined by dividing the number of channel termination points in North Carolina by the total number of channel termination points.

- *Call center cap*

The gross receipts tax on interstate telecommunications service that originates outside North Carolina, terminates in North Carolina, and is provided to a call center that has a North Carolina direct pay certificate may not exceed $50,000 in a calendar year. This cap applies separately to each legal entity [G.S. § 105-164.4C(f)].

- *Credit*

A taxpayer who pays a tax legally imposed by another state on a telecommunications service taxable in North Carolina is allowed a credit against the 6% telecommunications services tax [G.S. § 105-164.4C(g)].

- *Direct pay permits*

Persons who purchase telecommunications services and call centers that purchase certain interstate telecommunications services may apply for direct pay permits. See explanation at ¶ 1812.

- *Local restrictions*

Counties and cities may not impose a license, franchise, or privilege tax on companies that provide telecommunications services [G.S. §§ 153A-152(b), 160A-211(c)(2)].

¶ 1720 Prepaid Telephone Calling Service

- *Imposition*

The sale or recharge of prepaid telephone calling service is taxable at the general rate of tax [G.S. § 105-164.4(a)(4d)]. The tax also applies to a service that is sold in conjunction with prepaid wireless calling service. The tax applies regardless of whether tangible personal property (e.g., card, telephone) is transferred. Prepaid telephone calling service taxed under this provision is not subject to tax as a telecommunications service.

- *Prepaid telephone calling service*

The term "prepaid telephone calling service" includes (a) prepaid calling service or prepaid wireless calling service [G.S. § 105-164.3(27)].

- *Prepaid calling service*

A "prepaid calling service" is a right that meets all of the following requirements [G.S. § 105-164.3(26b)]:

    (1) It authorizes the exclusive purchase of telecommunications service.

    (2) It must be paid for in advance.

(3) It enables the origination of calls by means of an access number, authorization code, or another similar means, regardless of whether the access number or authorization code is manually or electronically dialed.

(4) It is sold in predeterminded units or dollars whose number or dollar value declines with use and is known on a continuous basis.

• *Prepaid wireless calling service*

A "prepaid wireless calling service" is a right that meets all of the following requirements [G.S. § 105-164.3(27a)]:

(1) It authorizes the purchase of mobile telecommunications service, either exclusively or in conjunction with other services.

(2) It must be paid for in advance.

(3) It is sold in predetermined units or dollars whose number or dollar value declines with use and is known on a continuous basis.

Prepaid wireless telecommunications 911 service charge: Effective July 1, 2013, a 70¢ 911 service charge is imposed (in addition to the sales tax) on each in-state retail purchase of prepaid wireless telecommunications service made for any purpose other than resale [G.S. § 62A-43].

• *Sourcing*

Prepaid telephone calling service is taxable at the point of sale, not the point of use [G.S. § 105-164.4(a)(4d)]. If the sale or recharge does not take place at a retailer's place of business, the sale or recharge is considered to have taken place at one of the following: (1) the customer's shipping address, if an item of tangible personal property is shipped to the customer as part of the transaction; or (2) the customer's billing address or, for mobile telecommunications service, the customer's service address, if no tangible personal property is shipped to the customer as part of the transaction.

¶1721 Video Programming

The combined general rate applies to the gross receipts derived from providing video programming to a subscriber in North Carolina, including any separately stated charges billed to a customer for repair, maintenance and installation services or a contribution in aid of construction. Taxable video programming includes cable service and direct-to-home satellite service [G.S. § 105-164.4(a)(6)]. "Video programming" is programming provided by, or generally considered comparable to programming provided by, a television broadcast station, regardless of the method of delivery [G.S. § 105-164.3(50c)].

¶1722 Spirituous Liquors

The sale of spirituous liquors in ABC stores is subject to the combined general rate of tax [G.S. § 105-164.4(a)(7)]. "Spirituous liquors" means distilled spirits or ethyl alcohol, including spirits of wine, whiskey, rum, brandy, gin, and all other distilled spirits and mixtures of cordials, liqueur, and premixed cocktails, in closed containers for beverage use regardless of their dilution [G.S. § 18B-101(14)]. "Mixed beverage" means either (1) a drink composed in whole or in part of spirituous liquor and served in a quantity less than the quantity contained in a closed package, or (2) a premixed cocktail served from a closed package containing only one serving [G.S. § 18B-101(10)].

¶1723 Internet Data Centers

Sales of electricity for use at an eligible Internet data center and eligible business property to be located and used at an eligible Internet data center are exempt from the North Carolina sales and use tax [G.S. § 105-164.13(55)].

• *Eligible business property*

"Eligible business property" is property that is capitalized for tax purposes under the Internal Revenue Code and is used for one of the following purposes:

(1) For the provision of a service included in the business of the primary user of the datacenter, including equipment cooling systems for managing the performance of the property [G.S. § 105-164.13(55)a.].

(2) For the generation, transformation, transmission, distribution, or management of electricity, including exterior substations and other business personal property used for these purposes [G.S. § 105-164.13(55)b.].

(3) To provide related computer engineering or computer science research [G.S. § 105-164.13(55)c.].

• *Eligible Internet datacenter*

An "eligible Internet data center" is a facility that satisfies all of the following conditions [G.S. § 105-164.e(8e)]:

(1) *Use:* The facility is used primarily or is to be used primarily by a business in software publishing included in industry 511210 of NAICS or an Internet activity included in industry 519130 of NAICS [G.S. § 105-164.3(8e)].

(2) *Composition:* The facility comprises a structure or series of structures located or to be located on a single parcel of land or on contiguous parcels of land that are commonly owned or owned by affiliation with the operator of that facility [G.S. § 105-164.3(8e)b.].

(3) *Location:* The facility is located or to be located in a county that was designated (at the time of application for written determination, see (4) below) either an enterprise tier one, two, or three area, regardless of any subsequent change in county enterprise or development tier status [G.S. § 105-164.3(8e)c.].

(4) Written determination: The Secretary of Commerce has made a written determination that at least $250,000,000 in private funds has been or will be invested in real property or eligible business property (or a combination of both) at the facility within five (5) years after the commencement of construction of the facility [G.S. § 105-164.3(83)d.].

• *Forfeiture [G.S. §105-164.13(55)]*

Failure to make enough investment: If a taxpayer fails timely to make the required level of investment ($250,000,000) within the required time period (five years from time construction began), this exemption is forfeited.

Business property not located and used at an eligible data center: If the level of required investment is timely made but any specific eligible business property is not located and used at an eligible Internet datacenter, this exemption for eligible business property is forfeited.

Electricity not used at an eligible data center: If the level of required investment is timely made but any portion of the electricity is not used at an eligible Internet data center, the exemption provided for electricity is forfeited.

Recovery of past taxes: A taxpayer that forfeits this exemption is liable for all past taxes avoided as a result of the forfeited exemption, computed from the date the taxes would have been due if the exemption had not been allowed, plus interest at the established rate (see ¶3205).

Interest period: If the forfeiture is triggered due to the lack of a timely investment, interest is computed from the date the taxes would have been due if the exemption had not been allowed. For all other forfeitures, interest is computed from the time as of which the eligible business property or electricity was put to a disqualifying use.

Due date for taxes and interest: The past taxes and interest are due 30 days after the date the exemption is forfeited. A taxpayer that fails to pay the past taxes and interest by the due date is subject to the penalties under G.S. § 105-236 (see ¶3205).

¶1724 Heavy Equipment—Gross Receipts Tax

• *County*

Imposition: A county may elect to impose a tax on the gross receipts derived by equipment lessors from short-term leases of heavy equipment delivered from business locations within the county. The tax is imposed in lieu of subjecting such equipment to property tax [G.S. § 153A-156.1(b), effective August 2, 2008]and was intended to help alleviate inequities and administrative difficulties in applying the property tax to easily movable equipment.

The tax is imposed on taxpayers whose principal business is the short-term lease of heavy equipment if the place of business from which the property is delivered is located in the county [G.S. § 153A-156.1(b)]. A person is not considered to be in the short-term lease or rental business if the majority of the person's lease and rental gross receipts are derived from leases and rentals to a person who is a related person under G.S. § 105-163.010 [G.S. § 153A-156.1(b)]. The tax applies to gross receipts even if those receipts are subject to taxation at a special rate under G.S. § 105-164.4(a)(2). See table at ¶1605. The tax becomes effective on the date set in the resolution imposing the tax, which must be the first day of a calendar quarter and at least two months after the date the resolution is adopted [G.S. § 153A-156.1(e)].

Heavy equipment: "Heavy equipment" for this purpose means mobile earthmoving, construction, or industrial equipment that weighs at least 1,500 and is either a self-propelled vehicle that is not designed to be driven on a highway or industrial lift equipment, industrial material handling equipment, industrial electrical generation equipment, or a similar piece of industrial equipment [G.S. § 153A-156.1(a)(1)]. The term includes an attachment for heavy equipment, regardless of the weight of the attachment [G.S. § 153A-156.1(a)(1)].

¶1724

Rate: The rate of tax is 1.2% [G.S. § 153A-156.1(b)]. A short-term lease or rental is one other than a lease made under a written agreement to lease or rent property to the same person for a period of at least 365 continuous days [G.S. § 105-187.1(3)].

Payment: A person whose principal business is the short-term lease or rental of heavy equipment is required to remit the tax to the county finance officer. The tax is payable quarterly and is due by the last day of the month following the end of the quarter. The tax is intended to be added to the amount rent charged by the taxpayer [G.S. § 153A-156.1(c)].

Enforcement: The penalties and collection remedies that apply to the payment of sales and use taxes apply to this tax [G.S. § 153A-156.1(d)]. Sales and use taxes penalty and collection are discussed in Chapter 19.

Repeal: A county may, by resolution, repeal this tax. The repeal is effective on the date set in the resolution. The date must be the first day of a calendar quarter and may not be sooner than the first day of the calendar quarter that begins at least two months after the date the resolution is adopted [G.S. § 153A-156.1(f)].

¶1725 Certain Digital Property

The general sales tax rate applies to retail sales of certain digital property. The tax applies regardless of whether the purchaser has a right to use the property permanently or to use it without making continued payments [G.S. § 105-164.4(a)(1)b]. Note that the requirement that digital property is taxable only if it would be taxable if sold in a tangible medium has been repealed [S.L. 2019-169, § 3.2]. The holding of SUPLR 2011-10 that digital property with no tangible counterpart is not taxable is thus overturned.

¶1726 Accommodations

• *In general*

North Carolina imposes a sales tax at the general rate on the gross receipts derived from the rental of an accommodation (see ¶1603 for definition) [G.S. § 105-164.4F(b)]. The gross receipts derived from the rental of an accommodation include the sales price of the rental, which is determined as if the rental were a rental of tangible personal property [G.S. § 105-164.4F(b)].

• *Retailer*

The retailer liable for the tax is generally the person who collects the rental payment. This is typically the provider of the accommodation (but see below regarding accommodation facilitators), and if the person who collects the payment cannot be determined or is a third party (other than an accommodation facilitator), the provider is considered the retailer [G.S. § 105-164.4F(b1)].

• *Exceptions*

The tax does not apply to (1) a private residence or cottage that is rented for fewer than 15 days in a calendar year (unless the rental is made by an accommodation facilitator), (2) an accommodation that is supplied to the same person for 90 or more consecutive days, or (3) an accommodation arranged or provided to a person by a school, camp, or similar entity where a tuition or fee is charged to the person for enrollment in the school, camp or similar entity [G.S. § 105-164.4F(e)]. The exemption for 90-day rentals is available even though the guest checks out and checks back in on the same day to take advantage of promotional discounts. *See* SUPLR 2017-0002.

• *Accommodation facilitators*

If an accommodation facilitator (see ¶ 1603 for definition) collects the rental payment for an accommodation, the accommodation facilitator is considered the retailer. If each of the provider and the accommodation facilitator collects a portion of the rental payment, each is considered a retailer and is liable to collect and remit tax from that portion of the rental payment its collects. The sales price of an accommodation rental made by an accommodation facilitator includes any charges or fees charged by the accommodation facilitator to the purchaser of the accommodation that are necessary to complete the rental [G.S. § 105-164.4F(b) and (b1)]. An accommodation facilitator must file an annual report by March 31 of each year covering the accommodation rentals it made during the previous calendar year. The report must be made electronically and include the property owner's name and mailing address, the physical location of the accommodation and the gross receipts for the rentals [G.S. § 105-164.4F(c1)].

• *Hotel-affiliated accommodation facilitators*

Certain hotel-affiliated accommodation facilitators are not treated as retailers and are subject to special rules. Specifically, these provisions apply to an accommodation facilitator that (1) is operated by or on behalf of a hotel or hotel corporation, (2) facilitates the rental of hotel accommodations solely for the hotel or the hotel corporation's owned or managed hotels and franchisees, and (3) collects payment, or a portion of the payment, for the rental of an accommodation. A hotel-affiliated accommodation facilitator must send the retailer the tax due on the portion of the sales price it collects within 10 days after the end of each calendar month. If it fails to do so it becomes liable for the amount of tax it fails to send. The hotel-affiliated accommodation facilitator is not liable for tax it sends to the retailer if the retailer fails to remit the tax to the Secretary. Tax payments received by a retailer from a hotel-affiliated accommodation facilitator are held in trust by the retailer for remittance to the Secretary. A retailer that receives a tax payment from a hotel-affiliated accommodation facilitator must remit the amount received to the Secretary, but the retailer is not liable for tax due but not received from the hotel-affiliated accommodation facilitator [G.S. § 105-164.4F(c)].

¶1727 Items Given Away by Merchants

If a retailer engaged in the business of selling food or drink for immediate on-premises consumption also gives away food or drink to patrons or employees, the food or drink given away is considered sold along with the food or drink sold.

If a retailer gives an item of inventory to a customer on the condition that the customer purchase a similar or related item, the item given away is considered sold along with the item sold.

In all other cases, items given away or used by any retailer or wholesale merchant are not considered sold, whether or not the retailer or wholesale merchant recovers its cost of the items given away or used from sales of other items [G.S. § 105-164.12C].

¶1727

¶1728 Admission Charges to Entertainment Events

The general sales tax rate applies to the gross receipts derived from admission charges to an entertainment activity [G.S. §§ 105-164.4(a)(10) and 105-164.4G(b)]. For general guidance on the sales tax on admission charges before the 2014 amendments to the tax, *see Directive SD-13-4.*

- *Retailer*

The retailer liable for the tax or admission charges is the operator of the venue where the entertainment activity occurs, the person that provides the entertainment and receives the admission charges directly from the purchaser, or any other person who receives gross receipts derived from an admission charge sold at retail [G.S.§ 105-16.4G(b)].

- *Admission facilitators*

An admission facilitator must report to the retailer the admission charges it receives from consumers and must send the retailer the gross receipts it owes the retailer and the tax due within 10 days after the end of each calendar month. The retailer holds the taxes received from the admission facilitator in trust and must remit such taxes to the Secretary. If the admission facilitator does not send the taxes due to the retailer, the admission facilitator is liable for such tax, and the retailer is relieved of liability. The admission facilitator is not liable for any taxes it sends to the retailer but which the retailer fails to remit to the Secretary. These requirements are considered terms of the contract between the admission facilitator and the retailer [G.S. § 105-164.4G(c)].

- *Dual remittance arrangements*

An admission facilitator may elect to remit tax under a dual remittance option along with the venue operator. Under this option, the admission facilitator may pay part of the taxes due to the operator for remittance to the Secretary and remit the balance of the taxes due to the Secretary directly. An admission facilitator electing this dual remittance option must obtain a certificate of registration from the Department and becomes subject to the provisions of Article 9 of Chapter 105 (dealing with administration of the revenue laws and assessment and refunds) [G.S. § 105-164.4G(d)].

- *Sourcing rule*

An admission charge to an entertainment activity is sourced to the location where admission to the activity may be gained. Where this location is not known when the gross receipts are received, the general sourcing rules of G.S. § 105-164.4B(a) apply [G.S. § 105-164.4G(g)].

- *Exceptions and exemptions*

The tax on gross receipts from admissions to entertainment activities does not apply to:

Participation in sporting events: Amounts paid solely for the right to participate (other than as a spectator) in sporting activities, including bowling fees, greens fees and gym memberships [G.S. § 105-164.4G(e)(1)].

Instructional fees: Tuition, registration fees or charges to attend instructional seminars, conferences or workshops for educational purposes (even if entertainment activities are offered as an ancillary purpose of the event) [G.S. § 105-164.4G(e)(2)].

Political contributions [G.S. § 105-164.4G(e)(3)].

Leases: Charges for lifetime seat rights, leases or rentals of seats or boxes, provided the charge is separately stated on an invoice or similar billing document given to the purchaser at the time of sale [G.S. § 105-164.4G(e)(4)].

Transportation charges: Amounts paid solely for transportation [G.S. § 105-164.4G(e)(5)].

Miscellaneous activities: Amounts paid for the right to participate (other than as a spectator) in the following activities (1) rock climbing, (2) skating, (3) skiing, (4) snowboarding, (5) sledding, (6) zip lining, (7) instruction relating to the foregoing, (8) riding on carriage, boats, trains, buses, chairlifts or similar riding activities, and (9) amusement rides, including waterslides [G.S. § 105-164.4G(e)(6)].

Charitable contributions: A donation that is deductible, including the portion of a membership charge that is deductible, as a charitable contribution under Code § 170 or that is not deductible but described in Code § 170(l)(2). [G.S. § 105-164.4G(f)(1) and (2)].

Charges for amenities: Charges for amenities that are separately stated on a billing document given to the purchaser at the time of sale. If the charges are not separately stated, the sale is treated as a bundled transaction (provided that the 10% test of G.S. § 105-164.4D(a)(3) does not apply) [G.S. § 105-164.4G(f)(3)]. *See also Important Notice: Recent Changes for Admission Charges to Entertainment Activities* (June 25, 2014).

School events: Gross receipts from an event sponsored by an elementary or secondary school (for this purpose a "school" is an entity regulated under Chapter 115C of the General Statutes) [G.S. § 105-164.4G(f)(4)].

Nonprofit events: Gross receipts from an event sponsored solely by a nonprofit that is exempt from North Carolina income tax, provided (1) all the proceeds are used exclusively for the entity's nonprofit purposes, (2) the entity does not declare dividends, receive profits or pay compensation to any member or individual, and (3) the entity does not compensate any person for participating, performing or placing in the event or for producing the event [G.S. § 105-164.4G(f)(5)].

Farmer sponsored events: Admission charges to an event sponsored by a farmer are exempt if the event takes place on farmland and is related to farming activities. Examples include corn mazes and farm operation tutorials. The farmer must hold a qualifying farmer sales tax exemption certificate, and the farmland must be enrolled in the property tax present use value program [G.S. § 105-164.4G(f)(6)].

- *When tax is due*

The tax on admission charges is due when the charges are received even when the entertainment activity is scheduled for a future date. When season tickets are billed and paid for in advance, the tax is due for the period in which the payment is made. *See Important Notice: Recent Changes for Admission Charges to Entertainment Activities* (June 25, 2014).

• *Resellers*

Before May 29, 2014, a ticket reseller engaged in the business of reselling tickets to live events in North Carolina on or after January 1, 2014 was required to remit sales tax on the reseller's mark-up. Effective May 29, 2014, the reseller is liable for tax on the full price charged by the reseller, and the reseller may provide a certificate of exemption to avoid tax on tickets purchased for resale. *Important Notice: Recent Changes for Admission Charges to Entertainment* (June 25, 2014).

• *Effective date*

The sales tax on entertainment events is effective January 1, 2014 and applies to gross receipts derived from an admission charge sold at retail on or after that date. For admissions to a live event, the tax applies to the initial sale or resale of tickets occurring on or after January 1, 2014. If the initial sale or resale occurred before January 1, 2014, admission receipts are taxed under the former 3% privilege tax regardless of when received. Gross receipts derived from an admission charge sold at retail to a live event occurring on or after January 1, 2015, are taxable under G.S. § 105-164.4G regardless of when the initial sale of a ticket to the event occurred [S.L. 2013-316, § 5(f), as amended by S.L. 2014-3, § 5.1(f)].

¶1729 Service Contracts

• *Imposition of tax*

The sales price of or the gross receipts from a service contract or the renewal of a service contract sold at retail is subject to tax at the general rate. The general sourcing rules of G.S. § 105-164.4B (discussed at ¶1602) and reporting and payment provisions of G.S. § 105-164.16 (discussed at ¶1901) apply to service contracts [G.S. § 105-164.4I(a)]. For general advice on the sales taxation of service contracts before the 2014 amendments to the sales tax law, *see* Directive SD-13-5. *See also* Directive SD-14-1 (regarding application of the sales tax to optional service contracts for portable toilettes before the 2014 amendments).

• *Retailer of a service contract*

The retailer of a service contract is the person obligated under the contract to provide the services if such person is the retail seller of the contract to the purchaser [G.S. § 105-164.4I(a)(1)]. In some cases service contracts are sold by service contract facilitators. In such cases the service contract facilitator is treated as the retailer unless an agreement between the service contract facilitator and the service provider states that the service provider is responsible for paying the tax, in which case the service provider is treated as the retailer [G.S. § 105-164.4I(a)(2) and (3)]. Where such an agreement exists, the service contract facilitator must send the tax due on the contract to the service provider within 10 days after the end of each calendar month. The service provider holds payments received from the service contract facilitator in trust for remittance to the Secretary. The service provider must remit the tax received to the Secretary, and the service contract facilitator is not liable for any tax sent to the service provider that the service provider fails to remit. If the service contract facilitator fails to send the tax due to the service provider the service contract facilitator is liable for the tax it failed to send, and the service provider is not liable for such tax the service contract facilitator failed to send. These requirements are considered part of the agreement between the service contract facilitator and the service provider [G.S. § 105-164.4I(a)(3)].

• *Mixed service contracts*

A mixed service contract is a service contract for real property that includes two or more services, one of which is taxable and one of which is not. The general rule is that the entire contract is taxable. However, if the taxpayer can determine an allocated price for the taxable portion of the contract based on a reasonable allocation of revenue supported by business records kept in the ordinary course of business, only the allocated price of the taxable portion of the contract is taxable. If the allocated price of the taxable portion of the contract does not exceed 10% of the price of the contract, then the entire contract is nontaxable [G.S. § 105-164.4I(a1)].

• *Accounting and payment*

Retailers must report sales of or gross receipts from service contracts on the accrual basis even if they report other retail sales on the cash method. The tax is due at the time of the sale even if all or part of the sale was financed, in which case subsequent receipt of the financed portion of the sales price or gross receipts is not taxable if the financed portion is separately stated in the contract and on the billing statement or other documentation given to the purchaser at the time of sale [G.S. § 105-164.4I(d)].

¶1730 Manufactured and Modular Homes

• *Definitions*

See ¶1603 for the definitions of "manufactured home," "modular home," and "modular homebuilder."

• *Taxable sale or use*

The sales taxation of manufactured homes is governed, like items of tangible personal property, by the general definition of a "retail sale."

The sales taxation of modular homes is governed by a special rule providing that the retail sale of a modular home occurs when a modular home manufacturer sells a modular home to a modular homebuilder or directly to the end user of the modular home even if modular home is used to fulfill a real property contract [G.S. § 105-164.4(a)(1a)]. A modular homebuilder is not required to collect sales or use tax on charges to a customer for a modular home. Consequently, a modular homebuilder should not indicate on an invoice, bill, or similar document issued to the customer that sales tax is due on the transaction. If the modular homebuilder presents a customer with a list of the costs or expenses associated with the modular home transaction, the amount of sales or use tax paid by the modular homebuilder may be shown as a cost or expense, but the itemization should not indicate that the modular homebuilder is charging and collecting sales or use tax on the transaction with the customer. *See* Directive SD-13-3.

¶1730

A modular homebuilder or end user that purchases a modular home from an out-of-state retailer that does not collect sales or use tax is liable for North Carolina use tax on the purchase price of the modular home including all accessories attached to the modular home at the time of purchase. *See* Directive SD-13-3.

• *Rate, credit and exemption*

The general sales tax rate applies to the sales price of each modular and manufactured home sold at retail, including all accessories attached to the home when it is delivered to the purchaser [G.S. §§105-164.4(a)(1a)]. Sales of modular homes and manufactured homes are not subject to local sales and use taxes [G.S. §105-467(a)].

A person who sells a modular home at retail is allowed a credit for sales or use tax paid to another state on tangible personal property incorporated in the modular home [G.S. §105-164.4(a)(1a)]. Similarly, a modular homebuilder that purchases a modular home from an out-of-state retailer is allowed a credit for any state sales and use tax paid to the other state. *See* Directive SD-13-3.

For sales of manufactured and modular homes made on or after September 1, 2014, 50% of the sales price of the home, including all accessories attached at the time of delivery, is exempt [G.S. §105-164.13(64); S.L. 2014-100 §37.3].

• *Sales price*

The sales price of a modular or manufactured home is governed by the general definition of "sales price" (discussed at ¶1704). In Directive SD-13-2, the Department asserted that the following items are included in the sales price of a manufactured home:

(1) Any furniture, appliances, or accessories placed in or attached to the home by the manufacturer or the retailer that are a part of the sale of the home when it is delivered to the purchaser.

(2) Charges by the retailer for anchor bolts, tie-downs, skirting, prefabricated steps, central air-conditioning units, window air-conditioning units, and HVAC systems (excluding central air-conditioning units or HVAC systems installed by a third party pursuant to a performance contract) that are to be attached to the home when title or possession passes to the customer or when the home is installed by the retailer, even if such charges are separately stated on the invoice, bill of sale, or similar document given to a purchaser.

(3) Permit charges that are imposed on the retailer to deliver the home, even if such charges are separately stated on the invoice, bill of sale, or similar document given to the purchaser.

(4) Any charge by the retailer for running gear upon which the home is delivered.

(5) Other charges by the retailer necessary to complete the sale of the home.

(6) The retailer's profit from the sale of the home.

Similarly, in Directive SD-13-3, the Department asserted that the following items are included in the sales price of a modular home even if such charges are separately stated in the invoice, bill of sale, or similar document given to the purchaser by the modular home manufacturer or other person at the time of the sale:

(1) Carrier deposit fees.

(2) Freight charges.

(3) Engineering fees.

(4) Labeling fees imposed by the N.C. Department of Insurance.

(5) Other charges by the modular home manufacturer necessary to complete the sale.

Directives SD-13-2 and SD-13-3 provide that the following items charged in conjunction with the retail sale of a modular or manufactured home are not part of the sales price and so are not taxable if such items are separately stated on the invoice, bill of sale, or similar document given to the purchaser by the retailer at the time of a sale:

(1) Installation charges (*but See Important Notice: Repeal of Installation Charges Exemption* (January 11, 2016)).

(2) Charges for clearing and grading real property.

(3) Building, electrical, plumbing and other similar permit fees.

(4) A central air-conditioning unit or a HVAC system installed by a third party pursuant to a performance contract.

(5) Well installation charges.

(6) Sidewalk and driveway installation charges.

(7) Brick foundations installed by a third party pursuant to a performance contract.

(8) Wooden decks installed by a third party pursuant to a performance contract.

• *Land/home packages*

A "land/home" package is an arrangement whereby a purchaser enters into a performance contract with a contractor under which the contractor agrees to provide a modular home or manufactured home and land in exchange for a lump-sum price, with the home and land transferred to the purchaser by deed. Like other performance contractors, a contractor under a land/sale package is treated as the consumer of tangible personal property and taxable services used to fulfill the contract. As such, the contractor is liable for the applicable state and local sales or use tax on such items, unless such items are otherwise exempt. Contractors are discussed at ¶1709.

When a contractor or subcontractor, who is a modular homebuilder, makes a taxable purchase of a modular home for use in a land/home package pursuant to a performance contract, the contractor or subcontractor must pay the applicable rate of sales or use tax on the sales price or purchase price of the modular home including all accessories attached to the modular home when it is delivered to the purchaser. If an out-of-state retailer or other person withdraws a modular home from an out-of-state inventory for use in fulfilling a performance contract for a land/home package in North Carolina, the retailer or other person must remit the sue tax due on the purchase price of the modular home and accessories attached to the modular home when it is delivered. *See* Directive SD-13-3.

¶1730

Similarly, when a contractor or subcontractor makes a taxable purchase of a manufactured home for use in a land/home package pursuant to a performance contract, the contractor or subcontractor must pay the applicable rate of sales or use tax on the sales price of the manufactured home including all accessories attached at the time of delivery. If a retailer withdraws a manufactured home from inventory for use in a land/home package where such retailer operates as the contractor, such retailer must remit the use tax due on the purchase price of the manufactured home. *See* Directive SD-13-2.

- *Other items sold at retail*

If the retailer of a modular or manufactured home makes a retail sale of tangible personal property not considered accessories of the home, including other freestanding structures such as storage buildings, the retailer must collect and remit sales tax at the applicable state and local rates on the sales price of such items. *See* Directives SD-13-2 and SD-13-3.

SALES AND USE TAXES

CHAPTER 18

EXEMPTIONS

¶1801 Introduction

Sales and use tax exemptions are allowed for specified property and services [G.S. § 105-164.13]. These exemptions are classified into "groups" [G.S. § 105-164.13]. In general, groups are classified by function (*e.g.*, agricultural, industrial). The largest group, however, is the "Unclassified Group." These groups are discussed separately in the following paragraphs. Property purchased for resale is the largest single item in the exempt category. Exemption certificates in general are discussed at ¶ 1811.

¶1802 Agricultural Group

In addition to the exemptions listed below, see ¶ 1810.

• *Farm products sold to manufacturers*

Cotton, tobacco, peanuts, or other farm products sold to manufacturers for further manufacturing or processing are exempt [G.S. § 105-164.13(4)].

• *Farm products sold by producers*

Farm products sold in their original state by the producer of the products are exempt if the producer is not primarily a retail merchant [G.S. § 105-164.13(4b)].

• *Forestry and mine products*

Products of forests and mines in their original or unmanufactured state when such sales are made by the producer in the capacity of producer are exempt [G.S. § 105-164.13(3)].

• *Ice*

Ice used to preserve agriculture, aquaculture, and commercial fishery products until the products are sold at retail is exempt [G.S. § 105-164.13(4b)].

• *Logging machinery*

Sales to a person engaged in the commercial logging business of the following are exempt: (1) logging machinery used to harvest raw forest products for transport to first market; (2) attachments and repair parts for logging machinery; (3) lubricants applied to logging machinery; and (4) fuel used to operate logging machinery [G.S. § 105-164.13(4f)].

• *Stone*

Sales of equipment (including attachments and repair parts) used in cutting, shaping, polishing and finishing rough cut slabs and blocks of natural or engineered stone and stone-like products are exempt if sold to a company primarily engaged in the business of providing made-to-order countertops, walls or tubs [G.S. § 105-164.13(5p)].

¶1803 Industrial Group

• *Boats and supplies*

The sales of boats, fuel oil, lubricating oils, machinery, equipment, nets, rigging, paints, parts, accessories, and supplies sold to any of the following are exempt [G.S. § 105-164.13(9)]:

(1) The holder of a standard commercial fishing license for principal use in commercial operations.

(2) The holder of a shellfish license for principal use in commercial use of the boat.

(3) The operator of a for-hire boat (as defined in G.S. § 113-174) for principal use in the commercial use of the boat.

The industrial group of exemptions comprises tangible personal property involved in the following: (1) manufacturing; (2) production of seafood; (3) generation of electricity; (4) commercial fishing operations; (5) and commercial laundry operations [G.S. § 105-164.13(5)-(10)]. The following sales and uses in the "industrial group" are specifically exempted from the sales and use taxes.

• *Broadcasting equipment*

The following broadcasting equipment is exempt:

(1) Sales of towers, broadcasting equipment, and parts and accessories attached to the equipment to a radio or television company licensed by the Federal Communications Commission [G.S. § 105-164.13(5c)].

(2) Sales of broadcasting equipment and parts and accessories attached (but not including cable) to the equipment to a cable service provider [G.S. § 105-164.13(5d)].

• *Commercial fishing*

Sales of boats, fuel oil, lubricating oil, machinery, equipment, nets, rigging, paints, parts, accessories, and supplies to persons for use principally in commercial fishing operations, *except* when the property is for use by persons principally to take fish for recreation or personal use or consumption, are exempt. A "commercial fishing operation" for this purpose means any activity preparatory to, during, or subsequent to the taking of any fish, the taking of which is subject to regulation by the Marine Fisheries Commission, either with the use of commercial fishing equipment or gear, or by any means if the purpose of the taking is to obtain fish for sale [G.S. § 105-164.13(9)].

"Commercial fishing operation" does not include (1) the taking of fish as part of a recreational fishing tournament, unless commercial fishing equipment or gear is used, or (2) the taking of fish under a Recreational Commercial Gear License (RCGL) [G.S. § 113-168(1)]. "Fish" for this purpose means all marine mammals; all shellfish; all crustaceans; and all other fishes [G.S. § 113-129(7)].

• *Fish and seafood*

Sales of products of waters in their original or unmanufactured state when the sales are made by the producer in the capacity of producer are exempt. Fish and seafoods are also exempt when sold by a fisherman in that capacity [G.S. § 105-164.13(7)].

• *Fuel and piped natural gas sold to a small power production facility*

Sales to a small power production facility of fuel and piped natural gas used by the facility to generate electricity are exempt. A "small power production facility" is a facility described in 16 U.S.C. § 796(17)(A) [G.S. § 105-164.13(8a)].

• *Laundry operation items*

Sales to commercial laundries or to pressing and dry cleaning establishments of the following items are exempt [G.S. § 105-164.13(10)]:

(1) Articles or materials used for the identification of garments being laundered or dry cleaned, wrapping paper, bags, hangers, starch, soaps, detergents, cleaning fluids, and other compounds or chemicals applied directly to the garments in the direct performance of the laundering or the pressing and cleaning service.

(2) Laundry and dry cleaning machinery, parts and accessories attached to the machinery, and lubricants applied to the machinery.

(3) Fuel (other than electricity) and piped natural gas used in the direct performance of the laundering or the pressing and cleaning service.

• *Manufactured products*

Manufactured products produced and sold by manufacturers or producers to other manufacturers, producers, or registered retailers or wholesale merchants, for the purpose of resale, are exempt except as modified by G.S. § 105-164.3(51) (relating to wholesale merchants). This exemption does not extend to or include retail sales to users or consumers not for resale [G.S. § 105-164.13(5)].

• *Mill machinery and similar items*

Mill machinery and certain other items were formerly subject to a privilege tax under Article 5F. Such items were correspondingly exempt from sales tax. Article 5F was repealed effective July 1, 2018, and new sales tax exemptions were enacted for the items formerly taxed under Article 5F, also effective July 1, 2018 [S.L. 2017-57, § 38.8]. Specifically, the following items are exempt:

Mill machinery. Sales of mill machinery or mill machinery parts or accessories (not including electricity) to a manufacturing industry or plant or to a contractor or subcontractor if the purchase is for use in the performance of a contract with a manufacturing industry or plant or with a general contractor that has a contract with a manufacturing industry or plant. A manufacturing industry or plant does not include a production company or a restaurant or similar retailer that is principally engaged in the retail sale for consumption of food it prepares [G.S. § 105-164.13(5e)].

"Manufacturing" defined

There is no statutory definition of "manufacturing". Thus, the courts have resorted to the dictionaries to ascertain its generally accepted meaning and have then undertaken to determine its application to the circumstances of the particular case. There are many holdings and statements to the effect that to constitute manufacturing, the operation, process, or activity in question must produce a new and different commodity or work a substantial change in the basic material [*Master Hatcheries, Inc. v. Coble*, 286 N.C. 518, 212 S.E.2d 150 (1975)]. Manufacturing has been defined as the production of a new article by the application of skill and labor to raw materials of which it is composed [*Duke Power Co. v. Clayton*, 274 N.C. 505, 164 S.E.2d 289 (1968)], as the change of one commodity into another commodity or the creation of a new commodity [*Sayles Biltmore Bleacheries, Inc. v. Johnson*, 266 N.C. 692, 147 S.E.2d 177 (1966)], and as the application of skill and labor to raw materials to create a new and more valuable property [*Master Hatcheries, Inc. v. Coble*, 286 N.C. 518, 212 S.E. 2d 150 (1975)]. Taxpayers who fabricate or extract materials for their own uses are not treated as manufacturers. See Secretary's Decision No. 2006-114 (August 14, 2006) (contractor fabricated gutters and other items for use in its contracting business); Secretary's Decision No. 2005-209 (March 6, 2006) (grading contractor extracted sand from sand pits for its contracting business).

The table below contains examples of activities that have been held to be manufacturing or not to be manufacturing.

Product or Activity	Manufacturing	Authority
Commercial egg hatchery	Yes	*Master Hatcheries, Inc. v. Coble*, 286 N.C. 518 (1975)
Engraving print cylinders owned by customers	No	*Secretary's Decision No. 2002-501* (December 19, 2002); *Secretary's Decision No. 2002-502* (December 19, 2002), *aff'd*, Tax Review Board Administrative Decision No. 450 (July 7, 2004)
Coal—heating and carbonizing	Yes	*Duke Power Co. v. Clayton*, 274 N.C. 505 (1968)
Electricity, generation of	Yes	*Duke Power Co. v. Clayton*, 274 N.C. 505 (1968)
Mining	Yes	*Campbell v. Currie*, 251 N.C. 329 (1959)
Rebuilding racing engines	No	*Secretary's Decision No. 2001-397* (January 22, 2002)
Repackaging manufactured goods	No	*Secretary's Decision No. 2002-152* (July 9, 2002); *Secretary's Decision No. 2003-68* (June 4, 2003)

Product or Activity	Manufacturing	Authority
Assembling beauty products into gift baskets	Yes	Secretary's Decision No. 2006-154 (April 9, 2007)
Sifting sand after extraction	No	Secretary's Decision No. 2006-178 (November 3, 2006)
Restaurant—preparation of food	No	HED, Inc. v. Powers, 84 N.C. App. 292, rev. denied, 319 N.C. 458 (1987)
Textile refinishing	Yes	Sayles Biltmore Bleacheries, Inc. v. Johnson, 266 N.C. 692 (1966)
Transforming natural stone into granite countertop	No	SUPLR 2017-0004
Secondary metal recycling	Yes	N.C. Department of Revenue v. Tri-State Scrap Metal, Inc., 18 CVS 10357 (N.C. Business Court 2019)
Landfill methane collection	No	MEPLR 2018-0002

Major recycling facility items. Sales to a major recycling facility of any of the following items for use in connection with the facility: (a) cranes, structural steel crane support systems, and related foundations; (b) port and dock facilities; (c) rail equipment; and (d) material handling equipment [G.S. § 105-164.13(5f)].

R&D items. Sales of equipment (or an attachment or repair part for equipment) to a company primarily engaged at the establishment in research and development activities in the physical, engineering, and life sciences included in industry group 54171 of NAICS if the item is capitalized for federal income tax purposes and is used at the establishment in the research and development of tangible personal property [G.S. § 105-164.13(5g)].

Software publishing items. Sales of equipment (or an attachment or repair part for equipment) to a company primarily engaged at the establishment in software publishing activities included in industry group 5112 of NAICS if the item is capitalized for federal income tax purposes and is used at the establishment in the research and development of tangible personal property [G.S. § 105-164.13(5h)].

Industrial machinery refurbishing items. Sales of equipment (or an attachment or repair part for equipment) to a company primarily engaged at the establishment in industrial machinery refurbishing activities included in industry group 811310 of NAICS if the item is capitalized for federal income tax purposes and is used at the establishment in repairing or refurbishing tangible personal property [G.S. § 105-164.13(5i)].

Port facility items. Sales of the following to a company located at a ports facility for waterborne commerce: (a) machinery and equipment that is used at the facility to unload or to facilitate the unloading or processing of bulk cargo to make it suitable for delivery to and use by manufacturing facilities and (b) parts, accessories, or attachments used to maintain, repair, replace, upgrade, improve, or otherwise modify such machinery and equipment [G.S. § 105-164.13(5j)].

Secondary metal recycling items. Sales of the following to a secondary metals recycler: (a) equipment (or an attachment or repair part for equipment, but excluding motor vehicles and motor vehicle attachments and repair parts) that is capitalized for federal income tax purposes and used in the secondary metals recycling process, and (b) fuel, piped natural gas, or electricity for use at the person's facility at which the primary activity is secondary metals recycling [G.S. § 105-164.13(5k)].

Precious metal extraction items. Sales of equipment (or an attachment or repair part for equipment) to a company primarily engaged at the establishment in processing tangible personal property for the purpose of extracting precious metals to determine their value for potential purchase if the item is capitalized for federal income tax purposes and is used in the process described above [G.S. § 105-164.13(5*l*)].

Metal work fabrication items. Sales of equipment (or an attachment or repair part for equipment) to a company that is engaged in the fabrication of metal work and that has annual gross receipts (including the gross receipts of related persons) from the fabrication of metal work of at least $8,000,000 if the item is capitalized for federal income tax purposes and is used at the establishment in the fabrication or manufacture of metal products or used to create equipment for the fabrication or manufacture of metal products [G.S. § 105-164.13(5m)].

Ready-mix concrete items. Sales of repair or replacement parts for a ready-mix concrete mill to a company that primarily sells ready-mix concrete, regardless of whether the mill is freestanding or affixed to a motor vehicle [G.S. § 105-164.13(5n)].

• *Products of waters*

Sales of products of waters in their original or unmanufactured state when sales are made by the producer in the capacity of producer. Fish and seafood are also exempt when sold by the fisher man in that capacity [G.S. § 105-164.13(7)].

• *Tangible personal property that becomes part of manufactured product*

Sales of tangible personal property to a manufacturer that enters into or becomes an ingredient or component part of tangible personal property that is manufactured are exempt [G.S. § 105-164.13(8)]. Electricity is a form of energy, not tangible personal property. Thus, this exemption does not apply to electricity. See, for example, *Secretary's Decision No.* 97-1058 (August 11, 1998).

• *Telephone equipment*

Sales to a telephone company regularly engaged in providing telecommunications service to subscribers on a commercial basis of central office equipment, switchboard equipment, private branch exchange equipment, terminal equipment (other than public pay telephone terminal equipment) and parts and accessories attached to the equipment are exempt [G.S. § 105-164.13(5b)].

• *Wood chipper*

A wood chipper that meets all of the following requirements is exempt [G.S. § 105-164.13(4g)]:

(1) It is designed to be towed by a motor vehicle.

(2) It is assigned a 17-digit vehicle identification number by the National Highway Transportation Safety Association.

(3) It is sold to a person who purchases a motor vehicle in North Carolina that is to be registered in another state and who uses the purchased motor vehicle to tow the wood chipper to the state in which the purchased motor vehicle is to be registered.

¶1803

¶1804 Motor Fuels Group

• *Alternative fuel*

Alternative fuel taxed under Article 36D of Chapter 105 is exempt, unless a refund of that tax is allowed [G.S. § 105-164.13((11)b)]. See ¶2909 for discussion of the alternative fuels tax.

• *Aviation fuel*

Sales of aviation gasoline and jet fuel to an interstate air business for use in a commercial aircraft (as defined in G.S. § 105-164.13(45a)) are exempt. This exemption also applies to aviation gasoline and jet fuel purchased for use in a commercial aircraft in interstate or foreign commerce by a person whose primary business is scheduled passenger air transportation. This exemption expires January 1, 2024 [G.S. § 105-164.13(11b)].

• *Diesel fuel*

Sales of diesel fuel to railroad companies for use in rolling stock other than motor vehicles are exempt [G.S. § 105-164.13(11a)].

• *Major recycling facility, sales to*

Sales of the following to major recycling facilities are exempt [G.S. § 105-164.13(10a)]:

(1) Lubricants and other additives for motor vehicles or machinery and equipment used at the facility.

(2) Materials, supplies, parts, and accessories (other than machinery and equipment) that are not capitalized by the taxpayer and are used or consumed in the manufacturing and material handling processes at the facility.

(3) Electricity used at the facility.

• *Motor fuel*

Motor fuel taxed under Article 36C of Chapter 105 [G.S. § 105-449.60 et seq.] (other than motor fuel for which a refund of the per gallon excise tax is allowed) is exempt [G.S. § 105-164.13((11)a)]. "Motor fuel" for this purpose means gasoline, diesel fuel, and blended fuel [G.S. § 105-449.60(31)].

¶1805 Medical Group

The medical group includes medical equipment and supplies, drugs, certain nutritional supplements, and medical devices of various kinds [G.S. § 105-164.13(12)-(13c)].

• *Diapers and incontinence underpads*

Sales of diapers and incontinence underpads on prescription by an enrolled Medicaid/Health Choice provider are exempt if sold for use by beneficiaries of the State Medicaid program when the provider is reimbursed by the State Medicaid program or a Medicaid managed care organization [G.S. § 105-164.13(13d)].

• *Drugs*

All of the following drugs (including their packaging materials and any instructions or information about the drugs included in the package with the drugs, but not including pet food or animal feed) are exempt:

(1) Drugs required by federal law to be dispensed only on prescription [G.S. § 105-164.13(13)a].

(2) Over-the-counter drugs sold on prescription (not including over-the-counter drugs purchased by medical facilities for the treatment of patients) [G.S. § 105-164.13(13)b].

(3) Insulin [G.S. § 105-164.13(13)c].

• *Medical devices, equipment, and supplies*

The following are specifically exempt from the North Carolina sales and use tax:

(1) Prosthetic devices for human use [G.S. § 105-164.13(12)a].

(2) Mobility-enhancing equipment sold on a prescription [G.S. § 105-164.13(12)b].

(3) Durable medical equipment sold on prescription [G.S. § 105-164.13(12)c].

(4) Durable medical supplies sold on prescription [G.S. § 105-164.13(12)d]. *See Feeling Great, Inc. v. Department of Revenue,* 14 CVS 11139 (N.C.B.C. 2015), *reversing,* 13 REV 18080 and 18081 (supplies purchased and consumed by a sleep testing clinic in performing sleep tests prescribed for patients did not qualify for exemption where the supplies were not purchased by the patients). *See also,* SUPLR 2018-0012 (computer controlled therapy units, and other wound therapy products entitled to exemption).

(5) Human blood, including whole blood, plasma and derivatives [G.S. § 105-164.13(12)e].

(6) Human tissue, eyes, DNA and organs [G.S. § 105-164.13(12)f]. *See* SUPLR 2018-0007 for an application of this exemption.

• *Nutritional supplements*

Nutritional supplements sold by a chiropractic physician at a chiropractic office to a patient as part of the patient's plan of treatment as authorized by G.S. § 90-151.1, which authorizes a chiropractic physician to sell nutritional supplements to a patient as part of the patient's plan of treatment, are exempt [G.S. § 105-164.13(13c)]. This exemption is repealed effective for sales made on or after January 1, 2014 [S.L. 2013-316, § 3.2(a) and (d)]. *See also* Directive SD-98-5 as modified on December 6, 2013.

• *Orthopedic appliances*

Orthopedic appliances designed to be worn by the purchaser or user are exempt [G.S. § 105-164.13(12c)].

¶1805

¶1806 Printed Materials Group

• *Public school books*

Public school books on the adopted list, the selling price of which are fixed by State contract are exempt [G.S. § 105-164.13(14)]. This is the only item in the "printed materials group."

¶1807 Transactions Group

The "transactions group" includes provisions relating to worthless accounts and repossessed articles [G.S. § 105-164.13(15), (16)].

• *Worthless accounts*

When a worthless account upon which the sales and use tax has been previously paid is charged off for income tax purposes, a deduction from gross retail sales is allowed for the amount of the worthless account. A "worthless account" is one that would be treated as a "bad debt" under Code Section 166, but the amount of the bad debt must be adjusted to exclude financing charges, interest, sales or use taxes, uncollectible amounts on property that remains in the seller's possession, collection expenses and repossessed property. If the worthless account is later recovered, it must be added to gross sales [G.S. § 105-164.13(15)]. *See also Tax Directive* SD-03-2 (October 15, 2003). The deduction is allowed only to the retailer who made the sales that generated the worthless accounts. It is not available to a factor purchasing the accounts from the retailer [*Secretary's Decision No.* 2001-276 (February 28, 2002)]. A taxpayer may not deduct worthless accounts belonging to a third party lender extending credit to the taxpayer's customers (such as a bank issuing private label credit cards to the taxpayer's customers). Final Agency Decision 09 REV 4211 (January 13, 2011). In the case of a municipality that sells electricity, the account may be deducted if it meets all the conditions for charge-off that would apply if the municipality were subject to income tax [G.S. § 105-164.13(15)].

• *Repossessed articles*

Sales of articles repossessed by vendors are exempt if tax was paid on the sales price of the article [G.S. § 105-164.13(16)]. The exemption was not available to a finance company that repossessed articles and resold them, because the finance company was not the original vendor [*Secretary's Decision No.* 2002-63 (July 11, 2002), *aff'd, Tax Review Board Administrative Decision No.* 426 (March 23, 2004)].

¶1808 Exempt Status Group

Sales that a state would be without power to tax under the limitations of the Constitution or laws of the United States or under the Constitution of North Carolina are exempt from the sales and use tax [G.S. § 105-164.13(17)]. Sales of tangible personal property that the vendor delivers to the purchaser at a point outside the State, or that the vendor delivers to a common carrier or to the mails for transportation and delivery to the purchaser at a point outside the State, are exempt under this provision as sales in interstate commerce, provided the property is not returned to North Carolina. Vendors have the burden of proving that property was in fact delivered to points outside the state. See, e.g., Secretary's Decision No. 2006-218 (January 10, 2007) (sales to out-of-state customers taxable where taxpayer could not produce documentary evidence of delivery outside North Carolina). The most acceptable forms of proof of transportation and delivery to a point outside the State include: a waybill or bill of lading made out to the seller's order calling for delivery, an insurance or registry receipt issued by the United States Postal Service, or a postal service receipt, or a trip sheet that is signed by the seller's delivery agent and shows the signature and address of the person who received the delivered goods outside the State. *See Sales and Use Tax Technical Bulletins* § 42-1.A. Note, however, that sales of tangible personal property delivered in North Carolina to the buyer or his agent, if such agent is not a common carrier, are subject to tax notwithstanding that the buyer may subsequently transport the property out of this State. *See Sales and Use Tax Technical Bulletins* § 42-1.D. *See also Secretary's Decision No. 2005-145*(September 12, 2005) (sale of property delivered to buyer's agent for shipment to a point outside the state was taxable). In addition, a retailer is required to collect tax notwithstanding the fact that (1) the retailer solicits the sale through a catalogue or other written advertisement and the purchase order or sales contract is transmitted to the retailer outside North Carolina; (2) the purchase order or sales contract is approved or accepted outside North Carolina or before any tangible or certain digital property that is part of the order enters North Carolina; (3) the purchase order or sales contract provides that the property is to be (or the property is in fact) procured or manufactured outside North Carolina and shipped directly to the purchaser from the point of origin; (4) the property is mailed to the purchaser in North Carolina or to a point outside North Carolina or delivered to a carrier outside North Carolina and directed to the purchaser in North Carolina; (5) the property is delivered directly to the purchaser outside North Carolina; or (6) any combination of any two of the foregoing factors if it is intended that the property be brought into North Carolina for storage, consumption or use [G.S. § 105-164.8(a)].

¶1809 Unclassified Group

The "unclassified group" includes a large number of sales and uses that are exempt and do not belong to any of the other groups.

• *Accommodation rentals*

Gross receipts from the rental of certain accommodations are exempt [G.S. § 105-164.13(70)]. See discussion at ¶1727.

• *Advertising supplements*

Advertising supplements and any other printed matter ultimately to be distributed with or as part of a newspaper are exempt [G.S. § 105-164.13(36)].

• *Air business*

Sales to an interstate air business of tangible personal property that becomes a component part of or is dispensed as a lubricant into commercial aircraft during its maintenance, repair, or overhaul are exempt [G.S. § 105-164.13(45a)]. For this purpose, the term "commercial aircraft" includes only aircraft that has a certified maximum take-off weight of more than 12,500 pounds and is regularly used to carry for compensation passengers, commercial freight, or individually addressed letters and packages.

¶1809

• *Air carriers*

Sales of aircraft lubricants, aircraft repair parts, and aircraft accessories to an interstate passenger air carrier for use at its hub are exempt [G.S. § 105-164.13(45)]. In addition, sales of aircraft simulators to a company for flight crew training and maintenance training are exempt [G.S. § 105-164.13(45c)].

• *Air couriers*

Sales of the following items to an interstate air courier for use at its hub are exempt [G.S. § 105-164.13(45b)]:

(1) Aircraft lubricants, aircraft repair parts, and aircraft accessories.

(2) Materials-handling equipment, racking systems, and related parts and accessories for the storage or handling and movement of tangible personal property at an airport or in a warehouse or distribution facility.

• *Art museum (State)*

Sales to the North Carolina Museum of Art of paintings and other objects or works of art for public display are exempt if the purchases are financed in whole or in part by gifts or donations [G.S. § 105-164.13(29)].

• *Audiovisual masters*

Sales of audiovisual masters made or used by a production company in making visual and audio images for first generation reproduction are exempt. For this purpose an "audio visual master" is an audio or video film, tape, or disk or other audio or video storage device from which all other copies are made [G.S. § 105-164.13(22a)]. A "production company" is a person engaged in the business of making motion picture, television, or radio images for theatrical, commercial advertising, or educational purposes [G.S. § 105-164.3(30)].

• *Blind merchants*

Sales by blind merchants operating under supervision of the Department of Health and Human Services are exempt [G.S. § 105-164.13(20)].

• *Bread sold at bakery thrift store*

Bread, rolls, and buns sold at a bakery thrift store are exempt. A "bakery thrift store" is a retail outlet of a bakery that sells at wholesale over 90% of the items it makes and sells at the retail outlet day-old bread, rolls, and buns, returns to it by retailers [G.S. § 105-164.13(27a)]. This exemption is repealed effective for sales made on or after July 1, 2014 [S.L. 2013-316, § 3.4(a) and (e)].

• *Charitable, civic, educational, scientific, literary, or fraternal organizations—annual fund raising*

Sales by *nonprofit* charitable, civic, educational, scientific, literary, or fraternal organizations are exempt when all three of the conditions listed below are met. This exemption does not apply to gross receipts from admission charges to an entertainment activity [G.S. § 105-164.13(35)]:

¶1809

(1) The sales are conducted only on an annual basis for the purpose of raising funds for the organization's activities [G.S. § 105-164.13(35a)].

(2) The proceeds of the sale are actually used for the organization's activities [G.S. § 105-164.13(35b)].

(3) The products sold are delivered to the purchaser within 60 days after the first solicitation of any sale made during the organization's annual sales period [G.S. § 105-164.13(35c)].

- *Cherokee Indian Reservation*

Sales on the Cherokee Indian Reservation by merchants authorized to do business on the Reservation and paying the tribal gross receipts levy to the Tribal Council are exempt [G.S. § 105-164.13(25)].

- *Coin, currency and bullion*

Coins and paper currency of the United States or foreign governments with more than nominal value and elementary precious metals in bullion form are exempt effective July 1, 2017 [G.S. § 105-164.13(69); S.L. 2017-181].

- *Computer software*

Computer software is exempt if it is (1) purchased to run on an enterprise server operating system, (2) sold to a datacenter operator and is used within the datacenter, or (3) sold to a provider of cable, telecommunications, or video programming service and is used to provide ancillary service, cable service, Internet access service, telecommunications service or video programming. The exemption described in (1) includes a purchase or license of software for high-volume simultaneous use on multiple computers that is housed or maintained on an enterprise server or end-user's computers. The exemption includes software designed to run a computer system, an operating program or application software [G.S. § 105-164.13(43a)]. In addition, computer software or certain digital property that becomes a component part of other computer property or certain digital property that is offered for sale or of a service that is offered for sale [G.S. § 105-164.13(43b)].

- *Custom computer software*

Custom computer software and the portion of prewritten computer software that is modified or enhanced are exempt if the modification or enhancement is designed and developed to the specifications of a specific purchaser and the charges for the modification or enhancement are separately stated on the invoice or similar billing document given to the purchaser at the time of sale [G.S. § 105-164.13(43)].

- *Department of Transportation*

Sales to the Department of Transportation are exempt [G.S. § 105-164.13(40)].

- *Deposits on beverage containers*

An amount charged as a deposit on a beverage container that is returnable to the vendor for reuse when the amount is refundable or creditable to the vendee is exempt, whether or not the deposit is separately charge [G.S. § 105-164.13(47)].

¶1809

• *Deposits on replacement parts*

An amount charged as a deposit on an aeronautic, automotive, industrial, marine, or farm replacement part that is returnable to the vendor for rebuilding or remanufacturing when the amount is refundable or creditable to the vendee is exempt, whether or not the deposit is separately charged. This exemption does not include tires or batteries [G.S. § 105-164.13(48)].

• *Direct mail delivery*

Delivery charges for delivery of direct mail are exempt if the charges are separately stated on an invoice or similar billing document given to the purchaser at the time of sale [G.S. § 105-164.13(49a)].

• *Donated tangible personal property*

Tangible personal property that is purchased by a retailer or wholesale merchant for resale and then withdrawn from inventory and donated to (i) a governmental entity or (ii) a nonprofit organization is exempt if the contribution is deductible as a charitable contribution for federal income tax purposes [G.S. § 105-164.13(42)].

• *Electricity and business property used at Internet data centers*

Sales of electricity for use at an eligible Internet data center and eligible business property to be located and used at an eligible Internet data center are exempt [G.S. § 105-164.13(55)]. See discussion at ¶1723. This exemption has been upheld against a challenge that it violates the public purpose clause and other clauses of the North Carolina Constitution. *See Munger v. State*, 202 N.C. App. 404, 689 S.E.2d 230 (2010).

• *Exports*

Tangible personal property purchased solely for export to a foreign country for exclusive use in that or some other country, either in the direct performance or rendition of professional or commercial services, or in the direct conduct or operation of a trade or business, all of which purposes are actually consummated, or purchased by the government of a foreign country for export and actually exported are exempt. "Export" includes the acts of possessing and marshalling such property, by either the seller or the purchaser, for transportation to a foreign country but does not include devoting such property to any other use in North Carolina or in the United States. "Foreign country" does not include any territory or possession of the United States. The purpose of this exemption is to encourage the flow of commerce through North Carolina ports that is now moving through out-of-state ports, but it is not intended that property acquired for personal use or consumption by the purchaser, including gifts, shall be exempt under this provision [G.S. § 105-164.13(33)].

Affidavit of export: In order to qualify for this exemption, the purchaser must submit to the seller (and the seller must retain) an affidavit of export. The affidavit must contain express provision that the purchaser has recognized and assumed the tax liability in the event the export purposes are not consummate [G.S. § 105-164.13(33)].

Export purposes not consummated: If the export purposes are not consummated, the purchaser is liable for the tax that was avoided by the execution of an affidavit of export and is subject to applicable penalties and interest [G.S. § 105-164.13(33)].

¶1809

• *Film for exhibition*

The lease or rental of motion picture films used for exhibition purposes is exempt where the lease or rental of such property is (1) an established business; (2) part of an established business; or (3) incidental or germane to the lessee's business [G.S. § 105-164.13(21)].

• *Film, transcriptions, and recordings for radio and television*

The lease or rental of films, motion picture films, transcriptions, and recordings to radio stations and television stations operating under a certificate from the Federal Communications is exempt [G.S. § 105-164.13(22)].

• *Food served in State or private educational institutions*

Food and prepared food served to students in dining rooms regularly operating by State or private educational institutions or student unions thereof are exempt [G.S. § 105-164.13(27)]. This exemption is repealed effective for sales made on or after January 1, 2014 [S.L. 2013-316, § 3.2(a) and (d)].

• *Food sold by church and religious organizations*

Sales of food and prepared food by nonprofit church or religious organizations are exempt if the sale proceeds are actually used for religious activities [G.S. § 105-164.13(31a)].

• *Food sold in school cafeterias*

Food sold within school buildings: Sales of food and prepared food, within school buildings during the regular school day are exempt, For this purpose a "school" is an entity regulated under Chapter 115C of the General Statutes [G.S. § 105-164.13(26)].

Food sold to child care centers: Sales of food and prepared food by public school cafeterias to child care centers that participate in the Child and Adult Care Food Program of the Department of Health and Human Services are exempt if the sales are not for profit [G.S. § 105-164.13(26a)].

• *Food and other items sold to benefit elementary or secondary schools*

Sales of food, prepared food, soft drinks, candy and other tangible personal property sold not for profit for or at an event sponsored by an elementary or secondary school are exempt if the net proceeds will be given to the school or a nonprofit charitable organization for the benefit of the school [G.S. § 105-164.13(26b)].

• *Food sold under prepaid meal plans*

Food and prepared food provided to a person entitled to the food under a prepaid meal plan subject to sales tax is exempt. This exemption applies to packaging (such as wrapping paper, labels, plastic bags, cartons, packages, containers, paper cups, napkins, straws and similar items) that are used for packaging, shipment or delivery of the food or prepared food, constitute part of the sale and are delivered with the food or prepared food [G.S. § 105-164.13(63)].

- *Food stamps, Special Supplemental Food Program*

Food and other products lawfully purchased under the Supplemental Nutrition Assistance Program [7 U.S.C. §2001] and supplemental foods lawfully purchased with a food instrument issued under the Special Supplemental Nutrition Program [42 U.S.C. §1786] are exempt [G.S. §105-164.13(38)].

- *Fuel, electricity and piped natural gas sold to manufacturers and secondary metal recyclers*

Fuel, electricity and piped natural gas sold to a manufacturer for use in connection with the operation of a manufacturing facility, provided that the exemption for electricity applies only if manufacturing is the primary activity at the facility. In addition, the exemption does not apply to fuel or piped natural gas that is used solely for comfort heating at a manufacturing facility where there is no use of fuel or piped natural gas in a manufacturing process [G.S. §105-164.13(57)]. Fuel, electricity and piped natural gas sold to a secondary metals recycler on or before July 1, 2018 are exempt if such items are sold for use in recycling at a facility of the recycler if the primary activity at the facility if recycling [G.S. §105-164.13(57a)].

- *Installation charges*

Installation charges that are a part of the sales price of tangible personal property purchased by a real property contractor to fulfill a real property contract are exempt. To be exempt the installation charges must be for the installation of an item that is installed or applied to real property, and the installation charges must be separately stated and identified as such on documentation such as an invoice provided to the real property contractor at the time of the sale. This exemption extends to a retailer-contractor's installation charges under a real property contract and includes the retailer-contractor's labor costs including employee wages and labor purchased from a third party [G.S. §105-164.13(61c)].

- *Interior design services*

Interior design services provided in conjunction with the sale of tangible personal property are exempt [G.S. §105-164.13(59), effective August 1, 2008].

- *Land surveyor purchases*

Sales to a professional land surveyor of tangible personal property on which custom aerial survey data are stored in digital form or are depicted in graphic form are exempt [G.S. §105-164.13(53)]. A set of data is custom if it was created to the specifications of the professional land surveyor purchasing the property. A professional land surveyor is a person licensed as a surveyor under Chapter 89C of the General Statutes.

- *Large fulfillment facility purchases*

Sales of equipment, or an accessory, an attachment, or a repair part for equipment, to a large fulfillment facility are exempt if the item is used at the facility in the distribution process. The distribution process includes receiving, inventorying, sorting, repackaging, and distributing finished retail products. The exemption does not apply to sales of electricity [G.S. §105-164.13(5o)]. A "large fulfillment facility" is a facility that is used primarily for receiving, inventorying, sorting, repackaging, and distributing finished retail products for the purpose of fulfilling customer orders. In addition, the Secretary of Commerce must have certified (i) that an investment of private funds of at least $100,000,000 has been or will be made in real and tangible personal property for the facility within five years after the date on which the first property investment is made and (ii) that the facility will employ at least 400 workers within five years after the date the facility is placed into service and will maintain that employment level throughout its operation [G.S. § 105-164.3(16f)]. If the investment or employment requirement is not timely satisfied, the exemption is forfeited on all purchases. If the investment and employment requirements are initially satisfied, but the facility does not maintain the required level of employment, then the exemption is forfeited for those purchases occurring on or after the date the employment level falls below the require threshold. A taxpayer that forfeits the exemption is liable for all past sales and use taxes avoided as a result of the forfeiture, computed at the applicable State and local rates from the date the taxes would otherwise have been due, plus interest at the statutory rate from the date the sales or use tax would otherwise have been due. The past taxes and interest are due 30 days after the date of forfeiture. A taxpayer that fails to pay the past taxes and interest by the due date is subject to penalties [G.S. § 105-164.13(5o)]. This exemption is effective July 1, 2017 and applies to sales made on or after that date [S.L. 2017-57, § 38.9.(c)].

- *Life and Health Insurance Guaranty Association*

Sales of items to the North Carolina Life and Health Insurance Guaranty Association are exempt [G.S. § 105-164.13(71)].

- *Manufactured and modular homes*

One half of the sales price of a manufactured or modular home, including all accessories attached to the home when delivered to the purchaser, is exempt [G.S. § 105-164.13(64); S.L. 2014-100 § 37.3].

- *Meals for elderly and incapacitated*

Sales of meals delivered to elderly and incapacitated persons at their homes by nonprofit charitable or religious organizations qualifying under G.S. § 105-164.14(b) are exempt if the meals are not sold for profit [G.S. § 105-164.13(31)].

- *Mobile classrooms*

Sales of mobile classrooms to local boards of education or to local boards of trustees of community colleges are exempt [G.S. § 105-164.13(41)].

- *Motorsports racing team items*

The following items sold, before January 1, 2024 to a professional motorsports racing team or a related member of such a team for use in competition in a sanctioned race series are exempt: (i) the sale, lease or rental of an engine, (ii) the sales price or gross receipts from a service contract or repair, maintenance and installation services for a transmission, an engine, rear-end gears and any tangible personal property that is purchased, leased or rented and that is exempt or entitled to a refund, (iii) the gross receipts derived from an agreement to provide an engine where the agreement does not meet the definition of a "service contract" as defined in G.S. § 105-164.3 but may meet the definition of "lease or rental" as defined in that section. This exemption expires January 1, 2020 [G.S. § 105-164.13(65)].

¶1809

In addition, an engine or a part to build or rebuild an engine for the purpose of providing an engine under an agreement to a professional motorsports racing team or a related member of such a team for use in competition in a sanctioned race series is exempt. This exemption also expires January 1, 2024 [G.S. § 105-164.13(65a)].

• *Motor vehicles and chassis temporarily in North Carolina*

The following are exempt: (1) sales of motor vehicles (including a park model RV); (2) the sale of a motor vehicle body to be mounted on a motor vehicle chassis when a certificate of title has not been issued for the chassis; and (3) the sale of a motor vehicle body mounted on a motor vehicle chassis that temporarily enters North Carolina so the manufacturer of the body can mount the body on the chassis [G.S. § 105-164.13(32)].

• *Motor Vehicle Service contracts*

Motor vehicle service contracts are exempt from tax [G.S. § 105-164.13(61)]

• *Motor vehicle storage*

Storage of a motor vehicle is exempt if the storage charge is separately stated on documentation such as an invoice provided to the purchaser at the time of sale [G.S. § 105-164.13(66)].

• *Newspapers*

Newspaper sales: Sales of newspapers by newspaper street vendors, by newspaper carriers making door-to-door deliveries, and by means of vending machines are exempt [G.S. § 105-164.13(28)]. This exemption is repealed effective for sales made on or after January 1, 2014 [S.L. 2013-316, §3.2.(a) and (d)]. Newspapers sold through coin-operated vending machines remain 50% exempt pursuant to G.S. § 105-164.13(50).

• *Ocean-going vessels*

Sales of fuel and other tangible personal property for use or consumption by or on ocean-going vessels that ply the high seas in interstate or foreign commerce in the transport of freight and/or passengers exclusively for hire when delivered to an officer or agent of the vessel are exempt. However, sales of fuel and other items of tangible personal property made to officers, agents, crew members, or passengers for their personal use are not exempt [G.S. § 105-164.13(24)].

• *Packaging containers*

A container that is used as packaging by the owner of the container or another person to enclose tangible personal property for delivery to a purchaser of the property if it is required to be returned to its owner for reuse [G.S. § 105-164.13(23b)]. *See Parkdale Am., LLC v. Hinton*, 200 N.C. App. 275, 684 S.E.2d 458 (2009) (holding that an industrial yarn container qualified for exemption even though it did not enclose the yarn on all sides).

• *Packaging*

The following are exempt: wrapping paper, labels, wrapping twine, paper, cloth, plastic bags, cartons, packages and containers, cores, cones or spools, wooden boxes, baskets, coops and barrels, paper cups, napkins and drinking straws and like articles sold to manufacturers, producers, and retailers to be used for packaging, shipment, or delivery of tangible personal property that is sold either at wholesale or retail if such articles constitute a part of the sale of such tangible personal property and are delivered with the property to the customer [G.S. § 105-164.13(23a)].

• *Periodicals, free*

Sales of paper, ink, and other tangible personal property to commercial printers and commercial publishers for use as ingredients or component parts of free distribution periodicals are exempt. Also, sales by printers of free distribution periodicals to the publishers of these periodicals are exempt. A "free distribution periodical" means a publication that is continuously published on a periodic basis monthly or more frequently, is provided without charge to the recipient, and is distributed in any manner other than by mail [G.S. § 105-164.13(39)].

• *Permitted items*

Items purchased under an exemption certificate for resale of under a direct pay permit are exempt [G.S. § 105-164.13(61b)].

• *Qualified aircraft and qualified jet engines repair parts*

Parts and accessories for use in the repair or maintenance of a qualified aircraft or qualified jet engine are exempt [G.S. § 105-164.13(45d)].

• *Qualifying datacenter electricity and support equipment*

Exemption. Sales of electricity for use at a qualifying datacenter and sales of datacenter support equipment located and used at a qualifying datacenter are exempt [G.S. § 105-164.13(55a)].

Qualifying datacenter. For the definition of "qualifying datacenter" *see* ¶ 1603.

Datacenter support equipment. Datacenter support equipment is property that is capitalized for federal income tax purposes and that is (1) used to provide a service or function included in the business of an owner, user or tenant of the datacenter, (2) used to generate, transform, transmit, distribute or manage electricity, (3) HVAC or mechanical system equipment, (4) hardware or software for distributed and mainframe computers and servers, data storage devices, network connectivity equipment or peripheral components and equipment or (5) used to provide related computer engineering or computer science research [G.S. § 105-164.13(55a)].

Forfeiture. The exemption for qualifying datacenter electricity and support equipment is forfeited in the following circumstances: (1) if the investment requirement included in the definition of "qualified datacenter" is not satisfied, the entire exemption is forfeited; (2) if specific equipment or electricity is put to a disqualifying use the exemption for that equipment or electricity is forfeited. If an exemption is forfeited, the taxpayer is liable for all past taxes avoided as a result of the forfeited exemption plus interest. The interest is computed from the date the taxes would have been due absent the exemption if the forfeiture is caused by a failure to satisfy the investment requirement. In other case, interest is computed from the date the equipment or electricity was put to a disqualifying use. The taxes and interest are due 30 days after the date of forfeiture [G.S. § 105-164.13(55a)].

¶1809

• *Railroad intermodal equipment*

Sales to the owner or lessee of an eligible railroad intermodal facility of intermodal cranes, intermodal hostler trucks, and railroad locomotives that reside on the premises of the facility and are used at the facility are specifically exempt from the sales and use tax [G.S. § 105-164.13(56)]. Railroad intermodal facilities are discussed at ¶ 1103.

• *Repair, maintenance and installation services*

The sales price or gross receipts derived from certain repair, maintenance and installation services are exempt [G.S. § 105-164.13(61a)]:

(1) A motor vehicle emissions and safety inspection fee required by G.S. § 20-183.7, provided the fee is separately stated on the invoice or other documentation provided to the purchaser at the time of the sale.

(2) A service performed for a person by a related member.

(3) Cleaning services for real property, except where the service constitutes a part of the gross receipts derived from the taxable rental of an accommodation or for a pool, fish tank, or other similar aquatic feature. This exemption covers custodial services, window washing, mold remediation, carpet cleaning, gutter cleaning, duct cleaning and powerwashing (other than for a pool).

(4) A service on roads, driveways, parking lots, and sidewalks.

(5) Removal of waste, trash, debris, grease, snow, and other similar tangible personal property from property, other than a motor vehicle. This exemption applies to trash collection and septage removal but does not include removal of waste from portable toilets.

(6) The following inspections: (i) inspections the results of which are included in a real property sale or financing report, (ii) a real property structural integrity report if the charge is separately stated, (iii) an inspection of a capital improvement system that is provided to fulfill a safety requirement if the charge is separately stated.

(7) Alteration and repair services for clothing (other than belts and shoes), except where the service constitutes a part of the gross receipts derived from the taxable rental of clothing.

(8) A Pest control service.

(9) A moving service.

(10) Self service vehicle wash or vacuum and a limited-service vehicle wash.

(11) Repair, maintenance and installation services and service contracts on qualified aircraft, qualified jet engines and (effective July 1, 2019) aircraft with a take-off weight of more than 2,000 pounds.

(12) A service performed on a transmission, distribution or other network asset on land owned by a service provider or on a right-of-way or easement in favor of the service provider. This exemption does not apply to charges billed to a customer for repair, maintenance and installation services or a contribution in aid of construction and included in gross receipts subject to the combined general rate.

(13) A funeral-related service, including a burial service (but not the sale of tangible personal property such as caskets and head stones)

(14) A service performed on an animal such as hoof shoeing and microchipping a pet.

(15) A service and a service contract for an item exempt from tax, other than water for a pool, fishtank or other aquatic feature or a motor vehicle. Note that an item used to fulfill a service or a contract on exempt items is also exempt.

(16) A security or similar monitoring contract for real property, not including services to repair security and monitoring equipment.

(17) A contract to provide a certified operator of a wastewater system.

• *Service contract property and services*

An item, including repair, maintenance and installation services, purchased or used to fulfill a service contract is exempt if the purchaser of the service contract is not charged for the item. For purposes of this exemption, an "item" does not include a tool, equipment, supply or similar tangible personal property that is not a component or repair part of the tangible personal property, real property or certain digital property that is the subject of the service contract. This exemption does not apply to tangible personal property or certain digital property purchased to fulfill a service contract for real property if the charge would otherwise be taxable as part of a real property contract [G.S. § 105-164.13(62)].

• *State agency purchases*

Direct purchases exempt: Items purchased by a State agency for its own use (except electricity, telecommunications service, and ancillary service as defined in G.S. § 105-164.3) with a sales tax exemption number pursuant to G.S. § 105-164.29A are exempt if (1) they are purchased pursuant to a valid purchase order; (2) they are paid for with a State-issued check, electronic deposit credit card, procurement card, or credit account of the State agency; and (3) they meet sales tax exemption number requirements [G.S. § 105-163.13(52)].

Sales tax exemption number required: To be eligible for the exemption for direct purchases, a State agency must obtain from the Department of Revenue a sales tax exemption number. The exemption application must (1) be in the form required by the Secretary of Revenue; (2) be signed by the head of the State agency, and (3) contain any information required by the Secretary. Upon submission of a proper application, the Secretary will assign a sales tax exemption number to the State agency. Occupational licensing boards and the agencies listed in G.S. § 105-164.14(c) are not eligible for these exemption numbers [G.S. § 105-164.29A(a)].

Liability: A State agency that does not use the items purchased with its exemption number must pay the tax that should have been paid on the items purchased, plus interest calculated from the date the tax would otherwise have been paid [G.S. § 105-164.29A(b)].

Purchases not made by agency-issued purchase order: For all purchases other than by an agency-issued purchase order, the agency must provide the retailer with an exemption number or have its exemption number on file with the retailer [G.S. § 105-164.13(52c)].

¶1809

• *Tangible personal property delivered out of state by common carrier or USPS*

Tangible personal property sold by a retailer to a purchaser is exempt if the retailer delivers the property in North Carolina to a common carrier or to the United States Postal Service for delivery to the purchaser or the purchaser's designees outside North Carolina and the purchaser does not subsequently use the property in North Carolina. This exemption includes printed material sold by a retailer to a purchaser when the printed material is delivered directly to a mailing house, common carrier or the postal service for delivery to a mailing house in North Carolina that will address and sort the material and deliver it to a common carrier or the postal service for delivery to recipients outside North Carolina designated by the purchaser [G.S. § 105-164.13(33a)].

• *Tangible personal property purchased with certain disaster relief debit cards*

Tangible personal property purchased with a client assistance debit card issued for disaster assistance relief by a State agency or a federal agency or instrumentality is exempt [G.S. § 105-164.13(58), effective August 1, 2008, and applicable to purchases made on or after that date].

• *Telecommunications services and charges*

The following telecommunications services and charges are exempt [G.S. § 105-164.13(54)]:

(1) Telecommunications service that is a component part of or is integrated into a telecommunications service that is resold. This exemption does not apply to service purchased by a pay telephone provider who uses the service to provide pay telephone service.

(2) Pay telephone service.

(3) 911 charges.

(4) Charges for telecommunications service made by a hotel, motel, or another entity whose gross receipts are taxable if the charges are incidental to the occupancy of the entity's accommodations.

(5) Telecommunications service purchased or provided by a State agency or a until of local government for the State Network or another data network owned or leased by the State or unit of local government.

• *Towing services*

Towing services are exempt if the towing charge is separately stated on documentation such as an invoice provided to the purchaser at the time of sale [G.S. § 105-164.13(67)].

• *Vending machines*

Fifty percent (50%) of the sales price of tangible personal property sold through coin-operated vending machines (other than tobacco and newspapers) is exempt [G.S. § 105-164.13(50)].

• *Warranty items*

The following items are exempt if provided under a manufacturer's or dealer's warranty with respect to tangible personal property or a motor vehicle: (1) replacement items, (2) repair parts, and (3) repair, maintenance and installation services. A dealer's warranty is an explicit warranty extended by the seller of an item to the purchaser as part of the purchase price. A manufacturer's warranty is an explicit warranty extended by the manufacturer of an item to the purchaser as part of the purchase price of the item [G.S. § 105-164.13(62a)].

• *Wastewater dispersal products*

Sales of wastewater dispersal products approved by the N.C. Department of Health and Human Services [G.S. § 105-164.13(68)].

• *Water*

Sales of water delivered by or through main lines or pipes for either commercial or domestic use or consumption are not taxable [G.S. § 105-164.13(51)].

¶1810 Exemptions for Farmers

A number of sales tax exemptions for farm and agricultural supplies are available to farmers who (1) had at least $10,000 in annual income from farming operations for the preceding calendar year or (2) had at least $10,000 in an average annual income from farming operations for the three preceding taxable years ("qualifying farmers"). "Income from farming operations" means sales plus any other amounts from farming operations that are treated as gross income under the Code. A qualifying farmer includes a dairy operator, a poultry farmer, an egg producer, a livestock farmer, a farmer of crops, a farmer of an aquatic species and a person who boards horses. The exemption is available only if the item is used by the farmer primarily in farming operations. An item is used in farming operations if it is used for planting, cultivating, harvesting or curing farm crops, in the production of dairy products, eggs or animals or by a person who boards horses [G.S. § 105-164.13E(a)]. A qualifying farmer may obtain an exemption certificate (discussed at ¶1811). Conditional exemption certificates [discussed at ¶1811] are available to new farmers.

The items listed below are exempt if purchased by a qualifying farmer and used in farming operations [G.S. §§ 105-164.13(l); 105-164.13E]. Note that an exemption is also available for the items described in (6) below when purchased by someone other than a farmer to fulfil a service for a farmer [G.S. § 105-164.13E(c1)].

(1) Fuel, piped natural gas and electricity if separately metered and not used for household purposes such as preparing food and heating a dwelling.

(2) Commercial fertilizer, lime, land plaster, plastic mulch, plant bed covers, potting soil, baler twine and seeds.

(3) Farm machinery, including implements with moving parts or that are operated or drawn by an animal but not including implements operated wholly by hand or motor vehicles required to be registered. Attachment and repair parts for farm machinery and lubricants applied to farm machinery are also exempt.

(4) Containers used in planting, cultivating, harvesting or curing crops; producing dairy products, eggs or animals; or transporting the farmer's products for sale.

(5) Grain, feed or soybean storage facilities and attached parts and accessories.

(6) The following substances if purchased for use on animals or plants held or produced for commercial purposes:

a. Remedies, vaccines, medications, litter materials and animal feeds.

b. Rodenticides, insecticides, herbicides, fungicides and pesticides.

c. Defoliants for use on crops.

d. Plant growth inhibitors, regulators, or stimulators, including systemic and contact or other sucker control agents for crops.

e. Semen.

(7) Baby chicks and poults sold for commercial poultry or egg production.

(8) Commercially manufactured facilities used for commercial purposes for housing, raising, or feeding animals or for housing equipment necessary for the housing, raising or feeding of animals, including commercially manufactured equipment, parts and accessories for such equipment, if used in the facility. *See* SUPLR 2018-0001 (exemption not applicable to sheds for storage of manure).

(9) Building materials, supplies, fixtures and equipment that are used in the construction, repair or improvement of an enclosure or structure specifically designed, constructed and used to house, raise or feed animals or to house equipment necessary for the housing, raising or feeding of animals if the items become a part of the enclosure or structure. The exemption also applies to commercially manufactured equipment and parts and accessories for the equipment, if used in the enclosure or structure.

(10) A bulk tobacco barn or rack, parts and accessories attached to the tobacco barn or rack, and any similar apparatus, part or accessories used to cure or dry tobacco or any other crop.

(11) Repair, maintenance and installation services.

A contractor who purchases an item listed in (5), (8), (9) or (10) above from a retailer to use in fulfilling a contract with a qualified farmer who holds an exemption certificate or conditional exemption certificate is exempt from tax on the purchase to the same extent as the qualified farmer, provided the contractor provides the retailer with an exemption certificate that includes the name of the qualified farmer and the qualified farmer's exemption certificate number. [G.S. § 105-164.13E(c)]. A contractor who paid sales tax on exempt items on or after July 1, 2014 may request a refund from the retailer, and the retailer may, after refunding the tax to the contractor, request a refund from the Department [S.L. 2015-6, § 2.13.(b)]. See also Department of Revenue, Important Notice: Certain Purchases by a Contractor to Fulfill a Contract with a Qualifying or Conditional Farmer (May 28, 2015).

¶1810

¶1811 Exemption Certificates

An exemption certificate is a certificate issued by the Secretary that authorizes a retailer to sell an item to the holder of the certificate and either collect tax at a preferential rate or not collect tax on the sale. The Department must issue a preferential rate or use-based exemption number to a person who qualifies for the preferential rate or exemption. A person who no longer qualifies for a preferential rate or use-based exemption number must notify the Secretary within 30 days to cancel the number. An exemption certificate authorizes a retailer to sell an item to the holder of the certificate and either collect tax at a preferential rate or not collect tax on the sale, as appropriate. A person who no longer qualifies for an exemption certificate must notify each seller that may rely on the certificate on or before the next purchase. A person who purchases an item under an exemption certificate is liable for any tax due on the purchase if the Department of Revenue determines that the person is not eligible for the certificate or if the person purchased items that do not qualify for an exemption under the certificate. The liability is relieved when the seller obtains the purchaser's name, address, type of business, reason for exemption and exemption number in lieu of obtaining an exemption certificate. These rules also apply to conditional exemption certificates (relating to qualifying farmer exemptions, discussed below) ¶1812.

Records: An exemption certificate should be prepared in duplicate and a copy retained by both the purchaser and the vendor in their permanent records. A copy of the completed certificate should not be sent to the Department of Revenue unless requested by the Department [*Tax Directive SD-04-1* (June 1, 2004), § VI].

• *Streamlined Sales Tax Agreement Certificate of Exemption (Form E-595E)*

Vendors and purchasers must use Form E-595E. In general, a purchaser will be required to enter a sales and use tax registration number or an exemption number on the certificate, depending on the type of transaction [*Tax Directive SD-04-1*]. To obtain a sales and use tax registration number, a taxpayer should submit Form AS/RP1. to obtain an exemption number, a taxpayer should submit a Form E-595 EA [*Tax Directive SD-04-1* (June 1, 2004), § VI].

Occasional or infrequent purchases: If a purchaser makes occasional or infrequent purchases of tangible personal property that is eligible for an exemption, the purchaser should furnish a copy of the exemption certificate with each purchaser order [*Tax Directive SD-04-1* (June 1, 2004), § VI].

Frequent purchases of same type property: If a purchaser makes frequent purchases of the same type property from a vendor, the purchaser is only required to issue a single certificate to that vendor [*Tax Directive SD-04-1* (June 1, 2004), § VI].

• *Entities not required to furnish exemption certificates*

Certain purchasers, such as the United States Government or the State of North Carolina, are not required to furnish Form E-595E. Purchase requisitions, affidavits from purchasing officers, and applicable credit cards issued by the United States Government are acceptable documentation for exempting purchases by federal agencies and instrumentalities. Purchases by State agencies are exempt from sales or use tax, and purchase orders or other documentation bearing the assigned State agency exemption number are acceptable [*Tax Directive No. SD-04-1* (June 1, 2004), § VII].

¶1811

Warning to Purchaser

Form E-595E is a multi-state form. Not all states allow all exemptions listed on the form. Purchasers are responsible for knowing if they qualify to claim exemption from tax in the state that is due tax on a sale. The state that is due tax on a sale will be notified that the taxpayer claimed exemption from sales tax. The taxpayer will be held liable for any tax and interest, as well as civil and criminal penalties imposed by the member state, if the taxpayer is not eligible to claim the exemption. Sellers may not accept a certificate of exemption for sales sourced within the state if an exemption does not apply in the seller's state [Form E-595E].

• Sales for resale

A purchaser of property for resale should present Form E-595E to a vendor in order to exclude the sale from sales or use tax. A purchaser's sales and use tax registration number and other information required under G.S. § 105-164.28 must be entered on the Form E-595E [*Tax Directive No. SD-04-1* (June 1, 2004), § II].

Refunds to Certain Entities

Interstate carriers, hospitals, educational institutions, churches, charitable institutions, and certain governmental agencies do not use exemption certificates. Instead, they must pay tax on purchases and apply for refunds [G.S. § 105-164.14]. Certificates of resale cannot be used by any nonprofit entity in making purchases of tangible personal property for its own use. Nonprofits must use Form E-585, *Nonprofit and Governmental Entity Claim for Refund State and County Sales and Use Tax*, when filing the refund authorized by G.S. § 105-164.14(b) [*Sales and Use Tax Technical Bulletins*, § 17-2.A].

• Sales to manufacturers

A manufacturer should issue Form E-595E to a vendor when making a purchase of property that is exempt from tax (*e.g.*, ingredient or component materials or packaging materials that become part of the sale of a product). A manufacturer must enter its sales and use tax registration number on the Form E-595E. A manufacturer that is not liable for remitting sales or use tax to the Department of Revenue is required to register with the Department of Revenue for the purposes of obtaining a sales and use tax registration by submitting Form AS/RP1 [*Tax Directive No. SD-04-1* (June 1, 2004), § III].

• Sales to qualifying farmers

A qualifying farmer (discussed at ¶ 1810) may obtain an exemption certificate, which will remain valid until the holder ceases to engage in farming operations or fails to satisfy the qualifying farmer income threshold for three consecutive years [G.S. § 105-164.13E(a)]. A person who does not meet the definition of a qualifying farmer may apply for a conditional exemption certificate, which permits the person to purchase items exempt from sales tax as if the person were a qualified farmer. To obtain the conditional exemption certificate, the person must certify its intent to engage in farming operations and that it will timely file state and federal income tax returns that reflect income and expenses from farming operations during the taxable years that the conditional exemption certificate is valid. The certificate is valid for the taxable year in which it is issued and the following two taxable years, provided the holder is engaged in farming and provides copies of its state and federal income tax returns to the Department within 90 days following the due date of an income tax return for each taxable year covered by the certificate (including an extension granted by the Secretary). A conditional exemption certificate may not be renewed beyond its three-year period, (except that a one-year extension may be granted in certain cases where a weather-related disaster prevents the farmer from satisfying the farming operations income requirement). A person may not obtain a conditional exemption certificate if it had been issued a prior conditional exemption certificate during the prior 15 years. The holder of a conditional exemption certificate must maintain documentation of the items purchased with the certificate and copies of its federal and state income tax returns for the years covered by the certificate for three years after the expiration of the certificate. The Secretary may require the holder of a conditional exemption certificate to produce additional information to verify the holder's qualification to use the certificate. A person who fails to provide such information in a timely manner or who otherwise fails to comply with the conditional exemption certificate rules is liable for any taxes for which a qualifying farmer exemption was claimed. The taxes become due when the certificate expires, with interest from the date of purchase. In addition, if the holder does not timely provide information requested by the Secretary, each person who sold items to such person is liable for the penalty for misuse of an exemption certificate (G.S. § 105-236(a)(5a)) [G.S. § 105-164.13E(b)].

• *Liability*

When a customer makes a qualifying purchase as indicated on the exemption certificate and furnishes a properly completed certificate to a vendor, the vendor is relieved of the liability for any additional tax that is subsequently determined to be due; and the purchaser is liable to the additional tax. If the vendor does not have proper documentation to support a full or partial exemption from tax, the vendor is liable for any additional tax determined to be due [*Tax Directive SD-04-1* (June 1, 2004), § VI]. See also G.S. § 105-164.28, regarding the liability of a vendor who accepts a Certificate of Exemption.

Remote sales: For a sale for resale, a remote vendor is relieved of liability for any additional tax that is subsequently determined to be due when the vendor secures a sales and use tax registration number from a purchaser that matches the number of the Department's registry, in lieu of obtaining a completed exemption certificate. For a sale subject to a preferential rate of tax or exempt from tax other than as a sale for resale, the remote vendor's liability is relieved if the vendor secures the information as to a purchaser's type of business, reason for exemption, and identification number in lieu of obtaining an exemption certificate. The registry of sales and use tax registration numbers and a registry of exemption numbers is available on the Department's website at www.dor.state.nc.us [*Tax Directive SD-04-1* (June 1, 2004), § VI].

• *Misuses of exemption certificates*

Misuse of an exemption certificate by a purchaser subjects the purchaser to a penalty of $250 [G.S. § 105-236(5a)].

¶1811

• *Seller's responsibilities*

A seller is not liable if the Secretary determines that the purchaser improperly claimed an exemption or if, within 90 days of the sale, the seller meets the following requirements [G.S. § 105-164.28(a)]:

(1) For a sale made in person, the seller obtains a certificate of exemption. If the purchaser provides a paper certificate (including a fax), the certificate must be signed by the purchaser and state the purchaser's name, address, and registration number, reason for exemption and the type of business. If the purchaser does not provide a paper certificate, the seller must obtain and maintain the same information.

(2) For a sale made over the Internet or by other remote means, the seller obtains the purchaser's name, address, registration number, reason for exemption and type of business and maintains this information in a retrievable format in its records. If the certificate of exemption is provided electronically, it must meet the requirements of a paper exemption certificate except that it does not have to be signed.

(3) For a drop shipment sale, a third party vendor may obtain a certificate of exemption from its customer or any other "acceptable" information evidencing qualification for the resale exemption regardless of whether the customer is registered to collect sales tax in North Carolina.

• *Substantiation Request*

If the Secretary determines that a certificate of exemption or other data collected by the seller are incomplete, the Secretary may request substantiation from the seller, and the seller can avoid liability if within 120 days, the seller obtains a completed exemption certificate from the purchaser provided in good faith or other information that establishes the transaction was exempt. The good faith requirement is satisfied if the claimed exemption was available in North Carolina by statute as of the date of sale, the exemption "could be" applicable to the item in question and the exemption is reasonable for the purchaser's type of business. Note that the seller is not required to verify that the purchaser's registration number is correct [G.S. § 105-164.28(b)].

• *Effect of Fraudulent Activity*

The liability relief provided by the procedures discussed above is not available if the seller fraudulently fails to collect tax, solicits purchasers to unlawfully claim exemptions, knew or had reason to know that the exemption information provided by the purchaser was materially false, or knowingly participated in an activity intended to evade tax. In addition, liability relief is not available when the purchaser claims an entity-based exemption that is not available in North Carolina if the purchaser receives the item sold at a location operated by the seller [G.S. § 105-164.28(c)].

• *Blanket exemptions*

If a seller has a recurring business relationship with a purchaser, the seller may accept a blanket exemption certificate from the purchaser. The Secretary may not require a seller to review a blanket exemption certificate or update exemption certificate information for such a purchaser. A recurring business relationship exists when the seller and purchaser engage in transactions no more than 12 months apart [G.S. § 105-164.28(a)(i) and (e)].

• *Purchaser's liability*

A purchaser who does not resell an item purchased under a Certificate of Exemption is liable for any tax subsequently determined to be due on the sale [G.S. § 105-164.28(b)].

¶1812 Direct Pay Permits

• *General*

A general direct pay permit authorizes its holder to purchase certain items without paying tax to the seller and relieves the seller of the obligation to collect any tax on a sale to the permit holder. A person who purchases an item under a direct pay permit is liable for use tax due on the purchase. The tax is payable when the property is placed in use or the service is received. A direct pay permit does not apply to purchases of electricity, piped natural gas, video programming, spirituous liquor or the rental of accommodations taxable under G.S. § 105-164.4. In addition, a general direct pay permit may not be used to purchase direct mail, a qualified jet engine, items purchased for boats, aircraft and qualified jet engines and telecommunications services for which specialized permits are available as described below [G.S. § 105-164.27A(a)].

• *Direct mail*

A person who purchases direct mail may apply for a direct pay permit for the purchase of direct mail. A direct pay permit issued for direct mail does not apply to purchases other than purchases of direct mail. A person who purchases direct mail under a direct mail permit must file a return and pay the tax monthly or quarterly [G.S. § 105-164.27A(a1)].

• *Qualified jet engines*

A person who purchases a qualified jet engine may apply for a direct pay permit and pay a use tax directly to the Secretary. The maximum use tax on a qualified jet engine acquired under a direct pay permit is $2,500. The use tax return and the use tax are due monthly. The direct pay permit does not apply to any other purchase [G.S. § 105-164.27A(a2)].

• *Certain items purchased with respect to boats, aircraft and qualified jet engines*

A taxpayer may apply for a direct pay permit for the purchase of tangible personal property, certain digital property or repair, maintenance and installation services for a boat, aircraft or qualified jet engine. In addition, the holder of such a permit is entitled to a use tax exemption for (1) separately stated installation charges that are part of the sales price of the tangible personal property or certain digital property purchased under the permit and (2) the sales price or gross receipts derived from the provision of repair, maintenance and installation services provided for a boat or aircraft purchased under the permit to the extent such charges or receipts exceed $25,000. In lieu of using the direct pay permit, the purchaser may elect to have the seller collect and remit the tax on his behalf. In this case, the purchaser's liability for the tax is extinguished upon the receipt of an invoice showing the proper amount of tax. If the seller does not separately state installation charges that are part of the sales price of the property for a boat, aircraft or qualified jet engine, tax is due on the total sales price. [G.S. §§ 105-164.27A(a3); 105-164.13(62b)].

- *Telecommunications service*

A direct pay permit for telecommunications service authorizes its holder to purchase telecommunications service and ancillary service without paying tax to the seller and relieves the seller of the obligation to collect any tax on a sale to the permit holder. A person who purchases telecommunications service and ancillary service under a direct pay permit must file a return and pay the tax due monthly or quarterly. A direct pay permit for telecommunications service does not apply to any tax other than the tax on telecommunications service and ancillary service [G.S. § 105-164.27A(b)]. Telecommunications services are discussed at ¶ 1719.

- *Call centers*

A call center that purchases interstate telecommunications service that originates outside North Carolina and terminates in North Carolina may apply for a direct pay permit for telecommunications service. A "call center" is a business that is primarily engaged in providing support services to customers by telephone to support products or services of the business. A business is primarily engaged in providing support services by telephone if at least 60% of its calls are incoming [G.S. § 105-164.27A(b)].

- *Applications*

An application for a direct pay permit must be made on a form provided by the Secretary and contain the information required by the Secretary. The Secretary may grant the application upon finding that the applicant complies with the sales and use tax laws and that the applicant's compliance burden will be greatly reduced by use of the permit [G.S. § 105-164.27A(c)].

- *Status of property uncertain*

If the taxable status of an item cannot be determined because (1) the place of business where the item will be used is not known at the time of the purchase and a different tax consequence applies depending on where the item is used or (2) the manner in which the item will be used is not known at the time of the purchase and one or more of the potential uses is taxable but others are not taxable, the purchaser may apply for a direct pay permit [G.S. § 105-164.27A(a)].

- *Revocation*

A direct pay permit is valid until it is returned to the Secretary or revoked by the Secretary. A direct pay permit may be revoked if (1) the certificate holder does not file a timely sales and use tax return, (2) does not pay sales and use tax on time, or (3) otherwise fails to comply with the sales and use tax laws [G.S. § 105-164.27A(d)].

- *Misuse of direct pay permit*

Misuse of an exemption permit by a purchaser subjects the taxpayer to a penalty of $250 [G.S. § 105-246(5a)].

¶1813 Casual Sales

Embedded in the definition of "business" is the statement that the term "business" does not include occasional and isolated sales or transactions by a person who does not hold himself or herself out as being engaged in business [G.S. § 105-164.3(1k)]. *See* SUPLR 2018-0002 for an example of the application of this definition. This is the authority for exemption of casual sales. The frequency of the transactions, not the number of customers, determines whether a taxpayer's sales qualify as occasional or isolated sales [*Tax Review Board Administrative Decision No. 382* (2002)]. Sales will also not be considered occasional or isolated simply because they produce relatively little of the taxpayer's revenues [*Secretary's Decision No. 2002-63* (July 11, 2002) (denying occasional or isolated sale exemption to finance company whose sales of repossessed articles accounted for only 3.2% of the "dollar volume")].

¶1814 Computer Services

• *Systems and programming services*

Services involved in the analysis, design and programming of an electronic data processing system are exempt, whether the services are used for the initial development or modification of the computer software or the data processing system. Persons providing the preceding exempt services for their customers are liable for the applicable sales or use taxes on all purchases of tangible personal property used to provide such services, notwithstanding the fact that some part of the property may later be transferred to the customer with the exempt service [*Sales and Use Tax Technical Bulletins*, § 28-3(A)].

Modifications: Charges for services to modify or update existing software, to meet additional processing procedures or new procedures being employed by the users of the software program, are not subject to sales or use tax.

Analysis and design: When a programmer goes to a customer's location to analyze a customer's requirements and designs a program to solve a problem, and after a program is written it is keypunched by the customer and introduced into his own computer system for use, the charge therefor is for services rendered which are not subject to sales or use tax.

• *Time sharing*

Charges made to customers for the use of a computer to which the customer has access through a remote terminal device are not deemed to be a taxable transfer of possession of the computer [*Sales and Use Tax Technical Bulletins*, § 28-3(B)].

• *Data processing services*

Information services are commonly provided by data processing centers. An information service may consist of a data processing company using its own facilities to process its customers' data to record information. The data may be provided to the data processing company in source document forms, as machine readable medium or entered directly into the company's computer facilities by devices located at the customers' premises. Information services are not subject to tax when the output is personal or individual in nature to the purchaser and the object of the transaction is to obtain the information and not to obtain tangible personal property for use or consumption [*Sales and Use Tax Technical Bulletins*, § 28-3(C)].

- *Support services*

When a firm furnishes support services only, such as training and consulting personnel, to train employees of customers to use computer software, such services are not taxable [*Sales and Use Tax Technical Bulletins*, § 28-3(D)].

- *Cloud-based services*

Licence revenues from subscription agreements for access to cloud-based software is not subject to sales tax. *See* SUPLR 2018-0005.

¶1815 Gift Certificates

Charges by vendors for gift certificates that can be exchanged for merchandise are not subject to sales tax. When the holders of such gift certificates exchange the certificate for merchandise, the transaction is subject to the general State tax and any applicable local sales or use tax. The basis for the tax is the sales price of the property [*Sales and Use Tax Technical Bulletins*, § 44-2].

¶1816 Prepaid Telephone Calls

The sale or recharge of prepaid telephone calling service is taxable at the general rate of tax, but calls placed using prepaid calling service are not taxed [G.S. § 105-164.4B(c)(2)]. Prepaid telephone calling service is discussed at ¶1720.

SALES AND USE TAXES

CHAPTER 19

RETURNS, PAYMENT OF TAX, ADMINISTRATION AND PROCEDURES

¶1901 Returns and Payment of Tax

• *General rules*

Sales and use taxes are payable when a return is due. A return is due monthly or quarterly (see discussion below). Taxpayers who are consistently liable for at least $20,000 per month must pay semimonthly and file monthly. Returns must be (1) filed with the Secretary on forms prescribed by the Secretary, (2) in the manner required by the Secretary, and (3) signed by the taxpayer or the taxpayer's agent [G.S. § 105-164.16(a)]. If no return is filed, or a filed return is grossly incorrect, the Secretary must estimate the tax due and assess tax based on the estimate [G.S. § 105-164.32].

• *Personal liability when certain taxes not paid*

Each responsible person in a business entity is personally and individually liable for the principal amount of all sales and use taxes collected by the business entity upon its taxable transactions and all sales and use taxes due upon taxable transactions of the business entity but upon which it failed to collect the tax. See ¶ 3211.

• *Use tax on out-of-state purchases*

Use tax payable by an individual who purchases an item other than a boat or aircraft outside North Carolina for a nonbusiness purpose is due on an annual basis [G.S. § 105-164.16(d)].

For individuals who are not required to file North Carolina individual income tax returns, the annual reporting period ends on the last day of the calendar year, and a use tax return is due by the following April 15. For individuals who are required to file North Carolina individual income tax returns, the annual reporting period ends on the last day of the individual's income tax year, and the use tax must be paid with the individual's income tax return [G.S. § 105-164.16(d)].

Payment of Use Tax with Individual Income Tax Return

An individual who owes use tax that is payable on an annual basis and who is required to file a North Carolina individual income tax return must pay the use tax with the individual income tax return for the taxable year [G.S. § 105-269.14]. Appropriate space and information for reporting use tax on out-of-state purchases are provided on forms and instructions.

• *Quarterly returns*

Taxpayers who are consistently liable for less than $100 a month in State and local sales and use taxes must file returns and remit the tax quarterly [G.S. § 105-164.16(b)]. Quarterly returns cover a calendar quarter and are due by the last day of the month following the end of the quarter.

• *Monthly returns*

Taxpayers who are consistently liable for at least $100 but less than $10,000 a month ($20,000, effective October 1, 2011) in State and local sales and use taxes must file returns and remit the taxes due on a monthly basis. Monthly returns are due by the 20th day of the month following the calendar month covered by the return [G.S. § 105-164.16(b1)].

• *Monthly filing with prepayment*

A taxpayer who is consistently liable for at least $15,000.00 a month ($20,000 effective October 1, 2011) in State and local sales and use taxes must make a monthly prepayment of the next month's liability when filing their monthly return due on or before the 20th day of each month.

The prepayment must equal at least 65% of any of the following:

    (1) The amount of tax due for the current month.

    (2) The amount of tax due for the same month in the preceding year.

    (3) The average monthly amount of tax due in the preceding calendar year.

Penalties or interest will not be due on an underpayment of a prepayment if one of these three calculation methods is used. Payments must be made by Electronic Funds Transfer or online.

• *Prepayment*

Taxpayers who are consistently liable for at least $20,000 a month in State and local sales and use taxes must make monthly prepayments of the next month's tax liability instead of paying twice a month [G.S. § 105-164.16(b2)]. The prepayment is due on the date a monthly return is due. The prepayment must equal at least 65% of any of the following:

    (1) The amount of tax due for the month covered by the return.

    (2) The amount of tax due for the same month in the preceding year.

    (3) The average monthly amount of tax due in the preceding calendar year.

• *Special due date rules*

When the last day for filing a sales or use tax return or doing any other act required or permitted under the sales and use tax laws (including the local sales and use tax law) falls on a Saturday, Sunday or holiday, the return or other act is considered timely if done on the next business day. If the Federal Reserve Bank is closed on a due date and a person is thereby prohibited from making a payment by ACH as required by the sales and use tax law, the payment is considered timely if made on the next day the Federal Reserve Bank is open [G.S. § 105-164.45].

• *Utility services*

Returns for taxes levied on electricity and telecommunications are due monthly on or before the last day of the month following the month in which the taxes accrue, except the return for taxes that accrue in May, which is due by June 25 [G.S. § 105-164.16(c)]. Retailers that are required to file monthly returns may file an estimated return for the first month, the second month (or both) in a quarter. However, a retailer is not subject to interest on or penalties for an underpayment submitted with an estimated monthly return if the retailer timely pays at least 95% of the amount due with a monthly return and includes the underpayment with the retailer's return for the third month in the same quarter.

• *Determination of filing schedules*

It is the responsibility of the Secretary to monitor the amount of State and local sales and use taxes paid by a taxpayer or estimate the amount of taxes to be paid by a new taxpayer and must direct each taxpayer to pay tax and file returns in accordance with the appropriate schedule [G.S. § 105-164.16(b3)]. In determining the amount of taxes due from a taxpayer, the Secretary must consider the total amount due from all places of business owned or operated by the same person as the amount due from that person. A taxpayer must file a return and pay tax in accordance with the Secretary's direction until notified in writing to file and pay under a different schedule.

• *Electronic funds transfer*

The Department reviews tax payment history annually and advises those tax-payers who are required to remit payment by EFT. Taxpayers that consistently remit $20,000 or more per month in sales and use tax or utilities and municipalities sales tax are required to remit their payment by EFT when instructed to do so by the Department of Revenue. Taxpayers who pay by EFT are still required to timely file required reports and schedules.

• *Method of accounting*

Except as noted below, a retailer may make application to the Secretary to report sales on either the cash or accrual basis of accounting. Permission by the Secretary to report on a selected basis continues in effect until (1) revoked by the Secretary or (2) the taxpayer receives permission from the Secretary to change the method of account-ing [G.S. § 105-164.20].

Certain retailers must report sales on the accrual basis. These retailers are: (1) retailers who sell electricity, piped natural gas or telecommunications service (a sale of electricity, piped natural gas or telecommunications service is considered to accrue when the retailer bills its customer for the sale), (2) retailers who derive gross receipts from a prepaid meal plan (even if the retailer reports other sales on the cash basis and even if the prepaid meal plan revenue has not been recognized for accounting purposes), and (3) retailers who derive gross receipts from a service contract [G.S. § 105-164.20].

¶1901

- *Reporting option for prepaid meal plans*

When a retailer enters into an agreement with a food service contractor under which the contractor agrees to provide food or prepared food under a prepaid meal plan and the contractor is also a sales tax retailer, the parties may agree that the contractor is liable for reporting and remitting tax on the gross receipts derived from the meal plan on behalf of the retailer. The agreement must provide that the tax applies to the allocated sales price of the meal plan paid by or on behalf of the person entitled to the food or prepared food under the plan and not the amount charged by the contractor to the retailer under the agreement. A retailer who elects this option must report to the contractor the gross receipts paid to the retailer for the plan using the accrual method of accounting, and the retailer must send the contractor the tax due on such receipts. The contractor must hold the tax payments received from the retailer in trust and must remit such payments to the Secretary. If the retailer does not send the tax payments to the contractor, the retailer and not the contractor is liable for the tax due [G.S. § 105-164.16A].

- *Extension of time*

The Secretary, for good cause, may extend the time for filing any sales and use tax return and grant additional time to file the return. [G.S. § 105-164.19].

¶ 1902 Records

- *Presumption of taxability*

It is presumed that (1) all gross receipts of wholesale merchants and retailers are taxable until the contrary is established by proper records; (2) tangible personal property sold by a person for delivery in North Carolina is sold for storage, use, or other consumption in North Carolina; (3) tangible personal property delivered outside North Carolina and brought to North Carolina by the purchaser is for storage, use, or consumption in North Carolina; (4) certain digital property sold for delivery or access in North Carolina is sold for storage, use, or consumption in North Carolina, and (5) a service purchased for receipt in North Carolina is purchased for storage, use, or consumption in North Carolina [G.S. § 105-164.26].

- *Records to be kept*

Retailers, wholesale merchants, facilitators, real property contractors and consumers must keep records that establish their sales and use tax liability. The Secretary may inspect these records at any reasonable time during the day [G.S. § 105-164.22]. Note that the former three-year limit on this record retention requirement has been repealed *See* S.L. 2016-5, § 3.15.

A retailer's records must include records of the retailer's gross income, gross sales, net taxable sales, all items purchased for resale, and reports or records related to transactions with any facilitators with whom it has a contract. Failure to keep records that establish a sale as exempt subjects the retailer to liability for tax on the sale [G.S. § 105-164.22]. *See also* Secretary's Decision No. 2001-507 (November 7, 2001) (where retailer failed to maintain records of gross sales, tax will be based upon Secretary's estimate of sales based on best information available).

A facilitator's records must include the facilitator's gross income, gross sales, net taxable sales, all items purchased for resale, any reports or records related to transactions with any retailer with whom it has a contract, and any other records that establish its tax liability. Failure to keep records that establish a sale is exempt subjects the facilitator to liability for tax on the sale.

A real property contractor's records must include substantiation that a transaction is a real property contract or a mixed transaction contract. Failure to keep records that establish a real property contract subjects the real property contractor to liability for tax on the sale.

A wholesale merchant's records must include the bill of sale for each customer that contains the name and address of the purchaser, the date of the purchase, the item purchased, and the sales price. Failure to keep records that establish that a sale is exempt subjects the wholesale merchant to liability for tax at the rate that applies to a retail sale of the item [G.S. § 105-164.22].

A consumer's records must include an invoice or other statement of the purchase price of an item the consumer purchased from inside or outside North Carolina and any sales or use tax paid thereon. Failure to keep these records subjects the consumer to liability for tax on the purchase price of the item, as determined by the Secretary [G.S. § 105-164.22].

¶1903 Refunds

• *In general*

In general, refunds of overpayments of sales and use taxes must conform to the general provisions of Article 9 of Chapter 105. See ¶3203. Refunds applied for more than three years after the due date are barred [G.S. § 105-164.14(d)].

Special refunds: Special sales and use tax refund provisions that apply to refunds to certain entities are discussed at ¶1904. Economic incentive refunds are discussed at ¶1905.

• *Refunds to retailer on rescinded sales and cancelled services*

A retailer is allowed a refund of sales tax remitted on a sale when the purchaser rescinds the sale by returning the item purchased to the retailer and receives a full or partial refund of the sales price paid, including a refund of sales tax collected on the refunded portion of the sales price. A retailer is also allowed a refund of sales tax remitted on a service when the service is cancelled by terminating the service and refunding all or a portion of the sales price paid, including a refund of sales tax collected on the refunded portion of the sales price. In the case of a rescinded sale or a cancelled service, once the tax has been refunded to the purchaser, the retailer may either request a refund under the general refund procedure discussed in ¶3203 or reduce taxable receipts by the taxable amount of the refund for the period in which the refund occurs. The retailer's records must clearly reflect and support the claim for refund or adjustment to taxable receipts [G.S. § 105-164.11A(a)].

• *Special rule for refunds to purchasers of cancelled service contracts*

If a service contract is cancelled the purchaser may receive a refund from the retailer of the sales price paid, including the sales tax collected on the refunded sales price, under the rules discussed above. In some cases, however, the purchaser may cancel a service contract and receive a refund of the sales price from a third party other than the retailer (e.g., a facilitator who had an agreement with the service provider for the service provider to remit the tax due). In such cases, the refund provided to the purchaser by the third party would not have to include the sales tax collected on the refunded sales price since the retailer, rather than the third party making the refund, would have remitted the tax. In such cases, the purchaser may, within 30 days of receiving a refund of the sales price, apply to the Secretary for a refund of the tax paid on the refunded portion of the sales price. Late applications are barred. The application must be made on a form provided by the Secretary and supported by documentation on the taxable amount of the refunded portion of the sales price. Taxes for which a refund is allowed to the purchaser under this rule do not accrue interest [G.S. § 105-164.11A(b)].

¶1904   Special Refunds to Certain Entities

• *In general*

Sales to interstate carriers, hospitals, educational institutions, churches, charitable institutions, and certain governmental agencies are taxable, but the purchasers may apply for refunds [G.S. § 105-164.14]. These refunds are discussed below. The refunds authorized by G.S. § 105-164.14 do not apply to purchases of alcoholic beverages [G.S. § 105-164.14(d1)]. In addition, a city subject to G.S. § 160A-340.5 (regarding city-owned communications networks) are not allowed refunds of sales and use taxes paid on purchases related to the provision of communications service [G.S. § 105-164.14(d2)]. Taxes for which a refund is allowed under G.S. § 105.164.14 are not overpayments for taxes and do not accrue interest [G.S. § 105-164.14(p)].

• *Interstate carriers*

An interstate carrier is allowed a refund of part of the sales and use taxes paid by it on the purchase in North Carolina of railway cars and locomotives, fuel, lubricants, repair parts, accessories, service contracts and repair maintenance and installation services purchased in North Carolina for a motor vehicle, railroad car, locomotive, or airplane the carrier operates. An "interstate carrier" is a person who is engaged in transporting persons or property in interstate commerce for compensation [G.S. § 105-164.14(a)]. Requests for refund under G.S. § 105-164.14(a1) are due within six months after the end of the calendar year for which the refund is claimed and must be in writing and contain all required information and documentation [G.S. § 105-164.14(a1)].

Application for refund: An application for refund must contain the following information and any proof of the information required by the Secretary:

    (1) A list identifying the items purchased by the applicant inside or outside North Carolina during the refund period for which a refund is available [G.S. § 105-164.14(a)(1)].

    (2) The purchase price of the tangible personal property and services listed that are taxable in North Carolina [G.S. § 105-164.14(a)(2)].

    (3) The sales and use taxes paid in North Carolina on the listed items [G.S. § 105-164.14(a)(3)].

    (4) The number of miles the applicant's motor vehicles, railroad cars, locomotives, and airplanes were operated both inside and outside North Carolina during the refund period. Airplane miles are not in North Carolina if the airplane does not depart or land in North Carolina [G.S. § 105-164.14(a)(4)].

    (5) Any other information required by the Secretary [G.S. § 105-164.14(a)(5)].

Refund periods: The Secretary prescribes the periods of time, whether monthly, quarterly, semiannually, or otherwise, with respect to which refunds may be claimed and the time within which, following such a period, an application for refund may be made [G.S. § 105-164.14(a)].

Computation of refund: The Secretary does the computation of the refund amount as follows:

> Step 1: Determine the mileage ratio. The numerator of the mileage ratio is number of miles the applicant operated its motor vehicles, railroad cars, locomotives, and airplanes in North Carolina during the refund period. The denominator of the mileage ratio is the number of miles it operated them both inside and outside North Carolina during the refund period.

> Step 2: Determine the applicant's proportional liability for the refund period by multiplying this mileage ratio by the purchase price of the tangible personal property and services entitled to refund and then multiplying the resulting product by the applicable tax rate.

> Step 3: Refund to the applicant the excess of the amount of sales and use taxes the applicant paid in North Carolina during the refund period on these items over the applicant's proportional liability for the refund period.

- *Utility companies*

A utility company is allowed a refund of part of the sales and use taxes paid by it on the purchase in North Carolina of railway cars and locomotives and accessories for a railway car or locomotive the utility company operates. The Secretary is authorized to prescribe the periods with respect to which refunds may be claimed and the periods within which an application for refund may be made [G.S. § 105-164.14(a2)].

Amount of refund: The amount of the refund is calculated by applying the North Carolina sales tax rate to the purchase price of all the taxpayer's purchases of railway cars, locomotives, and accessories for a given refund period, whether purchased inside or outside of North Carolina and then multiplying that number by the ratio of the number of miles the taxpayer's railway cars and locomotives were operated in North Carolina to the total number of miles the taxpayer's cars and locomotives were operated.

Credit Is Refundable

> If the amount of credit as calculated above is more than the sales tax the taxpayer paid on its North Carolina purchases, the excess is refundable to the taxpayer. This formula appears to be designed to ensure that the taxpayer does not suffer if it buys proportionately more of its locomotives, cars, and accessories in North Carolina.

- *Nonprofit entities and hospital drugs*

Certain nonprofit entities must pay sales or use tax on their purchases but are entitled to refunds of any tax paid. The nonprofit entities identified below are entitled to a semiannual refund of sales and/or use taxes paid by them in North Carolina on their direct purchases (including reimbursements to an authorized person of the entity) of tangible personal property and services used in carrying on their nonprofit work. Sales and use taxes indirectly incurred by a nonprofit entity through reimbursement to an authorized person of the entity for the purchase of tangible personal property and services for use in carrying on the work of the entity are considered direct purchases by the entity. These refund provisions apply to the following entities:

¶1904

(1) Hospitals not operated for profit, including hospitals and medical accommodations operated by an authority or other public hospital described in the Hospital Authorities Law (Article 2 of Chapter 131E of the General Statutes) [G.S. § 105-164.14(b)(1)].

(2) An organization that is exempt from income tax under IRC § 501(c)(3), other than an organization that is properly classified in any of the following major group areas of the National Taxonomy of Exempt Entities [G.S. § 105-164.14(b)(2)]:

(a) Community Improvement and Capacity Building.

(b) Public and Societal Benefit.

(c) Mutual and Membership Benefit.

(3) A single member LLC that is a disregarded entity for income tax purposes owned by an organization exempt under IRC § 501(c)(3) if the LLC is a nonprofit entity that would qualify for exemption under IRC § 501(c)(3) if it were not a disregarded entity and provided the LLC would not be properly classified in any of the major group areas identified in (2) above.

(4) A volunteer fire department or volunteer emergency medical services squad that is exempt from income tax under the Code or financially accountable to a city, county or group of cities and counties [G.S. § 105.164.14(b)(2a)].

(5) Qualified retirement facilities whose property is excluded from property tax under G.S. § 105-278.6A [G.S. § 105-164.14(b)(1)]. See ¶ 2210.

(6) A university affiliated nonprofit organization that procures, designs, constructs, or provides facilities to, or for use by, a constituent institution of The University of North Carolina. This includes an entity exempt from taxation as a disregarded entity of the nonprofit organization [G.S. § 105-164.14(b)(5), retroactive to January 1, 2004].

No Need for Independent Determination of Charitable Status

The 2008 amendment to the exemption provision for nonprofits (S.L. 2008-107 § 28.22.(a)) entitles any charitable organization that has received a federal determination of 501(c)(3) status and that does not fall into one of the identified non-exempt classifications to refunds without an independent determination of charitable status under state law. Before amendment, an organization had to be able to establish that it qualified under state law as a "charitable or religious institution," a phrase that was undefined under the sales tax law. For applications of the prior law, see, e.g., *Lynnwood Found. v. N.C. Dept. of Revenue*, 190 N.C. App. 593, 660 S.E.2d 611 (2008) (historic mansion museum held to be charitable); *Southminster, Inc. v. Justus*, 119 N.C. App. 669, 459 S.E.2d 793 (1995) (retirement community held to be charitable); *Tax Review Board Administrative Decision No. 398* (2002) (youth soccer league held to be charitable).

Proof for direct purchases: A claim for refund must be supported by adequate documentation (*i.e.*, an invoice or copy of an invoice that sets out the item purchased, the date of the purchase, the cost of the item, and the amount of sales or use tax paid) [17 NCAC 7B:1602(b)].

Contractor purchases: A nonprofit entity listed above may file a claim for refund of sales or use tax paid indirectly by it on building materials, supplies, fixtures, and equipment that become part of a building it owns or leases and uses to conduct its nonprofit activity. A claim for refund for taxes paid indirectly must be supported by a certified statement from the contractor or subcontractor that purchased the item [G.S. § 105-164.14(b); 17 NCAC 7B.1602].

Nonprofits owned by governmental entities: The refunds for nonprofit entities do not apply to organizations, corporations, and institutions that are owned and controlled by the United States, the State, or a unit of local government except hospitals created under the Municipal Hospital Act [Part 1, Article 2, G.S. Chapter 131E] [G.S. § 105-164.14(b)]. There are special provisions that apply to certain governmental entities (see "Certain governmental entities," below).

Medicines and drugs: Hospitals that are not eligible for refunds under G.S. § 105-164.14(b) are allowed a semiannual refund of sales and use taxes paid by them on over-the-counter drugs purchased for use in carrying out its work [G.S. § 105-164.14(b)].

City or county medical facilities: Sales or use taxes paid on purchases by hospitals and other medical facilities that are agencies of a county or city or refundable to the same extent as sales or use taxes paid on purchases by other nonprofit hospital. However, the county or city must file the refund claim unless (1) the facility has submitted a written request to the Secretary to file a semiannual refund claim on its own behalf rather than having its purchases included in the county or city annual refund claim and (2) the request has been approved. An approved request becomes effective on the date set by the Secretary and applies to sales and use taxes paid on or after the effective date [17 NCAC 7B.1802(b)]. Hospitals and other medical facilities that are not nonprofits and are not agencies of a city or county are not eligible for sales and use tax refunds [17 NCAC 7B.1802(c)].

Resale exemption: Nonprofit entities registered for sales and use tax purposes may purchase the tangible personal property that they resell without paying tax to their suppliers if they have a Certificate of Resale. Certificates of resale, however, may not be used by nonprofit entities in making purchases of tangible personal property to be used or consumed by them [*Sales and Use Tax Technical Bulletins* § 17-2]. See also discussion of exemption certificates at ¶ 1811.

Request for refund: A request for a refund by a nonprofit entity must be in writing and include any information and documentation required by the Secretary. Refund requests for the first six months of a calendar year must be made on or before October 15 of the following year; refund requests for the second six months of a calendar year must be made on or before the following April 15 [G.S. § 105-164.14(b)]. A claim for refund applies to taxes paid during the period for which the refund claim is filed [17 NCAC 7B.1602(a)].

Nonrefundable items: These refund provisions do not apply to the following items:

(1) Purchases of electricity, telecommunications service, ancillary service, piped natural gas, video programming or prepaid meal plans [G.S. § 105-164.14(b)].

(2) Occupancy taxes levied and administered by certain counties and cities in North Carolina [17 NCAC 7B.1602(d)(2)].

(3) Prepared food and beverage taxes levied by various local governments in North Carolina [17 NCAC 7B.1602(d)(3)].

(4) Highway use taxes paid on the purchase, lease, or rental of motor vehicles [17 NCAC 7B.1602(d)(4)].

(5) The white goods disposal tax levied on new tires [17 NCAC 7B.1602(d)(5)].

(6) The scrap tire disposal tax levied on new tires [17 NCAC 7B.1602(d)(6)].

(7) The dry-cleaning solvent tax levied on dry-cleaning solvent purchased by a dry-cleaning facility [17 NCAC 7B.1602(d)(7)].

(8) Reimbursed employee expenses. The refund provisions of G.S. § 105-164.14(b) do not apply to sales taxes incurred by employees on purchases of food, lodging, or other taxable travel expenses paid by employees and reimbursed by a nonprofit entity. These expenses are personal to the employee because the contract for food, shelter, and travel is between the employee and the provider and payment of the tax is by the employee individually and personally. In this circumstance, a nonprofit entity has not incurred any sales tax liability and has not paid any sales tax; instead, it has chosen to reimburse a personal expense of the employee [17 NCAC 7B.1602(d); *Sales and Use Tax Technical Bulletins* § 17-2].

Cap: The aggregate annual refund allowed to an entity under G.S. § 105-164.14(b) for the State's fiscal year may not exceed $31,700,000 [G.S. § 105-164.14(b)].

- *Certain governmental entities*

Certain governmental entities are allowed an *annual* refund of sales and use taxes paid by it on direct purchases of tangible personal property and services. Sales and use tax liability indirectly incurred by a governmental entity on building materials, supplies, fixtures, and equipment that become a part of or annexed to any building or structure that it owns or leases and that is under construction, alteration, or repair for use by the governmental entity is considered a sales or use tax liability incurred on direct purchases by the governmental entity itself [G.S. § 105-164.14(c)]. *See, Franklin County Board of Education v. Department of Revenue,* 09-CV-20861 (N.C. Business Court, June 21, 2010) (local board of education entitled to refund for indirectly incurred taxes even though contractors were paid from funds maintained on the boards behalf in an account controlled by the county rather than the local board of education). This refund provision does not apply to purchases of electricity, telecommunications service, ancillary service, piped natural gas, video programming or prepaid meal plans [G.S. § 105-164.14(c)].

Governmental entities entitled to refunds: The governmental entities entitled to refunds under this provision are listed in G.S. § 105-164.14(c).

Governmental entities not eligible for refunds: The following governmental entities are not eligible for a refund:

(1) An alcoholic beverage control board [17 NCAC 7B.1704(1)].

(2) A community college established under G.S. § 115D [17 NCAC 7B.1704(2)].

(3) A drainage district [17 NCAC 7B.1704(3)].

(4) A housing authority [17 NCAC 7B.1704(4)].

(5) The North Carolina Civil Air Patrol, a State agency created by G.S. § 143B-490 [17 NCAC 7B.1704(5)].

Nonrefundable taxes: These refund provisions are not applicable to the following taxes [*Sales and Use Tax Technical Bulletins* § 18-2.D]:

(1) Tax paid on taxable sales made by governmental entities.

(2) Reimbursed employee expenses.

¶1904

(3) States sales tax on sales by a utility of electricity and local, toll, or private telecommunications services [G.S. § 105-164.14(c)].

(4) Occupancy taxes levied and administered by certain counties and cities in North Carolina.

(5) Prepared food and beverage taxes levied by various governments in North Carolina.

(6) Highway use taxes paid on the purchase, lease, or rental of motor vehicles.

(7) Scrap tire disposal tax paid on new tires.

(8) White goods disposal tax paid on new white goods.

(9) Dry-cleaning solvent tax levied on dry-cleaning solvent purchased by a dry-cleaning facility.

(10) The excise tax paid on piped natural gas.

(11) Other states' sales and use tax.

(12) Sales and use tax paid on purchases of alcoholic beverages.

Request for refund: Refund requests by a governmental entity must be in writing and must include any information and documentation required by the Secretary. A request for a refund is due within six months after the end of the governmental entity's fiscal year [G.S. § 105-164.14(c)].

• *State agencies*

Direct purchases: State agencies are exempt from taxes on items (other than electricity and telecommunications) purchased for their own use [G.S. § 105-164.13(52)]. See discussion of "State agency purchases" at ¶ 1809.

Indirect purchases: The State is allowed quarterly refunds of local sales and use taxes paid indirectly by a State agency on building materials, supplies, fixtures, and equipment that become a part of or annexed to a building or structure owned or leased by the State agency that is under construction, alteration, or repair for use by the State agency. This provision does not apply to a state agency that is ineligible for a sales and use tax exemption number [G.S. § 105-164.14(e)].

State building projects: A person who pays local sales and use taxes on building materials or other tangible personal property for a State building project must give the State agency for whose project the property was purchased a signed statement containing all of the following information: (1) date of purchase; (2) type of property purchased; (3) project for which the property was used; (4) county in which property was purchased (whether or not purchased in North Carolina); (5) the amount of sales and use taxes paid. If the property was purchased in North Carolina, a copy of the sales receipt must be attached to the statement [G.S. § 105-164.14(e)].

Refund applications: State agencies must file a written application for a refund of taxes paid during the quarter within 15 days after the end of each calendar quarter. The application must contain all information required by the Secretary. Refunds granted to State agencies are credited directly to the General Fund [G.S. § 105-164.14(e)].

¶ 1904

¶1905 Economic Incentive Refunds

• *In general*

Refund allowed. Certain taxpayers are allowed annual economic incentive refunds of sales and use tax paid [G.S. § 105-164.14A(a)]. Taxes for which refunds are allowed are not treated as overpayments and do not accrue interest [G.S. § 105-164.14A(d)].

Refund request. A request for a refund must be in writing and must include any information and documentation required by the Secretary. A request for a refund is due within six months after the end of the State's fiscal year. Refunds applied for after the due date are barred [G.S. § 105-164.14A(b)].

• *Major recycling facility*

Refund allowed. An owner of a major recycling facility is allowed a refund of the sales and use tax paid by it on building materials, building supplies, fixtures, and equipment that become a part of the real property of the recycling facility. Liability incurred indirectly by the owner for sales and use taxes on these items is considered tax paid by the owner [G.S. § 105-161.14A(a)(2)].

• *Motorsports team or sanctioning body*

Refund allowed. A professional motorsports racing team, a motorsports sanctioning body, or a related member of such a team or body is allowed a refund of the sales and use tax paid by it in North Carolina on aviation gasoline or jet fuel that is used to travel to or from a motorsports event in North Carolina, to travel to a motorsports event in another state from a location in North Carolina, or to travel in North Carolina from a motorsports event in another state [G.S. § 105-164.14A(a)(4)].

"Motorsports event" defined. For purposes of this refund a "motorsports event" includes a motorsports race, a motorsports sponsor event, and motorsports testing [G.S. § 105-164.14A(a)(4)].

Sunset. This refund is repealed for purchases made on or after January 1, 2024 [G.S. § 105-164.14A(a)(4)].

• *Professional motorsports team*

Refund allowed. A professional motorsports racing team or a related member of such a team or body is allowed a refund of 50% of the sales and use tax paid by it in North Carolina on tangible personal property (other than tires or accessories) that comprises any part of a professional motorsports vehicle [G.S. § 105-164.14A(a)(5)].

"Motorsports accessories" defined. For purposes of this refund, "motorsports accessories" includes instrumentation, telemetry, consumables, and paint [G.S. § 105-164.14A(a)(5)].

Sunset. This refund is repealed for purchases made on or after January 1, 2024 [G.S. § 105-164.14A(a)(5)].

• *Railroad intermodal facility*

Refund allowed. The owner or lessee of an eligible railroad intermodal facility is allowed a refund of sales and use tax paid by it on building materials, building supplies, fixtures, and equipment that become a part of the real property of the facility. Liability incurred indirectly by the owner or lessee of the facility for sales and use taxes on these items is considered tax paid by the owner or lessee [G.S. § 105-164.14A(a)(7)]. Railroad intermodal facilities are discussed at ¶1103.

Sunset. This refund is repealed for purchases made on or after January 1, 2038 [G.S. § 105-164.14A(a)(7)].

• *Transformative projects*

The owner or lessee of a business that is the recipient of a grant under the Job Development Investment Grant Program on or before June 30, 2019, for a transformative project is allowed a refund of the sales and use tax paid (directly or indirectly) on building materials, building supplies, fixtures, and equipment that become a part of the real property of the facility [G.S. § 105-164.14A(a)(8)]. A "transformative project" is a project involving the investment of $1 billion in private funds and the creation of at least 3,000 jobs [G.S. 143B-437.51(9a)]. This refund provision is effective July 1, 2017, and applies to purchases made on or after that date [S.L. 2017-57, § 38.9A.(b)].

¶1906 Special Relief Provisions

• *Reliance on databases maintained by the Secretary*

A person that relies on information regarding tax rates and the boundaries of taxing jurisdictions included in a database developed by the Secretary is not liable for underpayments of tax attributable to errors in those databases until 10 business days after the date of notification by the Secretary. If the Secretary develops a taxability matrix that provides information on the taxability of certain items or certain tax administrative practices, a person who relies on the matrix is not liable for underpayments attributable to erroneous information in the matrix until 10 business days after notification by the Secretary. Further, if the State fails to provide at least 30 days between the enactment and effective date of a rate change, a retailer is not liable (absent fraud) for an underpayment attributable to the rate change if the retailer collects tax at the old rate, provided the retailer's failure to collect tax at the new rate does not extend for more than 30 days after the enactment or effective date of the new rate [G.S. § 105-164.42L].

• *Grace period to comply with sales tax base expansion provisions*

The Department is prohibited from taking any action to assess any tax due for a filing period beginning on or after March 1, 2016 and ending before January 1, 2019 in various circumstances arising from taxpayer mistakes in complying with recent expansions of the sales tax base. To be eligible for this relief, the taxpayer must not have received specific written advice on the issue in question from the Department. In addition, the grace period does not prevent the Department from assessing use taxes on the purchasers of goods or services on which the seller erroneously failed to collect tax. Further, the grace period does not prevent the Department from assessing taxpayers for sales taxes they collected but failed to remit, or, generally, for taxes on amounts included in the definition of "sales price" on which the taxpayer erroneously failed to collect tax [G.S. § 105-244.3].

• *Abatement and waiver of tax and penalty on vacation rental linen charges*

The sales tax applies to the gross receipts from the rental of an accommodation [G.S. § 105-164.4F]. The Department has taken the position that these gross receipts include charges for vacation rental linens. Where a linen rental company rents linens to a property management company, that rental is itself a taxable rental of tangible personal property [G.S. § 105-164.4(a)(1)]. When the property manager then charges the vacationer for the same linens as part of the accommodation rental, the same linens are subject to tax twice. To mitigate this potential liability, the Secretary is permitted to abate 90% of the amount of such an assessment and waive all associated penalties for periods ending before January 1, 2018. To be eligible for the abatement and waiver the taxpayer must (i) have remitted during the period under audit all taxes collected during that period, (ii) not have been informed of the issue in a prior audit, (iii) not have requested a private letter ruling on the issue from the Department, and (iv) request an abatement within 45 days of a proposed assessment along with its written request for departmental review of the proposed assessment [G.S. § 105-244.4].

• *Prepaid Items*

A retailer who pays sales and use tax on an item that is separately stated on an invoice or similar document given to the retailer at the time of sale and later resells the item at retail, without first using it, must collect tax on the resale but may recover the tax paid on the purchase of the item by reducing taxable receipts for the period in which the resale occurs by the purchase price of the items in question. A retailer who takes advantage of this recovery provision is not entitled to a refund of the tax originally paid. If the amount of tax to be recovered exceeds the tax due for the reporting period in which the recovery is claimed, the excess is not refundable but may be carried forward to later reporting periods. The retailer must maintain records that clearly reflect and support the recovery adjustment [G.S. § § 105-164.11B and 105-164.11(b)].

¶ 1907 Advertising Absorption of Tax Is Illegal

It is unlawful for a retailer to advertise that the tax will be absorbed or is not considered an element in the price to the purchaser. A retailer who violates this provision is guilty of a Class 1 misdemeanor, and any violations reported to the Secretary will be forwarded to the North Carolina Attorney General for the purpose of bringing such violations to the attention of the solicitor of the court of the county or district responsible for prosecution of misdemeanors. It is the duty of the solicitor to investigate alleged violations and prosecute the violators upon finding that the violations have occurred [G.S. § 105-164.9].

¶ 1908 Successor Liability Rules

The sales and use tax is a lien upon all personal property of any person who is required to obtain a license to engage in business and stops engaging in the business by (1) transferring the business, (2) transferring the stock of goods of the business, or (3) going out of business. A person who stops engaging in business must file a return within 30 days after (1) transferring the business, (2) transferring the stock of goods of the business, or (3) going out of business [G.S. § 105-164.38].

Successor: A person to whom the business or stock of goods is transferred (the successor) must withhold from the consideration paid for the business or stock of goods an amount sufficient to cover the taxes due until the seller produces a statement from the Secretary showing that the taxes have been paid or that no taxes are due. If the successor fails to withhold an amount sufficient to cover the taxes and the taxes remain unpaid after the 30-day period allowed, the successor becomes personally liable for the unpaid taxes to the extent of the greater of (1) the consideration paid by the successor for the business or stock of goods, or (2) the fair market value of the business or stock of goods. The fact that the successor becomes liable for such unpaid taxes does not, however, relieve the transferor from liability. *See Secretary's Decision No. 2004-359* (March 7, 2005).

Period of limitations: The period of limitations for assessing liability against a successor expires one year after the end of the period of limitations for assessment against the seller.

Administrative provisions: In general, the liability of a successor who buys a business or stock of goods if subject to the general administrative rules to the same extent as if the successor had incurred the original tax liability [G.S. § 105-164.38].

PART VIII

PROPERTY TAXES

CHAPTER 21

IMPOSITION OF TAXES

¶2101 Imposition of Tax

• *Generally*

The General Assembly grants each *county* in North Carolina the power to levy taxes on property having a situs within the county under the rules according to the procedures prescribed in the Machinery Act [G.S. § 153A-149(a)]. The General Assembly also grants each *city* (defined in G.S. § 160A-1) in North Carolina the power to levy taxes on property having a situs within the city under the rules according to the procedures prescribed in the Machinery Act [G.S. § 160A-209(a)]. Thus, property tax in North Carolina is imposed and collected by the local taxing units. The North Carolina Department of Revenue does not send property tax bills or collect property taxes. The property tax provisions are imposed by Subchapter II of Chapter 105 of the North Carolina General Statutes, often referred to as the Machinery Act [G.S. § 105-271].

• *Administration*

The North Carolina Department of Revenue is charged by statute with the duty to exercise general and specific supervision over the valuation and taxation of property by taxing units throughout North Carolina [G.S. § 105-289]. The Property Tax Division of the North Carolina Department of Revenue is the division of the Department that is responsible for the administration of the North Carolina property tax provisions.

• *Classification by General Assembly*

Only the General Assembly has the power to classify property for taxation, and that power is to be exercised only on a statewide basis and is not to be delegated. No class of property can be taxed except by uniform rule, and every classification must be made by general law uniformly applicable in every county, city and town, and other unit of local government [North Carolina Constitution, Article V, § 2(2)]. Property can only be classified by the General Assembly. Thus, while the courts have the power to review legislative classifications, they have no power to create classifications in response to taxpayer challenges [*In re Estate of Battle*, 166 N.C. App. 240, 601 S.E.2d 253 (2004)].

The "classification" exercised by the General Assembly is the classification as a special class of property. For example, intangible personal property is designated as a special class under authority of Article V, §2(2), of the North Carolina Constitution and shall not be listed, appraised, assessed, or taxed [G.S. §105-275(31)].

- *Exemptions—Constitutional rules*

Only the General Assembly has the power to grant property tax exemptions. Property belonging to the State, counties, and municipal corporations is exempt from taxation by the North Carolina Constitution. The General Assembly may exempt the following:

(1) Cemeteries.

(2) Property held for educational, scientific, literary, cultural, charitable, or religious purposes.

(3) Personal property to a value not exceeding $300.

(4) Up to $1,000 in value of property held and used as the place of residence of the owner.

Every exemption must be on a statewide basis and must be made by general law uniformly applicable in every county, city and town, and other unit of local government [North Carolina Constitution, Article V, §2(3)].

- *Uniformity*

The intent of the North Carolina General Assembly is to make the property tax provisions (*i.e.*, the Machinery Act) uniformly applicable throughout North Carolina. To assure the intended uniformity, no "local act" to become effective on or after July 1, 1971, shall be construed to repeal or amend any section of Subchapter II (cited as the Machinery Act) in whole or in part unless it is expressly provided by specific reference to the section to be repealed or amended. For this purpose "local act" means any act of the General Assembly that applies to one or more counties by name, to one or more municipalities by name, or to all municipalities within one or more named counties [G.S. §105-272].

- *Minimal taxes and refunds*

The governing body of a taxing unit that collects its own taxes may, by resolution, direct its assessor and tax collector not to collect minimal taxes charged on the tax records and receipts. Minimal taxes are the combined taxes and fees of the taxing unit and any other units for which it collects taxes, due on a tax receipt in an amount not to exceed $5.00 [G.S. §105-321(f)]. The governing body of a taxing unit that collects its own taxes may also adopt a resolution directing that refunds of less than $15.00 be applied to the taxpayer's tax liability for the next year instead of being mailed to the taxpayer. The taxpayer can, however, obtain the refund by requesting it in person before the end of the fiscal year in which the refund becomes due [G.S. §105-321(g)].

- *When due date falls on a weekend or holiday*

When the last day for doing an act required or permitted under the property tax law falls on a Saturday, Sunday or holiday, the act is considered timely if it is done on the next business day. The same rule applies if the last day for doing an act falls during a declared disaster. To qualify under this rule, a disaster declaration must have been made by the Governor, the county or the municipality, the tax office must be closed, and the taxpayer must certify that in writing that the U.S. Postal Service did not provide service to the taxpayer's address [G.S. §105-395.1].

¶2102 Taxable Property

The North Carolina property tax is imposed on all property, real and personal, "within the jurisdiction of the State" unless the property is excluded under the authority of Article V, §2(2) or Article V, §2(3) of the North Carolina Constitution

[G.S. § 105-274(a)]. These exclusions are discussed at ¶ 2201.The extension of the taxing power to all property within the state's jurisdiction is presumed to mean that North Carolina taxes all property it has the power to tax under the United states Constitution. See J. Ferrell & M. Smith, State Jurisdiction to Tax Tangible Personal Property, 56 N.C.L.Rev., 807 (1978).

Property situated in North Carolina that belongs to a foreign corporation is not exempt unless specifically exempted by the General Assembly [G.S. § 105-274(b)]. Thus, all real and personal property situated in North Carolina is subject to the property tax unless it is specifically exempted [G.S. § 105-274]. Since 1997, all intangible personal property except leasehold interests in exempted real property is exempt from property tax. Leasehold interests in exempt real property are exempt as of July 1, 2019 [G.S. § 105-275(31)]. Exempt property is discussed at ¶ 2202. Certain categories of real and personal property are subject to special rules (*e.g.*, property owned by public service companies). See ¶ 2104 for discussion of property subject to special rates. Property subject to special assessment is discussed at ¶ 2304.

NOTE: Much of the material in ¶ 2201 is contained in the Department of Revenue's *Business Personal Property Manual*. This manual is published on the Department of Revenue's web site (*http://www.dor.state.nc.us*).

Not only can property be classified as real or personal; it can be subdivided as business or personally used. Thus, we can have four classes of real and personal property:

(1) Personally used real property (*e.g.*, residence).

(2) Business real property (*e.g.*, manufacturing facility).

(3) Personally used personal property, also referred to as "non-business property" (*e.g.*, family automobile).

(4) Business personal property (*e.g.*, machinery and equipment).

Note

The classification of property as real or personal is not the same kind of classification as a special class of taxation that can be made only by the General Assembly; it is merely a process of categorizing property for the purpose of determining the appropriate tax treatment of the asset in question. See "Classification by General Assembly."

The tax treatment of personally used property (either real or personal) is different from the tax treatment of business property (either real or personal). For example, personally used property is not depreciable; most business property is depreciable, especially business personal property. The tax treatment of business real property and business personal property also differs. For example, business personal property usually has more favorable depreciation treatment than business real property. Thus, in this section the authors concentrate of the classification of business property as business real property or business personal property. Since intangible personal property is not subject to taxation, the discussion focuses on tangible personal property.

• *Business personal property*

Frequently, it is difficult to draw a fine line between what is treated as real property and what is treated as personal property for ad valorem tax purposes. There are no hard and fast rules. Generally, business personal property includes, but is not limited to, (1) inventories; (2) depreciable property; and (3) leasehold interests in exempt realty (the only item of intangible personal property subject to property tax). Often, the way property is used is determinative, and the appraiser must examine leases and other documents to determine the intent of the owner of the property or rely on the owner's statement of intent. The appraiser may have to determine how the property is affixed to the realty and/or whether the property is there for the benefit of the process or for the benefit of the employees or the building. Sometimes, items that appear to be permanently attached to realty should be classified as personalty.

The following are examples of items that may appear to be realty but should be classified as personal property *in certain situations* [*Business Personal Property Manual,§ 3*]:

(1) Boilers and furnaces.

(2) Special climate control—special (*e.g.,* heating and air conditioning systems associated with particular equipment or product).

(3) Conveyors.

(4) Flooring.

(5) Leasehold improvements (owned by lessee).

(6) Shelving and displays.

(7) Venting.

(8) Wiring.

• *Certain computer software*

In general, computer software is not taxable. However, computer software and related documentation are taxable if they meet one or more of the following descriptions [G.S. § 105-275(40)]:

(1) *It is embedded software.* "Embedded software" means computer instructions, known as microcode, that reside permanently in the internal memory of a computer system or other equipment and are not intended to be removed without terminating the operation of the computer system or equipment and removing a computer chip, a circuit, or another mechanical device.

(2) *It is purchased or licensed from a person who is unrelated to the taxpayer, and it is capitalized on the books of the taxpayer in accordance with generally accepted accounting principles (GAAP).* A person is unrelated to a taxpayer if (a) the taxpayer and the person are not subject to any common ownership (directly or indirectly), and (b) neither the taxpayer nor the person has any ownership interest (directly or indirectly) in the other. However, effective for taxable years beginning on or after July 1, 2014, this exception does not apply to software or software modifications developed or modified to meet a customer's specific needs, whether the software or modifications were made internally or by a third party. *See* S. L. 2013-259. This change effectively reverses the position previously held by the Department of Revenue that custom modifications to taxable software were themselves taxable.

• *Motor vehicles*

Motor vehicles are classified as a special class of property for purposes of North Carolina property taxation. Property taxation of motor vehicles is discussed at ¶ 2106.

• *Public service companies [G.S. § § 105-333–105-344]*

"Public service company" means a railroad company, a pipeline company, a gas company, an electric power company, an electric membership corporation, a telephone company, a bus line company, an airline company, a motor freight carrier company, a mobile telecommunications company or a tower aggregator company. The term also includes any company performing a public service that is regulated by the U.S. Department of Energy, the U.S. Department of Transportation, the Federal Communications Commission, the Federal Aviation Agency, or the North Carolina

Utilities Commission, except that the term does not include a water company, a cable television company, or a radio or television broadcasting program [G.S. § 105-333(14)].

General appraisal rule for public service company property: The Department of Revenue appraises the property of railroad companies, pipeline companies, gas companies, electric power companies, electric membership corporations and telephone companies by (1) appraising the true value of the taxpayer's system property, whether located inside or outside of North Carolina, as of January 1 of each year and apportioning a fair and reasonable share of such value to North Carolina and allocating the share apportioned to North Carolina among local taxing units, (2) appraising the true value of the taxpayer's non-system tangible personal property in North Carolina as of January 1 of each year and assigning such value to the taxing units in which the property is located, and (3) appraising the true value of the taxpayer's non-system real property in North Carolina in accordance with the appraisal schedules of the counties where such property is situated and assigning such value to the taxing units in which the property is situated [G.S. § § 105-335, 105-337, 105-338 and 105-339].

System property: System property is real and personal property used by a public service company in its public service activities, including property under construction on the day as of which the property is assessed which will be used in such activities when completed [G.S. § 105-333(17)]. Leased property is also included in system property if necessary to ascertain the true value of the taxpayer's system property [G.S. § 105-335(b)(1)]. In valuing a public service company's system property the Department must consider (1) the market value of the taxpayer's capital stock and debt (taking into account the influence of any non-system property), (2) the book value of the property, (3) the replacement cost of the property less depreciation, (4) the taxpayer's gross receipts and operating income, and (5) any other factor or information the Department determines has a bearing on the value of such property [G.S. § 105-336(a)]. If the public service company operates inside and outside North Carolina, the Department must apportion a fair and reasonable share of the value of the taxpayer's system property to North Carolina by applying one or more of the business, mileage and property factors to such value [G.S. § 105-337]. The business factor is the ratio the taxpayer's business in North Carolina bears to its total business based on data that reflects the use of the taxpayer's property such as gross revenue, net income, tons of freight carried, revenue ton miles, passenger miles, car miles, and ground hours [G.S. § 105-337(1)]. The mileage factor is a ratio of the taxpayer's mileage in North Carolina to its total mileage based on factual information as to the linear miles of track, wire, lines, pipe, routes and similar operational routes and factual information as to the miles traveled by the company's rolling stock [G.S. § 105-337(2)]. The property factor is a ratio of the taxpayer's property in North Carolina to its total property based on gross or net investment or other reasonable figures reflecting the company's investment in property [G.S. § 105-337(3)]. Rules for allocating the value of the taxpayer's system property apportioned to North Carolina among local taxing units are set out in G.S. § 105-338.

Non-system personal property: Non-system personal property is tangible personal property owned by a public service company but not used in its public service activities [G.S. § 105-333(12)]. Such property is appraised only if it has a taxable situs in North Carolina and is appraised at its true value as of January 1 [G.S. § 105-335(b)(2)]. The Department must assign the appraised value of non-system personal property to the taxing units in which the property is situated by certifying the valuations to the appropriate counties and municipalities [G.S. § 105-339]. Each local taxing unit must assess the property at the values certified by the Department and tax the assessed values at the rates levied against other property subject to tax [G.S. § 105-339].

Non-system real property: Non-system real property is real property owned by a public service company but not used in its public service activities [G.S. § 105-333(12)]. Such property is appraised only if it has a taxable situs in North Carolina and is appraised at its true value based on the appraisal schedules applicable to other real property in the counties where such property is situated [G.S. § 105-335(b)(3)]. The Department must assign the appraised value of non-system real property to the taxing units in which the property is situated by certifying the valuations to the appropriate counties and municipalities [G.S. § 105-339]. Each local taxing unit must assess the property at the values certified by the Department and tax the assessed values at the rates levied against other property subject to tax [G.S. § 105-339].

Special appraisal rules for bus lines, motor freight carriers, airlines, mobile telecommunications companies and tower aggregator companies: The general appraisal rules described above do not apply to bus lines, motor freight carriers, airlines, mobile telecommunications companies or tower aggregator companies. Instead, the properties owned by these public service companies are listed, appraised and assessed under the general rules applicable to other taxpayers, except for the special rules described below [G.S. § 105-335(a)].

Bus line company rolling stock: The Department must appraise, as of each January 1, the true value of the rolling stock owned or leased by or operated under the control of a bus line that is either domiciled in North Carolina or regularly engaged in business in North Carolina [G.S. § 105-335(c)(1)]. A bus line is a company engaged in the business of transporting passengers and property by motor vehicle for hire over the public highways of North Carolina (but excluding companies operating primarily within a single local taxing unit), whether the transportation is wholly within North Carolina or partly within and partly without the state [G.S. § 105-333(2)]. In appraising bus line company rolling stock, the Department must consider the property's book value and the cost of replacing or reproducing the property in its existing condition [G.S. § 105-336(b)].

Motor freight carrier company rolling stock: The Department must appraise, as of each January 1, the true value of the rolling stock owned by a motor freight carrier company or leased by such a company and operated by its employees if the company is either domiciled in North Carolina or regularly engaged in business in the state at a terminal owned or leased by the company [G.S. § 105-335(c)(2)]. A motor freight carrier is a company engaged in the business of transporting property by motor vehicle for hire over the public highways of North Carolina. As to intrastate carriers, the term only includes carriers that transport property by tractor trailer to or from two or more terminals in North Carolina owned or leased by the carrier. As to interstate carriers domiciled outside North Carolina, the term includes carriers that regularly move property by tractor trailer to or from one or more terminals in North Carolina owned or leased by the carrier. As to interstate carriers domiciled in North Carolina, the term includes carriers that regularly move property by tractor trailer (1) to or from one or more terminals owned or leased by the carrier outside North Carolina or (2) to or from two or more terminals inside North Carolina. The term can also include an interstate carrier domiciled in North Carolina with no terminals outside North Carolina but whose operations outside the state are sufficient to require the payment of ad valorem taxes on its rolling stock to one or more taxing units outside the state [G.S. § 105-333(10)]. In appraising motor freight carrier rolling stock, the Department must consider the property's book value and the cost of replacing or reproducing the property in its existing condition [G.S. § 105-336(b)].

Flight equipment: The Department must appraise, as of each January 1, the true value of the flight equipment owned or leased by or operated under the control of an airline company that is domiciled in North Carolina or regularly engaged in business at an airport in the state [G.S. § 105-335(c)(3)]. An airline company is a company engaged in the business of transporting passengers and property by aircraft for hire within North Carolina or to or from points within the state [G.S. § 105-333(1)]. Flight equipment consists of aircraft fully equipped for flying and used in any operation within the State [G.S. § 105-333(7)]. In appraising flight equipment, the Department must consider the property's book value and the cost of replacing or reproducing the property in its existing condition [G.S. § 105-336(b)].

Mobile telecommunication company property: Effective for taxable years beginning on or after July 1, 2015, the Department must appraise, as of each January 1, the true value of the tangible personal property of a mobile telecommunications company [G.S. § 105-335(c)(4)]. A mobile telecommunications company is a company providing mobile telecommunications service as defined for sales tax purposes (discussed at ¶ 1603) [G.S. § 105-333(9a)]. The tangible personal property of a mobile telecommunications company includes all the tangible personal property located in North Carolina that is owned by the company or leased to the company and capitalized on its books in accordance with generally accepted accounting principles. The term includes cellular towers, cellular equipment shelters, and site improvements at cellular tower locations. The term does not include FCC licenses or authorizations or other intangible property [G.S. § 105-333(17a)]. In appraising such property (other than towers), the Department must consider the original cost of the property as reflected in the company's GAAP books, and may consider the cost of replacing or reproducing the property. In either case, the Department must make an appropriate deduction for all forms of depreciation including physical deterioration, functional obsolescence and external or economic obsolescence [G.S. § 105-336(c)]. In appraising a tower, the Department must consider the replacement or reproduction cost of the property, based on tower height and type, as determined by a nationally recognized cost service normally used by appraisers, and must make an appropriate deduction for all forms of depreciation, including physical deterioration, functional obsolescence, and external or economic obsolescence [G.S. § 105-336(d)].

Tower aggregator company property: Effective for taxable years beginning on or after July 1, 2015, the Department must appraise, as of each January 1, the true value of the tangible personal property of a tower aggregator company [G.S. § 105-335(c)(5)]. A tower aggregator company is a company that provides tower infrastructure for broadcasting and mobile telephony and that leases space on the tower infrastructure to mobile telecommunications companies [G.S. § 105-333(22)]. The tangible personal property of such a company includes all tangible personal property located in North Carolina that is owned by the company or leased to the company and capitalized on its books in accordance with generally accepted accounting principles. The term includes cellular towers, cellular equipment shelters, and site improvements at cellular tower locations [G.S. § 105-333(17b)]. In appraising the tangible personal property of tower aggregator companies other than towers, the Department must consider the original cost of the property as reflected on the company's GAAP books and may also consider the cost of replacing or reproducing the property. In appraising the towers of a tower aggregator company, the Department must consider the same information required to be considered in appraising towers of a mobile telecommunications company. For all tower aggregator company property, the Department must make an appropriate deduction for all forms of depreciation, including physical deterioration, functional obsolescence and external or economic obsolescence [G.S. § 105-336(d)].

Apportionment of rolling stock and flight equipment. The Department is required to apportion to North Carolina a fair and reasonable share of the value of the rolling stock and flight equipment of bus lines, motor freight carriers and airlines that operate within and without the State by reference to the taxpayer's business, property and mileage factors in the same manner as the apportionment of the system property of public service companies subject to appraisal by the Department under G.S. § 105-335(a) [G.S. § 105-337].

Allocation of value among taxing units: The Department of Revenue must allocate the valuations of public service company property among local taxing units in accordance with the rules set forth below.

System property of railroad companies. The distributable system property of a railroad company is allocated among local taxing units based on the ratio of the miles of track in the local taxing unit to the total miles of track in North Carolina with adjustments to reflect the density of traffic in the local taxing unit [G.S. § 105-338(b)(1)]. Distributable system property is all real and personal property owned or used by a railroad company other than (1) land other than rights-of-way, (2) depots, (3) machine shops, (4) warehouses, (5) office buildings, (6) other structures and (7) the contents of any of the foregoing structures [G.S. § 105-333(3) and (11)].

System property of telephone companies. The system property of a telephone company is allocated among local taxing units by (1) dividing all system property located in North Carolina into Class 1 property (central office equipment, large P.B.X equipment, motor vehicles, tools and work equipment, office furniture and equipment, materials and supplies, and land and buildings including towers and other structures) and Class 2 property (all other system property located in the State); (2) determining the original cost of all Class 1 property and all Class 2 property; (3) determining the percentage of the aggregate original cost of all Class 1 and Class 2 property represented by the Class 1 property (the Class 1 percentage) and the percentage of the aggregate original cost represented by the Class 2 property (the Class 2 percentage); (4) multiplying the appraised value of the company's system property apportioned to North Carolina by each of the Class 1 and Class 2 percentages to determine the appraised value of Class 1 property and the appraised value of Class 2 property; (5) allocating the appraised value of Class 1 property among local taxing units in which such property was situated on January 1 pursuant to the ratio of the original cost of such property in the taxing unit to the original cost of such property in the State; and (6) allocating the appraised value of the Class 2 property among local taxing units in which the company operates in the proportion that the miles of the company's single aerial wire and single wire in cables (including single tube in coaxial cable) in the taxing unit bears to the total of such wire miles of the company in the State [G.S. § 105-338(b)(2)].

System property of pipeline companies, gas companies, electric power companies and electric membership corporations. The appraised value of system property of pipeline, gas, and electric power companies and electric membership corporations is allocated among the local taxing units in which the taxpayer operates in the proportion that the original cost of the taxable system property located in the taxing unit on January 1 bears to the original cost of all such property in the State [G.S. § 105-338(b)(3)].

Bus line company rolling stock. The appraised value of a bus line company's rolling stock is allocated among local taxing units according to the ratio of the company's scheduled miles in each unit during the preceding calendar year to the company's total scheduled miles in the State for such year [G.S. § 105-338(c)(1)].

Motor freight carrier rolling stock. The appraised value of the rolling stock (other than locally assigned rolling stock) owned or leased by a motor freight carrier company is allocated among the local taxing units in which the company has a terminal according to the ratio of the tons of freight handled in the preceding calendar year at the company's terminals located in the taxing unit to the total tons of freight handled by the company in the State during such year. If a North Carolina interstate motor freight carrier has no terminals outside North Carolina but has been required to pay ad valorem taxes to one or more taxing units outside the State, a reduction is allowed in the North Carolina valuation measured by the ratio of the rolling stock subject to tax outside the State to all the company's rolling stock [G.S. § 105-338(c)(2)].

¶2102

Airline flight equipment. The appraised value of an airline company's flight equipment is allocated among the local taxing units in which an airport used by the company is situated according to the ratio obtained by averaging (1) the ratio of the company's ground hours in the taxing unit during the preceding calendar year to the company's total ground hours in the State during such period and (2) the ratio of the company's gross revenue in the taxing unit during the preceding calendar year to the company's total gross revenue in the State during such year [G.S. § 105-338(c)(3)].

Certification. The Department of Revenue must assign the appraised valuations of public service company property to the appropriate local taxing units by certifying such valuations to the appropriate counties and municipalities, which must assess the respective taxpayers' property using the certified valuations and tax such property at the rate of tax levied against other property subject to tax in such county or municipality [G.S. §§ 105-339, 105-340 and 105-341].

Right to information. A public service company subject to appraisal by the Department of Revenue may make a written request to the Department to be informed of the elements the Department considered in its appraisal of the company's property, the result in dollars produced by each element, the factors and ratios used in apportioning the appraised values and factors and calculations used in allocating the appraised values to the local taxing units. Local taxing units may also make written requests to obtain this information with respect to any public service company whose property is subject to appraisal by the Department [G.S. § 105-342(a)].

Review of appraisal and apportionment. As soon as practicable after the Department has determined the appraised value of public service company property and share of such value apportioned to North Carolina, the Department must give written notice to the taxpayer of such figures. The taxpayer has 20 days after the date on which the notice was mailed to submit a written request to the Property Tax Commission for a hearing on the appraisal, apportionment or both. If a timely hearing request is not made, the appraisal and apportionment become final and conclusive at the close of the 20-day notice period. If a timely hearing request is made, the Property Tax Commission must schedule a hearing and provide the taxpayer at least 20 days written notice of the hearing [G.S. § 105-342(b)]. At the hearing the Property Tax Commission must hear the taxpayer's evidence, may obtain additional pertinent evidence on its own motion, make findings of fact and conclusions of law, issue an order embodying its decision and serve written notice of its decision on the taxpayer as soon as practicable [G.S. § 105-342(c)].

¶2103 Rates and Base

• *Rates*

Each year the tax levying authorities of counties and municipalities determine the rates of taxes that are necessary to meet the general and other legally authorized expenses of the taxing units. The tax rates cannot be in excess of any constitutional or statutory limits [G.S. § 105-347]. Counties are authorized to create economic development and training districts and levy an additional North Carolina property tax in those districts [S.L. 2003-418 (S.B. 168)]. See ¶2107 for discussion of economic development and training districts.

• *Base*

The property tax is levied annually on the assessed value of the taxable property (the base) at the applicable rate. North Carolina imposes uniform assessment and appraisal standards. All property, real and personal must, as far as it is feasible, be appraised or valued at its true value in money. "True value" means market value, that is, the price estimated in terms of money at which the property would change hands between a willing and financially able buyer and a willing seller, neither being under any compulsion to buy or to sell and both having reasonable knowledge of all the uses to which the property is adapted and for which it is capable of being used. This is commonly referred to as "fair market value." In the case of acquisition of an interest in land by an entity having the power of eminent domain, it is not considered competent evidence of the true value in money of comparable land [G.S. § 105-283].

• *Assessment and appraisal*

Definitions: "Appraisal" means both the true value of property and the process by which true value is ascertained. "Assessment" means both the tax value of property and the process by which the assessment is determined [G.S. § 105-273(2), (3)].

Appraisal: North Carolina imposes uniform appraisal standards. All property, real and personal must, as far as it is feasible, be appraised or valued at its true value in money (*i.e.*, market value). See ¶ 2302 and ¶ 2303 for discussion of assessment and appraisal.

Assessment: North Carolina imposes a uniform assessment standard. All property must be assessed for taxation at its true value or use value as determined under G.S. § 105-283, and taxes levied by all counties and municipalities must be levied uniformly on these assessments [G.S. § 105-284]. Present-use value is discussed at ¶ 2309. Assessment and appraisal are discussed at ¶ 2302 and ¶ 2303.

¶2104 Special Valuation Rules

• *Indebtedness on fertilizer and fertilizer materials:* All bona fide indebtedness incurred in the purchase of fertilizer and fertilizer materials owing by a taxpayer as principal debtor may be deducted from the total value of all fertilizer and fertilizer materials that are held for the taxpayer's own use in agriculture during the current year [G.S. § 105-277(d)].

• *Buildings with solar energy systems:* Buildings equipped with solar energy heating and/or cooling systems are designated a special class of property for property taxation purposes. Such buildings are assessed for taxation in accordance with each county's schedules of value for buildings equipped with conventional heating or cooling systems, and no additional value is assigned for the difference in cost between a solar energy heating or cooling system and a convention system typically found in the county. The term "system" includes all controls, tanks, pumps, heat exchangers, and other equipment used directly and exclusively for the conversion of solar energy for heating or cooling. It does not, however, include any land or structural elements of the building such as walls and roofs or other equipment ordinarily contained in the structure [G.S. § 105-277(g)].

• *Private water companies—contributions in aid of construction and acquisition adjustments:* In assessing the property of any private water company, that portion of the investment of the company represented by contributions in aid of construction and by acquisition adjustment that is designated a special class of property is excluded. "Investment," "contributions in aid of construction," and "acquisition adjustment" have the meanings as those terms are defined in the Uniform System of Accounts specified by the North Carolina Utilities Commission for use by such private water companies [G.S. § 105-277(h)].

• *Real property inside certain roadway corridors*

Unimproved property. Real property that lies within a transportation corridor marked on an official map filed under Article 2D of Chapter 136 of the North Carolina General Statutes is designated a special class of property and is taxable at 20% of the appraised value of the property if the property meets both of the following criteria [G.S. § 105-277.9]: (1) As of January 1, no building or other structure is located on the property. (2) The property has not been subdivided since it was included in the corridor. See G.S. § 105-153A-335 or G.S. § 105-160A-376 for the definition of "subdivision" for this purpose.

- *Improved property*

Real property on which a building or other structure is located and that lies within a transportation corridor marked on an official map filed under Article 2E of Chapter 136 (requiring official transportation corridor maps to be filed with the register of deeds) of the General Statutes is designated a special class of property and is taxable at 50% of the appraised value of the property if the property has not been subdivided (as defined in G.S. § 153A-335 or G.S. § 160A-376) since it was included in the corridor [G.S. § 105-277.9A(a)].

Sunset: This provision is repealed effective for taxes imposed for taxable years beginning on or after July 1, 2021 [G.S. § 105-277.9A(b)].

- *Annual review of transportation corridors*

The assessor must annually review the transportation corridor official maps and amendments to them filed with the register of deeds and indicate on all tax maps maintained by the county or city that portion of the properties within a transportation corridor, noting any variance granted for the property. The assessor must tax the property within a transportation corridor as required under G.S. §§ 105-277.9 and 105-277.9A [G.S. § 105-296(m)].

¶2105 Definitions

When used in the context of the North Carolina property tax, the terms below have the meaning given unless the context requires a different meaning [G.S. § 105-273].

Abstract: The document on which the property of a taxpayer is listed for ad valorem taxation and on which the appraised and assessed values of the property are recorded.

Appraisal: Both the true value of property and the process by which true value is ascertained.

Assessment: Both the tax value of property and the process by which the assessment is determined.

Code: "Code" for this purpose is defined in G.S. § 105-228.90 [G.S. § 105-273(4a)]. For the current definition of the Code, see ¶103.

Collector (or tax collector): Any person charged with the duty of collecting taxes for a county or municipality.

Contractor: A taxpayer who is regularly engaged in building, installing, repairing, or improving real property.

Corporation: Nonprofit corporations and every type of organization having capital stock represented by shares.

Discovered property: All of the following are discovered property: (1) property that was not listed during a listing period; (2) property that was listed but the listing included a substantial understatement; and (3) property that has been granted an exemption or exclusion and does not qualify for the exemption or exclusion.

"To discover property" means to determine that property was not listed, was listed with a substantial understatement, or was granted an exemption or exclusion for which the property did not qualify.

Documents: Books, papers, records, statements, accounts, maps, plats, films, pictures, tapes, objects, instruments, and any other things conveying information.

Failure to list property: All of the following are failures to list property: (1) failure to list property during a listing period; (2) a substantial understatement of listed property; (3) failure to notify the assessor that property granted an exemption or exclusion under an application for exemption or exclusion does not qualify for the exemption or exclusion.

Intangible personal property: Patents, copyrights, secret processes, formulae, goodwill, trademarks, trade brands, franchises, stocks, bonds, cash, bank deposits, notes, evidences of debt, leasehold interests in exempted real property, bills and accounts receivable, and other like property.

Inventories: Any of the following:

(1) Goods held for sale in the regular course of business by manufacturers, retail and wholesale merchants, and construction contractors.

(2) As to manufacturers, the term includes raw materials, goods in process, and finished goods, as well as other materials or supplies that are consumed in manufacturing or processing, or that accompany and become a part of the sale of the property being sold. The term also includes crops, livestock, poultry, feed used in the production of livestock and poultry, and other agricultural or horticultural products held for sale, whether in process or ready for sale. The term does not include fuel used in manufacturing or processing, nor does it include materials or supplies not used directly in manufacturing or processing.

(3) As to retail and wholesale merchants and contractors, the term includes, in addition to articles held for sale, packaging materials that accompany and become a part of the sale of the property being sold.

(4) The term also includes a modular home that is used as a display model and held for eventual sale at the retail merchant's place of business.

(5) Goods held by construction contractors to be furnished in the course of building, installing, repairing, or improving real property.

List or listing: When used as a noun the term "list" means "abstract" (see above).

Local tax official: Any of the following is a local tax official:

(1) A county assessor.

(2) An assistant county assessor.

(3) A member of a county board of commissioners.

(4) A member of a county board of equalization and review.

(5) A county tax collector.

(6) The municipal equivalents of these officials.

Manufacturer: A taxpayer who is regularly engaged in the mechanical or chemical conversion or transformation of materials or substances into new products for sale or in the growth, breeding, raising, or other production of new products for sale. The term does not include delicatessens, cafes, cafeterias, restaurants, and other similar retailers that are principally engaged in the retail sale of foods prepared by them for consumption on or off their premises.

Municipal corporation or municipality: City, town, incorporated village, sanitary district, rural fire protection district, rural recreation district, mosquito control district, hospital district, metropolitan sewerage district, watershed improvement district, or other district or unit of local government by or for which *ad valorem* taxes are levied. The terms also include a consolidated city-county. A "consolidated city-county" means any county where the largest municipality in the county has been abolished and its powers, duties, rights, privileges and immunities consolidated with those of the county [G.S. § 105-160B-2(1)].

¶2105

Person: Any individual, trustee, executor, administrator, other fiduciary, corporation, limited liability company, unincorporated association, partnership, sole proprietorship, company, firm, or other legal entity.

Real property: "Real property," "real estate," and "land" mean not only the land itself, but also buildings, structures, improvements, and permanent fixtures thereon, and all rights and privileges belonging or in any wise appertaining thereto. This term also means a manufactured home as defined in G.S. § 143-143.9(6) (see above). The term also includes a modular home that is used as a display model and held for eventual sale at the retail merchant's place of business.

Retail merchant: A taxpayer who is regularly engaged in the sale of tangible personal property (acquired by a means other than manufacture, processing, or producing by the merchant) to users or consumers.

Substantial understatement: The omission of a material portion of the value, quantity, or other measurement of taxable property. The determination of materiality in each case shall be made by the assessor, subject to the taxpayer's right to review of the determination by the county board of equalization and review or board of commissioners and appeal to the Property Tax Commission.

Tangible personal property: All personal property that is not intangible and that is not permanently affixed to real property.

Tax and taxes: The principal amount of any tax, costs, penalties, and interest imposed upon property tax or dog license tax.

Taxing unit: A county or municipality authorized to levy ad valorem property taxes.

Taxpayer: Any person whose property is subject to ad valorem property taxation by any county or municipality and any person who has a duty to list property for taxation.

Valuation: Appraisal and assessment.

Wholesale merchant: A taxpayer who is regularly engaged in the sale of tangible personal property (acquired by a means other than manufacture, processing, or producing by the merchant) to other retail or wholesale merchants for resale or to manufacturers for use as ingredient or component parts of articles being manufactured for sale.

¶2106 Motor Vehicles

All motor vehicles (except those specifically excluded) are designated a special class of property under authority of Article V, §2(2) of the North Carolina Constitution, and taxes on classified motor vehicles are listed, assessed, and collected under the provisions of Article 22A of Chapter 105 of the North Carolina General Statutes [G.S. §§ 105-330 *et seq.*].

• *Classified motor vehicles*

A "classified motor vehicle" is one that is classified under Article 22A of Chapter 105 of the North Carolina General Statutes. A "motor vehicle" for this purpose includes every vehicle that is self-propelled and every vehicle designed to run on the highways that is pulled by a self-propelled vehicle [G.S. §§ 105-330(2), 20-4.01(23)]. This term, however, does not include mopeds [G.S. § 20-4.01(23)]. A "registered classified motor vehicle" is a classified motor vehicle that has a current registration plate or that has been transferred to a new owner who has applied for a plate [G.S. § 105-330(4)].

- *Motor vehicles excluded from special classification*

The following motor vehicles are not classified as a special class of property:

(1) Motor vehicles exempt from registration pursuant to G.S. § 20-51 [G.S. § 105-330.1(b)(1)].

(2) Manufactured homes, mobile classrooms, and mobile offices [G.S. § 105-330.1(b)(2)].

(3) Semitrailers or trailers registered on a multiyear basis [G.S. § 105-330.1(b)(3)].

(4) Motor vehicles owned or leased by a public service company and appraised under G.S. § 105-335 [G.S. § 105-330.1(b)(4)]. For the definition of public service company see ¶2102.

(5) Motor vehicles registered under the International Registration Plan [G.S. § 105-330.1(b)(6)]. The term "International Registration Plan" is not defined anywhere in the General Statutes, but refers to a registration reciprocity agreement among the states of the United States and the Canadian provinces. See www.irponline.org.

(6) Motor vehicles issued permanent plates under G.S. § 20-84 [G.S. § 105-330.1(b)(7)].

(7) Self-propelled property-carrying vehicles issued three-month registration plates at the farmer rate under G.S. § 20-88 [G.S. § 105-330.1(b)(8)].

(8) Motor vehicles owned by participants in the Address Confidentiality Program authorized under Chapter 15C of the General Statutes (intended to protect the confidentiality of victims of domestic violence, sexual offense, stalking or human trafficking) [G.S. § 105-330.1(b)(9)].

- *Application for exempt status*

The owner of a classified motor vehicle who claims an exemption or exclusion from tax has the burden of establishing that the vehicle is entitled to exemption or exclusion and may establish prima facie entitlement by filing an application for exempt status with the assessor within 30 days of the date taxes on the vehicle are due. When an approved application is on file, the assessor will omit the vehicle from the tax records [G.S. § 105-330.3(b)]. An application is not required for vehicles qualifying for exemptions or exclusions listed in G.S. § 105-282.1(a)(1). Owners of classified vehicles that have been omitted from the tax records must report to the assessor any classified motor vehicles registered in their name or owned by them but not registered in their names that do not qualify for exempt status for the current year. This report must be made within 30 days after the renewal of registration or initial registration of a registered vehicle or, in the case of an unregistered vehicle, on or before January 31 of the listing year. Classified motor vehicles that do not qualify for exempt status but have been omitted from the tax records are subject to discovery, except that in lieu of the discovery penalties, a penalty of $100 for each elapsed registration period will be assessed [G.S. § 105-330.3(c)]. Discovery is discussed in Chapter 24.

- *Ownership, situs, and taxability*

Registered vehicles: The ownership, situs, and taxability of a registered classified motor vehicle is determined annually as of the day on which a new registration is applied for or the day on which the current vehicle registration is renewed (without regard to whether or not the registration has expired). The situs may not be changed until the next registration date [G.S. § 105-330.2(a)].

Unregistered vehicles: The ownership, situs, and taxability of an unregistered classified motor vehicle are determined as of January 1 of the year in which the registration of the motor vehicle expires without renewal or in which the motor vehicle is transferred to an owner who does not apply for a new registration [G.S. § 105-330.2(a1)].

¶2106

• *Motor vehicle tax year*

The tax year for a classified motor vehicle registered under the staggered system begins on the first day of the first month following the date on which the former registration expires or on which an application for new registration is made and ends on the last day of the month in which the current registration expires. The tax year for a classified motor vehicle registered under the annual system begins on the first day of the month following the date on which the registration expires or on which application for new registration is made and ends the following December 31. The tax year for an unregistered classified motor vehicle is the fiscal year that opens in the calendar year in which the vehicle is required to be listed [G.S. § 105-330.6(a)].

Credit for change in tax year: If the tax year for a classified motor vehicle changes because of a change in its registration for a reason other than the transfer of its registration plates to another classified motor vehicle pursuant to G.S. § 20-64, and the new tax year begins before the expiration of the vehicle's original tax year, the taxpayer may receive a credit (in the form of a release) against the taxes on the vehicle for the new tax year. The amount of the credit is computed by multiplying the taxes paid on the vehicle for the original tax year multiplied by a fraction, the numerator of which is the number of full calendar months remaining in the original tax year and the denominator of which is the number of months in the original tax year. To obtain this credit, a taxpayer must apply within 30 days after the taxes for the new tax year are due and must provide the county tax collector information establishing (1) the original tax year of the vehicle, (2) the amount of taxes paid on the vehicle for that year, and (3) the reason for the change in registration [G.S. § 105-330.6(a1)].

• *Transfer or surrender of plates*

Transfer of plates: If the owner of a registered classified motor vehicle transfers the registration plates from the listed vehicle to another classified motor vehicle pursuant to G.S. § 20-64 during the listed vehicle's tax year, the vehicle to which the plates are transferred is not required to be listed or taxed until the current registration expires or is renewed [G.S. § 105-330.6(b)].

Surrender of plates: If the owner of a registered classified motor vehicle either transfers the motor vehicle to a new owner or moves to another state and registers the vehicle in another jurisdiction, and the owner surrenders the registration plates from the listed vehicle to the Division of Motor Vehicles (DMV), the owner may apply for a release or refund of taxes on the vehicle for any full calendar months remaining in the vehicle's tax year after the date of surrender. To apply for a release or refund, the owner must present to the county tax collector within one year after surrendering the plates the receipt received from the DMV accepting the surrender of the registration places. If the taxes have not been paid at the date of application, the county tax collector makes a release of the prorated taxes and credits the owner's tax notice with the amount of the release. If the taxes have been paid at the date of application, the prorated taxes must be refunded [G.S. § 105-330.6(c)].

• *Listing*

Registered vehicles: Assessors must list a registered classified motor vehicle for county, municipal, and special district taxes each year in the name of the owner of record as of the day on which the current registration is renewed or the day on which an application for a new registration is made by a new owner [G.S. § 105-330.3(a)]. The owners of vehicles listed by an assessor do not have to list the vehicle themselves under the requirement of G.S. § 105-306. The rules with respect to discovered property (discussed in Chapter 24) do not apply to registered vehicles.

Unregistered vehicles: The owner of an unregistered classified motor vehicle must list the vehicle for taxes by filing an abstract with the assessor of the county in which the vehicle is located on or before January 31 following the date the unregistered vehicle is acquired or, in the case of a registration that is not renewed before January 31 following the date the registration expires and on or before January 31 of each succeeding year that the vehicle is unregistered. If an unregistered vehicle required to be listed under this provision is registered before the end of the fiscal year for which it was required to be listed, it is taxed as a registered vehicle and any tax assessed for the fiscal year in which the vehicle was required to be listed will be released or refunded. For any period for which the vehicle was not taxed between the date its registration expired and the start of the registered vehicle tax year the vehicle is taxed as an unregistered vehicle with its value determined as of January 1 of the year in which the taxes are computed. A vehicle required to be listed pursuant to this provision that is neither listed by January 31 or registered before the end of the fiscal year for which it was required to be listed is subject to discovery [G.S. § 105-330.3(a1)]. Discovery is discussed in Chapter 24.

- *Appraised value*

A classified motor vehicle is appraised at its true value in money (discussed at ¶ 2302). The sales price of a classified motor vehicle purchased from a dealer, including the price of all accessories attached at the time of delivery, but excluding any highway use tax, is considered the true value [G.S. § 105-330.2(b)]. The value of a registered classified motor vehicle is determined as of January 1 of the current year for a registration expiring or an application for a new registration submitted between January 1 and August 31 and as of January 1 of the following year for a registration expiring or an application for a new registration submitted between September 1 and December 31. The value of a new registered classified motor vehicle for which there is no expiring registration or new application is its value as of the date that model of motor vehicle is first offered for sale at retail in North Carolina. The value of a registered classified motor vehicle that cannot be valued as of the date determined under any of the above rules is valued using the most currently available January 1 retail value [G.S. § 105-330.2(a)]. The value of an unregistered classified motor vehicle is determined as of January 1 of the year the vehicle is required to be listed [G.S. § 105-330.2(a1)].

- *Valuation appeal*

The owner of a classified motor vehicle may appeal the appraised value of the vehicle by first paying the tax due and then filing a request for appeal with the assessor within 30 days of the date taxes are due on the vehicle. A lessee who is required to pay the tax on the leased vehicle under the terms of the lease is considered the owner of the vehicle for purposes of filing an appeal. Appeals proceed in the same manner as appeals of discovered property [G.S. § 105-330.2(b1)].

- *Exemption or exclusion appeal*

The owner of a classified motor vehicle may appeal the vehicle's eligibility for an exemption or exclusion by filing a request for appeal with the assessor within 30 days of the assessor's initial decision on the exemption or exclusion application filed by the owner. Appeals proceed in the same manner as appeals of discovered property [G.S. § 105-330.2(b2)].

- *Notice and computation of tax*

Registered vehicles: The Property Tax Division of the Department or a third-party contractor selected by the Property Tax Division must prepare a combined tax and registration notice for each registered classified motor vehicle that includes (1) the appraised value of the vehicle, (2) the tax rate of each taxing unit, (3) a statement that the appraised value and taxability of the vehicle may be appealed to the assessor in writing within 30 days of the due date, (4) the registration fee imposed by the Division of Motor Vehicles and any other information required by the Division of Motor Vehicles and (5) instructions for payment. If the vehicle has a temporary or limited registration plate, the notice must state that the registration fees for the plate have been paid and that the registration becomes valid for the remainder of the year upon payment of the taxes and fees that are due. A notice that includes the required information on a vehicle with a limited registration plate serves as the registration certificate for the vehicle [G.S. § 105-330.5(a)]. In computing the taxes, the assessor appraises the motor vehicle at its true value (discussed at ¶ 2302) and uses the tax rates and any additional motor vehicle taxes of the various taxing units in effect on the date the taxes are computed. The tax on the motor vehicle is the product of a fraction and the number of months in the motor vehicle tax year. The numerator of the fraction is the product of the appraised value of the motor vehicle and the tax rate of the various taxing units. The denominator of the fraction is 12. This procedure constitutes the listing and assessment of each classified motor vehicle for taxation [G.S. § 105-330.5(a)].

Unregistered vehicles: The owner of an unregistered classified motor vehicle must list the vehicle by filing an abstract with the assessor of the county in which the vehicle is located on or before January 31 following the date the owner acquired the unregistered vehicle or, in the case of a registration that is not renewed, January 31 following the date the registration expires, and on or before January 31 of each succeeding year that the vehicle is unregistered. If a classified motor vehicle required to be registered before the end of the fiscal year for which it was required to be listed, the requirements of G.S. § 105-330.3(a1)(1), (2), and (3) [G.S. § 105-330.3(a1)]. The assessor must prepare and send a tax notice for each unregistered classified motor vehicle before September 1 following the January 31 listing date. The notice must include all county and special district taxes due. In computing the taxes, the assessor must use the tax rates of the taxing units in effect for the fiscal year that begins in July 1 following the January 31 listing date. Municipalities must list, assess and tax unregistered classified motor vehicles in the same manner as they do for other property [G.S. § 105-330.5(c)].

• *Proration of tax*

When a new registration is obtained for a vehicle registered under the annual system, the assessor must prorate the taxes due for the remainder of the calendar year. The amount of prorated taxes due is the amount of tax due for the year multiplied by a proration fraction, the numerator of which is the number of full months remaining in the calendar year following the date of application for registration and the denominator of which is 12 [G.S. § 105-330.5(a1)].

• *Due dates of tax payment*

Registered vehicles: Taxes on registered classified motor vehicles are due each year on the following dates:

(1) For a vehicle registered under the staggered system, taxes are due on the date the owner applies for a new registration or the fifteenth day of the month following the month the registration renewal sticker expires [G.S. § 105-330.4(a)(2)].

(2) For a vehicle registered under the annual system, taxes are due on the date the owner applies for a new registration or 45 days after the registration expires [G.S. § 105-330.4(a)(3)].

(3) For a vehicle that has a temporary registration plate or a limited registration plate, the taxes are due on the last day of the second month following the date the owner applies for the plate [G.S. § 105-330.4(a)(4)].

Unregistered vehicles: Taxes on an unregistered classified motor vehicle are due on September 1 following the date by which the vehicle was required to be listed [G.S. § 105-330.4(a)(j)].

¶2106

• *No registration without payment of tax*

A classified motor vehicle may not be registered unless the taxes for the motor vehicle's tax year that begins after issuance of the registration are paid or a temporary tag is issued. Similarly, a classified motor vehicle's registration may not be renewed unless the taxes for the year beginning after the current registration expires have been paid. If registration is renewed before the date the taxes are due, the taxes must be paid as if they were due [G.S. § 105-330.4(a)].

• *Timely payment by mail*

Tax payments submitted by mail are deemed to be received as of the date shown on the postmark affixed by the United States Postal Service. If no date is shown on the postmark or if the postmark is not affixed by the United States Postal Service, the tax payment is deemed to be received when the payment is received by the collecting authority. In any dispute, the burden of proof is on the taxpayer to show that the payment was timely made [G.S. § 105-330.3(d)].

• *Interest*

Registered vehicles: Interest on unpaid taxes and registration fees on registered classified motor vehicles accrues at the rate of 5% for the remainder of the month following the month the taxes were due and $3/4$% beginning the second month following the due date and for each month thereafter until the taxes are paid, unless the tax notice for the vehicle is prepared after the taxes are due. In that case, the interest accrues beginning the second month following the date of the notice until the taxes are paid [G.S. § 105-330.4(b)].

Unregistered vehicles: Taxes on unregistered vehicles paid on or after January 6 following the due date are delinquent and subject to interest, which accrues as follows: (1) for the period January 6 to February 1, at the rate of 2%; and (2) for the period February 1 until the principal amount of the taxes, the accrued interest, and any penalties are paid, at the rate of $3/4$% a month or fraction thereof [G.S. § § 105-330.4(b), 105-360(a)]. Discounts are allowed as provided in G.S. § 105-360(c).

• *Enforcement remedies*

Unpaid taxes on unregistered classified motor vehicles may be collected by using the remedies available for the enforcement of property taxes, including levying on the motor vehicle taxed or on any other personal property of the taxpayer pursuant to G.S. § § 105-366 and 105-367, or by garnishment of the taxpayer's property pursuant to G.S. § 105-368 [G.S. § 105-330.4(c)]. A person who willfully attempts to evade or defeat the motor vehicle tax, or who willfully aids or abets another person to do so, by removal or concealment of a vehicle or otherwise, is guilty of a Class 2 misdemeanor [G.S. § 105-330.3(d)]. Enforcement remedies apply to unpaid taxes on an unregistered classified motor vehicle; they do not apply to unpaid taxes on a registered classified motor vehicle for which the tax year begins on or after August 1, 2013 [G.S. § 105-330.4(c)].

• *Antique automobiles*

Antique automobiles are designated a special class of property under Article V, § 2(2) of the North Carolina Constitution and are assessed for taxation at the lower of (1) true value or (2) $500 [G.S. § 105-330.9(b)]. The term "antique automobile" means a motor vehicle that meets all of the following conditions:

(1) It is registered with the Division of Motor Vehicles and has an historic vehicle special license plate under G.S. § 20-79.4 [G.S. § 105-330.9(a)(1)].

(2) It is maintained primarily for use in exhibitions, club activities, parades, and other public interest functions [G.S. § 105-330.9(a)(2)].

(3) It is used only occasionally for other purposes [G.S. § 105-330.9(a)(3)].

(4) It is owned by an individual (including direct or indirect ownership by an individual through one or more pass-through entities) [G.S. § 105-330.9(a)(4)].

(5) It is used by the owner for a purpose other than the production of income and is not used in connection with a business [G.S. § 105-330.9(a)(5)].

• *Deadlines not extended*

Except as specifically provided in Article 22A, the provisions of G.S. §§ 105-395.1 and 103-5 (providing for extensions of deadlines when the deadline dates fall on a Saturday, Sunday, or holiday); 105-321(f) (authorizing taxing authorization not to collect minimal taxes (but see G.S. § 105-330.5(e) discussed above)) and 105-360 (setting forth due dates and interest charges for property tax purposes) do not apply to the deadlines established in Article 22A [G.S. § 105-330.8].

¶2107 Economic Development and Training Districts

The board of commissioners of any county may define a county economic development and training district (as defined in G.S. § 153A-317.12) to finance, provide, and maintain for the district a skills training center in cooperation with its community college branch in or for the county. An economic development and training district is a special tax area under § 2(4) of Article V of the North Carolina Constitution [G.S. § 153A-317.11].

• *Taxes authorized on property in economic development and training districts*

A county may levy property taxes within an economic development and training district (in addition to those levied throughout the county) for the purposes listed in G.S. § 153A-317.11 within the district in addition to or to a greater extent than the same purposes provided for the entire county [G.S. § 153A-317.17]. Property subject to taxation in a newly established district or in an area annexed to an existing district is subject to property tax valuation as of the preceding January 1.

• *Rate*

Additional property taxes imposed in an economic development and training district cannot exceed the rate of 8¢ on each $100 of taxable valuation [G.S. § 153A-317.17].

PROPERTY TAXES

CHAPTER 22

NONTAXABLE PROPERTY

¶2201 In General

All property (real and personal) within the jurisdiction of the State of North Carolina is subject to property taxation unless it meets one of the following criteria [G.S. § 105-274(a)]:

(1) It is excluded from the tax base by a statute of statewide application enacted under the classification power of the General Assembly granted by Article V, § 2(2) of the North Carolina Constitution. Most of the properties that are exempt from the property tax due to designation as special classes are enumerated in G.S. § 105-275 and are discussed at ¶2203.

(2) It is exempted from taxation by the North Carolina Constitution or by a statute of statewide application enacted under the authority granted the General Assembly by Article V, § 2(3) of the North Carolina Constitution. These exempt properties are designated by sections of Chapter 105 other than G.S. § 105-275 and are discussed at ¶2204—2212.

County rosters: County assessors must maintain rosters of all county property that is granted tax relief through classification or exemption, and the rosters must contain the following information [G.S. § 105-282.1(d)]:

(1) The name of the property owner.

(2) A brief description of the property.

(3) How the property is used.

(4) The property value.

(5) The total value of exempt property in the county and in each municipality in the county.

Exemption vs. Exclusion

The practical effect of exemption and exclusion is the same. The difference between exemption and exclusion is a function of the authority granted to the North Carolina General Assembly under § 2(2) and (3) of Article V of the North Carolina Constitution. Subsection 2(3) specifically provides for the "exemption" of a *limited* number of specified properties (*e.g.,* property belonging to the State, counties, and municipal corporations; cemeteries; property held for educational, scientific, literary, cultural, charitable, or religious purposes).

The General Assembly has the power, under the authority of Article V, § 2(2), to provide different tax rules for different classes of property by declaring it a special class of property subject to special rules. For example, the General Assembly has classified agricultural and horticultural land and historic properties as special classes of taxation and subjected them to tax at favorable rates (see ¶ 2305). When the General Assembly decides that other classes of property should not be taxed, it resorts to its power to classify property for special treatment under subsection 3. For example, qualified retirement facilities are not charitable organizations and cannot, therefore, be exempted under subsection 3. The General Assembly, however, has classified it as a special type of property and "excluded" it from taxation (see ¶ 2210).

• *Annual review of exempted or excluded property*

The assessor must annually review at least one-eighth of the parcels in the county exempted or excluded from taxation to verify that the parcels qualify for the exemption or exclusion [G.S. §§ 105-282.1(e), 105-296(l)]. The assessor may require the owner of exempt or excluded property to make available for inspection any information reasonably needed to verify the property's qualification for exemption or exclusion. The owner has 60 days from the date of a written request for information to submit the information to the assessor. If the assessor determines that the owner failed to make the information requested available in the time required without good cause, the property loses exemption or exclusion. If the property loses its exemption or exclusion for failure to provide the requested information, the assessor must reinstate the property's exemption or exclusion when the owner makes the requested information available within 60 days after the disqualification unless the information disclosed that the property is no longer eligible for the exemption or exclusion [G.S. § 105-296(l)].

¶2201

¶2202 Applications for Property Tax Exemption or Exclusion

- *Generally*

Property owners seeking exemption or exclusion from North Carolina property taxes have the burden of establishing that the property is entitled to exemption or exclusion [G.S. § 105-282.1]. With certain exceptions (see below), an owner claiming exemption or exclusion must file an *annual* application for exemption or exclusion during the listing period. This paragraph contains a discussion of the application requirements of G.S. § 105-282.1.

- *Where to file application*

Property appraised by the Department of Revenue: If the property for which the owner is seeking exemption or exclusion is appraised by the Department of Revenue, the application must be filed with the Department [G.S. § 105-282.1(a)]. See ¶2302 for discussion of appraisal procedures.

Property not appraised by the Department of Revenue: If property is not appraised by the Department of Revenue, applications for exemption or exclusion must be filed with the assessor of the county in which the property is situated [G.S. § 105-282.1(a)]. Appraisal procedures are discussed at ¶2302.

- *Contents of applications*

All applications for exemption or exclusion must (1) contain a complete and accurate statement of the facts that entitle the property to the exemption or exclusion and (2) indicate the municipality (if any) in which the property is located [G.S. § 105-282.1(a)].

- *Application forms*

Applications filed with the Department of Revenue must be submitted on forms approved by the Department. Application forms may be obtained from the assessor and the Department, as appropriate [G.S. § 105-282.1(a)].

- *Action on applications*

The Department of Revenue or the assessor to whom an application is submitted will review the application and either approve or deny it. Approved applications are filed and made available to all appropriate taxing units. If the Department denies an application, it must notify the taxpayer, who may appeal the denial to the Property Tax Commission [G.S. § 105-282.1(b)].

- *Applications handled separately by a municipality*

The governing body of a municipality may deny an application that has been approved by the assessor or by the county board if the owner's rights to notice and hearing are not abridged. Applications handled separately by a municipality must be filed in the office of the person designated by the governing body or, in the absence of a governing body, in the office of the chief fiscal officer of the municipality.

- *Appeal of denial of exemption or exclusion*

Denial by Department of Revenue: If the Department of Revenue denies an application for exemption or exclusion, it must notify the taxpayer, who has the right to appeal to the Property Tax Commission [G.S. § 105-282.1(b)].

Denial by assessor: If an assessor denies an application for exemption or exclusion, the assessor must notify the owner in time for the owner to appeal to the board of equalization and review (see ¶2503) and from the county board to the Property Tax Commission (see ¶2505). If the property is located with a municipality, the assessor must also notify the municipality's governing body. The municipal governing body will then advise the owner whether it will adopt the county board's decision of require the owner to file a separate appeal with the municipality. If the owner is required to apply to the municipality and receives an adverse decision, the owner may then appeal to the Property Tax Commission (see ¶2505).

• *Failure to make timely application*

If a taxpayer fails to make a timely application for exemption or exclusion, an application filed after the close of the listing period may be approved by the Department of Revenue, the board of equalization and review, the board of county commissioners, or the governing body of a municipality, as appropriate. An untimely application so approved applies only to property taxes levied by the county or municipality in the calendar year in which the untimely application is filed [G.S. § 105-282.1(a1)]. The purpose of the application requirement has been stated to be to inform the county in a timely manner of a taxpayer's intention to claim an exemption for its property. Where the county is otherwise on notice of the taxpayer's plans, failure to make a timely application may not prevent exemption. *See In re Appeal of Valley Proteins,* 128 N.C. App. 151, 494 S.E.2d 111 (1997). Thus, a charitable organization that was given a grant by Wake County to purchase a new headquarters and that failed to file an application for exemption for the headquarters facility was nevertheless held to be entitled to exemption. *See In re Urban Ministries of Wake County,* 08 PTC 088 (August 26, 2008). In *In re Appeal of David H. Murdock Research Inst.,* 220 N.C. App. 377, 725 S.E.2d 619 (2012), the court affirmed the Property Tax Commission's decision reversing the county's denial of a late application where the facts showed that (1) the county knew of the taxpayer's exempt status, (2) the county had denied the late application request because of the large value of the subject property and the impact the exemption of the property would have on the county's budget and (3) the county's history of accepting late applications in other cases. *See also In re Appeal of Rowland,* 15 PTC 453 (2016) (Property Tax Commission approved late application for disability exclusion because taxpayer's disabilities were the cause of her late application); *In re Appeal of Christ Church Greensboro, Inc.,* 16 PTC 0405 (2017) (Property Tax Commission approved late application where county sent tax bill to property address, which had no mailbox, instead of office address.) *But see In re Appeal of Rowan Museum, Inc.,* 11 PTC 972 (December 4, 2012), where County denied retroactive exemption due to late application despite fact that County had itself conveyed the property at issue to the taxpayer. *See also In re Appeal of Community Outreach of Archdale-Trinity, Inc.,* 14 PTC 053 (2014) (Property Tax Commission not authorized to grant exemption for year before year in which application is filed); *In re Appeal of DG Solar Lessee, LLC,* 14 PTC 391 (2015) (late application denied where taxpayer's late application in another county in a prior year showed taxpayer had knowledge of application requirement); *In re Appeal of Rock Solar Energy Plant LLC,* 14 PTC 188 (2015) (late application denied where taxpayer's only explanation for untimely application was ignorance of application requirement).

• *Failure to list and make application*

If the owner of property that may be eligible for exemption or exclusion neither lists the property nor files an application for exemption or exclusion, the assessor or the Department of Revenue, as appropriate, is required to discover the property [G.S. § 105-282.1]. Discovery of the property by the Department or the county automati-

¶2202

cally constitutes a discovery by any taxing unit in which the property has a taxable situs. Discoveries are discussed in ¶ 2401. If, upon appeal, the owner demonstrates that the property meets the conditions for exemption or exclusion, the exemption or exclusion may be approved by the appeal body [G.S. § 105-282.1(c)].

The Property Tax Commission has also held property to be entitled to exemption despite the taxpayer's failure to file a timely application because the County sent the property tax bill to the wrong address. The Commission noted that the taxpayer's intention to seek an exemption constituted "sufficient communication" between the County and the taxpayer to put the County on notice of the taxpayer's plans *See, In re Appeal of North Carolina Episcopal Diocese, Inc.,* 08 PTC 090 (February 4, 2010). *See also In re Appeal of Stedman Baptist Church,* 11 PTC 076 (April 24, 2012); *In re Appeal of Christ Church Greensboro, Inc.,* 14 PTC 0405 (2017).

• *Owners not required to file applications for exemption*

Owners of the following exempt or excluded property do not need to file an application for the exemption or exclusion to be entitled to receive it [G.S. § 105-282.1(a)(1)]:

(1) Real and personal property owned by the following entities:

(a) The United States.

(b) The State of North Carolina and its counties and municipalities.

(2) Burial property that is exempted under G.S. § 105-278.2.

(3) Certain special classes of property, as follows:

(a) Standing timber, pulpwood, seedlings, saplings, and other forest growth that are excluded under G.S. § 105-275(15).

(b) Nonbusiness property that is excluded under G.S. § 105-275(16).

(c) Certain tangible personal property manufactured in North Carolina for a nonresident customer that is excluded under G.S. § 105-275(26).

(d) Intangible personal property other than a leasehold interest that is in exempted real property and is not excluded as a leasehold interest in real property used to provide affordable housing for government employees. See item (i) below.

(e) Inventories that are excluded under G.S. § 105-275(32a), (33), and (34).

(f) Poultry and livestock and feed used in the production of poultry and livestock that are excluded under G.S. § 105-275(37).

(g) Computer software and documentation that is excluded under G.S. § 105-275(40).

(h) A vehicle that is offered at retail for short-term lease or rental that is excluded under G.S. § 105-275(42).

(i) Free samples of prescription drugs excluded under G.S. § 105-275(44).

(4) Buildings equipped with a solar energy heating or cooling system that are classified for taxation at a reduced rate under G.S. § 105-277(g).

(5) Property inside certain roadway corridors that is classified for taxation at a reduced valuation under G.S. § 105-277(g).

NOTE: Property exempt (excluded) under G.S. § 105-275 is discussed at ¶ 2203.

• *Owners required to file only one application*

The owners of the following property, after receiving approval for exemption or exclusion, are not required to file an application in subsequent years unless (1) new or additional property is acquired or improvements are added or removed, necessitating a change in the property valuation or (2) there is a change in the use of the property or the qualifications or eligibility of the taxpayer necessitating a review of the exemption or exclusion [G.S. § 105-282.1(a)(2)]:

(1) Property (real and personal) used for religious purposes that is exempted under G.S. § 105-278.3.

(2) Property (real and personal) used for educational purposes that is exempted under G.S. § 105-278.4.

(3) Property (real and personal) of religious educational assemblies used for religious and educational purposes that is exempted under G.S. § 105-278.5.

(4) Property (real and personal) used for charitable purposes that is exempted under G.S. § 105-278.6.

(5) Property (real and personal) used for educational, scientific, literary, or charitable purposes that is exempted under G.S. § 105-278.7.

(6) Property (real and personal) used for charitable hospital purposes that is exempted under G.S. § 105-278.8.

(7) Special classes of excluded property:

(a) Property (real and personal) owned by nonprofit water or nonprofit sewer associations or corporations that is excluded under G.S. § 105-275(3).

(b) Property (real and personal) owned by certain nonprofit corporations and charitable organizations and used for public parks and drives that is excluded under G.S. § 105-275(7).

(c) Property (real and personal) used for pollution control and recycling that is excluded under G.S. § 105-275(8).

(d) Real property owned by a nonprofit corporation or association for educational and scientific purposes as a protected area that is excluded under G.S. § 105-275(12).

(e) Property (real and personal) belonging to certain veterans' organizations that is excluded under G.S. § 105-275(17).

(f) Property (real and personal) belonging to certain lodges, orders, and shrines that is excluded under G.S. § 105-275(18).

(g) Property (real and personal) belonging to certain civic organizations (*e.g.*, Elks, Moose) used for meeting and lodge purposes that is excluded under G.S. § 105-275(19).

(h) Property (real and personal) belonging to Goodwill Industries and similar charitable organizations that is excluded under G.S. § 105-275(20).

(i) Severable development rights that are excluded under G.S. § 105-275(35).

(j) Property (real and personal) belonging to the North Carolina Low-Level Radioactive Waste Management Authority that is excluded under G.S. § 105-275(36).

(k) Property (real and personal) belonging to the North Carolina Hazardous Waste Management Commission that is excluded under G.S. § 105-275(38).

(l) Property (real and personal) that is (1) owned by a qualified nonprofit corporation, (2) leased to a qualified unit of local government, and (3) used for a public purpose and that is excluded under G.S. § 105-275(39).

(m) Solar energy electric system property partially excluded under G.S. § 105-275(45).

(n) Health care facilities financed under the Health Care Facilities Finance Act and described in G.S. § 131A-21.

(o) Real property occupied by a charter school and wholly and exclusively used for educational purposes that is excluded under G.S. § 105-275(46).

(p) Energy mineral interests excluded under G.S. § 105-275(47)

(q) Real and personal property located on Cherokee Indian land excluded under G.S. § 105-275(48).

(r) Mobile classrooms and modular units excluded under G.S. § 105-275(49).

(8) Special classes of property classified for taxation at a reduced rate:

(a) Property owned by private water companies that qualify for special valuation under G.S. § 105-277(h).

(b) Residential and commercial property held by a builder as inventory that qualifies for special valuation under G.S. § 105-277.02.

(c) The first $20,000 in appraised value of an owner-occupied permanent resident that is excluded under G.S. § 105-277.1.

(d) The first $45,000 in appraised value of a residence excluded under G.S. § 105-277.1C.

(e) Precious metals used in manufacturing or processing that qualify for special valuation under G.S. § 105-277.10.

(f) Qualifying improvements on brownfields properties that qualify for special valuation under G.S. § 105-277.13.

(g) Working waterfront property described in G.S. § 105-277.14.

(h) Wildlife conservation land described in G.S. § 105-277.15.

(i) Community land trust property described in G.S. § 105-277.17.

(j) Historic properties that qualify for special valuation under G.S. § 105-278.

(9) Property owned by a nonprofit homeowners' association where the value of the property is included in the appraisals of property owned by members of the association under G.S. § 105-277.8.

¶2203 Property Excluded Under G.S. § 105-275

The following classes of property are designated special classes under the authority of Article V, § 2(2) of the North Carolina Constitution and shall not be listed, appraised, assessed or taxed [G.S. § 105-275].

- *Air cleaning and waste disposal*

Real and personal property that is used or (if under construction) to be used exclusively for air cleaning or waste disposal or to abate, reduce, or prevent the pollution of air or water (including, but not limited to, waste lagoons and facilities owned by public or private utilities built and installed primarily for the purpose of providing sewer service to areas that are predominantly residential or areas that lie outside territory already having sewer service) is exempt. In order to qualify for this exemption the property must be certified by the Department of Environmental Quality or a local air pollution control program [G.S. § 105-275(8)a]. This exemption applies to animal waste management systems only if they meet the new requirements of G.S. § 105-275(8)al. See "Animal waste management," below.

- *Aircraft*

Aircraft that is owned or leased by an interstate air courier that is apportioned to the courier's hub in North Carolina and used in the air courier's operations in North Carolina is exempt [G.S. § 105-275(24a)].

- *Animal waste management*

Animal waste management systems qualify for exclusion under G.S. § 105-275(8)a (see "Air cleaning and waste disposal," above) only if the Environmental Management Commission determines that the animal waste management system will accomplish all of the following [G.S. § 105-275(8)a1]:

(1) It will eliminate the discharge of animal waste to surface waters and groundwater through direct discharge, seepage, or runoff.

(2) It will substantially eliminate atmospheric emissions of ammonia.

(3) It will substantially eliminate the emission of odor that is detectable beyond the boundaries of the parcel or tract of land on which the farm is located.

(4) It will substantially eliminate the release of disease-transmitting vectors and airborne pathogens.

(5) It will substantially eliminate nutrient and heavy metal contamination of soil and groundwater.

- *Capital lease property*

Real or tangible personal property subject to a capital lease pursuant to G.S. § 115C-531 (relating to capital leases of school buildings) is excluded from tax [G.S. § 105-275(43)]. Note that G.S. § 115C-531 was repealed effective July 1, 2015.

- *Cargo containers*

Cargo containers and container chassis used for the transportation of cargo by vessels in ocean commerce are exempt [G.S. § 105-275(24)].

- *Charitable and nonprofit organizations*

Real and personal property owned either (1) by a bona fide charitable organization or (2) by a nonprofit corporation formed under the provisions of Chapter 55A of the General Statutes that meets either of the following criteria is exempt [G.S. § 105-275(7)]:

(a) The property is either operated by the owning charitable organization or nonprofit or leased to another such nonprofit corporation or charitable organization [G.S. § 105-275(7)a].

(b) The property is appropriated exclusively for public parks and drives [G.S. § 105-275(7)b].

¶2203

- *Charter school property*

Real and personal property occupied by a charter school and wholly and exclusively used for educational purposes as defined in G.S. § 105-278.4(f). If these requirements are met the exclusion is available regardless of who owns the property [G.S. § 105-275(46)].

- *Cherokee Indian property*

Real and personal property located on lands held in trust by the United States for the Eastern Band of the Cherokee Indians, regardless of ownership, is excluded from tax effective July 1, 2016 [G.S. § 105-275(48)]. This provision resolves uncertainties about the ability of the state to tax personal property located on Indian lands but not owned by tribe members.

- *Computer software*

Computer software and any documentation related to the computer software are exempt. For this purpose, the term "computer software" means any program or routine used to cause a computer to perform a specific task or set of tasks, including system and application programs and database storage and management programs [G.S. § 105-275(40)]. See "Certain computer software" at ¶2102 for discussion of certain computer software that is taxable.

- *Conservation property*

Real property that is owned by a nonprofit corporation or association organized to receive and administer lands for conservation purposes is exempt if (1) it is exclusively held and used for one or more of the qualifying purposes (see below) and (2) produces no income or produces income that is incidental to and not inconsistent with the purpose(s) for which the land is held and used [G.S. § 105-275(12)]. For an example of property held to qualify under this exclusion, see *In re Appeal of Grandfather Mountain Stewardship Foundation, Inc.*, 11 PTC 068 (June 24, 2013).

Qualifying purposes: To qualify for the exemption, the conservation property must be any of the following:

(1) Used for an educational or scientific purpose as a nature reserve or park in which wild nature, flora and fauna, and biotic communities are preserved for observation and study. For this purpose the terms "educational purpose" and "scientific purpose" has the same meaning as those discussed at ¶2211 [G.S. § 105-275(12)a].

(2) Managed under a written wildlife habitat conservation agreement with the North Carolina Wildlife Resources Commission [G.S. § 105-275(12)b].

(3) Managed under a forest stewardship plan developed by the Forest Stewardship Program [G.S. § 105-275(12)c].

(4) Used for public access to public waters or trails [G.S. § 105-275(12)d].

(5) Used for protection of water quality and subject to a conservation agreement under the provision of the Conservation and Historic Preservation Agreements Act (Article 4, Chapter 121 of the General Statutes) [G.S. § 105-275(12)e].

(6) Held by a nonprofit land conservation organization for sale or transfer to a local, state, or federal government unit for conservation purposes [G.S. § 105-275(12)f].

Lien on property: The taxes that would otherwise be due on conservation property are a lien on the real property of the taxpayer. The taxes are to be carried forward on the records of the taxing unit as deferred taxes. The deferred taxes for the preceding five fiscal years become due and payable when the property loses its eligibility for deferral as the result of a disqualifying event, in accordance with the uniform rules for the payment of deferred taxes (see ¶ 2311). A disqualifying event occurs when the property (i) is no longer held and used for a qualifying purpose, (ii) produces income that is not incidental to and consistent with the purpose for which the land is held and used, (iii) is sold or transferred without recordation of an easement requiring perpetual use for a qualifying purpose and prohibiting any use that would generate income that is not incidental to and consistent with the purpose for which the land is held or used. The lien imposed on the property is extinguished if the property is sold or transferred to a local, state or federal government unit for conservation purposes or subject to an easement requiring perpetual use of the land for a qualifying purpose [G.S. § 105-275(12)].

• *Correctional facilities*

A correctional facility located on state-owned land and constructed pursuant to a contract with the state is excluded from tax. The exclusion covers construction in progress and leasehold interests in state-owned land on which the facility is located [G.S. § 105-275 (39a)].

• *Cotton dust*

Tangible personal property that is used or (if being installed) is to be used exclusively for the prevention or reduction of cotton dust inside a textile plant in accordance with OSHA standards adopted by the State of North Carolina is exempt [G.S. § 105-275(8)c]. Notwithstanding the exclusive-use requirement, all parts of a ventilation or air conditioning system that are integrated into a system used for the prevention or reduction of cotton dust (except for chillers and cooling towers) are excluded [G.S. § 105-275(8)c].

• *Damaged commercial property*

Real and personal property that meets the following requirements is exempt:

(a) The property is a contiguous tract of land previously used primarily for commercial or industrial purposes and damaged significantly as the result of fire or explosion.

(b) The property was donated to a North Carolina nonprofit corporation formed by an entity other than an affiliate as defined in G.S. § 105-163.010.

(c) No portion of the property may have been leased or sold by the nonprofit corporation [G.S. § 105-275(7a)].

The statutory language is crafted to apply only to property donated by ConAgra to the Garner Economic Development Corporation as a result of the 2009 explosion of the ConAgra facility in Garner. This exclusion expires for taxable years beginning on or after July 1, 2021.

¶2203

- *Development rights*

Severable development rights when severed and evidenced by a deed recorded in the office of the register of deeds are exempt [G.S. § 105-275(35)]. "Severable development right" means the potential for the improvement or subdivision of part or all of a parcel of real property, as permitted under the terms of a zoning and/or subdivision ordinance, expressed in dwelling unit equivalents or other measures of development density or intensity or a fraction or multiple of that potential that may be severed or detached from the parcel from which they are derived and transferred to one or more other parcels located in receiving districts where they may be exercised in conjunction with the use or subdivision of property [G.S. § 136-66.11(a)].

- *Energy minerals*

An energy mineral interest in property for which a drilling permit has not been issued under G.S. § 113-395 is exempt [G.S. § 105-275(47)]. An "energy mineral" is defined in G.S. § 105-187.71. See ¶ 2916.

- *Foreign trade zone*

Tangible personal property imported from outside the United States and held in a Foreign Trade Zone for the purpose of sale, manufacture, processing, assembly, grading, cleaning, mixing, or display, and tangible personal property produced in the United States and held in a Foreign Trade Zone for exportation, either in its original form or as altered by any of the above processes, is exempt [G.S. § 105-275(23)].

- *Forest growth*

Standing timber, pulpwood, seedlings, saplings, and other forest growth (on the date on which each county's next general reappraisal of real property becomes effective) are exempt [G.S. § 105-275(15)].

- *Fraternal orders*

Real and personal property belonging to the Loyal Order of Moose, the Benevolent and protective Order of Elks, the Knights of Pythias, the Odd Fellows, the Woodmen of the World, and similar fraternal or civic orders and organizations operated for nonprofit benevolent, patriotic, historical, charitable, or civic purposes, when used exclusively for meeting or lodge purposes, is exempt [G.S. § 105-275(19)]. Despite the reference in the statute to the exclusive use of fraternal order lodge facilities for lodge purposes, the Property Tax Commission has ruled that the incidental use of such facilities by nonmembers does not defeat the exemption [In re ENC Woodmen Youth Camp, Inc., 04 PTC 22 (2005]. See also In re New Bern Shrine Club, 04 PTC 21 (2005) (incidental use of Masonic lodge facilities by nonmembers did not defeat exemption under G.S. § 105-275(18)).

- *Fraternities and sororities*

Improvements to real property owned by social fraternities and sororities and similar college, university and high school organizations that are located, owned by, or allocated to the University of North Carolina or one of its constituent institutions are exempt [G.S. § 105-275(19a), effective for taxes imposed for taxable years beginning on or after July 1, 2013 (S.L. 2013-375. § 3.(b))].

- *Historic districts*

Land within an historic district held by a nonprofit corporation organized for historic preservation purposes for use as a future site for an historic structure that is to be moved to the site from another location, but not for more than five years, is exempt. This classification is made for no more than five years, and the deferred taxes become due if an historic structure is not moved to the site within five years. All liens arising under G.S. § 105-275(29a) are extinguished upon the location of an historic structure on the site within the time period allowed [G.S. § 105-275(29a)]. See ¶ 2311 for a discussion of payment of deferred taxes following a disqualifying event.

• *Historic preservation*

Real property and easements wholly and exclusively held and used for nonprofit historic preservation purposes by a nonprofit historical association or institution are exempt [G.S. § 105-275(29)].

• *Imported tangible personal property*

Tangible personal property that is imported from a foreign country through a North Carolina seaport terminal and that is stored at the North Carolina terminal while awaiting further shipment for the first 12 months of storage is exempt [G.S. § 105-275(2)].

• *Intangible personal property*

Intangible personal property, other than computer software not exempt under G.S. § 105-275(40), is exempt [G.S. § 105-275(31)]. Leasehold interests in exempt real property were taxable for taxable years beginning before July 1, 2019 [G.S. § 105-275(31); S.L. 2018-98, § 1].

The right to a club membership that taxpayers were required to purchase when they purchased a home in a retirement community was held not to be intangible property, and the cost of the membership was properly included in the taxable value of the home. See *In re Appeal of Tillman*, 187 N.C. App. 739, 653 S.E.2d 911 (2007).

• *Inventories*

Inventories owned by contractors, manufacturers, and merchants (retail and wholesale) are exempt [G.S. § 105-275(32a), (33), (34)]. *See In re Appeal of Michelin North America, Inc.*, ___ N.C. App. _____, ___ S.E. 2d ___ (2016) (tire manufacturer's prototype and test tires qualified as inventory); *In re Appeal of Corporate Fleet Services LLC*, 11 PTC 635 (2015) (use of aircraft owned by aircraft brokerage firm for demonstration purposes did not result in loss of inventory status where demonstration use was beneficial in mitigating maintenance costs); *In re Appeal of Aaron's, Inc.*, 16 PTC 0124 (2018), *aff'd* ___ N.C. App. ___ (2019) (furniture and household articles held for lease were not inventory despite lesee's option to purchase).

• *Leased vehicles*

General rule: A vehicle that is offered at retail for short-term lease or rental and is owned or leased by an entity engaged in the business of leasing or renting vehicles to the general public for short-term lease or rental is exempt [G.S. § 105-275(42)]. "Short-term lease or rental" means a lease or rental that is for a period of fewer than 365 continuous days. "Vehicle" has the meaning assigned in G.S. §§ 153A-156(e)(1) and 160A-215.1(e)(1).

Heavy equipment: Heavy equipment on which a gross receipts tax may be imposed under G.S. § 153A-156.1 and G.S. § 160A-215.2 (discussed at ¶ 1724) [G.S. § 105-275(42a)].

- *Lodges*

Real and personal property belonging to the Grand Lodge of Ancient Free and Accepted Masons of North Carolina, the Prince Hall Masonic Grand Lodge of North Carolina, and their subordinate lodges and appendant bodies when used exclusively for meeting or lodge purposes, is exempt [G.S. § 105-275(18)]. Despite the reference in the statute to the exclusive use of lodge facilities for lodge purposes, the Property Tax Commission has ruled that the incidental use of lodge facilities by nonmembers, including renting parts of the lodge to nonmembers for a fee, does not defeat the exemption. *See In re New Bern Shrine Club*, 04 PTC 21 (2005); *see also In re ENC Woodmen Youth Camp, Inc.*, 04 PTC 22 (2005) (incidental use of fraternal order facilities by nonmembers did not defeat exemption under G.S. § 105-275(19)).

- *Major recycling facility*

Real or personal property that is used or (if under construction) is to be used by a major recycling facility (defined in G.S. § 105-129.25) predominantly for recycling or resource recovering of or from solid waste if properly certified by the Department of Environmental Quality is exempt [G.S. § 105-275(8)d].

- *Mobile classrooms or modular units*

Mobile classrooms or modular units occupied by a school and used exclusively for educational purposes are exempt, regardless of who owns the property. A "school" for this purpose includes a public school, a regional school, a non-profit non-public school and a community college [G.S. § 105-275(49)].

- *Motor vehicle chassis*

Motor vehicle chassis belonging to nonresidents that temporarily enter North Carolina for the purpose of having a body mounted thereon are exempt [G.S. § 105-275(14)].

- *Nonbusiness property*

Personal property that is used by the owner for a purpose other than the production of income and that is not used in connection with a business is exempt. The term "nonbusiness property" includes household furnishings, clothing, pets, lawn tools, and lawn equipment. The term does not include motor vehicles, mobile homes, aircraft, watercraft, or engines for watercraft [G.S. § 105-275(16)].

- *Nonprofit water or sewer organizations*

Real and personal property owned by nonprofit water or nonprofit sewer associations or corporations is exempt [G.S. § 105-275(3)].

- *Nonresident customers*

For the tax year immediately following transfer of title, tangible personal property manufactured in North Carolina for the account of a nonresident customer and held by the manufacturer for shipment is exempt [G.S. § 105-275(26)].

- *Nuclear materials*

Special nuclear materials held for or in the process of manufacture, processing, or delivery by the manufacturer or processor are exempt. The terms "manufacture" and "processing" do not include the use of special nuclear materials as fuel. The term "special nuclear materials" includes (1) uranium 233, uranium enriched in the isotope 233 or 235 and (2) any material artificially enriched by uranium, thorium, or any combination of uranium and thorium, provided that to qualify for this exemption no nuclear materials can be discharged into any river, creek, or stream in North Carolina. The term, "special nuclear materials," however, does not include "source material," which is any material except special nuclear material that contains by weight one-twentieth of one percent (0.05%) or more of uranium, thorium, or any combination thereof. An exclusion will be denied to any manufacturer, fabricator, or processor who permits either of the following [G.S. § 105-275(6)]:

> (1) Burial of special nuclear materials in North Carolina.

> (2) Discharge of special nuclear materials into the air or into any river, creek, or stream in North Carolina if the discharge would contravene in any way the applicable health and safety standards established and enforced by the Department of Health and Human Services, the North Carolina Department of Environmental Quality, or the Federal Atomic Energy Commission. The most stringent of these standards will govern.

• *Poultry and livestock*

Poultry and livestock and feed used in the production of poultry and livestock are exempt [G.S. § 105-275(37)].

• *Prescription drugs given as free samples*

Free samples of drugs that are required by federal law to be dispensed only on prescription and are given to physicians and other medical practitioners to dispense free of charge in the course of their practice are exempt [G.S. § 105-275(44)].

• *Public-purpose property*

Real and personal property that is (1) owned by a nonprofit corporation organized upon the request of a local government unit for the sole purpose of financing projects for public use; (2) leased to a unit of local government whose property is exempt from taxation under G.S. § 105-278.1 (relating to property owned by governmental units); and (3) used in whole or in part for a public purpose by the local governmental unit is exempt. If only part of the property is used for a public purpose, only that part is exempt from tax. The property is not exempt if any distributions are made to members, officers, or directors of the nonprofit corporation [G.S. § 105-275(39)].

• *Recycling*

Real or personal property that is used or (if under construction) to be used exclusively for recycling or resource recovering of or from solid waste, if properly certified by the Department of Environmental Quality, is exempt [G.S. § 105-275(8)b)].

• *Repair and service*

Tangible personal property shipped into North Carolina for the purpose of repair, alteration, maintenance, or servicing and reshipment to the owner outside North Carolina is exempt [G.S. § 105-275(25)].

• *Solar energy electric systems*

Eighty percent (80%) of the appraised value of a solar energy electric system is exempt. For this purpose, the term "solar energy electric system" means all equipment used directly and exclusively for the conversion of solar energy to electricity [G.S. § 105-275(45)]. A solar energy electric system under construction may qualify for the exemption. *See In re Appeal of Snow Camp, LLC*, 16 PTC 0765 (2018). This decision of the Property Tax Commission was affirmed by an unpublished decision of the North Carolina Court of Appeals. *See In re Appeal of Highwater Solar 1, LLC* (COA18-396) (Nov. 20, 2018).

• *Training and rehabilitation*

Real and personal property belonging to Goodwill Industries and other charitable organizations organized for the training and rehabilitation of disabled persons when used exclusively for training and rehabilitation, including commercial activities directly related to such training and rehabilitation, is exempt [G.S. § 105-275(20)]. *See also In re Appeal of Johnston County Industries, Inc.,* 09 PTC 1011 (June 30, 2011) (unused wooded acreage surrounding property used by charitable organization for training and rehabilitation purposes did not qualify for exemption).

• *Veterans*

Organizations: Real and personal property belonging to the American Legion, Veterans of Foreign Wars, Disabled American Veterans, or to any similar veterans organizations chartered by the Congress of the United States or organized and operated on a statewide or nationwide basis, and any post or local organization thereof, when used exclusively for meeting or lodge purposes, is exempt [G.S. § 105-275(17)].

Vehicles: Vehicles that the United States government gives to veterans because of disabilities they suffered in World War II, the Korean Conflict, or the Vietnam Era so long as they are owned by (1) a person to whom the vehicle was given or (2) another person entitled to receive such a gift are exempt [G.S. § 105-275(5)].

Vehicles of disabled veterans: A motor vehicle owned by a disabled veteran that is altered with special equipment to accommodate a service-connected disability is exempt. For this purpose a "disabled veteran" means a person as defined in 38 U.S.C. § 101(2) who is entitled to special automotive equipment for a service-connected disability, as provided in 38 U.S.C. § 3901 [G.S. § 105-275(5a)].

¶2204 Property Owned by Units of Government

• *Generally*

For purposes of this exemption a specified unit of government (federal, State, or local) includes its departments, institutions, and agencies [G.S. § 105-278.1(a)(1)].

• *Federal government property*

Real and personal property owned by the United States and, by virtue of federal law, not subject to State and local taxes is exempt [G.S. § 105-278.1(a)]. *See also Atl. Marine Corps Cmtys., LLC v. Onslow County,* 497 F. Supp. 2d 743 (E.D.N.C. 2007) (discussing exemption of property held by public-private partnership on federal enclave under Article I, § 8, cl. 17 of the U.S. Constitution); *In re Appeal of Fontana Village, Inc.,* 10 PTC 149 (July 12, 2011) (holding that a private concessioner's leasehold interest in land owned by the federal government was exempt under the Supremacy Clause of the United States Constitution); *In re Appeal of Novartis Vaccines and Diagnostics, Inc.,* 10 PTC 434 and 11 PTC 028 (June 30, 2011) (holding that where the federal government entered into a contract with a private company to jointly fund the construction of a manufacturing facility and where the contract provided that the parties would jointly own the facility in accordance with their funding percentages, the federal government's percentage interest in the facility's real and personal property was exempt).

• *State government property*

Real and personal property belonging to the State, counties and municipal corporations is exempt from taxation [NC Constitution, Art. V, §2.(3); G.S. §105-278.1(b)]. The following are examples of boards, commissions, authorities, and institutions that are considered units of North Carolina government and the property of which is therefore exempt [G.S. §105-278.1(c)(2)]:

(1) The State Marketing Authority established by G.S. §106-529 (relating to the promotion of orderly and efficient marketing of products of the home, farm, sea, and forest).

(2) The Board of Governors of the consolidated University of North Carolina incorporated under the provisions of G.S. §116-3 (relating to the organization, governance, and property of the University) and known as "the University of North Carolina." *See also* G.S. §116-16 (exempting property of the University of North Carolina from all forms of public taxation).

(3) The North Carolina Museum of Art made an agency of the State under G.S. §140-5.12.

Equitable Title to Property Held in Trust for the State

Property held in trust by a nonprofit student housing corporation for Appalachian State University (a constituent university of the consolidated University North Carolina) was exempt from property tax. The Court ruled that neither the North Carolina Constitution (Art. V, §2) nor G.S. §105-278.1(b) requires the State to have legal title in order to exempt the property from taxation; the equitable title held by Appalachian State University was sufficient to show that the property belongs to the State of North Carolina [*In re Appeal of Appalachian Student Hous. Corp.*, 165 N.C. App. 379, 598 S.E.2d 701 (2004), *appeal dismissed*, 359 N.C. 58, 604 S.E.2d 307 (2004)]. While this case was pending, the General Assembly enacted a specific exemption for student housing property owned by a nonprofit for the University of North Carolina or North Carolina Community colleges. *See* S.L. 2004-174; G.S. §105-278.4(a)(1)b. *See also In re Appeal of Fayette Place*, 193 N.C. App. 744, 668 S.E.2d 354 (2008) (property owned by for-profit entity owned in turn by a county housing authority qualified for exemption).

• *Local government property*

Real and personal property belonging to the counties and municipalities of North Carolina is exempt from taxation [G.S. §105-278.1(b)]. The following are examples of boards, commissions, authorities, and institutions that are units of local government of North Carolina [G.S. §105-278.1(c)(3)]:

(1) Airport authorities, boards, or commissions created as a separate and independent body corporate and politic (a) by an act of the North Carolina General Assembly or (b) by one or more counties or municipalities or combinations thereof under the authority of an act of the North Carolina General Assembly.

(2) Hospital authorities created under G.S. §131E-17.

(3) Housing authorities created under G.S. §157-4 or 157-4.1.

(4) Municipal parking authorities created under G.S. §160-477. Note that G.S. §160-477 has been repealed and transferred.

(5) Veterans' recreation authorities created under G.S. §165-26.

¶2205 Burial Property

Real property set apart for burial purposes is exempted from taxation unless it is owned and held for purposes of (1) sale or rental, or (2) sale of burial rights therein [G.S. § 105-278.2(a)]. *See* ¶2304 for special assessment of taxable burial property. "Real property" for this purpose includes land, tombs, vaults, monuments, and mausoleums, and the term "burial" includes entombment [G.S. § 105-278.2(c)]. A county may not deny the exemption for burial property merely because the owner lacks a survey or plat of the property [G.S. § 105-278.2(a)].

¶2206 Real Property Used for Religious Purposes

• *Requirements*

Buildings, the land they occupy, and additional adjacent land reasonably necessary for the convenient use of the buildings are exempt from property taxation if they are wholly owned by a qualified agency (see definition below) and if (1) they are wholly and exclusively used by owners for religious purposes or (2) they are occupied gratuitously by one other than the owners and exclusively used by the occupant for religious, charitable, or nonprofit educational, literary, scientific, or cultural purposes [G.S. § 105-278.3(a)].

Unimproved Land Does Not Qualify

The North Carolina Court of Appeals has held that unimproved land does not qualify for exemption even where the land is used for outdoor worship services. Under the language of the statute, land is exempt only to the extent necessary for the convenient use of buildings used for religious purposes [*In re Appeal of the Church of Yahshua the Christ*, 160 N.C. App. 236, 584 S.E.2d 827 (2003); *cert. denied*, 357 N.C. 505, 587 S.E.2d 421 (2003)].

• *Religious purpose defined*

A religious purpose is one that pertains to practicing, teaching, and setting forth a religion. Worship is the most common religious purpose but the term encompasses other activities that demonstrate and further the beliefs and objectives of a given church or religious body (*e.g.*, ownership and maintenance of a general or promotional office or headquarters; ownership and maintenance of residences for clergy, rabbis, priests, or nuns assigned to a unit of a religious body; residences for clergy on furlough or unassigned). The ownership and maintenance of residences for employees other than clergy, rabbis, priests, or nuns is not a religious purpose. However, if part of exempt property is made available as a residence for an individual who provides guardian, janitorial, and custodial services for the property or who oversees and supervises qualifying activities upon and in connection with the property, the entire property is exempt [G.S. § 105-278.3(d)(1)].

• *Exclusive-use exceptions*

The following are exceptions to the exclusive-use requirement for real property used for religious purposes:

(1) If part of a property that otherwise meets the requirements for exemption is used for an exempt purpose that would require exemption if the entire

property were so used, the valuation of the part used for an exempt purpose is exempted from taxation [G.S. § 105-278.3(g)(1)].

(2) The fact that a building or facility is incidentally available to and patronized by the general public does not defeat the exemption so long as there is no material amount of business or patronage with the general public [G.S. § 105-278.3(f)].

(3) Any parking lot wholly owned by a qualifying agency may be used for parking without removing the tax exemption if the total charge for parking does not exceed that portion of the actual maintenance expenditures for the parking lot reasonably estimated to have been made on account of the parking [G.S. § 105-278.3(g)(2)].

(4) A building and the land occupied by the building is exempt if the building is under construction and intended to be wholly and exclusively used by the owner for religious purposes upon completion. A building is under construction from the date a building permit is issued until the earlier of 90 days after a certificate of occupancy is issued or 180 days after the end of active construction [G.S. § 105-278.3(g)(3)]. This provision effectively overturns the decision of the North Carolina Court of Appeals in *In re Vienna Baptist Church*, 241 N.C. App. 268, 773 S.E. 2d 97 (2015).

• *Qualifying agencies*

The following agencies, when the other requirements are met, may obtain exemption for their properties:

(1) Congregations, parishes, missions, or similar local units of a church or religious body.

(2) Conferences, associations, presbyteries, dioceses, districts, synods, or similar units of local units of a church or religious body.

¶2207 Real and Personal Property Used for Educational Purposes

Buildings, the land they actually occupy, and additional land reasonably necessary for the convenient use of the buildings are exempt from taxation if all of the following requirements are met [G.S. § 105-278.4(a)]:

(1) They are owned by one of the following:

(a) An educational institution.

(b) A nonprofit entity for the sole benefit of a constituent or affiliated institution of The University of North Carolina, a community college, a nonprofit postsecondary educational institution described in G.S. § 116-22 (regarding eligibility for state-funded need-based scholarships), or a combination of these.

(2) The owner is not organized or operated for profit and no officer, shareholder, member, or employee of the owner or any other person is entitled to receive pecuniary profit from the owner's operations except reasonable compensation for services.

¶2207

(3) They are of a kind commonly employed in the performance of those activities naturally and properly incident to the operation of an educational institution.

(4) They are wholly and exclusively used for educational purposes by the owners or occupied gratuitously by another nonprofit educational institution and wholly and exclusively used by the occupant for nonprofit educational purposes.

Day Care Center Denied Educational Exemption

A nonprofit day care center was not entitled to a property tax exemption under G.S. §105-278.4 because it provided custodial care as well as education and, therefore, did not have a "wholly and exclusively educational" purpose. It also had a custodial purpose, and G.S. §105-278.4 does not specifically mention an exemption for custodial institutions such as day care facilities [*In re Appeal of Chapel Hill Day Care Ctr., Inc.*, 144 N.C. App. 649, 551 S.E.2d 172 (2001), *appeal dismissed*, 355 N.C. 492, 563 S.E.2d 564 (2002)]. But see *In re Carolina Friends School*, 03 PTC 276 (2/23/05), holding that property owned by an institution providing educational programs for three -and four-year-olds with a curriculum taught by qualified teachers with degrees in early childhood development was wholly and exclusively used for educational and not custodial purposes.

• *Educational institutions*

The term "educational institution" includes the following [G.S. §105-278.4(a)(1)]:

(1) A university.

(2) A college.

(3) A school.

(4) A seminary.

(5) An academy.

(6) An industrial school.

(7) A public library.

(8) A museum.

(9) Similar institutions.

• *Educational purpose*

An educational purpose is one that has as its objective the education or instruction of human beings; it includes the transmission of information and the training or development of the knowledge or skills of individual persons [G.S. §105-278.4(f)]. The operation of the following is an educational purpose regardless of the extent to which the property is also available to and patronized by the general public [G.S. §105-278.4(f)(2)]:

(1) A student housing facility.

(2) A student dining facility.

(3) A golf course.

(4) A tennis court.

(5) A sports area.

(6) A similar sport property or recreational sport property for the use of students or faculty.

¶2207

However, a sorority house not owned by an educational institution was held not to be entitled to exemption, because the operation of the house to recruit sorority members was held not to be an educational purpose [*In re Appeal of Alpha Chapter of Pi Beta Phi House Corporation*, 08 PTC 207 (July 24, 2009)]. *But see* G.S. § 105-275(19a).

Incidental Public Use Does Not Defeat Exemption

The fact that a building or facility is incidentally available to and patronized by the general public does not defeat the exemption *if* there is no material amount of business or patronage with the general public [G.S. § 105-278.4(d)]. Note, however, that the operation one of the facilities listed in G.S. § 105-278.4(f)(2), *e.g.*, a tennis court, is exempt regardless of the extent to which the property is used by the public (see "*Educational purpose*," above).

• *Exempt land and improvements*

Land (exclusive of improvements), improvements other than buildings, the land actually occupied by such improvements, and additional land reasonably necessary for the convenient use of any such improvement shall be exempted from taxation if they meet the following three requirements [G.S. § 105-278.4(b)]:

(1) They are owned by an educational institution that owns real property entitled to exemption.

(2) They are of a kind commonly employed in the performance of those activities naturally and properly incident to the operation of an educational institution.

(3) They are wholly and exclusively used for educational purposes by the owner or occupied gratuitously by another nonprofit educational institution and wholly and exclusively used by the occupant for nonprofit educational purposes.

• *Exempt personal property*

Personal property owned by a church, a religious body, or an educational institution is exempt if it meets the following two requirements [G.S. § 105-278.4(e)]:

(1) The owner is not organized or operated for profit, and no officer, shareholder, member, or employee of the owner, or any other person is entitled to receive pecuniary profit from the owner's operations except reasonable compensation for services.

(2) The personal property is used wholly and exclusively for educational purposes by the owner or held gratuitously by a church, religious body, or nonprofit educational institution other than the owner, and wholly and exclusively used for nonprofit educational purposes. There are no exceptions to the exclusive-use requirement for personal property.

• *Partial exemption*

Notwithstanding the exclusive-use requirements of G.S. § 105-278.4(a) and (b) (with respect to exempt buildings and land), if a part of a property that otherwise meets the requirements of one of those subsections is used for a purpose that would require exemption if the entire property were so used, the valuation of the part used for educational purposes is exempt from taxation [G.S. § 105-278.4(c)].

¶2208 Real and Personal Property of Religious Educational Assemblies Used for Religious and Educational Purposes

• *Exempt property*

Buildings, the land they actually occupy, and additional adjacent land reasonably necessary for the convenient use of the buildings or for the religious educational programs of the owner are exempt if they meet the following four requirements [G.S. § 105-278.5(a)]:

(1) They are owned by a religious educational assembly, retreat, or similar organization.

(2) No officer, shareholder, member, or employee of the owner or any other person is entitled to receive pecuniary profit from the owner's operations *except* reasonable compensation for services.

(3) They are of a kind commonly employed in those activities naturally and properly incident to the operation of a religious educational assembly.

(4) They are wholly and exclusively used for (a) religious worship or (b) purposes of instruction in religious education.

• *Exclusive-use exceptions*

The following are exceptions to the exclusive-use requirement for real property of religious educational assemblies:

(1) If part of a property that otherwise meets the requirements for exemption is used for an exempt purpose that would require exemption if the entire property were so used, the valuation of the part used for an exempt purpose is exempted from taxation [G.S. § 105-278.3(e)].

(2) The fact that a building or facility is incidentally available to and patronized by the general public does not defeat the exemption so long as there is no material amount of business or patronage with the general public [G.S. § 105-278.3(f)].

(3) Any parking lot wholly owned by a qualifying agency may be used for parking without removing the tax exemption if the total charge for parking does not exceed that portion of the actual maintenance expenditures for the parking lot reasonably estimated to have been made on account of the parking [G.S. § 105-278.3(g)].

• *Exempt personal property*

Personal property owned by a religious educational assembly, retreat, or similar organization is exempt from taxation if it is exclusively maintained and used in connection with exempt real property used for the exempt purpose [G.S. § 105-278.4(c)]. There are no exceptions to the exclusive-use requirement for personal property. *See In re Habitat for Humanity of Charlotte, Inc.*, 06 PTC 242 (May 11, 2007) (Habitat for Humanity warehouse and construction material intake facility entitled to full exemption despite incidental use of the facility to sell donated items not suitable for organization's charitable purposes).

¶2209 Exemptions for Specific Charitable Organizations

Property owned by the following charitable organizations is specifically exempt [G.S. § 105-278.6(a)]:

(1) A YMCA or similar organization.

(2) A home for the aged, sick, or infirm.

(3) An orphanage or similar home.

(4) A Society for the Prevention of Cruelty to Animals.

(5) A reformatory or correctional institution.

(6) A monastery, convent, or nunnery.

(7) A nonprofit, life-saving, first aid, or rescue squad organization.

(8) A nonprofit organization providing housing for individuals or families with low or moderate incomes.

To qualify for exemption, the owner must not be organized or operated for profit. Note that low income housing property owned by a limited partnership claiming federal tax credits could qualify for exemption when, after the tax credits expired, the for-profit partners transferred their interests in the partnership to the nonprofit general partner, which then became the sole owner of the property. *See In re Appeal of The Elderly Housing Corporation of Kinston, North Carolina,* 11 PTC 106 (October 8, 2013). In addition, real property must be exclusively occupied and used for charitable purposes and personal property must be exclusively occupied and used for charitable purposes. In *In re Appeal of Haliwa-Saponi Indian Tribe,* 13 PTC 742 and 14 PTC 0010 (2015), property was found to qualify for exemption where it was used to provide housing for low-income families pending future conversion of the property into a school.

• *Additional requirements*

To qualify for exemption, the owner must not be organized or operated for profit. In addition, real property must be actually and exclusively occupied and used for charitable purposes and personal property must be entirely and completely used for charitable purposes [G.S. § 105-278.6(a)].

• *Charitable purpose defined*

A charitable purpose is one that has humane (including humane treatment of animals) and philanthropic objectives; it is an activity that benefits humanity or a significant rather than limited segment of the community without expectation of pecuniary profit or reward [G.S. § 105-274.6(b)]. The fact that a building or facility is incidentally available to and patronized by the general public does not defeat the charitable exemption provided that there is no material amount of business or patronage with the general public [G.S. § 105-278.6(c)]. A house next to an exempt YMCA camp and owned by the camp and used as a residence for the camp director who was on call seven days a week was held to be used for a charitable purpose [*In re Appeal of YMCA of Greensboro, Inc.,* 08 PTC 096 (December 5, 2008)].

Residential Treatment Center

A residential treatment center was held to be used wholly and exclusively for a charitable purpose even though it charged $12,500 for its four-week program [*In re Appeal of Pavillon Int'l,* 166 N.C. App. 194, 601 S.E.2d 307 (2004)]. Polk County, where the center was located, conceded that the facility served a useful and beneficial purpose but contended that the cost of treatment limited the segment of the community it benefited such that it could not be considered charitable. The court held, however, that the facility was a charitable organization because (1) its fee was much less than the fee charged by private for-profit institutions; (2) it provided a considerable amount of free care when compared to the client fees it generated; (3) no one had been turned away for financial reasons; (4) the facility's work benefited a large segment of the community in ways other than caring for indigents and those incapable of paying the full price (*e.g.*, provision of free training to mental health care professionals across the State); and (5) the facility would be unable to continue operations without charitable contributions that helped subsidize client fees.

- *Ownership requirement*

In order to satisfy the requirements of G.S. §105-278.6(a), property must be owned by a qualified entity. Legal title, however, is not determinative of ownership for this purpose. While some actual ownership interest is required, even a diminutive interest is sufficient if other evidence supports the qualifying entity's interest in the property. Such evidence includes the qualifying entity's (1) control of operations on the property, (2) status as trustee of the property, (3) possible future increased ownership interest (such as a right of first refusal) and (4) intent with respect to the property. *See In re Appeal of Blue Ridge Housing of Bakersville LLC*, 226 N.C. App. 42, 738 S.E.2d 802 (2013) (0.1% actual ownership sufficient where other factors supported the qualifying entity's interest).

- *Future site of low- and moderate-income property*

Real property held by a nonprofit organization providing low-or moderate-income housing is held for a charitable purpose if it is held for as a future site for low- or moderate-income housing. The taxes that would otherwise be due on exempt housing real property are a lien on the property as provided in G.S. §105-355(a). The taxes are carried forward as deferred taxes in the records of the taxing unit and become due and payable if the organization fails to construct low-or moderate-income housing within 10 years of the first day of the fiscal year the property was classified under this provision. All liens arising under this provision are extinguished when the property is used for low-or moderate-income housing within the 10-year period [G.S. §105-278.6(e)]. Before July 1, 2011, the qualifying period was five years. The uniform provisions for payment of deferred taxes are discussed at ¶2311.

- *Other charitable use property*

See also the discussion of the general exemption for property used for educational, scientific, literary, or charitable purposes at ¶2211.

¶2210 Qualified Retirement Facilities

Buildings, the land they actually occupy, additional adjacent land reasonably necessary for the convenient use of the buildings, and personal property owned by a qualified retirement facility and used in the operation of that facility are exempt if the property meets all requirements for exemption [G.S. §105-278.6A(a)].

- *Requirements for total exclusion*

A retirement facility qualifies for total exemption if it meets all six (6) of the following requirements [G.S. §105-278.6A(c)]:

(1) It is exempt from North Carolina income tax (either corporate or individual) [G.S. § 105-278.6A(c)(1)].

(2) Private shareholders do not benefit from its operations [G.S. § 105-278.6A(c)(1)].

(3) All of its revenues (less operating and capital expenses) are applied to providing uncompensated goods and services to the elderly and to the local community, or are applied to an endowment or a reserve for these purposes [G.S. § 105-278.6A(c)(2)].

(4) Its charter provides that in the event of dissolution, its assets will revert or be conveyed to an entity that is organized exclusively for charitable, educational, scientific, or religious purposes, and it is an exempt organization under IRC § 501(c)(3) [G.S. § 105-278.6A(c)(3)].

(5) It has an active program to generate funds through one or more sources (*e.g.,* gifts, grants, trusts, devises, endowment, annual giving program) to assist the retirement facility in serving persons who might not be able to reside there without financial assistance or subsidy [G.S. § 105-278.6A(c)(5)].

(6) It meets at least one of the following conditions:

(a) The facility serves all residents without regard to their ability to pay [G.S. § 105-278.6A(c)(6)a.].

(b) At least five percent (5%) of the facility's resident revenue for the financial reporting period is provided in charity care to its residents, in community benefits, or in both [G.S. § 105-278.6A(c)(6)b.].

• *Partial exclusion*

A retirement facility qualifies for a partial exclusion if it meets the first four of the conditions for total exclusion (see above) *and* at least one percent (1%) of its resident revenue for the financial reporting period is provided in charity care to its residents, in community benefits, or in both. The percentage of the retirement facility's assessed value that is excluded from taxation based on the minimum percentage of its resident revenue that it provides in charity care to its residents, in community benefits, or in both [G.S. § 105-278.6A(d)]. The applicable percentage of partial exclusion is shown in the table below.

Partial Exclusion	Minimum Percentage of Resident Revenue
80%	4%
60%	3%
40%	2%
20%	1%

• *Application for exclusion*

See ¶ 2202 for procedures for applying for this exemption.

• *Definition of terms*

(1) *Charity care:* The unreimbursed costs to the facility of providing health care, housing, or other services to a resident who is uninsured, underinsured, or otherwise unable to pay for all or part of the services rendered [G.S. § 105-278.6A(b)(1)].

¶2210

(2) *Community benefits:* The unreimbursed costs to the facility of providing the following:

(a) Services (including health, recreation, community research, and education activities) provided to the community at large, including the elderly [G.S. § 105-278.6A(b)(2)a].

(b) Charitable donations [G.S. § 105-278.6A(b)(2)b].

(c) Donated volunteer services [G.S. § 105-278.6A(b)(2)c].

(d) Donations and voluntary payments to government agencies [G.S. § 105-278.6A(b)(2)d].

(3) *Financial reporting period:* The calendar year or tax year ending prior to the date the retirement facility applies for an exclusion [G.S. § 105-278.6A(b)(3)].

(4) *Resident revenue:* Annual revenue paid by a resident for goods and services and one year's share of the initial resident fee amortized in accordance with generally accepted accounting principles [G.S. § 105-278.6A(b)(4)].

(5) *Retirement facility:* A community that meets all of the following conditions:

(a) It is licensed under Article 64 of Chapter 58 of the North Carolina General Statutes [G.S. § 105-278.6A(b)(5)a].

(b) It is designed for elderly residents [G.S. § 105-278.6A(b)(5)b].

(c) It includes independent living units for elderly residents [G.S. § 105-278.6A(b)(5)c].

(d) It includes a skilled nursing facility or an adult care facility [G.S. § 105-278.6A(b)(5)d].

(6) *Unreimbursed costs:* The costs a facility incurs for providing charity care or community benefits after subtracting payment or reimbursement received from any source for the care or benefits. Unreimbursed costs include costs paid from funds generated by a program described in G.S. § 105-278.6A(c)(5) (*e.g.,* gifts, grants, bequests, annual giving program) [G.S. § 105-278.6A(b)(6)].

¶2211 Real and Personal Property Used for Educational, Scientific, Literary, or Charitable Purposes

• *Real property*

Buildings, the land they actually occupy, and additional adjacent land necessary for the convenient use of the buildings are exempted from taxation if they meet all three of the following requirements [G.S. § 105-278.7(a)]:

(1) They are wholly owned by a qualifying agency (see "Qualifying agencies," below) [G.S. § 105-278.7(a)(2)].

(2) They are wholly and exclusively used by their owners for nonprofit educational, scientific, literary, charitable, or cultural purposes [G.S. § 105-278.7(a)(2)]. See "Purpose," below. The fact that a building or facility is incidentally available to and patronized by the general public does not defeat this exemption if there is no material amount of business or patronage with the general public [G.S. § 105-278.7(e)].

(3) They are occupied gratuitously by a qualifying agency other than the owner and wholly and exclusively used by the occupant for nonprofit educational, scientific, literary, or charitable purposes. "Qualifying agencies" and "purpose" are explained below.

Partial exemption: Notwithstanding the exclusive-use requirement above, if part of real property that otherwise qualifies for exemption is used for a purpose that would require exemption if the entire property were used for the exempt purpose, the valuation of the part used for the exempt purpose is exempt from taxation [G.S. § 105-278.7(d)].

• *Personal property*

Personal property is exempted from taxation if it meets both of the following requirements [G.S. § 105-278.7(a)]:

(1) It is wholly owned by a qualifying agency (see "Qualifying agencies," below).

(2) It is wholly and exclusively used by its owner for nonprofit educational, scientific, literary, or charitable purposes or gratuitously made available to a qualifying agency other than the owner and wholly and exclusively used by the possessor for nonprofit educational, scientific, literary, or charitable purposes. See above for definitions of these purposes. See "Purpose," below.

NOTE: There is no partial exemption for personal property.

• *Qualifying agencies*

The following agencies are qualified to receive exemption for real and personal property used for educational, scientific, literary, or charitable purposes [G.S. § 105-278.7(c)]:

(1) Charitable associations or institutions.

(2) Historical associations or institutions.

(3) Scientific associations or institutions.

(4) Literary associations or institutions.

(5) Benevolent associations or institutions.

(6) Nonprofit community or neighborhood organizations.

Property owned by a corporation and leased to a qualifying agency was found to be effectively owned by the qualifying agency where the agency was the sole shareholder of the corporation. *See In re Appeal of Grandfather Mountain Stewardship Foundation, Inc.,* 11 PTC 068 (June 24, 2013).

• *Purpose*

Educational purpose: An "educational purpose" is one that has as its objective the education or instruction of human beings, including the transmission of information and the training or development of the knowledge or skills of individual persons [G.S. § 105-278.7(f)(1)]. See discussion at ¶ 2207.

Scientific purpose: A "scientific purpose" is one that yields knowledge systematically through research, experimentation, or other work done in one or more of the natural sciences [G.S. § 105-278.7(f)(2)].

¶2211

Literary purpose: A "literary purpose" is one that is related to letters or literature, especially writing, publishing, and the study of literature. It includes the literature of the stage and screen as well as the performance or exhibition of works based on literature [G.S. § 105-278.7(f)(3)].

Charitable purpose: A "charitable purpose" is one that has humane and philanthropic objectives (including the humane treatment of animals). It is an activity that benefits humanity or a significant rather than a limited segment of the community without expectation of pecuniary profit or reward [G.S. § 105-278.7(f)(4)]. Real property owned by a nonprofit corporation and used as a business incubator that, providing tenants with free utilities, internet service, conference facilities, and certain legal and accounting assistance, but which charged competitive rates for office space, was held not to be used for charitable purposes [*In re Appeal of Empowerment, Inc.,* 03 PTC 355 (2/23/05), *but see In re Appeal of Empowerment, Inc.,* 07 PTC 381 (May 18, 2009) (same facility qualified for exemption in later tax year)]. On the other hand, a nonprofit organization that provided residential treatment for people with addictions, disorders and life crises on a fee-for-service basis was entitled to real and personal property tax exemptions despite the relatively high cost of the services [*In re Appeal of Pavillon Int'l,* 166 N.C. App. 194, 601 S.E.2d 307 (2004)]. In that case, the Court of Appeals rejected the County's claim that the fees charged by the taxpayer limited the segment of the community benefited by the taxpayer's services to such an extent that the taxpayer could not be considered to operate "wholly and exclusively" for charitable purposes. The evidence showed that (1) the taxpayer's fees were less than those charged for similar services by for-profit organizations, (2) the taxpayer provided free services over a three-year with a value equal to 36% of the taxpayer's fee income over the same period, (3) the taxpayer had not refused service to anyone based on inability to pay, (4) the taxpayer provided other free services (such as training) to the community, and (5) the taxpayer depended on donations to support its activities and could not have supported its operations through its fees alone. The Property Tax Commission has ruled that a nonprofit daycare facility qualified as a charitable organization where the facility provided subsidized quality day care to children to permit their parents to seek and maintain employment and where the facility offered social service programs to families in the evenings. *See In re Totsland Preschool, Inc.,* 04 PTC 91 (2005) *aff'd* 180 N.C. App. 160, 636 S.E.2d 292 (2006). The County unsuccessfully argued on appeal that the daycare center lacked a charitable purpose because it received most of its funding from government sources rather than private contributions. The Court of Appeals ruled that where "a nonprofit corporation receives government funding, which it in turn uses for a charitable purpose, we hold the purpose of the activities and the actual use of the funds to be the controlling factors, rather than the source of the funds." See also discussion at ¶2209. On the other hand, the Property Tax Commission has ruled that a summer camp did not have a charitable purpose where the camp charged market rates, devoted less than 2% of its revenues to financial aid and accumulated substantial surpluses. *See In re Appeal of Eagles Nest Foundation,* 06 PTC 200 (December 12, 2007), *aff'd,* 194 N.C. App 770, 671 S.E.2d 366 (2009). In addition, a non-profit custodial care center that charged market rates for custodial care was held not to be a charitable or educational organization [*In re Appeal of Watch Me Grow, Inc.,* 07 PTC 1053 (October 27, 2008)]. *See also In re Appeal of Avalon Farm,* 13 PTC 778 (2014) (horse farm charging market rates not charitable). In *In re Appeal of Grandfather Mountain Stewardship Foundation, Inc.,* ___ N.C. App. ___, 762 S.E.2d 364 (2014) property was held not to be used wholly and exclusively for charitable purposes where significant rates were charged and substantial revenues were generated from admissions and commercial activities such as gift shops and restaurants.

Cultural purpose: A "cultural purpose" is one that is conducive to the enlightenment and refinement of taste acquired through intellectual and aesthetic training, education, and discipline [G.S. § 105-278.7(f)(5)]. In *In re Appeal of Home Health and Hospice Care, Inc.*, 09 PTC 105 (July 12, 2011), the Property Tax Commission ruled that a building used by a hospice provider to house its accounting and administrative operations (and not used for direct patient services) qualified for exemption because the administrative activities were essential to the provision of patient services. In *In re Appeal of Haliwa-Saponi Indian Tribe*, 13 PTC 742 and 14 PTC 0010 (2015) property was found to qualify for exemption when the building on the property was used to provide low-income housing and the surrounding land was used for harvesting plants, growing animals, gathering clay for educational and cultural classes.

¶2212 Real and Personal Property Used for Charitable Hospital Purposes

Real and personal property held for or owned by a hospital organized and operated as a nonstock, nonprofit, charitable institution (without profit to members or their successors) is exempted from taxation if it is actually and exclusively used for charitable hospital purposes [G.S. § 105-278.8(a)]. In *In re Appeal of Home Health and Hospice Care, Inc.*, 09 PTC 105 (July 12, 2011), the Property Tax Commission ruled that a building used by a hospice provider to house its accounting and administrative operations (and not used for direct patient services) qualified for exemption because the administrative activities were essential to the provision of patient services.

A "charitable hospital purpose" is a hospital purpose that has humane and philanthropic objectives; it is a hospital activity that benefits humanity or a significant rather than limited segment of the community without expectation of pecuniary profit or reward. However, the fact that a qualifying hospital charges patients who are able to pay for services rendered does not defeat the exemption [G.S. § 105-278.8(c)].

Notwithstanding the exclusive-use requirements above, if part of a property that otherwise meets the requirements for exemption is used for a purpose that would require exemption if the entire property were so used, the valuation of the part so used is exempted from taxation [G.S. § 105-278.8(b)].

¶2214 Property Tax Homestead Exclusion

A permanent residence owned and occupied by a qualifying owner is designated a special class of property and is subject to a special property tax homestead exclusion. The exclusion is the greater of $25,000 or half (50%) of the appraised value of the residence ($20,000 prior to July 1, 2008). An owner who receives this exclusion may not receive other property tax relief (effective July 1, 2009) [G.S. § 105-277.1(a)]. *Property tax relief* means the property tax homestead exclusion (discussed in this paragraph), the property tax homestead circuit breaker (discussed at ¶2216), or the disabled veteran property tax homestead exclusion (discussed at ¶2215) [G.S. § 105-277.1(b)(3a)].

• *Permanent residence*

A "permanent residence" for this purpose is a person's legal residence and includes the dwelling, the dwelling site (not to exceed one acre) and related improve-ments. The dwelling may be a single-family residence, a unit in a multi-family residential complex, or a manufactured home [G.S. § 105-277.1(b)(3)].

• *Qualifying owner*

A "qualifying owner" is an owner who meets all three of the following requirements as of January 1 preceding the taxable year for which the exclusion is claimed:

(1) The owner is at least 65 years of age or totally and permanently disabled. A person is "permanently and totally disabled" if the person has a physical or mental impairment that substantially precludes him or her from obtaining gainful employment and appears reasonably certain to continue without substantial improvement throughout his or her life [G.S. § 105-277.1(b)(4)].

(2) The owner has an income for the preceding calendar year of not more than the income eligibility limit. See discussion of "Income eligibility limit," below. "Income" for this purpose means adjusted gross income as defined in IRC § 62, plus all other moneys received from every source other than gifts or inheritances received from a spouse, lineal ancestor, or lineal descendant. For married applicants residing with their spouses, the income of both spouses must be included, whether or not the property is in both names [G.S. § 105-277.1(b)(1)(1a)].

(3) The owner is a North Carolina resident. An otherwise qualifying owner will not lose the benefit of this exclusion because of a temporary absence from the permanent resident for reasons of health, or because of an extended absence while confined to a rest home or nursing home, so long as the residence is (a) unoccupied or (b) occupied by the owner's spouse or other dependent. For this purpose "owner" means the person who holds legal or equitable title, whether individually, as a tenant by the entirety, a joint tenant, or a tenant in common, or as the holder of a life estate or an estate for the life of another. A manufactured home jointly owned by spouses is considered property held by the entirety [G.S. § 105-277.1(b)(1)(1b)]. A taxpayer may qualify for the exclusion despite extended periods of absence in other states to care for a family member. *In re Appeal of Pellerin*, 15 PTC 0012 (2015).

Ownership by spouses: A permanent residence owned and occupied by husband and wife is entitled to the full benefit of the homestead exclusion even though only one of them meets the age or disability requirements [G.S. § 105-177.1(d)].

Other multiple owners: The homestead exclusion is applicable to co-owners who are not husband and wife, but each co-owner must apply separately for the exclusion [G.S. § 105-277.1(e)]. When one or more co-owners qualify for the homestead exclusion and none qualifies for the disable veteran property tax homestead exclusion (discussed at ¶2215), each co-owner is entitled to the full amount of the homestead exclusion. The exclusion allowed to one co-owner may not exceed the co-owner's proportionate share of the valuation of the property, and the amount of the exclusion allowed to all the co-owners may not exceed the total homestead exclusion.

When one or more co-owners qualifies for the homestead exclusion and one or more co-owners qualifies for the disabled veteran property tax homestead exclusion, each co-owner who qualifies for the homestead exclusion is entitled to the full amount of the exclusion. The exclusion allowed to one co-owner may not exceed the co-owner's proportionate share of the valuation of the property, and the amount of the exclusion allowed to all co-owners may not exceed the greater of the homestead exclusion and the disabled veteran property tax homestead exclusion.

Temporary absence: An otherwise qualifying owner does not lose the benefit of this exclusion because of a temporary absence from his or her permanent residence because of health, or because of an extended absence while confined to a rest home or nursing home, so long as the residence is unoccupied or occupied by the owner's spouse or other dependent [G.S. § 105-277.1(a1)].

• *Income eligibility limit*

On or before July 1 of each year, the Department of Revenue must determine the income eligibility amount to be in effect for the taxable year beginning the following July 1 and notify all county assessors of the amount to be in effect for that taxable year [G.S. § 105-277.1(a2)]. For the taxable year beginning on July 1, 2009, the income eligibility limit is $25,000. For taxable years beginning on or after July 1, 2008, the income eligibility limit is the amount for the preceding year, adjusted by the same percentage of this amount as the percentage of any cost-of-living adjustment made to the benefits under Titles II and XVI of the Social Security Act for the preceding calendar year, rounded to the nearest one hundred dollars ($100) [G.S. § 105-277.1(a1)]. For this purpose "income" means all moneys received from every source other than gifts or inheritances received from a spouse, lineal ancestor, or lineal descendant. For married applicants residing with their spouses, the income of both spouses must be included, whether or not the property is in both names [G.S. § 105-277.1(b)(1a)].

• *Application for exclusion*

An application for the permanent residence exclusion should be filed during the regular listing period, but it may be filed and must be accepted at any time up to and through June 1 preceding the tax year for which the exclusion is claimed. When property is owned by two or more persons other than spouses and only one qualifies for this exclusion, each owner must apply separately for his/her proportionate share of the exclusion [G.S. § 105-277.1(c)]. The application form for the property tax homestead exclusion (Form AV-9) is available from county tax offices.

Once an application has been approved, the owner does not need to file an application in subsequent years unless one of the following occurs: (1) new or additional property is acquired; (2) improvements are added or removed, necessitating a change in the valuation of the property; (3) there is a change in the use of the property or the qualifications or eligibility of the taxpayer necessitating a review of the benefit [G.S. § 105-282.1(a)(2)].

Elderly taxpayers: Persons 65 years of age or older may apply by entering the appropriate information on a form made available by the assessor [G.S. § 105-277.1(c)(1)].

Disabled taxpayers: Persons who are totally and permanently disabled may apply for this exclusion by (1) entering the appropriate information on a form made available by the assessor and (2) furnishing acceptable proof of their disability (*i.e.,* a certificate from a physician licensed to practice medicine in North Carolina or from a governmental agency authorized to determine qualification for disability benefits). After a disabled applicant qualifies, no additional certificate is required unless the applicant's disability is reduced to the extent the applicant no longer qualifies for the taxation at reduced valuation [G.S. § 105-277.1(c)(2)].

• *Other exclusions for real property*

Disabled veterans: The first $38,000 in assessed value of housing and necessary accompanying land that is owned and used as a residence by a disabled veteran who receives federal compensation for permanent and total service-connected disability under 38 U.S.C. § 2101 is excluded [G.S. § 105-275(21)]. Note that G.S. § 105-275(21) is

¶2214

repealed for taxable years beginning July 1, 2009. This exclusion has been replaced with a property homestead exclusion for disabled veterans, discussed at ¶2215. Exemptions for veterans are discussed at ¶2203.

Land use: Property owners who grow agricultural, horticultural, or forestry products on their land are entitled to land-use exclusions. These exclusions are discussed at ¶2305.

¶2215 Disabled Veteran Property Tax Homestead Exclusion

Effective for taxable years beginning on or after July 1, 2009, qualified disable veterans may apply for a special property tax homestead exclusion.

• *Authorization of exclusion*

A permanent residence owned and occupied by a qualifying owner is designated a special class of property. The first $45,000 of appraised value of the residence is excluded from taxation. A qualifying owner who receives this exclusion may not receive other property tax relief [G.S. § 105-277.1C(a)].

• *Ownership by spouses*

A permanent resident owned and occupied by husband and wife is entitled to the full benefit of this exclusion even if only one of them meets the requirements for the exclusion [G.S. § 105-277.1C(d)].

• *Other multiple owners*

This exclusion is available to co-owners who are not husband and wife. Each co-owner of a permanent residence must apply separately for this exclusion [G.S. § 105-277.1C(e)].

When one or more co-owners of a permanent residence qualify for the property homestead exclusion and none qualifies for the exclusion allowed under G.S. § 105-277.1 (discussed at ¶2214), each co-owner is entitled to the full amount of the exclusion, but not to exceed the co-owner's proportionate share of the valuation of the property. The amount of the exclusion allowed to all the co-owners may not exceed the allowable exclusion.

When one or more co-owners of a permanent residence qualify for this exclusion and one or more qualify for the property homestead exclusion allowed under G.S. § 105-277.1 (discussed at ¶2214), each co-owner who qualifies for this exclusion is entitled to the full amount of the exclusion, but the exclusion allowed to one co-owner may not exceed the co-owner's proportionate share of the valuation of the property. The amount of the exclusion allowed to all the co-owners may not exceed the greater of the disabled veteran property tax homestead exclusion and the property homestead exclusion allowed under G.S. § 105-277.1.

• *Application*

An application for this exclusion should be filed during the regular listing period, but may be filed and must be accepted at any time up to and through June 1 preceding the Tax year for which the exclusion is claimed. An applicant must establish eligibility for the exclusion by providing a copy of the veteran's disability certification or evidence of benefits received under 38 U.S.C. § 2101 [G.S. § 105-277.1C(f)].

• *Definitions*

The following terms are defined in G.S. § 105-277.1C(b):

Disabled veteran: A veteran of any branch of the U.S. Armed Forces whose character of service at separation was honorable or under honorable conditions and who satisfies one of the following requirements:

(1) As of January 1 preceding the taxable year for which this exclusion is claimed, received benefits under 38 U.S.C. § 2101.

(2) Has a veteran's disability certification (*i.e.*, a certification by the United States Department of Veterans Affairs or another federal agency that a veteran has a permanent total disability that is service-connected).

(3) The veteran is deceased and the United States Department of Veterans Affairs or another federal agency has certified that, as of January 1 preceding the taxable year for which the exclusion is claimed, the veteran's death was the result of a service-connected condition, as defined in 38 U.S.C. § 101.

Permanent residence: Defined in G.S. § 105-277.1.

Qualifying owner: An owner (as defined in G.S. § 105-277.1) who is a North Carolina resident and is either a disabled veteran or the unremarried surviving spouse of a disabled veteran.

• *Temporary absence*

An owner does not lose the benefit of this exclusion because of a temporary absence from his or her permanent residence for reasons of health or because of an extended absence while confined to a rest home or nursing home, so long as the residence is unoccupied or occupied by the owner's spouse or other dependent [G.S. § 105-277.1C(c)].

¶2216 Property Tax Homestead Circuit Breaker

A permanent residence owned and occupied by a qualifying owner is designated a special class of property and is subject to a special provision called the property tax homestead circuit breaker [G.S. § § 105-277.1B(a)]. The property tax homestead circuit breaker is not, however, an exclusion; it is a deferral of taxes.

• *Qualifying owner*

A qualifying owner for purposes of the property tax homestead circuit breaker is an owner who meets all of the following requirements as of January 1 preceding the taxable year for which the benefit is claimed [G.S. § 105-277.1B(d)]:

(1) The owner has an income for the preceding calendar year of not more than 150% of the income eligibility limit.

(2) The owner has owned the property as a permanent residence for at least five consecutive years and has occupied the property as a permanent residence for at least five years.

(3) The owner is at least 65 years of age or totally and permanently disabled.

(4) The owner is a North Carolina resident.

Temporary absence: An otherwise qualifying owner does not lose the benefit of the circuit breaker because of a temporary absence from his or her permanent residence because of health, or because of an extended absence while confined to a rest home or nursing home, so long as the residence is unoccupied or occupied by the owner's spouse or other dependent [G.S. § 105-277.1B(g)].

Multiple owners: A permanent residence owned and occupied by a husband and wife is entitled to the full benefit of the property tax homestead circuit breaker even if only one spouse meets the length of occupancy and ownership requirements and the age or disability requirement. When a permanent residence is owned and occupied by two or more persons other than husband and wife, no property tax homestead circuit breaker is allowed unless all of the owners qualify and elect to defer taxes [G.S. § 105-277.1B(e)].

* *Application for tax relief*

An application for property tax homestead circuit breaker relief should be filed during the regular listing period but may be filed and must be accepted at any time up to and through June 1 preceding the tax year for which the relief is claimed. Persons may apply for this property tax relief by filling out a form made available by the assessor [G.S. § 105-277.1B(n)]. Once an application has been approved, the owner does not need to file an application in subsequent years unless one of the following occurs: (1) new or additional property is acquired; (2) improvements are added or removed, necessitating a change in the valuation of the property; (3) there is a change in the use of the property or the qualifications or eligibility of the taxpayer necessitating a review of the benefit [G.S. § 105-282.1(a)(2)].

* *Income eligibility limit*

The income eligibility limit is $25,000 with an annual cost of living adjustment [G.S. § 105-277.1B, 1(a2)]. For this purpose "income" means all moneys received from every source other than gifts or inheritances received from a spouse, lineal ancestor, or lineal descendant. For married applicants residing with their spouses, the income of both spouses must be included, whether or not the property is in both names [G.S. § 105-277.1(b)(1a)].

* *Tax limitation*

A qualifying owner may defer the portion of the principal amount of tax imposed on his or her permanent residence for the current year if it exceeds a percentage of the qualifying owner's income as indicated in the following table:

Income	Percentage
Up to the income eligibility limit	4.0%
Over the income eligibility limit up to 150% of the income eligibility limit	5.0%

If a permanent residence is subject to tax by more than one taxing unit and the total tax liability exceeds the tax limit then both the taxes due and the taxes deferred must be apportioned among the taxing units based on the ratio each taxing unit's tax rate bears to the total tax rate of all units [G.S. § 105-277.1B(f)].

* *Deferred taxes*

The difference between the taxes due under the circuit-breaker provision and the taxes that would have been payable in the absence of the circuit-breaker provision are a lien on the real property of the taxpayer. The difference in taxes is carried forward in the records of the taxing unit(s) as deferred taxes. The deferred taxes for the preceding three fiscal years are due and payable in accordance with G.S. § 105-277.1C when the property loses its eligibility for deferral because of the occurrence of a disqualifying event. On or before September 1 of each year, the collector must send to the mailing address of a deferred-tax residence a notice stating the amount of deferred taxes and interest that would be due on the occurrence of a disqualifying event [G.S. § 105-277.1B(h)]. Property tax homestead circuit breaker relief does not affect the attachment of a lien for personal property against a tax-deferred residence [G.S. § 105-277.1B(m)].

• *Disqualifying events*

Taxes deferred under the circuit-breaker provisions are payable within nine (9) months after a disqualifying event. The tax for the fiscal year that opens in a calendar year in which deferred taxes become due is computed as if the property was not eligible for property tax relief under the circuit-breaker provisions. The following are disqualifying events [G.S. § 105-277.1B(i)]:

(1) The owner transfers the residence except for certain transfers between spouses and co-owners.

(2) The owner dies unless the owner's share passes to a co-owner of the residence or to his or her spouse who occupies or continues to occupy the property as his or her permanent residence.

(3) The owner ceases to use the property as a permanent residence.

• *Gap in deferral*

If an owner of a residence on which taxes have been deferred is not eligible for continued deferral for a tax year, the taxes deferred are carried forward until a disqualifying event occurs. If the owner of the residence qualifies for deferral after one or more years in which the owner did not qualify for deferral and a disqualifying event occurs, the years in which the owner did not qualify are disregarded in determining the preceding three years for which the deferred taxes are due [G.S. § 105-277.1B(j)].

• *Creditor limitations*

A mortgagee or trustee that elects to pay any tax deferred by the owner of a residence subject to a mortgage or deed of trust does not acquire a right to foreclose as a result of the election. Except for requirements dictated by federal law or regulation, any provision in a mortgage, deed of trust, or other agreement that prohibits the owner from deferring taxes on property under the circuit-breaker provisions is void [G.S. § 105-277.1B(l)].

¶2217 Inventory Property Tax Deferral

Repeal

The deferral provisions for residential builder inventory are repealed for taxes imposed for taxable years beginning on or after July 1, 2013. Notwithstanding the repeal residences that are receiving the property tax benefit provided in the year immediately prior to the repeal do not become due by virtue of the repeal but remain eligible for this benefit for subsequent taxable years until the occurrence of one of the triggering events described above [S.L. 2010-95, § 21; S.L. 2009-308, § 4].

• *Deferral*

A residential builder (or a business entity of which the builder is a member) may defer the portion of real property taxes due on lots owned by the builder attributable to the improvements constructed by the builder. This provision applies only to new residential construction (not to remodeling or refinishing jobs, or to renovations or rehabilitations) [G.S. § 105-277.1D(a)].

• *Period of deferral*

Taxes cannot be deferred for more than three years and also cannot be deferred for more than five years from the time the improvements first became subject to listing. In addition, the deferred taxes become due and payable when the owner transfers or occupies the residence or when someone other than the owner occupies the residence with the builder's consent [G.S. § 105-277.1D(b)].

• *Application for deferral*

To claim the benefit of deferral, the owner must file an application for deferral during the regular listing period. An application filed after the end of the listing period will be accepted if the owner can show good cause (as determined by the board of equalization or the board of county commissioners) for filing a late application. A decision of the county board rejecting a late application can be appealed to the Property Tax Commission [G.S. § 105-277.1D].

• *Protection against foreclosure*

Any provision in a mortgage, deed of trust or other agreement that prohibits an owner from deferring taxes on property is void, unless the provision is dictated by federal law or regulation. In addition, a mortgagee or trustee does not acquire a right to foreclose on property on which taxes have been deferred by paying the deferred tax [G.S. § 105-277.1D(c)].

• *Lien provisions*

The taxes deferred are a lien on the property [G.S. § 105-277.1D(b)]. The deferral of real property taxes on a residence under this provision does not affect the attachment of a lien for personal property taxes against the residence [G.S. § 105-277.1D(d)].

PROPERTY TAXES

CHAPTER 23

LISTING, APPRAISAL, ASSESSMENT, AND PAYMENT

¶2301 Listing

All property subject to ad valorem taxation, that is, all property that North Carolina has the Constitutional power to tax, must be listed annually, ordinarily during the period beginning on the first business day of January and ending on January 31 [G.S. §§ 105-285 and 105-307(a)]. If the taxing jurisdiction allows electronic listing of property, the property may be listed electronically. See discussion of electronic listing below.

• *Place for listing*

Real property: Real property must be listed in the county in which the property is situated regardless of its actual location on the listing date [G.S. § 105-304(c)]. To help ensure accurate real property appraisals, every deed conveying real property (other than deeds of trust, deeds of release and similar instruments) must include the name and mailing address of each grantor and grantee and a statement whether the property includes the primary residence of any grantor, although the failure to comply with these absence of such information will not affect the validity of the deed [G.S. § 105-317.2; S.L. 2009-454, § 3].

Tangible personal property: Subject to the exceptions noted below, tangible personal property is listed at the residence of the owner regardless of its actual location on the listing date [G.S. § 105-304(c)]. Thus, an aircraft was required to be listed at the residence of the taxpayer despite that fact that the taxpayer had purchased the aircraft outside North Carolina, had had the aircraft flown directly to other locations outside the state for painting and upfitting and had never brought the aircraft into the state. *See In re Appeal of SAS Institute, Inc.,* 07 PTC 209 (March 10, 2008), *aff'd* 200 N.C. App 238, 684 S.E.2d 444 (2009).

If an individual has two or more dwelling places in North Carolina, his residence is the place at which he dwelt for the longest period of time during the calendar year immediately preceding the listing date [G.S. § 105-304(c)(1)].

The residence of a domestic or foreign taxpayer other than an individual is the place at which its principal North Carolina place of business is located [G.S. § 105-304(c)(2)]. Thus, carnival amusement rides stored in Pender county during the winter months and otherwise used outside the state and owned by a corporation headquartered in New York had a taxable situs in Pender County [*In re Appeal of Amusements of Rochester, Inc.*, 07 PTC 820 (Sept. 16, 2008), *aff'd*, 201 N.C. App. 419, 689 S.E.2d 451 (2009)]. *See also In re Appeal of Marathon Holdings, LLC*, 09 PTC 308 (March 17, 2010) (aircraft owned by limited liability company taxable at the company's principal place of business).

Intangible property: Intangible property is defined to include intellectual property, goodwill, choses in action, leasehold interests in exempt real property "and other like property." G.S. § 105-273(8). However, all intangible property except for certain computer software is exempt from property taxation. See G.S. § 105-275(31).

Place for Listing Computer Software

G.S. § 105-275(31) provides that the property tax exemption for intangible property "does not affect the taxation of software" not otherwise exempt from tax. The implication of this provision is that such software should be treated either as tangible personal property or as taxable intangible property. If non-exempt software is treated as tangible personal property it should be listed in accordance with the rules set forth in G.S. § 105-304. If it is treated as intangible property, the place for listing is less clear, since the rules for listing intangible property were repealed in 1997. *See* S.L. 1997-456, § 43(a). This may indicate a legislative intent to treat non-exempt computer software as tangible personal property.

Submission of abstracts: Any abstract (*i.e.*, listing) may be submitted in person, by mail and, if the county has provided for electronic listing of personal property, by electronic listing. In no event, however, will an abstract submitted by mail be accepted unless the affirmation on the abstract is signed by the person whose duty it is to list the property. An electronic listing may be signed electronically using an electronic signature method approved by the Department. Mailed abstracts are considered filed as of its United States Postal Service postmark date. If an abstract does not have a United States Postal Service postmark, it is considered filed when received in the assessor's office. Abstracts submitted electronically are considered filed when received in the assessor's office. The burden of proof is on the taxpayer to show that an abstract was timely filed [G.S. § 105-311(b)].

Electronic Listing of Personal Property

A board of county commissioners may, by resolution, allow electronic listing of business personal property (*i.e.*, the electronic filing of the abstract and affirmation required by G.S §§ 105-309 and 105-310) in accordance with procedures established by the Department after consultation with the counties and may delegate its authority to provide for electronic listing to the county assessor [G.S. § 105-310.1]. If the board of county commissioners allows electronic listing of personal property, the assessor must publish this information, including the timetable and procedures for electronic listing, in the notice required by G.S. § 105-296(c). *See* ¶ 2303, "Powers and Duties of County Assessors," for notice requirements. If a county has provided for electronic listing of personal property, the listing period for electronic listing of business personal property may be extended up to June 1. A resolution providing a general extension of time for the electronic listing of personal property continues in effect until revised or rescinded unless otherwise stated in the resolution [G.S. § 105-307(b)(3)]. Nonbusiness personal property would still have to be listed (whether electronically or otherwise) by January 1.

• *Exceptions to normal situs rules for tangible personal property*

As noted above, the default rule for listing tangible personal property is that such property is listed at the residence of the owner, regardless of where the property is actually located. However, a number of broad exceptions to this general rule require most articles of tangible personal property to be taxed where such property is actually situated or used.

Property of Nonresidents: Tangible personal property of nonresident individuals and entities with no North Carolina principal office is taxable where it is more or less permanently located [G.S. § 105-304(d)].

Property Associated with Temporary or seasonal dwellings: Tangible personal property more or less permanently located at or used in connection with a seasonal or temporary dwelling is taxable at the location of the dwelling [G.S. § 105-304(f)(1)]. The temporary absence of the tangible personal property on the listing date does not affect this rule. However, the presence of tangible personal property at a location on the listing date is prima facie evidence that it is situated at or commonly used in connection with that location [G.S. § 105-304(f)(4)].

Property Associated with business premises: Tangible personal property more or less permanently located at or commonly used in connection with a business premises hired, occupied or used by the owner of the personal property (or his agents) is taxable at such business premises. This includes property that may be used by the general public or that is used to sell or vend merchandise to the public. G.S. § 105-304(f)(2). The temporary absence of the tangible personal property on the listing date does not affect this rule. However, the presence of tangible personal property at a location on the listing date is prima facie evidence that it is situated at or commonly used in connection with that location [G.S. § 105-304(f)(4)]; *See In re Tri-Star Aviation & Development LTD*, 05 PTC 712 (2006) (aircraft owned by corporation with principal office in Beaufort County but used primarily in Dare County taxable in Dare County).

Leased property: Tangible personal property in the possession of a person other than the owner under a commercial lease, bailment for hire, consignment, or similar business arrangement and more or less permanently located at or commonly used in connection with premises owned, hired, occupied, or used the possessor is taxable at the location of the possessor's premise [G.S. § 105-304(f)(3)]. The temporary absence of the tangible personal property on the listing date does not affect this rule. However, the presence of tangible personal property at a location on the listing date is prima facie evidence that it is situated at or commonly used in connection with that location [G.S. § 105-304(f)(4)].

Farm products: Farm products produced in North Carolina, and owned by their producer, are taxable at the place where they were produced [G.S. § 105-304(e)].

Decedents: Tangible personal property of a decedent whose estate is in the process of administration or has not been distributed is taxable at the place at which it would be taxable if the decedent were still alive and still residing at the place at which s/he resided when s/he died [G.S. § 105-304(g)].

Property held by fiduciaries: Tangible personal property within the jurisdiction of North Carolina held by a trustee, guardian, or other fiduciary (resident or nonresident) having legal title to the property is taxable as follows:

(1) If any beneficiary is a North Carolina resident, an amount representing his/her portion of the property is taxable at the place at which it would be taxable if s/he were the owner of his/her portion [G.S. § 105-304(h)(1)].

(2) If any beneficiary is a nonresident of North Carolina, an amount representing his/her portion of the property is taxable at the place at which it would be taxable if the fiduciary were the beneficial owner of the property [G.S. § 105-304(h)(2)].

Caution: Changes to Real Property

While owners of taxable property are generally required to list such property during the listing period, there is no duty to list taxable real property that is subject to a permanent listing system [G.S. §§ 105-302(a), 105-303(b)]. Accordingly, such real property is not subject to being discovered [G.S. § 105-303(b)(2)]. However, the owners of real property listed under a permanent listing system must inform the assessor during the listing period of any improvements on or separate rights in the real property, and failure to provide such information can lead to discovery of the improvements or separate rights [G.S. § 105-303(b)].

• *Extensions of time for listing*

A board of county commissioners may by resolution extend the listing period [G.S. § 105-307(b)]. Any action by the board of county commissioners extending the listing period must be recorded in the minutes of the board, and notice must be published as required by G.S. § 105-296(c). See ¶ 2303 for these notice requirements. The entire period for listing, including extensions, is considered the regular listing period for a particular year.

Nonrevaluation years: The listing period may be extended for up to 30 additional days.

Octennial appraisal: In years of octennial appraisal of real property, the listing period may be extended for up to 60 additional days.

Electronic listing: If the county has provided for electronic listing of business personal property, the period for electronic listing may be extended up to June 1.

Individual extensions: The board of county commissioners must grant individual extensions of time for listing upon written request and for good cause shown [G.S. § 105-304(c)]. In order to be timely filed, written requests for extension of time for listing must be filed with the assessor no later than the ending date of the regular listing period. The board may delegate authority to grant extensions to the assessor. Individual extensions cannot extend beyond April 15 except in the cast of electronic listings [G.S. § 105-307(c)].

¶2301

• *Reports by Custodians*

Every person who has custody of tangible personal property entrusted to him for storage, sale, rental or any other business purpose must furnish the assessor of the county in which the property is situated a report as of January 1 of each year that includes a description of the property, the quantity of the property and the amount of money (if any) advanced against the property by the custodian. This requirement applies to, among others, warehouses, cooperative growers and marketing associations, consignees, factors, commission merchants and brokers. It does not apply to a person having custody of exempt inventories owned by contractors, manufacturers or retail and wholesale merchants [G.S. § 105-315].

• *County assessors*

County assessors are appointed by the boards of county commissioners [G.S. § 105-294(a)]. A county assessor has general charge of the listing, appraisal, and assessment of all property in the county [G.S. § 105-296(a)]. In general, cities and towns must accept the county appraisals and assessments [G.S. § 105-327]. Appeals from decisions of a county assessor may be made to the county board of equalization and review or the county tax commission if the county has one. See Chapter 25 for discussion of taxpayers' remedies. Powers and duties of county assessors are discussed in more detail at ¶ 2303.

Discovered property: A county assessor has the duty to see that all property not properly listed during the regular listing period be listed, assessed, and taxed (called discovered property) [G.S. § 105-312(b)]. "Discovered property includes (1) property not listed during a listing period; (2) property listed with a substantially understated value; and (3) property exercising an invalid exemption or exclusion [G.S. § 105-273(6a)]. Discovered property is listed, assessed, and taxed under the special provisions of G.S. § 105-312. Discovered property is taxed for the year in which it is discovered and for any of the preceding five years in which it escaped taxation. If the discovery is based upon an understatement, the tax is computed on the additional valuation and the penalty computed at the rate of 10% on the basis of the additional tax. For discovered property that has not been listed, each year's taxes are computed separately at the rate of 10% [G.S. § 105-312(g)].

¶ 2302 Appraisal

• *Generally*

"Appraisal" means both the true value of property and the process by which true value is ascertained. North Carolina imposes a uniform assessment standard. All property must be assessed for taxation at its true value or use value as determined under G.S. § 105-283, and taxes levied by all counties and municipalities must be levied uniformly on these assessments [G.S. § 105-284]. The regular appraisal and listing date for real and personal property is January 1 [G.S. § 105-285]. Accordingly, property that is present in the taxing county on January 1 is taxable even if it is destroyed or removed from the county immediately thereafter. See also G.S. § 105-365.1(b) (discussed at ¶ 2312) regarding liability for delinquent taxes of successive owners where property is transferred after the listing date.

General rule: Each county must reappraise all real property in accordance with the provision of G.S. § 105-283 (relating to uniform appraisal standards) and G.S. § 105-317 (relating to adoption of schedules, standards, and rules as of January 1 of the year according to the schedule set out in G.S. § 105-286(a)(1) and every eighth year thereafter, unless the county is required to advance the date (mandatory advancement) or chooses to advance the date (optional advancement) [G.S. § 105-286(a)].Counties are divided into eight divisions whose reappraisal years are staggered in such a way that there are county reappraisals conducted every year [G.S. § 105-286(a)(1)].

Exception: If a tract of land has been subdivided into lots and more than five acres of the tract remain unsold by the owner of the tract, the assessor may appraise the unsold portion as land acreage rather than as lots [G.S. § 105-287(d)].

• *Elements to be considered*

Land. In appraising land, at least the following elements must be considered with respect to each tract, parcel, or lot separately listed [G.S. § 105-317(a)(1)]: (1) location, (2) zoning, (3) quality of soil, (4) waterpower, (5) water privileges, (6) dedication as a nature preserve, (7) conservation or preservation agreements, (8) mineral, quarry, or other valuable deposits, (9) fertility, (10) adaptability for agricultural, timber-producing, commercial, industrial, or other uses, (11) past income, (12) probable future income, (13) and any other factors that may affect its value except growing crops of a seasonal or annual nature.

Building. In appraising buildings or other improvements, at least the following elements must be considered [G.S. § 105-317(a)(2)]: (1) location, (2) type of construction, (3) age, (4) replacement cost, (5) cost, (6) adaptability for residence, commercial, industrial, or other uses, (7) past income, (8) probable future income, (9) and any other factors that may affect its value. In addition, partially completed buildings must be appraised in accordance with the degree of completion on January 1.

Personal property. In appraising personal property, at least the following elements must be considered with respect to each item or lot of similar items [G.S. § 105-317.1(a)]: (1) the replacement cost of the property, (2) the sale price of similar property, (3) the age of the property, (4) the physical condition of the property, (5) the productivity of the property, (6) the remaining life of the property, (7) the effect of obsolescence on the property, (8) the economic utility of the property, that is, its usability and adaptability for industrial, commercial, or other purposes, and (9) any other factor that may affect the value of the property. In addition, in appraising personal property held and used in connection with the taxpayer's business, the appraiser must consider any information reflected on the taxpayer's records and reported to the Department of Revenue and to the Internal Revenue Service for income tax purposes, taking into account the accuracy of the taxpayer's records, the taxpayer's method of accounting, and the level of trade at which the taxpayer does business [G.S. § 105-137.1(b)].

Farm Equipment. The Department of Revenue is required to publish on its Web site a depreciation schedule for farm equipment, and a county that uses the cost approach to appraise farm equipment must use this depreciation schedule [G.S. § 105-317.1(b1), effective July 1, 2019].

• *Mandatory advancement of reappraisal*

A county whose population is 75,000 or greater according to the most recent annual population estimates certified to the Secretary by the State Budget Officer must conduct a reappraisal of real property when the county's sales assessment ratio determined under G.S. § 105-289(h) (*i.e.,* the ratio of the appraised value of real property in the county to its true value) is less than 0.85 or greater than 1.15. A mandatory reappraisal must become effective no later than January 1 of the earlier of (1) the third year following the year the county received the notice or (2) the eighth year following the year of the county's last reappraisal [G.S. § 105-286(a)(2)].

● *Optional advancement of reappraisal*

A county may conduct a reappraisal of real property earlier than otherwise required if the county commissioners adopts a resolution providing for advancement of the reappraisal. The resolution must designate the effective date of the advanced reappraisal and may designate a new reappraisal cycle that is more frequent than the octennial cycle.

A more frequent reappraisal cycle continues in effect after a mandatory reappraisal unless the board of county commissioners adopts another resolution designating a different date for the nest reappraisal [G.S. § 105-286(a)(3)].

● *Years in which no reappraisals or adjustments are made*

Permitted reasons for changing property values: In a year in which a general reappraisal of real property in a county is not made, the assessor increases or decreases the appraised value of real property to recognize a change in the property's value resulting from one or more of the following reasons [G.S. § 105-287(a)]:

(1) To correct a clerical or mathematical error.

(2) To correct an appraisal error resulting from a misapplication of the schedules, standards, and rules used in the county's most recent general reappraisal. *See In re Appeal of Ocean Isle Palms LLC,* 366 N.C. 351, 749 S.E.2d 439 (2013) (county's "resetting" of values of underdeveloped parcels in non-revaluation year to eliminate application of a "condition factor" to the base value of such parcels was not the correction of an appraisal error but the unlawful institution of a new revaluation system); *In re Appeal of Lowe's Home Centers, LLC,* 17 PTC 0146, 0147 and 0148 (2018) (county's change in value based on its conclusion that previously assessed value was based on flawed comparables was not a misapplication of schedule of values).

(3) To recognize an increase or decrease in the value of the property resulting from a conservation or preservation agreement subject to Article 4 of Chapter 121 of the General Statutes [Conservation and Historic Preservation Agreements Act].

(4) To recognize an increase or decrease in the value of the property resulting from a physical change to the land or to the improvements on the land, other than a change prohibited by G.S. § 105-287(b). *See In re Appeal of JC Rock Properties LLC,* 09 PTC 260 (June 29, 2011) (renovations transforming properties from boarded-up vacant units to rentable houses justified non-octennial revaluation); *In re Appeal of Warehouse Solutions LLC,* 12 PTC 636 (August 1, 2013) (theft and vandalism resulting in total destruction of electrical wiring and power infrastructure and substantial harm to HVAC systems justified non-octennial revaluation).

(5) To recognize an increase or decrease in the value of the property resulting from a change in the legally permitted use of the property.

(6) To recognize an increase or decrease in the value of the property resulting from a factor other than one prohibited by G.S. § 105-287(b).

An increase or decrease in the appraised value of real property permitted as listed above must be made in accordance with the schedules, standards, and rules used in the county's most recent general reappraisal. Such a change is effective as of January 1 of the year in which it is made and is not retroactive. The reason for an increase or decrease in appraised value for the permitted reasons listed above need not be under the control or at the request of the owner of the affected property [G.S. § 105-287(c)]. A county may not increase the appraised value of property in a year in which a general reappraisal is not made because of a misclassification of the property in the general reappraisal year. *See In re Pace/Dowd Props. Ltd.*, 233 N.C. App. 7, 755 S.E.2d 401 (2014). *See also In re Appeal of Shore*, 11 PTC 943 (November 21, 2013) (County could not arbitrarily increase valuation above value determined on appeal of reappraisal year assessed value). A challenge to an assessment in a nonreappraisal year that does not site one of the reasons listed above will be dismissed. *See In re Appeal of Slaughter*, 15 PTC 114 (2016).

Taxpayers Must Satisfy Evidentiary Requirements

Where the taxpayer challenges the valuation of property in a nonappraisal year based on an alleged appraisal error by the assessor, it is essential that the taxpayer introduce sufficient evidence of the County's schedules, standards and rules. Without such evidence, the court will not be able to determine whether the alleged error resulted from a misapplication of such schedules, standards, and rules as required by G.S. § 105-287(a). See *In re Schwartz & Schwartz, Inc.*, 166 N.C. App. 744, 603 S.E.2d 852 (2004).

Reasons for changing property values that are not permitted under G.S. § 105-287(b): In a year in which a general reappraisal of real property in a county is not made, the assessor is not permitted to increase or decrease the appraised value of real property to recognize a change in value caused by the following:

(1) Normal, physical depreciation of improvements.

(2) Inflation, deflation, or other economic changes affecting the county in general. *See In re Appeal of Jahrstorfer*, 09 PTC 410 (July 6, 2011) and *In re Appeal of Kasianowicz*, 09 PTC 411 (July 6, 2011) (developer's bankruptcy was symptom of general economic downturn and did not justify change in value in non-reappraisal year).

(3) Betterments to the property made by the following:

(a) Repainting buildings or other structures.

(b) Terracing or other methods of soil conservation.

(c) Landscape gardening.

(d) Protecting forests against fire.

(4) Impounding water on marshland for noncommercial purposes to preserve or enhance the natural habitat of wildlife.

Conveyances and Divisions of Property

While the transfer of an entire, unchanged parcel of real estate is not a factor that triggers revaluation under G.S. § 105-287 [*In re Allred*, 351 N.C. 1, 519 S.E.2d 52 (1999)], the division of a single parcel into two or more parcels is such a factor [*In re Appeal of Corbett*, 355 N.C. 181, 558 S.E.2d 82 (2002)].

¶2302

• *Methods of valuation (appraisal)*

All property must be assessed for property tax purposes at its true value or use value as determined under G.S. § 105-283. True value in money, the basis of the property tax, is determined by application of standard appraisal methods. The most commonly used appraisal methods in North Carolina, are (1) the cost approach, (2) the income approach, and (3) the comparable sales approach. The unit valuation method is applied to property in certain highly regulated industries that cross jurisdictions. See CCH NORTH CAROLINA TAX REPORTS, ¶ 20-635.

Cost approach: In the cost approach, the "cost" of the land and the cost of improvements are separately calculated. The "cost" used in this approach is usually replacement value, not the original cost of the property. After initial replacement cost is determined, deductions are made for physical depreciation and, in the case of business property, obsolescence. See CCH NORTH CAROLINA TAX REPORTS, ¶ 20-620. Depreciation applied to business personal property should reflect installed costs. *See In re Appeal of Harris Teeter LLC*, 16 PTC 0060 (2019). Because the cost approach may not effectively reflect market conditions, the cost approach has been held to be better suited for valuing specialty property or newly developed property and is often used when no other method will yield a realistic result. See *In re Appeal of Belk-Broome Co.*, 119 N.C. App. 470, 458 S.E.2d 921 (1995), *aff'd*, 342 N.C. 890, 467 S.E.2d 242 (1996), and *In re The Greens of Pine Glen Ltd.*, 356 N.C. 642, 576 S.E.2d 316 (2003); *In re Appeal of Target Corporation*, 08 PTC 783 (2010); *In re Appeal of Harris Teeter, LLC*, 16 PTC 0060 (2019). The Courts have indicated, however, that special use property is not required to be valued exclusively under the cost approach. *See In re Appeal of Corning, Inc.*, ___ N.C. App. 786, S.E.2d 816 (2016) (upholding a blended cost-sale approach). *See also In re Appeal of Tryon-Columbus Retirement Associates, LLC*, 09 PTC 843 (May 11, 2012) (cost approach most appropriate method for valuing assisted and independent living housing development). Thus, a county's reliance on the cost approach to the exclusion of the other methods in valuing investment property was held to yield an arbitrary and illegal appraisal that substantially exceeded the true value of the property [*In re Weaver Inv. Co.*, 165 N.C. App. 198, 598 S.E.2d 591, *rev. denied*, 359 N.C. 188, 606 S.E.2d 695 (2004), *In re Appeal of Lowe's Home Centers, LLC*, ___ N.C. App. ___ (2018)]. Similarly, an assessment will be upheld despite a failure to take into account the taxpayer's cost of acquiring the property where the property was acquired at a bulk repossession sale, since the price paid at such a sale did not reflect the property's true value. See *In re Oliver*, 190 N.C. App. 674, 661 S.E.2d 788 (2008).

Income approach: The income method of valuation involves the determination of the present value of the income from the property at an appropriate rate of return. This method is often used for residential and commercial rental properties.

> **Example:** Louise owns a building and leases it to Lester, who operates a craft shop in the building. Lester pays Louise a market rent of $600 per month. The current market rate for borrowed funds is 6%. The simplest application of the present-value method is to value the income in perpetuity and involves simply dividing the income by the appropriate interest rate. In this case the annual income is $7,800, and the appropriate rate is 6%. The "true value" of the building using the income approach is $120,000 [$7,200/.06].

The income approach is typically applied using market rates of income, rather than the income the taxpayer's property actually generates, since actual income may be above or below market and thus not indicate the property's true value. See, e.g., *In re Property of Greens of Pine Glen Ltd.*, 356 N.C. 642, 576 S.E.2d 316 (2003) (low-income housing rent restrictions disregarded); *In re Pine Raleigh Corp.*, 258 N.C. 398, 128

S.E.2d 855 (1963) (long-term below-market lease disregarded) However, in *In re Appeal of Belk-Broome*, 119 N.C. App. 470, 458 S.E.2d 921 (1995), *aff'd*, 342 N.C. 890, 467 S.E.2d 242, the Court of Appeals held that the value of space in a shopping mall leased to an anchor department store should be determined by reference to the subsidized contract rent paid by the department store, since the subsidized rental arrangement was typical of and integral to the market. This reasoning was extended in *In re Appeal of Westmoreland-LG&E*, 174 N.C. App. 692, 622 S.E.2d 124 (2005), where the taxpayer's electricity generating facilities were valued using the income the taxpayer actually earned under a long-term power purchase agreement rather than the lower spot market rates for electricity on the theory that the power purchase agreement was typical of and integral to the electricity market. The income approach also requires consideration of the capitalization rate applied to the property's income stream. *See In re Appeal of Hull Story Retail Group*, 8 PTC 240 (November 30, 2012) (direct capitalization method appropriate to value mall property).

Use of Income Method

The income method is generally considered the most accurate measure of the value of investment property. While the cost method is sometimes used in conjunction with the income method to establish a ceiling on the property's value, the Court of Appeals has held that the use of the income approach alone without resort to the cost approach is not per se improper [*In re Winston-Salem Joint Venture*, 144 N.C. App. 706, 551 S.E.2d 450, *rev. denied*, 354 N.C. 217, 555 S.E.2d 277 (2001)]. Failure to consider the income approach for rental property has been held to be arbitrary even where the property consists of multiple, separately platted parcels capable of being sold as separate single-family units. *In re Appeal of Villas at Peacehaven*, LLC, 10 PTC 011 (on remand 2015). On the other hand, the Court has upheld a determination by the Property Tax Commission that the use of the income method to value an older, large, multistory, owner-occupied manufacturing facility was arbitrary [*In re Appeal of Lane Company-Hickory Chair Div.*, 153 N.C. App. 119, 571 S.E.2d 224 (2002)].

Comparable sales approach: The market data method involves the comparison of property to prices at which comparable properties have recently been sold. While the courts and the Property Tax Commission have rejected the use of post-octennial sales data of the property being valued in determining value under the comparable sales method (*In re Allred*, 351 N.C. 1, 519 S.E.2d 52 (1999); *In re Appeal of Kilaru*, 10 PTC 698 (2011); *In re Appeal of Sexton*, 10 PTC 697 (2011), *In re Appeal of* McKean, 14 PTC 033 (2015)) they have permitted the use of post-octennial sales data of comparable properties, adjusted to account for changing values over time [*In re Lane Company-Hickory Chair Div.*, 153 N.C. App. 119, 571 S.E.2d 224 (2002)]. The Property Tax Commission has rejected foreclosure sale prices as reliable comparable sales. *See In re Steintiz*, 03 PTC 815 (2006); *In re Carter*, 03 PTC 816 (2006). The Property Tax Commission has held that failure to give predominant weight to the comparable sales approach in cases where there is an active market is arbitrary and illegal. *See In re Appeal of McLane Foodservice, Inc.*, 10 PTC 788 (2012). The Property Tax Commission has held that the comparable sales approach is the most reliable approach in valuing older manufacturing facilities. *See In re Appeal of Parkdale America, LLC*, 15 PTC 87 (2016).

Unit valuation approach: The unit valuation method is appropriate when "the whole is greater than the sum of its parts." For example, in the landmark case *Cleveland, C., C. & S.L. Ry. Co. v. Backus*, 154 U.S. 439 (1894), the United States Supreme Court stated: "The true value of a line of railroad is something more than an aggregation of the values of separate parts of it, operated separately. It is the aggregate of those values plus that arising from a connected operation of the whole, and each part of the road contributes not merely the value arising from its independent operation, but its mileage proportion of that flowing from a continuous and connected operation of the whole. This is no denial of the mathematical proposition that the whole is equal to the sum of all its parts, because there is a value created by and resulting from the combined operation of all its parts as one continuous line. This is something which does not exist, and cannot exist, until the combination is formed." In the case of property that is used in multiple jurisdictions, the aggregate value will be apportioned among the jurisdictions. The unit valuation method is commonly used for companies such as airlines, telegraph and telephone companies, pipelines, and electric companies. See CCH NORTH CAROLINA TAX REPORTS, ¶ 20-635.

¶2303 Assessment

• *Generally*

"Assessment" means both the tax value of property and the process by which the assessment is determined [G.S. § 105-273(2), (3)]. North Carolina imposes uniform appraisal standards. All property (real and personal) must, as far as it is feasible, be appraised or valued at its true value in money.

Most property subject to the North Carolina property tax is assessed by county assessors.

Motor Vehicles, Public Service Companies, and Discovered Property

Motor vehicles, the property of public service companies, and discovered property are subject to special assessment rules. The property of public service companies is appraised by the Department of Revenue, and discovered property (discussed at ¶ 2401) must be "discovered" by county assessors; both are listed under special rules.

• *Powers and duties of county assessors*

In general: The county assessor has general charge of the listing, appraisal, and assessment of all property in the county in accordance with statutory provisions and must perform all duties legally imposed on county assessor. County assessors have, and may exercise, all powers reasonably necessary to perform his/her duties not inconsistent with the laws or Constitution of North Carolina [G.S. § 105-296(a)]. An assessor may conduct preparatory work before the listing period begins but cannot make a final appraisal of property before the listing date [G.S. § 105-304(d)].

Allocation of responsibility: The county assessor (within budgeted appropriations) may employ listers, appraisers, and clerical assistants necessary to carry out the required listing, appraisal, assessing, and billing functions. The county assessor may allocate responsibility among employees by territory, subject matter, or any other reasonable basis [G.S. § 105-296(b)].

Employment of Experts: The board of county commissioners may employ experts, such as appraisal and mapping firms, to assist the assessor, provided that any person so employed may not be compensated in whole or in part on a contingent fee basis or on the basis of any similar method that may impair the assessor's independence or the perception of the assessor's independence by the public [G.S. § 105-299].

Required notices: At least ten (10) days before the date on which property is to be listed, the county assessor must advertise in a newspaper of having general circulation in the county and post in at least five (5) public places in each township in the county a notice contain at least the following information [G.S. § 105-296(c)]:

(1) The date as of which property is to be listed.

(2) The date on which listing will begin.

(3) The date on which listing will end.

(4) The times between the beginning and ending listing dates during which lists will be accepted.

(5) The place(s) at which lists will be accepted.

(6) A statement that all persons who own taxable property on the listing date must list the property within the period set forth in the notice and that failure to list taxable property will be subject to the penalties prescribed by law. See discussion of penalties at ¶ 2403.

Power of subpoena: The county assessor has the power to subpoena persons and documents whenever there are reasonable grounds for the belief that such persons have knowledge or such documents contain information pertinent to the discovery or valuation of any taxable property. Persons who fail to respond to such subpoenas are guilty of a Class 1 misdemeanor [G.S. § 105-296(g)].

Detailed financial statements: Only after the abstract (*i.e.,* list or listing) has been carefully reviewed can an assessor require any person operating a business enterprise to submit a detailed inventory, statement or assets and liabilities, or other similar information pertinent to the discovery or appraisal in the county. Information on detailed financial statements required by a county assessor that are not required to be shown on the abstract itself are not available for inspection by the public but must be made available, upon request, to representatives of the Department of Revenue or the Department of Employment Security. Any assessor, county official, or employee who discloses information contained in detailed financial statements shall be guilty of a Class 3 misdemeanor, punishable only by a fine not exceeding $50 [G.S. § 105-296(h)].

• *True value*

"True value" means market value, that is, the price estimated in terms of money at which the property would change hands between a willing and financially able buyer and a willing seller, neither being under any compulsion to buy or to sell and both having reasonable knowledge of all the uses to which the property is adapted and for which it is capable of being used. This is commonly referred to as "fair market value." In the case of acquisition of an interest in land by an entity having the power of eminent domain, it is not considered competent evidence of the true value in money of comparable land [G.S. § 105-283].

Unique property: Despite the requirement that property be valued at market values, counties will sometimes value unique property for which there is no ready market at its value in use (*i.e.,* at its value to the present owner) rather than its value to a willing buyer.

¶2303

There are also situations in which there may be no willing buyer when property is appraised. In one case, contamination of property by pollutants left the property owners without a willing buyer. In that case, the North Carolina Court of Appeals said that the contamination and the cost of remediation are factors to be considered [*In re Camel City Laundry Co.,* 123 N.C. App. 210, 472 S.E.2d 402 (1996), *rev. denied,* 354 N.C. 342, 483 S.E.2d 402 (1996)]. The following are additional examples of circumstances that have been held to affect the true value of property: the property was subject to an historic preservation agreement that prevented alterations to the property (*In re Appeal of Williams,* 06 PTC 119 (July 3, 2008); the property was custom designed in a way that limited future renovations (*In re Appeal of Isenhour,* 07 PTC 459 (July 31, 2008)); the property was being used for a dune restoration project and thus was temporarily unbuildable (*In re Appeal of Neithold,* 06 PTC 390 (January 2, 2008)).

¶2304 Property Subject to Special Assessment

• *Agricultural land, horticultural land, and forestland*

Agricultural land, horticultural land, and forestland (discussed at ¶2305) are designated special classes of property and are subject to special assessment at their present-use value (discussed at ¶2309).

• *Antique airplanes*

Antique airplanes are assessed for taxation at the lower of (1) true value or (2) $5,000 [G.S. § 105-277.12(b)]. An "antique airplane" is an airplane that meets all four of the following requirements of G.S. § 105-277.12(a):

(1) It is registered with the Federal Aviation Administration and is a model year 1954 or older.

(2) It is maintained primarily for use in exhibitions, club activities, air shows, and other public interest functions.

(3) It is used only occasionally for other purposes.

(4) It is used by the owner for a purpose other than the production of income.

• *Brownfields properties*

Definition: Property that is abandoned, idled, or underused because of actual or possible environmental contamination and that is or may be subject to remediation under specified state or federal remediation programs is known as "brownfields property" [G.S. § 130A-310.31(b)(3)].

Brownfields agreements: Brownfields property often remains undeveloped, because the cost of remediation to normal standards is prohibitive. As a result, the Brownfields Property Reuse Act [S.L. 1997-357, H.B. 1121] permits a developer to enter into an agreement, known as a "brownfields agreement," with the North Carolina Department of Environmental Quality under which the developer agrees to undertake limited remediation and to develop the property for a use that is safe to the public. In exchange, the developer is absolved from liability for failing to undertake more extensive remediation efforts. See generally, G.S. § 130A-310.30 *et seq.*

Exclusion: As an added incentive to brownfields redevelopment, the owner of a brownfields property is entitled to exclude a portion of the appraised value of qualifying improvements made to the property for the first five years after their completion [G.S. § 105-277.13(a)].

To qualify for the partial exclusion, the property must meet the following two requirements:

(1) The property must be subject to a brownfields agreement; and

(2) The improvements to the property must be made after July 1, 2000, and after the date of the brownfields agreement [G.S. § 105-277.13(a)].

In addition, the improvements must be appraised annually during the five-year exclusion period [G.S. § 105-277.13(a)].

Amount of exclusion: The following table shows the percentage of the appraised value of the qualified improvements that is excluded during the five-year exclusion period [G.S. § 105-277.13(c)]:

Year	Percent of Appraised Value Excluded
1	90%
2	75%
3	50%
4	30%
5	10%

- *Burial property*

In general, real property set apart for burial purposes is exempt from property taxation. See ¶ 2205. However, real property set apart for burial purposes is taxable if it is owned and held for purposes of (1) sale or rental, or (2) sale of burial rights there [G.S. § 105-278.2(a)]. "Real property" for this purpose includes land, tombs, vaults, monuments, and mausoleums, and the term "burial" includes entombment [G.S. § 105-278.2(c)].

Taxable real property set apart for human burial purposes is designated a special class of property and is assessed for taxation taking into consideration the following three factors [G.S. § 105-278.2(b)]:

(1) The effect on its value by division and development into burial plots.

(2) Whether it is irrevocably dedicated for human burial purposes by plat recorded with the Register of Deeds in the county in which the land is located.

(3) Whether the owner is prohibited or restricted by law or otherwise from selling, mortgaging, leasing, or encumbering the land.

- *Community land trust property*

Community land trust property is classified as a special class of property subject to special valuation. Community land trust property is an improvement to real property that meets the following requirements [G.S. § 105-277.17(b)]:

(1) The improvements are developed by a non-profit entity exempt from federal income tax under Code § 501(c)(3).

(2) The developer conveys an interest in the property to a North Carolina resident (the qualifying owner) who occupies the improvements as a permanent residence and who is part of a household with an annual income, at the time of

transfer and adjusted for family size, of not more than 100% of the local area median income (as determined by reference to HUD publications).

(3) The interest conveyed to the qualifying owner may be either a fee interest in the improvements together with a ground lease of the underlying land or a lease of the land and improvements, provided that in either case, the lease must be of at least 99-years duration. The lease must include the right to ingress to and egress from the dwelling and an undivided interest in common areas.

(4) The developer retains an interest in the property pursuant to the deed or ground lease and the deed or ground lease restricts the price at which the property can be transferred by the qualifying owner to ensure that low-priced housing is available to subsequent qualifying owners.

If property qualifies as community land trust property, its appraised value in the year it first qualifies as community land trust property is the actual sales price paid by the qualifying owner, less the amount of any "silent mortgage," *i.e.*, the amount of any debt incurred by the qualifying owner secured by the property but that accrues no interest and requires no payment until the qualifying owner either pays off any interest-bearing debt on the property or transfers the property. This initial value is referred to as the initial investment basis [G.S. § 105-277.17(c)].

In subsequent general reappraisals, the value of the property may not exceed the sum of (1) the initial investment basis and (2) the "restricted capital gain amount." The restricted capital gain amount is the market value of the property but not in excess of the maximum sales price permitted under the resale restrictions contained in the deed or ground lease and reduced by the initial investment basis and any silent mortgage amount [G.S. § 105-277.17(c)].

• *Farm products classified to taxation at reduced valuation*

Farm products (including crops but excluding poultry and other livestock) held by or for a cooperative stabilization or marketing association or corporation to which they have been delivered, conveyed, or assigned by the original producer for the purpose of sale are designated a special class of property. Before being assessed for taxation, the appraised valuation of farm products in the designated classification is reduced by the amount of any unpaid loan or advance made or grated thereon by the United States government, an agency of the United States government, or a cooperative stabilization or marketing association or corporation [G.S. § 105-277.01].

• *Historic properties*

Real property designated as historic property by a local ordinance (under the authority of former G.S. § 160A-399.4) or designated as an historic landmark by a local ordinance (under the authority of former G.S. § 160A-400.5) is taxed uniformly as a class in each local taxing unit on the basis of 50% of the true value of the property [G.S. § 105-278(a)]. The amount by which the taxes on the property are reduced under this provision are a lien on the property and are carried forward as deferred taxes. The deferred taxes for the preceding three fiscal years are due and payable in accordance with G.S. § 105-277.1D (discussed at ¶2308) when the property loses its classification as a result of a disqualifying event. A disqualifying event occurs when there is a change in the relevant ordinance or a change in the property (other than by fire or natural disaster) that substantially impairs its historical significance. No deferred taxes are due and all liens arising under this provision are extinguished when the property's historical significance is lost or substantially impaired due to fire or other natural disaster [G.S. § 105-278(b)].

• *Lessees and users of tax-exempt cropland or forestland*

When cropland or forestland owned by the United States, North Carolina, a county, or a municipal corporation is leased, loaned, or otherwise made available to and used by a person in connection with a business conducted for profit, the lessee or user of the property is eligible for the benefit of special-use valuation. This does not apply to cropland or forestland for which payments in lieu of taxes are made in amounts equivalent to the amount of tax that could otherwise be lawfully assessed. The purpose of a tax on lessees and users of cropland or forestland is to eliminate the competitive advantage accruing to profit-making enterprises from the use of tax-exempt property, and it is levied on the privilege of leasing or otherwise using tax exempt cropland or forestland in connection with a business conducted for profit [G.S. § 105-282.7].

• *Low-income housing developments*

A North Carolina low-income housing development to which the North Carolina Housing Finance Agency allocated a low-income housing federal tax credit under IRC § 42 is designated a special class of property and must be appraised, assessed, and taxed as follows [G.S. § 105-277.16]:

> (1) The assessor must use the income approach as the method of valuation.

> (2) The assessor must take rent restrictions that apply to the property into consideration in determining the income attributable to the property.

> (3) The assessor may not consider federal or state low-income tax credits received under IRC § 42 or G.S. § 105-129.42.

Note that property that continues to be used as low-income housing may qualify for exemption under G.S. § 105-278.6(a)(6) if, after the tax credits expire, it becomes wholly-owned by a nonprofit organization. *See In re Appeal of The Elderly Housing Corporation of Kinston, North Carolina*, 11 PTC 106 (October 8, 2013).

• *Nonprofit homeowners' associations*

General: The value of real and personal property owned by a nonprofit home-owners' association is not included in the appraisals of property owned by members of the association and is not assessed against the association if the following three requirements are met (but see "Exception" below) [G.S. § 105-277.8(a)]:

> (1) All property owned by the association is held for the use, benefit, and enjoyment of all association members equally.

> (2) All association members have an irrevocable right to use and enjoy, on an equal basis, all property owned by the association, subject to any restrictions imposed by the instruments conveying the right or the rules, regulations, or bylaws of the association.

> (3) Each irrevocable right to use and enjoy all property owned by the association is appurtenant to taxable real property owned by a member of the association.

Exception: The value of extraterritorial common property shall be subject to taxation only in the jurisdiction in which it is entirely contained and only in the amount of the local tax of the jurisdiction in which it is entirely contained. The value of any property taxed pursuant to this subsection, as determined by the latest schedule of values, shall not be included in the appraisals of property owned by members of the association that are referenced in subsection (a) of this section or otherwise subject to taxation. The assessor for the jurisdiction that imposes a tax pursuant to this subsection shall provide notice of the property, the value, and any other information to the assessor of any other jurisdiction so that the real properties owned by the members of the association are not subject to taxation for that value. The governing board of a nonprofit homeowners' association with property subject to taxation under this subsection shall provide annually to each member of the association the amount of tax due on the property, the value of the property, and, if applicable, the means by which the association will recover the tax due on the property from the members [G.S. § 105-277.8(a1)].

Nonprofit homeowners' association: "Nonprofit homeowners' association" means a homeowners' association as defined in IRC § 528(b). The assessor may allocate the value of the association's property among the property of the association's members on any fair and reasonable basis [G.S. § 105-277.8(a)].

Extraterritorial common property: "Extraterritorial common property" means real property that is (i) owned by a nonprofit homeowners' association that meets the requirements of subdivisions (1) through (3) of subsection (a) of this section and (ii) entirely contained within a taxing jurisdiction that is different from that of the taxable real property owned by members of the association and providing the appurtenant rights to use and enjoy the association property [G.S. § 105-277.8(b)]. Extraterritorial common property taxed pursuant to G.S. § 105-277.8 shall be assessed, pro rata, among the lot owners based on the number of lots in the association [G.S. § 47F-1-105].

- *Precious metals used in manufacturing or processing*

Precious metals, including rhodium and platinum, used or held for use directly in manufacturing or processing by a manufacturer as part of industrial machinery is a special class of property and is assessed at the lower of (1) its true value or (2) the manufacturer's original cost less depreciation. See "Base," above, for definition of "true value." The "original cost" of the classified property is adjusted by the index factor, if any, that applies in assessing the industrial machinery with which the property is used, and the "depreciable life" of the classified property is the life assigned to the industrial machinery with which the property is used. The "residual value" of the classified property may not exceed 25% of the manufacturer's original cost [G.S. § 105-277.10].

- *Property tax homestead exclusion*

A permanent residence owned and occupied by a qualifying owner is designated a special class of property, and the amount of the appraised value of the residence equal to the exclusion amount is excluded from property taxation [G.S. § 105-277.1(a)]. This exclusion is discussed at ¶ 2214.

- *Wasteland and woodland*

Agricultural land and horticultural land include woodland and wasteland that is a part of the farm or horticultural unit, but the woodland and wasteland included in the unit must be appraised under the use-value schedules as woodland or wasteland

[G.S. § 105-277.2(1), (3)]. Forestland includes wasteland that is a part of the forest unit, but the wasteland included in the unit must be appraised under the use-value schedules as wasteland [G.S. § 105-277.2(2)].

• *Wildlife conservation land*

Taxed like agricultural land: Effective for taxable years beginning on or after July 1, 2010, wildlife conservation land is designated as a special class of property and must be appraised, assessed, and taxes as if it were classified as agricultural land (discussed above) [G.S. § 105-277.15(b)].

Requirements: Land qualifies as wildlife conservation if it meets the following requirements [G.S. § 105-277.15(c)]:

(1) The land consists of at least 20 contiguous acres.

(2) The land is owned by an individual, a family business entity, or a family trust and has been owned by the same owner for the previous five years, except as follows:

(a) If the land is owned by a family business entity, the land meets the ownership requirement if the land was owned by one or more members of the family business entity for the required time.

(b) If the land is owned by a family trust, the land meets the ownership requirement if the land was owned by one or more beneficiaries of the family trust for the required time.

(c) If an owner acquires land classified as wildlife conservation land when it was acquired and the owner continues to use the land as wildlife conservation land, the land meets the ownership requirement if the new owner files an application and signs the wildlife habitat conservation agreement in effect for the property within 60 days after acquiring the property.

(3) The land must meet all of the following use requirements:

(a) The land must be managed under a written wildlife habitat conservation agreement with the North Carolina Wildlife Resources Commission that is in effect as of January 1 of the year for which the special classification benefit is claimed and that requires the owner to (i) protect an animal specials that lives on the land and, as of January 1 of the year for which the special classification is claimed, is on a North Carolina protected animal list published by the Commission under G.S. § 113-333 ("protection" land); (ii) conserve any of the following priority animal wildlife habitats: longleaf pine forest, early successional habitat, small wetland community, stream and riparian zone, rock outcrop, or bat cave ("conservation" land); or (iii) create and actively and regularly use the land as a reserve for hunting, fishing, shooting, wildlife observation or wildlife activities, provided that the land is inspected every five years by a certified wildlife biologist ("reserve" land).

(b) Except for reserve land, the land must have been classified under G.S. § 105-277.3 when the wildlife habitat conservation agreement was signed or the owner must demonstrate to both the Wildlife Resources Commission and the assessor that the owner used the land for a purpose specified in the signed wildlife habitat conservation agreement for three years preceding January 1 of the year for which special classification is claimed.

¶2304

Restrictions: The following restricts apply to special classification as wildlife conservations land [G.S. § 105-277.15(d)]:

> (1) No more than 100 acres (800 acres in the case of reserve land) of an owner's land in a county may be classified as wildlife conservation land.

> (2) Land owned by a business entity is not eligible for classification as wildlife conservation land it is a corporation whose shares are publicly traded or one of its members is a corporation whose shares are publicly traded.

Deferred taxes: The difference between taxes that are due on wildlife conservation land and that would be due if the land were taxed on the basis of its true value is a lien on the property. This difference must be carried forward as deferred taxes. The deferred taxes for the preceding fiscal years are due and payable when the land loses its eligibility for deferral as a result of a disqualifying event (*i.e.*, when the property no longer qualifies as wildlife conservation land [G.S. § 105-277.15(e)]. Notwithstanding these provisions, if land loses its eligibility for deferral solely due to one of the following reasons, no deferred taxes are due and the lien for the deferred taxes is extinguished [G.S. § 105-255.15(g)]:

> (1) The property is conveyed by gift to a nonprofit organization and qualifies for exclusion from the tax base under G.S. § 105-275(12) (relating to certain property owned by a nonprofit corporation or association) or G.S. § 105-275(29).

> (2) The property is conveyed by gift to the State, a political subdivision of the State, or the United States.

Exceptions to payment: No deferred taxes are due in the following circumstances and the deferred taxes remain a lien on the land [G.S. § 105-277.15(f)]:

> (1) When the owner of land previously classified as agricultural land before the wildlife habitat conservation agreement was signed does not transfer the land and the land again becomes eligible for classification as agricultural land. In this circumstance, the deferred taxes are payable in accordance with the rules for agricultural land.

> (2) When land classified as wildlife conservation land is transferred to an owner who signed the wildlife habitat conservation in effect for the land at the time of the transfer and the land remains classified as wildlife conservation land. In this circumstance the deferred taxes are payable in accordance with the wildlife conservation provisions.

Administration: An owner who applies for classified of land as wildlife conservation land must attach a copy of the owner's written wildlife habitat agreement. An owner who fails to notify the county assessor when land classified as wildlife conservation land loses its eligibility for special classification is subject to a penalty of 10% of the total amount of the deferred taxes and interest for each listing period for which the failure to report continues [G.S. §§ 105-277.15(h), 105-277.5].

- *Working waterfront property*

Working waterfront property (discussed at ¶2306) is designated a special class of property and is subject to special assessment at its present-use value (discussed at ¶2309).

¶2304

¶2305 Agricultural, Horticultural, Land, and Forestland

If they meet all requirements, agricultural land, horticultural land, and forestland are designated special classes of property and are appraised at their present-use value [G.S. §105-277.3(a)]. Certain exceptions to the general rules apply. For discussion of exceptions, see "Exceptions to ownership requirements;" "Exception for Conservation Reserve Program;" "Exception for conservation easements;" and "Exception for turkey disease," below. Present-use valuation for agricultural, horticultural, and forestland is discussed at ¶2309.

• *Agricultural land*

"Agricultural land" defined: "Agricultural land" is land that is part of a farm unit that is actively engaged in the commercial production or growing of crops, plants, or animals (including the rearing, feeding, training, caring and management of horses) under a sound management program (see "Sound management programs for agricultural and horticultural land," below). Agricultural land includes woodland and wasteland that is part of the farm unit, but the woodland and wasteland included in the unit must be appraised under the use-value schedules as woodland or wasteland. If the agricultural land includes fewer than 20 acres of woodland, the woodland portion is not required to be under a sound management program. Also, a woodland is not required to be under a sound management program if it is determined that the highest and best use of the woodland is (1) to diminish wind erosion of adjacent agricultural land, (2) to protect water quality of adjacent agricultural land, or (3) to serve as buffers for adjacent livestock or poultry operations [G.S. §105-277.2(1)]. A farm unit may consist of more than one tract of agricultural land, but at least one of the tracts must meet the requirements for special classification as agricultural land. Further, the tracts comprising the farm unit must have a "rational relationship with each other." *See In re Frizzelle,* 151 N.C. App. 552, 566 S.E.2d 506 (2002) (tracts lying more than 100 miles apart in different counties not part of the same farm unit).

Requirements for special assessment as agricultural land: In order to be qualify for special assessment as agricultural land, land must meet the following requirements:

(1) It must be "agricultural land" as defined above [G.S. §105-277.3(a)(1)].

(2) It must be individually owned [G.S. §105-277.3(a)(1)].

(3) It must consist of one or more tracts, one of which satisfies the following requirements. For agricultural land used as a farm for aquatic species (as defined in G.S. §106-758) the tract must meet the income requirement for agricultural land and must consist of at least five (5) acres in actual production or produce at least 20,000 pounds of aquatic species for commercial sale annually, regardless of acreage. For all other agricultural land, the tract must meet the income requirement for agricultural land and must consist of at least 10 acres that are in actual production. Land in actual production includes land under improvements used in the commercial production or growing of crops, plants, or animals [G.S. §105-277.3(a)(1)].

(4) To meet the income requirement, agricultural land must, for the three (3) years preceding January 1 of the year for which special classification is claimed, it must have produced an average gross income of at least $1,000. "Gross income" for this purpose includes income from the sale of the agricultural products produced from the land, grazing fees for livestock, the sale of bees or products derived from beehives other than honey, and any payments received under a governmental soil conservation or land retirement program, and buyout

payments received pursuant to the Fair and Equitable Tobacco Reform Act of 2005 (P.L. 108-357) [G.S. § 105-277.3(a)(1)]. The Court of Appeals has rejected the argument that each 10 acres of the land in active production must produce at least $1,000 of gross income [*In re Appeal of Briarfield Farms*, 147 N.C. App. 208, 555 S.E.2d 621 (2001), *rev. denied*, 355 N.C. 211 (2002)]. The Property Tax Commission has ruled that when a tract of agricultural land is divided, each parcel must individually satisfy the income requirement. *In re Appeal of McCraw*, 07 PTC 253 (July 31, 2008)].

(5) The land must satisfy the applicable ownership requirements (see "Ownership requirements," below) [G.S. § 105-277.3(b), (b1)].

• *Horticultural land*

"Horticultural land" defined: "Horticultural land" is land that is a part of a horticultural unit that is actively engaged in the commercial production or growing of fruits or vegetables or nursery or floral products under a sound management program (see "Sound management programs for agricultural and horticultural land," below). Horticultural land includes woodland and wasteland that is a part of the horticultural unit, but the woodland and wasteland included in the unit must be appraised under the use-value schedules as woodland or wasteland. If the horticultural land includes fewer than 20 acres of woodland, the woodland portion is not required to be under a sound management program. Also, woodland is not required to be under a sound management program if the best use of the woodland is (1) to diminish wind erosion of adjacent horticultural land or (2) to protect water quality of adjacent horticultural land. Land used to grow horticultural and agricultural crops on a rotating basis, or where the horticultural crop is set out or planted and harvested within one growing season, may be treated as agricultural land when there is determined to be no significant difference in the cash rental rates for the land [G.S. § 105-277.2(3)]. A horticultural unit may consist of more than one tract of horticultural land, but at least one of the tracts must meet the requirements for special assessment as horticultural land.

Requirements for special assessment as horticultural land: In order the qualify for special assessment as horticultural land, land must meet the following requirements [G.S. § 105-277.3(a)(2)]:

(1) It must be "horticultural land" as defined above [G.S. § 105-277.3(a)(2)].

(2) It must be individually owned [G.S. § 105-277.3(a)(2)].

(3) It must consist of one or more tracts, one of which meets the following criteria [G.S. § 105-277.3(a)(2)].

(a) It consists of at least five (5) acres that are in actual production. "Land in actual production" for this purpose includes land under improvements used in the commercial production or growing of fruits or vegetables, or nursery or floral products.

(b) For the three (3) years preceding January 1 of the year for which special classification is claimed, it must meet the applicable minimum gross income requirement.

(4) The land must satisfy the applicable ownership requirements (see "Ownership requirements," below) [G.S. § 105-277.3(b), (b1)].

Applicable minimum gross income requirement: The applicable minimum gross income is established by the Department of Revenue, for land that has been used to produce evergreens intended for use as Christmas trees. For all other horticultural land, the minimum income requirement is an average gross income of at least $1,000. "Gross income" includes income from the sale of the horticultural products produced from the land and any payments received under a governmental soil conservation or land retirement program [G.S. § 105-277.3(a)(2)].

• *Forestland*

"Forestland" defined: "Forestland" is land that is a part of a forest unit that is actively engaged in the commercial growing of trees under a sound management program. Forestland includes wasteland that is a part of the forest unit, but the wasteland included in the unit must be appraised under the use-value schedules as wasteland. A forest unit may consist of more than one tract of forestland, but (1) each tract must be under a sound management program and (2) at least one of the tracts must meet the requirements for special assessment as forestland [G.S. § 105-277.2(2)].

Sound Management Programs for Forestland

The sound management program requirements for forestland differ from those for agricultural and horticultural land (discussed at "Sound management programs for agricultural and horticultural land," below). Forestland is operated under a sound management program if the owner demonstrates that the forestland complies with a written sound forest management plan for the production and sale of forest products [G.S. § 105-277.3(g)].

Requirements for special assessment as forestland: In order the qualify for special assessment as forestland, land must meet the following requirements:

(1) It must be "forestland" as defined above [G.S. § 105-277.3(a)(3)].

(2) It must be individually owned [G.S. § 105-277.3(a)(3)].

(3) It must consist of one or more tracts, one of which consists of at least 20 acres that are in actual production and are not included in a farm unit [G.S. § 105-277.3(a)(2)].

(4) The land must satisfy the applicable ownership requirements (see "Ownership requirements," below) [G.S. § 105-277.3(b), (b1)].

In *In re Appeal of Miller*, 14 PTC 15 (2016), the Property Tax Commission held that a taxpayer's listing of forestland for sale and its temporary suspension of logging operations did not disqualify the property for present-use valuation where the property otherwise satisfied these requirements.

• *Sound management programs for agricultural and horticultural land*

Agricultural or horticultural land is considered to be operated under a sound management program if the property owner demonstrates any one of the following factors [G.S. § 105-277.3(f), added by S.L. 2002-184 (S.B. 1161), § 2]:

(1) Enrollment in and compliance with an agency-administered and approved farm management plan.

(2) Compliance with a set of best management practices.

(3) Compliance with a minimum gross income per acre test.

(4) Evidence of net income from the farm operation.

(5) Evidence that farming is the farm operator's principal source of income.

(6) Certification by a recognized agricultural or horticultural agency with the county that the land is operated under a sound management program.

(7) Evidence of other similar factors.

Before the enactment of G.S. § 105-277.3(f), the Court of Appeals had ruled that agricultural property could meet the sound management program requirement even where the farm manager had no prior farm operation experience, was not trained in agricultural science, and did not consult the local county extension officer, and even though the farm produced only minimal income [*In re Appeal of Briarfield Farms*, 147 N.C. App. 208, 555 S.E.2d 621 (2001), *rev. denied*, 355 N.C. 211 (2002)].

Farm Operator vs. Property Owner

If a farm operator meets the sound management requirements, it is irrelevant whether the property owner received income or rent from the farm operator [G.S. § 105-277.3(f)].

• *Ownership requirements*

The ownership requirements for classification as agricultural, horticultural, or forestland depend on the who owns the land—a natural person, a business entity, or a trust.

Individual ownership requirements: In order to be classified as agricultural, horticultural, or forestland, the land must, if owned by an individual, also satisfy one of the following conditions [G.S. § 105-277.3(b)]:

(1) It is the owner's place of residence.

(2) It has been owned by the current owner or a relative of the current owner for the four (4) years preceding January 1 of the year for which special assessment is claimed.

(3) At the time of transfer to the current owner, it qualified for classification in the hands of a business entity or trust that transferred the land to the current owner who was a member of the business entity or a beneficiary of the trust.

However, see "Exceptions to ownership requirements," below.

Business entity ownership requirements: In order to be classified as agricultural, horticultural, or forestland, the land, if owned by a business entity, must have been owned by one or more of the following for the four (4) years immediately preceding January 1 of the year for which the benefit is claimed [G.S. § 105-277.3(b1)(1)]:

(1) The business entity.

(2) A member of the business entity.

(3) Another business entity whose members include a member of the business entity that currently owns the land.

However, see "Exceptions to ownership requirements" below.

Land owned by a trust: In order to be classified as agricultural, horticultural, or forestland, the land, if owned by a trust, must have been owned by the trust or by one or more of its creators for the four (4) years immediately preceding January 1 of the year for which special classification is claimed [G.S. § 105-277.3(b1)(2)]. However, see "Exceptions to ownership requirements" below.

- *Exceptions to ownership requirements*

Notwithstanding the natural person or business entity ownership requirements (discussed above), land may qualify as agricultural, horticultural, or forestland, if all of the conditions in either of the following are met [G.S. § 105-277.3(b2)]:

(1) *Continued use:* If the land qualifies for classification in the hands of the new owner under the provisions of G.S. § 105-277.3(b2)(1), any deferred taxes remain a lien on the land under G.S. § 105 277.4(c), the new owner becomes liable for the deferred taxes, and the deferred taxes become payable if the land fails to meet any other condition or requirement for classification. Land qualifies for classification in the hands of the new owner if all of the following conditions are met:

(a) The land was appraised at its present-use value at the time title to the land passed to the new owner.

(b) The new owner acquires the land for agricultural, horticultural, or forestland purposes and continues to use the land for the purpose for which it was classified while under previous ownership.

(c) The new owner has timely filed an application for classification (see "Application for classification," below) and has certified that the new owner (a) accepts liability for any deferred taxes, and (b) intends to continue the present use of the land [G.S. § 105-277.3(b2)(3)].

(2) *Expansion of existing unit:* The land qualifies for classification in the hands of the new owner if, at the time title passed to the new owner, the land was not appraised at its present-use value but was being used for the same purpose and was eligible for appraisal at its present-use value as other land already owned by the new owner and classified under subsection G.S. § 105-277.3(a). The new owner must timely file an application as required by G.S. § 105 277.4(a) [G.S. § 107-277.3(b2)(2); *see also In re Appeal of Pridgen*, 06 PTC 179 (June 8, 2007)].

Liability for deferred taxes: If land qualifies for classification in the hands of the new owner under the ownership requirements exception, the deferred taxes remain a lien on the land, the new owner becomes liable for the deferred taxes, and the deferred taxes become payable if the land fails to meet any other condition or requirement for classification [G.S. § 105-277.3(b2)]. See "Deferred taxes" in see also ¶ 2309 below.

- *Exception for Conservation Reserve Program*

Land enrolled in the federal Conservation Reserve program authorized by 16 U.S.C. Chapter 58 is considered to be in actual production, and income derived from participation the federal Conservation Reserve Program may be used in meeting the minimum gross income requirements either separately or in combination with income from actual production. Land enrolled in the federal Conservation Reserve Program must be assessed as agricultural land if it is planted in vegetation other than trees or as forestland if it is planted in trees [G.S. § 105-277.3(d)].

¶2305

• *Exception for conservation easements*

Property that is appraised at its present-use value continues to qualify for appraisal, assessment, and taxation as agricultural, horticultural, or forestland as long as the property is subject to a qualifying conservation easement that meets the requirements of the conservation grant program under G.S. § 113A-232 (without regard to actual production or income requirements and the taxpayer received no more than 75% of the fair market value of the donated property interest in compensation [G.S. § 105-277.3(d1)].

• *Wildlife exception*

When an owner of land classified as agricultural land, horticultural land, or forestland does not transfer the land and the land becomes eligible for classification as wildlife conservation land under G.S. § 105-277.15, no deferred taxes are triggered. Instead, the deferred taxes remain a lien on the land and are payable when the land no longer qualifies as wildlife conservation land [G.S. § 105-277.3(d2)].

• *Exception for turkey disease*

Agricultural land that meets all of the following conditions is considered to be in actual production and to meet the minimum gross income requirements if it meets the following requirements [G.S. § 105-277.3(e)]:

(1) The land was in actual production in turkey growing within the preceding two (2) years and qualified for present-use valuation while in actual production.

(2) The land was taken out of actual production in turkey growing solely for health and safety considerations due to the presence of Poult Enteritis Mortality Syndrome among turkeys in the same or a neighboring county.

(3) The land is otherwise eligible for present-use valuation.

• *Definition of terms*

Business entity: A corporation, general partnership, limited partnership, or limited liability company [G.S. § 105-277.2(1a)].

Individually owned: Owned by one of the following:

(1) An individual.

(2) A business entity that meets all of the following conditions:

(a) Its principal business is farming agricultural land, horticultural land, or forestland. *See In re Appeal of Green Gardens, Inc.,* 06 PTC 093 (May 27, 2009) (a corporation that leased land to a lessee that used the land to grow nursery plants was engaged in farming and so qualified for special use valuation); *In re Appeal of Farriers Ridge Development, LLC,* 09 PTC 186 (2010) (land held by LLC that filed annual report stating "housing subdivision" as principal business and that recorded a subdivision plat and marketed and sold other property was not primarily engaged in agriculture). The entity's principal business is presumed to satisfy this requirement if the entity has been approved for present-use valuation in another county. If the assessor rebuts this presumption, the rebuttal does not affect the classification of the entity's property in the other county.

(b) All of its members are, directly or indirectly, individuals who are actively engaged in farming agricultural land, horticultural land, or forestland or a relative of one of the individuals who is actively engaged. An individual is indirectly a member of a business entity that owns the land if the individual is a member of a business entity or a beneficiary of a trust that is part of the ownership structure of the business entity that owns the land.

(c) It is not a corporation whose shares are publicly traded, and none of its members are corporations whose shares are publicly traded.

(d) If it leases the land, all of its members are individuals and are relatives. Under this condition, "principal business" and "actively engaged" include leasing.

(3) A trust that meets all of the following conditions:

(a) It was created by an individual who owned the land and transferred the land to the trust.

(b) All of its beneficiaries are, directly or indirectly, individuals who are the creator of the trust or a relative of the creator. An individual is indirectly a beneficiary of a trust that owns the land if the individual is a beneficiary of another trust or a member of a business entity that has a beneficial interest in the trust that owns the land.

(4) A testamentary trust that meets all of the following conditions:

(a) It was created by an individual who transferred to the trust land that qualified in his or her hands as agricultural land, horticultural land or forestland.

(b) At the date of the creator's death, the creator had no relatives.

(c) The trust income (less reasonable administrative expenses) is used exclusively for educational, scientific, literary cultural, charitable, or religious purposes.

(5) Tenants in common, if each tenant would qualify as an owner if the tenant were the sole owner. Tenants in common may elect to treat their individual shares as owned by them individually. The ownership requirements of G.S. § 105-277.3(b) apply to each tenant in common who is an individual, and the ownership requirements of G.S. § 105-277.3(b1) apply to each tenant in common who is a business entity or a trust.

Member: A shareholder of a corporation, a partner of a general or limited partnership, or a member of a limited liability company [G.S. § 105-277.2(4a)].

Present-use value: The value of land in its current use as agricultural land, horticultural land, or forestland, based solely on its ability to produce income and assuming an average level of management. *See In re Appeal McLamb,* 218 N.C. App. 485, 721 S.E.2d 285 (2012) (in appraising present use value property assessor not required to consider the factors set forth in G.S. § 105-317(a) which are applicable only to "true value" appraisals). A rate of 9% must be used to capitalize the expected net income of forestland. The capitalization rate for agricultural and horticultural land is determined by the Use-Value Advisory Board [G.S. § 105-277.2(5)].

Relative: Any of the following [G.S. § 105-277.2(5a)]:

(1) A spouse (including a surviving spouse) or the spouse's lineal ancestor or descendant.

(2) A lineal ancestor or lineal descendant.

(3) A brother or sister (including stepbrother or stepsister) or the lineal descendant of a brother or a sister.

(4) An aunt or an uncle.

(5) The spouse of an individual listed in (1) through (4).

For this purpose, an adoptive or adopted relative is a relative.

Sound management program: A program of production designed to obtain the greatest net return from the land consistent with its conservation and long-term improvement [G.S. § 105-277.2(6)].

Unit: One or more tracts of agricultural land, horticultural land, or forestland. Multiple tracts must be under the same ownership and be of the same classification. If the multiple tracts are located within different counties, they must be within 50 miles of a tract that qualifies for special classification [G.S. § 105-277.2(7)]. Unity of ownership was lost where, for instance, the individual owner of multiple tracts conveyed all but one tract to a living trust. *See In re Appeal of Capps,* 11 PTC 917 (August 23, 2012).

¶2306 Working Waterfront Property

• *Classification*

Working waterfront property is designated a special class of property and must be assessed at its present-use value rather than on its true value [G.S. § 105-277.14(b)].

• *Working waterfront property defined*

Working waterfront property is any of the following property that has, for the most recent three-year period, produced an average gross income of at least $1,000 [G.S. § 105-277.14(a)(4)]:

(1) A pier that extends into coastal fishing waters and limits access to those who pay a fee.

(2) Real property that is adjacent to coastal fishing waters and is primarily used for a commercial fishing operation or fish processing, including adjacent land that is under improvements used for one of these purposes.

Working waterfront property includes land reasonably necessary for the convenient use of the property [G.S. § 105-177.14(b)].

• *Deferred taxes*

The difference between the taxes that are due on working waterfront property taxed on the basis of its present use and that would be due if the property were taxed on the basis of its true value is a lien on the property. The difference in taxes must be carried forward in the records of each taxing unit as deferred taxes. The deferred taxes for the preceding three fiscal years are due and payable in accordance with G.S. § 105 277.1D when the property loses its eligibility for deferral as a result of a disqualifying event. A disqualifying event occurs when the property no longer qualifies as working waterfront property [G.S. § 105-277.14(c)]. The uniform provisions for payment of deferred taxes are discussed at ¶ 2311.

¶2307 Site Infrastructure Land

• *Classification*

Site infrastructure land is designated a special class of property and is subject to special appraisal, assessment and taxation [G.S. §105-277.15A(a)]. The deferral program for site infrastructure land permits the owner of land that is rezoned for industrial or office use to defer taxes on increases in value attributable to the rezoning and site improvements. See also the builders' inventory exclusion discussed at ¶2308.

• *Requirements*

Site infrastructure land is land consisting of at least one hundred contiguous acres that is zoned for industrial use, office use or both, which lacks any primary building or structure. In addition, no building permit for a primary building or structure may have been issued for the property [G.S. §105-277.15A(b)]. The term "primary building or structure" is not defined.

• *Deferred Taxes*

The owner of site infrastructure land may defer that portion of the tax imposed on the land that is attributable to the value of improvements made to the land, if any, as well as that portion of the taxes imposed on the land that represents the difference between the true value of the land as it is currently zoned and the value of the land as if it were zoned as in the calendar year before the time the application for deferral as site infrastructure land was filed. The deferred taxes are a lien on the property and are carried forward in the records of the taxing unit as deferred taxes [G.S. §105-227.15A(c)].

The deferred taxes are due and payable upon the occurrence of one of the following disqualifying events [G.S. §105.227.15A(c)]:

(1) If an amount equal to the deferred taxes are not invested in improvements to make the land suitable for industrial use, office use or both within five years from the day of the fiscal year the property was classified as site infrastructure land, the deferred taxes for the previous five years become due and payable.

(2) If the land has been classified as site infrastructure land for ten years, the deferred taxes for the previous five years becomes due and payable. In other words, the building of a primary structure must commence or a building permit for such a structure must be issued within ten years.

(3) If some or all of the site infrastructure land is rezoned for use other than industrial use, office use, or both, all deferred taxes become due and payable.

(4) If the land is transferred or a building permit for a primary building or structure for the land is issued, the deferred taxes for the preceding year become due and payable.

The uniform provisions for the payment of deferred taxes are discussed at ¶2311.

• *Notices*

On or before September 1 of each year, the tax collector of the taxing unit must notify each owner of site infrastructure land in the deferral program of the accumulated deferred taxes and interest.

An owner must notify the county assessor when land classified as site infrastructure land loses its eligibility. An owner who fails to provide this notice is subject to a penalty equal to 10% of the total amount of deferred taxes and interest thereon [G.S. § 105-227.15A(b)].

• *Application*

An owner wishing to apply for the site infrastructure land deferral program should file an application during the regular listing period. Applications are made on forms to be provided by the assessor. An application may be filed after the regular listing period upon a showing of good cause by the applicant for failure to make a timely application. A late application may be approved by the Board of Equalization and Review or, if the board is not in session, by the Board of County Commissioners. An untimely application that is approved applies only to property taxes levied by the county or municipality in the calendar year in which the untimely application is filed. Decisions of the county board may be appealed to the Property Tax Commission. An application may not be approved for any portion of site infrastructure land which previously lost its eligibility for the deferral program [G.S. § 105-277.15A(f)].

¶2308 Builders' Inventory Exclusion

Residential and commercial real property held for sale by a builder is designated a special class of property subject to special valuation as described below.

• *Residential real property*

Any increase in the value of residential real property held for sale by a builder is excluded from taxation if the increase in value is attributable to (1) the subdivision of the property, (2) land improvements to the property (such as grading, streets and utilities) or (3) the construction of either a new single family home or a duplex on the property by the builder.

This exclusion does not extend more than three years from the time the improved property was first subject to being listed for taxation by the builder.

For this purpose, "residential real property" means real property that is intended to be sold and used as an individual's residence immediately or after construction of a residence. The term does not include property occupied by a tenant or used for commercial purposes (such as a model home shown to prospective buyers) [G.S. § 105-277.02(a)].

• *Commercial real property*

Any increase in the value of commercial real property held for sale by a builder is excluded from taxation if the increase in value is attributable to (1) the subdivision of the property or (2) improvements to the property by the builder.

This exclusion ends at the earliest of (1) five years from the time the improved property was first subject to being listed for taxation by the builder, (2) issuance of a building permit, or (3) sale of the property. Because the exclusion ends upon the issuance of a building permit, the exclusion does not cover structural improvements.

For this purpose, "commercial real property" means real property that is intended to be sold and used for commercial purposes immediately or after improvement [G.S. § 105-277.02(b)].

• *Application*

The builder is required to apply for an exclusion for residential or commercial property held for sale only once [G.S. § 105-277.02(c)].

• *Assessor's appraisal*

The assessor must specify what portion of the value of property is attributable to an increase in value that is excluded under this provision [G.S. § 105-277.09(d)].

¶2309 Present-Use Value—Agricultural Land, Horticultural Land, and Forestland

Agricultural land, horticultural land, and forestland are eligible for taxation on the basis of the value of the property in its present use if a timely and proper application is filed with the county assessor [G.S. § 105-277.4(a)]. For business entities and trusts, certain ownership requirements must be met. See below.

A rate of 9% is used to capitalize the expected net income of forestland. The capitalization rate for agricultural land and horticultural land is determined by the Use-Value Advisory Board [G.S. § 105-277.2(5)].

Working Waterfront Property

Working waterfront property is also assessed at its present-use value. See the discussion of working waterfront property at ¶2306.

• *Ownership requirements for business entities and trusts*

Business entities: In order to be classified as agricultural, horticultural, or forestland, land owned by a business entity must have been owned by one or more of the following for the four (4) years immediately preceding January 1 of the year for which the benefit is claimed [G.S. § 105-277.3(b1)(1)]:

(1) The business entity.

(2) A member of the business entity.

(3) Another business entity whose members include a member of the business entity that currently owns the land.

Trusts: Land owned by a trust must have been owned by the trust or by one or more of its creators for the four (4) years immediately preceding January 1 of the year for which the benefit is claimed [G.S. § 105-277.3(b1)(2)].

• *Application*

In general, a taxpayer must file a timely and proper application with the county assessor of the county in which the property is located. The application must clearly show that the property comes within one of the classes and contain any other relevant information required by the assessor to make a proper appraisal of the property at its present-use value. An initial application must be filed during the regular listing period of the year for which the benefit is first claimed or within 30 days of the date shown on a notice of a change in valuation. A new application is not required unless the property is transferred or becomes ineligible for use-value appraisal because of a change in use or acreage [G.S. § 105-277.4(a)]. An application required due to transfer of the land must be submitted within 60 days of the date of the property's transfer [G.S. § 105-277.4(a)]. Upon a showing of good cause by the applicant for failure to make a timely application, an application may be approved by the board of equalization and review or, if that board is not in session, by the board of county commissioners. An untimely application approved in this manner applies only to property taxes levied by the county or municipality in the calendar year in which the untimely application is filed. Decisions of the county board denying late applications may be appealed to the Property Tax Commission [G.S. § 105-277.4(a1)]. The statute does not prescribe a particular application form, and the Property Tax Commission has ruled that a new owner's written expression of intent to keep property enrolled in the present-use valuation program within 60 days of the transfer was timely notice. *See In re Appeal of Holmes Land & Timber LLC*, 16 PTC 0193 (2018).

Late applications: County boards of equalization and review are permitted to consider late applications of property tax exemptions or exclusions. Prior to June 29, 2006, county boards were not authorized to consider late applications for present-use valuation. Now county boards of equalization and review may review and accept late applications for present-use valuation if the applicant demonstrates good cause for the delay. A decision of the county board denying late application may be appealed to the Property Tax Commission [G.S. § 105-277.4(a1)]. *See In re Appeal of Umberger*, 17 PTC 0182 (2018) (good cause shown where widow filed late application shortly after the end of the listing period and demonstrated impact of husband's death on management of the property); *But see In re Appeal of Brice*, 17 PTC 0087 (2018) (inability to obtain forest management plan not good cause).

• *Deferred taxes*

The difference between the taxes due on the present-use basis and the taxes that would have been payable in the absence of this classification, plus interest, penalties, or costs, are a lien on the taxpayer's property and carried forward in the records of the taxing unit as deferred taxes. The deferred taxes for the three preceding years are due and payable when the property loses its eligibility for deferral as a result of a disqualifying event. A disqualifying event occurs when the land fails to meet any requirement for classification or when an application is not approved [G.S. § 105-277.4(c)]. The uniform provisions for payment of deferred taxes are discussed at ¶ 2311.

Exceptions: There are two exceptions to this rule [G.S. § 105-277.4(d) and (d1)]. First, no deferred taxes are due and the lien for the deferred taxes is extinguished if property loses its eligibility for present-use value classification solely due to a change in income caused by enrollment of the property in the federal conservation reserve program. Second, if the property loses its eligibility for present-use classification because the property is conveyed by gift to a nonprofit organization and qualifies for exclusion from the tax base as a "protected natural area", or as land within a qualifying historic district (see ¶ 2203), or the property is conveyed by gift to North Carolina, a political subdivision of North Carolina, or the United States, then no deferred taxes are due and the lien is extinguished if the property was conveyed at or below its present-use value. If the property was conveyed for more than its present-use value, then a portion of the deferred taxes for the three preceding fiscal years becomes due and payable. The portion due is the lesser of the deferred taxes and the deferred taxes multiplied by a fraction the numerator of which is the sales price in excess of the present-use value and the denominator of which is the true value of the property in excess of the present-use value.

Despite the failure to meet any of these exceptions, the land may qualify for classification in the hands of the new owner if both of the following conditions are met: (1) the land was appraised at its present-use value or was eligible for appraisal at its present-use value at the time title to the land passed to the new owner; and (2) at the time title to the land passed to the new owner, the new owner acquires the land for and continues to use the land for the purposes it was classified while under previous ownership. If the land ceases to qualify because of a transfer to a new owner, no relief is available. *See In re Appeal of Terrell,* 16 PTC 0768 (2017) (transfer of portion of 30-acre forest land tract left transferor and transferee with less than required 20-acres). If the land qualifies for classification in the hands of the new owner, the new owner becomes liable for the deferred taxes, which become payable if the land fails to meet any other condition or requirement for classification [G.S. § 105-277.3(b2)]. Land may also qualify if the conditions for exception to ownership requirements are met. See "Exceptions to ownership requirements," at ¶ 2305.

Exception for certain easements on qualified conservation lands: Property that is appraised at its present-use value continues to qualify for special classification as long as (i) the property is subject to a qualifying conservation easement that meets the requirements of G.S. § 113A-232 without regard to actual production or income requirements and (ii) the taxpayer received no more than 75% of the fair market value of the donated property interest in compensation [G.S. § 105-277.3(d1)].

Exception for site infrastructure land. Deferred taxes on present-use value property are not triggered if the land becomes eligible for classification as site infrastructure land or if the owner transfers the property and the property becomes eligible for such classification within six months of the transfer [G.S. § 105-277.3(d3)]. For site infrastructure land see ¶ 2307.

Computation of deferred tax: In determining the amount of deferred taxes, the assessor uses the appraised valuation established in the county's last general revaluation except for any changes made under G.S. § 105-287, relating to errors and changes in value resulting from changes in value of the property [G.S. § 105-277.6(a)]. When a general reappraisal is made, the new appraised value is used [G.S. § 105-277.6(b)].

• *Use-Value Advisory Board*

The Use-Value Advisory Board is established under the supervision of the Agricultural Extension Service of North Carolina State University and chaired by the Director of the Agricultural Extension Service of North Carolina State University. Eight additional members of the Board represent various State departments and agencies [G.S. § 105-277.7(a)]. The Board must annually submit to the Department of Revenue a recommended use-value manual [G.S. § 105-277.7(b)]. However, counties are not required to adopt the values set forth in the manual. *See In re Appeal of McLamb,* 218 N.C. App. 485, 721 S.E.2d 285 (2012). The Department of Revenue is responsible for preparing and distributing annually to each assessor the manual developed by the Use-Value Advisory Board that establishes the cash rental rates for agricultural and horticultural lands and the net income ranges for forestland [G.S. § 105-289(a)(5)].

• *Assessor's annual review of present-use value*

The assessor is required to review the eligibility of all parcels classified for taxation at present-use value in an eight-year period [G.S. § 105-296(j)]. To accomplish this, assessor must annually review one-eighth of the parcels in the county classified for taxation at present-use. The period of the review process is based on the average

¶2309

of the preceding three (3) years' data. The assessor may request assistance from the Farm Service Agency, the Cooperative Extension Service, the North Carolina Forest Service of the Department of Agriculture and Consumer Services, or other similar organizations [G.S. § 105-296(j)]. The board of county commissioners may employ experts to assist the assessor and may also assign to county agencies, or contract with State or federal agencies, for any duties involved with the approval or auditing of use-value accounts [G.S. § 105-299].

The assessor may require the owner of classified property to submit any information needed to verify the property's qualification for present-use valuation (including sound management plans for forestland). The owner has 60 days from the date of a written request for information to submit the information to the assessor. If the assessor determines that the owner failed to make the information requested available in the time required without good cause, the property loses its present-use value classification, and the property's deferred taxes become due and payable. If the property loses its present-use value classification for failure to provide the requested information, the assessor must reinstate the property's present-use value classification when the owner submits the requested information within 60 days after the disqualification unless the information discloses that the property no longer qualifies for present-use value classification. When a property's present-use value classification is reinstated, it is reinstated retroactively; and any deferred taxes paid as a result of the revocation must be refunded to the property owner. The owner may appeal the final decision of the assessor to the county board of equalization and review as provided in G.S. § 105 277.4(b1) [G.S. § 105-296(j)]. *See In re Appeal of RGS Properties, Inc.,* 14 PTC 114 (2015) (assessor's removal of property from present use valuation for taxpayer's failure to respond to audit notice was improper where taxpayer claimed it did not receive the notice and where assessor did not otherwise attempt to verify the property's qualification).

In determining whether property is operating under a sound management program, the assessor must consider any weather conditions or other acts of nature that prevent the growing or harvesting of crops or the realization of income from cattle, harvesting of crops, or the realization of income from cattle, swine, or poultry operations. The assessor must also allow the property owner to submit additional information before making this determination [G.S. § 105-296(j)].

• *Appeal*

Decisions of the assessor regarding the qualification or appraisal of property at its present-use value may be appealed to the county board of equalization and review. If that board is not in session, the taxpayer may appeal to the board of county commissioners. An appeal must be made within 60 days after the decision of the assessor. If an owner submits additional information to the assessor pursuant to G.S. § 105-296(j), the appeal must be made within 60 days after the assessor's decision based on the additional information. Decisions of the county board may be appealed to the Property Tax Commission [G.S. § 105-277.4(b1)]. See Chapter 25 for discussion of taxpayers' remedies.

¶2310 Payment of Tax

In general, property is listed with the county assessor during January, and the taxes on the property are due on September 1. Taxes due on September 1 become delinquent on January 6 of the next calendar year. Taxes are payable at the office of the tax collector or at a financial institution with which the taxing unit has contracted for receipt of payment of taxes. A financial institution, however, cannot issue a receipt for any tax payments it receives [G.S. § 105-321(e)]. See ¶ 2106 for treatment of motor vehicles.

Taxes are payable in cash, but the tax collector may accept checks and electronic payment. Deeds, notes, payments in kind, and other similar documents will not be accepted; and taxing units cannot permit the payment of taxes by offset of any bill, claim, judgment, or other obligation owed to the taxpayer by the taxing unit. However, the prohibition against payment of taxes by offset does not apply to offset of an obligation arising from a lease or another contract entered into between the taxpayer and the taxing unit before July 1 of the fiscal year for which the unpaid taxes were levied [G.S. § 105-357(a)].

For the convenience of taxpayers, the governing body may require the tax collector to be present to collect taxes in person or by deputy at their designated places within the taxing unit at times prescribed by the governing body; and the tax collector must give timely notice of when and where he will be present. This notice must be published in a newspaper having general circulation in the taxing unit and posted at three or more public places within the taxing unit [G.S. § 105-353].

Military Personnel Deployed in Iraq

Military personnel deployed in Iraq are allowed 90 days after the end of their deployment to pay property taxes, at par, for any property taxes that became due or delinquent during the term of deployment. For these individuals, the taxes for the relevant tax year do not become delinquent until after the end of the 90-day period; and an individual who pays the property taxes before the end of the 90-day period is not liable for interest on the taxes for the relevant year. If the individual does not pay the taxes before the end of the 90-day period, interest accrues on the taxes as through the taxes were unpaid as of the date the taxes would have become delinquent without benefit of the 90-day grace period [S.L. 2003-300 (S.B. 936), § 4(a)].

• *Payment required before recording conveyance deeds*

The board of commissioners of certain counties may, by resolution, require the register of deeds not to accept any deed transferring real property for registration unless the county tax collector has certified that no delinquent taxes with which the collector is charged (*e.g.*, ad valorem county taxes, ad valorem municipal taxes) are a lien on the property described in the deed [G.S. § 161-31(a)].

This provision applies only to the following counties: Alleghany, Anson, Beaufort, Bertie, Cabarrus, Camden, Carteret, Cherokee, Chowan, Clay, Cleveland, Currituck, Davidson, Duplin, Durham, Forsyth, Gaston, Gates, Graham, Granville, Harnett, Haywood, Henderson, Hertford, Hyde, Iredell, Jackson, Lee, Macon, Madison, Martin, Montgomery, Northampton, Pasquotank, Perquimans, Person, Pitt, Polk, Rockingham, Rowan, Rutherford, Stanly, Swain, Transylvania, Vance, Warren, Washington, and Yadkin [G.S. § 161-31(b)]. In addition, the General Assembly has enacted special legislation that prohibits a register of deeds from registering a deed unless the tax collector has certified that no delinquent taxes are due. Those special provisions apply to Alleghany County, Ashe County, Avery County, Mitchell County, and the Towns of Bakersville, Banner Elk, Newland, and Spruce Pine.

¶**2310**

Uncertified Deeds

If a county has adopted a resolution to require the register of deeds to refuse registration of a deed without certification from the county tax collector, the register of deeds must nevertheless accept an uncertified deed that is submitted under the supervision of a closing attorney and that contains a statement that delinquent taxes will be paid out of closing proceeds [G.S. § 161-31(a)(1)].

¶2311 Uniform Provisions for Payment of Deferred Taxes

• *Programs covered*

G.S. § 105-277.1F provides uniform rules for the payment of taxes under the following deferred tax programs:

(1) Real property owned by a nonprofit corporation held as a protected natural area [G.S. § 105-275(12)f]. See ¶2203.

(2) Historic district property held as a future site of an historic structure [G.S. § 105-275(29a)]. See ¶2203.

(3) The property tax homestead circuit breaker [G.S. § 105-277.1B]. See ¶2215.

(4) The residential homebuilder inventory tax deferred [G.S. § 105-277.1D]. See ¶2217.

(5) Present-use value property [G.S. § 105-277.4(c)]. See ¶2309.

(6) Working waterfront property [G.S. § 105-277.14]. See ¶2306.

(7) Wildlife conservation land [G.S. § 105-277.15]. See ¶2304.

(8) Site infrastructure land [G.S. § 105-277.15A]. See ¶2307.

(9) Historic property [G.S. § 105-278(b)]. *See* ¶2304.

(10) Nonprofit property held as the future site of low- or moderate-income housing [G.S. § 105-278.6(e)]. See ¶2203.

• *When deferred taxes become due*

Taxes deferred under one of these programs are due and payable on the day the property loses its eligibility as a result of a disqualifying event. If only part of the property loses its eligibility for deferral, the assessor must determine the amount of the deferred taxes that apply to the ineligible part, and the amount so determined is due and payable. A lien for deferred taxes is extinguished when the taxes are paid [G.S. § 105-277.1D(b)].

• *Interest*

Interest accrues on deferred taxes as if they had been payable on the dates on which they would have originally become due [G.S. § 105-277.1D(b)].

• *Taxes for the year of disqualification*

The tax for the fiscal year that begins in the calendar year in which the deferred taxes are due is computed as if the property had not been classified for that year [G.S. § 105-277.1D(b)].

• *Voluntary payment*

All or part of the deferred taxes that are not due and payable may be paid to the tax collector at any time without affecting the property's eligibility for deferral. Any partial payment is applied first to accrued interest [G.S. § 105-277.1D(b)].

¶2312 Tax Liens

A lien for taxes attaches to property on the listing date. All penalties, interest, and costs allowed by law are added to the amount of the lien and are regarded as attaching at the same time as the lien for the principal amount of the taxes [G.S. § 105-355(a)]. For discussion of the general rules for tax liens, see ¶330.

• *Lien on real property*

Regardless of the time at which liability for a tax for a given fiscal year may arise or the exact amount of the tax may be determined, the lien for taxes levied on a parcel of real property attaches to the parcel as of the listing date [G.S. § 105-355(a)]. Listing is discussed at ¶2301.

Life tenants: Taxes levied on real property listed in the name of a life tenant is a lien on the fee as well as the life estate [G.S. § 105-355(a)(1)].

Improvements or separate rights: Taxes levied on improvements on or separate rights in real property owned by one other than the owner of the land (whether or not listed separately from the land) is a lien on both the improvements or rights and on the land [G.S. § 105-355(a)(2)].

Presumption of Notice

Anyone who has acquired or who may acquire any interest in property, real or personal, that may be or may become subject to a lien for taxes are charged with notice that such property is or should be listed for taxation, that taxes are or may become a lien thereon, and that if taxes are not paid the proceedings allowed by law may be taken against such property. This notice is conclusively presumed, whether or not such persons have actual notice [G.S. § 105-348].

• *Lien on personal property*

Taxes levied on real and personal property (including penalties, interest, and costs allowed by law) are a lien on personal property from and after levy or attachment and garnishment of the personal property levied upon or attached [G.S. § 105-355(b)].

• *Priority of tax liens on real property*

The priority of tax liens on real property is determined in accordance with the following rules:

(1) Subject to the provisions of the Revenue Act prescribing the priority of the lien for State taxes, the lien of taxes under the property tax laws is superior to all other liens, assessment, charges, rights, and claims of any and every kind in and to the real property to which the lien attaches regardless of the claimant and regardless of whether acquired prior or subsequent to the attachment of the lien for taxes [G.S. § 105-356(a)(1)].

¶2312

(2) The liens of taxes of all taxing units are of equal dignity [G.S. § 105-356(a)(2)].

(3) The priority of tax liens is not affected by transfer of title to the real property after the lien has attached, nor is it affected by the death, receivership, or bankruptcy of the owner of the property to which the lien attaches [G.S. § 105-356(a)(3)].

• *Priority of tax liens on personal property*

The priority of liens on personal property is determined in accordance with the following rules:

(1) A tax lien that attaches to personal property is, insofar as it represents taxes imposed upon the property to which the lien attaches, superior to all other liens and rights whether they are prior or subsequent to the tax lien in point of time [G.S. § 105-356(b)(1)].

(2) A tax lien on personal property is, insofar as it represents taxes imposed upon property other than that to which the lien attaches, inferior to prior valid liens and perfected security interests and superior to all subsequent liens and security interests [G.S. § 105-356(b)(2)].

(3) With respect to tax liens of different taxing units, the tax lien that attaches first is superior [G.S. § 105-356(b)(3)].

• *Discovered property*

Tax receipts prepared for discovered property have the same force and effect as if they had been delivered to the collector at the time of the delivery of the regular tax receipts for the current year, and the taxes charged in the receipts are a lien upon the property in the same manner as other real property [G.S. § 105-312(j)].

• *Advertisement of tax liens on real property*

In February of each year, the tax collector must report liens on real property to the governing body. The governing body must then order the tax collector to advertise the tax liens [G.S. § 105-369(a)]. The county tax collector must advertise tax liens by posting a notice of the liens at the county courthouse and by publishing each lien at least one time in one or more newspapers having general circulation in the taxing unit. Municipal tax liens must be advertised by posting a notice of the liens at the city or town hall and by publishing each lien at least one time in one or more newspapers having general circulation in the taxing unit. Advertisement of tax liens must be made during the period March 1 through June 30 [G.S. § 105-369(c)]. No tax lien is void because the real property to which the lien attached was listed or advertised in the name of a person other than the person in whose the name should have been listed if the property was in other respects correctly described on the abstract or in the advertisement [G.S. § 105-369(f)].

• *Notice to owners of tax liens*

After the governing body orders the tax collector to advertise the tax liens, the collector must send a notice to the listing owner and to the record owner of each affected parcel of property, as determined as of the date the taxes became delinquent. The notice must be send to each owner's last known address by first-class mail at least 30 days before the date the advertisement is to be published [G.S. § 105-369(b)]. At any time during the advertisement period, any parcel may be withdrawn from the list by payment of the taxes plus accrued interest and a proportionate part of the advertising fee to be determined by the tax collector [G.S. § 105-369(e)].

Collection Against Purchasers of Real Property

The "taxpayer" against whom collection remedies for delinquent real property taxes can be enforced means the record owner of the real property on the date the taxes become delinquent and any subsequent record of the real property who takes title after the delinquent date [G.S. §§ 105-273(17), 105-369, 105-374(c), and 105-375(i)]. Note that the law requires property taxes on real property being sold to be prorated between the seller and buyer of the property on a calendar-year basis unless otherwise provided by contract [G.S. § 39-60].

• *Foreclosure on tax liens*

If a tax is not paid within 30 days after the taxpayer was given notice of final assessment, the Secretary may issue a warrant for the sale of the taxpayer's real property in the county in which the real property is situated. This warrant is executed in the same manner of court judgments. This is an action in the nature of an action to foreclose on a mortgage; and the Secretary may advertise the sale in any reasonable manner and for any reasonable period of time to effect an adequate bid for the property [G.S. § 105-242(a)].

Methods of foreclosure: North Carolina statute provides for two methods of fore-closure: (1) mortgage foreclosure [G.S. § 105-274]; and (2) *in rem* foreclosure [G.S. § 105-275]. An action to foreclose a mortgage may be instituted in the appropriate division of the general court of justice in the county in which the real property is situated. *In rem* foreclosure is a simple and inexpensive alternative method of enforcing payment of taxes necessarily levied for the requirements of local governments in North Carolina. *In rem* foreclosure is also available as a method of foreclosing the lien of special assessments. For an unsuccessful due process challenge to the in rem foreclosure method, *see Da Dai Mai v. Carolina Holdings, Inc.*, 205 N.C. App. 659, 696 S.E.2d 769 (2010).

Court action: No court may enjoin the collection of any tax, the sale of any tax lien, or the sale or any property for nonpayment of tax except upon a showing that the tax (or some part thereof) is illegal or levied for an illegal or unauthorized purpose [G.S. § 105-379(a)].

Date of delinquency: A tax collector may proceed to collect a tax using levy, garnishment, foreclosure and the other collection remedies available to the tax collector under G.S. §§ 105-366 through 105-375 on or after the day the tax becomes delinquent. A tax is delinquent as follows [G.S. § 105-365.1(a)]:

    (1) Deferred on property under the property tax homestead circuit breaker program that lost its eligibility due to the death of the owner become delinquent on the first day of the ninth month following the date of death.

    (2) Other deferred taxes become delinquent the day a disqualifying event occurs.

    (3) Taxes other than deferred taxes become delinquent the day the tax begins to accrue interest.

Against whom collection remedies may be enforced: The tax collector shall enforce collection remedies against the following taxpayers [G.S. § 105-365.1(b)]:

¶2312

(1) Delinquent taxes on real property may be enforced against the owner of record as of the date of delinquency and any subsequent owner of record. Since taxes are generally delinquent when interest accrues and since interest begins to accrue on January 6 (*see* ¶2402), the owner of record on January 6 is the party against whom the taxes may be enforced.

(2) Delinquent taxes on personal property may be enforced against the owner of record as of January 1 of the calendar year in which the fiscal year of taxation begins.

(3) Delinquent taxes on a registered motor vehicle may be enforced against the owner of record as of the date on which the current vehicle registration is renewed or the date on which a new registration is applied for.

Limitations on actions: Counties and municipalities are barred from enforcing tax liens (other than liens for special assessments) or taking other enforcement action if more than ten years have elapsed since the taxes became due [G.S. § 105-378(a)]. The county tax collector may not enforce a tax lien or take other collection action (other than sending an initial bill or notice to the taxpayer) with respect to an assessment that has been appealed to the county board of equalization and review or the Property Tax Commission until the appeal has been finally adjudicated [G.S. § 105-378(d)].

PROPERTY TAXES

CHAPTER 24

DISCOVERIES, INTEREST, AND PENALTIES

¶2401 Discoveries

• *Discovered property*

Discovered property is (1) property that was not listed during a listing period; (2) property that was listed but the listing included a substantial understatement; or (3) property that has been granted an exemption or exclusion and does not qualify for the exemption or exclusion. "To discover property" means to determine that property was not listed, was listed with a substantial understatement, or was granted an exemption or exclusion for which the property did not qualify [G.S. § 105-273(6a), (6b)].

Caution: Changes to Real Property

While owners of taxable property are generally required to list such property during the listing period, there is no duty to list taxable real property that is subject to a permanent listing system [G.S. §§ 105-302(a), 105-303(b)]. Accordingly, such real property is not subject to being discovered [G.S. § 105-303(b)(2)]. However, the owners of real property listed under a permanent listing system must inform the assessor during the listing period of any improvements on or separate rights in the real property, and failure to provide such information can lead to discovery of the improvements or separate rights [G.S. § 105-303(b)].

• *Duty to discover and assess*

It is the duty of the assessor to see that all property not properly listed during the regular listing period be listed, assessed, and taxed as required. The assessor must file reports of discoveries with the board of commissioners in the manner required by the board [G.S. § 105-312(b)].

• *Application of discovery rules*

The discovery provisions apply to all cities, towns, and other municipal corporations having the power to tax property. Governmental units that have the power to tax property must designate an appropriate municipal officer to exercise the discovery powers and duties assigned to the assessor. The powers and duties assigned to the board of county commissioners must be exercised by the governing body of the unit. When the assessor discovers property having a taxable situs in a municipal corporation, the assessor must send a copy of the notice of discovery to the governing body of the municipality along with any other information that may be necessary to enable the municipality to proceed. The governing board of a municipality may, by resolution, delegate the power to compromise, settle, or adjust discovery tax claims to the county board of equalization and review [G.S. § 105-312(l)].

• *Carrying forward real property*

At the close of the regular listing period each year, the assessor must compare the submitted tax lists with the lists for the preceding year and carry forward to the lists of the current year all real property that was listed in the preceding year. The assessor must list the property carried forward in the name of the taxpayer who listed it in the preceding year unless, under the provisions of G.S. § 105-302, it must be listed in the name of another taxpayer.

Real property carried forward is considered discovered property and is subject to discovered property procedures unless the property discovered is listed in the name of the taxpayer who listed it for the preceding year and the property is not subject to appraisal under either G.S. § 105-286 or G.S. § 105-287, in which case no notice of listing and valuation need be sent to the taxpayer [G.S. § 105-312(c)]. See "Discovered property procedures," below. Appraisal is discussed at ¶ 2302.

• *Discovered property procedures*

Owner: Taxable real property must be listed in the name of the owner on the required listing day, and it is the duty of the owner to list the property [G.S. § § 105-302, 105-306]. The assessor must list discovered real property in the name of the owner.

Date of discovery: The discovery is deemed to have been made on the date that the abstract is made or corrected. See "Records of discovered property," below.

Tentative appraisal: The assessor, upon discovering property, must made a tentative appraisal of the discovered property in accordance with the best information available to the assessor.

Notice of discovery: When a discovery is made, the assessor must mail a notice to the person in whose name the discovered property has been listed [G.S. § 105-312(d)]. *See In re Appeal of Enforge, LLC,* 12 PTC 658 (2014) (discovery notice improperly delivered when sent to an address different from address used in all provisions and subsequent communications between the county and the taxpayer). The notice must contain the following information:

> (1) The name and address of the person in whose name the property is listed.

> (2) A brief description of the property.

> (3) A tentative appraisal of the property.

> (4) A statement to the effect that the listing and appraisal will become final unless written exception is filed with the assessor within 30 days from the date of the notice.

• *Appeals*

When an assessor receives a timely exception to a notice of discovery, the assessor must arrange a conference with the taxpayer to afford the taxpayer the opportunity to present any evidence of argument regarding the discovery [G.S. § 105-312(d)]. Within 15 days after the conference, the assessor must give written notice to the taxpayer of the final decision unless the taxpayer signs an agreement accepting the listing and appraisal. If agreement is not reached, the taxpayer has 15 days from the notice date to request a review of the assessor's decision by the Board of Equalization and Review. If the Board of Equalization and Review is not in session, the taxpayer may request a review by the county board of commissioners. Unless a request for review by the county board is given at the conference, it must be made in writing to the assessor. Upon receipt of a timely request for review, the Board of Equalization and Review or the board of commissioners must follow the appropriate procedures. The Board of Equalization and Review is discussed at ¶ 2503. The board of county commissioners is discussed at ¶ 2504.

¶ 2401

• *Records of discovered property*

When property is discovered, the taxpayer's original abstract (if one was submitted) may be corrected or a new abstract may be prepared to reflect the discovery. If a new abstract is prepared, it may be filed with the abstracts that were submitted during the regular listing period, or it may be filed separately with abstracts designated "Late Listings." Regardless of how it is filed, the listing has the same force and effect as if it had been submitted during the regular listing period [G.S. § 105-312(e)].

• *Presumptions*

When property is discovered and listed to a taxpayer in any year, it is presumed that it should have been listed by the same taxpayer for the preceding five (5) years unless the taxpayer produces satisfactory evidence that (1) the property was not in existence; (2) the property was actually listed for taxation; or (3) it was not the taxpayer's duty to list the property during these years (or some of them) under the provisions of G.S. § § 105-302 and 105-306 [G.S. § 105-312(f)].

If it is shown that the property should have been listed by some other taxpayer during some or all of the preceding years, the property must be listed in the name of the appropriate taxpayer for the proper years. The discovery, however, is still deemed to have been made as of the date that the assessor first listed it [G.S. § 105-312(f)].

• *Taxation of discovered property*

When property is discovered, it is taxed for the year in which discovered and for any of the preceding five (5) years for which it escaped appropriate taxation. If the discovery is based upon an understatement of value, quantity, or other measurement rather than an omission from the tax list, the tax will be computed on the additional valuation, and appropriate penalties will be applied [G.S. § 105-312(g)]. Each year's tax is computed separately.

• *Penalties for discovered property*

After computing each year's taxes separately, penalties are applied. There is a penalty of ten percent (10%) of the amount of the tax for the earliest year in which the property was not listed, plus an additional ten percent (10%) of the same amount for each subsequent listing period that elapsed before the property was discovered. This penalty shall be computed separately for each year in which a failure to list occurred; and the year, the amount of the tax for that year, and the total of penalties for failure to list in that year shall be shown separately on the tax records; but the taxes and penalties for all years in which there was a failure to list shall be then totalled on a single tax receipt [G.S. § 105-312(h)].

Exception for certain real property: The penalty for failure to list does not apply to real property if there have been no improvements to the property or change in ownership since its last listing [G.S. § 105-312(h)].

Collection of penalties: For purposes of tax collection and foreclosure, the total amount of penalties is deemed to be a tax for the fiscal year beginning on July 1 of the calendar year in which the property was discovered, and the schedule of discounts for prepayment and interest for late payment applicable to taxes for the fiscal year apply when the total figure on the single tax receipt is paid. Any property owner required to pay taxes on discovered property is entitled to a refund of any taxes erroneously paid on the same property to other taxing jurisdictions in North Carolina. Claims for refund must be filed in the counties where tax was erroneously paid [G.S. § 105-312(i)].

Tax receipts charged to collector: Tax receipts prepared (as required by G.S. § 105-312(h) and (i)) for taxes and penalties imposed upon discovered property are delivered to the tax collector, who is charged with their collection. These receipts have the same force and effect as if they had been delivered to the collector at the time of the delivery of the regular tax receipts for the current year, and the taxes charged in the receipts become a lien upon the property in accordance with the provisions of G.S. § 105-355 [G.S. § 105-312(j)].

Power to compromise: After a tax receipt computed and prepared as required by subsections (g) and (h) of G.S. § 105-312 has been delivered and charged to the tax collector, the board of county commissioners, upon the petition of the taxpayer, may compromise, settle, or adjust the county's claim for taxes. The board of commissioners may, by resolution, delegate this authority to the board of equalization and review [G.S. § 105-312(k)].

¶2402 Interest and Refunds

• *Interest on delinquent property taxes*

Taxes are due and payable at par if paid before January 6 following the due date. The governing unit is authorized to give discounts for early payment [G.S. § 105-360(c)]. Taxes paid on or after the due date are subject to interest charges [G.S. § 105-360(a)]. Interest accrues on taxes paid on or after January 6 as follows:

(1) For the period January 6 to February 1, interest accrues at the rate of 2%.

(2) For the period February 1 until the principal amount of tax, interest, and penalties are paid, interest accrues at the rate of $3/4$% a month or fraction thereof.

• *Interest on overpayments upon reduction of value or removal of property from tax lists*

When an order of the county board of equalization of review reduces the valuation of property or removes the property from the tax lists and, based on the order, the taxpayer has paid more tax that is due on the property, the taxpayer is entitled to receive interest on the overpayment at the rate set under G.S. § 105-360(a) from the date the interest begins to accrue until a refund is paid. Interest accrues from the later of the date the tax was paid and the date the tax would have been considered delinquent under G.S. § 105-360. A refund is considered paid on a date determined by the governing body of the taxing unit that is no sooner than five (5) days after a refund check is mailed [G.S. § 105-360(e)].

• *Refunds*

Request for refund: Any taxpayer asserting a valid defense to the enforcement of the collection of a tax assessed upon his/her property may seek a release of the tax claim or a refund. If a tax has not been paid, the taxpayer may make a demand for the release of the tax claim by submitting to the governing body of the taxing unit a written statement of his/her defense and a request for release of the tax at any time prior to payment. If a tax has been paid, the taxpayer, at any time within the later of (1) five years after the tax became due, or (2) six months from the date of payment, may make a demand for a refund by submitting to the governing body of the taxing unit a written statement of his/her defense and request for a refund [G.S. § 105-381]. For this purpose, a "valid defense" includes the following:

(1) A tax imposed through clerical error.

(2) An illegal tax.

(3) A tax levied for an illegal purpose.

Action of governing body: Upon receiving a taxpayer's written statement of defense and request for release or refund, the governing body of the taxing unit must, within 90 days after receipt of the refund request, determine whether the taxpayer has a valid defense to the tax imposed or any part of it. They must either release or refund that portion of the amount determined to be in excess of the correct tax liability or notify the taxpayer in writing that no release or refund will be made [G.S. § 105-381(b)].

Suit for recovery: If within 90 days after receiving a release request for an unpaid tax, the governing body has failed to grant the release or has denied the request, the taxpayer must pay the tax. If still dissatisfied, the taxpayer may bring civil action against the taxing unit at any time within three years from the date of payment of tax. In the case for a request for refund of taxes already paid, if the governing body has denied the request for refund or has taken no action on the request, the taxpayer may bring a civil action against the taxing unit for the amount claimed at any time within three years from the expiration of the period in which the governing body is required to act [G.S. § 105-381(c)]. Civil actions brought to recover property taxes must be brought to the appropriate division of the general court of justice of the county in which the taxing unit is located. If the court determines that the tax or any part of it was illegal or levied for an illegal purpose, or excessive as the result of a clerical error, judgment will be rendered therefor with interest at 6% per annum, plus costs [G.S. § 105-381(d)].

¶2403 Penalties

Failure to list: Any person who willfully fails or refuses to list property will, in addition to all other penalties prescribed by law, be guilty of a Class 2 misdemeanor punishable by a fine not to exceed $500 or imprisonment not to exceed six months The failure to list is *prima facie* evidence that the failure was willful. Anyone who willfully aids or abets another in any way to evade property taxes (or attempts to do so) is also guilty of a Class 2 misdemeanor [G.S. § 105-308].

Insufficient funds: The penalty for presenting in payment of taxes a check or electronic funds transfer that is returned or not completed because of insufficient funds or nonexistence of an account of the drawer or transferor is the greater of (1) twenty-five dollars ($25) or (2) 10% of the amount of the check, subject to a maximum of $1,000 [G.S. § 105-357(b)(2)]. The penalty does not apply, however, if the tax collector finds that the drawer had sufficient funds in an account to make payment and, by inadvertence, the drawer of the check or transferor of the funds failed to draw the check or initiate a transfer on the account that had sufficient funds. This penalty shall be added to and collected in the same manner as the taxes for which the check or electronic payment was given [G.S. § 105-357(b)(2)]. A tax collector may reduce or waive the penalty imposed on giving a worthless check [G.S. § 105-358(a)].

Other penalties: The North Carolina statutes provide for penalties in other situations. There are penalties for failures to file required reports for the following:

(1) Persons having custody of another's tangible personal property [G.S. § 105-315].

(2) House trailer parks, marinas, and aircraft storage facility operators [G.S. § 105-316].

(3) Apartment complex owners [G.S. § 105-316].

(4) Public service companies [G.S. § 105-344].

(5) Failure to obtain permit to move mobile home [G.S. § 105-316].

Information Obtained from Web Sites

If a taxing unit maintains an Internet web site on which current information on the amount of taxes, special assessments, penalties, interest, and costs due on any real or personal property is available, the taxing unit's governing body may adopt an ordinance to allow a person to rely on information obtained from the web site as if it were a written certificate issued by the tax collector. A taxpayer who relies on the web site information must keep and present a copy of the information as necessary or appropriate [G.S. § 105-361(e)].

PROPERTY TAXES

CHAPTER 25

TAXPAYER REMEDIES

¶2501 In General

North Carolina provides two basic routes for challenging a property tax assessment: administrative review followed by judicial review in the Court of Appeals and direct review in the district or superior court. *See Johnston v. Gaston County,* 71 N.C. App. 707, 709, 323 S.E.2d 381, 382 (1984), *cert. denied,* 313 N.C. 508, 329 S.E.2d 392 (1985). The first route involves an appeal to the county board of equalization [G.S. § 105-322(g)(2)] with an appeal to the Property Tax Commission [G.S. § 105-290(b) and (c)] and a further appeal to the Court of Appeals [G.S. § 105-345]. The second route involves paying the tax due and requesting a refund from the governing body of the taxing unit [G.S. § 105-381(a)(3)]followed by a civil action against the taxing unit in district or superior court [G.S. § 105-381(c)(2) and (d)]. As a variant of this second route, the taxpayer may, without first paying the tax, demand that the governing body of the taxing unit release its tax claim, and, if the claim is denied, pay the tax and bring a civil action to recover the tax in the district or superior court [G.S. § 105-381(a)(2), (c)(1) and (d)]. The grounds for redress under these alternative procedures are not, however, the same, as discussed below. In addition, special rules are provided for appealing the value, situs or taxability of personal property. These rules are discussed at ¶ 2506 below. These remedial avenues are exclusive, and a taxpayer may not, for instance, apply to the courts for a writ of mandamus ordering the local board to correct a valuation or other error. *See Villages at Red Bridge, LLC v. Weisner,* 209 N.C. App. 604, 704 S.E.2d 925 (2011). In addition, the governing body of a taxing unit may not release, refund or compromise any tax levied on property within its jurisdiction except in accordance with these procedures, and members of a governing body who vote for such an improper release, refund or compromise may be held personally liable for the tax [G.S. § 105-380]. An exception to this rule (which expires July 1, 2016) requires a governing body to release taxes levied on property that was deannexed by the municipality if (1) the property was within the corporate limits of the municipality for six months or less and (2) no notice of the tax has been sent to the taxpayer [G.S. § 105-380(e)].

¶2502 Board of Equalization and Review

The board of equalization and review of each county is composed of the members of the board of county commissioners unless the board of commissioners adopts a resolution appointing a special board to serve that function [G.S. § 105-322(a)]. In counties that have a tax commission or comparable agency, the tax commission or agency performs all the duties required by the board of equalization and review and the board of county commissioners, except for levying taxes [G.S. § 105-300].

- *Duty to review tax lists*

The duty of the board of equalization and review is to examine and review the tax lists of the county for the current year to ensure that all taxable property is (1) listed on the abstracts and county tax records, and (2) meets the uniform appraisal standards of G.S. § 105-283. Appeals of appraisals are not required to be made in the year the county reappraises property, though any adjustment to the property's value as a result of the appeal made in a later year will not be retroactive to the reappraisal year. *See In re Appeal of Ocean Isle Palms LLC,* 219 N.C. App. 81, 723 S.E.2d 543 (2012), *rev'd on other grounds,* 366 N.C. 351, 749 S.E.2d 439 (2013). The board of equalization and review has broad authority to list, appraise and assess any property omitted from the tax lists, correct errors in the abstracts, increase or decrease appraised values and generally to take any actions necessary to make the lists and tax records conform to the requirements of the Machinery Act [G.S. § 105-322(g)(1)].

- *Duty to hear appeals*

In addition, the board has the duty to hear any taxpayer who owns or controls property taxable in the county with respect to the listing or appraisal of the taxpayer's property or the property of others [G.S. § 105-322(g)(2)]. A request for a hearing must be made to the board in writing or by personal appearance before its adjournment. and before any deadline established by the board [G.S. §§ 105-322(e) and (g)(2) as interpreted by *In re Appeal of Dixie Bldg., LLC,* 235 N.C. App. 61, 760 S.E.2d 769 (2014)]. However, if a taxpayer requests a review of a board decision made under G.S. § 105-322(g)(1) (relating to the review and correction of the tax lists) notice of which was mailed fewer than fifteen days before the board's adjournment, the taxpayer may request a hearing on that decision within fifteen days after the notice of the board's decision was mailed [G.S. § 105-322(g)(2)a]. At the hearing, the board shall hear any pertinent evidence offered by the appellant, the assessor and other county officials. Upon the appellant's request, the board shall subpoena witnesses or documents if there is a reasonable basis for believing they may have pertinent information [G.S. § 105-322(g)(2)c]. After the hearing, the board may order the appraisal under appeal to be reduced, increased or confirmed and may order the property at issue to be listed or removed from the tax lists and must notify the appellant by mail of the action taken within thirty days after the board's adjournment [G.S. § 105-322(g)(2)d].

- *Meetings and adjournment*

Each year the board of equalization and review must hold its first meeting not earlier than the first Monday in April and not later than the first Monday in May. In years in which a county does not conduct a real property revaluation, the board must complete its duties on or before the third Monday following its first meeting unless, in its opinion, a longer period of time is necessary or expedient to a proper execution of its responsibilities. The board cannot, however, sit later than July 1 except to hear and determine timely requests for review. In the year in which a county conducts a real property revaluation, the board must complete its duties on or before December 1, except to hear and determine timely requests for review. The place and time of the meetings after the first meeting are within the discretion of the board [G.S. § 105-322(e)]. Proper notice of meetings and adjournments must be published [G.S. § 105-322(f)].

- *Duties after adjournment*

Following adjournment upon completion of its duties, the Board may continue to meet for the following purposes [G.S. § 105-322(g)(5)]:

    (1) To hear and decide all appeals relating to discovered property.

    (2) To hear and decide all appeals relating to appraisal, situs, and taxability of classified motor vehicles.

¶2502

(3) To hear and decide all appeals relating to audits of property classified at present-use value and property exempted or excluded from taxation.

(4) To hear and decide appeals relating to personal property.

¶2503 Property Tax Commission

The Property Tax Commission consists of five members, three appointed by the Governor and two appointed by the General Assembly [G.S. § 105-288(a)]. In its capacity as the State Board of Equalization and Review, the Property Tax Commission hears and adjudicates appeals from boards of county commissioners and county boards of equalization and review [G.S. § 105-290(a)]. These appeals are of two types: appeals from decisions concerning the listing, appraisal or assessment of property [G.S. § 105-290(b)] and appeals from orders adopting schedules of values, standards and rules [G.S. § 105-290(c)]. It also hears appeals from the appraisal and assessment of the property of public service companies [G.S. § 105-288(b)]. Public service companies are discussed at ¶2102.

• *Appeals of decisions concerning listing, appraisal and assessment*

Any property owner within a county may appeal an order of the county board of equalization and review or the county board of commissioners concerning the listing, appraisal, or assessment of property to the Property Tax Commission. Persons who have an ownership interest in the taxable property may file a joint appeal or separate appeals, as they elect [G.S. § 105-290(b)(1)].

Collection Activity Pending Appeal

When the board of county commissioners or municipal governing body delivers a tax receipt to a tax collector for any assessment that has been or is subsequently appealed to the Property Tax Commission, the tax collector may not seek collection of taxes or enforcement of a tax lien resulting from the assessment until the appeal has been finally adjudicated. The tax collector, however, may send an initial bill or notice to the taxpayer so that the taxpayer may, if the taxpayer chooses, pay the amount due and stop the running of interest on the amount in dispute [G.S. § 105-378].

• *Appeals from orders adopting schedules of values, standards and rules*

Before each revaluation of real property, the assessor must prepare schedules of values, standards and rules to be used in appraising real property at its true value and at its present-use value. The schedules must be sufficiently detailed to enable appraisers to adhere to them in making appraisals. The schedules must be reviewed and approved by the board of county commissioners before January 1 of the year they are to be applied [G.S. § 105-317(b)(1), (c)]. The courts have liberally construed these requirements and have upheld schedules that did not include standards for every factor that appraisers are required to consider under G.S. § 105-317(a), that included standards for government restrictions on the use of property without specifically listing each potential government restriction, and that did not contain sufficient detail to permit property owners (as opposed to appraisers) to understand the standard of value under which their property was appraised. *See In re Appeal of Parker*, 191 N.C. App. 313, 664 S.E.2d 1 (2008). A taxpayer who objects to a schedule of standards, values and rules must file an appeal under G.S. § 105-290(c) and will not be permitted to challenge the schedules in an appeal of an assessment based on those schedules. *See In re Appeal of Haney*, 08 PTC 330 (December 23, 2009).

• *Notice of appeal*

A notice of appeal filed with the Property Tax Commission must be in writing and must state the grounds for the appeal. A property owner who files a notice of appeal must send a copy of the notice to the appropriate county assessor [G.S. § 105-290(f)]. A notice of appeal from an order of a board of county commissioners, other than an order adopting a schedule of values, or from a board of equalization and review must be filed with the Property Tax Commission within 30 days after the date the board mailed a notice of its decision to the property owner [G.S. § 105-290(e)]. A notice of appeal from an order adopting a schedule of values must be filed within 30 days of the date when the order adopting the schedules, standards, and rules was first published [G.S. § 105-290(e)]. A notice of appeal submitted to the Property Tax Commission by United States mail is considered to be filed on the date shown on the postmark stamped by the United States Postal Service. A notice submitted by any other means is considered to be filed on the date it is received in the office of the Commission. If an appeal submitted by United States mail is not postmarked or the postmark does not show the date of mailing, the appeal is considered to be filed on the date it is received in the Commission office. The burden of proving timely filing is on the taxpayer [G.S. § 105-290(g)].

Incomplete Notice May Not Be Amended

A notice of appeal filed within the 30-day notice period but that fails to set forth any grounds for appeal is ineffective and may not be amended to state grounds for appeal after the notice period has run. *See In re Estate of Battle,* 166 N.C. App. 240, 601 S.E.2d 253 (2004).

• *Acknowledgment of notice and application for hearing*

Once a notice of appeal has been filed, the Property Tax Commission will send the appellant a written acknowledgment of the notice of appeal and an application for a hearing [17 NCAC 11.0212(a)]. Unless an extension has been requested and granted, the application for hearing must be filed within 30 days of the date of the letter of acknowledgment or the appeal may be dismissed. A copy of the completed application for hearing must also be sent to the county attorney at the same time [17 NCAC 11.0212(b)]. The county attorney is allowed 20 days from the receipt of the completed application for hearing to file a written Answer to the appeal, but the county's failure to file an Answer does not constitute a waiver of the county's rights or an admission of the appellant's allegations [17 NCAC 11.0212(c)].

• *Documents must be furnished*

At least 10 days prior to the date of the hearing, each party to the appeal must furnish the Commission with six copies of all documents to be introduced at the hearing [17 NCAC 11.0213]. Failure to furnish required documents may lead to dismissal of the appeal. *See, e.g., In re Appeal of Fayetteville Hotel Assocs.,* 117 N.C. App. 285, 450 S.E.2d 568 (1994), *aff'd per curiam,* 342 N.C. 405, 464 S.E.2d 298 (1995).

• *Requirement of pre-hearing order*

Parties must enter into a pre-hearing order before the appeal is set for hearing. This order will include stipulations as to parties, exhibits, witnesses, issues, and any other matters that can be stipulated by the parties [17 NCAC 11.0214].

Failure to Follow Rules Leads to Dismissal of Appeal

The appeal of a North Carolina property tax assessment was properly dismissed because the taxpayer failed to enter into a pre-hearing order with stipulations as to the parties, witnesses, issues, and other matters relating to the appeal [*In re the Appeal of Hershner,* N.C. App., No. COA03-861, April 20, 2004]. Another taxpayer's appeal was dismissed for failure to follow the Commission's rules with respect to furnishing copies of documents as well as failure to enter into a pre-hearing order [*In re Phillips,* 161 N.C. App. 173, 587 S.E.2d 465 (2003)]. *See also In re Appeal of Fayetteville Hotel Assocs.,* 117 N.C. App. 285, 450 S.E.2d 568 (1994), aff'd per curiam, 342 N.C. 405, 464 S.E.2d 298 (1995)], regarding dismissal of appeal for failure to furnish documents.

• *Representation by attorneys*

Individual taxpayers may present their own cases, but are encouraged to hire an attorney. Corporations and other business entities, which formerly were required to be represented by an attorney (see *In re Schwartz & Schwartz, Inc.,* 166 N.C. App. 744, 603 S.E.2d 852 (2004)), may now be represented by (1) an officer, (2) a manager or member-manager (in the case of a limited liability company), (3) a W-2 employee or (4) a 25% owner. In the case of a W-2 employee or 25% owner, the entity must authorize the representation in writing. Authority for and prior notice of non-attorney representation must be made in writing, under penalty of perjury, to the Property Tax Commission on a form to be provided by the Commission [G.S. § 105-290(d2)]. Counties are required to have an attorney [G.S. § 105-290(d2); 17 NCAC 11.0216)].

¶2504 Taxpayer's Burden of Proof — A Two-Pronged Test

The taxpayer's burden of proof in challenging an appraisal must meet the two-pronged test established by the North Carolina Supreme Court in *Appeal of AMP, Inc.,* 287 N.C. 547, 215 S.E.2d 752 (1975). The Court said that it is a sound and fundamental principle of law in this state that *ad valorem* tax assessments are presumed to be correct. Therefore, when *ad valorem* assessments are attacked or challenged, the taxpayer must produce "competent, material and substantial" evidence that tends to show that the county used an arbitrary or illegal method of valuation and that the assessment substantially exceeded the property's true value in money.

• *Presumption of correctness*

While assessments are presumed to be correct, the fact that the county applied its schedule of values in valuing the property at issue does not preclude a taxpayer from overcoming this presumption. *See, e.g., In re Blue Ridge Mall LLC,* 214 N.C. App. 263, 713 S.E.2d 779 (2011). *See also In re Appeal of Elkins,* 14 PTC 315 (2015) (presumption of correctness applies even where taxpayer seeks increased valuation). In addition, if a county abandons its assessed value in favor of a higher valuation offered by its expert in proceedings challenging the assessement, the presumption of correctness is lost. *See In re Appeal of Lowe's Center, LLC,* ___ N.C. App. ___ (2018).

• *Illegal or arbitrary methods*

An illegal or arbitrary appraisal method is one that will not result in true value. *See In re Appeal of Southern Ry. Co.,* 313 N.C. 177, 328 S.E.2d 235 (1985); *In re Lane Company-Hickory Chair Div.* 153 N.C. App. 119, 571 S.E.2d 224 (2002).

For examples of arbitrary methods of valuation, *see In re Appeal of Wenger,* 160 N.C. App. 250, 584 S.E.2d 108 (2003) (New Hanover County's method of assigning a value of $200,000 to any buildable waterfront property in a certain area and permitting a 50% reduction for unbuildable lots, regardless of other factors (*e.g.,* size, height above sea level, the presence of wetlands), held to be arbitrary); *In re Appeal of Performance Fibers, Inc.,* 05 PTC 690 (January 16, 2007) (Chatham County held to have used arbitrary method to value business personal property that taxpayer purchased in preceding year where County appraisal exceeded the appraised value of the same property in the preceding year in the hands of the seller), *In re Appeal of Murray,* 179 N.C. App. 780, 635 S.E.2d 477 (2006) (Durham County held to have used arbitrary or illegal appraisal method in appraising manufactured home located on land leased for less than 20 years using real property schedule of values, standards and rules); *In re Appeal of Speedway TBA, LLC,* 07 PTC 250 (June 26, 2009) (county valued racetrack in reliance on the cost method without taking obsolescence into account); *In re Appeal of Hendricks,* 08 PTC 070 (March 4, 2009) (county assigned a uniform value to all coastal lots located on dirt roads and did not take distance from beach into account); *In re Appeal of Edwards,* 07 PTC 891 (October 6, 2009) (county failed to adjust for land subject to right-of-way easement); *In re Appeal of Redman,* 07 PTC 980 (August 13,

2009) (county failed to apply its own schedule of standards, values and rules by not considering neighborhood quality, water and view quality and failed to consider that property lacked septic tanks); *In re Appeal of Daniel G. Kamin Westgate LLC*, 08 PTC 779 (2010) (county failed to apply its own schedule of standards, values and rules since there were errors as to grade, square footage and depreciation); *In re Appeal of Tryon-Columbus Retirement Associates, LLC*, 09 PTC 843 (May 11, 2012) (county misapplied its schedule of standards, values and rules in applying the cost method, and its schedule of standards, values and rules did not include any income model for applying the income method to the type of property at issue (assisted and independent living facility)); *In re Appeal of Maddrey*, 07 PTC 1032 (January 15, 2010) (county failed to consider location and topography of lot, fact that lot was not within a subdivision protected by restrictive covenants and failed to consider dangers associated with nearby lake levels); *In re Appeal of Thomas*, 08 PTC 123 (April 27, 2010) (county valued lot in uncompleted subdivision as if subdivision were completed); *In re Appeal of Wingate*, 08 PTC 460 (December 23, 2009) (county failed to consider the personal property factors set out in G.S. § 105-317.1 when valuing a mobile home); *In re Appeal of Davis*, 08 PTC 529 (February 25, 2010) (county valued subdivision lot at $205,000 where comparable lots in the same subdivision were valued at $146,000); *In re Appeal of May*, 09 PTC 065 (April 22, 2010), (county valued tract of land at $133,380 and valued adjacent tract comparable in size, location and desirability at $82,500); *In re Appeal of Reyner*, 09 PTC 714 (June 29, 2011) (county failed to consider reduction in value of lots due to incapacity to support suitable septic systems); *In re Appeal of Pace/Dowd Props. Ltd.*, 233 N.C. App. 7, 755 S.E.2d 401 (2014) (county failed to consider availability of water and sewer service to residential tract as required by G.S. § 105-317); *In re Appeal of Ballantyne Village Parking LLC*, 14 PTC 336 (2015) (county failed to consider perpetual easement granted by parking deck owner in favor of adjacent shopping center; value of parking deck reduced to zero); *In re Appeal of DLP Wilson Medical Center, Inc.*, 14 PTC 423 (2016) (county failed to consider super adequacy of hospital facilities); *In re Appeal of Corning, Inc.*, ___ N.C. App. ___, 786 S.E. 2d 816 (2016) (county incorrectly valued property as special purpose property rather than limited market property); *In re Appeal of Reynolds Mineral Inc.*, 15 PTC 0138 (2016) (appraisal of mineral rights arbitrary where county failed to consider size of parcels or quality of mineral deposits); *In re Appeal of Ravenswood of Wilson LLC*, 15 PTC 178 (2016) (county appraisal arbitrary where county derived its vacancy and capitalization rates from a prior non-appealed final decision of the Property Tax Commission involving a different taxpayer in lieu of an independent appraisal). *In re Appeal of Parkdale America, LLC*, 15 PTC 87 (2016) (county failed to give priority to sales comparison method in valuing older manufacturing facility and to consider obsolescence factors). *In re Appeal of Heirs of P.F. Mumford*, 15 PTC 0050 (2017) (county failed to consider absence of utility hook-ups and interior wiring); *In re Appeal of Shannon*, 16 PTC 0056 (2017) (county failed to consider costs of removing contamination caused by unauthorized dumping); *In re Appeal of Monbarren Family Partnership, Ltd*, 16 PTC 249 (2017) (county's comparable sales occurred two years before general reappraisal); *In re Appeal of Aluri*, 16 PTC 0044 (2017) (county failed to consider location of residential property near busy street or to rebut taxpayers' comparable sales); *In re Appeal Shelby Mall, LLC*, 16 PTC 0462 (2018) (county failed to provide convincing support of capitalization rate in valuing shopping mall using the income method); *In re Appeal of Shannon*, 16 PTC 0056 (2018) (county failed to consider that landfill property produced no income and that state environmental regulations required owner to clean up the site).

In the following cases, the taxpayers were not able to demonstrate that the county employed an arbitrary or illegal method: *In re Appeal of Kimberly-Clark Corporation*, 07 PTC 298 (March 13, 2009) (county's method of valuing 22-year old manufacturing plant was not arbitrary despite lack of discount for functional or economic obsolescence where no buildings had been torn down due to technological innovations and plant was otherwise functioning at 95% capacity); *In re Appeal of Gurganus,* 08 PTC 310 (February 25, 2010) (taxpayer failed to satisfy its burden where it produced a valuation of the subject property as of March 11 rather than January 1 of relevant tax year); *In re Appeal of Proctor,* 07 PTC 732 (2010) (taxpayer failed to demonstrate that lake level fluctuations and dredging activity affected value of lake-front property); *In re Appeal of Cash,* 09 PTC 270 (2010) (developer's failure to complete promised amenities and infrastructure did not justify reduction in assessed value); *In re Appeal of Liles,* 09 PTC 137 (2010) (taxpayer failed to demonstrate that purchase price paid for land and improvements near subject property at a foreclosure sale justified lower valuation of subject property); *In re Appeal of Geissler,* 10 PTC 320 (June 29, 2011) (taxpayer failed to demonstrate that purchase price paid for subject property at foreclosure sale after the valuation date justified lower valuation); *In re Appeal of Interstate Outdoor Inc.,* 763 S.E. 2d 172 (2014) (taxpayer failed to demonstrate that county valuation of road signs based on Department of Revenue's billboard valuation schedules was arbitrary or illegal where taxpayer's evidence involved similar properties rather than the specific properties in question); *In re Appeal of Lowes Home Centers, LLC,* 13 PTC 904 (2016) (taxpayer's appraiser considered only comparable properties that subject to restrictions prohibiting their highest and best use); *In re Appeal of Perdue Products Inc.,* 13 PTC 736 (2016) (taxpayer's appraiser considered only comparable properties that, unlike the subject property, were dark, closed or fore-closed and in different markets).

• *Appraisal substantially in excess of true value*

While there is no objective test of when an over-appraisal will be viewed as substantially in excess of true value, there is evidence that the Property Tax Commission may not view a appraisal that exceeds true value by only 5% to be substantial. *See In re Appeal of Harris,* 08 PTC 338 (2010).

• *Burden of production, not persuasion*

In *In re Appeal of IBM Credit Corp.,* 186 N.C. App. 223, 650 S.E.2d 828 (2007), *aff'd per curiam* 362 N.C. 228, 657 S.E.2d 355 (2008), the Court of Appeals, relying on *In re Appeal of Southern Ry. Co.,* 313 N.C. 177, 328 S.E.2d 235 (1985), held that the taxpayer's burden is one of production only and not persuasion. The taxpayer must offer evidence that the government's appraisal relies on illegal or arbitrary methods. In a second appeal, the Court of Appeals held that the taxpayer had satisfied its burden of production by producing a third-party valuation of the computer equipment at issue, offering expert testimony that the county's depreciation schedule did not properly account for functional and economic obsolescence and offering evidence that rapid changes in technology caused the equipment to depreciate rapidly in value. *See In re Appeal of IBM Credit Corp.,* 201 N.C. App. 343, 689 S.E.2d 487 (2009). *See also In re Appeal of Villas at Peacehaven, LLC,* __ N.C. App. __, 760 S.E. 2d 773 (2014) (taxpayer satisfied burden of production by introducing evidence that multi-unit residential property owned and operated by a single owner should have been valued as income-producing property rather than as separate parcels on a cost basis). For other examples of taxpayers who have satisfied the burden of production, *see, e.g., In re Appeal of Horton,* 10 PTC 053 (November 30, 2012) (evidence that county failed to consider that residential properties had no access to public sewers); *In re Appeal of Sara Lee Corporation,* 10 PTC 306 (December 21, 2012) (expert testimony of cost and comparable sales with respect to manufacturing facility); In re Appeal of King, 11 PTC 838 (June 21, 2013) (residential property owner's own testimony that county failed to consider "watershed issues"); *In re Appeal of Larson Place LLC,* 12 PTC 510 (July 30, 2013) (testimony of taxpayer's managing member that county's comparables were superior in quality to taxpayer's townhouses); *In re Appeal of Mebane Mill Lofts, LLC,* 12 PTC 561 (June 28, 2013) (expect testimony that county did not follow requirements of G.S. § 105-277.16 in valuing low-income housing units); *In re Appeal of Calderbank,* 12 PTC 588 (May 31, 2013) (testimony as to income capitalization value of apartment building and issues regarding ingress and egress and mail delivery). In some cases it may be sufficient for the taxpayer to satisfy its burden by producing an appraisal showing a value substantially below the assessed value. *See, e.g., In re Appeal of Smith*, 09 PTC 606 (June 30, 2011); *In re Appeal of Old Towne Yacht Club, Inc.*, 07 PTC 761 (2010).

Once the taxpayer has produced this evidence, the burden of proof then shifts to the taxing authority to persuade the tribunal that its methods would in fact produce true values. At this point the trier of fact must test the validity of the premises underlying the county's appraisal methodology. *See In re Appeal of IBM Credit Corp.*, 201 N.C. App. 343, 689 S.E.2d 487 (2009). The critical inquiry is whether the county's appraisal methodology was the proper means, given the characteristics of the property, of determining true value. The Property Tax Commission must do more than merely accept the county's valuation. It must hear and evaluate evidence from both sides, and its order should include findings of fact and conclusions of law supporting the application of these burdens. If it does not, the case may be remanded for further development. *See In re Parkdale Mills & Parldate Am.*, 225 N.C. App. 713, 741 S.E.2d 416 (2013). *See also In Parkdale Mills*, 240 N.C. App. 130, 770 S.E. 2d 152 (2015) (Property Tax Commission not required to hold further hearings on remand where the court had directed that such hearings be held "as necessary"). *See also In re IBM Credit Corp.*, 222 N.C. App. 418, 731 S.E.2d 444 (2012) (county failed to introduce evidence to support its valuation and court adopted taxpayer's valuation despite flaws in taxpayer's evidence).

• *Immaterial irregularities*

Immaterial Irregularities in the listing, appraisal and assessment of property or in the levy or collection of tax due will not invalidate the tax imposed [G.S. § 105-394]. Section 105-394 contains a list of irregularities that are considered immaterial, including the failure to assess property within the time permitted by law. This has been interpreted to permit a county to collect nine years of property tax plus interest on property that the taxpayer properly listed but which the county failed to timely assess through its own negligence. *In re Appeal of Morgan*, 362 N.C. 339, 661 S.E.2d 733 (2008), *rev'g* 186 N.C. App. 567, 652 S.E.2d 655 (2007).

¶2505 Judicial Appeal

Any party may appeal from a final order or decision of the Property Tax Commission to the Court of Appeals by filing a notice of appeal within 30 days after the entry of the order or decision. The notice of appeal must set out specifically the grounds for appeal and the errors alleged to have been committed by the Commission [G.S. § 105-345(a)]. A notice of appeal that fails to set out grounds for appeal may not be remedied by filing an amended notice after the running of the 30-day notice period. *See In re Estate of Battle*, 166 N.C. App. 240 (2004). The procedure for the appeal is provided by the rules of appellate procedure. Interlocutory orders of the Commission may not be appealed. *See In re Becky King Properties, LLC*, 234 N.C. App. 699, 760 S.E.2d 292 (2014). Failure to appeal the Commission's decision may result in further challenges to the property's valuation being barred as *res judicata, see In re Appeal of Black*, 14 PTC 432 (2015).

• *Condition precedent to judicial appeal*

No party to a Property Tax Commission proceeding may appeal a final order of the Commission unless a notice of appeal and exceptions is made within 30 days after the Property Tax Commission enters its final order or decision. The notice must set forth specifically the ground or grounds on which the aggrieved party considers the Property Tax Commission's decision or order to be unlawful, unjust, unreasonable, or unwarranted (including errors alleged to have been committed by the Property Tax Commission [G.S. § 105-345(a)]. The Property Tax Commission may set the exceptions to the final order upon which such appeal is based for further hearing before the commission [G.S. § 105-345(c)]. The aggrieved party must also mail a copy of the notice to each party to the proceeding at the addresses as they appear in the files of the Commission in the proceeding. However, the failure of any party, other than the Commission, to be served with or to receive a copy of the notice of appeal does not affect the validity or regularity of the appeal [G.S. § 105-345(b)].

• *Standard of review*

In reviewing decisions by the Property Tax Commission, the Court of Appeals applies the "whole record test" under which the decision of the Commission will be sustained if its findings and conclusions are supported by substantial evidence (*i.e.,* evidence that a reasonable mind might accept as adequate to support a conclusion). Under this standard of review, the Court must affirm the Commission's finding and conclusions if they are supported by substantial evidence, even if there is evidence that would have supported a contrary finding [G.S. § 105-345.2(c). See also, *e.g., In re Maharishi Spiritual Ctr. of Am.,* 357 NC 152, 579 S.E.2d 249 (2003) (adopting dissenting opinion in *In re Maharishi Spiritual Ctr. of Am.,* 152 N.C. App. 269, 569 S.E.2d 3, (2002); *In re Univ. for the Study of Human Goodness & Creative Group Work,* 159 N.C. App. 85, 582 S.E.2d 645 (2003); *In re North Wilkesboro Speedway, Inc.,* 158 N.C. App. 669, 582 S.E.2d 39 (2003); *In re Master's Mission,* 152 N.C. App. 640, 568 S.E.2d 208 (2002)].

¶2506 Special Rule for Personal Property

The first level of appeals concerning the value, situs, or taxability of personal property may be made to the county assessor, and appeals of the assessor's decision may be made to the board of equalization and review or, if that board is not in session, to the board of county commissioners [G.S. § 105-317.1(c)].

A taxpayer who owns personal property taxable in a county may appeal the value, situs, or taxability of the property within 30 days after the date of the initial notice of value. If the assessor does not give separate written notice of the value to the taxpayer at the taxpayer's last known address, the bill serves as notice of the value of the personal property. The notice must contain a statement that the taxpayer may appeal the value, situs, or taxability of the property within 30 days after the date of the notice.

When the assessor receives a timely appeal, the assessor must arrange a conference with the taxpayer to afford the taxpayer the opportunity to present any evidence or argument with regard to the value, situs, or taxability of the property.

Within 30 days after the conference, the assessor must give notice to the taxpayer of the assessor's final decision. Written notice is not required if the taxpayer signs an agreement accepting the value, situs, or taxability of the property. If an agreement is not reached, the taxpayer has 30 days from the date of the notice of the assessor's final decision to request review by the board of equalization and review or, if that board is not in session, by the board of county commissioners. Unless the request for review is given at the conference, it must be made in writing to the assessor.

PART IX

PRIVILEGE TAXES

CHAPTER 26

PRIVILEGE TAXES

¶2601 Privilege Taxes in General

Article 2 of Chapter 105 of the North Carolina General Statutes imposes privilege taxes on certain specified occupations, businesses or activities. Privilege taxes are administered by the Excise Tax Division of the Department of Revenue.

• *Change of name or ownership*

Neither a change in the name of a firm, partnership, or corporation nor the taking in or withdrawal of a new partner is considered as commencing business (thus requiring a new license). If any one or more of the partners remain in the firm, or if there is a change in ownership of less than a majority of the stock of a corporation, the business is regarded as continuing [G.S. § 105-106].

• *Penalties*

The penalties imposed by Article 9 apply to the State privilege taxes. Penalties are discussed at ¶ 3204. The same penalty provisions apply to local license taxes [G.S. § 105-109(d) and (e)].

• *Property used in a license business*

A State license shall not be construed to exempt property used in a licensed business from other forms of taxation [G.S. § 105-108].

• *Liability on transfer*

The transferee of any business or property subject to an Article 2 privilege tax must make diligent inquiry into whether the tax has been paid. However, an innocent purchase of such business or property for value and without notice that the tax has not been paid takes such business or property without any lien for such taxes [G.S. § 105-33(h)].

¶2602 Privilege License Tax on Professionals

Every individual in North Carolina who practices a profession or engages in a business in the list below must obtain from the Secretary a statewide license for the privilege of practicing the profession or engaging in the business. This license is not transferable to another person and is imposed at the flat rate of $50 [G.S. § 105-41(i)]. Licenses issued under G.S. § 105-41 are issued as personal privilege licenses and are not issued in the name of a firm or corporation [G.S. § 105-41(e)]. Obtaining a personal privilege license by itself does not authorize the practice of a profession, business, or trade for which a State qualification license is required [G.S. § 105-41(i)].

The businesses and professions that are subject to a license tax under G.S. § 105-41 are as follows:

(1) *Attorney-at-law* [G.S. § 105-41(a)(1)];

(2) *Physician, veterinarian, surgeon, osteopath, chiropractor, chiropodist, dentist, ophthalmologist, optician, optometrist, massage and bodywork therapist* or *another person who practices a professional art of healing* [G.S. § 105-41(a)(2)]. Licensed respiratory therapists working as employees under the direction of a physician are not subject to the privilege tax. See PTPLR 2018-1;

(3) *Professional engineer* [G.S. § 105-41(a)(3)]. A "professional engineer" is a person who has been duly licensed as a professional engineer by the North Carolina State Board of Examiners for Engineers and Surveyors [G.S. § 89C-3(8)];

(4) *Registered land surveyor* [G.S. § 105-41(a)(4)]. A person who has been licensed as a professional land surveyor by the North Carolina State Board of Examiners for Engineers and Surveyors [G.S. § 89C-3(9)];

(5) *Architect* [G.S. § 105-41(a)(5)];

(6) *Landscape architect* [G.S. § 105-41(a)(6)];

(7) *Photographer, canvasser for any photographer,* or *agent of a photographer in transmitting photographs to be copied, enlarged, or colored* [G.S. § 105-41(a)(7)]. A licensed photographer having a located place of business in North Carolina is liable for a license tax on each agent or solicitor employed for soliciting business [G.S. § 105-41(e)];

(8) *Real estate broker* [G.S. § 105-41(a)(8)]. A "real estate broker" is any person, partnership, corporation, limited liability company, association, or other business entity who, for a compensation or valuable consideration (or promise thereof) engages in real estate activities [G.S. § 93A-2(b)];

(9) *Real estate appraiser* [G.S. § 105-41(a)(9)]. A "real estate appraiser" is a person who (for a fee or valuable consideration) develops and communicates real estate appraisals or otherwise gives an opinion of the value of real estate or any real estate interest [G.S. § 93E-1-4(11)];

(10) *A person who solicits or negotiates loans on real estate as agent for another* for a commission, brokerage, or other compensation [G.S. § 105-41(a)(10)];

(11) *Funeral directors, etc.* [G.S. § 105-41(a)(11)]. A funeral director, embalmer or funeral service licensee licensed under G.S. § 90-210.25 by the North Carolina Board of Mortuary Science;

(12) *Home inspectors* [G.S. § 105-41(a)(12)]licensed under Article 9F of Chapter 143, effective for taxable years beginning on or after July 1, 2008; and

(13) *Accountant* [G.S. § 105-41(c)]. An "accountant" for this purpose is a person engaged in the public practice of accounting as a principal or as a manager of the business of public accountant [G.S. § 105-41(c)]. In addition to a license fee of $50, accountants must pay a license fee of $12.50 for each person

employed who is engaged in the capacity of supervising or handing the work of auditing, devising, or installing systems of accounts [G.S. § 105-41(c)].

Local Taxation Prohibited

Counties and cities are not authorized to levy any license tax on the businesses or professions taxable under G.S. § 105-41 [G.S. § 105-41(h)].

Exempt persons: The following persons are exempt from the foregoing privilege license tax:

(1) *Elderly person* [G.S. § 105-41(b)(1)]. An "elderly person" for this purpose is an individual who is at least 75 years old;

(2) *Religious healer* [G.S. § 105-41(b)(2)]. A "religious healer" for this purpose is a person who practices the professional art of healing for a fee or reward who (i) is an adherent of an established church or religious organization and (ii) confines the healing practice to prayer or spiritual means; and

(3) *Blind person* [G.S. § 105-41(b)(3)]. A "blind person" for this purpose is any person who is totally blind or whose central visual acuity does not exceed 2/200 in the better eye with correcting lenses, or where the widest diameter of visual field subtends an angle no greater than 20 degrees. The exemption applies only to a blind person who is engaged in a trade or business as a sole proprietor.

NOTE: The exemption does not extend to any sole proprietor who permits more than one person (other than the proprietor) to work regularly in the trade or profession for compensation of any kind, unless the other person in excess of one is a blind person [G.S. § 105-41(b)(3)].

• *Due date*

The tax is imposed for the fiscal year that begins on the July 1 due date of the return. The full amount of a license tax applies to a person who, during a fiscal year, begins to engage in an activity which requires a license. Before a person engages in an activity for which a license is required, the person must obtain the license. The tax is due by July 1 of each year [G.S. § 105-33(b)].

• *Obtaining Licenses*

Before a person may engage in a business, trade, or profession for which a license is required, the person must be licensed by the Department of Revenue [G.S. § 105-109(b)]. It is unlawful to operate without a required license. No person is allowed the privilege of exercising any business, trade, employment, profession, or the doing of any act taxed under Article 2 throughout North Carolina under one license, except under a statewide license [G.S. § 105-103]. To obtain a license, a person must submit an application to the Department for the license and pay the required tax. An application for a license is considered a return. The Department must issue a license to a person who files a completed application and pays the required tax [G.S. § 105-109(b)]. A person, firm, or corporation must have a license for each separate business, trade, employment, or profession [G.S. § 105-105]. A license must be displayed conspicuously at the location of the license business, trade, or profession [G.S. § 105-109(b)]. If a person engages in more than one business, profession or activity subject to a privilege license tax, the tax must be paid for each separate business, trade or profession [G.S. § 105-105].

¶2602

¶2603 Privilege Tax on Loan Agencies

• *Imposition and rate*

Every person, firm, or corporation engaged in any of the following businesses must pay for the privilege of engaging in that business an annual tax of $250 for each location at which the business is conducted [G.S. § 105-88(a)]:

(1) The business of making loans or lending money, accepting liens on, or contracts of assignments of, salaries or wages, or any part thereof, or other security or evidence of debt for repayment of such loans in installment payment or otherwise.

(2) The business of check cashing regulated under Article 22 of Chapter 53 of the North Carolina General Statutes.

(3) The business of pawnbroker regulated under Part I of Article 45 of the North Carolina General Statutes.

Local Jurisdictions

Counties, cities, and towns may levy a loan agency license tax generally not in excess of $100 [G.S. § 105-88(e)].

• *Exemptions*

The loan agency license fee does not apply to banks, industrial banks, trust companies, savings and loan associations, cooperative credit unions, the business of negotiating loans on real estate described above, or insurance premium finance companies licensed under Article 35 of Chapter 58 of the North Carolina General Statutes. No real estate mortgage broker is required to obtain a loan agency license merely because the broker advances his/her own funds and takes a security interest in real estate to secure the advances and who has arranged, or intends to arrange, to sell or discount the obligation [G.S. § 105-88(b)].

• *Requirement of written agreement*

The person or officer of the firm or corporation making the loan must, at the time the loan is made, give to the borrower in writing in convenient form a statement showing the amount received by the borrower, the amount to be paid back by the borrower, the time in which the amount is to be paid, and the rate of interest and discount agreed upon [G.S. § 105-88(c)].

• *Loan made without license*

A loan made by a person who does not comply with the loan agency privilege license tax requirements is not collectible at law in North Carolina [G.S. § 105-88(d)].

¶2604 Privilege Tax on Installment Paper Dealers

• *Impositions*

A privilege tax is imposed on every person engaged in the business of dealing in, buying, or discounting installment paper, notes, bonds, contracts, or evidences of debt for which, at the time of or in connection with the execution of the instruments, a lien is reserved or taken upon personal property located in North Carolina to secure the payment of the obligations. The tax is imposed at the rate of 0.237% of the face amount of the obligation [G.S. § 105-83(a)].

• *Nexus*

The tax is imposed on the privilege of dealing in installment paper. Although a dealer in installment paper must secure repayment of the obligations by acquiring a lien on personal property located in North Carolina, no other connection to North

Carolina is required. The North Carolina Court of Appeals has specifically ruled that the taxpayer need not engage in any business activity in North Carolina to become subject to the tax [*Navistar Fin. Corp. v. Tolson*, 176 N.C. App. 217, 625 S.E.2d 852, *rev. denied*, 360 N.C. 482, 632 S.E.2d 176 (2006). *See also Administrative Decision No. 418* (2003)]. Under a prior version of the installment paper dealer privilege tax, some activity incident to the sale and purchase was required to takes place in North Carolina in order to subject the dealer to tax. *See Chrysler Fin. Co., LLC v. Offerman*, 138 N.C. App 268, 531 S.E.2d 223, *rev. denied*, 352 N.C. 588, 544 S.E.2d 777 (2000). See also the discussion of the term "dealing" for corporate income tax purposes in *A&F Trademark, Inc. v. Tolson*, 167 N.C. App. 150, 605 S.E.2d 187 (2004), *appeal dismissed*, 359 N.C. 320 (2005), *cert. den.*, 546 U.S. 821 (2005).

• *Reports and payment of tax*

The taxpayer must submit quarterly reports to the Secretary no later than January 20, April 20, July 20, and October 20 of each year [G.S. § 105-83(a)]. A person who fails to pay the tax cannot bring an action in a North Carolina court to enforce collection of an installment paper until the tax is paid, with penalties and interest [G.S. § 105-83(c)]. Counties and cities are not authorized to levy any license tax on businesses subject to the installment payer dealer tax [G.S. § 105-83(c)]. This tax does not apply to savings and loan associations or corporations liable for the bank privilege tax (see above) [G.S. § 105-83(d)].

¶2605 County Privilege License Taxes

• *General authority*

Counties have no authority to levy privilege license taxes except as specifically authorized by statute [S.L. 2014-3, § 12.3(a)].

• *Specific authority*

A county may impose privilege taxes on malt beverage and wine retailers [G.S. § 105-113.78] and pets [G.S. § 153A-153].

¶2606 City Privilege License Taxes

• *General authority*

Cities have no authority to levy privilege license taxes except as specifically authorize by statute [S.L. 2014-3 § 12.1].

• *Specific authority*

A city may impose privilege taxes on malt beverage and wine retailers [G.S. § 105-113.77], beer and wine wholesalers [G.S. § 105-113.79], pets [G.S. § 160A-212], motor vehicles [G.S. § 20-97], and taxicab and limousine services [G.S. § 20-97].

PART X

EMPLOYMENT SECURITY TAX

CHAPTER 27

STATE UNEMPLOYMENT TAX

¶2701 In General

Unemployment insurance is a joint federal-state program that provides benefits to employees during periods of temporary unemployment. The program is financed through federal and state taxes on employers. The federal rate is 6% of a taxable wage base capped at $7,000. Employers are entitled to a credit against their federal unemployment tax liability for contributions to state unemployment insurance funds. The credit may not exceed 90% of the federal tax due. As a result, the effective federal tax rate for most employers is 0.6% of taxable wages. Federal unemployment taxes are used to fund administration of the program, while state unemployment taxes are used to fund unemployment benefits.

Taxes on employers under North Carolina's unemployment tax are referred to as "contributions" and are paid into the Unemployment Insurance Fund [G.S. § 96-9.1]. The tax is a direct tax on employers and is not withheld from employee wages [G.S. § 96-9.2(a)]. Amounts paid into the Unemployment Insurance Fund are transferred to the federal Unemployment Trust Fund established under the Social Security Act and credited to North Carolina's account in that fund. The State requisitions moneys held in the State's account in the Unemployment Trust Fund to pay unemployment benefits [G.S. § 96-6].

Title XII of the Social Security Act provides for automatic advances from the federal government to the states if state unemployment insurance funds are insufficient. Federal advances are repaid by automatic reductions in the credit against the federal unemployment tax for employer contributions to state unemployment insurance funds.

An employer must make an unemployment insurance contribution to North Carolina's Unemployment Insurance Fund each calendar year. The amount of the contribution is determined by multiplying the "taxable wages" paid by the "employer" to "employees" for "services performed in North Carolina" by the employer's "contribution rate" [G.S. § 96-9.2(a)]. Each of these terms is discussed below.

¶2702 Employers and Employees

All "employers" are required to make contributions to the State Unemployment Insurance Fund [G.S. §96-9.2(a)]. An "employer" is defined as (1) an employer as defined in section 3306 of the Code, (2) a State or local governmental unit required to provide unemployment compensation coverage to its employees under section 3309 of the Code, (3) a nonprofit organization required to provide unemployment compensation coverage to its employees under section 3309 of the Code or (4) an Indian tribe required to provide unemployment compensation coverage to its employees under section 3309 of the Code [G.S. §96-1(b)(11)].

For purposes of the state unemployment tax, the term "employee" has the meaning set forth in Code section 3306 [G.S. §96-1(b)(10)].

See ¶3312 for disaster-response relief provisions.

¶2703 Taxable Wages

"Wages" has the meaning set forth in Code section 3306 without regard to the $7,000 wage base cap of Code section 3306(b)(1) [G.S. §96-1(b)(28)].

The "taxable wages" of an employee is an amount equal to the greater of (1) the federal taxable wages set forth in section 3306 of the Code or (2) 50% of the average yearly insured wage, rounded to the nearest multiple of $100. The average yearly insured wage is the average weekly wage on the "computation date" multiplied by 52 [G.S. §96-9.3(a)]. The average weekly wage is the weekly rate obtained by dividing the total wages reported by all insured employers for a calendar year by the average monthly number of individuals in insured employment during that year and then dividing that quotient by 52 [G.S. §96-1(b)(2)]. The "computation date" is August 1 of each year [G.S. §96-1(b)(7)].

An employer is not liable for contributions on wages paid to an employee in excess of taxable wages [G.S. §96-9.3(a)]. The following wages are included in determining whether the amount of wages paid to an individual in a single calendar year exceeds taxable wages: (1) wages paid to an individual in North Carolina by an employer that made contributions in another state upon the wages paid to the individual because the work was performed in the other state, and (2) wages paid by a successor employer to an individual if (i) the individual was an employee of the predecessor and was taken over as an employee by the successor as a part of the organization acquired, (ii) the predecessor employer paid contributions on the wages paid to the individual while in the predecessor's employ during the year of acquisition and (iii) the account of the predecessor is transferred to the successor [G.S. §96-9.3(b)].

The Department of Commerce's Division of Employment Security is required to determine the taxable wages for each calendar year [G.S. §96-9.3(a)].

¶2704 Services Performed in North Carolina

Only taxable wages for services performed in North Carolina are taken into account in computing an employer's contribution [G.S. §96-9.2(a)]. A service is performed in North Carolina if it meets one or more of the following descriptions [G.S. §96-9.5]:

(1) The service is localized in North Carolina, *i.e.*, it is performed entirely inside North Carolina or it is performed both inside and outside the State, but the service performed outside the State is incidental to the service performed inside the State (as where the service performed outside the State is temporary or transitory in nature or consists of isolated transactions).

(2) Some of the service is performed in North Carolina, and one or more of the following applies: (i) the base of operations is in North Carolina, (ii) there is

no base of operations and the place from which the service is directed or controlled is in North Carolina, or (iii) the service is not performed in any state that has a base of operations or a place from which the service is directed or controlled and the individual who performs the service is a resident of North Carolina.

(3) The service is performed anywhere within the United States or Canada, the service is not covered under the employment security law of any other state or Canada, and the place from which the service is directed or controlled is in North Carolina.

(4) The service is performed outside the United States or Canada by a citizen of the United States in the employ of an American employer (as defined in Code section 3306) and at least one of the following applies: (i) the employer's principal place of business in the United States is located in North Carolina; (ii) the employer has no place of business in the United States, but the employer is an individual who is a resident of North Carolina, a corporation that is organized under the laws of North Carolina, a partnership or a trust if more of its partners or trustees are residents of North Carolina than of any other state, or a limited liability company if more of its members are residents of North Carolina than of any other state; (iii) the employer has elected coverage in North Carolina in accordance with G.S. § 96-9.9; or (iv) the employer has not elected coverage in any state and the employee has filed a claim for benefits under the law of North Carolina based on the service provided to the employer.

¶2705 Contribution Rate

Employer contributions to the state Unemployment Insurance Fund are computed by multiplying the employer's taxable wages for services performed in North Carolina by the employer's contribution rate [G.S. § 96-9.2(a)]. The Division of Employment Security must notify an employer of the employer's contribution rate for a calendar year by January 1 of that year. The contribution rate becomes final unless the employer files an application for review and redetermination before May 1 following the effective date of the contribution rate. The Division of Employment Security may redetermine the contribution rate on its own motion within the same time period [G.S. § 96-9.2(d)].

• *Contribution rate for beginning employer*

The contribution rate for a beginning employer is 1%. A beginning employer is any employer until the employer's account has been chargeable with benefits for at least 12 calendar months ending July 31 immediately preceding the August 1 computation date. An employer's account has been chargeable with benefits for at least 12 calendar months if the employer has reported wages paid in four completed calendar quarters and these quarters are in two consecutive calendar years [G.S. § 96-9.2(b)].

• *Contribution rate for experience-rated employer*

For experience-rated employers, *i.e.*, all employers not treated as beginning employers, the contribution rate is determined as described below [G.S. § § 96-9.2(c) and 96-9.4].

First, the employer's "reserve ratio" is determined. The reserve ratio is the quotient, expressed as a percentage, obtained by dividing the employer's account balance on the computation date (August 1) by the total taxable payroll of the employer for the 36 calendar month period ending June 30 preceding the computation date. The employer's account balance, which is determined by the Division of Employment Security, is the total of all contributions and other amounts credited to the employer for all past periods reduced by the total amount of all benefits charged to the employer's account for all past periods. If the Division finds that an employer failed to file a report or finds that a report filed by an employer is incorrect or insufficient, the Division must determine the employer's account balance based upon the best information available to it and must notify the employer that it will use this balance to determine the employer's reserve ratio unless the employer provides additional information within 15 days of the date of the notice.

Second, the employer's reserve ratio is multiplied by 0.68 to produce the employer's "Employer Reserve Ratio Percentage" or "ERRP".

Third, the "UI Trust Fund Balance as a Percentage of Total Insured Wages" is determined by dividing the State's account in the Unemployment Trust Fund by the total wages reported by all insured employers for the 12-month period ending on July 31 preceding the August 1 computation date.

Fourth, the employer's rough contribution rate is determined based on the UI Trust Fund Balance as a Percentage of Total Insured Wages. If that percentage is less than or equal to 1%, the employer's rough contribution rate is 2.9% minus the employer's ERRP. If that percentage is greater than 1% but less than or equal to 1.25%, the employer's rough contribution rate is 2.4% minus the employer's ERRP. If that percentage is greater than 1.25%, the employer's rough contribution rate is 1.9% minus the employer's ERRP. This calculation is made as of September 1 following the computation date.

Fifth, the employer's rough contribution rate is rounded to the nearest one-hundredth percent (0.01%).

The employer's contribution rate is the rounded contribution rate computed as described above subject to the minimum and maximum contribution rates. The minimum contribution rate is 0.06%. The maximum contribution rate is 5.76%.

• *Additional contributions*

An employer may make a voluntary contribution to the Unemployment Insurance Fund in addition to its required contribution. An additional voluntary contribution is credited to the employer's account. An additional voluntary contribution made by an employer within 30 days after the date on an annual notice of its contribution rate is considered to have been made as of the previous July 31 [G.S. §96-9.2(e)].

¶2706 Surtax

Any employer who is required to make a contribution to the Unemployment Insurance Fund must also pay a surtax equal to 20% of the required contribution [G.S. §96-9.7]. The surtax is paid into a reserve fund used to repay interest and principal on federal advances to the State to make up for shortfalls in the State's Unemployment Insurance Fund [G.S. §96-6.1]. The surtax does not apply in a calendar year if, as of September 1 of the preceding calendar year, the amount in the State's account in the Unemployment Trust Fund equals or exceeds $1,000,000,000 [G.S. §96-9.7(b)].

¶2707 Reimbursing Employers

• *Applicability*

Code section 3309 requires states to permit governmental entities, nonprofit organizations, and Indian tribes to elect not to make contributions to the state unemployment insurance fund but instead to reimburse the fund for benefits paid attributable to covered service for such employers [G.S. §96-9.6(a)].

• *Election*

An employer entitled to elect the reimbursement option may do so by filing a written notice of its election with the Division of Employment Security at least 30 days before the January 1 effective date of the election. An Indian tribe may make separate elections for itself and each subdivision, subsidiary, or business enterprise wholly owned by the tribe. A new employer may make the election by filing a written notice of its election within 30 days after it receives notification from the Division that it is eligible to make a reimbursement election [G.S. § 96-9.6(b)].

Once made, an election is valid for a minimum of four years and is binding until the employer files a notice terminating its election. An employer must file a written notice of termination with the Division of Employment Security at least 30 days before the January 1 effective date of the termination [G.S. § 96-9.6(b)].

The Division must notify an employer of a determination of the effective date of an election and of any termination of the election. These determinations are subject to reconsideration, appeal, and review. An employer that makes a reimbursement election may not deduct the amount of any reimbursement payment any from the remuneration of the individuals it employs [G.S. § 96-9.6(b)].

• *Reimbursable amount*

A reimbursing employer must reimburse the Unemployment Insurance Fund for the amount of benefits that are paid to an individual for weeks of unemployment that begin within a benefit year established during the effective period of the employer's election and are attributable to service that is covered by section 3309 of the Code and was performed in the employ of the employer [G.S. § 96-9.6(c)].

• *Account*

The Division of Employment Security must establish a separate account for each reimbursing employer. The Division must credit payments made by the employer to the account. The Division must charge to the account benefits that are paid by the Unemployment Insurance Fund to individuals for weeks of unemployment that begin within a benefit year established during the effective period of the election and are attributable to service in the employ of the employer. All benefits paid must be charged to the employer's account except benefits paid through error [G.S. § 96-9.6(d)].

The Division must furnish an employer with a statement of all credits and charges made to its account as of the August 1 computation date before January 1 of the succeeding year. The Division may, in its sole discretion, provide a reimbursing employer with informational bills or lists of charges on a basis more frequent than yearly if the Division finds it is in the best interest of the Division and the affected employer to do so [G.S. § 96-9.6(d)].

• *Annual reconciliation*

A reimbursing employer must maintain an account balance equal to 1% of its taxable wages. The Division of Employment Security must determine the balance of each employer's account on the August 1 computation date. If there is a deficit in the account, the Division must bill the employer for the amount necessary to bring its account to 1% of its taxable wages for the four quarters immediately preceding July 1. Any amount in the account in excess of 1% of taxable wages is retained in the employer's account as a credit and is not refunded to the employer. The Division must send a bill as soon as practical. Payment is due within 30 days from the date a bill is mailed. Amounts unpaid by the due date accrue interest and penalties in the same manner as past-due contributions and are subject to the same collection remedies provided for past-due contributions [G.S. § 96-9.6(e)].

• *Quarterly wage reports*

A reimbursing employer must submit quarterly wage reports to the Division of Employment Security on or before the last day of the month following the close of the calendar quarter in which the wages are paid. During the first four quarters following an election to be a reimbursing employer, the employer must submit an advance payment with its quarterly report. The amount of the advance payment is equal to 1% of the taxable wages reported on the quarterly wage report. The Division must remit the payments to the Unemployment Insurance Fund and credit the payments to the employer's account [G.S. § 96-9.6(f)].

• *Change in election*

The Division of Employment Security must close the account of an employer that has been paying contributions and then elects to become a reimbursing employer. A closed account may not be used in any future computation of a contribution rate. The Division must close the account of an employer that terminates its election to be a reimbursing employer. An employer that terminates its election to be a reimbursing employer is treated as a beginning employer [G.S. § 96-9.6(g)].

• *Noncompliance by Indian tribes*

A reimbursing Indian tribe that fails to comply with the rules applicable to reimbursing employers may be required to become a contributing employer or may lose covered employment [G.S. § 96-9.6(h)]. Specifically:

An employer that fails to pay an amount due within 90 days after receiving a bill and has not paid this liability as of the computation date loses the option to make reimbursable payments in lieu of contributions for the following calendar year. An employer that loses the option to make reimbursable payments in lieu of contributions for a calendar year regains that option for the following calendar year if it pays its outstanding liability and makes all contributions during the year for which the option was lost.

Services performed for an employer that fails to make reimbursing payments, including interest and penalties, after all collection activities considered necessary by the Division of Employment Security have been exhausted, are no longer treated as "employment" for the purpose of unemployment security coverage. An employer that has lost coverage regains coverage for services performed if the Division determines that all contributions, payments in lieu of contributions, penalties, and interest have been paid. The Division must notify the Internal Revenue Service and the United States Department of Labor of any termination or reinstatement of coverage.

¶2708 Voluntary Contributions

Several classes of employers may elect to be subject to the contribution requirement and thereby provide benefit coverage for their employees. Specifically [G.S. § 96-9.8(a)]:

(1) An employer that is not otherwise liable for contributions may elect to make contributions to the same extent as an employer that is liable for those contributions.

(2) An employer that pays for services that are not otherwise subject to the contribution requirement may elect to make contributions on those services performed by individuals in its employ in one or more distinct establishments or places of business.

(3) An employer that employs the services of an individual who resides within North Carolina but performs the services entirely outside the State may elect to have the individual's service constitute employment subject to contributions if no contributions are required or paid with respect to the services under an employment security law of any other state or of the federal government.

• *Election*

Employers who elect to make contributions must file an application with the Division of Employment Security. An election is effective on the date stated by the

Division in a letter approving the election. An election is irrevocable for the two-year period beginning on the effective date [G.S. § 96-9.8(b)].

• *Termination of coverage*

Termination by Division of Employment Security. The Division of Employment Security may, on its own motion, terminate the coverage of an employer who has elected to make contributions as described above. This termination may occur within the two-year minimum election period. The Division must give the employer 30 days written notice of a decision to terminate an election. The notice must be mailed to the employer's last known address [G.S. § 96-9.8(c)].

Termination by employer. An employer that has elected coverage may, after the two-year minimum election period, terminate the election by filing a notice of termination with the Division of Employment Security. The notice must be given before the first day of March following the first day of January of the calendar year for which the employer wishes to cease coverage [G.S. § 96-9.8(c)].

¶2709 Reports and Payments

• *Reports*

An "Employer's Quarterly Wage and Tax Report" is due on or before the last day of the month following the close of the calendar quarter in which the wages are paid [G.S. § 96-9.15(a) and (d)].

An employer or an agent of an employer that reports wages for at least 25 employees (10 employees beginning January 1, 2019) must file the portion of the "Employer's Quarterly Tax and Wage Report" that contains the name, social security number, and gross wages of each employee in a format prescribed by the Division of Employment Security. An employer that fails to comply with the reporting requirements is subject to a penalty of $25. An agent of an employer who fails to comply with the reporting requirements may be denied the right to report wages and file reports for that employer for a period of one year following the calendar quarter in which the agent filed the improper report. The Division may reduce or waive a penalty for good cause shown [G.S. § 96-9.15(d)].

The Division may authorize an employer of domestic service employees to file an annual report and to file that report by telephone. An annual report is due on or before the last day of the month following the close of the calendar year in which the wages are paid. A domestic service employer that files a report by telephone must contact either the tax auditor assigned to the employer's account or the Division of Employment Security and report the required information to that auditor or to that section by the date the report is due [G.S. § 96-9.15(f)].

• *Payments*

Contributions are payable when a report is due. If the amount of the contributions shown to be due after all credits is less than $5.00, no payment need be made [G.S. § 96-9.15(a)].

An employer may pay contributions by electronic funds transfer. When an electronic funds transfer cannot be completed due to insufficient funds or the nonexistence of an account of the transferor, the Division of Employment Security may assess a penalty equal to 10% of the amount of the transfer, subject to a minimum of $1 and a maximum of $1,000. The Division may waive this penalty for good cause shown [G.S. § 96-9.15(c)].

The Division may also allow an employer to pay contributions by credit card. An employer that pays by credit card must include an amount equal to any fee charged by the Division for the use of the card. A payment of taxes that is made by credit card and is not honored by the card issuer does not relieve the employer of the obligation to pay the taxes [G.S. § 96-9.15(c)].

An employer that does not pay by electronic funds transfer or by credit card must pay by check or cash. A check must be drawn on a United States bank and cash must be in currency of the United States [G.S. § 96-9.15(c)].

• *Overpayment*

If an employer remits an amount in excess of the amount of contributions due, including any applicable penalty and interest, the excess amount remitted is considered an overpayment. The Division of Employment Security must refund an overpayment unless the amount of the overpayment is less than $5. Overpayments of less than $5 may be refunded only upon receipt of a written demand for the refund from the employer within the time allowed under G.S. § 96-10(e) [G.S. § 96-9.15(b)].

• *Jeopardy assessment*

The Secretary may immediately assess and collect a contribution the Secretary finds is due from an employer if the Secretary determines that collection of the tax is in jeopardy and immediate assessment and collection are necessary in order to protect the interest of the State and the Unemployment Insurance Fund [G.S. § 96-9.15(e)].

¶2710 Administration of Accounts

• *Employer accounts*

The Division of Employment Security must maintain a separate account for each employer. The Division must credit the employer's account with all contributions paid by the employer or on the employer's behalf and must charge the employer's account for benefits paid. The Division must prepare an annual statement of all charges and credits made to the employer's account during the 12 months preceding the August 1 computation date. The Division must send the statement to the employer when the Division notifies the employer of the employer's contribution rate for the succeeding calendar year. The Division may provide a statement of charges and credits more frequently upon a request by the employer [G.S. § 96-11.1].

• *Allocation of charges to base period employers*

Benefits paid to an individual are charged to an employer's account quarterly. Benefits paid to an individual must be allocated to the account of each base period employer in the proportion that the base period wages paid to the individual in a calendar quarter by each base period employer bears to the total wages paid to the individual in the base period by all base period employers. The amount allocated to an employer that pays contributions is multiplied by 120% and charged to that employer's account. The amount allocated to a reimbursing employer is the amount of benefits charged to that employer's account [G.S. § 96-11.2]. The base period is the first four of the last five completed calendar quarters immediately preceding the first day of an individual's benefit year [G.S. § 96-1(b)(3)]. An individual's benefit year is the fifty-two week period beginning with the first day of a week with respect to which an individual first files a valid claim for benefits and registers for work [G.S. § 96-1(b)(5)].

• *Noncharging of benefits*

Benefits paid to an individual under a claim filed for a period occurring after the date of the individual's separation from employment may not be charged to the account of the employer by whom the individual was employed at the time of the separation if the separation occurs because (1) the individual left work without good cause attributable to the employer, (2) the employer discharged the individual for misconduct in connection with the work, (3) the employer discharged the individual solely for a bona fide inability to do the work for which the individual was hired and the individual's period of employment was 100 days or less, or (4) the separation is a disqualifying separation under G.S. §96-14.7 (*e.g.*, the separation is due to a labor dispute or to the employee's failure to obtain a necessary license). The employer must promptly notify the Division of Employment Security of the reason for the separation [G.S. §96-11.3(a)].

Benefits paid to an individual also may not be charged to the account of an employer of the individual if the benefits (1) were paid to an individual who is attending a vocational school or training program approved by the Division of Employment Security, (2) were paid to an individual for unemployment due directly to a disaster covered by a federal disaster declaration, (3) were paid to an individual who left work for good cause, or (4) were paid as a result of a decision by the Division and the decision is ultimately reversed upon final adjudication [G.S. §96-11.3(b)].

At the request of the employer, no benefit charges may be made to the account of an employer that has furnished work to an individual who, because of the loss of employment with one or more other employers, is eligible for partial benefits while still being furnished work by the employer on substantially the same basis and substantially the same wages as had been made available to the individual during the individual's base period. This prohibition applies regardless of whether the employments were simultaneous or successive [G.S. §96-11.3(c)].

- *No relief for errors resulting from noncompliance*

An employer's account may not be relieved of charges relating to benefits paid erroneously from the Unemployment Insurance Fund if the Division of Employment Security determines that (1) the erroneous payment was made because the employer, or the agent of the employer, was at fault for failing to respond timely or adequately to a written request from the Division for information relating to the claim for unemployment compensation, and (2) the employer or agent has a pattern of failing to respond timely or adequately to requests from the Division for information relating to claims for unemployment compensation. An employer or agent may not be determined to have a pattern of failing to respond if the number of failures during the year prior to the request is fewer than two or less than 2% of the total requests made to that employer or agent, whichever is greater. An employer may appeal an adverse determination by the Division in the same manner as other determinations by the Division with respect to the charging of employer accounts [G.S. §96-11.4].

- *Contributions credited to wrong account*

When contributions are credited to the wrong account, the erroneous credit may be adjusted only by refunding the employer who made the payment that was credited in error. This applies regardless of whether the employer to whom the payment was credited in error is a related entity of the employer to whom the payment should have been credited. An employer whose payment is credited to the wrong account may request a refund of the amount erroneously credited by filing a request for refund within five years of the last day of the calendar year in which the erroneous credit occurred. Failure of the Division to credit the correct account for contributions does not affect the contribution rate for either the employer whose account should have been credited for the contributions or the employer whose account was credited. No prior contribution rate for either of the employers may be adjusted even though the contribution rates were based on incorrect amounts in their account. An employer is liable for contributions determined under those rates for the five calendar years preceding the year in which the error is determined, regardless of whether the employer acted in good faith [G.S. §96-11.5].

- *Acquisition of employer and transfer of account to another employer*

Acquisition of a business. When an employer acquires all of the business of another employer, the account of the predecessor must be transferred as of the date of the acquisition to the successor for use in the determination of the successor's contribution rate. This provision does not apply when there is no common ownership between the predecessor and the successor and the successor acquired the assets of the predecessor in a sale in bankruptcy [G.S. § 96-11.7(a)].

Acquisition of a portion of a business. When a distinct and severable portion of an employer's business is transferred to a successor employer and the successor employer continues to operate the acquired business, the portion of the account attributable to the transferred business may, with the approval of the Division of Employment Security, be transferred by mutual consent to the successor as of the date of transfer [G.S. § 96-11.7(b)].

A successor employer that is a related entity of the transferring employer is eligible for a transfer from the transferring employer's account only to the extent permitted by rules adopted by the Division [G.S. § 96-11.7(b)].

No transfer may be made to the account of an employer that has ceased to be an employer under G.S. 96-11.9 [G.S. § 96-11.7(b)].

If a transfer of part or all of an account is allowed, the successor employer requesting the transfer may make a request for transfer by filing an application for transfer with the Division within two years after the date the business was transferred [G.S. § 96-11.7(b)].

Acquisition by a related party. If an employer transfers all or a portion of its business to a person who, at the time of transfer, is under substantially common ownership, management or control with the transferor, the portion of the account attributable to the transferred business must be transferred to the transferee as of the date of the transfer for use in determining the transferee's contribution rate [G.S. § 96-11.7(c)].

Acquisition to obtain a lower rate. If the Division of Employment Security finds that a person formed or acquired a business solely or primarily to obtain a lower contribution rate, the predecessor employer's account will not be transferred [G.S. § 96-11.7(c1)].

Effect on contribution rate. If an account is transferred after the computation date for the calendar year, the Division of Employment Security must recalculate the transferor's and the transferee's contribution rates based on their account balances on the date of transfer [G.S. § 96-11.7(d)].

Successor liability for contributions. An employer that, by operation of law, purchase, or otherwise is the successor to an employer liable for contributions becomes liable for contributions on the day of the succession. This provision does not affect the successor's liability as otherwise prescribed by law for unpaid contributions due from the predecessor [G.S. § 96-11.7(e)].

Deceased or insolvent employer. When the organization, trade, or business of a deceased person or of an insolvent debtor is taken over and operated by an administrator, executor, receiver, or trustee in bankruptcy, the new employer automatically succeeds to the account and contribution rate of the deceased person or insolvent debtor without the necessity of filing an application for the transfer of the account [G.S. § 96-11.7(f)].

Continuation of existing account. A transferee of an entire account may not request or maintain an account other than the account of the existing business. If such a transferee nevertheless receives a new account, the Division of Employment Security must recalculate the annual tax rates based on the combined annual account balances of the new employer and the existing business [G.S. § 96-11.7(g)].

PART XI

MISCELLANEOUS TAXES

CHAPTER 28

GROSS PREMIUMS TAX ON INSURANCE COMPANIES

¶2801 Imposition

Article 8B of Chapter 105 of the North Carolina General Statutes imposes a gross premiums tax on (1) insurers, (2) Article 65 corporations, (3) health maintenance organizations (HMOs), and (5) self-insurers. An insurer, HMO, or Article 65 corporation that is subject to the gross premiums tax is not subject to the corporation income tax or the franchise tax [G.S. § 105-228.5(a)]. See definition of terms at ¶ 2808.

In addition, North Carolina imposes the following on insurance companies:

(1) A regulatory charge.

(2) A retaliatory premium tax.

(3) An annual license fee.

• *Exempt companies*

The gross premiums tax is not levied on (1) farmers' mutual assessment fire insurance companies, (2) fraternal orders or societies that do not operate for a profit and do not issue policies on any person except members who are exempt from the gross premiums tax, (3) captive insurance companies taxed under G.S. § 105-228.4A, or (4) foreign captive insurance companies taxed on their gross premiums in a United States jurisdiction other than North Carolina [G.S. § 105-228.5(g)].

¶2802 Base

• *Generally*

The gross premiums tax is measured by the gross premiums of the taxpayer. The base (gross premiums) is defined differently for different insurance companies, as indicated below.

• *Insurers and health maintenance organizations (HMOs)*

The tax base for insurers and HMOs is measured by gross premiums from business done in North Carolina during the preceding calendar year [G.S. § 105-228.5(a)(1)]. The amount of gross premiums from business in North Carolina includes all gross premiums (1) received in North Carolina, (2) credited to policies written or procured in North Carolina, or (3) derived from business written in North Carolina in the preceding calendar year [G.S. § 105-228.5(b)(1)].

• *Article 65 corporations*

The tax base for Article 65 corporations is gross collections from membership dues, exclusive of receipts from cost plus plans, received by the corporation during the preceding calendar year [G.S. § 105-228.5(b)(3)].

• *Self-insurers*

The tax base for self-insurers is gross premiums that would be charged against the same or most similar industry or business, taken from the manual insurance rate then in force in North Carolina, applied to the self-insurer's payroll for the previous calendar year as determined under Article 36 of Chapter 58 of the General Statutes [G.S. § 105-228.5(b)(4)]. Premiums received from policies or contracts issued in connection with the funding of a pension, annuity, or profit-sharing plan qualified under IRC § 401, 403, 404, 408, 457, or 501 are excluded from the base [G.S. § 105-228.5(c)].

• *Business done in North Carolina*

Gross premiums received on life insurance contracts (including supplemental contracts providing for disability benefits or other special benefits that are not annuities, but not including reinsurance contracts) are treated as derived from business done in North Carolina if (1) the premiums on the policies were paid were by or credited to persons, firms, or corporations that are North Carolina residents, or (2) in the case of group policies, the premiums were paid on contracts covering North Carolina residents [G.S. § 105-228.5(b1)]. Gross premiums are deemed to have been collected for the amounts as provided in the policy contracts for the time in force during the year. The only deductions allowed are for premiums refunded on policies rescinded for fraud or breach of contract and refunds of pre-paid life insurance premiums [G.S. § 105-228.5(b1)].

Gross premiums for all other health care plans and contracts of insurance (including Workers' Compensation but not including reinsurance contracts) are treated as derived from business done in North Carolina if the premiums were written during the calendar year (or the equivalent thereof in the case of self-insurers under the Workers' Compensation Act) on contracts covering property or risks in North Carolina [G.S. § 105-228.5(b1)].

In determining the amount of gross premiums derived from business done in North Carolina, all gross premiums (1) received in North Carolina, (2) credited to policies written or procured in North Carolina, or (3) derived from business written in North Carolina shall be deemed to be contracts covering persons, property or risks resident in or located in North Carolina unless (1) the premiums are properly reported and allocated as being received from business done outside North Carolina or (2) the premiums are from policies written in federal areas for persons in military service who pay premiums by assignment of service pay [G.S. § 105-228.5(b1)]. Gross premiums from individual and group life insurance policies providing coverage for individuals living in North Carolina are treated as derived from business done in North Carolina even if the policyholder, policy owner or beneficiary (including a trust established by a corporation to hold policies on the lives of its employees) is a resident of another state. See *Directive CD-08-01* (January 23, 2008).

Returned premiums: If, for any tax year, returned premiums exceed gross premiums collected, insurers may reduce taxable premiums to zero. There is, however, no statutory provision for the carryforward of any unused returned premiums or the refund of premium taxes paid on any unused returned premiums. When insurers are ordered by the Department of Insurance to establish escrow accounts of possible premium overcharges, reductions in gross premiums are allowed after any refunds have been paid to insureds, not when the escrows are established [*Corporate Income, Franchise, and Insurance Tax Bulletin*, III.E (2018)].

Exclusions from gross premiums: Insurers may exclude all of the following from the gross amount of premiums, and the excluded amount is exempt [G.S. § 105-228.5(c)]:

(1) Premiums received on or after July 1, 1973, from policies or contracts issued in connection with the funding of a pension, annuity, or profit-sharing plan qualified or exempt under the Internal Revenue Code.

(2) Premiums or considerations received from annuities as defined in G.S. § 58-7-15.

(3) Funds or considerations received in connection with funding agreements as defined in G.S. § 58-7-16.

(4) The following premiums, to the extent federal law prohibits their taxation under North Carolina insurance tax laws of Article 8B of the General Statutes:

(a) Federal Employees Health Benefits Plan premiums; and

(b) Medicaid or Medicare premiums.

¶2803 Rates

• *Insurers*

The gross premiums rate on taxable premiums on contracts issued by insurers (except for contracts for liabilities under the Workers' Compensation Act) and health maintenance organizations is 1.9% [G.S. § 105-228.5(d)(2)].

• *Article 65 corporations*

The rate on gross premiums and gross collections from membership dues, exclusive of receipts from cost plus plans, received by Article 65 corporations (hospital, medical, and dental service corporations such as Blue Cross/Blue Shield and Delta Dental Corporation) is 1.9% [G.S. § 105-228.5(d)(2)].

• *Workers' compensation*

The tax rate on taxable gross premiums (or the equivalent thereof for self-insurers) on contracts applicable to liabilities under the Workers' Compensation Act is 2.5% [G.S. § 105-228.5(d)(1)].

• *Property coverage contracts*

Statewide: An additional tax rate applies to gross premiums on insurance contracts for property coverage. The rate is 0.74%. The tax is imposed on 10% of the gross premiums from automobile physical damage coverage contracts and 100% of the gross premiums from all other contracts for property coverage. This additional amount is considered a special purpose assessment based on gross premiums but not a gross premiums tax [G.S. § 105-228.5(d)(3)]. This has relevance for taxpayers claiming credits limited by a percentage of their gross premiums tax liability.

¶2804 Retaliatory Premiums Tax

When the laws of any other state impose premiums taxes upon North Carolina insurers doing business in the other state that are (in the aggregate) in excess of the premiums taxes directly imposed upon similar corporations by North Carolina, North Carolina imposes the same premiums taxes (in the aggregate) on companies chartered in other states doing business or seeking to do business in North Carolina. Retaliatory taxes must be reported and paid with the annual gross premiums tax return. The retaliatory tax must be included in the quarterly prepayment rules for premium taxes [G.S. § 105-228.8]. The retaliatory tax does not apply to (1) special purpose obligations or assessments based on premiums imposed in connection with particular kinds of insurance or (2) dedicated special purpose taxes based on premiums.

If the laws of another state retaliate against North Carolina companies on other than an aggregate basis, North Carolina will retaliate against companies chartered in that state on the same basis [G.S. § 105-228.8(f)].

¶2805 Regulatory Charge

An annual insurance regulatory charge is levied on insurance companies in addition to all other fees and taxes. The rate is established annually by the North Carolina General Assembly. The charge for insurance companies is due at the time the company remits its premiums tax. The percentage rate to be used in calculating the insurance regulatory charge under G.S. § 58-6-25 is 6.5% for the 2020 calendar year [S.L. 2014-100, § 20.2.(a)].

¶2806 Returns, Due Date, and Payment

Gross premiums annual reports for the preceding year are due on or before March 15. Payment of the tax is due with the annual report [G.S. § 105-228.5(e)]. Payment by electronic funds transfer (EFT) may be required if the taxpayer's required payments averaged at least $20,000 a month.

• *Installment payments required*

Taxpayers that are subject to the gross premiums tax and have a premiums tax liability (not including the additional local fire and lightning tax discussed below) of $10,000 or more in the immediately preceding year must remit three equal quarterly installments, each installment being equal to $33^1/3\%$ of the premium tax liability incurred in the immediately preceding taxable year. The quarterly installment payments are due on or before April 15, June 15, and October 15 of each taxable year. The taxpayer must remit the balance (if any) by the following March 15 [G.S. § 105-228.5(f)].

¶2807 Credits Against the Tax

• *Credit for assessments to IGA and LHIGA*

A member insurer who pays an assessment to an Association (see G.S. §§ 58-48-35 and 58-62-41) is allowed as a credit against the gross premiums tax in an amount equal to 20% of the amount of the assessment in each of the five taxable years following the year in which the assessment was paid [G.S. § 105-228.5A(b)]. If a member insurer ceases doing business, all assessments for which it has not taken a credit may be credited against its premiums tax liability for the year in which it ceases doing business. The amount of this credit may not exceed the member insurer's premium tax liability for the taxable year. Any amounts acquired by refund from the Association by member insurers that have previously been used as a credit against the gross premiums tax must be remitted to the State. The Association must notify the Secretary that refunds have been made [G.S. § 105-228.5A(c)].

"Association" for this purpose means (1) the North Carolina Insurance Guaranty Association (IGA), or (2) the North Carolina Life and Health Insurance Guaranty Association (LHIGA).

"Member insurer" means (1) any person who (a) writes any kind of insurance to which this Article applies under G.S. § 58-48-10, including the exchange of reciprocal or interinsurance contracts, and (b) is licensed and authorized to transact insurance in North Carolina [G.S. § 58-48-20(6)]; or (2) any insurer and any hospital or medical service corporation that is governed by Article 65 of Chapter 58 and that is licensed or that holds a license to transact in North Carolina any kind of insurance for which coverage is provided under G.S. § 58-62-21 except the following: (a) HMOs; (b) fraternal orders or benefit societies; (c) mandatory State pooling plans; (d) mutual assessment companies or any entities that operate on an assessment basis; (e) insurance exchanges; or (f) any entities similar to any of the foregoing [G.S. § 58-62-16(11)].

¶2808 Definition of Terms

Article 65 corporation: An "Article 65 corporation" is a corporation subject to Article 65 (regulating hospital, medical, and dental service corporations) of Chapter 58 of the General Statutes (The Insurance Law) [G.S. § 105-228.3(1)].

Insurer: An "insurer," "company," or "insurance company" is any corporation, association, partnership, society, order, individual or aggregation of individuals engaging or proposing or attempting to engage as principals in any kind of insurance business, including the exchanging of reciprocal or interinsurance contracts between individuals, partnerships and corporations. "Company" or "insurance company" or "insurer" does not mean the State of North Carolina or any county, city, or other political subdivision of the State of North Carolina [G.S. § 58-1-5(c)] or a group of employers who have pooled their liabilities pursuant to G.S. § 97-93 of the Workers' Compensation Act [G.S. § 105-228.3(2)].

Self-insurer: A "self-insurer" is an employer that carries its own risk pursuant to G.S. § 97-95 of the Workers' Compensation Act [G.S. § 105-228.3(3)].

¶2809 Administration and Procedures

The insurance company gross premiums tax is administered by the Corporate Tax Division of the North Carolina Department of Revenue.

¶2810 Captive Insurance Companies

• *Imposition*

Captive Insurance Companies doing business in North Carolina are subject to a tax on direct premiums and a tax on assumed reinsurance premiums. In the case of a branch captive insurance company, the tax applies only to the branch business of the company [G.S. § 105-228.4A(a)]. A branch captive insurance company is a captive insurance company licensed by a jurisdiction outside the United States and licensed by the Commissioner of Insurance to transact insurance business in North Carolina through a business unit with a principal place of business in North Carolina. The branch business of a branch captive insurance company consists of any insurance business transacted by the branch in North Carolina [G.S. § 58-10-340(6) and (7)]. Note that the tax on captive insurance companies does not apply to foreign captive insurance companies, *i.e.*, captive insurance companies formed and licensed under the laws of a jurisdiction within the United States other than North Carolina [G.S. §§ 105-228.4A(a) and 105-228.3(1b)].

• *Tax on direct premiums*

A tax at the rate of 0.4% is imposed on the direct premiums collected by a captive insurance company up to $20 million. Direct premiums collected by a captive insurance company of $20 million or more are subject to a tax at the rate of 0.3% [G.S. § 105-228.4A(e)]. In determining the amount of premiums subject to tax, the taxpayer may deduct amounts paid to policy holders as return premiums. Return premiums include dividends on unabsorbed premiums and premium deposits returned or credited to policy holders [G.S. § 105-228.4A(e)].

• *Tax on assumed reinsurance premiums*

A captive insurance company is subject to a tax at the percentages set forth below on assumed reinsurance premiums.

Premiums Collected	Rate of Tax
Up to $20 million	0.225%
$20 million to $40 million	0.150%
$40 million to $60 million	0.050%
$60 million and over	0.025%

The tax on assumed reinsurance premiums does not apply to premiums for risks or portions of risks that are subject to the direct premiums tax. The tax also does not apply to assets received in exchange for the assumption of loss reserves or other liabilities of one insurer by another insurer if the two insurers are under common control and the Commissioner of Insurance verifies (1) that the transaction between the insurers is part of a plan to discontinue the operations of one of the insurers and (2) the intent of the insurers is to renew or maintain business with the captive insurance company [G.S. § 105-228.4A(d)].

- *Total tax liability*

A captive insurance company's aggregate liability for the direct premiums tax and the assumed reinsurance premiums tax generally may not be less than $5,000 nor more than $100,000. A special rule applies to certain captive insurance companies that fund their liabilities to their participants through segregated accounts known as protected cells. The aggregate tax payable by such a protected cell captive insurance company with more than 10 cells may not be less than $10,000 nor more than the lesser of (1) $100,000 plus $5,000 for each cell in excess of 10 and (2) $200,000 [G.S. § 105-228.4A(f)].

- *Captive insurance companies under common ownership and control*

Two or more captive insurance companies under common ownership and control are taxed as a single taxpayer [G.S. § 105-228.4A(a)]. If a group of captive insurance companies under common ownership and control includes a special purpose financial captive, then several special rules apply. Specifically, (1) the amount of premium tax payable is allocated to each member of the group in the same proportion that the premium allocable to the member bears to the total premium of all members; (2) the aggregate amount of tax payable by the group is equal to the greater of the sum of the premium tax allocated to the members and $5,000; (3) if the total premium tax allocated to all members that are special purpose financial captives exceed $100,000, the total premium tax allocated to those members is $100,000; and (4) if the total premium tax allocated to all members that are not special purpose financial captives exceeds $100,000, the total premium tax allocated to those members is $100,000 [G.S. § 105-228.4A(f)]. A special purpose financial captive is a captive insurance company that has received a certificate of authority from the Commissioner of Insurance to facilitate the securitization of one or more risks as a means of accessing alternative sources of capital and achieving the benefits of securitization. *See* G.S. § 58-10-340(39) and G.S.§ 58-10-555 et seq.

- *Exemption from other taxes*

Captive insurance companies that are subject to the tax on direct premiums or assumed reinsurance premiums, as well as foreign captive insurance companies, are not subject to franchise taxes, income taxes, local privilege taxes, local taxes computed on the basis of gross premiums, or the insurance regulatory charge imposed by G.S. § 58-6-25 [G.S. § 105-228.4A(b)].

- *Administration*

A captive insurance company subject to the tax on direct premiums or assumed reinsurance premiums must file a report with the Secretary of Revenue on or before March 15 of each year showing the premiums contracted for or collected on policies or contracts of insurance written by the company during the preceding calendar year. In the case of a multi-year policy or contract, the premiums must be prorated among the years covered by the policy or contract. The taxes on direct and assumed reinsurance premiums are due with the report [G.S. § 105-228.4A(c)].

¶2810

MISCELLANEOUS TAXES

CHAPTER 29

MISCELLANEOUS TAXES

¶2901 Highway Use Tax

• *Imposition*

A highway use tax is imposed on the privilege of using the highways of North Carolina and is measured by the retail value of a motor vehicle for which a certificate of title is issued [G.S. § 105-187.2]. The tax is in addition to all other taxes and fees imposed and replaced the sales tax on motor vehicles in 1989.

• *Full exemptions*

The highway use tax does not apply when a certificate of title is issued as a result of the transfer of a motor vehicle in a transfer described below, except where the motor vehicle was licensed in another state at the time of transfer [G.S. § 105-187.6(d)].

(1) To the insurer of the vehicle under G.S. § 20-190.1 because the vehicle is a salvage vehicle [G.S. § 105-187.6(a)(1)].

(2) To a used motor vehicle dealer under G.S. § 20-109.1 because the vehicle is a salvage vehicle that was abandoned [G.S. § 105-187.6(a)(l)].

(3) To one of the following:

(a) A manufacturer, as defined in G.S. § 20-286 [G.S. § 105-187.6(a)(2)].

(b) A motor vehicle retailer for the purpose of resale [G.S. § 105-187.6(a)(2)].

(4) To the same owner to reflect a change or correction in the owner's name [G.S. § 105-187.6(a)(3)].

(5) To one or more of the same co-owners to reflect the removal of one or more other co-owners, when there is no consideration for the transfer [G.S. § 105-187.6(a)(3a)].

(6) By will or intestacy [G.S. § 105-187.6(a)(4)].

(7) By a gift between spouses, a parent and child, or a stepparent and a stepchild [G.S. § 105-187.6(a)(5)].

(8) By a distribution of marital or divisible property incident to a marital separation or divorce [G.S. § 105-187.6(a)(6)].

(9) To a local board of education for use in the driver education program of a public school when the motor vehicle is transferred.

(a) By a retailer and is transferred back to the retailer within 300 days after the transfer to the local board [G.S. § 105-187.6(a)(8)a].

(b) By a local board of education [G.S. § 105-187.6(a)(8)b].

(10) To a volunteer fire department or volunteer rescue squad that (i) is not part of a unit of local government, (ii) has no more than two (2) paid employees, and (iii) is exempt from State income tax, when the motor vehicle is one of the following:

(a) A fire truck, a pump truck, a tanker truck, or a ladder truck used to suppress fire [G.S. § 105-187.6(a)(9)a].

(b) A four-wheel drive vehicle intended to be mounted with a water tank and hose and used for forest fire fighting [G.S. § 105-187.6(a)(9)b].

(c) An emergency services vehicle [G.S. § 105-187.6(a)(9)c].

(11) To a State agency from a unit of local government, volunteer fire department or volunteer rescue squad to enable the State agency to transfer the vehicle to another unit of local government, volunteer fire department or volunteer rescue squad [G.S. § 105-187.6(a)(10)].

(12) To a revocable trust from an owner who is the sole beneficiary of the trust [G.S. § 105-187.6(a)(11)].

(13) To a 501(c)(3) charitable organization if the vehicle was donated to the charity solely for the purpose of resale [G.S. § 105-187.6(a)(12)].

• *Base and Rate*

The highway use tax is imposed at the rate of 3% on the sum of the retail value of a motor vehicle for which a certificate of title is issued and any fee regulated by G.S. § 20-101.1 (relating to administrative fees charged by motor vehicle dealers). The tax does not apply to the sales price of a service contract if the charge for the service contract is separately stated on the bill of sale or other similar documents given to the purchaser at the time of sale [G.S. § 105-187.3(a) and (a1)]. Some vehicles are subject to maximum taxes (discussed below). For definition of "retail value," see "Retail value," below.

¶2901

• *Maximum tax of $40*

A maximum tax of $40 applies when a certificate of title is issued as the result of a transfer of a motor vehicle:

   (1) To a secured party who has a perfected security interest in the motor vehicle [G.S. § 105-187.6(b)(1)].

   (2) To a partnership, limited liability company, corporation, trust or other person where no gain or loss arises on the transfer of the motor vehicle under IRC § 351 or IRC § 721 or because the transfer is treated under the Internal Revenue Code as being an entity that is not a separate entity from its owner or whose separate entity from its owner or whose separate existence is otherwise disregarded, or to a partnership, limited liability company, or corporation by merger, conversion, or consolidation in accordance with applicable law [G.S. § 105-187.6(b)(2)].

Note that this cap on tax liability does not apply if the motor vehicle was titled in another state at the time of transfer [G.S. § 105-187.6(d)].

• *Maximum tax of $250*

A maximum tax of $250 applies when a certificate of title is issued for a motor vehicle that, at the time of applying for a certificate of title, is and has been titled in another state for at least 90 days [G.S. § 105-187.6(c)].

• *Maximum tax of $2,000*

The tax may not be more than $2,000 for each certificate of title issued for a Class A or Class B commercial motor vehicle and for a recreational vehicle [G.S. § 105-187.3(a1)]. See G.S. § 20-4.01 for definitions of Class A and Class B motor vehicles [G.S. § 105-187.3(a)]. This maximum tax also applies to a continuous lease or rental of a Class A or Class B commercial motor vehicle to the same person [G.S. § 105-187.5(b)].

• *Retail value*

Sale by retailer: The retail value of a motor vehicle for which a certificate of title is issued because of a sale of the motor vehicle by a retailer is the sales price of the motor vehicle (including all accessories attached to the vehicle when it is delivered to the purchaser) less the amount of any allowance given by the retailer for a trade-in vehicle as a full or partial payment for the purchased motor vehicle [G.S. § 105-187.3(b)].

Sale by seller who is not a retailer: The retail value of a motor vehicle for which a certificate of title is issued because of a sale of the motor vehicle by a seller who is not a retailer is the market value of the vehicle less the amount of any allowance given by the seller for a trade-in vehicle as a full or partial payment for the purchased vehicle [G.S. § 105-187.3(b)].

Exchange of vehicles: A transaction in which two parties exchange motor vehicles is considered a sale with respect to whether either party gives additional consideration as part of the transaction. The retail value of a motor vehicle is the market value of the vehicle [G.S. § 105-187.3(b)].

Title issued for reason other than sale: The retail value of a motor vehicle for which a certificate of title is issued for a reason other than the sale of the vehicle is the market value of the vehicle [G.S. § 105-187.3(b)].

Market value: The market value of a vehicle is presumed to be the vehicle's value set in a schedule of values adopted by the Commissioner of Motor Vehicles, which must not exceed the wholesale values of motor vehicles published in a recognized automotive reference manual [G.S. § 105-187.3(b) and (c)].

Department of Defense vehicles: The retail value of a motor vehicle for which a certificate of title is issued because of a transfer by a State agency that assists the Department of Defense with purchasing, transferring or titling a vehicle to another State agency, a unit of local government, a volunteer fire department or a volunteer rescue squad is the sales price paid by the State agency, unit of local government, volunteer fire department or volunteer rescue squad [G.S. § 105-187.3(b1)].

• *Payment of tax*

The highway use tax is paid when a taxpayer applies for a certificate of title for a motor vehicle; the certificate of title will not be issued until the highway use tax has been paid. The tax may be paid in cash or by check [G.S. § 105-187.4(a)].

Sale by retailer: In the case of a sale by a retailer, the applicant for the certificate of title must attach a copy of the bill of sale to the application. A retailer may collect the tax from the purchases payable upon the issuance of a title for the vehicle, apply for a title on behalf of the purchaser, and remit the tax due on behalf of the purchaser [G.S. § 105-187.4(b)].

• *Alternate tax for limited possession commitments*

A retailer may elect not to pay the highway use tax when applying for a certificate of title for a motor vehicle purchased for limited possession commitment. A limited possession commitment includes a long-term lease or rental, a short-term lease or rental and a vehicle subscription (generally, an arrangement that allows a person to use and exchange vehicles from a fleet). A retailer who makes this election pays, in lieu of the highway use tax, a tax on the gross receipts of the limited possession commitment. The portion of billing or payment that represents any amount applicable to the sales price of a service contract (as defined in G.S. § 105-164.3) is not included in the gross receipts subject to the Highway Use Tax. Such amount must be separately stated on documentation given to the purchaser when the limited possession commitment agreement goes into effect or on the monthly billing statement or other documentation given to the purchaser. When a retailer sells a limited possession commitment to another retailer, the seller should provide the purchaser documentation showing that the service contract and applicable sales tax were separately stated when the limited possession commitment went into effect, and the purchaser must retain the information to support an allocation for tax computed on the gross receipts subject to the highway use tax. This alternate tax is also a tax on the privilege of using the highways of North Carolina. This alternate tax is imposed on retailers but is to be added to the limited possession commitment price of a motor vehicle, thereby being paid by the person who leases or rents the vehicle [G.S. § 105-187.5(a)]. A retailer who elects the alternate tax makes this election when applying for a certificate of title for the vehicle by completing a form provided by the Division of Motor Vehicles giving information needed to collect the alternate tax based on gross receipts. Rental car businesses typically elect to pay the gross receipts tax. Once made, this election is irrevocable [G.S. § 105-187.5(c)].

Rate: The tax rate on the gross receipts from the short-term lease or rental (fewer than 365 consecutive days) of a motor vehicle is 8%; the tax rate on the gross receipts from the long-term lease or rental of a motor vehicle is 3%; and the tax on the gross receipts from a vehicle subscription is 5%. Gross receipts does not include the amount of any allowance given for a motor vehicle taken in trade as a partial payment on the lease or rental price. The maximum tax (see above) applies to a continuous lease or rental of a motor vehicle to the same person [G.S. § 105-187.5(b)].

• *Credits against highway use tax*

Tax paid in another state: A person who, within 90 days before applying for a certificate of title for a motor vehicle on which the highway use tax is due, has paid a sales tax, an excise tax, or a tax substantially equivalent to the highway use tax to a taxing jurisdiction outside North Carolina is allowed a credit against the highway use tax due for the amount of tax paid to the other jurisdiction [G.S. § 105-187.7(a)].

Tax paid within one year: A person who applies for a title for a motor vehicle that is titled in another state but was formerly titled in North Carolina is allowed a credit for the amount of highway use tax paid by that person on the same vehicle within one year before the application for a certificate of title [G.S. § 105-187.7(b)].

• *Refunds on returns*

When a purchaser of a motor vehicle returns the motor vehicle to the seller of the motor vehicle within 90 days after purchase and receives a replacement vehicle or a refund of the price paid (whether from the seller or the manufacturer of the vehicle), the purchaser may obtain a refund of the highway use tax paid on the certificate of title issued for the returned motor vehicle. To obtain a refund, the purchaser must apply to the Division of Motor Vehicles for a refund within 30 days after receiving the replacement vehicle or refund of the purchase price [G.S. § 105-187.8].

• *Penalties and remedies*

Bad checks: The penalty for bad checks applies to the highway use tax (see ¶ 3204). If a bad check is returned and the tax plus penalty is not paid within 30 days after demand for payment, the Commissioner of Motor Vehicles may revoke the registration plate of the vehicle for which the check for tax was paid [G.S. § 105-187.10(a)].

Unpaid taxes: The remedies for collection of taxes in Article 9 of Chapter 105 apply to the highway use tax [G.S. § 105-187.10(b)].

Appeals: A taxpayer who disagrees with the presumed value of a motor vehicle must pay the tax based on the presumed value and appeal to the Commissioner of Motor Vehicles. A taxpayer who appeals the value must provide two estimates of the vehicle's value. If the Commissioner of Motor Vehicles finds that the vehicle's value is less than its presumed values, the Commissioner will refund any overpayment with interest at the established rate (see ¶ 3205) from the date of the overpayment [G.S. § 105-187.10].

• *Administration*

The highway use tax is administered by the Sales and Use Tax Division of the North Carolina Department of Revenue.

¶ 2902 Excise Taxes on Malt Beverages, Wine, and Liquor

North Carolina's Alcoholic Beverage Tax is covered in North Carolina General Statutes, Chapter 105, Article 2C, Alcoholic Beverage License and Excise Taxes. Current tax rates are [G.S. § 105-113.80]:

— malt beverages . . . . 61.71¢ per gallon

— unfortified wine . . . . 26.34¢ per liter

— fortified wine .... 29.34¢ per liter

— liquor .... 30% of retail price

Comprehensive coverage of taxation of alcohol, as well as licensing and distribution information is provided in Wolters Kluwer, CCH Liquor Control Law Reporter. For more information go to CCHGroup.com or contact an account representative at 888-CCH-REPS (888-224-7377).

¶2903 Alcoholic Beverage License Taxes

Comprehensive coverage of taxation of alcohol, as well as licensing and distribution information, is provided in Wolters Kluwer, CCH Liquor Control Law Reporter. For more information go to CCHGroup.com or contact an account representative at 888-CCH-REPS (888-224-7377).

¶2904 Cigarette Tax and Other Tobacco Products Tax

Article 2A of Chapter 105 of the North Carolina General Statutes imposes taxes on the distribution of cigarettes and other tobacco products.

• *Cigarette tax*

Tax on distributors and users: A tax is imposed on licensed distributors who sell cigarettes in North Carolina or possess cigarettes for sale in North Carolina at the rate of 2.25¢ per individual cigarette (45¢ per pack). The tax falls on the licensed distributor who first acquires or handles the cigarettes – generally the distributor who imports cigarettes manufactured outside North Carolina into the state or the distributor who is the first consignee of cigarettes manufactured outside the state [G.S. § 105-113.5]. A "distributor" includes both a manufacturer of cigarettes (including someone who is the exclusive purchaser of cigarettes under a contract manufacturing arrangement) and a person who buys non-tax-paid cigarettes from a manufacturer for storage, sale or other disposition [G.S. § 105-113.4(3) and (6)]. A use tax at the same rate is imposed on any person other than a distributor who sells, uses or consumes non-tax-paid cigarettes or possesses non-tax-paid cigarettes for sale, use or consumption in North Carolina.

Definitions

Definition of terms applicable to the cigarette tax are located in G.S. § 105-113.4].

Exemption for interstate sales: A licensed distributor engaged in interstate business is not required to pay tax on cigarettes sold in interstate sales, provided the distributor complies with the Secretary's administrative requirements including those concerning recordkeeping, reporting, and posting of a bond [G.S. § 105-113.9]. Generally, exempt interstate sales require the distributor to deliver the cigarettes to the nonresident purchaser's business location in another state. However, cigarettes delivered to a nonresident purchaser at the distributor's business location in North Carolina are also exempt if (1) the nonresident wholesaler or retailer has no place of business in North Carolina, (2) the nonresident wholesaler or retailer is registered with the Secretary, (3) the nonresident wholesaler or retailer purchases the cigarettes for the purpose of resale outside North Carolina, and (4) the distributor is also licensed as a distributor under the laws of the state of the nonresident wholesaler or retailer [G.S. § 105-113.9].

Manufacturer's exemption: A licensed manufacturer who sells cigarettes to a licensed distributor may apply to the Secretary to be relieved from the payment of the tax (but not from reporting requirements), in which case the tax is collected from the distributor. Even if a manufacturer is relieved from payment of the tax, it must be licensed as a distributor in order to make shipments, including drop shipments, to a retail dealer or ultimate user [G.S. § 105-113.10(a)].

Shipping for affiliated manufacturer: A manufacturer may, upon application to the Secretary and upon compliance with requirements prescribed by the Secretary, be relieved of paying cigarette taxes on cigarettes that are manufactured by an affiliated manufacturer and temporarily stored at and shipped from its facilities. The exemption does not relieve the manufacturer of reporting obligations [G.S. § 105-113.10(b)]. An affiliated manufacturer is a manufacturer licensed under G.S. § 105-113.12 who is an affiliate of a manufacturer licensed under G.S. § 105-113.12 [G.S. § 105-113.4(1a)]. An affiliate is a person who directly or indirectly controls, is controlled by, or is under common control with another person [G.S. § 105-113.4(4a)].

License required. Distributors engaged in business in North Carolina must obtain a license for each place of business (*i.e.*, each place where non-tax-paid cigarettes are received or stored) and pay a tax of $25 for each license [G.S. §§ 105-113.11, 105-113.12 and 105-113.4A]. It is unlawful for anyone to engage in business of selling (or offering to sell or possessing with intent to sell) cigarettes or other tobacco products without obtaining a license for each place of business required to be licensed [G.S. § 105-113.29.]The Secretary may investigate an applicant to confirm the accuracy of the information submitted by the applicant and the applicant's eligibility for a distributor's license. The Secretary may also require the applicant to post a bond to protect the State against loss if the distributor fails to pay the tax due. A distributor may substitute for such a bond an irrevocable letter of credit issued by a commercial bank provided that the bank and the form of the letter of credit are acceptable to the Secretary [G.S. § 105-113.13].

Vending machines: Cigarette vending machines must be marked to identify the owner in the manner required by the Secretary [G.S. § 105-113.17].

Returns. The following cigarette tax reports must be filed:

(1) *Distributor's report:* A licensed distributor must file a monthly report covering sales and other activities occurring in a calendar month and showing the quantity of all cigarettes transported into North Carolina for sales in the states. The distributor's report is due within 20 days after the end of the month covered by the report. The report must state the amount of tax due and identify any transactions to which the tax does not apply [G.S. § 105-113.18(1)].

(2) *Use tax report:* Every other person who has acquired non-tax-paid cigarettes for sale, use, or consumption within North Carolina must, within 96 hours after receipt of the cigarettes, file a report showing the amount of non-tax-paid cigarettes received and any other required information [G.S. § 105-113.18(2)].

(3) *Shipping report:* Any person (except a licensed distributor) who transports cigarettes upon the public highways, roads, or streets of North Carolina, upon notice from the Secretary, must file a report containing information required by the Secretary [G.S. § 105-113.18(3)].

Payments: Cigarette taxes are payable when a report is required to be filed [G.S. § 105-113.18].

Discounts: A licensed distributor who files a timely report and sends a timely payment may deduct from the amount due with the report a discount of two percent (2%). This discount is intended to cover expenses incurred in preparing the required records and reports and the expense of furnishing a bond [G.S. § 105-113.21(a1)]. The Secretary has ruled that the denial of the timely payment discount is not the equivalent of a penalty and that it therefore has no authority to offer the discount to taxpayers who do not strictly comply with to discount's requirements. See Secretary's Decision No. 2006-25 (taxpayer voluntarily enrolled in EFT program and with otherwise timely payment history was not entitled to discount where it failed to upload ACH data until date payment was due resulting in payment being credited one day late).

Refunds for unsalable cigarettes: A licensed distributor in possession of stale or otherwise unsalable cigarettes upon which tax has been paid may return the cigarettes to the manufacturer and apply for a refund of the tax. The refund request must be accompanied by an affidavit from the manufacturer stating the number of cigarettes returned. The amount of the refund is the tax paid on the unsalable cigarettes less any discount allowed. The distributor must return the cigarettes to the manufacturer of the cigarettes or to the affiliated manufacturer who is contracted by the manufacturer of the cigarettes to serve as the manufacturer's agent for the purposes of validating quantities and disposing of unsalable cigarettes [G.S. § 105-113.21(b)].

Non-tax-paid cigarettes: Distributors may not sell, borrow, loan or exchange non-tax-paid cigarettes to, from or with other distributors unless authorized by statute. No person may sell or offer for sale non-tax-paid cigarettes. The possession of more than 600 cigarettes on which tax has been paid to another state or country by a person other than a licensed distributor is prima facie evidence that cigarettes are possessed in violation of the statute [G.S. § 105-113.27]. Non-tax-paid cigarettes are subject to special regulation regarding transportation [G.S. § 105-113.31] and may be seized as contraband, and their possessors may be subject to arrest [G.S. § 105-113.32].

• *Other tobacco products tax*

Tax on wholesale and retail dealers: The tax on "other tobacco products" (i.e., products other than cigarettes, such as cigars, that contain tobacco and that are intended for inhalation or oral use) is imposed on the wholesale or retail dealer who first acquires or otherwise handles products subject to the tax. This includes a wholesale or retail dealer who brings a tobacco product made outside North Carolina into the state and a wholesale or retail dealer who is the original consignee of a tobacco product that is made outside North Carolina and shipped into the state [G.S. § 105-113.35(b)]. A retail dealer who acquires non-tax-paid other tobacco products from a wholesale dealer is liable for any tax due on such products [G.S. § 105-113.35(c)]. The rate of tax depends on the type of product acquired or handled. Beginning June 1, 2015 [S.L. 2014-3, § 15.1(g)], vapor products are taxed at the rate of 5¢ per fluid milliliter of consumable product. All other tobacco products (i.e., tobacco products other than cigarettes and vapor products) are taxed at the rate of 12.8% of the cost price of the product [G.S. § 105-113.35(a) and (a1)]. A "vapor product" is defined as a nonlighted, noncombustible product that employs a mechanical heating element, battery or electronic circuit that can be used to produce vapor from nicotine in a solution, including a vapor cartridge or other container of nicotine in a solution or other form intended to be used with or in an electronic cigarette or similar device. The term does not include any product regulated by the Food and Drug Administration under Chapter V of the federal Food, Drug and Cosmetic Act [G.S. § 105-113.4 (13a)]. For purposes of calculating the tax due on vapor products, "consumable product" means any nicotine liquid solution or other material containing nicotine that is depleted as a vapor product is used [G.S. § 105-113.4(1k)]. All invoices for vapor products issued by manufacturers must state the amount of consumable product in milliliters [G.S. § 105-113.35(a1)].

Limitations. The taxes on other tobacco products (including vapor products) do not apply to (1) products sold outside North Carolina, (2) products sold to the federal government or (3) sample products (other than cigarettes) distributed without charge (provided that such sample products may only be distributed in qualified adult-only facilities) [G.S. § 105-113-35(a2)].

Manufacturer's exemption: A manufacturer who is not a retail dealer and who ships other tobacco products to a licensed wholesale or retail dealer may apply to the Secretary to be relieved of paying the other tobacco products tax [G.S. § 105-113.35(d)]. A manufacturer that is not a retail dealer and that ships vapor products to a licensed wholesale or retail dealer may apply to be relieved of paying the tax on such vapor products [G.S. § 105-113.35(d)]. A manufacturer who sells other tobacco products exclusively to an affiliated wholesale dealer may take advantage of this provision, provided the affiliated wholesale dealer is not also a retail dealer [G.S. § 105-113.35(d)]. In addition, if a manufacturer of cigarettes is also a wholesale dealer of other tobacco products and the manufacturer obtains permission to be relieved of liability for the cigarette tax, it is also relieved of liability for the other tobacco products tax [G.S. § 105-113.35(d)].

License required: A wholesale or retail dealer must obtain a license for each place of business (*i.e.*, each place where non-tax-paid other tobacco products are made, received or stored) and pay a tax of $25 (for a wholesale dealer license) or $10 (for a retail dealer license) for each license [G.S. § 105-113.36]. The Secretary may require the applicant for a license to post a bond to protect the State against loss if the dealer fails to pay the tax due. A dealer may substitute for such a bond an irrevocable letter of credit issued by a commercial bank provided that the bank and the form of the letter of credit are acceptable to the Secretary [G.S. § 105-113.38].

Returns: A dealer must file a monthly report covering sales and other activities occurring in a calendar month. The report is due within 20 days after the end of the month covered by the report [G.S. § 105-113.37(a)]. In addition to monthly reports, any person who transports other tobacco products upon the public highways, roads, or streets of North Carolina, upon notice from the Secretary, must file a report containing information required by the Secretary [G.S. § 105-113.37(d)].

Payment: Other tobacco product taxes are payable when a report is required to be filed [G.S. § 105-113.37(a)]. However, a wholesale dealer is not required to pay tax on designated exempt sales when filing the monthly report [G.S. § 105-113.37(b)]. If the purchaser in the designated exempt sale does not in fact make an exempt sale of the product, that purchaser (but not the wholesale dealer) is liable for the tax and any penalties and interest due on the designated sale [G.S. § 105-113.37(b)].

Discounts: A wholesale or retail dealer of other tobacco products other than vapor products who files a timely report and sends a timely payment may deduct a discount of 2% from the amount due to cover the expenses incurred in preparing the records and reports and furnishing any bond required [G.S. § 105-113.39(a)]. A retail dealer who acquires non-tax-paid other tobacco products from a wholesale dealer and who thus becomes liable for the tax on such products may not deduct a discount from the amount of tax due when reporting the tax [G.S. § 105-113.35(c)].

Refunds: A wholesale or retail dealer (other than a retail dealer who becomes liable for the tax by acquiring non-tax-paid other tobacco products from a wholesale dealer) who is in possession of stale or otherwise unsalable other tobacco products upon which the tax has been paid may return the unsalable products to the manufacturer and apply for a refund of the tax. The refund request must be accompanied by a written certificate signed under penalty of perjury or an affidavit from the manufacturer listing the other tobacco products returned. The tax paid, less any discount allowed on the listed products, will be refunded [G.S. § 105-113.39(b)].

¶2904

Integrated wholesale dealers: A wholesale dealer affiliated with a manufacturer may not sell, borrow, loan or exchange non-tax-paid other tobacco products (other than cigarettes) to, from or with any other such wholesale dealer, except as provided by statute [G.S. § 105-113.35(d1)].

Use Tax: A person other than a licensed wholesale or retail dealer who sells other tobacco products or possesses other tobacco products for sale and any person who consumes other tobacco products on which the other tobacco products tax has not been paid is subject to a use tax at the other tobacco products tax rate.

• *Reduction in tax for modified risk tobacco products*

The tobacco products tax rate otherwise applicable to a tobacco product is reduced if the product is a modified risk tobacco product. A "modified risk tobacco product" is a tobacco product that is sold or distributed for use to reduce harm or the risk of tobacco-related disease. The rate reduction is (1) 50% for a modified risk tobacco product that has received a risk modification order by the United States Food and Drug Administration ("FDA") under 21 U.S.C. § 387k(g)(1) and (2) 25% for a modified risk tobacco product that has received an exposure modification order by FDA under 21 U.S.C. § 387k(g)(2). The taxpayer has the burden of substantiating that a product qualifies as a modified risk tobacco product. This can be done by providing the Department with a copy of the order issued by the FDA. Once the taxpayer provides the order to the Department, the tax is reduced effective on the first day of the next calendar month. If the FDA order is renewed, the taxpayer must provide the Department with a copy of the renewal order within 14 days. If the FDA order expires without renewal or is withdrawn by the FDA, the rate reduction is forfeited [G.S. § 105-113.4E].

• *Provisions common to cigarette tax and other tobacco products tax*

No double taxation: The cigarette and other tobacco products taxes may be collected only once on the same product [G.S. § 105-113.3(a)]

Increases in tax rates: A person subject to the cigarette tax or the other tobacco products tax who has any tobacco products in inventory on the effective date of a tax increase must file, within 20 days after the date of the increase, a complete inventory and remit an additional tax to the Secretary. The amount of tax due on the inventory is the difference between the tax computed at the former rate and the tax computed at the increased rate [G.S. § 105-113.4D]. Before September 1, 2009, this provision applied only to the cigarette tax. See S.L. 2009-451, § 27A.5.(b) and (f).

Administration: The administrative provisions of Article 9 of Chapter 105 apply to the cigarette and other tobacco products taxes [G.S. § 105-133.3(b)] The cigarette and other tobacco products taxes are administered by the Excise Tax Division of the North Carolina Department of Revenue.

Licenses: A cigarette or other tobacco products license is not transferable and must be displayed at the place of business for which it is issued [G.S. § 105-113.4A(a)]. The Secretary may summarily revoke a license where the holder incurs liability for tax after failing to pay a tax when due, provided that the Secretary must then notify the license holder and provide a hearing on the revocation. The Secretary may also revoke a license for any violation of the cigarette or other tobacco products tax after notice and a hearing. Violations justifying revocation of a license include willfully failing to file a return or pay tax due, making a false statement in an application or return, failing to keep required records, refusing to allow the Secretary to examine books and records, failing to disclose the correct amount of taxable products and failing to file required bonds. The Secretary may also cancel a license on the written request of the licensee and the return of the license to the Secretary [G.S. § 105-113.4B].

Records: Every person required to be licensed or to make reports under either the cigarette tax or other tobacco products tax must keep complete and accurate records of all purchases, sales, inventories, shipments, deliveries and other information in the form required by the Secretary. Such records must be open to inspection at all times and safely preserved for three years (unless the Secretary consents to their early destruction) in a manner to ensure their security and accessibility for inspection by the Department [G.S. § 105-113.26]. It is unlawful to fail to keep required records, to fail to make reports, to make false entries, or to refuse to produce records for inspection [G.S. § 105-113.30]. In addition, every person required to be licensed must keep records of its purchases, inventories, sales, shipments and deliveries of tobacco products, which it must keep open at all times for inspection and safely preserved for three years, [G.S. § 105-113.40].

Misdemeanor: Any person who violates any provision of the cigarette tax or other tobacco products tax is guilty of a Class I misdemeanor unless another punishment is specifically prescribed [G.S. § 105-113.33].

¶2905 Realty Transfer Tax

• *Imposition*

The realty transfer tax, or "excise tax on conveyances," is an excise tax levied on deeds and other instruments by which any person other than a governmental unit or an instrumentality of a governmental unit conveys an interest in real property (including timber deeds and contracts for the sale of standing timber) located in North Carolina, to another person [G.S. § § 105-228.28 and 105-228.30(a)].

• *Exemptions*

Transfers that occur by the following means are exempt from the realty transfer tax [G.S. § 105-228.29]:

(1) By operation of law.

(2) By lease for a term of years.

(3) By or pursuant to the provisions of a will.

(4) By intestacy.

(5) By gift.

(6) In which no consideration in property or money is due or paid by the transferee to the transferor.

(7) By merger or consolidation.

(8) By an instrument securing indebtedness.

• *Base and rate*

The realty transfer tax is levied at the rate of $1 on each $500 (or fractional part thereof) of the consideration or value of the property interest conveyed [G.S. § 105-228.30(a)].

• *Payment of tax*

The transferor must pay the tax to the register of deeds of the county in which the real estate is located before recording the instrument of conveyance. If the instrument transfers a parcel of real estate lying in two or more counties, the tax must be paid to the register of deeds of the county where the more valuable part of the real estate is located [G.S. § 105-228.30(a)]. A person presenting an instrument for registration must report to the register of deeds the amount of tax due [G.S. § 105-228.32]. It is thus the responsibility of the person presenting the instrument to determine the consideration paid for the property or the value of the property. Before the instrument may be recorded, the register of deeds must collect the tax due and mark the instrument to indicate that the tax has been paid and the amount of tax paid [G.S. § 105-228.32].

The county finance officer is required to credit half the tax proceeds to the county's general fund and remit the other half, less taxes refunded and a 2% handling fee, to the Department of Revenue [G.S. § 105-228.30(b)].

• *Taxes recoverable by action*

A county may recover unpaid realty transfer taxes in an action in the name of the county brought in the superior court of the county. The action may be filed if the taxes remain unpaid more than 30 days after the register of deeds has demanded payment. In such actions, costs of court will include a fee to the county of $25 for the expense of collection [G.S. § 105-228.33].

• *Administrative provisions*

The provisions of Article 9 of Chapter 105 apply to the realty transfer tax [G.S. § 105-228.35].

• *Refunds*

Refunds may be requested: A taxpayer who overpays the realty transfer tax may seek a refund by filing a written refund request with the board of county commissioners of the county where the tax was paid within six months of the date of payment explaining why a refund is due [G.S. § 105-228.37(a)]. Although the statute requires the transferor to pay the tax, a transferee may agree with his transferor to pay the tax. A transferee in such a case has no standing to seek a refund of an overpayment of the tax [*Am. Woodland Indus., Inc. v. Tolson*, 155 N.C. App. 624, 574 S.E.2d 55 (2002), *rev. denied*, 357 N.C. 61, 579 S.E.2d 283 (2003)].

Hearing must be held: The board must hold a hearing on the refund request. Within 60 days after a timely request for a refund has been filed and at least 10 days before the date set for the hearing, the board must notify the taxpayer in writing of the time and place at which the hearing will be conducted. The date set for the hearing must be within 90 days after the timely request for a hearing was filed or at a later date mutually agreed upon by the taxpayer and the board. The board must make a decision on the requested refund with 90 days after conducting the hearing [G.S. § 105-228.37(b)].

Process if refund granted: If the board of commissioners decides that a refund is due, it must refund the overpayment, together with any applicable interest to the taxpayer and inform the Department of Revenue of the refund. The Department of Revenue may assess the taxpayer for the amount of the refund if it disagrees with the board's decision [G.S. § 105-228.37(c)].

Process if refund denied: If the board of commissioners finds that no refund is due, the written decision of the board must inform the taxpayer and the taxpayer may request a departmental review of the denial in accordance with the procedures set out in G.S. § 105-241.11 [G.S. § 105-228.37(d)].

Before a refund can be made, the taxpayer must record a new instrument reflecting the correct amount of tax due, or, if no tax is due because the instrument was recorded in the wrong county, the taxpayer must record a document so stating, including the names of the grantors and grantees and the book and page number of the instrument being corrected. The taxpayer must also provide the register of deeds a copy of the refund decision granting the refund and showing the correct amount of tax [G.S. § 105-228.37(e)].

Interest on overpayments accrues 30 days after the filing of a refund request at the general rate of interest on overpayments and assessments established under G.S. § 105-241.21 [G.S. § 105-228.37(f)].

In Mecklenburg County, the county commissioners may delegate the authority to hear refund requests to the county manager. If the manager finds that a refund is due, the county must refund the overpayment with interest to the taxpayer. If the manager finds that no refund is due, the board of county commissioners must conduct a de novo hearing on the refund request [S.L. 2009-110, § 2].

¶2906 Public Utilities and Regulatory Fee

• *Public utility regulatory fee*

For the purpose of defraying the cost of regulating public utilities, every public utility subject to the jurisdiction of the North Carolina Utilities Commission is subject to a quarterly regulatory fee based on a percentage of the utility's jurisdictional revenues [G.S. § 62-302(a)]. The regulatory fee for noncompetitive jurisdictional revenues is 0.148%. The regulatory fee for subsection (h) competitive jurisdictional revenues is 0.04%. The regulatory fee for subsection (m) competitive jurisdictional revenues is 0.02%. These percentages applicable to non-competition revenues are subject to adjustment annually by the Utilities Commission but may not exceed 0.175% [G.S. § 62-302(b)]. The electric membership corporation regulatory fee is $200,000 [G.S. § 62-302(b1)].

• *Definitions*

Public utility. The term "public utility" means a person, whether organized under the laws of North Carolina or under the laws of any other state or county, that owns or operates equipment or facilities in North Carolina for the any of the purposes listed in G.S. § 62-3(23) [G.S. § 62-3(23)a]. The term includes light, heat, and power companies; water and sewerage companies; public transportation companies; oil and gas pipeline companies; and telecommunications companies. The term also includes all persons affiliated through stock ownership with a public utility doing business in North Carolina as parent corporation or subsidiary corporation to such an extent that the North Carolina Utilities Commission determines that such affiliation has an effect on the rate or service of the public utility [G.S. § 62-3(23)c].

Noncompetitive jurisdictional revenues. Noncompetitive jurisdictional revenues means all revenues derived from intrastate rates, tariffs or charges approved by the Utilities Commission other than tap-on fees and other contributions in aid of construction [G.S. § 62-302(b)(4)a].

Subsection (h) competitive revenues. Subsection (h) competitive revenues means revenue derived from retail services provided by local exchange companies and competing local providers that have elected to operate under G.S. § 62-133.5(h) [G.S. § 62-302(b)(4)b].

Subsection (m) competitive revenues. Subsection (m) competitive revenues means revenues derived from retail services provided by local exchange companies and competing local providers that have elected to operate under G.S. § 62-133.5(m) [G.S. § 62-302(b)(4)c].

¶2907 Freight Line Companies Excise Tax

Article 8A of Chapter 105 of the North Carolina General Statutes imposes an excise tax on freight line companies. For purposes of the excise tax on freight line companies, the property of freight line companies is declared to constitute a special class of property, and a gross earnings tax is imposed on freight line companies in lieu of all ad valorem taxes (both State and local) [G.S. § 105-228.2(a)].

• *Base and rate*

The excise tax on freight line companies is imposed on the total gross earnings received from all sources within North Carolina at a rate of 3% [G.S. § 105-228.2(c)].

A "freight line company" is any person or persons, joint-stock association or corporation (wherever organized or incorporated) engaged in the business of operating cars or engaged in the business of furnishing or leasing cars not otherwise listed for taxation in North Carolina, for the transportation of freight (whether the cars are owned by the leasing company or any other person or company), over any railway or lines (that the freight line company does not own), in whole or in part, within North Carolina. It does not matter whether the cars be termed box, flat, coal, ore, tank, stock, gondola, furniture, or refrigerator car, or by some other name [G.S. § 105-228.2(b)].

"Gross earnings received from all sources within North Carolina" means all earnings from the operation of freight cars within North Carolina for all car movements or business beginning and ending with North Carolina and a proportion (based on the proportion of car mileage with North Carolina to the total car mileage) or earnings on all interstate car movements or business passing through, or into or out of North Carolina [G.S. § 105-228.2(e)].

• *Reports and payment of tax*

Every railroad company using or leasing the cars of any freight line company must, when paying for the use or lease of cars, withhold the imposed freight lines tax. On or before March 1 of each year, a railroad company must file a statement showing the payment amount for the next preceding 12-month period ending December 31 and the amount of tax withheld. Payment of the tax withheld is due with the statements. If a railroad company fails to file a report or remit the withheld tax, the railroad company becomes liable for the tax and is not entitled to deduct from its gross earnings the amount paid by it to freight line companies [G.S. § 105-228.2(f)].

• *Administration*

The administrative provisions of Article 9 of Chapter 105 apply to the excise tax on freight line companies [G.S. § 105-228.2(i)]. The tax is administered by the Excise Tax Division of the North Carolina Department of Revenue.

¶2908 Gasoline Tax—Tax on Gasoline, Diesel, and Blends

• *Generally*

Currently there are three motor fuels taxes: (1) the gasoline tax—tax on gasoline, diesel, and blends (discussed in this paragraph); (2) the alternative fuels tax (discussed at ¶2909); and (3) the tax on carriers using fuel purchased outside North Carolina (discussed at ¶2910).

• *Imposition*

An excise tax (known as the "gasoline tax") is imposed on motor fuel. The state gasoline tax is included in the retail price paid by consumers at the pump and is thus paid by those who purchase and consume the fuel [G.S. § 105-449.62]. The gasoline tax is specifically imposed on the following motor fuels:

(1) Motor fuel that is removed from a refinery or terminal and, upon removal, is subject to the federal excise tax imposed by IRC § 4081 [G.S. § 105-449.81(1)]. If the fuel is removed from a refinery, the tax is payable by the refiner [G.S. § 105-449.82(a)]. If the fuel is removed from a terminal by a system transfer the tax is payable by the position holder or, if the position holder is not the terminal operator the tax is payable jointly and severally by the position holder and the terminal operator [G.S. § 105-449.82(b)]. If the fuel is removed at a terminal rack, the tax is payable by the person that first receives the fuel when it is removed from the terminal, provided that (1) the supplier of the fuel is also jointly and severally liable if the fuel is removed by an unlicensed distributor, (2) the terminal operator and the person selling the fuel are also jointly and severally liable if the fuel is sold by someone who is not a licensed supplier, (3) the terminal operator and the supplier are also jointly and severally liable if the shipping document states that the fuel is dyed diesel fuel but the fuel removed is not dyed diesel fuel. If the fuel is removed for export by an unlicensed exporter, the exporter is liable for the tax at the motor fuel rate and at the rate of the destination state, provided that a supplier who sells fuel to an unlicensed exporter is also jointly and severally liable for the tax due at the motor fuel rate [G.S. § 105-449.82(c)].

(2) Motor fuel that is imported by a system transfer to a refinery or a terminal and, upon importation, is subject to the federal excise tax imposed by IRC § 4081 [G.S. § 105-449.81(2)]. If the fuel is imported by a system transfer to a refinery, the tax is payable to the refinery. If the fuel is imported by a system transfer to a terminal, the tax is payable by the importer, provided that the terminal operator is also jointly and severally liable for the tax [G.S. § 105-449.83(a)].

(3) Motor fuel that is imported by a means of transfer outside the terminal transfer system for sale, use, or storage in this State and would have been subject to the federal excise tax imposed by Section 4081 of the Code if it had been removed at a terminal or bulk plant rack in this State instead of imported [G.S. § 105-449.81(3)]. If the fuel is removed from a terminal rack located in another state and North Carolina is the destination state (1) the tax is payable by the supplier if the importer is a licensed supplier and the fuel is removed for the supplier's own account for use in North Carolina; (2) the tax is payable to the supplier as trustee if the supplier is licensed in North Carolina as an elective supplier; and (3) otherwise the tax is payable by the importer when filing a return [G.S. § 105-449.83(b)]. If the fuel is removed from a bulk plant in another state, the tax is payable by the importer [G.S. § 105-449.83(c)].

(4) Fuel grade ethanol or biodiesel fuel if the fuel meets any of the following descriptions [G.S. § 105-449.81(3b)]:

(a) It is produced in North Carolina and is removed from the storage facility at the production location.

(b) It is imported to North Carolina by transport truck, railroad tank car, tank wagon or marine vessel where ethanol or biodiesel from the vessel is not delivered to a terminal that has been assigned a terminal control number by the IRS.

The tax on fuel grade ethanol is payable by the refiner or fuel alcohol provider. The tax on biodiesel fuel is payable by the refiner or biodiesel provider [G.S. § 105-449.83A].

(5) Blended fuel made in or imported to North Carolina [G.S. § 105-449.81(4)]. If the fuel is made in North Carolina, the tax is payable by the blender, and the number of gallons on which tax is due is the number of gallons of blended fuel made reduced by the number of gallons of previously taxed fuel used to make the blended fuel [G.S. § 105-449.84(a)]. If the fuel is imported into North Carolina, the tax is payable by the importer [G.S. § 105-449.84(b)].

(6) Motor fuel that is transferred within the terminal transfer system and, upon transfer, is subject to the federal excise tax imposed by IRC § 4081 or is transferred to a person who is not licensed under these provisions as a supplier [G.S. § 105-449.81(5)]. If the fuel is transferred within the terminal transfer system and is subject to the federal excise tax, the tax is payable by the supplier, the person receiving the fuel and the terminal operator all of whom are jointly and severally liable. If the fuel is transferred within the terminal transfer system by someone who is not a licensed supplier, the tax is payable by the person transferring the fuel, the person receiving the fuel and the terminal operator, all of whom are liable for the tax [G.S. § 105-449.84A].

• *Rate*

Beginning in 2017, the motor fuels excise tax rate is computed as the rate in effect for the prior year (which for 2017 is treated as 34¢ per gallon) multiplied by a percentage. The percentage is 100% plus or minus the sum of (1) 75% of the percentage change in population for the applicable calendar year (as estimated under G.S. § 143C-2-2) and (2) 25% of the annual percentage change in the Consumer Price Index for All Urban Consumers (or equivalent data as determined by the Secretary) [G.S. § 105-449.80(a)]. The rate in effect for the 2019 calendar year is $0.362 per gallon.

• *Tax on dyed diesel fuel*

An excise tax at the motor fuel rate is imposed on dyed diesel fuel acquired to operate any of the following:

(1) A local bus that is allowed by IRC § 4082(b)(3) to use dyed diesel fuel [G.S. § 105-449.86(a)(2)].

(2) A highway vehicle that is owned by or leased to an educational organization that is not a public school and is allowed by IRC § 4082(b)(1) or (b)(3) to use dyed diesel fuel [G.S. § 105-449.86(a)(3)].

Liability for tax: The distributor of taxable dyed diesel fuel is liable for the tax in the following circumstances:

(1) When the person acquiring the dyed diesel fuel has storage facilities for the fuel and is therefore a bulk-end use of the fuel.

(2) When the person acquired the dyed diesel fuel from a retail outlet of the distributor by using an access card or code indicating that the person's use of the fuel is taxable.

¶2908

If the dyed diesel fuel distributor is not liable for the tax on taxable dyed diesel fuel, the person that acquires the fuel is liable for the tax [G.S. § 105-449.86(b)].

Responsible person in business entity: Each responsible person in a business entity is personally and individually liable for all taxes due from the entity on fuels (under Articles 36C and 36D of Subchapter I of Chapter 105) and all fuel taxes payable by it to a supplier for remittance to North Carolina or another state [G.S. § 105-242.2(b)].

• *Marking requirements for dyed motor fuel storage facilities*

A person who is a dyed motor fuel retailer or who stores both dyed and undyed motor fuel must mark the storage facility for the dyed motor fuel as follows in a manner that clearly indicates the fuel is not to be used to operate a highway vehicle. The storage facility must be marked "Dyed Diesel, Nontaxable Use Only, Penalty For Taxable Use" or "Dyed Kerosene, Nontaxable Use Only, Penalty for Taxable Use" or a similar phrase that clearly indicates the fuel is not to be used to operate a highway vehicle. A person who intentionally fails to mark the storage facility as required is subject to a civil penalty equal to the excise tax at the motor fuel rate on the inventory held in the storage tank at the time of the violation. If the inventory cannot be determined, the penalty is calculated on the capacity of the storage tank [G.S. § 105-449.123(a)].

Place of marking: The following marking requirements must be met (see G.S. § 105-449.123(a)):

(1) The storage tank of the storage facility if the storage tank is visible.

(2) The fillcap or spill containment box of the storage facility.

(3) The dispensing device that serves the storage facility.

In addition, the retail pump or dispensing device at any level of the distribution system must comply with the marking requirements.

Exception: The marking requirements do not apply to a storage facility that (1) contains fuel used only for one of the purposes listed in G.S. § 105-449.105A(a)(1), relating to monthly refunds for kerosene (discussed below) and (2) is installed in a manner that makes use of the fuel for any other purpose improbable [G.S. § 105-449.123(b)].

• *Inspection tax*

The following fuels are subject to an inspection tax of one-fourth of one cent ($^1/_4$ of 1¢) per gallon regardless of whether the fuel is exempt from the gasoline tax (see "Exemptions," below) or the per-gallon alternative fuels tax (discussed at ¶ 2909) [G.S. § 119-18(a)]:

(1) Motor fuel.

(2) Alternative fuel used to operate a highway vehicle.

(3) Kerosene.

Definition of Terms

Definitions of terms used for gasoline tax purposes can be found in G.S. § 105-440.60.

• *Restrictions on local taxation of motor fuel*

A county or city may not impose a tax on the sale, distribution, or use of motor fuel, except motor fuel for which a refund of the per gallon excise tax is allowed under G.S. § § 105-449.105A or 105-449.107. The motor fuel taxes may be applied only once on the same motor fuel [G.S. § 105-449.61].

• *Exemptions*

The gasoline tax does not apply to the following:

(1) Motor fuel removed, by transport truck or another means of transfer outside the terminal transfer system, from a terminal for export, if (a) the motor fuel is removed by a licensed distributor or a licensed exporter and (b) the supplier of the motor fuel collects tax on it at the rate of the motor fuel's destination state [G.S. § 105-449.88(1)].

(2) Motor fuel removed by transport truck from a terminal for export if (a) the motor fuel is removed by a licensed distributor or licensed exporter; (b) the supplier that is the position holder for the motor fuel sells the motor fuel to another supplier as the motor fuel crosses the terminal rack; (c) the purchasing supplier or its customer receives the motor fuel at the terminal rack for export; and (d) the supplier that is the position holder collects tax on the motor fuel at the rate of the motor fuel's destination state [G.S. § 105-449.88(1a)].

(3) Motor fuel sold to the federal government for its use [G.S. § 105-449.88(2)].

(4) Motor fuel sold to the State of North Carolina for its use [G.S. § 105-449.88(3)].

(5) Motor fuel sold to a local board of education for use in the public school system [G.S. § 105-449.88(4)].

(6) Diesel that is kerosene and is sold to an airport [G.S. § 105-449.88(5)].

(7) Motor fuel sold to a charter school for use for charter school purposes [G.S. § 105-449.88(6)].

(8) Motor fuel sold to a community college for use for community college purposes [G.S. § 105-449.88(7)].

(9) Motor fuel sold to a county or a municipal corporation for its use [G.S. § 105-449.88(8)].

(10) Biodiesel that is produced by an individual for use in a private passenger vehicle registered in that individual's name [G.S. § 105-449.88(9)].

(11) Motor fuel sold to a hospital authority created by a city or county pursuant to G.S. § 131-E-17 [G.S. § 105-449.88(10)].

(12) Motor fuel sold to a joint agency created by interlocal government agreement to provide fire protection, emergency services, or police protection [G.S.§ 105-449.88(11)].

• *Licenses*

A person may not engage in any of the following businesses in North Carolina unless that person has a license issued by the Secretary authorizing the person to engage in that business:

(1) A refiner [G.S. § 105-449.65(a)(1)].

(2) A supplier [G.S. § 105-449.65(a)(2)].

(3) A terminal operator [G.S. § 105-449.65(a)(3)].

(4) An importer [G.S. § 105-449.65(a)(4)].

(5) An exporter [G.S. § 105-449.65(a)(5)]. An exporter that is not licensed as a distributor must have an exporter's license. An applicant for an exporter's license must meet the same licensing requirements as an applicant for a distributor's license, except the requirement of filing a bond [17 NCAC 12B.0102].

(6) A blender [G.S. § 105-449.65(a)(6)].

(7) A motor fuel transporter [G.S. § 105-449.65(a)(7)].

(8) A distributor who purchases motor fuel from an elective or permissive supplier at an out-of-state terminal for import into North Carolina [G.S. § 105-449.65(a)(10)].

Multiple activities: A person who is engaged in more than one activity for which a license is required must have a separate license for each activity [G.S. § 105-449.65(b)]. There are several exceptions to this rule:

(1) A person who is licensed as a supplier is considered to have a license as a distributor and as a blender.

(2) A person who is licensed as an occasional importer or a tank wagon importer is not required to obtain a separate license as a distributor unless the importer is also purchasing motor fuel, at the terminal rack, from an elective or permissive supplier who is authorized to collect and remit the tax to the State.

(3) A person who is licensed as a distributor is not required to obtain a separate license as an importer if the distributor acquires fuel for import only from an elective supplier or a permissive supplier and is not required to obtain a separate license as an exporter.

Other persons eligible to obtain licenses: Persons who are engaged in business as (1) distributors who are not required to be licensed under G.S. § 105-449.65 or (2) permissive suppliers may obtain licenses for that business [G.S. § 105-449.67].

License application: To obtain a license, an applicant must file an application with the Secretary on a form provided by the Secretary [G.S. § 105-449.69(a)]. An application must include the applicant's name, address, federal employer identification number, and any other information required by the Secretary. To be eligible for a license, an applicant must meet the requirements imposed by G.S. § 105-449.69.

Requirements for most license applicants: An applicant for a license as a refiner, a supplier, a terminal operator, an importer, a blender, a retailer of undyed diesel fuel, or a distributor must meet the following requirements:

(1) Corporate applicants must either be incorporated in North Carolina or be authorized to transact business in North Carolina [G.S. § 105-449.69(b)(1)].

(2) Limited liability company applicants must either be organized in North Carolina or be authorized to transact business in North Carolina [G.S. § 105-449.69(b)(2)].

(3) Limited partnership applicants must either be formed in North Carolina or be authorized to transact business in North Carolina [G.S. § 105-449.69(b)(3)].

(4) Individual applicants or general partnership applicants must designate an agent for service of process and give the agent's name and address [G.S. § 105-449.69(b)(4)].

Federal certificates: An applicant for a license as a refiner, a supplier, a terminal operator, a blender, or a permissive supplier must have a federal Certificate of Registry that is issued under IRC § 4101 and authorizes the applicant to enter into federal tax-free transactions in a taxable motor fuel in the terminal transfer system;

and the registration number of the certification must be included in the license application. An applicant for a license as an importer, an exporter, or a distributor that has a federal Certificate of Registry issued under IRC §4101 must include the registration number of the certificate on the license application [G.S. §105-449.69(c)].

Import activity: An applicant for a license as an importer or distributor must list on the license application each state from which the applicant intends to import motor fuel. If a state listed requires the applicant to be licensed or registered, the applicant must be licensed or registered for motor fuel tax purposes in that state, and the applicant must give its license or registration number in that state [G.S. §105-449.69(d)].

Export activity: An applicant for a license as an exporter or distributor must list on the license application each state to which the applicant intends to export motor fuel received in North Carolina by means of a transfer that is outside the terminal transfer system. If a state listed requires the applicant to be licensed or registered, the applicant must be licensed or registered for motor fuel tax purposes in that state, and the applicant must give its license or registration number in that state [G.S. §105-449.69(e)].

Bond or letter of credit required: An applicant for a license as a refiner, a terminal operator, a supplier, an importer, a blender, a permissive supplier, or a distributor must file a bond or an irrevocable letter of credit [G.S. §105-449.72(a)]. A bond or an irrevocable letter of credit must (1) be conditioned upon compliance with the requirements of Article 36C, (2) be payable to the State, and (3) be in the form required by the Secretary. The amount of the bond or irrevocable letter of credit is determined under G.S. §105-449.72. No bond or letter of credit is required of a distributor, importer, or transporter when the market for motor fuel is disrupted and emergency supplies are needed as determined by the Governor [G.S. §105-449.72(f)].

• *Issued licenses*

Upon approval of an application, the Secretary must issue a license to the applicant. A supplier's license must indicate the category of the supplier. An importer's license must indicate the category of the importer. A licensee must maintain and display a copy of the license issued in a conspicuous place at each place of business of the licensee. A license is not transferable and remains in effect until surrendered or cancelled [G.S. §105-449.74].

• *Denial of license for failure to pay tax or file return*

A license may be denied to an applicant if the applicant has, among other things, failed to file a return or pay a tax debt under either Chapter 105 or Chapter 199 [G.S. §105-449.73].

• *Discounts for licensed distributors and some licensed importers*

Amount of discount: A licensed distributor that pays tax due a supplier by the date the supplier must remit the tax to the State may deduct a discount of 1% of the amount of tax payable. A licensed importer that removes motor fuel from a terminal rack of a permissive or an elective supplier and pays the tax due the supplier by the date the supplier must remit the tax to the State may also deduct a discount of 1%. A supplier may not directly or indirectly deny this discount to a licensed distributor or licensed importer that pays the tax due to the supplier by the date the supplier must remit the tax to the State [G.S. §105-449.93(b)].

Refund: If the amount of the discount the licensed distributor or licensed importer receives under G.S. §105-449.93(b) is less than the amount that would have been received during the month if the distributor or importer had been allowed a discount on taxable gasoline purchased from a supplier under the distributor or importer is allowed a monthly refund of the difference [G.S. § 105-449.105B]:

Amount of Gasoline Purchased Each Month	Percentage Discount
First 150,000 gallons	2.0%
Next 100,000 gallons	1.5%
Amount over 250,000 gallons	1.0%

In determining the amount of discounts a distributor or importer received under G.S. § 105-449.93(b) for motor fuel purchased in a month, a distributor or importer is considered to have received the amount of any discounts the distributor or importer could have received but did not receive because the distributor or importer failed to pay the tax due to the supplier by the date the supplier had to pay the tax to the State.

- *Reports and payment of tax*

A gasoline tax return must be filed annually or monthly (as specified below) and must be filed with the Secretary of Revenue in the form required by the Secretary. Payment is due with the return [G.S. § 105-449.90(a)].

Annual filers: Terminal operators must file annual returns for tax on unaccounted for fuels [G.S. § 105-449.90(b)]. Annual returns are due within 45 days after the end of each calendar year and cover liabilities that accrue in the calendar preceding the due date of the return [G.S. § 105-449.90(a)].

Monthly filers: The following persons must file monthly returns [G.S. § 105-449.90(d)]:

(1) Refiners.

(2) Suppliers.

(3) Bonded importers.

(4) Blenders.

(5) Tank wagon importers.

(6) Persons that incurred a liability under G.S. § 105-449.86 during the preceding month for the tax on dyed diesel fuel used to operate certain highway vehicles.

(7) Persons that incurred a liability under G.S. § 105-449.87 during the preceding month for the backup tax on motor fuel.

Monthly returns (other than returns of occasional importers) are due within 22 days after the end of each month. A monthly return covers tax liabilities that accrue in the calendar month preceding the date the return is due [G.S. § 105-449.90(a)]. Occasional importers must file monthly returns by the 3rd day of each month. An occasional importer, however, is not required to file a return if all the motor fuel imported by the importer in a reporting period was removed at a terminal located in another state and the supplier of the fuel is an elective supplier or a permissive supplier [G.S. § 105-449.90(e)].

Reporting in the proper reporting period: All motor fuels transactions must be reported on the return for the month or other filing period in which the transaction occurred and may not be carried over to a return for a subsequent period. If a person, after filing a return, discovers information that affects the return, the person must file an amended return for the affected period and pay any tax, penalty, and interest due with the amended return [17 NCAC 12B.0301].

Tax collected by supplier on exported motor fuel: Tax collected by a supplier on exported motor fuel is payable by the supplier to the destination state. Payments due to the destination state are due on the date set by the law of the destination state [G.S. § 105-449.90A].

Requirements for Refund Applications

An application for a refund of gasoline tax must be filed with the Secretary and be in the form required by the Secretary. The application must state that the applicant has paid for the fuel for which a refund is claimed or that payment for the fuel has been secured to the seller's satisfaction. An application for an annual refund must state whether or not the applicant has filed a North Carolina income tax return for the preceding taxable year [G.S. § 105-449.108(b)].

• *Information returns*

A motor fuel transporter must file a monthly information return that shows motor fuel transported in North Carolina by the transporter during the month.

• *Refunds for exempt fuel*

The following entities may obtain motor fuel tax refunds [G.S. § 105-449.105(a)]:

(1) An entity whose use of motor fuel is exempt from tax may obtain a refund of any motor fuel excise tax it pays on its motor fuel.

(2) A person who sells motor fuel to an entity whose use of the fuel is exempt may obtain a refund of any motor fuel excise tax the person pays on motor fuel it sells to the entity.

(3) A credit card company that issues a credit card to an entity whose use of motor fuel is exempt may obtain a monthly refund of any tax the company pays on motor fuel the entity purchases using the credit card.

(4) A person may obtain a refund of tax paid by the person on exported fuel, including fuel whose shipping documents shows North Carolina as the destination state was diverted to another state in accordance with the diversion procedures established by the Secretary of Revenue [G.S. § 105-449.105(a)].

The amount of a refund allowed in the case of exempt fuel is the amount of the tax paid, less the amount of any discount allowed on the fuel under G.S. § 105-449.93 [G.S. § 105-449.105(e)].

• *Documenting sales to exempt entities*

A distributor or another vendor that sells motor fuel to an exempt entity may document the sales using third-party vendor lists or computer runs to document sales and must keep copies of sales invoices to support the exempt sales [17 NCAC 12B.0401].

• *Claims for refund for sales to exempt entities*

Claims for refund of tax on motor fuel sold to exempt entities are submitted on Form Gas-1206, which consists of three parts. A person who submits Form Gas-1206 must complete the applicable part of the form and submit copies of sales or purchases invoices, as appropriate, with the form [17 NCAC 12B.0402].

¶2908

• *Refunds for lost fuel*

A supplier, importer, or distributor that loses tax-paid motor fuel due to damage to a conveyance transporting the motor fuel, fire, a natural disaster, an act of war, or an accident may obtain a refund for the tax paid on the fuel [G.S. § 105-449.105(b)].

The amount of a refund allowed in the case of lost fuel is the amount of the tax paid, less the amount of any discount allowed on the fuel under G.S. § 105-449.93 [G.S. § 105-449.105(e)].

• *Refunds for fuel unsalable for highway use*

A person that accidentally combines any of the following may obtain a refund for the tax paid on the fuel [G.S. § 105-449.105(c)]:

(1) Dyed diesel fuel with tax-paid motor fuel.

(2) Gasoline with diesel fuel.

(3) Undyed diesel fuel with dyed kerosene.

The amount of a refund allowed in the case of fuel unsalable for highway use is the amount of the tax paid, less the amount of any discount allowed on the fuel under G.S. § 105-449.93 [G.S. § 105-449.105(e)]. A taxpayer's failure to tender to the Motor Fuels Tax Division invoices containing the information required by both the State Revenue Act (*i.e.,* Subchapter I of Chapter 105 of the North Carolina General Statutes) and the relevant administrative rules to substantiate a refund claim resulted in a denial of a refund [*Secretary's Decision No.* 2003-418 (March 12, 2004)].

• *Proportional refunds for off-highway use (annual)*

A person who purchases and uses motor fuel for a purpose other than to operate a licensed highway vehicle may, upon application, receive an annual refund for the excise tax paid on fuel used during the preceding calendar year. The amount of refund allowed is the amount of the flat cents-per-gallon rate in effect during the year for which the refund is claimed plus the average of the two variable cents-per-gallon rates in effect during that year, less the amount of sales and use tax due on the fuel [G.S. § 105-449.107(a)]. The amount of sales and use tax to be deducted from a motor fuel excise tax refund is determined under the sales and use tax provisions [G.S. § 105-449.107(c)].

Invoice requirements: An invoice for each purchase of motor fuel must be submitted with the claim for refund for purchases made for off-highway use during the refund period. A daily, weekly, or monthly statement of purchases is acceptable if it is prepared by the seller and shows all required information on each purchase. Invoices showing alterations or erasures are not acceptable. If no claim for refund was filed for the preceding refund period, an invoice or statement must be attached to substantiate inventory at the beginning of the refund period. Invoices must show the date of purchase, the names of the purchaser and seller, the number of gallons purchased, the purchase price and the amount paid [17 NCAC 12B.0404]. Refund claims supported by invoices that lack this information will be denied [*Secretary's Decision No.* 2003-418 (March 12, 2004)].

• *Proportional refund for use by certain vehicles with power attachments (annual)*

A person who purchases and uses motor fuel in certain vehicles may, upon application, receive an annual refund for the amount of fuel consumed by the vehicle in its mixing, compacting, or unloading operations, as distinguished from propelling the vehicle (considered to be $1/3$ of the amount of fuel consumed by the vehicle [G.S. § 105-449.107(b)].

The vehicles for which this refund is available are as follows:

(1) A concrete mixing vehicle.

(2) A solid waste compacting vehicle.

(3) A bulk feed vehicle that delivers feed to poultry or livestock and uses a power takeoff to unload the feed.

(4) A vehicle that delivers lime or fertilizer in bulk to farms and uses a power takeoff to unload the lime or fertilizer.

(5) A tank wagon that delivers alternative fuel (see ¶2909) or motor fuel or another type of liquid fuel into storage tanks and uses a power takeoff to make the delivery.

(6) A commercial vehicle that delivers and spreads mulch, soils, composts, sand, sawdust, and similar materials and that uses a power takeoff to unload, blow, and spread the materials.

(7) A commercial vehicle that uses a power takeoff to remove and dispose of sewage and for which an annual fee is required to be paid to the Department of Environmental Quality under G.S. § 130A 291.1.

(8) A sweeper.

The amount of refund allowed is $33^1/3$% of the following: the sum of the flat cents-per-gallon rate in effect during the year for which the refund is claimed and the average of the two variable cents-per-gallon rates in effect during that year, less the amount of sales and use tax due on the fuel [G.S. § 105-449.107(b)]. The amount of sales and use tax to be deducted from a motor fuel excise tax refund is determined under the sales and use tax provisions [G.S. § 105-449.107(c)].

• *Proportional refunds—filing and recordkeeping*

Operators of vehicles identified in G.S. § 105-449.107 (relating to proportional refunds) must file Form Gas-1220C to obtain a refund for motor fuel tax paid on fuel used in the operation of these vehicles [17 NCAC 12B.0412(a)]. Invoices for tax paid on motor fuel must be submitted with the claim for refund [17 NCAC 12B.0412(b)]. The following records must be kept to support a claim for refund [17 NCAC 12B.0412(c)]:

(1) Mileage records by vehicle (including odometer or hubmeter readings).

(2) Fuel records by vehicle.

(3) Records of the following deliveries:

(a) Cubic yards of concrete mix delivered, by vehicle.

(b) Tons of compacted waste hauled, by vehicle.

(c) Tons of bulk feed or fertilizer hauled, by vehicle.

(d) Tons of mulch, or other similar materials hauled, by vehicle.

(4) Records of withdrawals from bulk storage facilities (as required by 17 NCAC 12B.0405) if withdrawals of motor fuel from bulk storage are used to service vehicles for which a refund is requested.

• *Monthly refunds for kerosene*

Refund for undyed kerosene sold to an end user for non-highway use: A distributor who sells kerosene to an end user for one of the following purposes may obtain a monthly refund the excise tax (see "Amount of refund" below), if the distributor

¶2908

dispenses the kerosene into a storage facility of the end user that contains fuel used only for one of those purposes and the storage facility is installed in a manner that makes use of the fuel for any other purpose improbable [G.S. § 105-449.105A(a)]:

(1) Heating.

(2) Drying crops.

(3) A manufacturing process.

Amount of refund: The amount of the monthly refund is the excise tax the distributor paid on the kerosene, less the amount of any discount allowed under G.S. § 105-449.93 (see "Discounts for licensed distributors and some licensed importers" above) [G.S. § 105-449.105A(a)].

Liability: If the Secretary determines that the Department overpaid a distributor by refunding more tax to the distributor than is due, the distributor is liable for the amount of the overpayment [G.S. § 105-449.105A(b)].

- *Refunds to nonprofits*

A nonprofit organization listed below that purchases and uses motor fuel may, upon application, receive a quarterly refund for the gasoline tax paid during the preceding quarter:

(1) Private, nonprofit organizations that transport passengers under contract with or at the express designation of a local government unit.

(2) Volunteer fire departments.

(3) Volunteer rescue squads.

(4) Sheltered workshops recognized by the Department of Health and Human Services.

The refunds to nonprofits will be made at the tax rate in effect during the period for which the refund is claimed, less 1¢ per gallon [G.S. § 105-449.106(a)].

- *Refunds to operators of special mobile equipment*

A person who purchases and uses motor fuel for the off-highway operation of special mobile equipment registered under Chapter 20 of the General Statutes may, upon application, receive a quarterly refund, for the excise tax paid during the preceding quarter. This refund is made at the tax rate in effect during the period for which the refund is claimed, less the amount of sales and use tax due on the fuel under this Chapter, as determined in accordance with G.S. § 105-449.107(c) [G.S. § 105-449.106(c)].

Federal/State Difference

The North Carolina statutes allow special mobile equipment to use dyed diesel fuel when operating on the highway or to use undyed diesel fuel and apply for a quarterly refund. The Internal Revenue Service (IRS), however, does not allow dyed diesel fuel to be used in special mobile equipment. If the IRS takes a sample of fuel from a special mobile equipment tank and the fuel is dyed, the IRS may assess a $1,000 penalty [*Motor Fuels Tax Newsletter*, North Carolina Department of Revenue, June 2002].

- *Backup tax*

North Carolina imposes a "backup" tax on certain fuels. The backup tax is an excise tax imposed at the motor fuel tax rate on the following:

(1) Dyed diesel fuel that is used to operate a highway vehicle for a use that is not a taxable use under IRC § 4082(b) [G.S. § 105-449.87(a)(1)].

(2) Motor fuel that was allowed an exemption from the motor fuel tax and was then used for a taxable purpose [G.S. § 105-449.87(a)(2)].

(3) Motor fuel that is used to operate a highway vehicle after an application for a refund of tax paid on the motor fuel is made or allowed on the basis that the motor fuel was used for an off-highway purpose [G.S. § 105-449.87(a)(3)].

(4) Motor fuel that, based on its shipping documents, is destined for delivery to another state and is then diverted and delivered in North Carolina [G.S. § 105-449.87(a)(5)].

General liability: The operator of a highway vehicle that uses motor fuel that is taxable under G.S. § 105-449.87(a)(1), (2), or (3) is liable for the tax. If the highway vehicle that uses the fuel is owned by or leased to a motor carrier, the motor carrier is jointly and severally liable for the tax. If the end-seller of motor fuel subject to the backup tax knew or had reason to know that the motor fuel would be used for a taxable purpose, the end-seller is jointly and severally liable for the tax. If it is determined that a bulk end-user or retailer used or sold untaxed dyed diesel fuel to operate a highway vehicle when the fuel is dispensed from a storage facility or through a meter marked for nonhighway use, all fuel delivered into that storage facility is presumed to have been used to operate a highway vehicle. An end-seller of dyed diesel fuel is considered to have known or had reason to know that the fuel would be used for a taxable purpose if the end-seller delivered the fuel into a storage facility that was not marked as required [G.S. § 105-449.87(b)]. See *Secretary's Decision No. 2003-297* (December 15, 2003), where the lack of withdrawal records to demonstrate off-road fuel usage as required by 17 NCAC 12B.0502, coupled with the documented misuse of the fuel, resulted in imposition of a special fuels bulk user tax assessment and civil penalties upon the taxpayer. See, also, *Secretary's Decision No. 2003-298* (January 13, 2004), and *Secretary's Decision No. 2003-301* (January 29, 2004).

Diverted fuel: Anyone who authorizes a change in destination state of motor fuel from the state given on the fuel's shipping document to North Carolina is liable for the tax due on the motor fuel. If motor fuel is diverted from North Carolina to another state, only the person who authorized the diversion is eligible for a refund of the tax [G.S. § 105-449.87(c)].

• *Tax on "unaccounted for" fuel*

If unaccounted for motor fuel losses at a terminal exceed one-half of one percent (0.5%) of the number of net gallons removed from the terminal during the year by a system transfer or at a terminal rack, an excise tax is imposed on the unaccounted for fuel [G.S. § 105-449.85(a)]. To determine if this tax applies, the terminal operator of the terminal must determine the difference between the following:

(1) The amount of motor fuel in inventory at the terminal at the beginning of the year plus the amount of motor fuel received by the terminal during the year.

(2) The amount of motor fuel in inventory at the terminal at the end of the year plus the amount of motor fuel removed from the terminal during the year.

Liability: The terminal operator whose motor fuel is unaccounted for is liable for the tax on unaccounted for fuel and is liable for a penalty equal to the amount of tax payable. Motor fuel received by a terminal operator and not shown on an information return filed by the terminal operator with the Secretary as having been removed from the terminal is presumed to be unaccounted for. A terminal operator may

¶2908

establish that motor fuel received at a terminal but not shown on an information return as having been removed from the terminal was lost or part of a transmix and is therefore not unaccounted for [G.S. § 105-449.85(b)].

- *Recordkeeping requirements*

Persons subject to motor fuel tax audits must keep records of all shipping documents or other documents used to determine the information the person provides in a return or to determine the person's motor fuel transactions. The records must be kept for three (3) years from the due date of the return to which the records apply. If the records apply to a transaction not required to be reported in a return, the records must be kept for three (3) years from the date of the transaction [G.S. § 105-449.121].

- *Shipping documents required to transport by fuel wagon*

A person may not transport motor fuel by tank wagon unless that person has an invoice, bill of sale, or shipping document containing all required information [G.S. § 105-449.115A(a)]. A person to whom an invoice, bill of sale, or shipping document was issued must (1) carry the invoice, bill of sale, or shipping document in the conveyance for which it is issued when transporting the motor fuel described in it; and (2) show the invoice, bill of sale, or shipping document upon request when transporting the motor fuel described in it. Transporting motor fuel in a tank wagon without an invoice, bill of sale, or shipping document containing all required information is grounds for a civil penalty in the amount of $1,000, in addition to any motor fuel tax assessed. This penalty is payable by the person in whose name the tank wagon is registered [G.S. § 105-449.115A(b)].

- *Sanctions against transporters*

The following acts are grounds for a civil penalty:

(1) Transporting motor fuel in a railroad tank car or transport truck without a shipping document or with a false or incomplete shipping document [G.S. § 105-449.115(f)(1)].

(2) Delivering motor fuel to a destination state other than that shown on the shipping document [G.S. § 105-449.115(f)(2)].

This penalty is payable to the agency that assessed the penalty by the person in whose name the conveyance is registered, if the conveyance is a transport truck, and is payable by the person responsible for the movement of motor fuel in the conveyance, if the conveyance is a railroad tank car. The amount of this penalty is $5,000, in addition to any motor fuel tax assessed [G.S. § 105-449.115(f)].

- *Penalties*

The general penalties provided for in Article 9 of Chapter 105 of the General Statutes also apply to the gasoline tax [G.S. § 105-449.61(c)]. In addition, the following penalties apply specifically to the gasoline tax:

(1) *Highway use of dyed diesel or other non-tax-paid fuel:* It is unlawful to use dyed fuel in a highway vehicle that is licensed or required to be licensed under Chapter 20 of the General Statutes unless (a) that use is allowed under IRC § 4082 or (b) the tax has been paid. A person who violates this section is guilty of a Class 1 misdemeanor and is liable for a civil penalty. The amount of the penalty depends on the amount of fuel in the highway vehicle's supply tank and is the greater of (1) $1,000 or (2) five (5) times the amount of motor fuel tax payable on the fuel in the supply tank. This penalty is in addition to any motor

fuel tax assessed [G.S. § 105-449.117(a)]. The penalty is payable to the agency that assessed the penalty. This penalty may be assessed whenever the presence of dye is detected in a sample taken from the fuel tank of the vehicle [17 NCAC 12B.0503].

(2) *Buying or selling non-tax-paid motor fuel:* A person who dispenses (or allows to be dispensed) non-tax-paid motor fuel into the tank of a highway vehicle is subject to a civil penalty of $1,000. Failure to pay this penalty is grounds to withhold or revoke the registration plate of the motor vehicle into which the fuel was dispensed. The penalty is payable to the agency that assessed the penalty [G.S. § 105-449.118]. Prior to January 1, 2003, this penalty was based on the amount of motor fuel dispensed.

(3) *Refusal to allow sample to be taken:* A person who refuses to allow the taking of a motor fuel sample is subject to a civil penalty of $1,000. If the refusal is for a sample to be taken from a vehicle, the penalty is payable by the person to whom the vehicle is registered. If the refusal is for a sample to be taken from any other storage tank or container, the penalty is payable by the owner of the container [G.S. § 105-449.118A].

• *Review of civil penalty assessment*

A person who denies liability for a penalty may request the Secretary to waive the penalty. The Secretary may waive or reduce the penalty as provided in Article 9 of Chapter 105 [G.S. § 105-449.119].

• *Administration*

The gasoline tax is administered by the Motor Fuels Tax Division of the North Carolina. The administrative provisions of Article 9 of Chapter 105 apply to the gasoline tax [G.S. § 105-449.61(c)]. See Chapters 31 and 32 for discussion of administrative provisions.

¶2909 Alternative Fuels Tax

• *Imposition and liability for tax*

An alternative fuel tax is imposed on alternative fuels [G.S. § 105-449.136]. An "alternative fuel" is a combustible gas or liquid that can be used to generate power to operate a highway vehicle and that is not subject to the gasoline tax (discussed at ¶2908) [G.S. § 105-449.130(1)]. The tax is payable by a bulk end-user or retailer applies when fuel is withdrawn from the storage facility [G.S. § 105-449.137(a)].

A bulk end-user or retailer that stores highway and nonhighway alternative fuel in the same storage facility is liable for the alternative fuel tax; the alternative fuel provider that sells or delivers alternative fuel is liable for the tax on all other alternative fuels [G.S. § 105-449.137(a)]. A "bulk end-user" for this purpose is a person who maintains storage facilities for alternative fuel and uses part or all of the stored fuel to operate a highway vehicle [G.S. § 105-449.130(1a)].

• *Rates*

A tax at the gasoline tax rate is imposed on liquid alternative fuel used to operate a highway vehicle by means of a vehicle supply tank that stores fuel only for the purpose of supplying fuel to operate the vehicle. The tax on liquefied natural gas is imposed on each diesel gallon equivalent of liquefied natural gas (i.e., the energy equivalent of 6.06 pounds of liquefied natural gas). The tax on liquefied propane gas is imposed on each gas gallon equivalent of liquified propane gas (effective January

1, 2016). The tax on compressed natural gas is imposed on each gas gallon equivalent of compressed natural gas (i.e., the energy equivalent of 5.66 pounds of compressed natural gas) [G.S. §§ 105-449.136 and 105-449.130(1f), (1g) and (1h)]. A tax at the equivalent of the motor fuel rate (as determined by the Secretary of Revenue) is imposed on all other alternative fuel used to operate a highway vehicle [G.S. § 105-449.136]. The Secretary must determine the equivalent rate for all other non-liquid alternative fuels [G.S. § 105-449.136]. The rates of the gasoline tax (i.e., the motor fuel tax rates) are discussed at ¶ 2908.

- *Exemptions*

Fuel exempt from the gasoline tax under G.S. § 105-449.88 (discussed at ¶ 2908) is also exempt from the alternative fuels tax [G.S. § 105-449.136].

- *Licenses*

Persons may not engage in business in North Carolina as any of the following unless they have a license issued by the Secretary of Revenue authorizing them to engage in that business [G.S. § 105-449.131]:

(1) A provider of alternative fuel.

(2) A bulk end-user.

(3) A retailer.

License applicants must meet all the requirements of G.S. § 105-449.69 [G.S. § 105-449.132]. Licenses are not transferable and remain in effect until revoked or cancelled [G.S. § 105-449.135(a)].

License applications: To obtain a license, an applicant must file an application with the Secretary of Revenue on a form provided by the Secretary [G.S. § 105-449.132]. A bond or letter of credit is required as a condition of obtaining and keeping certain licenses [G.S. § 105-449.133]. The Secretary must issue a license to all applicants who applications are approved.

- *Returns and payment of tax*

Alternative fuel tax returns are due within 25 days after the end of each month. A monthly return covers liabilities that accrue in the calendar month preceding the date the return is due. The tax is payable when a return is due [G.S. § 105-449.137(b)].

- *Information returns*

Bulk end-users and retailers must file quarterly information returns that cover a calendar quarter and are due by the last day of the month that follows the quarter covered by the return [G.S. § 105-449.138(a)].

- *Storage of fuel*

Bulk end-user or retailers may store highway and nonhighway alternative fuel in separate storage facilities or in the same storage facility. If they are stored in separate storage facilities, the facility for the nonhighway fuel must be marked in accordance with the requirements for dyed diesel storage facilities (discussed at ¶ 2908). If they are stored in the same storage facility, the storage facility must be equipped with separate metering devices for the highway fuel and the nonhighway fuel. If it is determined that a bulk end-user or retailer used or sold alternative fuel to operate a highway vehicle when the fuel was dispensed from a storage facility or through a meter marked for nonhighway use, all fuel delivered into that storage facility is presumed to have been used to operate a highway vehicle [G.S. § 105-449.138(b)].

¶ 2909

• *Recordkeeping requirements*

Licensees must keep records of all documents used to determine the information provided in an alternative tax return and make them open to inspection during business hours. The records must be kept for three (3) years from the date of the return to which the records apply [G.S. § 105-449.139(a)].

• *Violations*

The misdemeanor acts listed in subdivisions (1) through (9) of G.S. § 105-449.120 apply to the alternative fuel tax [G.S. § 105-449.139(b)].

¶2910 Motor Fuels Tax on Motor Carriers

• *International Fuel Tax Agreement (IFTA)*

The International Fuel Tax Agreement (IFTA) is an agreement among states and Canadian provinces to simplify the reporting of fuel used by motor carriers operating in more than one jurisdiction. Currently, IFTA membership consists of all U.S. states except Alaska and Hawaii and the following Canadian provinces: Alberta, British Columbia, Manitoba, New Brunswick, Newfoundland, Nova Scotia, Ontario, Prince Edward Island, Quebec, and Saskatchewan. IFTA is a base jurisdiction fuel tax agreement. Upon application, a carrier's base jurisdiction issues the credentials (license and decals) that allow the IFTA licensee to travel in all IFTA member jurisdictions.

IFTA licensing offers several benefits to the interjurisdictional motor carrier, including the following: one application, one set of credentials for each qualified vehicle, one quarterly tax return that reflects the net tax or refund due, and one audit in most circumstances. IFTA carriers operating in non-IFTA jurisdictions must continue to follow the procedures and file the returns required by the statutes and regulations of those non-IFTA jurisdictions [*N.C. IFTA Compliance Manual*, § I].

More information: Additional information regarding IFTA can be found at the IFTA website at http://www.iftach.org.

N.C. IFTA Compliance Manual

Unless otherwise indicated, a reference to the *N.C. IFTA Compliance Manual* is a reference to the *International Fuel Tax Agreement Compliance Manual* issued by the Motor Fuels Tax Division of the North Carolina Department of Revenue. A copy of the *IFTA Compliance Manual* can be obtained from the Department of Revenue's web site at http://www.dornc.com/publications/compliancemanual.pdf#search=%22ifta%20compliance%20manual%22.

The Agreement is administered by the International Fuel Tax Association, Inc. More IFTA information is available on the Association's web site: http://www.iftach.org/index.php. All North Carolina IFTA inquiries should be directed to the Motor Fuels Tax Division of the North Carolina Department of Revenue.

• *Base jurisdiction in North Carolina*

North Carolina is a carrier's base jurisdiction (defined below) for IFTA licensing and reporting if the following requirements are met [*N.C. IFTA Compliance Manual*, § II]:

(1) The carrier has a qualified motor vehicle licensed with the North Carolina Division of Motor Vehicles.

¶2910

(2) The carrier maintains the operational control and records for qualified motor vehicles in North Carolina or can make those records available in North Carolina.

(3) The carrier has qualified motor vehicles that actually travel on North Carolina highways.

(4) The carrier operates in at least one other IFTA jurisdiction.

- *Definition of terms*

Base jurisdiction: The member jurisdiction where qualified motor vehicles are based for vehicle registration purposes and (1) where the operational control and operational records of the licensee's qualified motor vehicles are maintained or can be made available; and (2) where some travel is accrued by qualified motor vehicles within the fleet. The commissioners of two or more affected jurisdictions may allow a person to consolidate several fleets that would otherwise be based in two or more jurisdictions [*International Fuel Tax Agreement, § 212*].

International Fuel Tax Agreement: The Articles of agreement adopted by the International Fuel Tax Association, Inc., as amended as of January 1, 2017 [G.S. § 105-449.37(a)(1)].

Motor carrier: A person who operates (or causes to be operated) on any North Carolina highway a motor vehicle that is a qualified motor vehicle under the International Fuel Tax Agreement (IFTA). The term does not include the United States, a state, or a political subdivision of the State of North Carolina [G.S. § 105-449.37(a)(2)]. However, an intrastate carrier not subject to the IFTA is nevertheless subject to the motor carrier tax if it qualifies as a motor carrier [G.S. § 105-449.37(c)].

Motor vehicle: A motor vehicle as defined in G.S. § 20-4.01 [G.S. § 105-449.37(a)(3)].

Operations: The movement of a qualified motor vehicle by a motor carrier, whether loaded or empty and whether or not operated for compensation [G.S. § 105-449.37(a)(4)].

Person: An individual, a fiduciary, a firm, an association, a partnership, a limited liability company, a corporation, a unit of government, or another group acting as a unit. The term includes an officer or employee of a corporation, a member, a manager, or an employee of a limited liability company, and a member or employee of a partnership who, as officer, employee, member, or manager, is under a duty to perform an act in meeting the requirements of Subchapter I, V, or VIII of Chapter 105, of G.S. § 55-16-22, of Article 81 of Chapter 106 of the General Statutes, or of Article 3 of Chapter 119 of the General Statutes [G.S. § § 105-449.37(a)(25a), 105-228.90(b)(5)].

Qualified motor vehicle: A qualified motor vehicle as defined in the International Fuel Tax Agreement [G.S. § 105-449.37(a)(6)].

- *Imposition*

In addition to any other taxes imposed on motor carriers, a road tax for the privilege of using the streets and highways of North Carolina is imposed upon every motor carrier on the amount of motor fuel or alternative fuel used by the carrier in its operations within North Carolina [G.S. § 105-449.38]. A motor carrier that operates on one or more days of a reporting period is liable for the motor carrier tax for that reporting period and is entitled to the credits allowed (see below) for that reporting period [G.S. § 105-449.37(b)]. A motor carrier who operates a qualified motor vehicle in North Carolina must submit an application and obtain the appropriate decals for the vehicle [G.S. § 105-449.37(c)].

• *Rate*

The IFTA tax rate is imposed at (1) the gasoline tax rate imposed by G.S. § 105-449.80 (see ¶ 2908) or (2) the alternative fuel tax rate imposed by G.S. § 105-449.136 (see ¶ 2909), as appropriate. This tax is in addition to any other taxes imposed on motor carriers [G.S. § 105-449.38].

• *Base*

The North Carolina IFTA tax is based on the amount of motor fuel or alternative fuel used by a motor carrier in its operations within North Carolina [G.S. § 105-449.38]. The amount of motor fuel or alternative fuel that a motor carrier uses in its North Carolina operations for a reporting period is the number of miles the motor carrier travels in North Carolina during that period divided by the calculated miles per gallon for the motor carrier for all qualified vehicles [G.S. § 105-449.44(a)]. A motor carrier must report the operations of all qualified vehicles in its fleet when calculating fuel used in North Carolina. This requirement, however, does not apply to vehicles that operate exclusively intrastate and do not display an IFTA decal [17 NCAC 12A.0101].

The number of qualified motor vehicles of a motor carrier licensed under the North Carolina IFTA tax provisions is the number of sets of decals issued to the carrier. The number of qualified motor vehicles of a carrier not licensed under the North Carolina IFTA provisions is the number of qualified vehicles licensed by the motor carrier in the carrier's base state under the International Registration Plan [G.S. § 105-449.44(c)].

• *Presumption*

The Department checks IFTA returns filed by motor carriers against the weigh station records and other records of the Division of Motor Vehicles (DMV) of the Department of Transportation and the State Highway Patrol of the Department of Crime Control and Public Safety to determine if motor carriers operating in North Carolina are filing required returns [G.S. § 105-449.44(b)]. If a carrier did not file required returns or understated its North Carolina mileage by at least 25%, the Department may assess a motor carrier for the amount payable based on presumed mileage. A motor carrier is presumed to have mileage in North Carolina equal to 10 trips of 450 miles each for each of its qualified vehicles and to have fuel usage of four miles per gallon.

IFTA vs. IRP

The International Fuel Tax Agreement (IFTA) and the International Registration Plan (IRP) are programs that affect many of the same motor carrier companies. They are, however, different programs with different purposes. IRP is a registration reciprocity compact among jurisdictions (states and provinces) providing for payment of license fees of the basis of fleet miles operated in various jurisdictions. IRP allows registrants to do the following:

(1) Obtain one apportioned license plate from one jurisdiction (known as its base jurisdiction) for each apportionable vehicle for the purpose of paying registration fees for all member jurisdictions.

¶2910

(2) Obtain one cab card for each apportionable vehicle to satisfy intrastate and/or interstate credential requirements for registration fees with no further credential requirements for all member jurisdictions.

(3) Remit one annual application and payment to the base jurisdiction for the amount of registration fees due for all member jurisdictions.

• *Returns and payment of tax*

Motor carriers subject to the IFTA tax must report their operations on a form prescribed by the Secretary on a quarterly basis on or before the last days in April, July, October, and January [G.S. § 105-449.45(a)]. The IFTA tax is reported on North Carolina form GAS-1276 (International Fuel Tax Agreement Return). Payment of tax is due with the return. There is a $50 penalty for each failure to file a timely return, in addition to a penalty for failure to pay the tax on time. The license plates of anyone who fails to timely file and pay the IFTA tax are subject to revocation. Interest on overpayments and underpayments is determined using the interest rate adopted in the IFTA [G.S. § 105-449.45(e)].

Exception: A motor carrier is not required to file a quarterly return if either of the following applies:

(1) All of its operations during the quarter were made under a temporary permit (see above) [G.S. § 105-449.45(b)(1)].

(2) It is an intrastate motor carrier [G.S. § 105-449.45(b)(2)].

Informational returns: A motor carrier must file any informational returns that the Secretary requires [G.S. § 105-449.45(c)].

Bonds: The Secretary may require a motor carrier to furnish a bond when *any* of the following occurs [G.S. § 105-449.40(a)]:

(1) The motor carrier fails to timely file a report.

(2) The motor carrier fails to pay a tax when due.

(3) The Secretary determines, after auditing the motor carrier's records, that a bond is needed to protect the State from loss in collecting the tax.

Amount of bond: A required bond may not be more than the larger of (1) $500 or (2) four (4) times the motor carrier's average tax liability or refund for a reporting period [G.S. § 105-449.40(b)]. For motor carrier bonds exceeding $500, the amount of bond is rounded to the nearest $1,000. If the amount required is exactly between two $1,000 increments, the amount is rounded to the higher of the two [17 NCAC 12A.0302].

Electronic Filing

Taxpayers can use North Carolina's IFTA Internet Filing online resource to file quarterly IFTA returns, order credentials (license and decals) and remit payments. In order to participate in the program, a taxpayer must be registered with the Motor Fuels Tax Division as an IFTA carrier and have an access code that has not expired. The Department of Revenue has announced that taxpayers that have filed IFTA returns via the Internet for four (4) consecutive quarters will no longer receive paper returns or tax sheets [*Motor Fuels Tax Newsletter*, North Carolina Department of Revenue, March 2005].

Cessation of operations: If a company no longer exists or no longer owns or leases a vehicle for which a decal is required, it should indicate in the upper left corner of its

IFTA return the date the business was closed or notify the Department of Revenue in writing, including the name of the business, the IFTA account number, and the last date the company had operations. Accounts may also be closed via the Motor Carrier IFTA/Intrastate Online Filing Payment System at http://www.dor.state.nc.us. Turning in tags to the Division of Motor Vehicles does not close an IFTA account with the Department of Revenue. If a company with valid IFTA decals ceases to operate and fails to close its account, it continues to be liable for filing tax returns until the decals become invalid and is subject to a $50 late-filing penalty for each period that a return is not filed timely, even though there are no operations [*Motor Fuels Tax Newsletter*, North Carolina Department of Revenue, March 2005].

• *Credit against the tax*

A motor carrier subject to the IFTA tax is entitled to a credit on its quarterly return for tax paid on fuel purchased in North Carolina. The amount of the credit is determined using the tax rate in effect during the period covered by its report. To obtain a credit, the motor carrier must furnish satisfactory evidence that the tax for which the credit is claimed has been paid [G.S. § 105-449.39]. Satisfactory evidence can be established by a receipt or invoice, a credit card receipt, a microfilm/microfiche copy, or a computer image of the receipt or invoice that has been retained by the motor carrier [17 NCAC 12A.0201(b)]. If the amount of the credit exceeds a motor carrier's IFTA tax liability for a quarter, the excess. Refunds are discussed at ¶ 3203.

Withdrawals from bulk storage: A motor carrier maintaining bulk storage of North Carolina tax paid motor fuel is entitled to credit on the highway fuel use tax report based on the date the fuel is put into the motor vehicle, not on the date of purchase [17 NCAC 12A.0202(a)]. A motor carrier who withdraws fuel from bulk storage must maintain withdrawal records containing the following information [17 NCAC 12A.0202(b)]:

(1) Date of withdrawal.

(2) Number of gallons.

(3) Fuel type.

(4) Company unit number or vehicle licensee plate number and state.

(5) Purchase and inventory records to prove that tax was paid on all bulk purchases.

Adequate records must be kept to distinguish between fuel placed into qualified vehicles, non-qualified vehicles, and equipment. Separate records must be maintained for retail purchases and bulk storage withdrawals [*Motor Fuels Tax Newsletter*, North Carolina Department of Revenue, March 2005].

Upon application by the motor carrier, the State may waive the requirement of unit numbers if the carrier can show that adequate records are maintained to distinguish fuel placed into subject vehicles from that placed into non-subject vehicles [17 NCAC 12A.0202(c)].

• *Recordkeeping requirements*

Minimum documentation: A licensee must maintain records of all operations of qualified motor vehicles, and these records must support the information reported on the quarterly tax report. At a minimum, a licensee's system must include mileage data on each individual vehicle for each trip. The IVMR (Individual Vehicle Mileage Record) as required for the IRP (see "IFTA vs. IRP," above) is an acceptable source document for recording vehicle mileage information [*N.C. IFTA Compliance Manual*,

§ XI.A]. The Secretary and the Secretary's authorized agents and representatives have the right at any reasonable time to inspect the books and records of any motor carrier subject to the tax on carriers using fuel purchased outside North Carolina or the registration fee imposed by Article 3 of Chapter 20 of the General Statutes [G.S. § 105-449.46].

Supporting documentation: Supporting information should include the following documentation:

(1) Date of trip (starting and ending).

(2) Trip origin and destination (including city and state).

(3) Route of travel.

(4) Beginning and ending odometer or hubometer readings.

(5) Odometer or hubometer readings when crossing the jurisdiction line.

(6) Total trip miles.

(7) Mileage by jurisdiction.

(8) Vehicle unit number.

(9) Vehicle fleet number.

(10) Licensee's name.

GPS or Other Mileage Systems

The use of Global Position Satellite (GPS) or other mileage systems (*e.g.,* a mileage software system) does not automatically alleviate the requirement for maintaining individual vehicle mileage records. In order to eliminate any recordkeeping requirements, a waiver request must be submitted in writing to the Motor Fuels Tax Division of the Department of Revenue [*N.C. IFTA Compliance Manual,* § XI.A]. Thus, a taxpayer's challenge of proposed assessment for tax, penalty, and interest, calculated by the Department of Revenue using the best information available, was unsuccessful because it did not submit a written waiver request and receive approval before using a mileage software system instead of adhering to IFTA requirements [*Secretary's Decision No.* 2003-13 (August 20, 2003)].

Retail fuel purchase invoices: Motor carriers must maintain North Carolina retail fuel purchase invoices for a period of at least three (3) years for possible audit by an agent of the North Carolina Department of Revenue [17 NCAC 12A.0201(c)]. North Carolina retail fuel invoices must contain the following information [17 NCAC 12A.0201]:

(1) Date of purchase.

(2) Name and address of the seller.

(3) Number of gallons purchased.

(4) Type of fuel purchased.

(5) Price per gallon.

(6) Either the company unit number of the vehicle into which the fuel was placed or the vehicle's license plate designation and the state that issued the plate.

(7) Purchaser's name. In the case of a leased vehicle, either the lessee or the lessor can submit receipts as the purchaser if the person who submits the receipts can establish a legal connection to the person required to file a report.

- *BIA (best information available) audits*

If a licensee fails to make records available upon written request within a minimum of 30 days or fails to maintain records from which the licensee's true liability may be determined, the base jurisdiction will, on the basis of the best information available to it, determine the tax liability of the licensee for each jurisdiction. After adding the appropriate penalties and interest, the base jurisdiction will serve the assessment upon the licensee in the same manner as an audit assessment (discussed at ¶ 3208) or in accordance with the laws of the base jurisdiction. The assessment made by a base jurisdiction is presumed to be correct; and, in any case where the validity of the assessment is questioned, the burden is on the licensee to establish by a fair preponderance of evidence that the assessment is erroneous or excessive [*N.C. IFTA Compliance Manual*, § XII.E].

- *Refunds*

If the amount of a credit to which a motor carrier is entitled for a quarter exceeds the motor carrier's liability for that quarter, the Secretary must refund the excess [G.S. § 105-449.39]. The Secretary may make refunds without prior audit or without having been furnished bond if the motor carrier has complied with the motor fuel tax laws and rules. All credits of at least three dollars ($3) are automatically refunded. However, refunds of credits under three dollars ($3) must be requested in writing [17 NCAC 12A.0301].

- *License and decals*

Licensure: A motor carrier that operates a recreational vehicle that is considered a qualified motor vehicle cannot operate (or cause to be operated) in North Carolina any qualified motor vehicle (as defined above) unless both the motor carrier and at least one qualified motor vehicle are licensed with the Secretary of Revenue. A motor carrier that is subject to the IFTA must license with the motor carrier's base jurisdiction [G.S. § 105-449.47(a)].

This rule applies to a motor carrier that operates a recreational vehicle that is considered a qualified motor vehicle [G.S. § 105-449.47(a)].

Decals: When a motor carrier is licensed, the Secretary must issue a license for the motor carrier and a set of decals for each qualified motor vehicle. All decals remain the property of the State of North Carolina. Motor carriers must keep records of decals issued to it and be able to account for all of them. Licenses and decals are issued for a calendar year and remain the property of the State. A motor carrier must carry a copy of its license in each motor vehicle it operates when the vehicle is in North Carolina and clearly display an identification marker at all times. An identification marker must be affixed to the vehicle for which it was issued in the place. The Secretary may revoke a license or a decal when a motor carrier fails to comply with the fuel tax provisions of this article (36B), or Article 36C or 36D of Subchapter I of Chapter 105. A motor carrier must carry a copy of its license in each motor vehicle it operates when the vehicle is in North Carolina. A motor vehicle must clearly display a decal at all times. A decal must be affixed to the qualified motor vehicle for which it was issued in the place and manner designated by the authority that issued it [G.S. § 105-449.47(a1)].

¶2910

No Grace Zone Between Jurisdictions

The International Fuel Tax Agreement has no provision for a grace zone between jurisdictions. *Any* travel across jurisdictional lines by a qualified vehicle requires an IFTA license and decal or a temporary trip permit. If the qualified vehicle is licensed as IFTA, *all* miles must be reported on the IFTA tax return [*Motor Fuels Tax Newsletter*, North Carolina Department of Revenue, March 2005].

Denial of application: The Secretary can deny an application for a license and decals to an applicant that does not meet the requirements set out in G.S. § 105-449.69(b) or that has done any of the following [G.S. § 105-449.47A]:

(1) Had a license issued under Chapter 105 or Chapter 119 of the General Statutes cancelled by the Secretary for cause.

(2) Had a license issued by another jurisdiction, pursuant to the International Fuel Tax Agreement revoked by the Secretary.

(3) Been convicted of fraud or misrepresentation.

(4) Been convicted of any other offense that indicates that the applicant may not comply with Article 36B of Subchapter I of Chapter 105 if licensed and issued a decal.

(5) Failed to remit payment for any tax debt (as defined in G.S. § 105-243.1).

(6) Failed to file any required tax return.

(7) Failed to maintain the vehicle's registration.

Revocation: The Secretary of Revenue may revoke a registration or an identification marker when a motor carrier fails to comply with the North Carolina IFTA tax provisions [G.S. § 105-449.47(1a)]. Specifically, the Motor Fuels Tax Division may revoke a motor carrier's registration for failure to pay any of the following:

(1) Any motor fuels tax liability imposed under Subchapter V of Chapter 105 of the North Carolina Statutes [17 NCAC 12A.0502(1)].

(2) The liability imposed by another IFTA jurisdiction if the laws, administrative procedures, or reciprocal agreements of the other jurisdiction allow it to revoke a carrier based in that jurisdiction for failure to pay a similar liability imposed by North Carolina [17 NCAC 12A.0502(2)].

Exemption: The requirements of G.S. § 105-449.47 do not apply to the operation of a qualified motor vehicle (prior to January 1, 2009, "a vehicle") that is registered in another state and is operated temporarily in North Carolina by a public utility, a governmental or cooperative provider of utility services, or a contractor for one of these entities for the purpose of restoring utility services in an emergency outage [G.S. § 105-449.47(b)].

Fuel Decals

The Motor Fuels Tax Division issues two types of decals:

(1) International Fuel Tax Agreement (IFTA) decals.

(2) N.C. Highway Fuel Use Tax (NCHFUT) decals.

Carriers requesting IFTA decals must travel in at least two IFTA jurisdictions. The Division reviews completed returns from prior periods to ensure that carriers requesting IFTA licenses are traveling in more than one jurisdiction. NCHFUT decals are issued to carriers who operate vehicles that travel only in North Carolina. Any decals that are ordered but unused must not be destroyed or misplaced. Unused decals must be retained for audit purposes. Penalties may be imposed for failing to retain these decals [*Motor Fuels Tax Newsletter*, North Carolina Department of Revenue, December 2004].

• *Temporary permits*

A permitting service may (upon application and payment of a fee of $50) obtain a temporary permit authorizing a motor carrier to operate a vehicle for three (3) days in North Carolina without licensing the vehicle. The permitting service may sell the temporary permit to a motor carrier which may elect not to report its operation of the vehicle during the three-day period [G.S. § 105-449.49].

• *Leased motor vehicles*

Lessor in leasing business: A lessor regularly engaged in the business of leasing or renting motor vehicles without drivers for compensation is the motor carrier for a leased or rented motor vehicle unless the lessee gives the Secretary of Revenue written notice that the lessee is the motor carrier. If written notice is given by the lessee to the Department, the lessee is the motor carrier for the leased or rented motor vehicle. Before a lessee gives written notice to the Department, the lessee and lessor must have a written agreement for the lessee to be the motor carrier; and the lessee must, upon request, give a copy of that agreement to the Secretary of Revenue [G.S. § 105-449.42A(a)].

Independent contractor: The lessee of a motor vehicle leased from an independent contractor is the motor carrier for the leased motor vehicle unless one of the following applies [G.S. § 105-449.42A(b)]:

(1) The motor vehicle is leased for fewer than 30 days.

(2) The motor vehicle is leased for at least 30 days and the lessor gives the Secretary written notice that the lessor is the motor carrier. Before a lessor gives the Secretary written notice that the lessor is the motor carrier, the lessor and lessee must have a written agreement for the lessor to be the motor carrier; and, upon request of the Secretary, the lessor must give the Secretary a copy of that agreement.

If either of these circumstances applies, the lessor is the motor carrier for the leased motor vehicle [G.S. § 105-449.42A(b)].

Liability: An independent contractor who leases a motor vehicle to another for fewer than 30 days is liable for compliance with the North Carolina IFTA tax, and the person to whom the motor vehicle is leased is not liable. Otherwise, both the lessor and lessee of a motor vehicle are jointly and severally liable for compliance [G.S. § 105-449.42A(c)].

• *Civil penalties applicable to motor carriers*

A motor carrier who does any of the following is subject to a civil penalty [G.S. § 105-449.52(a)]:

(1) Operates (or causes to be operated) in North Carolina a qualified motor vehicle that either (a) fails to carry the required license or (b) fails to display a required decal. The amount of the penalty is $100.

¶2910

(2) Is unable to account for decals issued to it. The amount of the penalty is $200 for each identification marker for which the carrier cannot account [G.S. § 105-449.52(a)(2)].

(3) Displays a decal on a qualified motor vehicle operated by a motor carrier that was not issued to the carrier. The amount of the penalty is $1,000 for each identification marker unlawfully obtained. Both the licensed motor carrier to whom the decal was issued and the motor carrier displaying the unlawfully obtained decal are jointly and severally liable for this penalty.

Penalties are payable to the agency that assessed the penalty [G.S. § 105-449.52(a1)].

Waiver of penalties: The procedure set out in G.S. § 105-449.119 for requesting a waiver of a penalty applies to these penalties. See "Review of civil penalty assessment" at ¶ 2908.

- *Violations declared to be misdemeanors*

A person who operates or causes to be operated on a highway in North Carolina a qualified motor vehicle that does not carry a required license, does not properly display a required decal, or is not properly licensed commits Class 3 misdemeanor and is punishable by a fine of $200. Each day's operation in violation of these provisions constitutes a separate offense [G.S. § 105-449.51].

The tax on gasoline, diesel, and blends is discussed at ¶ 2908; and the alternative fuel tax is discussed at ¶ 2909.

- *Nonresident motor carriers*

By operating a motor vehicle on North Carolina highways, a nonresident motor carrier consents to the appointment of the Commissioner of Motor Vehicles as its attorney in fact and process agent for all summonses or other lawful process or notice in any action, assessment, or other proceeding under Chapter 105 of the North Carolina General Statutes [G.S. § 105-449.54].

¶ 2911 Unauthorized Substances Tax

Article 2D of Chapter 105 of the North Carolina General Statutes imposes an excise tax on controlled substances. The purpose of the tax is to generate revenue for State and local law enforcement agencies and for the General Fund. Nothing in Article 2D may in any manner provide immunity from criminal prosecution for a person who possesses an illegal substance [G.S. § 105-113.105].

- *Administration*

The unauthorized substances tax is administered by the Unauthorized Substances Tax Section of the Tax Enforcement Division of the North Carolina Department of Revenue.

- *Imposition and exemptions*

The unauthorized substances tax is imposed on controlled substances possessed, either actually or constructively, by dealers. An "unauthorized substance" is a controlled substance, an illicit mixed beverage, illicit spirituous liquor, or mash [G.S. § 105-113.107(a)]. The unauthorized substances tax does not apply to (1) a substance in the possession of a dealer who is authorized by law to possess the substance [G.S. § 105-113.107A(a)] and (2) certain marijuana parts [G.S. § 105-113.107A(b)]. The marijuana parts specifically exempt are as follows:

(1) Harvested mature marijuana stalks when separated from and not mixed with any other parts of the marijuana plant.

(2) Fiber or any other product of marijuana stalks, except resin extracted from the stalks.

(3) Marijuana seeds that have been sterilized and are incapable of germination.

(4) Roots of the marijuana plant.

The tax can also, of course, be avoided where the preponderance of the evidence indicates that the taxpayer did not have actual or constructive possession of the unauthorized substance. *See, e.g., Secretary's Decision No 2006-169* (June 18, 2007) and *Secretary's Decision No. 2006-239* (May 10, 2007).

• *Double jeopardy*

The North Carolina and federal appellate courts have reached contrary conclusions on the nature of the Unauthorized Substances Tax. In *Lynn v. West*, 134 F.3d 582 (4th Cir.), *cert. denied*, 525 U.S. 813 (1998), the United States Court of Appeals for the Fourth Circuit issued a declaratory judgment that the tax (then known as the Controlled Substances Tax) was a criminal penalty rather than a tax and could not be enforced without the constitutional safeguards that accompany criminal proceedings. However, in *Milligan v. State*, 135 N.C. App. 781, 522 S.E.2d 330, *appeal dismissed*, 351 N.C. 358, 543 S.E.2d 131 (2000), *cert. denied*, 531 U.S. 819 (October 2, 2000), the North Carolina Court of Appeals held that the tax was not a criminal penalty, that taxpayers subject to the tax were not entitled to the constitutional safeguards required for criminal prosecutions, and that the taxpayer in the case at hand was not entitled to a refund of taxes assessed and paid without regard to such safeguards. In reaching its decision in *Lynn*, the Fourth Circuit relied, in part, on the high rate of taxation imposed on the possession of cocaine ($200 per gram). Effective October 31, 1998, after the decision in *Lynn* was rendered, the General Assembly reduced the rate of tax on cocaine possession to $50 per gram. The authors understand that the North Carolina Department of Revenue takes the position that the *Lynn* decision therefore has no application to the statute as amended. With respect to cases governed by the pre-October 31, 1998, law, the authors understand that the Department has ceased all forced collection procedures.

Federal Appellate Decision Not Binding

Federal appellate decisions are not binding upon either the appellate or trial courts of North Carolina with the exception of decisions of the United States Supreme Court [*State v. Adams*, 132 N.C. App. 819, 513 S.E. 2d 588, *cert. denied*, 528 U.S. 1022 (1999)]. Absent modification by the North Carolina Supreme Court, a panel of the North Carolina Court of Appeals is bound by the prior decision of another panel addressing the same issue [*State v. Harris*, 157 N.C. App. 647 (2003)]. In the *Harris* case, the court held that the prosecution of a defendant for drug trafficking and possession after the defendant had been assessed with the North Carolina drug tax in a civil proceeding did not violate the Double Jeopardy Clause of the U.S. Constitution.

• *Rates*

The tax rates on unauthorized substances vary, depending on the substance. The rates are set out in G.S. § 105-113.107.

¶2911

The unauthorized substances excise tax is levied on controlled substances possessed by dealers at the following rates as follows [G.S. § 105-187.16(a)]:

Item	Rate
Harvested marijuana stems and stalks that have been separated from and are not mixed with any other parts of the plant	40¢ per gram or fraction thereof
Marijuana other than separated stems and stalks or synthetic cannabinoids	$3.50 per gram or fraction thereof
Cocaine	$50 per gram or fraction thereof
Any low-street value drug that is sold by weight[1]	$50 per gram or fraction thereof
Any other controlled substance sold by weight	$200 per gram or fraction thereof
Any low-street-value drug that is not sold by weight[1]	$50 for each 10 dosage units or fraction thereof
Any other controlled substance not sold by weight	$200 for each 10 dosage units or fraction thereof

[1] "Low-street-value drug" means anabolic steroids, depressants, hallucinogenic substances, stimulants, or controlled substances described in G.S. § 90-91(c), (d), or (e); G.S. § 90-92(a)(3) or (a)(5); or G.S. § 90-93(a)1 [G.S. § 105-113.106(4c)].

NOTE: A controlled substance is measured either by weight or dosage units. A quantity of marijuana or other controlled substance is measured by the weight of the substance whether pure or impure or dilute, or by dosage units when the substance is not sold by weight. A quantity of a controlled substance is dilute if it consists of a detectable quantity of pure controlled substance and any excipients or fillers [G.S. § 105-113.107(a1)].

Illicit mixed beverages: The tax rate on illicit mixed beverages is $20 on each four liters and a proportional sum on lesser quantities [G.S. § 105-113.107(d)].

Illicit spirituous liquor: The tax rate on illicit spirituous liquor is levied at the following rates: (1) $31.70 for each gallon, or fraction thereof, sold by the drink, or (2) $12.80 for each gallon, or fraction thereof, not sold by the drink [G.S. § 105-113.107(b)].

Mash: The tax rate on mash is $1.28 for each gallon, or fraction thereof [G.S. § 105-113.107(c)].

- *Reports and payment of tax*

The unauthorized substances tax is payable within 48 hours after a dealer acquires actual or constructive possession of a non-tax-paid unauthorized substance, exclusive of Saturdays, Sundays, and legal holidays in North Carolina, in which case the tax is payable on the next working day [G.S. § 105-113.109]. Dealers must report taxes payable at the time and on the return prescribed by the Secretary. When the tax is paid, the Secretary will issue stamps to affix to unauthorized substances to indicate payment of the tax [G.S. § 105-113.108].

Identification and Verification Not Required

Dealers are not required to give any identifying information (*e.g.*, name, address, social security number) on the return, and the return does not have to be verified by oath or affirmation [G.S. § 105-113.108(a)].

- *Definition of terms*

Controlled substance: A "controlled substance" is a drug, substance, or immediate precursor included in the six schedules contained in G.S. § 90-89 through G.S. § 90-94 [G.S. § § 105-113.106(1), 90-87(5)].

¶2911

¶2912 Scrap Tire Disposal Tax

Article 5B of Chapter 105 of the North Carolina General Statutes imposes a tax on new tires to provide funds for the disposal of scrap tires. A county may use the proceeds of the tax distributed to it only for the disposal of scrap tires or for the abatement of a nuisance created by a tire collection site [G.S. § 105-187.19]. A "scrap tire" is defined as a tire that is no longer suitable for its original, intended purpose because of wear, damage, or defect; a "tire" is defined as a continuous solid or pneumatic rubber covering or encircling a wheel [G.S. § 105-187.15].

• *Imposition*

The scrap tire disposal tax is levied on retailers, wholesalers, and purchasers of new tires [G.S. § 105-187.16(a)]. The scrap tire disposal tax provides for two privilege taxes and one excise tax, as follows:

(1) A privilege tax is imposed on a tire retailer at a percentage rate of the sales price of each new tire sold at retail by the retailer.

(2) A privilege tax is imposed on a tire retailer and on a tire wholesale merchant at the percentage rate of the sales price of each new tire sold by the retailer or wholesale merchant to a wholesale merchant or retailer for placement on a vehicle offered for sale, lease, or rental by the retailer or wholesale merchant.

(3) An excise tax is imposed on a new tire purchased for storage, use, or consumption in North Carolina or for placement in North Carolina on a vehicle offered for sale, lease, or rental at a percentage rate of the purchase price of the tire.

• *Exemptions*

The scrap tire disposal taxes do not apply to the following: (1) bicycle tires and other tires for vehicles propelled by human power; (2) recapped tires; and (3) tires sold for placement on newly manufactured vehicles [G.S. § 105-187.18(b)]. These are exemptions specific to the scrap tire disposal tax. Except for the exemption for sales that a state cannot constitutionally tax, the exemptions and refunds allowed for the sales and use tax do not apply to the scrap tire disposal tax [G.S. § 105-187.18(b)].

• *Rates*

The percentage rate of the taxes imposed under the scrap tire disposal provisions is currently based on the bead diameter of the new tire sold or purchased. The rates are as follows [G.S. § 105-187.16(a)]:

Bead Diameter of Tire	Percentage Rate
Less than 20 inches	2%
At least 20 inches	1%

• *Credits*

The privilege tax imposed on tire retailers who sell new tires at retail is an additional State sales tax, and the excise tax imposed on the storage, use, or consumption of a new tire in North Carolina is an additional State use tax. These taxes are collected and administered in the same manner as the State sales and use taxes; and the additional sales tax paid when a new tire is sold is a credit against the additional use tax imposed on the storage, use, or consumption of the same tire [G.S. § 105-187.17].

¶2912

The privilege tax imposed on tire retailers and wholesalers who sell new tires for placement in North Carolina on a vehicle offered for sale, lease, or rental is a tax on the wholesale sale of the tires. This tax and the excise tax imposed on a new tire purchased for placement in North Carolina on a vehicle offered for sale, lease, or rental is, to the extent practical, collected and administered as if they were additional State sales and use taxes. The privilege tax paid when a new tire is sold for placement on a vehicle offered for sale, lease, or rental is a credit against the use tax imposed on the purchase of the same tire for placement in North Carolina on a vehicle offered for sale, lease, or rental [G.S. § 105-187.17].

• *Administration*

The scrap tire disposal tax is administered by the Sales and Use Tax Division of the North Carolina Department of Revenue.

¶2913 Dry-Cleaning Solvent Tax

Article 5D of Chapter 105 of the North Carolina General Statutes imposes a privilege tax on a dry-cleaning solvent retailer at a flat rate for each gallon of dry-cleaning solvent sold by the retailer to a dry-cleaning facility, and an excise tax on dry-cleaning solvent purchased for storage, use, or consumption by a dry-cleaning facility in North Carolina [G.S. § 105-187.31]. "Dry-cleaning facility" means a place of business located in North Carolina and engaged in on-site dry-cleaning operations, other than a commercial uniform service or commercial linen supply facility. "Dry-cleaning solvent" means any hydrocarbon or halogenated hydrocarbon used as a solvent in a dry-cleaning operation or the degradation products from these solvents [G.S. § 143-215.104B]. The definitions for purposes of the sales and use tax contained in G.S. § 105-164.3 also apply for purposes of the dry-cleaning solvent tax [G.S. § 105-187.30].

• *Exemptions and refunds*

Except for the exemption for sales that a state cannot constitutionally tax, the exemptions and refunds allowed for sales and use tax purposes do not apply to the dry-cleaning solvent tax. The refunds allowed in G.S. § 105-164.14 do not apply to the dry-cleaning solvent tax [G.S. § 105-187.33].

• *Rates*

The dry-cleaning solvent tax is imposed at the rate of $10.00 for each gallon of dry-cleaning solvent that is chlorine-based and $1.35 for each gallon of dry-cleaning solvent that is hydrocarbon-based. These taxes are in addition to all other taxes [G.S. § 105-187.31].

• *Credit against the tax*

The privilege tax imposed on dry-cleaning solvent retailers is an additional State sales tax, and the excise tax imposed on the storage, use, or consumption of dry-cleaning solvent by a dry-cleaning facility in North Carolina is an additional use tax. Unless otherwise provided in Article 5D, these taxes are collected and administered in the same manner as the North Carolina sales and use taxes. The additional sales tax paid when dry-cleaning solvent is sold at retail is a credit against the additional State use tax imposed on the storage, use, or consumption of the same dry-cleaning solvent [G.S. § 105-187.32].

• *Administration*

The dry-cleaning solvent tax is administered by the Sales and Use Tax Division of the North Carolina Department of Revenue.

• *Sunset*

The dry-cleaning solvent tax is scheduled for sunset effective July 1, 2030 [G.S. § 105-187.35].

¶2914 White Goods Disposal Tax

Article 5C of Chapter 105 of the North Carolina General Statutes imposes a tax on the sale of new white goods [G.S. § 105-187.20]. For purposes of Article 5C "white goods" include refrigerators, ranges, water heaters, freezers, unit air conditioners, washing machines, dishwashers, clothes dryers, and other similar domestic and commercial large appliances [G.S. § § 105-187.20(2) and 130A-290(a)(44)]. A "sale" for this purpose has the same meaning as "sale" for sales and use tax purposes except that for purposes of the white goods disposal tax, "sale" does not include lease or rental [G.S. § 105-187.20].

• *Imposition*

A privilege tax is imposed on a white goods retailer at a flat rate for each new white good that is sold by the retailer. An excise tax is imposed on a new white good purchased for storage, use, or consumption in North Carolina [G.S. § 105-187.21].

• *Rate*

The rate of the privilege tax and the excise tax is $3.00. These tax rates are in addition to all other taxes [G.S. § 105-187.21].

• *Exemptions*

Except for the exemption for sales that a state cannot constitutionally tax, the exemptions and refunds allowed for sales and use tax purpose do not apply to the white goods disposal tax [G.S. § 105-187.23(a)].

• *Refunds*

In general, the refunds allowed for sales and use tax purposes do not apply to the white goods disposal tax. However, a person who buys at least 50 new white goods of any kind in the same sale or purchase is entitled to a refund equal to 60% of the amount of tax imposed if all of the white goods are purchased to be placed in new or remodeled dwelling units located in North Carolina and that do not contain the kind of white goods purchased.

• *Credit against the tax*

The privilege tax imposed on white goods retailers is an additional State sales tax, and the excise tax on the storage, use, or consumption of a new white good in North Carolina is an additional use tax. The additional States sales tax paid when a new white good is sold at retail is a credit against the additional State use tax imposed on the storage, use, or consumption of the same white good [G.S. § 105-187.22].

• *Administration*

The white goods disposal tax is administered by the Sales and Use Tax Division of the North Carolina Department of Revenue and is to be administered, except as otherwise provided in Article 5C, in the same manner as the sales and use tax [G.S. § 105-187.22].

• *Application to Real Property Contracts*

A real property contractor (see ¶ 1709) is the consumer of white goods it installs and that become part of real property and so is liable for the the tax when it purchases the white goods or, for items purchased out of state, when the item is withdrawn from inventory. A retailer-contractor (see ¶ 1709) is liable for the tax on white goods sold at retail. A retailer-contractor acting as a real property contractor who purchases white goods out of state is liable for the tax at the time of purchase rather than when the item is later withdrawn from inventory. A retailer-contractor acting as a real property contractor who purchases white goods in North Carolina to fulfill a real property contract in North Carolina is liable for the tax at the time of purchase, [Department of Revenue, Important Notice: White Goods Disposal Tax and Real Property Contracts (April 28, 2015)].

¶2915 Solid Waste Disposal Tax

An excise tax is imposed on the disposal of municipal solid waste and construction and demolition debris in a landfill permitted under Article 9 of Chapter 130A of the General Statutes and on the transfer of such waste and debris to a transfer station permitted under Article 9 of Chapter 130A of the General Statutes [G.S. § 105-187.61(a)].

• *Rate*

The tax is imposed at the rate of $2.00 per ton of waste [G.S. § 105-187.61(a)].

• *Tax liability*

The solid waste disposal tax is due on municipal solid waste and construction and demolition debris received from third parties and on municipal solid waste and construction demolition debris disposed by the owner or operator. The tax is payable by the owner or operator of each landfill and transfer station permitted under Article 9 of Chapter 130A of the General Statutes [G.S. § 105-187.61(b)]. An owner or operator may add the amount of the solid waste disposal tax due to the charges made to a third party for disposal of municipal solid waste or construction and demolition debris [G.S. § 105-187.62].

• *Returns and payment of tax*

The solid waste disposal tax is payable when a return is due. A return and payment are due on a quarterly basis. A quarterly return covers a calendar quarter and is due by the last day of the month following the end of the quarter [G.S. § 105-187.62(b)]. Until August 9, 2008 a solid waste disposal tax return was due to be filed and payable in the same manner as required under G.S. § 105-164.16 for sales and use tax [G.S. § 105-187.62].

• *Bad debt reduction*

If an owner or operator pays the tax on tonnage received from a customer and the customer's account is found to be worthless and charged off for income tax purposes, the owner or operator may recover the tax paid on the tonnage it received but for which it was never compensated. The tax is recovered by reducing the overall tonnage on which the owner or operator pays tax in a calendar quarter for which it was never compensated from the worthless account. If the owner or operator subsequently collects on an account that has been declared worthless, any tax recovered must be repaid in the next calendar quarter [G.S. § 105-187.62(c), effective August 9, 2008].

¶2916 Severance Tax on Energy Minerals

A severance tax is imposed on producers who sever energy minerals from the soil or water of North Carolina [G.S. §105-187-76 et seq.]. An energy mineral is any form of natural gas, oil or related condensates [G.S. §105-187.76(4)]. Severance occurs when the energy mineral is extracted or otherwise removed from the soil or water of the State [G.S. §105-187.76(17)]. A producer is the person who takes the energy mineral from the soil or water of the State [G.S. §105-187.76(13)].

- *Tax on condensates and oil*

A condensate is a liquid hydrocarbon that is or can be removed from gas by a separator or other means [G.S. §105-187.76(3)]. Oil means crude petroleum oil and other hydrocarbons, regardless of gravity, that are produced at the well in liquid form by ordinary production methods and that are not the result of condensation of gas after it leaves the reservoir [G.S. §105-187.76(10)]. The tax imposed on the severance of condensates and oil is 2% of the gross price paid, i.e., the total price paid by the first purchaser of the energy mineral from the producer at the wellhead [G.S. §§105-187.76(5) and (7) and 105-187.77(b) and (c)]. The rate increases to 3.5% on January 1, 2019 and 5% on January 1, 2021 [S.L. 2014.4 §§17(d) and 17(e)].

- *Tax on gas*

Gas is defined as all natural gas, including casinghead gas, and all other hydrocarbons not defined as condensates [G.S. §105-187.76(6)]. Casinghead gas is gas or vapor indigenous to an oil stratum and produced from the stratum with oil [G.S. §105-187.76(1)]. The tax imposed on the severance of gas is 0.9% of the "delivered to market" value of the gas [G.S. §105-187.77(b)(2) and (e)].

The rate of tax on the severance of gas is scheduled to increase as follows:

Delivered Market Value Between (per MCF)	From 7/1/15 through 12/31/18)	From 1/1/19 through 12/31/20	From 1/1/21 through 12/31/22	From and after 1/1/23
$0 – $3.00	0.9%	0.9%	0.9%	0.9%
$3.01 – $4.00	0.9%	1.9%	1.9%	1.9%
$4.01 – $5.00	0.9%	2.9%	2.9%	2.9%
$5.01 – $6.00	0.9%	2.9%	3.9%	3.9%
$6.01 – $7.00	0.9%	2.9%	4.9%	4.9%
$7.01 – $8.00	0.9%	2.9%	5.0%	5.9%
$8.01 – $9.00	0.9%	2.9%	5.0%	6.9%
$9.01 – $10.00	0.9%	2.9%	5.0%	7.9%
Over $10.00	0.9%	2.9%	5.0%	9.0%

The delivered to market value of gas is determined by subtracting the producer's actual costs to deliver the gas to the market from the producer's total gross cash receipts from the sale of the gas [G.S. §105-187.78(a)]. A producer receiving a cost reimbursement from the purchaser must include the reimbursement in gross cash receipts and may deduct actual delivery costs in determining the delivered to market value of the gas [G.S. §105-187.78(a)].

The costs to deliver gas to the market are the actual and reasonable costs incurred by the producer to get the gas from the mouth of the well to the first purchaser. Such costs are limited to (1) costs for compressing, dehydrating, sweetening, and treating the gas sold, (2) costs of delivering the gas to the purchaser, (3) reasonable charges for depreciating the facility used to deliver the gas to market (provided that if the facility is rented the actual rental fee is added), (4) costs of direct or allocated labor associated with the facility used to deliver the gas to market, (5) costs of materials, supplies, maintenance, repairs, and fuel associated with the facility used to deliver the gas to market, (6) property taxes paid on the facility used to deliver the gas to market and (7) charges for fees paid by the producer to any provider of dehydration, treating, compression and delivery services. For purposes of computing these costs, a facility used to deliver gas to market includes flow lines or gathering systems from the separator to the purchaser's transmission line, compressor stations, dehydration units, line heaters after the separator and treating facilities. Costs incurred in normal lease separation of the oil or condensate from the gas and costs associated with insurance premiums on facilities used to deliver the gas to market are not included in the costs to deliver the gas to market [G.S. § 105-187.78(c)].

A producer must maintain and make available for inspection any records the Secretary considers necessary to determine and verify the costs to deliver the gas to market that the producer wishes to deduct in computing the tax due. The producer has the burden of establishing these costs, and no delivery costs will be allowed to a producer that fails to maintain or make available for inspection adequate records [G.S. § 105-187.78(b)].

- *Tax on gas from marginal gas well*

A marginal gas well is a well incapable of producing more than 100 MCF per day as determined by the Mining and Energy Commissions using the current wellhead deliverability rate methodology used by the Commission during the calendar month for which a severance tax report is filed. An "MCF" is 1000 cubic feet of natural gas [G.S. § 105-187.76(8) and (9)]. A producer may apply to the Mining and Energy Commission for a determination that a proposed or existing well is a marginal gas well. If the Commission determines that a well is a marginal gas well, the producer may elect to compute the tax on gas produced at the well using either the gas rate or the marginal gas rate of 0.4% [G.S. § 105-187.77(d)]. The producer must provide the Secretary with proof that the Mining and Energy Commission has determined that a well qualifies as a marginal gas well [G.S. § 105-187.80(h)]. The marginal gas rate increases to 0.6% on January 1, 2019 and 0.8% on January 1, 2021 [S.L. 2014-4, § § 17.(d) and 17.(e)].

- *Exemption for on-site use*

Energy minerals that are severed by a producer from land or water legally or beneficially owned by the producer and used on the land from which they were taken by the producer in the use or improvement of the producer's homestead are exempt from the severance tax up to a market value of $1,200 [G.S. § 105-187.79]. To claim the exemption, the producer must apply to the Secretary for a determination of eligibility, and the Secretary must make the determination within 15 days of the receipt of all information required by the Secretary. The producer must attach the determination to its next severance tax return due [G.S. § 105-187.80(g)].

- *Returns and payment*

Severance tax returns are due on either a quarterly or monthly basis, depending on the amount of tax due. A producer who is consistently liable for less than $1000 a month in severance taxes must file a return on a calendar quarter basis by the 25th day of the second month following the end of the quarter. Otherwise, returns are due on a monthly basis by the 25th day of the second month following the month for which the return is due. The Secretary must notify the producer to file on a monthly or quarterly basis based on the total amount of taxes due from the producer for all places of business owner or operated by the producer and must monitor the producer's tax payments and notify it of any change in its required filing frequency [G.S.

§ 105-187.80(c), (d) and (e)]. Taxes are due when the return is due [G.S. § 105-187.80(a)]. The Secretary must prescribe a severance tax return form, which must require the producer to supply the gross amount of taxable energy minerals produced, the leases from which the minerals were produced and the name and address of the first purchasers of the minerals [G.S. § 105-187.80(a) and (f)]. A producer must file a bond or irrevocable letter of credit with the Secretary in the form required by the Secretary and conditioned on compliance with the severance tax requirements. The amount of the bond or letter of credit is twice the producer's average expected monthly severance tax liability, as determined by the Secretary, provided that the amount of the bond may not be less than $2,000 nor more than $2 million. The producer must file the bond or letter of credit within 30 days after receiving the Secretary's notification to do so [G.S. § 105-187.81].

The owner of a royalty interest must maintain and provide to the Secretary on request (1) a record of all money received as royalties from all producing leaseholds in the State and (2) a copy of all settlement sheets received from a purchaser or operator and a copy of any other statement showing the amount of energy materials for which a royalty was received and the amount of severance tax deducted [G.S. § 105-187.83].

• *Permit suspension for compliance failures*

The Secretary must notify the Secretary of Environmental Quality of any failure by any entity that fails to file any severance tax return or report or that fails to pay any severance tax or fee for 90 days after the due date of such report, return or payment. The Secretary of Environmental Quality must suspend the permits for oil and gas exploration using horizontal drilling and hydraulic fracturing issued to an entity pursuant to G.S. § 113-395 that fails to file a severance tax return and must immediately notify the entity by mail of such suspension [G.S. § 105-187.84].

• *No local taxation*

No city or county may impose a franchise privilege, license, income or excise tax on the severance, production, treating, processing, ownership, sale, storage, purchase, marketing or transportation of energy minerals produced in the State or on the business of doing any of the foregoing or on the ownership, operation or mainte-nance of plants, facilities, machinery, pipelines and gathering lines related to any of the foregoing. This prohibition does not preclude property taxation under Article 11 of Chapter 105 [G.S. § 105-187.85].

¶2917 Local Meal and Occupancy Taxes

• *Local meals taxes*

Certain local jurisdictions are authorized by the General Assembly to levy a meals tax. A meals tax is a tax on prepared food and drink [G.S. § § 153A-154.1(b) and 160A-214.1(c)(2)].

Penalties: The civil and criminal penalties that apply to State sales and use taxes apply to local meals taxes. The governing board of a taxing county or city has the same authority to waive the penalties for a local meals tax that the Secretary of Revenue has to waive the penalties for State sales and use taxes [G.S. § § 153A-154.1(a), 160A-214.1(a)]. Discussion of penalties that apply to State sales and use taxes is at ¶1906. Any inconsistent provision of any local act and any local act that purports to impose greater penalties are repealed [S.L. 2002-72 (S.B. 1160), § 3].

• *Local occupancy taxes*

Certain counties and municipalities are authorized by the General Assembly to levy a local occupancy tax on the rental of rooms and lodging in addition to any State or local sales tax. A room occupancy tax may be repealed or reduced by resolution of the governing body of the city or county that levied the tax [G.S. §§153A-155(f), 160A-215(f)].

Administration: Local room occupancy taxes are administered by the taxing county or city [G.S. §§153A-155(d), 160A-215(d)].

Reports and payment: A county room occupancy tax is due and payable to the county finance officer in monthly installments on or before the 20th day of the month following the month in which the tax accrues [G.S. §153A-155(d)]. A city room occupancy tax is due and payable to the city finance officer in monthly installments on or before the 20th day of the month following the month in which the tax accrues [G.S. §160A-215(d)].

Collection of tax: Retailers who are required to remit the sales tax on accommodations are required to remit a room occupancy tax to the taxing county on and after the effective date of the levy of the room occupancy tax. The room occupancy tax applies to the same gross receipts as the North Carolina sales tax on accommodations and is calculated in the same manner as that tax (see ¶1726). A rental agent or a facilitator (defined at ¶1603) has the same responsibility and liability under the room occupancy tax as the rental agent or facilitator has under the State sales tax on accommodations (see ¶1726). This provision effectively overturns the decision in *Pitt County v. Hotels.com, L.P.*, 553 F.3d 308 (4th Cir. 2009), where the court held that online hotel booking companies were not hotel operators or similar businesses and so were not required to collect the tax. *See also Wake County v. Hotels.com, L.P.*, ___ N.C. App. ___, 762 S.E.2d 477 (2014).

Taxing cities and counties must design and furnish to all appropriate businesses and persons the necessary forms for filing returns and instructions to ensure the full collection of the tax. A retailer who collects a room occupancy tax may deduct from the amount remitted to the taxing city or county a discount equal to the discount the State allows the operator for State sales and use tax [G.S. §§153A-155(c), 160A-215(c)].

Bundled Packages: If a taxable accommodation is furnished as part of a package, the bundled transaction provisions of G.S. §105-164.4D (discussed at ¶1715) apply in determining the sales price of the taxable accommodation. If those provisions do not address the type of package furnished, the person offering the package may allocate the price among the items in the package based on a reasonable allocation of revenue that is supported by the person's business records kept in the ordinary course of business [G.S. §§153A-155(c), 160A-215(c)].

Penalties: A taxpayer who fails to file a room occupancy tax return or to pay the tax when due is subject to the civil and criminal penalties established under G.S. §105-236 for failure to file a State sales or use tax return or to pay State sales or use tax (see ¶3205). The city or county governing body has the same authority to waive the penalties that the Secretary has to waive State sales and use tax penalties [G.S. §§153A-155(e), 160A-215(e)].

Use: The proceeds of a city or county room occupancy tax cannot be used for development or construction of a hotel or another transient lodging facility [G.S. §153A-155(f1) and G.S. §160A-215(f1)].

¶2917

¶2918 Local Vehicle Transit Authority Vehicle Rental and Registration Taxes

• *Regional Transit Authority Vehicle Rental Tax*

A regional public transportation authority or a regional transportation authority created pursuant to Articles 26 or 27 of Chapter 160A (*i.e.*, the Triangle Transit Authority or the Piedmont Authority for Regional Transportation) is authorized to levy a privilege tax not to exceed 5% of the gross receipts from the short-term (less than one-year) lease of motorcycles or U-drive-it vehicles (generally, private passenger vehicles and property-hauling vehicle of less than 7,000 pounds) derived by retailers located within the authority's territorial jurisdiction [G.S. § § 105-550(1), (2), (3), (6) and (7) and 105-551(a)]. No exemptions or refunds of lawfully collected rental taxes are permitted [G.S. § 105-553]. The taxing authority may use the revenues generated by the tax for any purpose for which the authority is authorized to use funds generally, including pledging such funds to secure the financing of a public transportation system or paying down the authority's obligations [G.S. § 105-554]. The tax is collected by the authority but is otherwise administered in the same manner as the optional gross receipts tax paid by motor vehicle lessors under G.S. § 105-187.5 (discussed at ¶2901), though the rental tax applies regardless of whether the retailer has in fact elected to pay the optional gross receipts tax [G.S. § 105-552(b)]. The penalties and remedies applicable to local government sales and use taxes (discussed at ¶1607) also apply to the regional transit authority vehicle rental tax [G.S. § 105-552(c)].

• *Regional Transit Authority Registration Tax*

The following entities are authorized to levy an annual license tax of $8.00 (or a smaller, whole-dollar amount) on motor vehicles with a tax situs within the entity's territorial jurisdiction: (1) a regional public transportation authority created pursuant to Article 26 of Chapter 160A, (2) a regional transportation authority created pursuant to Article 27 of Chapter 160A and (3) a municipal transit authority created pursuant to Article 25 of Chapter 160A that includes at least two counties [G.S. § § 105-560 and 105-561(a)]. The maximum license tax that may be levied by an entity other than a county is $8.00 per vehicle, while the license tax that may be levied by a county is capped at $7.00 [G.S. § 105-557(a)].

Only motor vehicles subject to state vehicle registration fees under G.S. § 20-87(1), (2), (4), (5), (6) and (7) and § 20-88 (for-hire passenger vehicles, U-drive-it vehicles, limousines, private passenger vehicles, private motorcycles and vehicles with dealer plates and property-hauling vehicles) are subject to the license tax, and the tax is due at the same time and subject to the same restrictions as the state registration fee [G.S. § 105-562(a) and (b)]. The license tax is to be prorated for partial years in the same manner as the state registration fee [G.S. § 105-562(b)].

The taxing authority may use the revenues generated by the tax for any purpose for which the authority is authorized to use funds generally (provided that counties levying the tax may use the revenues generated by the tax only to finance, construct, operate and maintain a public transportation system), but the revenues generated by the tax are intended to supplement rather than replace existing public transportation system funds or other resources [G.S. § 105-564].

If a regional transportation authority created pursuant to Article 26 or Article 27 of Chapter 160A has not levied the maximum license tax throughout its jurisdiction, it may create a special tax district consisting of one of the counties in its jurisdiction and levy the tax in that district, provided the license tax levied in the district, when combined with the license tax, if any, levied throughout the authority's territory, may not exceed the maximum tax of $8.00 per vehicle [G.S. § 105-561(d)]. The levy of the tax or the increase in the rate of tax levied in the special district must be approved by the county commissioners of the county within the district [G.S. § 105-561(d)]. The revenues generated by a special district tax may be used only for the benefit of the special district [G.S. § 105-561(d)].

The tax situs of a motor vehicle for purposes of the license tax is its property tax situs, or, if the vehicle is exempt from property tax, the property tax situs it would have if it were not exempt [G.S. § 105-562(c)].

A regional transit authority registration tax or an increase in such a tax applicable to a vehicle sold or leased by a dealer applies only to sales or leases after the effective date of the tax or tax increase (regardless of when the title and registration application is submitted to the DMV) [G.S. § 105-562(d)].

A license tax imposed throughout a county is collected and administered by the Division of Motor Vehicles. A tax imposed in only part of a county (because only part of the county is within the authority's jurisdiction) is collected and administered by the authority itself, which may contract with one or more local governments in its territory to collect the tax on its behalf [G.S. § 105-562(a)].

• *County Vehicle Registration Tax*

A county may levy an annual registration tax of $7.00 (or smaller whole-dollar amount) on motor vehicles with a tax situs within its territorial jurisdiction, but only if the county or a unit of local government within the county operates a public transportation system [G.S. § 105-570]. A county registration tax or an increase in such a tax applicable to a vehicle sold or leased by a dealer applies only to sales or leases after the effective date of the tax or tax increase (regardless of when the title and registration application is submitted to the DMV) [G.S. § 105-570(h)].

PART XIII

ADMINISTRATION AND PROCEDURE

CHAPTER 31

NORTH CAROLINA ADMINISTRATION

¶3101 The Power to Tax

• *Constitutional Provisions*

The North Carolina Constitution includes the following provisions specifically related to taxation.

(1) *Power of taxation reserved to the people.*

"The people of this State shall not be taxed or made subject to the payment of any impost or duty without the consent of themselves or their representatives in the General Assembly, freely given" [North Carolina Constitution, Article I, §8]. This limitation does not prohibit the authority of a private entity to set highway tolls, because tolls are not taxes. *See WIDENI77 v. NC. Department of Transportation,* __ N.C. App, __, 800 S.E 2d 441 (2017).

(2) *No retrospective taxation.*

"No law taxing retrospectively sales, purchases, or other acts previously done shall be enacted" [North Carolina Constitution, Article I, §16]. This provision has been held to prohibit the levy of a tax on pre-enactment purchases of merchandise [*Young v. Henderson,* 76 N.C. 420 (1877)] and the imposition of a tax incident on a taxpayer's pre-enactment status of being an employer [*Unemployment Compensation Comm. v. Wachovia Bank & Trust Co.,* 215 N.C. 491, 2 S.E.2d 592 (1939)] but not the retroactive increase in the personal income tax rate [*Coley v. State,* 173 N.C. App. 481, 620 S.E.2d 25 (2005), *aff'd,* 360 N.C. 493, *reh. denied,* 360 N.C. 582, 635 S.E.2d 430 (2006)].

(3) *Enactment of revenue laws.*

"No laws shall be enacted to raise money on the credit of the State, or to pledge the faith of the State directly or indirectly for the payment of any debt, or to impose any tax upon the people of the State, or to allow the counties, cities, or towns to do so, unless the bill for the purpose shall have been read three separate times in each house of the General Assembly and passed three separate readings, which readings shall have been on three different days, and shall have been agreed to by each house respectively, and unless the yeas and nays on the second and third readings of the bill shall have been entered on the journal" [North Carolina Constitution, Article II, §23]. This provision has been held not to apply to the legislation establishing the North Carolina lottery. See *Heatherly v. State,* 189 N.C. App. 213, 658 S.E.2d 11 (2008).

(4) *Prohibition on poll taxes.*

Prohibition on poll taxes. "No poll or capitation tax shall be levied by the General Assembly or by any county, city or town, or other taxing unit" [North Carolina Constitution, Article V, § 1].

(5) *Taxation for public purposes only.*

"The power of taxation shall be exercised in a just and equitable manner, for public purposes only, and shall never be surrendered, suspended, or contracted away" [North Carolina Constitution, Article V, § 2(1)]. This concept of a "public purpose" has been broadly construed to include any purpose that involves a reasonable connection with public convenience and necessity and that benefits the public generally rather than the special interests of particular persons [*Madison Cablevision, Inc. v. Morganton*, 325 N.C. 634, 386 S.E.2d 200 (1989)]. See also *Blinson v. State*, 186 N.C. App. 328, 651 S.E.2d 268 (2007), *rev. denied*, 362 N.C. 335, 661 S.E.2d 240 (2008) (state economic incentives); *Haugh v. County of Durham*, 208 N.C. App. 304, 702 S.E.2d 814 (2010) (same); *Parker v. New Hanover County*, 173 N.C. App. 644, 619 S.E.2d 868 (2005) (special assessment to fund inlet relocation); *Saine v. State*, 210 N.C. App. 594, 709 S.E.2d 379 (2011) (grants from the One North Carolina Fund). See also *Munger v. State*, 202 N.C. App. 404, 689 S.E.2d 230 (2010) (lack of taxpayer standing to challenge incentives based on discriminatory claims).

(6) *Just and equitable manner requirement*

The power of taxation must be exercised in a "just and equitable manner" [North Carolina Constitution, Article V, § 2(l)]. A city's amendment of its privilege tax on electronic gaming establishments from an annual flat tax of $12.50 to $5,000 per location plus $2,500 per computer terminal, resulting in a 59,900% increase in the minimum tax due, was held to violate the just and equitable manner requirement. *See IMT, Inc. v. City of Lumberton*, 366 N.C. 456, 738 S.E.2d 156 (2013). *See also Smith v. City of Fayetteville*, 227 N.C. App 563, 743 S.E.2d 662 (2013) (8,900% increase in electronic gaming privilege tax unjust and inequitable).

(7) *Requirement of uniformity.*

"Only the General Assembly shall have the power to classify property for taxation, which power shall be exercised only on a State-wide basis and shall not be delegated. No class of property shall be taxed except by uniform rule, and every classification shall be made by general law uniformly applicable in every county, city and town, and other unit of local government" [North Carolina Constitution, Article V, § 2(20)].

(8) *Exemptions.*

"Property belonging to the State, counties, and municipal corporations shall be exempt from taxation. The General Assembly may exempt cemeteries and property held for educational, scientific, literary, cultural, charitable, or religious purposes, and, to a value not exceeding $300, any personal property. The General Assembly may exempt from taxation not exceeding $1,000 in value of property held and used as the place of residence of the owner. Every exemption shall be on a State-wide basis and shall be made by general law uniformly applicable in every county, city and town, and other unit of local government. No taxing authority other than the General Assembly may grant exemptions, and the General Assembly shall not delegate the powers accorded to it by this subsection" [North Carolina Constitution, Article V, § 2(3)].

(9) *Special assessment districts.*

"Subject to the limitations imposed by Section 4, the General Assembly may enact general laws authorizing the governing body of any county, city, or town to define territorial areas and to levy taxes within those areas, in addition to those levied throughout the county, city, or town, in order to finance, provide, or maintain services, facilities, and functions in addition to or to a greater extent than those financed, provided, or maintained for the entire county, city, or town" [North Carolina Constitution, Article V, § 2(4)].

¶3101

(10) *Voter approval requirement.*

"The General Assembly shall not authorize any county, city or town, special district, or other unit of local government to levy taxes on property, except for purposes authorized by general law uniformly applicable throughout the State, unless the tax is approved by a majority of the qualified voters of the unit who vote thereon" [North Carolina Constitution, Article V, § 2(5)].

(11) *Limitations on income taxes.*

"The rate of tax on incomes shall not in any case exceed ten percent, and there shall be allowed personal exemptions and deductions so that only net incomes are taxed" [North Carolina Constitution, Article V, § 2(6)]. However, no particular deduction is required to be allowed, and the General Assembly has the authority to determine what deductions shall be allowed. *See Wal-Mart Stores East v. Hinton*, 197 N.C. App. 30, 676 S.E.2d 634 (2009).

(12) *Disclosure of objects of taxation.*

"Every act of the General Assembly levying a tax shall state the special object to which it is to be applied, and it shall be applied to no other purpose" [North Carolina Constitution, Article V, § 5].

• *Statutory Provisions*

The revenue laws of the State of North Carolina are contained in Chapter 105 of the General Statutes of North Carolina.

¶3102 Administration of Revenue Laws

• *Department of Revenue*

The revenue laws of the State of North Carolina are administered by the Department of Revenue. The Department of Revenue is a cabinet agency under the leadership of the Secretary of Revenue, the Deputy Secretary, and five Assistant Secretaries.

Article V, § 2(1) of the North Carolina Constitution provides that the State's taxing power cannot be surrendered, suspended, or contracted away. The General Assembly has declared that no provision of Subchapter I of Chapter 105 (under which estate, franchise, income, sales and use, and certain other taxes are levied) constitutes a contract, that such provision will remain in effect, and that any representation to such effect would be ineffective [G.S. § 105-1.1].

The main office of the Department of Revenue is located at 501 North Wilmington Street, Raleigh, NC 27604. Letters and other correspondence should be addressed to North Carolina Department of Revenue, P.O. Box 25000, Raleigh, NC 27640-0640. See Chapter 33.

• *Administrative divisions*

Each tax is administered by a Tax Division of the Department of Revenue. See discussion of individual taxes for information on tax administration.

• *Other administrative bodies*

(1) *Secretary of State*

Corporations Division: The Corporations Division of the North Carolina Department of the Secretary of State is responsible for the examination, custody and maintenance of the legal documents filed by more than 400,000 corporations, limited partnerships, and limited liability companies. The duty of the Secretary of State is to ensure uniform compliance with the statutes governing the creation of these entities, record the information required to be kept as a public record, and provide that information to the public. The Corporations Division acts in an administrative capacity only and cannot give legal advice [http://www.secretary.state.nc.us/Corporations].

Business License Information Office: The State of North Carolina has numerous business licenses, permits, regulations, and/or other approvals required for a planned business activity; and it does not have a single business license that ensures compliance with these numerous requirements, as well as local and federal requirements that may apply. The Business License Information Office (BLIO) was created to provide assistance to prospective business owners in identifying and meeting these requirements.

Securities Division: The Securities Division of the Department of the Secretary of State administers the Qualified Business Tax Credit Program.

(2) *Attorney General*

The attorney general participates in various revenue decisions and offers advice to the Secretary of Revenue.

(3) *Department of Commerce*

Employment Security Commission: The Employment Security Commission administers the North Carolina unemployment insurance program and collects the unemployment insurance tax.

Banking Commission: The Banking Commission is responsible for chartering and regulating North Carolina's state banks and trust companies, as well as registration and licensing of various financial institutions operating in the state [http://www.nccommerce.com/categories/deptorg.asp].

Savings Institutions Commission: The Savings Institutions Commission regulates and monitors the operations of all state-chartered savings institutions [http://www.nccommerce.com/categories/deptorg.asp].

(4) *Department of Insurance*—The Commissioner of Insurance administers and collects the surplus lines tax, the tax on risk retention groups not chartered in North Carolina and the tax on persons procuring insurance directly from unlicensed insurers.

(5) *Local taxing officers*—Local taxing officers levy and collect, with the Department of Revenue, the general property tax and the privilege tax on low-level radioactive and hazardous waste facilities.

For expedited rule-making procedures with respect to the Secretary's authority to redetermine a taxpayer's income under G.S. § 105-130.5A, *see* ¶ 1202.

• *Revenue law enforcement*

Summonses: The Secretary is authorized to examine personally or through agents any books, papers, records or other data that may be relevant or material to any inquiry into the correctness of any return or for the purpose of determining the liability of any person for a tax or for collecting any tax. The Secretary may also summon persons having possession, custody, care or control of books of account containing entries relevant or material to the income or expenditures of a taxpayer or any other person having knowledge in the premises to give testimony under oath and to produce documents and other data in order to determine the correctness of a return or otherwise to determine a taxpayer's tax liability [G.S. § 105-258(a)]. The Secretary's power to obtain information about taxpayers from third parties is, however, subject to constitutional limitations, including First Amendment protections against disclosures regarding the expressive content of taxpayer purchases. *See Amazon.com LLC v. Lay,* 758 F. Supp. 2d 1154 (W.D. Wash. 2010); *see also* S. Gaylord and A. Haile, *Constitutional Threats in the E-Commerce Jungle: First Amendment and Dormant Commerce Clause Limits on Amazon Laws and Use Tax Reporting Statutes,* 89 N.C. L. Rev. 2011 (2011). If a person refuses to comply with a summons issued by the Secretary, the Secretary may apply to the Superior Court of Wake County for an order to enforce the summons, and a person who refuses to obey such an order is subject to contempt proceedings [G.S. § 105-258(a)]. The North Carolina Supreme Court has held that the rules of civil procedure do not apply to the Secretary's summons enforcement actions but that the court has inherent authority to take reasonable actions to administer its duties in such actions, including the power to give third parties notice and an opportunity to assert privileges. *See In re Summons Issued to Ernst & Young, LLP*, 363 N.C. 612, 684 S.E.2d 151 (2009). *See also In re Summons Issued to Target Corporation and Affiliates*, 18 CVS 12841 (N.C. Business Court 2018) (allowing the Secretary's opposition to designation of summons enforcement action as a Mandatory Complex Business Case while declining to find that summons enforcement actions could never qualify for designation).

Criminal investigations: The Secretary of Revenue is authorized to appoint employees of the Criminal Investigations Division of the North Carolina Department of Revenue to serve as revenue law enforcement officers having the responsibility and subject matter jurisdiction to enforce the felony tax violations of the revenue laws. The Criminal Investigations Division reports to the Deputy Secretary of Revenue [G.S. § 105-236.1(a)].

Unauthorized substances: The Secretary of Revenue is authorized to appoint employees of the Unauthorized Substances Tax Division to serve as revenue law enforcement officers having the responsibility and subject matter jurisdiction to enforce the excise tax on unauthorized substances [G.S. § 105-236.1(a)]. The Unauthorized Substances Tax Division reports to the Assistant Secretary for Field Operations.

¶3103 Rules and Other Authority

Revised Interpretations

An interpretation by the Secretary that revises a prior interpretation or expands the scope of a tax or otherwise increases the amount of tax due may not become effective sooner than the following: (1) For a tax that is payable on a monthly or quarterly basis, the first day of a month that is at least 90 days after the date the revised interpretation is issued; (2) For a tax that is payable on an annual basis, the first day of a tax year that begins after the date the revised interpretation is issued [G.S. § 105-264(c)].

• *Administrative rules (regulations)*

North Carolina administrative rules are published in the North Carolina Administrative Code ("NCAC"). The administrative rules of the North Carolina Department of Revenue are contained in Title 17 of the NCAC. Administrative rules must be adopted pursuant to the procedures set forth in the North Carolina Administrative Procedure Act ("APA") [G.S. §§ 105-262(a), 150B-1 *et seq.*]. Those procedures require, among other things, that the Department publish the text of a proposed rule in the *North Carolina Register*, obtain a fiscal note from the Office of State Budget and Management where appropriate, and submit the rule to the Rules Review Commission for review. If the Rules Review Commission approves the rule, it may be included in the North Carolina Administrative Code but is subject to being disapproved by the General Assembly. The onerous procedures for adopting Rules make it more attractive for the Department to issue interpretive guidance in the form of Bulletins, Directives, or TAMs. Most of the current authoritative rulings, therefore, are now issued in the form of Bulletins, Directives, or TAMs. Note, however, that under the Administrative Procedure Act, the Department may not seek to implement or enforce against any person a policy, guideline, or other nonbinding interpretive statement that meets the Act's definition of a rule without complying with the Act's rulemaking procedures [G.S. § 150B-18].

• *Bulletins*

Bulletins are published for the purpose of presenting the administrative interpretation and application of the tax laws; they supplement but do not supersede the

Administrative Rules [http://www.dor.state.nc.us]. The Department publishes the following sets of Bulletins:

(1) *Corporate Income, Franchise, and Insurance Tax Bulletin:* This bulletin presents the administrative interpretation and application of North Carolina corporate income, franchise and insurance company gross premiums taxes.

(2) *Individual Income Tax, Pass-Through Entities, and Withholding Bulletin:* This bulletin presents the administrative interpretation and application of North Carolina income tax laws relating to individuals, partnerships, estates, and trusts and income tax withholding.

(3) *Sales and Use Tax Technical Bulletins:* These bulletins present the administrative interpretation and application of the North Carolina Sales and Use Tax Law. They also cover the following taxes: (a) the Highway Use Tax; (b) the Alternative Highway Use Tax on the lease or rental of motor vehicles; (c) the Scrap Tire Disposal Tax; (d) the White Goods Disposal Tax; (e) the Dry Cleaning Solvent Tax; (f) the certain Machinery and Equipment Tax, (g) the Solid Waste Disposal Tax and (h) the additional 1/2% Mecklenburg County Sales and Use Tax for Public Transportation.

(4) *Excise Tax Technical Bulletins:* These bulletins present the administration interpretation and application of North Carolina alcoholic beverages, piped natural gas, privilege license and tobacco product taxes.

• *Directives*

Directives are a form of written guidance on the tax laws issued for the following purposes (http://www.dor.state.nc.us):

(1) To set out the Department's interpretation of a new tax law.

(2) To explain the application of a tax law to stated facts.

(3) To clarify an issue on which the Department has received numerous questions.

Directives are issued with respect to the following taxes:

(1) Personal Taxes.

(2) Corporate Income and Franchise Taxes.

(3) Excise Taxes.

(4) Insurance Gross Premiums Tax.

(5) Privilege Taxes.

(6) Sales and Use Tax, Certain Machinery and Equipment Tax and Other Taxes Administered by the Sales and Use Tax Division.

• *Technical Advice Memoranda (TAMs)*

A Technical Advice Memorandum is issued to state or clarify the policy of the Department of Revenue regarding some tax issue (*e.g.,* interpretation of a statute). A TAM is given a number that indicates the Division that issued it, the year it was issued, and its order in the list of Directives issued by that Division for that year.

• *Private letter rulings*

The Department also issues advice in the form of private letter rulings addressed to taxpayers requesting specific advice under G.S. § 105-264(b) [G.S. § 105-264.2(e)(3)]. A private letter ruling is binding on the Department and, if erroneous, relieves a taxpayer from tax otherwise due plus penalties and interest. For the requirements that apply to a request for specific advice. *See* Department of Revenue, *Private Letter Rulings Policy.*

- *Redetermination private letter ruling*

A redetermination private letter ruling is written advice issued by the Secretary to a corporation pursuant to G.S. § 105-130.5A concerning whether a redetermination of the corporation's State net income is required or whether a combined return is required. A redetermination private letter ruling also includes a determination and agreement made jointly by the Secretary and the corporation for the use by the corporation of an alternative filing methodology that accurately reports State net income [G.S. § 105-264.2(e)(4)].

- *Alternative apportionment ruling*

An alternative apportionment ruling is written advice issued by the Secretary to a taxpayer pursuant to the taxpayer's written request to use an alternative apportionment method for corporate income or franchise tax purposes [G.S. § 105-264.2(e)(1)].

- *Written determinations*

Private letter rulings, redetermination private letter rulings and alternative apportionment rulings are referred to as "written determinations" [G.S. § 105-264.2(e)(5)]. Written determinations apply the tax law to a specific set of existing facts provided by the taxpayer and are applicable only to the taxpayers addressed. They have no precedential value to anyone other than the taxpayer to whom they are issued [G.S. § 105-264.2(a)]. The Department must publish on its web site a redacted version of each written determination within 90 days of the date it is provided to the taxpayer. Background documents are not required to be published [G.S. § 105-264.2(b)]. The Department is required to publish on its web site all written determinations issued since January 1, 2010. *See* S.L. 2016-103, § 8.

- *Fees*

The secretary may charge a fee for issuing a written determination at the request of a taxpayer. The Secretary may adopt a tiered fee structure based on the taxpayer's income or gross receipts, the complexity of the advice requested or the tax schedule for which advice is requested. The fee must be at least $500 and not more than $5,000 but may be waived by the Secretary [G.S. § 105-264(d)].

- *Presumption of correctness*

An "interpretation by the Secretary," presumably regardless of form, is *prima facie* correct [G.S. § 105-264]. The presumption of correctness undoubtedly applies to Rules adopted pursuant to the APA. See *Polaroid Corp. v. Offerman* [349 N.C. 290, 507 S.E.2d 284 (1998), *cert. denied*, 526 U.S. 1098 (1999)]. In addition, judicial notice can, and, in appropriate cases, shall, be taken of such Rules [G.S. § 150B-21.22]. Section 105-264 appears to extend the presumption of correctness to other forms of interpretive guidance issued by the Department, including Bulletins and Directives. However, the APA provides that any interpretive statement of general applicability, which would include the Department's Bulletins, Directives, and TAMs, is invalid or nonbinding unless issued under APA procedures [G.S. §§ 150B-2(8a), 150B-18]. *See also National Service Indus. Inc. v. Powers* [98 N.C. App. 504, 507, 391 S.E.2d 509, 511, *rev. denied*, 327 N.C. 431, 395 S.E.2d 685 (1990)], where it was ruled that interpretation contained in interoffice memo is not entitled to presumption of correctness.

- *Reliance by taxpayers*

Taxpayers are entitled to rely on the Secretary's interpretations of the tax laws, whether issued as Rules, Bulletins, or Directives. If the Secretary changes an interpretation, a taxpayer who relied on it before it was changed is not liable for any penalty or additional assessment on any tax that accrued before the interpretation was changed that was not paid in reliance on the former interpretation. Similarly, taxpayers who have requested in writing specific advice from the Department and received erroneous written advice in response are not liable for penalties or additional assessments attributable to the erroneous advice, provided the taxpayer's reliance on the advice was reasonable and the advice was based on adequate and accurate information furnished by the taxpayer [G.S. § 105-264]. Note that the taxpayer's request must be specific [*Secretary's Decision No.* 2000-7 (October 10, 2000)]. The Department's failure to address a particular issue in a past audit of the taxpayer does not constitute advice on that issue on which the taxpayer can rely [*Secretary's Decision Nos.* 2001-504 (January 14, 2002), 2002-63 (July 11, 2002)].

If a taxpayer requests specific advice from the Department of Revenue and receives erroneous advice in response, the taxpayer is not liable for any penalty or additional assessment attributable to the erroneous advice furnished by the Department to the extent that the following conditions are all satisfied [G.S. § 105-264(b)]:

(1) The advice was reasonably relied upon by the taxpayer.

(2) The penalty or additional assessment did not result from the taxpayer's failure to provide adequate or accurate information.

(3) The Department provided the advice in writing or the Department's records establish that the Department provided erroneous verbal advice.

Secretary's Duty to Document Oral Advice

The Department is required to document oral advice given to a taxpayer when (1) the taxpayer provides its identifying information (2) requests advice about the application of a tax to the taxpayer's situation and (3) requests the Department to document the advice in the taxpayer's records. This rule applies to in-person meetings and telephone conversations but does not apply to discussions that occur at presentations, conferences or other forums [G.S. § 105-258.2(a) and (b)]. The Secretary must also document advice given in a conversation with a person who is not registered as a retail or wholesale merchant for sales tax purposes when the person (1) provides his name and address, (2) describes the business in which he is engaged, (3) asks if he is required to register and (4) requests the Secretary to document the advice [G.S. § 105-258.2(c)].

• *Application to local laws*

An interpretation by the Secretary of a law administered by the Secretary applies to a local law administered by a unit of local government when the local law refers to State law to determine the application of the local law. A person who is subject to the local law or to the local government unit may request an interpretation form the Secretary of the State law that determines the application of the local law. The Secretary's interpretation in such a case provides the same protection against liability under the local law that it provides under State law [G.S. § 105-264.1].

¶3104 Taxpayers' Bill of Rights

At least once a year, the Secretary of Revenue must prepare and publish a statement of the Taxpayers' Bill of Rights, setting forth in simple and nontechnical terms the following [G.S. § 105-256(a)(5)]:

(1) The taxpayer's right to have tax information kept confidential.

(2) The rights of a taxpayer and the obligations of the Department during an audit.

(3) The procedure for a taxpayer to appeal an adverse decision of the Department at each level of determination.

(4) The procedure for a taxpayer to claim a refund for an alleged overpayment.

(5) The procedure for a taxpayer to request information, assistance, and interpretations or to make complaints.

(6) Penalties and interest that may apply and the basis for requesting waiver of a penalty.

(7) The procedures the Department may use to enforce the collection of a tax, including assessment, jeopardy assessment, enforcement of liens, and garnishment and attachment.

ADMINISTRATION AND PROCEDURE

CHAPTER 32

ASSESSMENTS AND REFUNDS

¶3201 Scope of Administrative Provisions of Article 9

Article 9 (G.S. §§ 105-228.90 through 105-269.15) of Subchapter I of Chapter 105 of the North Carolina General Statutes (relating to general administration, penalties, and remedies) applies to the following [G.S. § 105-228.90(a)]:

(1) Subchapter I (Levy of Taxes). Subchapter I contains the provisions relating to most North Carolina taxes, including corporate income and franchise taxes, personal income taxes, sales and use taxes, and estate and gift taxes. Note, however, that the provisions of Article 9 do not apply to the North Carolina property tax.

(2) Subchapter V (Motor Fuel Taxes).

(3) Subchapter VIII (Local Government Sales and Use Tax).

(4) The corporate annual report filing requirements of G.S. § 55-16-22.

(5) The primary forest product assessment levied under Article 81 of Chapter 106 of the General Statutes.

(6) Inspection taxes levied under Article 3 of Chapter 119 of the General Statutes (relating to gasoline and oil inspection and regulation).

(7) The Setoff Debt Collection Act codified in Chapter 105A of the North Carolina General Statutes.

¶3202 Definitions

The following definitions apply in Article 9 of Chapter 105 of the North Carolina General Statutes:

Charter school: A nonprofit corporation that has a charter under G.S. § 115C-218.5 to operate a charter school [G.S. § 105-228.90(b)(1)].

City: A city as defined by G.S. § 105-160A-1(2). The term also includes an urban service district defined by the governing board of a consolidated city-county as defined by G.S. § 160B-2(1) [G.S. § 105-228.90(b)(1a)].

Code: For the current definition of the Code, see ¶ 103.

County: Any one of the counties listed in G.S. § 153A-10 [G.S. § 105-228.90(b)(1c)]. North Carolina has 100 counties. The term "county" also includes a consolidated city-county. A "consolidated city-county" means any county where the largest municipality in the county has abolished and its powers, duties, rights, privileges and immunities consolidated with those of the county. Other municipalities in the county, if any, may or may not have been abolished and their powers, duties, rights, privileges and immunities consolidated with those of the county [G.S. § § 105-228.90(1c) and 160B-2(1)].

Department: The Department of Revenue.

Electronic funds transfer (EFT): A transfer of funds initiated by using an electronic terminal, a telephone, a computer, or magnetic tape to instruct or authorize a financial institution or its agent to credit or debit an account [G.S. § 105-228.90(b)(3)]. See ¶ 3304 for discussion of EFT.

Federal determination: A change or correction arising from an IRS audit or an agreement of the U.S. competent authority that has become final. A federal determination is final when it is not subject to administrative or judicial review. In addition, audit findings are considered final if the taxpayer does not timely file an administrative appeal with the IRS or if the taxpayer consented to any of the audit findings for the tax period through a form or other written agreement with the IRS [G.S. § 105-228.90(b)(3a)].

Income tax return preparer: Any person who prepares for compensation (or who employs one or more persons to prepare for compensation) any income tax return for individuals, estates and trusts, or corporations or any claim for refund for individuals, estates and trusts, or corporations. For purposes of this definition, the completion of a substantial portion of a return or claim for refund is treated as the preparation of the return or claim. The term "income tax return preparer" does not include a person merely because the person (1) furnishes typing, reproducing, or other mechanical assistance; (2) prepares a return or claim for refund of the employer, or an officer or employee of the employer, by whom the person is regularly and continuously employed; (3) prepares as a fiduciary a return or claim for refund for any person; or (4) represents a taxpayer in a hearing regarding a proposed assessment [G.S. § 105-228.90(b)(4)]. Person: An individual, a fiduciary, a firm, an association, a partnership, a limited liability company, a corporation, a unit of government, or another group acting as a unit. The term includes an officer or employee of a corporation, a member, a manager, or an employee of a limited liability company, and a member or employee of a partnership who, as officer, employee, member, or manager, is under a duty to perform an act in meeting the requirements of the statutory provisions within the scope of Article 9 of Chapter 105 of the North Carolina General Statutes [G.S. § 105-228.90(b)(5)]. For discussion of the scope of Article 9, see ¶ 3201.

Secretary: The Secretary of Revenue [G.S. § 105-228.90(b)(6)].

Tax: A tax that falls within the scope of Article 9 (see ¶3201) [G.S. § 105-228.90(b)(7)].

Taxpayer: A person subject to the tax or reporting requirements of the statutes within the scope of Article 9 (see ¶3201) [G.S. § 105-228.90(b)(8)].

¶3203 Refunds

• *Overpayments initiated by Department of Revenue*

The Department of Revenue must refund an overpayment made by a taxpayer if the Department discovers the overpayment before the expiration of the statute of limitations for obtaining a refund. Discovery occurs in any of the following circumstances [G.S. § 105-241.7(a)]:

(1) The automated processing of a return indicates the return requires further review. Note that "flagging" a return for further review is all that is required. Because returns are processed by the Department's computers almost immediately after they are received, the flagging of a return will almost always occur before the statute of limitations expires even if verification occurs afterwards.

(2) A review of a return by an employee of the Department indicates an overpayment.

(3) An audit of a taxpayer by an employee of the Department indicates an overpayment.

• *Overpayments initiated by taxpayer*

A taxpayer may request a refund of an overpayment by taking one of the following actions within the limitation period for refund claims [G.S. § 105-241.7(b)]:

(1) Filing an amended return reflecting an overpayment due the taxpayer.

(2) Filing a claim for a refund. The claim must identify the taxpayer, the type and amount of tax overpaid, the filing period to which the overpayment applies, and the basis for the claim. The taxpayer's statement of the basis of the claim in the claim for refund does not prevent the taxpayer from changing the basis of his claim at a later time.

Where the tax was paid by the manager of a business or partnership on behalf of a nonresident owner or partner, only the nonresident owner or partner, and not the manager, may request a refund [G.S. § 105-154(d)].

Voluntary Payment of Another Taxpayer's Tax Liability

A person who by voluntary agreement pays a tax imposed on another has no standing to seek a refund of the tax paid. *See Am. Woodland Indus. v. Tolson*, 155 N.C. App. 624, 574 S.E.2d 55 (2002), *rev. denied*, 357 N.C. 61, 579 S.E.2d 283 (2003) (denying standing to seek refund to transferee of timber contract who paid realty excise tax under agreement with transferor).

• *Period of limitation for refund claims*

General period of limitation on refund claims: Unless an exception applies, a taxpayer must file a refund claim before the later of (1) three (3) years after the due date of the return or (2) two (2) years after payment of the tax [G.S. § 105-241.6(a)].

• *Exceptions to the general period of limitation on refund claims*

The following exceptions apply to the general period of limitation on refund claims:

(1) *Waiver:* A taxpayer's waiver of the statute of limitations for making a proposed assessment extends the period in which the taxpayer can obtain a refund to the end of the period extended by the waiver [G.S. § 105-241.6(b)(2)].

(2) *Federal determination:* If a taxpayer files a return reflecting a federal determination and the return is filed within the statutory period, the period for requesting a refund is the later of (a) one (1) year after the return reflecting the federal determination is filed or (b) three (3) years after the original return was filed or due to be filed [G.S. § 105-421.6(b)(1)]. When a taxpayer files a timely return reflecting a federal determination that affects the amount of State tax payable and the general period of limitation for requesting a refund has expired, a taxpayer is allowed a refund only if the refund is the result of adjustments related to the federal determination [G.S. § 105-241.10]. While this language appears to permit a taxpayer to claim refunds unrelated to federal adjustments by deliberately failing to file a timely return reporting the federal determination, G.S. §§ 105-130.20, 105-159 and 105-163.6A provide that a taxpayer that fails to timely report a federal determination forfeits the right to any refund. See ¶ 3202 for the definition of a federal determination.

(3) *Worthless debts or securities:* For certain overpayments income taxes by individuals, trusts and estates attributable to bad debts and worthless securities, the special seven-year period of statute of limitations of IRC § 6511(d)(1) applies [G.S. § 105-241.6(b)(3)].

(4) *Capital loss and net operating loss carrybacks:* For purposes of income taxes on individuals, estates and trusts, the special three-year statute of limitations of IRC § 6511(d)(2) applies to overpayments attributable to a capital loss carryback under IRC § 1212(c) or net operating loss carrybacks under IRC § 172 [G.S. § 105-241.6(b)(4)].

(5) *Contingent events.* A taxpayer may not request a refund of an overpayment based on a contingent event until the event is resolved [G.S. § 105-241.7(b)]. If a taxpayer is subject to a contingent event and files a written notice with the Secretary, the period for requesting a refund may be extended one time until six months after the contingent event concludes. A contingent event generally means litigation or a state tax audit that prevents the taxpayer from filing an accurate and definite refund request. The required notice to the Secretary must be filed before the statute of limitations has otherwise expired (taking onto account the other exceptions to the general limitation period discussed above). The notice must also identify and describe the litigation or state tax audit, the type of tax, and the return or payment affected and state in clear terms the basis for and amount of the overpayment. A taxpayer who contends that an event or condition other than litigation or a state tax audit prevents the taxpayer from filing an accurate and definite refund request before the statute of limitations has otherwise expired (taking into account the other exceptions to the general limitation period discussed above) may request in writing that the Secretary extend the limitation period. The request must include clear and convincing proof that the contingency is beyond the taxpayer's control and prevents the taxpayer from filing a definite and accurate refund request. The Secretary's decision on the request is final and not subject to administrative or judicial review [G.S. § 105-241.6(b)(5)].

¶ **3203**

• *Action on refund requests*

When a taxpayer files an amended return or a claim for refund, the Department of Revenue must take one of the following actions within six (6) months after the date the amended return or claim for refund is filed [G.S. § 105-241.7(c)]:

(1) Send the taxpayer a refund of the amount shown due on the amended return or claim for refund [G.S. § 105-241.7(c)(1)].

(2) Adjust the amount of the of the requested refund by increasing or decreasing the amount shown due on the amended return or claim for refund and send the taxpayer a refund of the adjusted amount. If the adjusted amount is less than the amount shown due on the amended return or claim for refund, the adjusted refund must include a reason for the adjustment. The adjusted refund is considered a notice of proposed denial for the amount of requested refund that is not included in the adjusted refund [G.S. § 105-241.7(c)(2)].

(3) Deny the refund and send the taxpayer a notice of proposed denial [G.S. § 105-241.7(c)(3)].

(4) Send the taxpayer a letter requesting additional information concerning the requested refund. If a taxpayer does not respond to a request for information, the Department may deny the refund and send the taxpayer a notice of proposed denial. If a taxpayer provides the requested information, the Department must take one of the actions listed in (1) through (3) above within the later of the following [G.S. § 105-241.7(c)(4)]:

(a) The remainder of the six-month period.

(b) 30 days after receiving the information.

(c) A time period mutually agreed upon by the Department and the taxpayer.

Failure of the Department to act: If the Department does not take one of the required actions within six months after the amended return or claim for refund is filed, the inaction is considered a proposed denial of the requested refund [G.S. § 105-241.7(c)].

Requests regarding the statute of limitations: If the Department determines the amended return or refund request to be outside the statute of limitations, the Department must deny the refund and send the taxpayer a notice of denial [G.S. § 105-247.1(c1)].

Notice of proposed denial: A notice of a proposed denial of a request for refund (and a notice of denial based on a determination that the request was outside the statute of limitations) must contain (1) the basis for the denial or proposed denial and (2) the circumstances under which a proposed denial will become final. The statement of the basis of the denial in the notice of proposed denial does not prevent the Department from changing the basis of its denial later [G.S. § 105-247.1(d)].

Restrictions: The Department may not refund any of the following [G.S. § 105-247.1(e):

(1) An amount paid before the final return is filed.

(2) An overpayment setoff under Chapter 105A (Setoff Debt Collection Act) or under another setoff debt collection program authorized by law.

(3) An income tax overpayment the taxpayer has elected to apply to another purpose.

(4) An individual income tax overpayment of less than one dollar ($1.00) or another tax overpayment of less than three dollars ($3.00), unless the taxpayer files a written claim for the refund.

Refund does not prevent future assessment: A refund does not absolve a taxpayer of a tax liability that may in fact exist, and the Secretary may propose an assessment for any amount erroneously refunded [G.S. § 105-247.1(f)].

Proposed denial presumed correct: A denial or proposed denial of a refund by the Secretary is presumed to be correct [G.S. § 105-247.1(f)].

• *Result when taxpayer does not request a review*

If a taxpayer does not file a timely request for a Departmental review of a proposed denial, the proposed denial becomes final and is not subject to further administrative or judicial review. A taxpayer whose proposed denial becomes final may not file another amended return or claim for refund to obtain the denied refund [G.S. § 105-241.12(a)].

• *Requesting a review of proposed denial of refund*

A taxpayer who objects to a proposed denial of a refund may request a Departmental review of the proposed denial within 45 days after the date the notice of proposed denial was mailed or delivered if delivered in person. The request must be in the form prescribed by the Secretary and must include an explanation for the request. If the Department takes no action on the refund request for six months and is therefore deemed to have proposed a denial of the request under G.S. § 105-241.7(c), the taxpayer may request Departmental review of the deemed proposed denial any time after the running of the six month period without waiting for the Department to issue a notice of proposed denial. The taxpayer's right to request a review of the proposed denial in such a case does not terminate until 45 days after the Department actually mails or delivers its notice of proposed denial [G.S. § 105-241.11(a)]. A request for Departmental review of a proposed denial is considered filed as follows [G.S. § 105-241.11(b)]:

(1) On the date it is delivered, for a request that is delivered in person.

(2) In accordance with G.S. § 105-263 for a request that is mailed.

(3) The date the Department receives it if delivered by another method.

• *Action on request for review*

The procedures for resolving disputes over refund claims where the taxpayer timely requests a review of a proposed denial of the claim are discussed in ¶ 3210.

• *Interest on overpayments and underpayments*

Refunds bear interest at the established rate (discussed at ¶ 3205). The rate established by the Secretary may not be less than 5% per year and may not exceed 16% per year [G.S. § 105-241.21(a)].

¶3203

• *Special application of income tax refunds*

Any taxpayer whose income tax return shows that the taxpayer is entitled to a refund may elect to apply all or part of the refund to the taxpayer's estimated tax liability for the following year [G.S. § 105-269.4]. In addition, any taxpayer entitled to an income tax refund may elect to contribute all or part of the refund to the Wildlife Conservation Account. The taxpayer's election becomes irrevocable upon filing the return showing the refund [G.S. § 105-269.5]. Finally, individual taxpayers entitled to a personal income tax refund may elect to contribute all or part of the refund to the state Department of Health and Human Services to be used for the early detection of breast and cervical cancer. The election is available only for the 2017 through 2020 taxable years [G.G. § 105-269.8].

¶3204 Penalties

The North Carolina Statutes provide both civil and criminal penalties for failure to comply with the income tax laws. This paragraph provides a brief overview of the penalty provisions. These penalties do not apply to inheritance, estate, and gift tax deficiencies that are the result of valuation understatements [G.S. § 105-236(4)(e)].

Waiver of Penalties

The Secretary of Revenue, with the approval of the Attorney General, is authorized to reduce or waive any penalties for reasonable causes [G.S. § 105-237(a)]. Interest on the tax due, however, generally cannot be waived or reduced. Interest is discussed at ¶3205. A request for a waiver or reduction of penalty must be in writing and must include an explanation for the request. Interest on the tax cannot be waived or reduced. The Department's Penalty Waiver Policy and form to request waiver (Form North Carolina-5500) are available on the Department's web site, www.dornc.com The Secretary is also authorized to compromise on the amount of a taxpayer's liability. See ¶3301.

• *Bad checks*

If an uncertified check tendered to the Department of Revenue in payment of any obligation due to the Department is returned by the bank because of insufficient funds or the nonexistence of an account of the drawer, the person who tendered the check is subject to a penalty equal to 10% of the check, subject to a minimum of $1 and a maximum of $1,000. The penalty does not apply if, at the time the check was presented for payment, the drawer of the check had sufficient funds to pay the check in an account at the financial institution in North Carolina, but the financial institution failed to draw the check [G.S. § 105-236(a)(1)].

• *Bad electronic funds transfer (EFT)*

When an electronic funds transfer cannot be completed due to insufficient funds or the nonexistence of an account of the transferor, the transferor is subject to a penalty equal to 10% of the check, subject to a minimum of $1 and a maximum of $1,000 [G.S. § 105-236(a)(1a)].

• *Failure to file*

A taxpayer who fails to file a return on the due date, determined with regard to any extension of time for filing, is subject to a penalty equal to 5% of the amount of the tax if the failure is not for more than one month, with an additional 5% for each additional month, or fraction thereof, during which the failure continues, subject to 25% in the aggregate [G.S. § 105-236(9a)(3)]. Prior to January 1, 2014, the penalty is subject to a minimum of $5.00 [S.L. 2012-79 (S.B. 826), § 2.18(b)].

• *Failure to file informational returns*

A person who fails to timely file an information return with respect to withholding taxes, sales and use taxes, gasoline and alternative fuel taxes, tobacco product taxes, alcoholic beverage taxes, or income taxes is subject to a $50 per diem penalty up to a maximum of $1,000. A person who fails to file such a return in the form required by the Secretary is subject to a separate $200 penalty [G.S. § 105-236(a)(10)].

• *Failure to obtain a license*

A taxpayer who fails to obtain a license before engaging in a business, trade, or profession for which a license is required is subject to a penalty equal to 5% of the amount prescribed for the license per month or fraction thereof until paid, subject to a minimum of $5 and maximum of 25% of the prescribed license cost. In cases in which the taxpayer, after written notification by the Department of Revenue, fails to obtain a required license, the Secretary may assess a penalty of $1,000 [G.S. § 105-236(2)].

• *Failure to pay*

Failure to pay the tax when due results in a penalty of 10% of the tax [G.S. § 105-236(4)]. Prior to January 1, 2014, the penalty is subject to a minimum of $5.00 [S.L. 2012-79 (S.B. 826), § 2.18(b)]. This penalty does not apply in any of the following circumstances:

(1) When the amount of tax shown as due on an amended return is paid when the return is filed [G.S. § 105-236(a)(4)a.].

(2) When the Secretary proposes an assessment for tax due but not shown on a return and the tax due is paid within 45 days after the later of the following [G.S. § 105-236(a)(4)b.]:

(a) The date of the notice of proposed assessment of the tax, if the taxpayer does not file a timely request for a Departmental review of the proposed assessment.

(b) The date the proposed assessment becomes collectible under one of the following circumstances of G.S. § 105-241.22(3) through (6), if the taxpayer files a timely request for a Departmental review of the proposed assessment: (i) When a taxpayer and the Department agree of an settlement; (ii) When the Department sends a notice of final determination and the taxpayer does not file a timely petition for a contested case hearing on the assessment; (iii) When a final decision is issued on a proposed assessment of tax after a contested case hearing; (iv) When the Office of Administrative Hearings dismisses a petition for a contested case for lack of jurisdiction because the sole issue is the constitutionality of a statute and not the application of a statute.

(3) When a taxpayer files a consolidated or combined return at the request of the Secretary and the tax is paid within 45 days after the latest of the following: (i) the date the return is filed, (ii) the date of a notice of proposed assessment based on the return, if the taxpayer does not file a timely request for Departmental review, and (iii) the date the Departmental review ends, if the taxpayer files a timely request for Departmental review [G.S. § 105-236(a)(4)c].

(4) Consolidated or combined return: The amount of tax shown as due on a consolidated or combined return filed at the request of the Secretary is not considered a deficiency and is not subject to penalty unless one or more of the following applies [G.S. § 105-236(a)(5)f]:

(a) The return is an amended consolidated or combined return that includes the same corporations as the initial consolidated or combined return filed at the request of the Secretary. In this case the deficiency is the extent to which the amount shown as due on the amended return exceeds the amount shown as due on the initial return.

(b) The Secretary has adopted permanent rules under G.S. § 105-262 that describe the facts and circumstance under which a consolidated or combined return is required, and the Secretary requires the taxpayer file a consolidated or combined return because the taxpayer's facts and circumstances meet those described in the rules.

(c) Pursuant to a written request from a taxpayer, the Secretary has provided written advice to that taxpayer stating that a consolidated or combined return will be required under the facts and circumstances set out in the request, and the Secretary requires a taxpayer to file a consolidated or combined return because the taxpayer's facts and circumstances meet those described in the written advice.

• *Failure to report federal changes*

A taxpayer who fails to report federal changes within two years from the date he receives the federal revenue agent's report or other final determination of corrected net income is subject to the failure to file penalty (see above) and forfeits rights to any refund resulting from the federal changes. The failure to file penalty begins at the expiration of the two-year period [*2009—2010 Individual Income Tax Bulletins*, § XIII:4].

• *Frivolous returns*

Filing a frivolous return carries a penalty of up to $500. A frivolous return is one that meets both of the following requirements: (a) It fails to provide sufficient information to permit a determination of the correctness of the return or contains information that positively indicates that the return is incorrect; (b) It evidences an intention to delay, impede, or negate North Carolina revenue laws or purports to adopt a position that is lacking in seriousness [G.S. § 105-236(a)(10a)].

• *Fraud*

If there is a deficiency or delinquency in payment of any tax because of fraud with intent to evade the tax, the taxpayer is subject to a penalty of 50% of the total deficiency [G.S. § 105-236(6)]. When an examination of an income tax return is based on a federal audit report and the fraud penalty has been assessed for federal purposes, the 50% fraud penalty will be assessed for State purposes.

• *Identity theft*

A person who knowingly obtains, possesses or uses certain identifying information of another person, living or dead, with the intent to use that information in a fraudulent submission to the Department is guilty of a class G felony (or a class F felony if the person whose identifying information is used suffers any financial harm) [G.S. § 105-236(a)(9b)].

• *Misrepresentation of payment*

A person who receives money from a taxpayer with the understanding that the money is to be remitted to the State for application to the taxpayer's tax liability and who willfully fails to remit the money is guilty of a Class F felony [G.S. § 105-236(10b)].

• *Misuse of exemption certificate*

For misuse of an exemption certificate (including a conditional exemption certificate and a direct pay permit) by a purchaser, the penalty equal to $250 will be assessed [G.S. § 105-236(a)(5a)]. Exemption certificates are discussed at ¶1811.

• *Negligence*

(1) *Negligent failure to comply:* For negligent failure to comply with tax provisions, without intent to fraud, a taxpayer is subject to a penalty equal to 10% of the deficiency due to negligence [G.S. § 105-236(a)(5)].

(2) *Understatement of taxable income by individuals:* In the case of an individual who understates taxable income, by any means, by an amount equal to 25% or more of gross income (as defined in IRC § 61), the individual is subject to a penalty equal to 25% of the deficiency [G.S. § 105-236(a)(5)].

(3) *Understatement of tax liability by taxpayers other than individuals:* In the case of a tax other than the individual income tax, there is a penalty equal to 25% of the deficiency if the taxpayer understates tax liability by 25% or more [G.S. § 105-236(a)(5)].

No Double Penalty

If a fraud penalty is assessed, no penalty for negligence will be assessed with respect to the same deficiency [G.S. § 105-236(5)(d)]. However, other penalties for failure to file and for underpayment of estimated income tax will be assessed if applicable with respect to the same deficiency.

• *Payment in wrong form*

If a taxpayer makes a payment of tax that is not in the required form (i.e., in the national currency by cash, check, EFT, or other approved method), the taxpayer is subject to a penalty equal to 5% of the amount of the tax, subject to a minimum of $1 and a maximum of $1,000 [G.S. § 105-236(a)(1b)].

• *Road tax understatement*

For understatement of road tax by 25% or more, the penalty is equal to two times the amount of the deficiency [G.S. § 105-236(a)(5b)].

• *Willful evasion*

A taxpayer who willfully attempts in any manner to evade or defeat a tax or its payment is, in addition to other penalties provided by law, guilty of a Class H felony [G.S. § 105-236(a)(7)].

• *Willful failure to collect, withhold, or pay*

Any person required by law to collect, withhold, account for, and pay over any tax who willfully fails to collect or truthfully account for and pay over the tax is, in addition to other penalties provided by law, guilty of a Class 1 misdemeanor. Prosecution for a violation cannot be barred before the expiration of 6 years after the date of the violation [G.S. § 105-236(a)(8)].

• *Willful assistance with knowledge of falsity or fraud*

Any person who, pursuant to or in connection with the revenue laws, willfully aids, assists in, procures, counsels, or advises the preparation, presentation, or filing of a return, affidavit, claim, or any other document that the person knows is fraudulent or false as to any material matter is (whether or not the falsity or fraud is with the knowledge or consent of the person authorized or required to present or file the document) guilty of a felony. Income tax return preparers who assist in the preparation, presentation or filing, of false tax documents are guilty of (a) a class C felony if the amount of all taxes fraudulently evaded on returns filed in one taxable year equal or exceed $100,000 and (b) a class F felony if the amount of such taxes is less than $100,000. In all other cases the person who assists in the preparation, presentation or filing of false tax documents is guilty of a class H felony [G.S. § 105-236(a)(9a)].

• *Willful failure to file return, supply information, or pay tax*

Any person required to pay any tax, to file a return, to keep any records, or to supply any information who willfully fails to pay the tax, file the return, keep the records, or supply the information at the required time(s) is, in addition to being subject to other penalties provided by law, guilty of a Class 1 misdemeanor. Prosecution will not be barred before the expiration of 6 years after the date of the violation [G.S. § 105-236(a)(9)].

¶3205 Interest

• *Interest rate*

The interest rate on assessments and overpayments is set semiannually by the Secretary. On or before June 1 and December 1 of each year, the Secretary, after giving due consideration to current market conditions and to the federal rate that will be in effect under the Internal Revenue Code, will establish the interest rate to be in effect in the following six-month period (beginning July 1 or January 1). If no new rate is established, the rate in effect during the preceding six-month period continues to be in effect. The semiannual rate established by the Secretary cannot be less than 5% per year or more than 16% per year [G.S. § 105-241.21(a)].

Current interest rates are posted on the Department of Revenue's web site at http://www.dor.state.nc.us/taxes/rate.html.

The interest rate for periods between July 1, 2019 and December 31, 2019 is 5%.

• *Interest on underpayments*

Interest accrues on an underpayment of tax from the date set by the statute for payment of the tax until the tax is paid. Interest accrues only on the tax due and not on any penalty [G.S. § 105-241.21(b)]. Assessments are explained at ¶ 3208. See also G.S. § 105-241.1(i) (repealed effective January 1, 2008) [S.L. 2007-491 (S.B. 242), § 47.

• *Waiver of interest*

The Secretary is authorized to reduce or waive any interest on taxes imposed before or during a period for which the taxpayer has declared bankruptcy under Chapters 7, 11 or 13 of the federal bankruptcy code [G.S. § 105-237(a)].

• *Interest on overpayments*

Interest accrues on an overpayment of tax from the following specified times until the refund is paid [G.S. § 105-241.21(c)]:

(1) Franchise tax, individual and corporation income tax, and gross premiums tax: Interest on an overpayment of franchise tax payable on an annual basis and on an overpayment of income tax or gross premiums tax accrues from a date 45 days after the latest of the following dates:

(a) The date the final return was filed.

(b) The date the final return was due to be filed.

(c) The date of the overpayment. The date of an overpayment of income tax or gross premiums tax is determined in accordance with IRC § 6611(d),(f),(g), and (h)].

(2) *All other taxes:* Interest on an overpayment of any other tax accrues from a date that is 90 days after the date the tax was paid.

When a refund is paid: A refund sent to a taxpayer is considered paid on a date determined by the Secretary that is no sooner than five (5) days after a refund check is mailed. A refund set off against a debt pursuant to Chapter 105A of the General Statute is considered paid five (5) days after the Department mails the taxpayer a notice of the setoff, unless G.S. § 105A-5 or G.S. § 105A-8 requires the agency that requested the setoff to return the refund to the taxpayer. In this circumstance, the refund that was set off is not considered paid until five (5) days after the agency that requested the refund mails the taxpayer a check for the refund [G.S. § 105-241.21(d)].

¶ 3206 Voluntary Disclosure Program

The Department's Voluntary Disclosure Program is designed to promote compliance and to benefit taxpayers who discover a past filing obligation and liability that have not been discharged. It applies to taxpayers who have failed to file returns and pay any tax due to the Department. It applies to any tax administered by the Department and to any type of domestic or foreign taxpayer who is subject to tax in North Carolina. It does not apply to a taxpayer who is registered for payment of a tax but fails to file a return, and it does not apply to a taxpayer who files a return but underreports the tax due on the return.

Voluntary disclosure arises when a taxpayer contacts the Department (without any initial contact by the Department) about the filing of a return and the payment of a tax. Voluntary disclosure includes requests by taxpayers under the Multistate Tax Commission's National Nexus Program. The Multistate Tax Commission's National Nexus Program assists businesses involved in interstate commerce to voluntarily resolve potential problems with respect to state sales and use taxes, corporation income taxes, and franchise taxes; and a major component of the North Carolina Voluntary Disclosure Program is to resolve sales and use and corporate income and franchise tax liabilities when nexus is the central issue.

• *Multistate Tax Commission's National Nexus Program*

The Multistate Tax Commission's National Nexus Program is a voluntary disclosure program that allows taxpayers to resolve potential tax liabilities simultaneously with multiple states. Through this program, multistate businesses may anonymously approach any or all of the National Nexus Program member states to propose settlement of potential state sales and use tax and/or income and franchise tax liabilities arising from past activities within the states. North Carolina is a National Nexus Program Member. Taxpayers benefit by resolving potential state tax disputes before states issue prior year assessment of taxes, interest and penalties. Multistate resolution saves time and money, and the Commission staff performs most of the work at no cost to the taxpayer. To encourage voluntary compliance through this program, the Commission has adopted a policy where the Commission will not disclose the identities of taxpayers who voluntarily enter into settlements with those states that do not accept the taxpayer's proffer.

• *Benefits of voluntary disclosure*

A taxpayer whose application for a voluntary disclosure is approved will receive the following benefits:

(1) *Waiver of penalties and prosecution:* Waiver of civil penalties and an agreement by the Department not to pursue criminal prosecution unless the taxpayer collected a trust tax but did not pay it to the Department. If trust taxes were collected, the Department will waive all civil penalties, except the 10% civil penalty for failure to pay tax when due, and will not pursue criminal prosecution.

(2) *Simplified spreadsheet reporting:* The ability to file returns in a spreadsheet format, when applicable, instead of filing a return for every period involved. The spreadsheet must reflect liability in chronological order.

(3) *Time to prepare:* Thirty (30) days to determine the liability and prepare the returns.

(4) *Payment for look-back period:* A requirement to pay all tax due for the look-back period. The look-back period is three delinquent years plus the current year or, for taxes that do not have an annual filing frequency, the corresponding number of delinquent periods plus the current period. If the applicant has collected taxes and not reported them for periods beyond the look-back period, the look-back period will be extended to cover those periods. The look-back period for voluntary disclosure is shorter than the look-back period that applies when the Department discovers through examination that a taxpayer has failed to file returns and pay taxes due. The look-back period for taxpayers discovered through examination is five delinquent years plus the

current year or, for taxes that do not have an annual filing frequency, the corresponding number of delinquent periods plus the current period.

• *Qualifying for voluntary disclosure*

In order for a disclosure by a taxpayer to be voluntary, it must meet all of the following criteria:

(1) *No contact by Department:* The taxpayer has not been contacted by the Department of Revenue with respect to any tax for which the taxpayer is requesting voluntary disclosure.

(2) *No other tax liabilities:* The taxpayer does not have outstanding liabilities for other taxes.

(3) *No audit:* The taxpayer is not under audit for any tax.

(4) *Payment by taxpayer:* The taxpayer pays the tax due plus accrued interest. Upon request, the Department will calculate the interest due and notify the taxpayer.

(5) *Information supplied:* Upon request, the taxpayer makes records available for audit to verify the amount of the taxpayer's liability and the accuracy of the representations made by the taxpayer.

• *Application*

A request for a voluntary disclosure must be in writing and sent to the following address:

Voluntary Disclosure Program
North Carolina Department of Revenue
P.O. Box 871
Raleigh, NC 27602-0871

• *Information to be submitted—Business taxes*

The taxpayer or taxpayer's representative initiates contact with the Department of Revenue, which may be done anonymously, by writing a letter describing all of the following:

(1) The taxpayer's business.

(2) The nature and extent of the taxpayer's activities in North Carolina, including whether the taxpayer does any of the following:

(a) Owns or leases property in North Carolina.

(b) Has employees or independent sales representatives soliciting sales in North Carolina.

(c) Has inventory located in North Carolina.

(d) Makes deliveries into North Carolina and, if so, the means of transportation used.

(e) Engages third parties to install or repair property sold to North Carolina customers.

(f) Engages in other activities described in 17 NCAC 5C.0102 or in G.S. § 105-164.3(5) or § 105-164.8(b).

¶3206

(3) The length of time the taxpayer has been in business and the period of time it has conducted activities in North Carolina.

(4) The taxpayer's previous filing or payment history with the Department.

(5) Whether the taxpayer has been contacted by the North Carolina Department of Revenue or the Multistate Tax Commission regarding its liability.

(6) Whether the taxpayer has any outstanding liabilities for any tax administered by the Department.

(7) An explanation of why returns have not been filed and taxes have not been paid.

- *Information to be submitted—Personal taxes*

The taxpayer or taxpayer's representative initiates contact with the Department of Revenue, which may be done on an anonymous basis, by writing a letter describing the reason returns were not filed and taxes were not paid.

Withholding Taxes Not Personal Taxes

Withholding taxes are business taxes, not personal taxes, under the Voluntary Disclosure Program.

- *Review and approval*

An application will not be considered for approval until a full written disclosure has been made setting out all pertinent facts and circumstances concerning the information required by the Department. Based on the information submitted, the application (1) will be approved, (2) rejected, or (3) a counter proposal will be made. Once the application has been approved, the Department will sign a Voluntary Disclosure Agreement and send it to the taxpayer to sign, unless a letter is more appropriate. If the Department determines that the taxpayer or its representative misrepresented the information upon which the Agreement is based, the Agreement can be voided and the Department can take action as if the Agreement did not exist.

When the taxpayer is identified by signing the Agreement and returning it to the Department, the Division in the Department that signed the Agreement will check to determine if the taxpayer has an outstanding liability for any tax and if the taxpayer has a prior filing history. That Division will communicate with all appropriate Divisions to determine if the Department has previously contacted the taxpayer. Any returns and payments received will be processed, an account will be established, and Field Examinations will be notified to consider the taxpayer for examination.

- *Audits*

The Department reserves its right to audit a taxpayer's books and records, subject to statutory time. The audit may include all or part of a voluntary disclosure period. The Department will assess any tax determined to be due that was not discharged under the Voluntary Disclosure Agreement. All applicable penalties and interest will apply to additional taxes discovered to be due that have not been paid. If any of the factual representations made in the voluntary disclosure process are found to have been materially misrepresented or a material fact is found to have been omitted by the taxpayer or its representative, the Department may consider the Agreement null and void and proceed as though the Agreement never existed.

¶3206

• *Confidentiality*

The Department will not release the identity of a taxpayer who has entered into a Voluntary Disclosure Agreement or the terms of the Agreement unless the information must be released upon request under the provisions of G.S. § 105-259 or existing information exchange agreements.

¶3207 Collection of Tax

• *Collection of tax*

The Department may collect a tax in the following circumstances [G.S. § 105-241.22]:

(1) When a taxpayer files a return showing an amount due with the return and does not pay the amount shown due. Note that this provision is intended to permit the Department to collect tax, interest and penalties (not just tax) where the taxpayer files a no-remit return. This provision does not apply to a consolidated or combined return filed at the request of the Secretary.

(2) When the Department sends a notice of collection after a taxpayer does not file a timely request for a Departmental review of a proposed assessment of tax or in cases of taxpayer inaction under G.S. § 105-241.13A.

(3) When a taxpayer and the Department agree on a settlement concerning the amount of tax due.

(4) When the Department sends a notice of final determination concerning as assessment of tax and the taxpayer does not file a timely petition for a contested case hearing on the assessment.

(5) When a final decision is issued on a proposed assessment of tax after a contested case hearing.

(6) When a petition for a contested case in the Office of Administrative Hearings is dismissed and the period for timely filing a petition has expired.

• *Levy and sale of the taxpayer's tangible property*

If a taxpayer does not pay a tax within 30 days after it becomes collectible, as determined under G.S. § 105-241.22, the Secretary may issue a warrant to the sheriff of any county in North Carolina or to a revenue officer or other employee of the Department charged with the duty of collecting taxes [G.S. § 105-242(a)].

A warrant issued to a sheriff must direct the sheriff to levy upon and sell the taxpayer's real and personal property found within the county for purposes of paying the tax due plus the costs of executing the warrant and to return the money so collected to the Secretary within not less than 60 days from the date of the warrant. The procedures for executions issued against property upon judgments of a court apply to executions under the Secretary's warrant [G.S. § 105-242(a)(1)].

A warrant issued to a revenue officer or other employee of the Department charged with the duty to collect taxes must direct such person to levy upon and sell the taxpayer's personal property found within the state for the payment of the tax. The Secretary may sell the taxpayer's personal property levied upon and may advertise the sale in any reasonable manner and for any reasonable period of time to produce an adequate bid. Levy and sale fees and actual advertising costs must be added to and collected in the same manner as the delinquent taxes. The Secretary is not required to file a report of sale with the clerk of superior court if the sale is otherwise publicly reported. The levy and sale of personal property by an officer or employee of the Department is otherwise subject to the laws governing the sale of property levied upon under execution [G.S. § 105-242(a)(1)].

• *Attachment and garnishment of the taxpayer's intangible property*

Intangible property that belongs to the taxpayer or that is owed to the taxpayer by a third party, or that a third party has received from the taxpayer under circumstances that would permit it to be levied upon if it were tangible property, is subject to attachment and garnishment in payment of a tax that is collectible under G.S. § 105-241.22. A third party in possession of intangible property subject to attachment and garnishment is known as the "garnishee" and is liable for the amount the taxpayer owes up to the amount of taxpayer's property in the garnishee's possession reduced by any amount the taxpayer owes the garnishee [G.S. § 105-242(b)].

Intangible property subject to attachment and garnishment includes bank deposits, rent, salaries and wages (including salaries and wages of an employee of the United States, North Carolina or a political subdivision of North Carolina), property held in the State's escheat fund, and any other property incapable of manual levy or delivery. No more than 10% of a taxpayer's wages or salary is subject to attachment and garnishment [G.S. § 105-242(b)].

The Secretary may require a financial institution to assist it in identifying property subject to attachment and garnishment by providing the financial institution, on a quarterly (or, with the consent of the financial institution, more frequent) basis with information that identifies the taxpayer and the amount of the tax debt. The financial institution must then determine the amount, if any, of the taxpayer's property that it holds and inform the Secretary. The Secretary must reimburse the financial institution for its costs of compliance with this procedure, not to exceed the amount payable to the institution under G.S. § 110-139 for providing information for use in locating a noncustodial parent [G.S. § 105-242(b)].

The procedure for attachment and garnishment begins with a notice of garnishment from the Department sent in accordance with G.S. § 105-240.1 (or electronically if the garnishee agrees). The notice must set forth the taxpayer's name, social security or federal identification number, the amount of tax, penalties and interest the taxpayer owes, an explanation of the garnishee's liability for the taxes owed and an explanation of the garnishee's responsibility concerning the notice. The garnishee must comply with the garnishment notice or file a written response to the notice within 30 days (20 days for financial institutions). Upon receipt of a written response, the Department must contact the garnishee and schedule a conference to discuss the response or inform the garnishee of the Department's position concerning the response. If the Department and garnishee do not agree on the garnishee's liability, the Department may enforce the garnishee's liability by sending the garnishee a notice of proposed assessment. A notice of garnishment is released when the Department sends the garnishee a notice of release stating the name and identifying number of the taxpayer to whom the release relates, provided that a financial institution is released from a garnishment notice when it complies with the notice [G.S. § 105-242.1].

• *Certificate of Tax Liability*

Certificate a lien. The Secretary is authorized to file a certificate of tax liability stating the taxpayer's name and the type and amount of tax owed with the clerk of the superior court of any county in which the taxpayer resides or has property (or in Wake County if the taxpayer does not reside in or have property in North Carolina). A recorded certificate of tax liability is considered a judgment and is enforceable in the same manner as other judgments. The tax stated on a certificate is a lien on real and personal property from the date the certificate is recorded. Interest accrues on the principal amount of tax stated in the certificate at the legal rate set forth in G.S. § 24-1 [G.S. § 105-242(c)].

Ten-year enforcement period. The Secretary may enforce a certificate of tax liability for a period of ten years from the date it is recorded. If the certificate is not satisfied within this period, the remaining liability of the taxpayer is abated and the Department must cancel the certificate. There are a number of exceptions to the ten-year enforcement period. First, an execution sale initiated before the end of the ten-year period may be completed after the end of this period, regardless of whether resales are required because of the posting of increased bids. Second, the Secretary may accept tax payments made after a certificate has expired, regardless of whether any collection actions were taken before the certificate expired. Third, a taxpayer may waive the ten-year period for enforcement of the certificate for either a definite or an indefinite time. Finally, the ten-year period in which a certificate of tax liability is enforceable is tolled during the following periods:

(1) While the taxpayer is absent from the State. The period is tolled during the taxpayer's absence plus one year after the taxpayer returns.

(2) Upon the death of the taxpayer. The period is tolled while the taxpayer's estate is administered plus one year after the estate is closed.

(3) While an action is pending to set aside a conveyance made by the taxpayer as a fraudulent conveyance.

(4) While an insolvency proceeding against the taxpayer is pending.

(5) During the period of any statutory or judicial bar to the enforcement of the certificate.

(6) The period for which a taxpayer has waived the ten-year period [G.S. § 105-242(c)].

• *Release of Lien*

The Secretary must release a tax lien on a taxpayer's property if the liability for which the lien attached has been satisfied. In addition, the Secretary may release a tax lien on all or part of a taxpayer's property if (1) the liability for which the lien attached has become unenforceable due to lapse of time, (2) the lien is creating an economic hardship due to the financial condition of the taxpayer, (3) the fair market value of the property exceeds the tax liability and release of the lien on part of the property would not hinder collection of the liability, or (4) release of the lien will probably facilitate, expedite, or enhance the State's chances for ultimately collecting a tax due [G.S. § 105-242(c1)].

• *Remedies Cumulative*

The collection remedies set forth in G.S. § 105-242 (*i.e.,* levy and sale, attachment and garnishment, certificate of tax liability) are cumulative and in addition to all other remedies provided by law for the collection of taxes [G.S. § 105-242(d)].

¶3207

- *Exempt Property*

The following property (and only the following property) is exempt from levy, attachment, and garnishment: (1) the taxpayer's principal residence, unless the Secretary approves of the levy in writing or the Secretary finds that collection of the tax is in jeopardy, (2) tangible personal property and intangible property that is exempt from federal levy as provided in section 6334 of the Code, and (3) 90% of the taxpayer's salary or wages per month [G.S. § 105-242(e)].

- *Uneconomical Levy*

The Secretary may not levy against any property if he estimates that the expenses that would be incurred by the Department in levying against the property would exceed the property's fair market value [G.S. § 105-242(f)].

- *Erroneous Lien*

A taxpayer who believes a certificate of tax liability was erroneously filed against him may appeal to the Secretary to withdraw the certificate. Upon receipt of such an appeal, the Secretary must make a determination of such an appeal as quickly as possible, and if the Secretary finds that the certificate was erroneously filed, he must withdraw the lien as quickly as possible by issuing a certificate of withdrawal [G.S. § 105-242(g)].

- *Intergovernmental tax collection agreements*

There are a number of agreements among governmental agencies to provide for assistance in tax collection, both between the Internal Revenue Service and the states, and among the states themselves.

Agreement with IRS Abusive Tax Avoidance Transactions (ATAT) Memorandum of Understanding: The Small Business/Self-Employed Division of the Internal Revenue Service signed ATAT Memorandums of Understanding with 40 states (including North Carolina) and the District of Columbia on September 16, 2003, that provide for information sharing on abusive tax avoidance transactions (*Memorandum of Understanding,* Internal Revenue Service). The Memorandum authorizes the IRS and North Carolina to do the following:

(1) Exchange tax returns and return information.

(2) Share audit results from ATAT participant cases.

(3) Exchange information on identified types of ATAT schemes.

(4) Share audit technique guides.

The IRS will provide states with a list of participants in a particular ATAT scheme on a semiannual basis on July 31 and January 31. The IRS generally refers to an abusive tax shelter arrangement as the promise of tax benefits with no meaningful change in the taxpayer's control over or benefit from the taxpayer's income or assets.

- *Extraterritorial enforcement*

The Secretary of Revenue, with the assistance of the Attorney General, is authorized to bring suits in courts of other states to collect taxes legally due North Carolina [G.S. § 105-269(a)]. The officials of other states that extend a like comity to North Carolina are empowered to sue for the collection of their taxes in North Carolina courts. If the Secretary deems it expedient to employ local counsel to assist in bringing suit in other states, the Secretary, with the concurrence of the Attorney

¶3207

General, may employ local counsel on the basis of a negotiated retainer or in accordance with prevailing commercial law league rates.

- *Bankruptcy and receivership*

A lien for all North Carolina taxes due attaches to the property of a taxpayer and of an insolvent's estate as of the date and time of the execution of an assignment for the benefit of creditors by the taxpayer or of the institution of receivership or other insolvency proceeding [G.S. § 105-141].

- *Installment payments*

After a proposed assessment of a tax becomes final, the Secretary may enter into an agreement with the taxpayer for payment of the tax in installments [G.S. § 105-237(b)].

The agreement may include a waiver of penalties but not a waiver of liability for tax or interest due. The Secretary may modify or terminate the agreement if one or more of the following findings is made:

(1) Information provided by the taxpayer in support of the agreement was inaccurate or incomplete.

(2) Collection of tax to which the agreement applies is in jeopardy.

(3) The taxpayer's financial condition has changed.

(4) The taxpayer has failed to pay an installment when due or to pay another tax when due.

(5) The taxpayer has failed to provide information requested by the Secretary.

A taxpayer who has entered into an installment agreement must be given at least 30 days' written notice, specifying the basis of the finding of change in financial condition, before modification or termination of the agreement on the grounds that the taxpayer's financial condition has changed. Such notice is required unless the taxpayer failed to disclose or concealed assets or income when the agreement was made or the taxpayer has acquired assets since the agreement was made that can satisfy all or part of the tax liability.

- *Transferee liability*

Property transferred for an inadequate consideration at a time when the transferor is insolvent or is rendered insolvent by the transfer to a donee, heir, devisee, distributee, stockholder of a liquidated corporation, or any other person is subject to a lien for any state taxes the transferor owed at the time of the transfer, without regard to whether the taxes had been ascertained or assessed at the time of the transfer. If the property cannot be subjected to the state's tax lien because the transferee has disposed of it, the transferee is personally liable for the difference between the fair market value of the property at the time of the transfer and the actual consideration, if any, paid to the transferor by the transferee [G.S. § 105-239.1(a)].

Procedure: The Department may proceed to enforce a lien that arises against property transferred by a taxpayer to another or to hold that person liable for the tax due by sending the person a notice of proposed assessment [G.S. § 105-239.1(b)]. Proposed assessments are discussed at ¶ 3208.

¶3207

Proceeds: When property transferred by a taxpayer to another person is sold to satisfy the lien, the person is entitled to receive from the proceeds of the sale the amount of consideration, if any, the person paid for the property. The proceeds must be applied for this purpose before they are applied to satisfy the lien [G.S. § 105-239.1(c)].

¶3208 Assessments

• *Proposed Assessments*

The Secretary of Revenue may propose an assessment against a taxpayer for tax due from the taxpayer. The proposed assessment must be based on the best information available and is presumed to be correct [G.S. § 105-241.9(a)]. The Secretary must give a taxpayer written notice of a proposed assessment, which must contain the following information [G.S. § 105-241.9(c)]:

(1) The basis for the proposed assessment (which may be changed by the Department).

(2) The amount of tax, interest, and penalties included in the proposed assessment, stated separately.

(3) The date a failure to pay penalty will apply to the proposed assessment if the proposed assessment is not paid by that date and the amount of the penalty. If the proposed assessment is not paid by the specified date, the failure to pay penalty is considered to be assessed and applies to the proposed assessment without further notice.

(4) The circumstances under which the proposed assessment will become final and collectible.

Effect of Extensions

Under prior law, if the taxpayer had been granted an extension for filing the return, the due date of a return, for purposes of determining the period of limitation on assessments, was the extended due date. Thus, the Department had three years from the end of the extension period to propose an assessment even if the taxpayer filed the return earlier in the extension period [Directive CD-06-1, Scenario 3 (October 25, 2006)]. The Department will presumably interpret the new law in the same fashion.

• *General period of limitation on proposed assessments*

Unless an exception applies, the Secretary must propose an assessment before the expiration of the general period of limitation on assessments [G.S. § 105-241.9(b)]. The general period of limitation on assessments is the later of three years from the date on which the return was due or the date on which the return was filed [G.S. § 105-241.8(a)].

• *Exceptions to the general period of limitation on proposed assessments*

The following are exceptions to the general period of limitation on proposed assessments:

(1) *Waiver:* If the taxpayer waives the limitations period before it expires by agreeing in writing to extend the period, the Secretary may propose an assessment at any time within the time extended by the waiver. A waiver may be for a definite or indefinite period of time [G.S. § 105-241.9(b)].

(2) *Federal determination:* If a taxpayer timely files a return reflecting a federal determination, the period for proposing an assessment of any tax due is the later of one (1) year after the return is filed or three (3) years after the original return was filed or due to be filed. If there is a federal determination and the taxpayer does not file the return within the required time, the period for proposing an assessment of any tax due is three (3) years after the date the Secretary received the final report of the federal determination [G.S. § 105-241.8(b)(1)]. A return reflecting a federal determination is timely filed if it is filed within the time required by G.S. § 105-130.20 (corporate income taxes) G.S. § 105-159 (individual income taxes), G.S. § 105-160.8 (estate and trust income taxes), G.S. § 105-163.6A (withholding taxes), or G.S. § 105-197.1 (gift taxes) [G.S. § 105-241.10]. See ¶ 3202 for the definition of a federal determination.

Limited Effect of Extended Limitation Period Based on Federal Correction

When a taxpayer files a timely return reflecting a federal determination that affects the amount of State tax payable and the general period of limitation for proposing an assessment of the State tax has expired, a taxpayer is liable for additional tax only if the additional tax is the result of adjustments related to the federal determination. A proposed assessment may not include an amount that is outside the scope of this liability [G.S. § 105-241.10]. The Secretary retains authority to propose assessments unrelated to federal adjustments during the extended limitation period if the taxpayer does not timely report the federal determination.

---

(3) *Federal amended return:* If a taxpayer timely files a return resulting from the filing of a federal amended return, the period for proposing an assessment of any tax due is the later of one year after the return is filed or three years after the original return was filed or due. If the return is not timely, the period for proposing an assessment of any tax due is three years after the filing of the federal amended return. The federal amended return is presumed to be filed on the date recorded by the Internal Revenue Service [G.S. § 105-241.8(b)(1a)].

(4) *Failure to file or filing false return:* There is no statute of limitations and the Secretary may propose an assessment of tax due from a taxpayer at any time if the taxpayer did not file a return, filed a fraudulent return, or attempted in any manner to fraudulently evade of defeat the tax [G.S. § 105-241.8(b)(2)].

(5) *Tax forfeiture:* If a taxpayer forfeits a tax credit or tax benefit, the period for proposing an assessment of any tax due as a result of the forfeiture is three (3) years after the date of the forfeiture [G.S. § 105-241.8(b)(3)].

(6) *Involuntary Conversions:* If a taxpayer elects under IRC § 1033(a)(2)(A) not to recognize gain from involuntary conversion of property into money, the period for proposing as assessment of any tax due as a result of the conversion or election is the applicable period provided under IRC § 1033(a)(2)(C) or IRC § 1033(a)(2)(D) [G.S. § 105-241.8(b)(4)].

• *Requesting review of proposed assessment*

A taxpayer who objects to a proposed assessment may request a Departmental review of the proposed assessment by filing a request for review within 45 days after the following [G.S. § 105-241.11(a)]:

(1) The date the notice of the proposed assessment was mailed to the taxpayer, if the notice was delivered by mail.

¶3208

(2) The date the notice of proposed assessment was delivered to the taxpayer, if the notice was delivered in person.

Filing: A request for a Departmental review of a proposed assessment is considered filed on the following dates [G.S. § 105-241.11(b)]:

(1) For a request that is delivered in person, the date it is delivered.

(2) For a request that is mailed, the date determined in accordance with G.S. § 105-263.

(3) For a request that is delivered by another method, the date the Department receives it.

Failure to Pay Penalty

A request for a Departmental review of a proposed assessment is considered a request for a Departmental review of a failure to pay penalty that is based on the assessment. A taxpayer who does not request a Departmental review of a proposed assessment may not request a Departmental review of a failure to pay penalty that is based on the assessment but that is assessed at a later date pursuant to a separate notice [G.S. § 105-241.11(c)].

- *Result when taxpayer does not request a review*

If a taxpayer does not file a timely request for a Departmental review of a proposed assessment, the proposed assessment is final and is not subject to further administrative or judicial review. However, upon payment of the tax, the taxpayer may request a refund of the tax [G.S. § 105-241.12(b)].

Notice of collection: Before the Department collects a proposed assessment that becomes final when the taxpayer does not file a timely request for a Departmental review, the Department must send the taxpayer a notice of collection that contains (1) a statement that the proposed assessment is final and collectible; (2) the amount of tax, interest, and penalties payable by the taxpayer; and (3) an explanation of the collection options available to the Department if the taxpayer does not pay the amount shown due on the notice; and (4) an explanation of any remedies available to the taxpayer concerning these collection options [G.S. § 105-241.12(b)].

- *Action on request for review*

The procedures for resolving disputes over proposed assessments where the taxpayer timely requests a review of the proposed assessment are discussed in ¶ 3210.

¶3209 Jeopardy Assessment and Collection

- *Action*

The Secretary may at any time within the statute of limitations immediately assess and collect any tax the Secretary finds is due from a taxpayer if the Secretary determines that collection of the tax is in jeopardy and immediate assessment and collection are necessary in order to protect the interest of the State. In making a jeopardy collection, the Secretary may use any of the collection remedies in G.S. § 105-242 (e.g., levy and sale, garnishment, attachment, certificate of tax liability) and is not required to wait any period of time before using these remedies. Within 30 days after initiating a jeopardy collection, the Secretary must give the taxpayer the notice of proposed assessment required by G.S. § 105-241.9 [G.S. § 105-241.23(a)]. Notices of proposed assessment are discussed at ¶ 3208.

• *Review by Department*

Within five (5) days after initiating a jeopardy collection that is not the result of a criminal investigation or a liability for unauthorized substances tax, the Secretary must provide the taxpayer with a written statement of the information upon which the Secretary relied in initiating the jeopardy collection. Within 30 days after receipt of this written statement or, if no statement is received, within 30 days after the statement was due, the taxpayer may request the Secretary to review the action taken. After receipt of this request, the Secretary must determine whether initiating the jeopardy collection was reasonable under all the circumstances and whether the amount assessed and collected was reasonable under all the circumstances. The Secretary must give the taxpayer written notice of this determination within 30 days after the request [G.S. § 105-241.23(b)]. The Secretary's failure to provide the taxpayer with information supporting the assessment within five days does not void the assessment, at least where the Secretary has undertaken the review required by the statute, thus providing the taxpayer with the statute's intended benefit [Secretary's Decision No. 2001-610 (October 18, 2001)].

• *Judicial review*

Within 90 days after the earlier of the date a taxpayer received or should have received a determination of the Secretary concerning a jeopardy collection, the taxpayer may bring a civil action seeking review of the jeopardy collection. The taxpayer may bring the action in the Superior Court of Wake County or in the county in North Carolina in which the taxpayer resides. Within 20 days after the action is filed, the court must determine whether the initiation of the jeopardy collection was reasonable under the circumstances. If the court determines that an action of the Secretary was unreasonable or inappropriate, the court may order the Secretary to take any action the court finds appropriate. If the taxpayer shows reasonable grounds why the 20-day limit on the court should be extended, the court may grant an extension of not more than 40 additional days [G.S. § 105-241.23(c)].

¶3210 Uniform Tax Appeal Procedure

This paragraph describes the uniform procedures to be followed when a taxpayer has timely filed a request for Departmental review of a proposed assessment or proposed denial of a refund claim ("proposed denial").

• *Request for Departmental Review*

If a taxpayer files a timely request for a Departmental review of a proposed assessment or proposed denial, the Department must conduct a review of the proposed assessment or proposed denial and take one or more of the following actions [G.S. § 105-241.13(a)]:

(1) Remove the assessment or grant the refund.

(2) Adjust the amount of tax due or refund owed.

(3) Request additional information from the taxpayer concerning the proposed assessment or proposed denial.

• *Termination of Departmental review process due to taxpayer inaction following request for additional information*

If the Department requests additional information it must give the taxpayer at least 30 days to respond. If the taxpayer fails to respond in a timely fashion, the Department must reissue the request and give the taxpayer at least another 30 days to respond. A partial response to a request for information or to the reissuance of the request is considered to be a response. However, if the taxpayer fails to make even a partial response to the request or the reissued request, the Department must send the taxpayer a notice of inaction. The proposed assessment or proposed refund denial becomes final ten days from the date of the notice unless the taxpayer responds. A proposed assessment or proposed refund denial that has become final due to taxpayer inaction is not subject to further administrative or judicial review, and, in the case of a refund request, the taxpayer may not file another refund request to obtain he same refund. In the case of an assessment, the taxpayer may pay the tax and file a refund request [G.S. §§ 105-241.13(a)(3) and 105-241.13A(a)]. Where a proposed assessment has become final due to taxpayer inaction, the Department must send the taxpayer a notice of collection before commencing to the collect the tax [G.S. § 105-241.13A(b)].

• *Termination of Departmental review process due to taxpayer payment*

If the taxpayer requests Departmental review of a proposed assessment and then pays the amount due (or the adjusted amount due if the Department adjusted the amount due), the Department may take no further action on the request. To continue the process of Departmental review, the taxpayer must inform the Department in writing that he wishes to continue the review process. Alternatively, the taxpayer, having paid the tax due, may file a refund request [G.S. § 105-241.13(a1)].

• *Termination of Departmental review process due to agreed resolution*

If the taxpayer and the Department agree that the taxpayer's objection has been resolved, the Department is not required to take any further action on the taxpayer's request [G.S. § 105-241.13(b)].

• *Conference*

When the taxpayer's request for Departmental review is not resolved due to the Department's removal of the assessment or granting of the refund, payment by the taxpayer or an agreement with the Department, the Department must schedule a conference with the taxpayer. The Department must set the time and place for the conference, which may include a conference by telephone, and send the taxpayer notice of the designated time and place. The Department must send the notice at least 30 days before the date of the conference unless the Department and taxpayer agree to a shorter notice period. The conference is an informal proceeding at which the taxpayer and the Department must attempt to resolve the case. Testimony under oath is not taken, and the rules of evidence do not apply. A taxpayer may designate a representative, who need not be an attorney, to act on the taxpayer's behalf. The taxpayer may present any objections to the proposed assessment or proposed denial at the conference and is not limited by the explanation set forth in the request for review [G.S. § 105-241.13(b)].

After conference: One of the following must occur after the Department conducts a conference on a proposed denial of a refund or a proposed assessment [G.S. § 105-241.13(c)]:

¶3210

(1) The Department and the taxpayer agree on a settlement.

(2) The Department and the taxpayer agree that additional time is needed to resolve the taxpayer's objection to the proposed assessment or proposed denial.

(3) The Department and the taxpayer are unable to resolve the taxpayer's objection to the proposed assessment or proposed denial. The Department and the taxpayer will be considered to be unable to resolve the taxpayer's objection if the taxpayer fails to attend a scheduled conference on the a proposed assessment or proposed denial without prior notice to the Department.

• *Final determination after Departmental review*

If the Department and the taxpayer are unable to resolve the taxpayer's object to the proposed assessment or proposed denial, the Department must send the taxpayer a notice of final determination concerning the proposed assessment or refund claim [G.S. § 105-241.14(b)]. The notice of final determination must be issued within nine months after the date the taxpayer filed a request for review unless the Department and the taxpayer agree to extend the time for attempting to resolve the taxpayer's objections, although a failure by the Department to issue the final determination within the required time does not affect the validity of the proposed assessment or refund denial [G.S. § 105-241.14(c)]. In the case of a proposed denial, the notice of final determination must state the basis for the determination and inform the taxpayer of the procedures for contesting the determination. The statement of the basis of the Department's determination does not prevent the Department from changing the basis for its determination later [G.S. § 105-241.14(a)]. In the case of a proposed assessment, the notice of final determination must contain the following information [G.S. § 105-241.14(b)]:

(1) The basis for the determination, stated on the notice or set out in a separate document. However, the Department is not precluded from changing the basis for its determination later.

(2) The amount of tax, interest, and penalties payable by the taxpayer.

(3) The procedure the taxpayer must follow to contest the final determination.

(4) A statement that the amount payable stated on the notice is collectible by the Department unless the taxpayer contests the final determination.

(5) An explanation of the collection options available to the Department if the taxpayer does not pay the amount shown due on the notice and any remedies available to the taxpayer concerning these collections.

• *Contested case*

A taxpayer who disagrees with a notice of final determination after a Departmental review and conference may file a petition for a contested case hearing at the Office of Administrative Hearings (OAH) under Article 3 of Chapter 150B [G.S. § 105-241.15]. Thus, a taxpayer who does not request a review of a proposed assessment or proposed denial or who does not attend a conference with the Department may not file a petition for a contested case.

¶3210

Independent Prepayment Forum

Under prior law, a taxpayer's only opportunity for a prepayment review of a proposed assessment was to request a hearing before the Secretary. In practice, the hearing was held before a hearing officer within the Department of Revenue designated by the Secretary. Under current law, the taxpayer's prepayment hearing is held before an Administrative Law Judge within the Office of Administrative Hearings, an independent agency established under Article III, Section 11 of the N.C. Constitution. Ex parte communications between the Department and the hearing officer, which were permitted under prior law, are specifically prohibited in OAH proceedings [G.S. § 150B-35].

Contested case petition: The petition to the OAH must be filed within 60 days of notice of the Department's final determination [G.S. 150B-23(f)]. The OAH lacks jurisdiction over the controversy if the petition is filed late and will dismiss the petition no matter how meritorious the claim. *See James v. Department of Revenue,* Final Decision 09 REV 0255 (March 16, 2009); *Otto v. Department of Revenue,* Final Decision 13 REV 20057 (April 15, 2014) Likewise, the OAH has no jurisdiction when the petition is filed before the Department issues a notice of final determination. *See Green v. Department of Revenue,* Final Decision, 11 REV 5139 (August 25, 2011). The requirements for the petition are set forth in G.S. 150B-23(a). The petition must state facts tending to establish that the Department has deprived the taxpayer of property, ordered the taxpayer to pay a fine or civil penalty or otherwise substantially prejudiced the taxpayer's rights and that the Department exceeded its authority or jurisdiction, acted erroneously, failed to use proper procedure, acted arbitrarily or capriciously, or failed to act as required by law or rule [G.S. 150B-23(a)].

Basis of claim: The North Carolina Business Court has ruled that while a taxpayer is free to change the basis of a refund claim during departmental review pursuant to G.S. § 105-241.7, once a final determination is issued and a petition for a contested case is filed at OAH, the taxpayer's ability to change the basis of its claim is limited by the Administrative Procedure Act and the Rules of Civil Procedure. *See Railroad Friction Products Corp. v. N.C. Department of Revenue,* 18 CVS 3868 (N.C. Business Court 2019). A similar limitation would presumably apply to the Secretary's right to change the basis of an assessment.

Venue: Hearings on all contested tax cases must be conducted in Wake County, unless the parties agree to hear the case in another county [G.S. 150B-31.1(c)].

Conduct of hearings: Hearings before the OAH are formal proceedings in which the parties have the opportunity to present arguments on issues of law and policy and to present evidence on issues of fact [G.S. § 150B-25(c)]. The rules of evidence applicable in civil trials generally apply [G.S. § 150B-29]. The petitioner in the contested case hearing bears the burden of proving that it is entitled to relief. *See, e.g., Midrex Technologies, Inc. v. N.C. Department of Revenue,* 13 REV 18654 (2014), *aff'd* 14 CVS 13996 (N.C. Bus. Ct. 2015); *aff'd,* __ N.C. __ (2016).

Representation: Individual taxpayers may represent themselves before the OAH, and the Chief Administrative Law Judge is specifically authorized to limit and simplify the procedures that apply to contested tax cases in which the taxpayer is not represented by counsel. Moreover, an Administrative Law Judge assigned to a contested tax case must make reasonable efforts to assist such taxpayers [G.S. § 150B-31.1(b)]. Corporations and other business entities, which formerly were required to be represented by an attorney (see *Chase Manhattan Mortgage Corp. v.*

¶3210

Department of Revenue, Final Decision 13 REV 10114 (June 19, 2013)), may now be represented by (1) an officer, (2) a manager or member-manager in the case of a limited liability company, (3) a W-2 employee or (4) a 25% owner. In the case of a W-2 employee or a 25% owner, the business entity must authorize the representation in writing. Authority for and prior notice of the representation by a non-attorney must be made in writing, under penalty of perjury to the OAH on a form to be provided by the OAH (G.S. § 150B-23(a)].

Decisions: The Administrative Law Judge must make a final decision or order based on the preponderance of the evidence, giving due regard to the demonstrated knowledge and expertise of the Department agency with respect to the facts and inferences within its specialized knowledge [G.S. § 150B-34(a)]. The final decision or order of the Administrative Law Judge must include findings of fact and conclusions of law [G.S. § 150B-34(a)]. The Administrative Law Judge may grant judgment on the pleadings or summary judgment on motions duly made in accordance with the rules of civil procedure, and decisions granting such motions need not include findings of fact or conclusions of law, except to the extent the Administrative Law Judge determines them to be required or allowed by the rules of civil procedure [G.S.§ 150B-34(e)].

• *Contested cases regarding the statute of limitations*

A taxpayer whose refund claim or amended return was denied by the Department as outside the statute of limitations may contest the denial by petitioning for a contested case hearing at the OAH on the sole issue of whether the taxpayer's claim was barred by the statute of limitations. A final decision by the administrative law judge is subject to judicial review. If the administrative law judge determines that the claim is not barred and judicial review is not sought, the administrative law judge must remand the case to the Department for consideration of the substantive issues. Similarly, if judicial review is sought and it is finally determined that the claim was not barred, the case must be remanded to the Department for consideration of the substantive issues. Any remand is regarded as a new, timely filed, claim for refund or amended return [G.S. § 105-241.15(b)].

• *Judicial review*

A party aggrieved by the final decision in a contested case commenced at the Office of Administrative Hearings may seek judicial review of the decision in accordance with Article 4 of Chapter 150B of the General Statutes. A petition for review must be filed within 30 days after the taxpayer is served with a copy of the final decision [G.S. § 150B-45]. The petition must be filed in the Superior Court of Wake County. If the party seeking review is the taxpayer, the taxpayer must first pay the tax, penalty and interest stated to be due in the final decision [G.S. § 105-241.16]. Failure to pay the tax before filing a petition for review deprives the court of subject matter jurisdiction and personal jurisdiction over the Department [*Lord Baltimore Capital Corp. v. Department of Revenue,* 17 CVS 3096 (N.C. Business Court 2018)].

Business Court Jurisdiction

Appeals of contested case decisions are classified as mandatory complex business cases under G.S. §7A-45.4(b)(7). Thus, either party to the case may file a Notice of Designation with the Superior Court in which the action has been filed, the Senior Business Court Judge and the Chief Justice of the North Carolina Supreme Court. If the Chief Justice approves of the designation, the case will be administered as a complex business case. However, within 30 days of filing the Notice of Designation, any other party may file an opposition to the designation of the case as a mandatory complex business case. Based upon such opposition, or on its own motion, the Business Court Judge may determine that the case should not be designated a complex business case. Any party may appeal the Business Court Judge's determination to the Chief Justice. If the Business Court Judge determines that the case should not be designated a complex business case a party may appeal the determination to the Supreme Court [G.S. §7A-45.4(e)]. For an example of a successful opposition to a notice of designation, *See In re Summons Issued to Target Corporation and Affiliates,* 18 CVS 12841 (N.C. Business Court 2018).

Standard of Review: The court may affirm, modify, or reverse the decision or remand the decision to the Department or the Administrative Law Judge for further action. In order to have a final decision reversed or modified, a taxpayer must generally show that his substantial rights have been prejudiced because the findings, inferences, conclusion or decisions contained in the final decision are (1) in violation of constitutional provisions, (2) in excess of the statutory authority or jurisdiction of the agency or the Administrative Law Judge, (3) made upon unlawful procedure, (4) affected by other errors of law, (5) unsupported by substantial evidence admissible in view of the entire record as submitted, or (6) arbitrary, capricious or an abuse of discretion. G.S. §150B-51(b). If the petitioner asserts that the final decision violates the constitution, exceeds statutory authority or jurisdiction, was made upon unlawful procedures or was affected by other error of law, the court must review the final decision using the *de novo* standard of review. If the petitioner asserts that the final decision was unsupported by substantial evidence or was arbitrary, capricious or an abuse of discretion, the court must review the final decision using the whole record standard of review [G.S. §150B-51].

- *Appeal of Business Court Decision*

A party may appeal a decision of the Business Court directly to the Supreme Court [G.S. §7A-27(a)].

- *Confidentiality in Contested Tax Cases*

G.S. §150B-31.1(e) provides that the record, proceedings, and decision in a contested tax case are confidential until the final decision is issued in the case. G.S. §105-256(a) provides that identifying taxpayer information must be redacted prior to publication. Once a case has been appealed to the Business Court, a taxpayer may seek a protective order to protect confidential or proprietary information under Business Court Rule 10.1.

- *Constitutional Challenges*

Under North Carolina law, quasi-judicial bodies such as the OAH lack the authority to rule on the constitutionality of a statute. *See Great American Ins. Co. v. Gold,* 254 N.C. 168, 118 S.E.2d 792 (1961), overruled on other grounds, *Smith v. State,* 289 N.C. 303, 222 S.E. 2d 412 (1976). However, a taxpayer asserting that a tax statute is unconstitutional is not permitted, as he was under prior law, to avoid the administrative review process by paying the tax due and proceeding directly to court. Instead, the taxpayer must exhaust his administrative remedies by receiving a final determination after a Departmental review and conference and commence a contested case within the OAH. If the taxpayer's only claim is that the statute is unconstitutional on its face, *i.e.,* without regard to the particular facts of the taxpayer's situation, the OAH will dismiss the case for lack of jurisdiction. *See, e.g., Kaestner 1992 Trust v. Department of Revenue,* Final Decision 11 REV 3547 (August 19,

2011). At that point the taxpayer must pay the tax, penalties and interest stated to be due in the final determination and seek resolution of the constitutional claim by filing a civil action as a mandatory business case within two years of dismissal of the OAH proceeding [G.S. § 105-241.17]. Any facial challenge to the validity of a statute must be heard and determined by a three-judge panel of the Wake County Superior Court [G.S. § 1-267.1(a1)].

If the taxpayer has other claims in addition to his constitutional claim, or if his claim is that the statute in question is unconstitutional as applied to his particular facts (rather than on its face), the taxpayer would proceed as with any other claim by exhausting his administrative remedies within the Department, filing a contested case petition with the OAH where a factual record will be established and his other claims resolved and then appealing the Secretary's final decision to the court within 30 days of being served with the decision.

• *Class Actions*

A class action may be brought against the State for the refund of taxes paid if (1) the action is grounded on an allegedly unconstitutional statute, (2) the requirements of Rule 23 of the North Carolina Rules of Civil Procedure are satisfied (generally providing that the class must be so numerous as to make it impracticable to bring all members before the court) and (3) the requirements of G.S. § 105-241.18 (discussed below) are satisfied [G.S. § 105-241.18(a)].

Class representative. A class action may be brought only by a taxpayer who has complied with all the conditions for bringing constitutional tax challenges under G.S. § 105-241.17 discussed above, *i.e.,* the taxpayer must exhaust his administrative remedies, pay the tax and bring a civil action as a mandatory business case within two years of the dismissal of his case by the OAH. In addition, the taxpayer's claim must be typical of the claims of members of the class [G.S. § 105-241.18(b)]. The class action commences on the later of the date the complaint is filed alleging the existence of a class or the date a previously filed complaint is amended to allege the existence of a class [G.S. § 105-241.18(a)].

Notice to eligible taxpayers. The court may order the Department to provide the class representative a list of the names and addresses of the taxpayers the department can "readily determine" are eligible to become class members. The court must then approve the contents of a notice of the class action, the method of distributing the notice and how eligible taxpayers may indicate their desire to join the class. The class representative must advance the costs of the notice [G.S. § 105-241.18(c)].

Class members. A taxpayer is eligible to become a member of the class if the taxpayer could have filed a claim for refund as of the date the class action was commenced or any later date set by the court. Thus, a taxpayer is generally eligible to become a member of the class if the class action was commenced within three years of the filing of the taxpayer's return or within two years of the date the taxpayer paid the tax. If the taxpayer is eligible to join the class, the taxpayer may join the class by expressing a desire to join the class in response to a notice of the class action. The taxpayer need not have actually filed a claim for refund or initiated administrative proceedings to join the class [G.S. § 105-241.18(b)].

Effect of class action on statute of limitations. The filing of a class action tolls the statute of limitations for all taxpayers who are eligible to become members of the class. For a taxpayer who joins the class, the tolling ends when the court enters a final

¶3210

judgment on the merits or a final order denying class certification, decertifying the class, or dismissing the class action without adjudicating the merits. For a taxpayer who does not join the class, the tolling ends when the period set by the court for becoming a member of the class ends [G.S. § 105-241.18(d)].

Effect of class action on non-class members. A taxpayer who does not become a member of the class may pursue his administrative remedies, subject to the otherwise applicable statute of limitations, without regard to the class action. The effect of a final adjudication of the class action on a non-class member is generally governed by the normal rules of issue and claim preclusion. However, if a final judgment is entered in favor of the class, then the following rules apply to a taxpayer who did not participate in the class [G.S. § 105-241.18(e)]:

(1) The taxpayer is not entitled to any monetary relief awarded to the class on account of taxes previously paid by the taxpayer.

(2) If the taxpayer has already been assessed for failure to pay the tax at issue but has not yet paid the tax, the assessment is abated.

(3) The taxpayer is relieved of any future liability for the tax that is the subject of the class action.

Note that the only way to obtain a refund for a tax already paid is to pursue an independent refund action or to opt in to the class. A taxpayer who does neither will not be entitled to a refund.

• *Declaratory judgments, injunctions, and other actions prohibited*

The remedies in G.S. § 105-241.11 through G.S. § 105-241.18 discussed above are the exclusive remedies for disputing a proposed assessment, proposed denial or the constitutionality of a tax statute. Any other action is barred. Neither an action for declaratory judgment, an action for an injunction to prevent the collection of a tax, nor any other action is allowed [G.S. § 105-241.19]. *See also Gust v. N.C. Dep't. of Revenue,* 231 N.C. App. 551, 753 S.E.2d 483 (2014) (dismissal of declaratory judgment action for lack of jurisdiction).

• *Secretary's general duty to correct tax liability*

Outside of the administrative and judicial review process, whenever the taxpayer presents the Department with information establishing that an assessment is incorrect or a refund is due, the Secretary must correct a taxpayer's tax liability and adjust the assessment or issue the refund, provided only that the information is presented to the Department within the applicable statute of limitations [G.S. § 105-251(b)].

¶3211 Responsible Person Liability

Each responsible person in a business entity is personally and individually liable for the principal amount of the taxes listed below that are owed by the entity. If the business entity does not pay the amount it owes after the amount becomes collectible, the Secretary may enforce the responsible person's liability by sending the responsible person a notice of proposed assessment. The taxes for which the responsible person is liable are [G.S. § 105-242.2(b)]:

(1) Sales and use taxes collected by the business entity upon its taxable transactions.

(2) Sales and use taxes due on taxable transactions of the business entity but upon which it failed to collect tax, but only if the responsible person knew, or in the exercise of reasonable care should have known, that the tax was not being collected.

(3) Gasoline and alternative fuel taxes of the business entity under Articles 36C and 36D of Chapter 105 and all taxes payable by the business entity under those articles to a supplier for remittance to North Carolina or another state.

(4) All income taxes required to be withheld by the business entity.

Business entity: A business entity is a corporation, a limited liability company, or a partnership regardless of whether the entity is suspended or dissolved [G.S. § 105-242.2(a)(2)].

Responsible person: The term "responsible person" means (1) the president, treasurer, and chief financial officer of a corporation, (2) the manager of a limited liability company, (3) any officer of a corporation, member or company official of a limited liability company or partner of a partnership who has a duty to deduct, account for, or pay over the tax in question, and (4) a partner who is liable for the debts and obligations of a partnership under G.S. § 59-45 or G.S. § 59-403 [G.S. § 105-242.2(a)(1)]. The Department has the burden of establishing that a person is a responsible person. FINAL AGENCY DECISION 10 REV 4058 (May 16, 2012). For examples of persons who have been treated as responsible persons see Secretary's Decision Nos. 2006-145 (November 7, 2006) and 2006-147 (February 6, 2007) and FINAL AGENCY DECISION 11 REV 13094 (September 18, 2012) (LLC managers held responsible person)]. However, a secretary of a corporation (as opposed to the president, treasurer or chief financial officer) is not a responsible person absent an actual duty to deduct, account for or pay the taxes in question [FINAL AGENCY DECISION 10 REV 4058 (May 16, 2012)].

The statute draws no distinction between for-profit and nonprofit taxpayers. Thus, the Secretary of Revenue has held that the volunteer treasurer of a church can be a responsible officer within the meaning of the statute [Secretary's Decision No. 2004-45 (June 25, 2004).

It is not necessary that the failure to collect and remit was willful; it is only necessary that the responsible officer failed to remit the tax withheld or required to have been withheld to the Secretary of Revenue. See, for example, *Secretary's Decision No. 98-297* (February 26, 1999), where a president and significant shareholder of a small, closely held corporation with few employees and limited assets was held personally liable for unpaid North Carolina individual income taxes withheld from employee wages because he had signatory authority over the corporate checking account and was in a position to control the finances of the corporation. The fact that other employees were paid to manage corporate tax affairs did not remove the corporate president's duty to remit the funds. In addition, even if the corporate president's signature had been forged on some returns and checks, he knew or could have easily determined the status of the corporation's financial affairs and discovered the forgeries.

A responsible person is not relieved of liability where new owners and managers take over the business and agree to discharge the business's delinquent tax liability but fail to do so even if the Department of Revenue knew of, but was not a party to, the agreement. *Slowin v. Department of Revenue,* Final Decision, 12 REV 2218 (February 11, 2013).

¶3211

Distributions: An officer, partner, trustee, or receiver of a business entity required to file a report who has custody of funds of the entity and who allows the funds to be paid out or distributed to the owners of the entity without having remitted any state taxes due is personally liable for payment of the taxes [G.S. § 105-242.2(d)].

Statute of limitations: The period of limitations for assessing a responsible person for unpaid taxes expires the later of one year after the expiration of the period of limitations for assessing the business entity or one year after the tax becomes collectible from the business entity [G.S. § 105-242.2(e)].

ADMINISTRATION AND PROCEDURE

CHAPTER 33

OTHER PROCEDURES

¶3301 Compromise Settlements

The Secretary of Revenue may compromise a taxpayer's liability for a tax that is collectible under G.S. §105-241.22 when the Secretary determines that the compromise is in the best interest of the State and makes one or more of the following findings [G.S. §105-237.1(a)]:

(1) There is reasonable doubt as to the amount of the taxpayer's liability.

(2) The taxpayer is insolvent and the Secretary probably could not otherwise collect an amount equal to or in excess of the amount offered in compromise. A taxpayer is considered insolvent only in one of the following circumstances:

(a) It is plain and indisputable that the taxpayer is clearly insolvent and will remain so in the reasonable future.

(b) The taxpayer has been determined to be insolvent in a judicial proceeding.

(3) Collection of a greater amount than that offered in compromise is improbable, and the funds or a substantial portion of the funds offered in the settlement come from sources from which the Secretary could not otherwise collect.

(4) A federal tax assessment arising out of the same facts has been compromised with the federal government on the same or a similar basis as that proposed to the State and the Secretary probably could not collect anything in excess of the amount offered in compromise.

(5) Collection of a greater amount than that offered in compromise would produce an unjust result under the circumstances.

(6) The taxpayer is a retailer or a person under the sales and use tax law, the assessment is for sales and use tax the taxpayer failed to collect or pay on entertainment events, service contracts, prepaid meal plans, real property contracts, certain sales of piped natural gas maintenance and installation services

the taxpayer made a good faith effort to comply and the assessment is for a reporting period ending before July 1, 2020.

(7) The assessment is for sales or use tax the taxpayer failed to collect or pay as a result of the change in the definition of retailer or the expansion of the sales tax base to include service contracts, repair maintenance or installation services or sales transactions of a person in retail trade if the Secretary determines that the taxpayer made a good faith effort to comply and the assessment was for any period beginning March 1, 2016 and ending December 31, 2022.

(8) The assessment is for sales tax the taxpayer failed to collect or use tax the taxpayer failed to pay on repair, maintenance and installation services provided by a real property manager under a property management contract if the Secretary determines the taxpayer made a good faith effort to comply with the law. A taxpayer will be treated as having made a good faith effort if there is no fraud or egregious activity and the taxpayer substantiated the time spent managing the real property for a billing or invoice period.

• *Written statement and Attorney General approval*

When the Secretary compromises a tax liability and the amount of the liability is at least $1,000, the Secretary must make a written statement that summarizes the compromise and sets out the findings on which the compromised was based. If the compromise settles a dispute in litigation, the Attorney General must approve the compromise before the Secretary accepts it, and the Attorney General must sign the summary [G.S. § 105-237.1(b)].

¶3302 Penalty Waiver Policy

The penalty waiver policy of the North Carolina Department of Revenue applies to requests for waiver or reduction of civil penalties. The North Carolina General Statutes require the Department of Revenue to impose certain civil penalties on taxpayers who do not comply with the tax laws and give the Secretary of Revenue the authority to waive or reduce all of these penalties [G.S. § 105-237(a)]. The current penalty waiver policy can be found on the Department's website.

¶3303 Timely Filing and Extensions of Time to File

G.S. § 105-263(a) provides that the federal "mail box rule" (Code §§ 7502 and 7503) governs when a return, report, payment or any other document that is mailed to the Department of Revenue is timely filed. Where a document is delivered after its due date and received by the Department it will be deemed to have been filed on the date of the post mark stamped on the envelope in which it was mailed or the date of registration if sent by registered or certified mail. If the Department does not have a record of timely receiving the document, the taxpayer must provide direct evidence that the document was in fact delivered or proof of proper use of registered or certified mail or IRS-approved private delivery service [Directive TA-18-1]. North Carolina will consider any document with a due date on a Saturday, Sunday or legal holiday as timely filed if delivered in person or mailed or electronically submitted on or before the next business day after the Saturday, Sunday or legal holiday. In addition, North Carolina will consider any tax payment due on a Saturday, Sunday or legal holiday as timely paid if delivered in person or mailed to the Department on the next business day after the Saturday, Sunday or legal holiday. Directive TA-16-1.

The Secretary is required to prescribe when a return or other document that is filed electronically is considered timely filed [G.S. § 105-263].

The Secretary may extend the time for filing a return or report [G.S. § 105-263(b)]. To obtain an extension, a taxpayer must generally comply with any application requirement set by the Secretary. An extension for filing a franchise tax, income tax, or gift tax return does not extend the time for paying the tax due or the time when a failure-to-pay penalty attaches. When an extension of time for filing extends the time for paying the tax expected to be due, interest at the established rate accrues from the original due date of the report or return to the date the tax is paid. Interest rates are discussed at ¶3205.

A person who is granted an automatic extension of time to file a federal income tax return, including a partnership return, is automatically granted an extension to file the corresponding North Carolina income and franchise tax return. When the person files the North Carolina return, he must certify that the federal extension was granted [G.S. §105-263(c)]This provision is effective for taxable years beginning in or after 2019 [S.L. 2018-5, §38.4.(b)].

¶3304 Electronic Funds Transfers (EFT)

Electronic funds transfer (EFT) is the transfer of funds using either the ACH Debit method or the ACH Credit method. See discussion of "Methods of Payment" below. The Department of Revenue receives electronic payments for the following taxes [EFT Information Booklet, p. 1, North Carolina Department of Revenue]:

(1) Withholding Tax.

(2) Corporate Estimated Tax.

(3) Utility Franchise Taxes.

(4) Utility & Liquor Sales & Use Tax.

(5) Piped Natural Gas Tax.

(6) Alcoholic Beverage Taxes.

(7) Sales & Use Tax (semimonthly filers only).

(8) Machinery, Equipment, & Manufacturing Fuel.

(9) Streamlined Sales Tax.

(10) Tobacco Products Taxes (cigarettes and other tobacco products).

(11) Motor Fuels Taxes (excluding Highway Use Tax).

(12) Insurance Premium Taxes.

• *Mandatory participation*

Payment by EFT is mandatory for the following taxpayers [G.S. §105-241(b)]:

(1) Corporations that are required to pay federal estimated corporate income tax by EFT [G.S. §105-241(b)(1)].

(2) Taxpayers required to prepay tax under G.S. §105-116 (repealed as of July 1, 2014) or G.S. §105-164.16 [G.S. §105-241(b)(2)].

(3) Taxpayers that file motor fuels returns electronically [G.S. §105-241(b)(2a)].

(4) Taxpayers with an average amount of required payments of at least $20,000 per month in a 12-month period, designated by the Secretary of Revenue preceding the imposition or review of the payment requirement. Mandatory payment by EFT remains in effect until suspended by the Secretary of Revenue. Every 12 months after requiring a taxpayer to make payment by EFT, the Secretary of Revenue must determine whether, during the applicable period for that tax, the average amount of the taxpayer's required tax payments was at least $20,000 per month. If it was not, the Secretary of Revenue must suspend the requirement that the taxpayer make payments by EFT and notify the taxpayer in writing that the requirement has been suspended. The $20,000 threshold applies separately to each tax [G.S. §105-241(b)(3)]. The Department is not required to notify a taxpayer whose status has not changed [17 NCAC 1C.0505(e)].

• *Voluntary participation*

A taxpayer that is not subject to mandatory participation in the EFT program may, with the approval of the Secretary of Revenue, voluntarily enroll to remit tax payment by EFT [17 NCAC 1C.0506(a)]. Taxpayers who voluntarily elect to participate in the EFT program must do so for a minimum of 12 months. A voluntary participant in the EFT program may stop making its tax payments by EFT by giving the Department of Revenue at least 45 days written notice [17 NCAC 1C.0506]. A voluntary participant in the EFT program is subject to the same requirements and penalties as a taxpayer who is required to make tax payments by EFT [17 NCAC 1C.0506(c)]. The Department of Revenue offers voluntary participation in the EFT program for the same taxes for which participation is mandatory [EFT Information Booklet, p. 3]. The penalty for making payment in the wrong form imposed by G.S. § 105-236(1b) is applicable is a taxpayer fails to make tax payments electronically after electing to participate in the EFT program [EFT Information Booklet, p. 3].

• *Registration*

Both mandatory and voluntary participants in the EFT program must register with the Department of Revenue. Registration is accomplished by submitting a completed Electronic Funds Transfer Authorization Agreement (AC-EFT-100) to the Department of Revenue [17 NCAC 1C.0507].

• *Methods of payment*

There are two methods of payment by EFT that are acceptable to the Department of Revenue: (1) the ACH Debit method and (2) the ACH Credit method. The ACH Debit payment is the preferred method used by taxpayers to make EFT payments [17 NCAC 1C.0508(a)]. The ACH Credit payment method is available to taxpayers with permission of the Department of Revenue, and the taxpayer must demonstrate a valid operational reason for using the ACH Credit payment method in lieu of the ACH Debit method and demonstrate the ability to meet all the criteria of the Department [17 NCAC 1C.0508(b)].

Wire Transfer

Wire transfer is not an EFT payment option. Wire transfer is used only on an emergency basis with prior authorization by the Department of Revenue [17 NCAC 1C.0508(d)].

ACH Debit method: Under this method, taxpayers authorize the Department of Revenue to place debit entries against a bank account that is designated by the taxpayer. Taxpayers using the ACH Debit method will be furnished the necessary instructions to complete the ACH Debit transactions.

ACH Credit method: Under this method, taxpayers elect to originate transactions through their financial institutions. Taxpayers choosing the ACH Credit method will be provided with the documentation for making the payment in the proper format.

• *Timely payment*

Taxpayers who participate in the EFT program must initiate transfers so that the amount due settles into the Department's bank account on or before the due date. Late EFT payments are subject to penalty for failure to pay a tax when due. If the tax due date falls on a Saturday, a Sunday, or a legal holiday, the deposit by EFT is required on or before the first banking day thereafter. If the due date falls on a Saturday, Sunday, State-observed holiday or a Federal Reserve Bank holiday, payment is timely if the Department receives the funds on or before the next Federal Reserve banking day. Directive TA-16-1.

¶3304

- *Timely filing*

The EFT method of payment does not change the filing requirements for tax reports and returns that are required to be filed except for withholding taxes and installment payments of corporate estimated income tax [17 NCAC 1C.0509(c)].

Taxpayer Assistance

Taxpayers who have questions about the EFT Program or need assistance in making electronic funds transfers may contact the EFT Helpline in the Raleigh area at 919-733-7307 or toll free at 1-877-308-9103 Option 1 then Option 1 again from 8:00 a.m. to 5:00 p.m. Eastern time Monday through Friday [*EFT Information Booklet*, p. 9, Department of Revenue].

¶3305 Outsourcing Collection of Overdue Tax Debts

- *Outsourcing*

The Secretary may contract for the collection of tax debts owed by nonresidents and foreign entities [G.S. § 105-243.1(b)].

- *Notification required*

At least 30 days before the Department submits a tax debt to a contractor for collection, the Department must notify the taxpayer by mail that the debt may be submitted for collection if payment is not received within 30 days after the notice was mailed [G.S. § 105-243.1(b)].

- *Overdue tax debt*

An "overdue tax debt" is any part of a tax debt that remains unpaid 90 days or more after it becomes collectible (discussed at ¶3207). A "tax debt" is the total amount of tax, penalty, and interest due for which a notice of final assessment has been mailed to a taxpayer after the taxpayer no longer has the right to contest the debt [G.S. § 105-243.1(a)(2)].

Wire Transfer

If a taxpayer (1) enters into an installment agreement for the tax debt under G.S. § 105-237 within 90 days after the notice of final assessment was mailed and (2) has not failed to make payments as due, the tax debt will not be considered an overdue tax debt [G.S. § 105-243.1(a)(1)]. Installment agreements are discussed at ¶3207.

- *Contractor secrecy required*

A contract for collection tax debts is conditioned on compliance with the secrecy requirements of G.S. § 105-259. If a contractor violates the secrecy requirements the Secretary must notify the contractor that the contract is terminated; and that contractor is not eligible for an award of another contract for tax collection for a period of five years from the termination. An offending contractor is also subject to the criminal penalties of G.S. § 105-259 [G.S. § 105-243.1(c)]. See ¶3104 for discussion of taxpayers' right to privacy under the Taxpayers' Bill of Rights. See ¶1201 and ¶3208 for discussion of confidentiality requirements of G.S. § 105-259.

- *Collection assistance fee*

The Department may impose a collection assistance fee on a tax debt that remains unpaid 60 days or more after the debt is deemed collectible. See ¶3207 for a discussion of when a tax is collectible. The amount of the fee is the actual cost of collection, not to exceed 20% of the amount of the overdue tax debt [G.S. § 105-243.1(d)]. A fee notice warns the taxpayer that a fee will be imposed if the tax debt is not paid in full within 60 days after the date the fee notice was mailed to the taxpayer. The fee is collectible as part of the tax debt. If a taxpayer pays only part of an overdue tax debt, the payment will be credited proportionally to fee revenue and tax revenue [G.S. § 105-243.1(d)].

• *Enforcement of payment*

The Secretary of Revenue, with the assistance of the Attorney General, is authorized to bring suits in courts of other states to collect taxes legally due North Carolina [G.S. § 105-269(a)]. The officials of other states that extend a like comity to North Carolina are empowered to sue for the collection of their taxes in North Carolina courts. If the Secretary deems it expedient to employ local counsel to assist in bringing suit in other states, the Secretary, with the concurrence of the Attorney General, may employ local counsel on the basis of a negotiated retainer or in accordance with prevailing commercial law league rates.

• *Disclosure of information*

An officer, employee, or agent of North Carolina who has access to tax information in the course of service to or employment by the State may disclose the information to contract for the collection of overdue tax debts [G.S. § 105-259(b)(26)]. See also discussion of the requirements of G.S. § 105-259 at ¶ 1201.

¶3306   Tax Relief for Combat Service and Disaster Areas

• *Combat*

Interest or penalties may not be assessed against a taxpayer for any period that is disregarded under IRC § 7508 (relating to service in combat zones) in determining the taxpayer's liability for a federal tax. A taxpayer is granted an extension of time to file a return or take another action concerning a State tax during this period [G.S. § 105-249.2(a)].

• *Disaster*

The penalties for failure to obtain a license, failure to file a return, or failure to pay tax when due may not be assessed for any period in which the time for filing a federal return or report or for paying a federal tax is extended under IRC § 7508A because of a presidentially declared disaster [G.S. § 105-249.2(b)]. For this purpose "presidentially declared disaster" means any disaster which, with respect to the area in which property is located, resulted in a determination by the President that the area warrants assistance by the federal government under the Disaster Relief and Emergency Assistance Act [G.S. § 105-249.2(b); IRC § 1033(h)(3)].

¶3307   Tax Liens

• *General rules*

The lien of a tax attaches to all real and personal property of a taxpayer on the date a tax owed by the taxpayer becomes due and continues until the tax and all interest, penalty, and costs associated with the tax are paid. A tax lien is not extinguished by the sale of the taxpayer's property [G.S. § 105-241(d)]. However, a tax lien is not enforceable against a bona fide purchaser for value or the holder of a duly recorded lien unless one of the following applies:

    (1) In the case of real property, a certificate of tax liability or a judgment was first docketed in the office of the clerk of superior court of the county in which the real property is located [G.S. § 105-241(d)(1)].

    (2) In the case of personal property, there has already been a levy on the property under an execution or a tax warrant [G.S. § 105-241(d)(2)].

Priority: The priority of these claims and liens is determined by the date and time of recording, docketing, levy, or bona fide purchase [G.S. § 105-241(d)].

Assignment or insolvency: If a taxpayer executes an assignment for the benefit of creditors or if insolvency proceedings are instituted against a taxpayer who owes a tax, the tax lien attaches to all real and personal property of the taxpayer as of the date and time the taxpayer executes the assignment or the date and time the insolvency proceedings are instituted. In these cases the tax lien is subject only to a prior recorded specific lien and the reasonable costs of administering the assignment or the insolvency proceedings [G.S. § 105-241(d)].

Exceptions to General Rules

These general rules for tax liens apply unless another Article of Chapter 105 of the General Statutes contains contrary provisions with respect to a lien for a tax levied in that Article [G.S. § 105-241(d)].

¶3308 Secrecy Required of Officials

An officer, an employee, or an agent of the State who has access to tax information in the course of service to or employment by the State may not disclose the information to any other person unless the disclosure is made for one of the purposes authorized by G.S. § 105-259(b)]. If the person committing the violation is an officer or employee, that person shall be dismissed from public office or public employment and may not hold any public office or public employment in North Carolina for five (5) years after the violation [G.S. § 105-259(c)].

• *Employee or officer defined*

The term "employee or officer" includes a former employee, a former officer, and a current or former member of a State board or commission [G.S. § 105-259(a)(1)].

• *Tax information defined*

The term "tax information" means any information from any source concerning a taxpayer's liability for a tax (as defined in G.S. § 105-228.90(b)(7)) and includes the following [G.S. § 105-279(a)(2)]:

(1) Information contained on a tax return, a tax report, or an application for a license for which a tax is imposed.

(2) Information obtained through an audit of a taxpayer or by correspondence with a taxpayer.

(3) Information on whether a taxpayer has filed a tax return or a tax report.

(4) A list of other compilation of the names, addresses, social security numbers, or similar information concerning taxpayers.

Exceptions: The term does not include (1) statistics classified so that information about specific taxpayers cannot be identified; (2) an annual report required to be filed under G.S. § 55-16-22 (relating to annual reports); or (3) information submitted to the Business License Information Office of the Department of Secretary of State on a master application form for various business licenses [G.S. § 105-259(a)(2)].

¶3309 Electronically Filed Returns

The General Assembly has instructed the Department to consider whether returns must or may be filed electronically and to permit electronic filing in cases where the Department determines that it is cost-effective to do so. By December 1 of each year, the Department must publish on its Web site a list of returns required or permitted to be filed electronically during the next calendar year. If the Department permits or requires a return to be filed electronically, it must establish and implement electronic filing procedures, including the form of an electronically filed return and how the taxpayer or return preparer is to signs an electronically filed return. Whenever the Department requires a return to be filed electronically, the Secretary may waive the electronic submission requirement upon showing of good cause [G.S. § 105-241A].

¶3310 Contributions to North Carolina Education Endowment Fund

Taxpayers may make a contribution to the North Carolina Education Endowment Fund by adding a contribution to income taxes shown to be due on a return or by electing to contribute all or any portion of the refund shown on the return. A contribution, including an election to contribute all or part of a refund, is irrevocable upon filing the return [G.S. § 105-269.7].

¶3311 Charter Suspensions

If a corporation or limited liability company fails to file any report or return or pay any tax or fee required by Subchapter I of Chapter 105 (generally any tax other than property and motor fuels taxes) within 90 days of the applicable due date, the Secretary of Revenue is directed to notify the Secretary of State, who is directed to suspend the entity's charter, which terminates the entity's powers, privileges and franchises. Any act the entity attempts to perform during suspension is invalid unless the Secretary of State reinstates the entity. However, suspension does not affect the entity's obligations to file returns and pay taxes due or relieve any responsible person of liability for trust fund taxes [G.S. § 105-230].

¶3312 Disaster Response Relief Provisions

"Nonresident businesses" and "nonresident employees" engaged in performing "disaster-related work" restoring "critical infrastructure" during a "disaster response period" following a gubernatorial disaster declaration are relieved from many tax-related obligations.

• *Definitions*

A "Nonresident business" is a foreign business entity or nonresident individual-owned sole proprietorship that has not been required to file a North Carolina income or franchise tax return for the prior three years (other than with respect to disaster response work during a tax year before the enactment of these relief provisions) [G.S. § 166A-19.70A(b)(7)].

A "nonresident employee" is a nonresident individual employed by a nonresident business or by a critical infrastructure company who is brought into the state to perform disaster-related work during a disaster response period [G.S. § 166A-19.70A(b)(8)].

"Disaster-related work" is work repairing, installing, renovating, building or performing services on critical infrastructure that has been damaged or destroyed by a disaster in an area covered by a disaster declaration [G.S. § 166A-19.70A(b)(4)].

"Critical infrastructure" is property and equipment owned or used by a regulated public utility or a regulated public communications provider for utility or communications transmission services provided to the public in North Carolina [G.S. § 166A-19.70A(b)(2)].

The "disaster response period" begins ten days before the first day of a disaster declaration and ends on the earlier of 60 days after the disaster declaration's expiration or 180 days from the date of the disaster declaration [G.S. § 166A-19.70A(b)(5)].

• *Relief Provisions*

Nonresident businesses and nonresident employees may qualify for the following tax-related relief provisions (as well as other regulatory relief):

¶3310

Franchise tax. A nonresident business that solely performs disaster-related work during a disaster response period at the request of a critical infrastructure company is not considered to be doing business in North Carolina for franchise tax purposes [G.S. § 105-114(d)].

Corporate income tax. A nonresident business that solely performs disaster-related work during a disaster response period at the request of a critical infrastructure company is not considered to be doing business in North Carolina for corporate income tax purposes [G.S. § 105-114(d)]. Note that a corporation that makes an otherwise deductible payment to an affiliate that is not subject to tax because of the disaster relief provisions must add the payment back to federal taxable income in computing state net income [G.S. § 105-130.5(a)(30)].

S corporations and partnerships. S corporations and partnerships that are not doing business in the state because they are nonresident businesses performing disaster-related work during a disaster response period at the request of a critical infrastructure company are not required to file S corporation or partnership returns but must furnish each shareholder or partner any information necessary for that person to properly file a North Carolina return [G.S. §§ 105-131.7(f) and 105-154(c)].

Individual income tax. An individual who is either a nonresident business or a nonresident employee is not subject to the individual income tax and is not required to file an income tax return if the individual's sole North Carolina source income attributable to a business, trade, profession or occupation carried on in the state is derived from performing disaster-related work during a disaster response period at the request of a critical infrastructure company [G.S. §§ 105-153.2(2) and 105-153.8(a)(2)].

Withholding. Amounts paid to a nonresident employee for performing disaster-related work during a disaster response period at the request of a critical infrastructure company are not treated as wages and so are not subject to income tax withholding [G.S. § 105-163.1(13)]. The employer in such a case is not required to file an information return reporting withheld amounts, but must furnish to an employee, upon request, any information necessary for that person to properly file a North Carolina income tax return [G.S. § 105-163.7(b)]. In addition, compensation paid by a nonresident business or a critical infrastructure company to an ITIN contractor who is a nonresident individual for the performance of disaster-related work during a disaster response period at the request of a critical infrastructure company is not subject to withholding [G.S. § 105-163.3(b)(5)].

Motor fuel license. The Secretary is authorized to issue temporary licenses for the import, export, distribution or transportation of motor fuel in North Carolina in response to a disaster declaration. The license expires upon the expiration of the disaster declaration. The license may be granted only if the licensee files an application within seven days after the disaster declaration, but the Secretary way waive the otherwise applicable requirements that the applicant file a bond or irrevocable letter of credit or obtain an authorization to transact business in the state [G.S. § 105-449.69A].

Unemployment insurance. Work performed by a nonresident employee for a nonresident business performing disaster-related work in North Carolina during a disaster response period at the request of a critical infrastructure company is not "employment" for unemployment insurance purposes [G.S. § 96-1(b)(12)b.5].

¶3312

PART XIV

DOING BUSINESS IN NORTH CAROLINA

CHAPTER 34

FEES AND TAXES

¶3401 Corporate Document Filing, Service, and Copying Fees

The Secretary of State collects the following fees when the following corporate documents are delivered to the Secretary for filing:

Document	Fee	G.S. §
Articles of incorporation	$125.00	55-1-22(a)(1)
Application for reserved name	30.00	55-1-22(a)(2)
Notice of transfer of reserved name	10.00	55-1-22(a)(3)
Application for registered name	10.00	55-1-22(a)(4)
Application for renewal of registered name	10.00	55-1-22(a)(5)
Corporation's statement of change of registered agent or registered office or both	5.00	55-1-22(a)(6)
Agent's statement of change of registered office for each affected corporation	5.00	55-1-22(a)(7)
Agent's statement of resignation	No fee	55-1-22(a)(8)
Designation of registered agent or registered office or both	5.00	55-1-22(a)(9)
Amendment of articles of incorporation	50.00	55-1-22(a)(10)
Restated articles of incorporation	10.00	55-1-22(a)(11)
—with amendment of articles	50.00	55-1-22(a)(10)
Articles of merger or share exchange	50.00	55-1-22(a)(12)
Articles of conversion (other than articles of conversion included as part of another document)	50.00	55-1-22(a)(12a)
Articles of dissolution	30.00	55-1-22(a)(13)
Articles of revocation of dissolution	10.00	55-1-22(a)(14)
Certificate of administrative dissolution	No fee	55-1-22(a)(15)
Application for reinstatement following administrative dissolution	100.00	55-1-22(a)(16)
Certificate of reinstatement	No fee	55-1-22(a)(17)
Certificate of judicial dissolution	No fee	55-1-22(a)(18)
Application for certificate of authority	250.00	55-1-22(a)(19)
Application for amended certificate of authority	75.00	55-1-22(a)(20)
Application for certificate of withdrawal	25.00	55-1-22(a)(21)
Certificate of revocation of authority to transact business	No fee	55-1-22(a)(22)
Annual report (paper)[1]	25.00	55-1-22(a)(23)
Annual report (electronic)	18.00	55-1-22(a)(23a)
Articles of correction	10.00	55-1-22(a)(24)
Application for certificate of existence or authorization (paper)	15.00	55-1-22(a)(25)
Application for certificate of existence or authorization (electronic)	10.00	55-1-22(a)(25a)
Any other document required or permitted to be filed by G.S. Chapter 55	10.00	55-1-22(a)(26)

Document	Fee	G.S. §
Service of process on the Secretary of Revenue[2]	10.00	55-1-22(b)
Copying or comparing a copy to the original	1.00 per page	55-1-22(c)(1)
Certifying a copy (paper certificate)	15.00	55-1-22(c)(2)
Certifying a copy (electronic certificate)	10.00	55-1-22(c)(3)

[1] The fee for the annual report in G.S. § 55-1-22(a)(23) is nonrefundable [G.S. § 55-1-22(d)].
[2] The party to a proceeding causing service of process is entitled to recover this fee as costs if the party prevails in the proceeding) [G.S. § 55-1-22(b)].

¶3402 Partnership Document Filing, Service, and Copying Fees

The Secretary of State collects the following fees when the following partnership documents are delivered to the Secretary for filing [G.S. § 59-35.2]:

Document	Fee	G.S. §
Application for reserved name	10.00	59-35.2(a)(1)
Notice of transfer of reserved name	10.00	59-35.2(a)(2)
Application for registered name	10.00	59-35.2(a)(3)
Application for renewal of registered name	10.00	59-35.2(a)(4)
Registered limited liability partnership's or foreign limited liability partnership's statement of change of registered agent or registered office or both	5.00	59-35.2(a)(5)
Agent's statement of change of registered office for each affected registered limited liability partnership or foreign limited liability partnership	5.00	59-35.2(a)(6)
Agent's statement of resignation	No fee	59-35.2(a)(7)
Designation of registered agent or registered office or both	5.00	59-35.2(a)(8)
Articles of conversion (other than articles of conversion included as part of another document	50.00	59-35.2(a)(9)
Articles of merger	50.00	59-35.2(a)(10)
Application for registration as a registered limited liability partnership	125.00	59-35.2(a)(11)
Certificate of amendment of registration as a registered limited liability partnership	25.00	59-35.2(a)(12)
Cancellation of registration as a registered limited liability partnership	25.00	59-35.2(a)(13)
Application for registration as a foreign limited liability partnership	125.00	59-35.2(a)(14)
Certificate of amendment of registration as a foreign limited liability partnership	25.00	59-35.2(a)(15)
Cancellation of registration as a foreign limited liability partnership	25.00	59-35.2(a)(16)
Application for certificate of withdrawal by reason of merger, consolidation, or conversion	10.00	59-35.2(a)(17)
Annual report	200.00	59-35.2(a)(18)
Articles of correction	10.00	59-35.2(a)(19)
Any other document required or permitted to be filed	10.00	59-35.2(a)(20)
Copying, or comparing a copy to the original	1.00 per page	59-35.2(c)(1)
Certifying a copy (paper certificate)	15.00	59-35.2(c)(2)
Certifying a copy (electronic certificate)	10.00	59-35.2(c)(3)

¶3403 Limited Liability Company Document Filing, Service and Copying Fees

The Secretary of State collects the following fees when the following limited liability company documents are delivered to the Secretary for filing [G.S. § 57D-1-22]:

Document	Fee	G.S. §
Articles of organization	$125.00	57D-1-22(a)(1)
Application for reserved name	10.00	57D-1-22(a)(2)
Notice of transfer of reserved name	10.00	57D-1-22(a)(3)
Application for registered name	10.00	57D-1-22(a)(4)
Application for renewal of registered name	10.00	57D-1-22(a)(5)
Statement of change of registered agent or registered office or both	5.00	57D-1-22(a)(6)
Agent's statement of change of registered office	5.00	57D-1-22(a)(7)
Agent's statement of resignation	No fee	57D-1-22(a)(8)
Designation of registered agent or registered office or both	5.00	57D-1-22(a)(9)
Amendment of articles of organization	50.00	57D-1-22(a)(10)
Restated articles of organization without amendment of articles	10.00	57D-1-22(a)(11)
Restated articles of organization with amendment of articles	50.00	57D-1-22(a)(12)
Articles of conversion (other than articles of conversion included as part of another document)	50.00	57D-1-22(a)(13)
Articles of merger	50.00	57D-1-22(a)(14)
Articles of dissolution	30.00	57D-1-22(a)(15)
Cancellation of articles of dissolution	10.00	57D-1-22(a)(16)
Certificate of administrative dissolution	No fee	57D-1-22(a)(17)
Application for reinstatement following administrative dissolution	100.00	57D-1-22(a)(18)
Certificate of reinstatement	No fee	57D-1-22(a)(19)
Certificate of judicial dissolution	No fee	57D-1-22(a)(20)
Application for certificate of authority	250.00	57D-1-22(a)(21)
Application for amended certificate of authority	50.00	57D-1-22(a)(22)
Application for certificate of withdrawal	10.00	57D-1-22(a)(23)
Certificate of revocation of authority to transact business	No fee	57D-1-22(a)(24)
Articles of correction	10.00	57D-1-22(a)(25)
Application for certificate of existence or authorization (paper)	15.00	57D-1-22(a)(26)
Application for certificate of existence or authorization (electronic)	10.00	57D-1-22(a)(27)
Annual report	200.00	57D-1-22(a)(28)
Any other document required or permitted to be filed	10.00	57D-1-22(a)(29)
Copying or certifying a copy of an original	1.00 per page	57D-1-22(c)(1)
Certifying a copy (paper certificate)	15.00	57D-1-22(c)(2)
Certifying a copy (electronic certificate)	10.00	57D-1-22(c)(3)

¶3404 Other Requirements

• *Submission of documents to the Secretary of State for filing*

To be entitled to filing by the Secretary of State, a document must satisfy the following requirements of G.S. § 55D-10 (as well as any other section of the General Statutes that adds to or varies these requirements) [G.S. § 55D-10(a)]:

(1) The document must be one that is required or permitted by Chapter 55, 55A, 55B, 57D, or 59 of the General Statutes to be filed in the office of the Secretary of State [G.S. § 55D-10(b)(1)].

(2) The document must contain the information required by Chapter 55, 55A, 55B, 57D, or 59 of the General Statutes for that document. It may also contain other information [G.S. § 55D-10(b)(2)].

(3) The document must be typewritten, printed, or in an electronic form acceptable to the Secretary of State [G.S. § 55D-10(b)(3)].

(4) The document must be in the English language. There are, however, two exceptions: (i) A name does not have to be in English if it is written in English letters or Arabic or Roman numerals; and (ii) the certificate of existence required of foreign corporations, foreign nonprofit corporations, foreign limited liability companies, and foreign limited liability partnerships does not have to be in English if it is accompanied by a reasonably authenticated English translation [G.S. § 55D-10(b)(4)].

(5) A document submitted by an entity must be executed by a person authorized to execute documents under one of the following statutes:

(a) G.S. § 55-1-20 if the entity is a domestic or foreign corporation [G.S. § 55D-10(b)(5)(i)].

(b) G.S. § 55A-1-20 if the entity is a domestic or foreign nonprofit corporation [G.S. § 55D-10(b)(5)(ii)].

(c) G.S. § 57D-1-20 if the entity is a domestic or foreign limited liability company [G.S. § 55D-10(b)(5)(iii)].

(d) G.S. § 59-204 if the entity is a domestic or foreign limited partnership [G.S. § 55D-10(b)(5)(iv)].

(e) G.S. § 59-35.1 if the entity is any other partnership as defined in G.S. § 59-36 whether or not formed under the laws of North Carolina [G.S. § 55D-10(b)(5)(v)].

(6) The person executing the document must sign it and state, beneath or opposite the person's signature, the person's name and the capacity in which the person signs. Any signature may be a facsimile or an electronic signature if it is in a form acceptable to the Secretary of State. The document may (but need not) contain a seal, attestation, acknowledgment, verification, or proof [G.S. § 55D-10(b)(6)].

(7) The document must be in or on the prescribed form if the Secretary of State has prescribed a mandatory form for the document [G.S. § 55D-10(b)(7)].

(8) The document must be delivered to the office of the Secretary of State for filing and must be accompanied by the applicable fees [G.S. § 55D-10(b)(8)].

• *Forms*

The Secretary of State may promulgate and furnish on request forms for the following:

(1) An application for a certificate of existence [G.S. § 55-1-21(a)].

(2) A foreign corporation's application for a certificate of authority to transact business in North Carolina [G.S. § 55-1-21(b)].

(3) A foreign corporation's application for a certificate of withdrawal [G.S.§ 55-1-21(c)].

If the Secretary of State so requires, use of these forms is mandatory [G.S. § 55-1-21(a)].

Other forms and documents: The Secretary of State may promulgate and furnish on request forms for other documents required or permitted to be filed. However, the use of forms not promulgated or furnished under G.S. § 55-1-21(a) is not mandatory [G.S. § 55-1-21(b)].

• *Expedited filings*

A person submitting a document for filing may request an expedited filing only at the time the document is submitted. If the document is in proper form and accompanied by all applicable fees, the Secretary of State will guarantee the expedited filing of the document [G.S. § 55D-11]. Applicable fees include the following:

(1) $200.00 for the filing by the end of the same business day of a document received by 12:00 noon [G.S. § 55D-11(1)].

(2) $100.00 for the filing of a document within 24 hours after receipt, excluding weekends and holidays [G.S. § 55D-11(2)].

Notice of fees required: A person who requests an expedited filing when submitting a document must be informed of the fees prior to the filing. If the Secretary of State does not inform the person of the required fees prior to filing, the Secretary of State cannot collect the fees [G.S. § 55D-11].

• *Effective time and date of document*

A document that is accepted for filing is effective as follows:

(1) At the time of filing on the date it is filed, as evidenced by the Secretary of State's date and time endorsement on the filed document [G.S. § 55D-13(a)(1)].

(2) At the time specified in the document as its effective time on the date it is filed [G.S. § 55D-13(a)(2)].

Exception for specified delayed effective time and date: A document may specify a delayed effective time and date, and if it does, the document becomes effective at the time and date specified. If a delayed effective date but no time is specified, the document is effective at 11:59:59 p.m. on that date. A delayed effective date for a document may not be later than the 90th day after it is filed [G.S. § 55D-13(b)].

Validity: The fact that a document has become effective under this section does not determine its validity or invalidity or the correctness or incorrectness of the information contained in the document [G.S. § 55D-13(c)].

• *Correcting filed document*

A document that was filed in the office of the Secretary of State may be corrected if (i) it contains a statement that is incorrect and was incorrect when the document was filed or (ii) it was defectively executed, attested, sealed, verified, or acknowledged [G.S. § 55D-14(a)]. A document is corrected by delivering to the Secretary of State for filing articles of correction that do all three of the following:

(1) Describe the document (including its filing date) or have attached to them a copy of the document [G.S. § 55D-14(b)(1)].

(2) Specify the incorrect statement and the reason it is incorrect or the nature of the defect [G.S. § 55D-14(b)(2)].

(3) Correct the incorrect statement or defect [G.S. § 55D-14(b)(3)].

Effective time and date: Articles of correction are effective as of the effective time and date of the document they correct except as to persons relying on the uncorrected document and adversely affected by the correction. As to those persons, articles of correction are effective when filed [G.S. § 55D-14(c)].

• *If Secretary of State refuses to file a document*

If the Secretary of State refuses to file a document delivered for filing, the person on whose behalf the document was submitted for filing may, within 30 days after the date of the refusal, appeal the refusal to the Superior Court of Wake County [G.S. § 55D-16(a)]. The Court's final decision may be appealed as in other civil proceedings [G.S. § 55D-16(c)].

• *Evidentiary effect of copy of filed document*

A certificate attached to a copy of a document filed by the Secretary of State, bearing the Secretary of State's signature and the seal of office (both of which may be in facsimile or in any approved electronic form) and certifying that the copy is a true copy of the document, is conclusive evidence that the original document is on file with the Secretary of State. A photographic, microfilm, optical disk media, or other reproduced copy of a document, when certified by the Secretary, is considered an original for all purposes and is admissible in evidence like an original [G.S. § 55D-17].

• *Penalty for signing false document*

The signing of a document the signer knows is false in any material respect with intent that the document be delivered to the Secretary of State for filing is a Class 1 misdemeanor [G.S. § 55D-18].

DOING BUSINESS IN NORTH CAROLINA

CHAPTER 35

NORTH CAROLINA RESOURCES

Department of Revenue, PO Box 25000, Raleigh, NC 27640-0640
General Information 877-252-3052
Forms 877-252-3052
Electronic Services Helpline 877-308-9103
Internet: www.ncdor.gov
The main office of the Department of Revenue is located at 501
N. Wilmington St., Raleigh, NC 27604.

Department of Administration - Division of Purchase and Contract
Phone: 919-807-2425
Mailing address: NC Department of Administration
Office of the Secretary
1301 Mail Service Center
Raleigh, NC 27699-1301
Internet: www.ncdor.gov

Small Business and Technology Development Center
Small Business and Technology Development Center
5 West Hargett Street, Suite 600
Raleigh, NC 27601-1348
phone 919.715.7272
phone 800.258.0862 (*in North Carolina only*)
Internet: www.sbtdc.org

Frank H. Kenan Institute of Private Enterprise
CB# 34400, The Kenan Ctr. Chapel Hill, NC 27599-3440 919-962-8201
Internet: http://www.kenan-flagler.unc.edu/KI/

PART XV

UNCLAIMED PROPERTY

CHAPTER 36

UNCLAIMED PROPERTY

¶3601 Unclaimed Property

Generally, property that is unclaimed by its rightful owner is presumed abandoned after a specified period of years following the date upon which the owner may demand the property or the date upon which the obligation to pay or distribute the property arises, whichever comes first.

What is unclaimed property?

Property is unclaimed if the apparent owner has not communicated in writing or by other means with the holder concerning the property or the account in which the property is held and has not otherwise indicated an interest in the property.

CCH Comment: Escheat is an area of potential federal/state conflict

A federal statute may preempt state escheat provisions, as for instance Sec. 514(a) of the Employee Retirement Income Security Act of 1974 (ERISA). Pursuant to this provision, the Department of Labor and Workforce Development has been of the opinion that funds of missing participants in a qualified employee benefit plan must stay in the plan despite a state escheat provision because ERISA preempts application of the state escheat laws with respect to such funds (Advisory Opinion 94-41A, Department of Labor, Pension and Welfare Benefit Administration, Dec. 7, 1994). Some states have challenged the federal position on this and similar narrowly delineated situations. In the case of federal tax refunds, IRC Sec. 6408 disallows refunds if the refund would escheat to a state.

Practitioners are thus advised that a specific situation where federal and state policy cross on the issue of escheat may, at this time, be an area of unsettled law.

What are the dormancy periods for unclaimed property?

General rule. Generally, property that is held, issued or owing in the ordinary course of a holder's business is presumed abandoned if remained unclaimed by the owner for more than five years after the owner's right to demand the property or the obligation to pay or distribute the property arises, whichever occurs first.

Checks and drafts. Money orders, cashier's checks, teller's checks, and certified checks are presumed abandoned seven years after issuance.

Bank accounts. A demand or savings deposit is presumed abandoned five years after the date of the last indication by the owner of interest in the property. A time deposit, including a deposit that is automatically renewable, is presumed abandoned 10 years after the later of initial maturity or the date of the last indication by the owner of interest in the property.

Property distributable in the course of demutualization or related reorganization of an insurance company. Property distributable in the course of a demutualization or related reorganization of an insurance company is considered abandoned three years after the date prescribed for payment or delivery.

Gift certificates, gift cards and credit memos. A gift certificate or electronic gift card bearing an expiration date and remaining unredeemed or dormant for more than three years after its sale is deemed abandoned. The amount abandoned is deemed to be 60% of the unredeemed portion of the face value of the gift certificate or electronic gift card. Money or credit owed to a customer as a result of a retail business transaction is presumed abandoned three years after the obligation accrued.

Stock and other intangibles. A security or other intangible ownership interest in a business association is presumed abandoned three years after the earlier of:

the date of a cash dividend or other distribution unclaimed by the apparent owner;

the date a second consecutive mailing, notification, or communication from the holder to the apparent owner is returned to the holder as unclaimed by or undeliverable to the apparent owner; or

the date the holder discontinued mailings, notifications, or communications to the apparent owner.

Other dormancy periods. Most states also have specified dormancy periods for:

Business association dissolutions/refunds,

Insurance policies,

IRAs/retirement funds,

Money orders,

Proceeds from class action suits,

Property held by fiduciaries,

Safe deposit boxes,

Shares in a financial institution,

Traveler's checks,

Utilities,

Wages/salaries, and

Property held by courts/public agencies.

Is there a business-to-business exemption for unclaimed property?

Yes, North Carolina has a business-to-business exemption for unclaimed property.

What are the notice requirements for unclaimed property?

A holder of property presumed abandoned must mail a notice to the last-known address of the apparent owner not more than 120 days or less than 60 days before filing an abandoned property report for: (1) security or other business association equity interest valued at least $25 or more, or (2) other property, including a security entitlement, valued at $50 or more.

What are the reporting requirements for unclaimed property?

General requirements. Holders of abandoned property must file a report with the Treasurer before November 1 of each year that covers property for the 12 months prior to July 1 of that year, except that a report with respect to a life insurance company must be filed before May 1 of each year for the previous calendar year. The Treasurer may extend the time to file a report upon written request.

Negative reporting. North Carolina does not require negative reporting. (Form ASD-NEG)

Minimum reporting. There is no minimum amount required to file in North Carolina.

Aggregate reporting. Holders may report property amounting to less than $50 in the aggregate without specifying the name, address, or other identifying information of the owner.

Electronic reporting. Holders of abandoned property with 50 or more property owner records are required to file a report electronically.

Record keeping. A holder of abandoned property must maintain records for five years (three years in the case of traveler's checks and money orders) after the holder files the report.

CASE TABLE

A

B

HEA

M

N

Q

R

S

T

U

V

W

Y

UNE

Finding Lists

Department of Revenue Tax Directives

Property Tax Commission Decisions

Secretary of Revenue Hearing Decisions

Tax Review Board Administrative Decisions

Final Agency Decisions

LAW AND RULE LOCATOR

This finding list shows where sections of North Carolina statutory law and administrative rules referred to in the *Guidebook* are discussed.

LAW
North Carolina Constitution